PLATINUM EDITION

Series Director: Diane Larsen-Freeman

GRAMMAR DIMENSIONS

TEACHER'S EDITION

Jan Frodesen
University of California
Santa Barbara

Janet Eyring
California State University
Fullerton

Heinle & Heinle
Thomson Learning™

Australia • Canada • Denmark • Japan • Mexico • New Zealand
Philippines • Puerto Rico • Singapore • Spain • United Kingdom • United States

Acquisitions Editor: Eric Bredenberg
Senior Developmental Editor: Amy Lawler
Production Editor: Michael Burggren
Senior Marketing Manager: Charlotte Sturdy
Manufacturing Coordinator: Mary Beth Hennebury
Composition/Project Management: The PRD Group, Inc.
Text Design: Sue Gerould, Perspectives
Cover Design: Hannus Design Associates

For permission to use material from this text, contact us:
web   www.thomsonrights.com
fax   1-800-730-2215
phone   1-800-730-2214

Heinle & Heinle Publishers
20 Park Plaza
Boston, MA 02116

AUSTRALIA/NEW ZEALAND:
Nelson/Thomson Learning
102 Dodds Street
South Melbourne
Victoria 3205 Australia

CANADA:
Nelson/Thomson Learning
1120 Birchmount Road
Scarborough, Ontario
Canada M1K 5G4

UK/EUROPE/MIDDLE EAST:
Thomson Learning
Berkshire House
168-173 High Holborn
London, WC1V 7AA, United Kingdom

LATIN AMERICA:
Thomson Learning
Seneca, 53
Colonia Polanco
11560 México D.F. México

SPAIN:
Thomson Learning
Calle Magallanes, 25
28015-Madrid
Espana

ASIA (excluding Japan):
Thomson Learning
60 Albert Street #15-01
Albert Complex
Singapore 189969

JAPAN:
Thomson Learning
Palaceside Building, 5F
1-1-1 Hitotsubashi, Chiyoda-ku
Tokyo 100 0003, Japan

ISBN: 0-8384-0292-5

 This book is printed on acid-free recycled paper.

Printed in the United States of America
2 3 4 5 6 7 8 9 04 03 02 01

Teacher's Edition Contents

WORLDWIDE LANGUAGE INSTITUTE
609 WEST HASTINGS STREET
VANCOUVER, B.C.   V6B 4W4
TEL: 604-696-9954 FAX: 604-696-9956
www.wwli.ca

Contents

Unit 4   Passive Verbs   56

Unit 5   Article Usage   76

CONTENTS   **xi**

xiii

Introduction

A Word from Diane Larsen-Freeman, Series Director

Before ***Grammar Dimensions*** was published, teachers would always ask me, "What is the role of grammar in a communicative approach?" These teachers recognized the importance of teaching grammar, but they associated grammar with form and communication with meaning, and thus could not see how the two easily fit together. ***Grammar Dimensions*** was created to help teachers and students appreciate the fact that grammar is not just about form. While grammar does indeed involve form, in order to communicate, language users also need to know the meaning of the forms and when to use them appropriately. In fact, it is sometimes not the form, but the *meaning* or *appropriate use* of a grammatical structure that represents the greatest long-term learning challenge for students. For instance, learning when it is appropriate to use the present perfect tense instead of the past tense, or being able to use two-word or phrasal verbs meaningfully, represent formidable challenges for ESL students.

The three dimensions of form, meaning, and use can be depicted in a pie chart with their interrelationship illustrated by the three arrows:

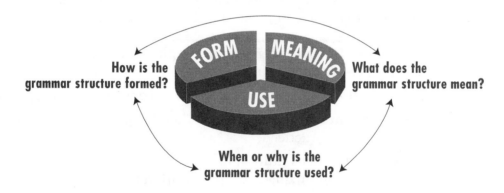

How is the grammar structure formed?

What does the grammar structure mean?

When or why is the grammar structure used?

Helping students learn to use grammatical structures accurately, meaningfully, and appropriately is the fundamental goal of ***Grammar Dimensions.*** It is consistent with the goal of helping students to communicate meaningfully in English, and one that recognizes the undeniable interdependence of grammar and communication.

Enjoy the Platinum Edition!

To learn more about form, meaning, and use, read ***The Grammar Book: An ESL/EFL Teacher's Course,*** Second Edition, by Marianne Celce-Murcia and Diane Larsen-Freeman, also from Heinle & Heinle. It helps both prospective and practicing teachers of ESL/EFL enhance their understanding of English grammar, expand their skills in linguistic analysis, and develop a pedagogical approach to teaching English grammar that builds on the three dimensions. ISBN: 0-8384-4725-2.

Welcome to Grammar Dimensions, Platinum Edition!
The most comprehensive communicative grammar series available.

Updated and revised, *Grammar Dimensions, Platinum Edition,* makes teaching grammar easy and more effective than ever. Clear grammar explanations, a wealth of exercises, lively communicative activities, technology resources, and fully annotated Teacher's Editions help both beginning and experienced teachers give their students the practice and skills they need to communicate accurately, meaningfully, and appropriately.

Grammar Dimensions, Platinum Edition is:

Communicative	• Students practice the **form, meaning,** and **use** of each grammar structure. • **Improved! A variety of communicative activities** helps students practice grammar and communication in tandem, eliciting self-expression and personalized practice. • Students learn to communicate accurately, meaningfully, and appropriately.
Comprehensive	• **Improved!** Grammar is presented in **clear charts.** • **A wealth of exercises** helps students practice and master their new language. • **The Workbook** provides extra practice and helps students prepare for the TOEFL® Test. • **Engaging listening activities** on audiocassette further reinforce the target structure. • **New! Enclosed CD-ROM** includes over 500 activities and gives students even more practice in mastering grammar and its use in language. **FREE!**
Clear	• **Improved! Simplified grammar explanations** help both students and teachers easily understand and comprehend each language structure. • **Improved! A fresh new design** makes each activity engaging. • **New! Communicative activities** ("the Purple Pages") are now labeled with the skill being practiced. • **New!** The Teacher's Edition has **page references** for the Student Book and Workbook, minimizing extra preparation time.

User Friendly for Students	• **Contextualized grammar explanations and examples** help students understand the target language. • **New! Goals** at the beginning of each unit focus students' attention on the learning they will do. • **Sample phrases and sentences** model the appropriate use of the structure.
User Friendly for Teachers	• **New!** Teacher's Edition now contains answers, tests, tape scripts, and complete, **step-by-step teaching suggestions** for every activity. • **New!** "Purple Page" activities are now labeled with the skill. • **Improved! A tight integration** among the Student Book, the Workbook, and the Teacher's Edition make extension activities easy to do.
Flexible	• Instructors can use the units in order or as set by their curriculum. • Exercises can be used in order or as needed by the students. • "Purple Page" activities can be used at the end of the unit or interspersed throughout the unit.
Effective	Students who learn the form, meaning, and use of each grammar structure will be able to communicate more accurately, meaningfully, and appropriately.

Grammar Dimensions, Platinum Edition

In *Grammar Dimensions, Platinum Edition,* students progress from the sentence level to the discourse level, and learn to communicate appropriately at all levels.

	Grammar Dimensions Book 1	Grammar Dimensions Book 2	Grammar Dimensions Book 3	Grammar Dimensions Book 4

Sentence level → Discourse level

	Grammar Dimensions, Book 1	Grammar Dimensions, Book 2	Grammar Dimensions, Book 3	Grammar Dimensions, Book 4
Level	High beginning	Intermediate	High intermediate	Advanced
Grammar level	Sentence and subsentence level	Sentence and subsentence level	Discourse level	Discourse level
Primary language and communication focus	Semantic notions such as *time* and *place*	Social functions, such as *making requests* and *seeking permission*	Cohesion and coherence at the discourse level	Academic and technical discourse
Major skill focus	Listening and speaking	Listening and speaking	Reading and writing	Reading and writing
Outcome	Students form accurate, meaningful, and appropriate structures at the sentence level.	Students form accurate, meaningful, and appropriate structures at the sentence level.	Students learn how accurate, meaningful, and appropriate grammatical structures contribute to the organization of language above the simple sentence.	Students learn how accurate, meaningful, and appropriate grammatical structures contribute to the organization of language above the simple sentence.

Unit Organization

Used with or without the Workbook and the *Grammar 3D* CD-ROM, ***Grammar Dimensions*** Student Book units are designed to be clear, comprehensive, flexible, and communicative.

Goals	• **Focus students' attention** on the learning they will do in each chapter.
Opening Task	• **Contextualizes** the target grammatical structure. • **Enables teachers to diagnose** their students' performance and identify the aspect of the structure with which their students have the most difficulty. • **Provides a roadmap** for the grammar points students need to work on in that unit.
Focus Boxes	• **Present the form, meaning,** or **use** of a particular grammatical structure. • **Focus students' attention** to a particular feature of the target structure. Each rule or explanation is preceded by examples, so teachers can have students work inductively to try to discover the rule on their own.
Exercises	• Provide a wealth of opportunity to **practice** the form and meaning of the grammar structures. • Help students develop the skill of **"grammaring"**—the ability to use structures accurately, meaningfully, and appropriately. • Are varied, thematically coherent, but purposeful. • Give students many opportunities to personalize and own the language.
Communicative Activities ("The Purple Pages")	• Help students practice **grammar and communication in tandem.** • **Are engaging!** • Encourage students to **use their new language** both inside and outside the classroom. • Provide an opportunity to **practice reading, writing, listening, and speaking skills,** helping students realize the communicative value of the grammar they are learning.

Student Book Supplements

Audiocassettes	• **Provide listening activities for** each unit so students can practice listening to **grammar structures in context.**
Workbooks	• **Provide additional exercises** for each grammar point presented in the student text.
	• Offer question types found on the **TOEFL**® Test.
CD-ROM	• *Grammar 3D* **provides additional practice** for 34 of the key grammar structures found in the text series.
	• Offers over **500 activities** for beginning to advanced students.
	• **Provides an instructional "help page"** that allows students to access grammar explanations at any point.
	• **Provides feedback** that helps students understand their errors and guides them toward correct answers.
	• **Free** with each Student Book!
Teacher's Editions	• **Facilitate teaching** by providing in one place notes and examples, answer keys to the Student Book and Workbook, page references to all of the components, the tapescript for the audiocassette activities, and tests with answer keys for each unit.
	• **Minimize teacher preparation time** by providing step-by-step teaching suggestions for every focus box and activity in the Student Book.

The *Grammar Dimensions, Platinum Edition* Student Books and the additional components help teachers teach and students learn to use English grammar structures in communication accurately, meaningfully, and appropriately.

Acknowledgments

Series Director Acknowledgments

This edition would not have come about if it had not been for the enthusiastic response of teachers and students using the previous editions. I am very grateful for the reception **Grammar Dimensions** has been given.

I am also grateful for all the authors' efforts. To be a teacher, and at the same time a writer, is a difficult balance to achieve . . . so is being an innovative creator of materials, and yet, a team player. They have met these challenges exceedingly well in my opinion. Then, too, the Heinle & Heinle team has been impressive. I am grateful for the leadership exercised by Erik Gundersen, formerly of Heinle & Heinle. I also appreciate all the support from Charlotte Sturdy, Eric Bredenberg, Mike Burggren, Mary Beth Hennebury, and Marianne Bartow. Deserving special mention are Amy Lawler and Nancy Jordan, who never lost the vision while they attended to the detail with good humor and professionalism.

I have also benefited from the counsel of Marianne Celce-Murcia, consultant for the first edition this project, and my friend. Finally, I wish to thank my family members, Elliott, Brent, and Gavin, for not once asking the (negative yes–no) question that must have occurred to them countless times: "Haven't you finished yet?"

Author Acknowledgments

With this edition of *Grammar Dimensions,* as with the previous one, we are grateful for the thoughtful comments and suggestions from ESL teachers and students who have used Book 4. We especially hope that teachers will find the annotated Teacher's Edition useful and that the teaching suggestions will inspire creative ways to help their students meet learning challenges.

As always, we appreciate the guidance, expertise and ongoing support of Diane Larsen-Freeman, our series director. We thank the Heinle and Heinle team for their constant support of the *Grammar Dimensions* series. Many thanks to our editor, Amy Lawler, for her patience and flexibility, as well as her valuable assistance with annotations for the Teacher's Edition. The PRD Group, Inc. deserves thanks for so smoothly managing the final stages of this project.

To the *Grammar Dimensions* authors of Books 1, 2 and 3—Carolyn, Victoria, Heidi, Gin, and Steve— we extend special thanks. The friendship and understanding of the author team resulting from shared efforts have meant a great deal to us over the last decade.

Once again we end with thanks to our family members, friends and colleagues for their continuous support and good will.

About the Teacher's Edition

The Teacher's Edition includes the following:

- General suggestions for teaching with *Grammar Dimensions Platinum*.
- Detailed teaching suggestions and answer keys for each unit in the Student Book. The following icons appear in this section:

 This icon signals a time when you could present a grammar point on the board.

 The pairwork icon appears when an exercise can be done in pairs.

 The groupwork icon appears when an exercise can be done in a group.

 This icon appears when a corresponding Workbook exercise or exercises can be assigned. The exercise and page number(s) in the Workbook are supplied next to the icon. The answers for the Workbook exercises appear in the Workbook Answer Key section of this Teacher's Edition. The page number for the answers to each exercise appear as part of each Workbook anno.

 This icon and an accompanying anno appear in the "Use Your English" section when there is an audio activity.

 Tests. A 15-minute test is included for each unit. You can administer it after each unit or combine with other units to create longer tests. You are welcome to photocopy the tests for student use. This icon appears when a test can be given.

- Answer key for the tests.
- Answer key for Workbook exercises.
- Tapescripts for the Listening Activities that appear in the "Use Your English" communicative activities section (purple pages) for each unit of the Student Book.

General Teaching Suggestions

OPENING TASK

Our time with our students is very precious. We must seek ways to put it to their best advantage. In order to do this, you need to learn what your students know and don't know how to do. This will allow you to target what you teach to what your students don't know, and therefore, need to learn. This is the major purpose of the opening task. You should be able to obtain invaluable information about your students' learning needs from "reading" (closely observing) your students as they go about doing the task. Each task has been constructed so that students will need to use the target structures in order to complete it.

As the students are focused on completing the task, you are freed to learn as much as you can about your students' learning needs. It will probably be best if after you have introduced the task (making sure students know what they are being asked to do), you have the students carry out as much of the task as they can by themselves. This will allow you to more closely observe your students' performance.

One way of doing this is to circulate in the classroom and "eavesdrop" on small group discussions. Take mental or written notes on your observations. Pay particular attention to how accurate, meaningful, and appropriate your students' use of the target structures is. Hold up the form, meaning, and use pie chart in your mind and see if you can determine where they have been successful, and where they need help. At this point, it is probably better if you refrain from any error correction. The tasks are supposed to encourage students to work meaningfully without concern that they will be interrupted, evaluated, or corrected. The only exception might be the need to remind students to work in English if they are using another language.

Sometimes the tasks involve individual written performances. When this is the case, study carefully what your students write. It, too, can provide valuable clues about what they can and cannot do. In many cases, students will want to hear each other's solutions to the questions or problems posed in the task. This provides yet another excellent opportunity for you to listen to your students and learn what has been easy for them and what has been difficult.

Of course, as with anything, different difficulties are likely to arise for different students. To cope with differing learning needs, you may consider grouping students with similar problems in class and giving each group different exercises to work through and/or different homework assignments. Another possibility is to group students in such a way that students who already know certain aspects of the target structure are grouped with other students who don't. In this way, students can learn from one another as they work through the focus boxes and exercises. If you do group students in this manner, however, it is important that each student be given a role in the group, so that students who are struggling with the content can still be contributing members of the group. For example, give these students the assignment of recording the group's answers, or reporting them to another group or to the whole class.

Obviously, if students demonstrate no ability to use the target structures required in completing the task, you will need to work systematically through the unit. It may be the case, though, that you will discover that students do not need to attend to all the focus boxes or do all the exercises; this makes your teaching more efficient.

Don't hesitate to alter tasks to fit your timetable. For example, have your students do only part of the task, or have them do one of the communicative activities at the end of the unit, if you feel that the opening task would not work as well. Other teachers have found it helpful to have students do the task twice—first for diagnostic purposes and second after students have worked through a unit in order to determine how much they have progressed.

All in all, what we are trying to achieve is an optimal use of the time we have available by identifying teachable moments when the students need to and are ready to learn.

FOCUS BOXES

The focus boxes feature the form, meaning, and use facts concerning the target structure that are appropriate for students at a given level of instruction. By treating one aspect of the structure at a time, followed by exercises providing practice, the focus boxes allow students to develop step-by-step a better understanding of, and an ability to use, the structure accurately, meaningfully, and appropriately.

Use student performance on the opening task as a bridge to the focus boxes. One way to do this is to write students' responses to the task on the blackboard, eliciting or supplying the target structures as they are needed. By going back and pointing out the target structures and asking questions about their form, meaning, or use, you may be able to induce the rules in the focus boxes (not all at once, of course). At this point, you may want students to consult the relevant focus box in order to confirm the generalizations they have just made. On the other hand, if the students have arrived at the generalizations you feel they need to know, you may simply want to call their attention to the appropriate focus boxes for them to refer to for homework or when needed.

If you prefer a more deductive approach, you could go right to the first or appropriate focus box after the students have completed the task. You could present it orally to students or read it while they listen or read along silently with you. Alternatively, you could have the students read the focus boxes for homework or silently in class. You could help them when they do not understand something. You could check their understanding by asking students to come up with additional examples to supplement the ones in the focus box or asking them to compare how the material in this focus box differs from one earlier in the unit or from those in a related unit that they have completed.

A variation on this is to ask students individually or in pairs to present the information in a focus box to another pair of students, or even to the whole class, adding a few new examples of their own. Teaching something to others is a great way to learn!

Another possible way of teaching the focus boxes is not to present them at all, but rather to assign students the exercises that go along with them. The focus boxes can be used for reference purposes as the students work their way through the exercises. In this way, the material becomes more meaningful to students because they will need to access and understand it in order to do something with it.

EXERCISES

At least one exercise follows each focus box. There is a wide variety of exercises in *Grammar Dimensions*. There are both comprehension and production exercises. Comprehension exercises work on students' awareness and understanding. Production exercises develop students' skill in using the structures.

There are exercises that are consistent with the theme of the task and ones that introduce students to new themes and vocabulary in order to provide variety and to foster students' ability to transfer their learning to new contexts. There are personalized exercises, in which students use their own background knowledge or opinions to answer questions, and ones where students use the information that is supplied in order to complete the exercise.

Then, too, although general directions are provided for each exercise, there is a great deal of flexibility in how the exercises can be handled. Some exercises, such as information gaps, call for pairwork. Others are amenable to many different student configurations: individual, pair, small group, whole class; so you will need to decide what works best for a particular exercise and particular group of students. For instance, some students prefer to work individually at first and then get together with others to go over their answers. The variety of possible student configurations that the exercises permit allows students' differing learning styles to be catered to.

Sometimes you can choose freely whether to have students do an exercise orally or in writing. At other times, an exercise will work better in one modality than another because of the modality in which the structure normally occurs. Some exercises may be done in class, others for homework, and still others skipped all together. Don't forget to consult the Workbook for additional exercises.

There are also many options for how exercise answers can be checked. For example:

1. You can circulate while students are doing an exercise in class and spot-check.
2. You can go over the exercise afterwards as a whole class with each student being called on to supply an answer.
3. Exercises can be done individually and then pairs of students can get together to check their answers with each other. Where a difference of opinion occurs, you (or another pair of students) can act as a referee.
4. Different students, pairs, or groups of students can be assigned different parts of an exercise. For example, the first group does #'s 1–5, the second group does #6–10, etc. The groups post their answers on newsprint or butcher block paper and everyone circulates at the end noting the answers and asking questions.
5. A variation of #4 is to have one student from each group get together and present to the other students the exercise answers that his or her group came up with.
6. You can prepare a handout with the answers, and each student corrects his or her answers individually.
7. You can collect the written work, and make a list of common errors. You can put the errors on an overhead transparency and show it to the students during the next class and have them correct the errors together.

There are both closed and open-ended answers to questions. With closed questions, there is a single right answer. This is the most common type of question in Books 1 and 2. In Books 3 and 4, while closed questions still prevail, sometimes open-ended questions, for which there are no definitive answers, are used. Nuances of the language and contextual differences are such that it is sometimes difficult to say definitively what the single best answer is. The point is that students should understand that they have choices, but they also need to understand the consequences of their choices, i.e., they should be able to explain why they have chosen a particular answer. In many of these cases a "most likely" interpretation (based on English native speaker responses) has been indicated in the answer key, but no feasible opinion offered by your students should be discounted. Giving students an opportunity to defend their answers encourages students to form their own hypotheses about the appropriate use of certain grammar structures and to test these hypotheses through continued observation and analysis.

"USE YOUR ENGLISH" ACTIVITIES

In the "Use Your English" activities section of each unit (the purple pages), students can apply the language discussed in the unit to wider contexts and integrate it with the language they already know. Many activities give students more control over what they want to say or write than the exercises, and offer them more opportunities to express their own points of view across a range of topics. Most of the activities are quite open-ended in that they lend themselves to being done with structures covered in the unit, but they do not absolutely require their use.

The activities section is also designed to give instructors a variety of options. Since time is limited, you probably will not be able to have students do all the activities. You might choose two to do or ask your students to choose ones that they would prefer. Perhaps different groups of students could do different activities and then report on their experience to the whole class. Like the exercises, the activities can be adapted for use with different group configurations and different modalities.

If you are teaching in a program that is skill-based, you might want to collaborate with your colleagues and distribute the activities among yourselves. For example, the writing teacher could assign the activities that involve a written report, the teacher of listening could work on the listening activities during his or her class periods, or the teacher of speaking could work with students on

activities where students are supposed to make an oral presentation.

Although the activities are meant to be culminating, it is also possible to intersperse them among the exercises. Sometimes an activity provides a particularly useful follow-up to an exercise. And we have already mentioned that certain activities might work well in place of the recommended opening task. Also, it may be useful to go back to a previous unit and do an activity for review purposes. This is especially useful at the beginning of a new, but related, unit.

The activities are an integral part of each unit because they not only provide students with opportunities to stretch their language use, but as with the opening task, they also provide you with the opportunity to observe your students' language use in action. In this way, activities can be informal holistic assessment measures encouraging students to show you how well they can use the target structures communicatively. Any persistent problems that still exist at this point can be noted for follow-up at a later time when students are more ready to deal with them.

As you can see, *Grammar Dimensions* is meant to provide you with a great deal of flexibility so that you can provide quality instruction appropriate for your class. We encourage you to experiment with different aspects of the material in order to best meet the needs of your unique group of students.

Unit 1

UNIT OVERVIEW

Unit 1 provides a review of the English verb system, including time frames (present, past, future) and aspects (simple, progressive, perfect, perfect progressive). Advanced students (Ss) will be familiar with the English verb system, but they will most likely still have problems with particular tenses (e.g., present perfect) and with the uses of tenses in contexts. Therefore, this unit also focuses on helping Ss understand and apply (1) principles of tense consistency and (2) the reasons why tenses and time frames shift within paragraphs in written texts.

UNIT GOALS

Review the goals listed on this page so Ss understand what they should be able to know by the end of the unit.

OPENING TASK

Note: The **Opening Task** allows Ss to use the target structures and allows teachers to notice what kinds of help they may need. For a more complete discussion of the Opening Task, see page xxiii of this Teacher's Edition.

In this task, Ss will use a wide range of verb tenses in discussing and writing about their "in-groups": various groups that an individual belongs to over the course of his/her life. Both spoken and written production will allow you to assess Ss' knowledge of verb forms and uses.

SETTING UP THE TASK

The beginning of this task defines the term "in-groups" and lists a number of examples, using a fictional Thai-American woman named Kay. Because in-groups include family, religious, social, and educational memberships and activities, all Ss will be able to identify some in-groups from their past and present.

CONDUCTING THE TASK

Step 1

Ask Ss if they have heard the term "in-groups" before. If they bring up the colloquial usage ("a popular group"), tell them in-group has a different meaning here. Have them read the definition and look at the list.

UNIT 1

VERB TENSES IN WRITTEN AND SPOKEN COMMUNICATION

UNIT GOALS:

- To use verb tenses correctly to describe events and situations
- To use verb tenses consistently
- To understand why tense and time frames may change

OPENING TASK
Describing In-Groups

STEP 1 Read the following information about *in-groups* and find the definition of this term.

Gordon Allport, a Harvard psychologist, used the term *in-groups* to describe the groups that individuals are part of at one time or another. We are born into some in-groups, such as our ethnic groups, our home-towns, and our nationalities. We join other in-groups through our activities, such as going to school, making friends, entering a profession, or getting married. Some in-groups, such as ethnic groups, are permanent, but others change as our activities, beliefs, and loyalties change.

EXPANSION

Bring in pictures of well-known persons—politicians, performing artists, etc. Ask Ss to state one or more in-groups to which these people belong or belonged (e.g., Michael Jordan, Chicago Bulls).

The following are some of the in-group memberships, both past and present, of Kay, a Thai-American woman in her mid-thirties.

the family she grew up in
her own family (husband Phil and
    child Andrea)
Thai (ethnic group)
native speakers of Thai
Bangkok (the city she was born in)
Chicago (where she lived from ages eight
    to eighteen)
Palo Alto, California (the city she lives
    in now)
her girlhood circle of friends

the Girl Scouts
her elementary and secondary school
Princeton University
Stanford Medical School
physicians (her profession)
the Buddhist religion
the National Organization for Women
her neighborhood volleyball team
the Sierra Club
the Democratic party
the United States

STEP 2 Make a list of some in-groups to which you belonged as a child (pick an age between five and twelve years old). Some of these groups might be the same as present ones. Next, make a list of in-groups that you belong to now. Finally, create a third list which includes your present in-groups that you believe will remain significant groups for you ten years from now.

STEP 3 Compare your lists with those of two or three other class members. Discuss which groups on your childhood lists have changed and which have remained important groups to you at the present time.

STEP 4 As an out-of-class assignment, write three paragraphs. For the first paragraph, describe a childhood in-group that was especially important to you. For the second paragraph, write about your current involvement in an in-group. In the third paragraph, speculate about what might be some new in-groups for you in the future—for example, a new school, a profession, your own family (as contrasted to your family of origin)—and when you think some of them might become a part of your life. Save your paragraphs for Exercise 2.

Step 2

SUGGESTION

To model the list Ss will generate, write your name on the board and a partial list of your own childhood in-groups. (Alternatively, use a student's name and in-groups.) Then have Ss work individually; assist where needed.

Step 3

As Ss discuss their lists, monitor production; note verb forms or uses that may need particular attention.

Step 4

You will probably want to collect Ss' paragraphs for diagnostic purposes at some point.

VARIATION

This assignment could be started in class. As a pre-writing activity, Ss could brainstorm ideas for each paragraph.

EXPANSION

1. During the next class, ask for volunteers to read paragraphs or read them aloud yourself. Have the class guess who the writer is. (Give clues after a few incorrect guesses.) You could do this as a "warm-up" in subsequent classes with different time frames.

Note: Focus boxes explain and give examples of each structure. For a more complete discussion of focus boxes, see page xxiv of this Teacher's Edition.

FOCUS 1

As stated earlier, the English verb system forms and meanings will be a review for advanced Ss. Since Units 1 and 2 offer a thorough review of forms and meanings of each time frame and aspect, it would be tedious to conduct lengthy verb tense "drills" for this focus box, which will serve as a reference chart. Tell Ss that the next two units will offer a lot of information about the various verb tenses and many opportunities for practice, so they shouldn't be intimidated by the overview chart or by grammar labels they're not familiar with.

SUGGESTION

To review briefly the twelve forms, use examples of your Ss' study habits or writing assignments to put the verbs *study* and *write* in contexts.

1. Draw a timeline on the board with present, past, and future time frames marked so that Ss can see tenses represented visually. Use this timeline to help Ss understand the terms *tense* and *aspect*.
2. Write sentences on the board or on a handout with blanks for the verbs. Examples for *study: Carlos _____ English two hours every day. Carlos _____ for two hours when his friend Sam called.*
3. As you work on tenses, review the grammar terms so that Ss will be more familiar with them. Help them make connections with other terms of labels they may know (e.g., *-ing verb* or *continuous* rather than *progressive*).

FOCUS **1**

FORM MEANING

The English Verb System: Overview

Verbs in English express how events take place in time. The verb tenses give two main kinds of information:

Time Frame When the event takes place: now, at some time in the past, or at some time in the future

Aspect The way we look at an action or state: whether it occurs at a certain point in time (for example, *study*) or lasts for period of time (for example, *speak*). (See Unit 2 for more detail.)

Time frame and **aspect** combine in twelve different ways in English.

	TIME FRAME		
ASPECT	**Present**	**Past**	**Future***
Simple Ø-aspect (at that point in time)	*study/studies* *speak/speaks* (simple present)	*studied* *spoke* (simple past)	*will study* *will speak* (simple future)
Progressive (in progress at that point in time)	*am/is/are studying* *am/is/are speaking* (present progressive)	*was/were studying* *was/were speaking* (past progressive)	*will be studying* *will be speaking* (future progressive)
Perfect (before that time)	*has/have studied* *has/have spoken* (present perfect)	*had studied* *had spoken* (past perfect)	*will have studied* *will have spoken* (future perfect)
Perfect Progressive (in progress during and before that time)	*has/have been studying* *has/have been speaking* (present perfect progressive)	*had been studying* *had been speaking* (past perfect progressive)	*will have been studying* *will have been speaking* (future perfect progressive)

*Please note that there are many ways to express the future time frame in English. The chart above gives examples of the future using *will* only. See Focus 7 in Unit 2 for other ways.

EXERCISE 1

In his autobiography, *The Hunger of Memory*, Richard Rodriguez describes his struggles growing up in two different worlds: Mexican culture and the American educational system. The following passages are from his book. Underline the verbs of main clauses in each sentence. Then identify the time frame for each passage: present, past, or future. Circle words and phrases that help to signal the time frame. The first one has been done as an example.

► **EXAMPLE:** **1.** (a) (From an early age) I <u>knew</u> that my mother and father could read and write both Spanish and English. (b) I <u>had observed</u> my father making his way through what, I now suppose, must have been income tax forms. (c) (On other occasions) I <u>waited</u> apprehensively while my mother read onion-paper letters air-mailed from Mexico with news of a relative's illness or death. (d) For both my parents, however, reading <u>was</u> something done out of necessity and as quickly as possible.

   Time frame: *past*

2. (a) Lately, I have begun to wonder how the family will gather even three times a year when [my mother] is not there with her phone to unite us. (b) For the time being, however, she presides at the table. (c) She—not my father, who sits opposite her—says the grace before meals. (d) She busies herself throughout the meal.

3. (a) Someday . . . you will all grow up and all be very rich. (b) You'll have lots of money to buy me presents. (c) But I'll be a little old lady. (d) I won't have any teeth or hair. (e) So you'll have to buy me soft food and put a blue wig on my head. (f) And you'll buy me a big fur coat. (g) But you'll only be able to see my eyes.

4. (a) The third of four children, I had been preceded to a neighborhood Roman Catholic school by an older brother and sister. (b) But neither of them had revealed very much about their classroom experiences. (c) Each afternoon they returned, as they left in the morning, always together, speaking in Spanish, as they climbed the five steps of the porch.

5. (a) Visiting the East Coast or the gray capitals of Europe during the long months of winter, I often meet people at deluxe hotels who comment on my complexion. (b) (In such hotels it appears nowadays a mark of leisure and wealth to have a complexion like mine.) (c) Have I been skiing? In the Swiss Alps? (d) Have I just returned from a Caribbean vacation? (e) No. I say no softly but in a firm voice that intends to explain: My complexion is dark.

6. (a) [My nephew] smiles. (b) I wonder: Am I watching myself in this boy? (c) In this face where I can scarcely trace a family resemblance? (d) Have I

Note: The exercises following each focus box provide meaningful practice with the grammar item presented in that particular box. For a more complete discussion of how to use the exercises, see page xxv of this Teacher's Edition.

Exercise 1

If your Ss have attended a secondary school in the U.S., they may have read parts of Richard Rodriguez's book as it has been extensively anthologized. Introduce the exercise by telling them that Richard Rodriguez went to school from an early age in the U.S., but his parents spoke mostly Spanish at home.

Like many of the exercises in *Grammar Dimensions 4*, this one provides authentic texts in which Ss can identify and analyze grammatical structures. This exercise focuses Ss' attention on the various time frames represented by verbs.

Ss will find many of the authentic materials in *Grammar Dimensions 4* challenging. If appropriate for your context, tell them that working with these authentic materials should help them prepare for future academic reading and writing tasks. Many of the texts offer excellent opportunities for academic vocabulary development as well as work on grammatical structures.

SUGGESTION

This would make a good pair or group work exercise if done in class. Before starting, help Ss distinguish between main clauses and subordinate (dependent) clauses since Ss are asked to find main clause verbs. Have them highlight dependent markers such as *who, that, where*.

Note: The phrase *On other occasions* often suggests past time periods, as in the example, although this phrase does occur also with habitual present meaning.

ANSWER KEY

Exercise 1

2. (a) have begun (b) presides (c) says (d) busies
Time frame: present. Time signals: lately, for the time being

3. (a) will grow up (b) will have (c) will be (d) won't have (e) will have to (f) will buy (g) will be able to
Time frame: future. Time signals: someday

4. (a) had been preceded (b) had revealed (c) returned
Time frame: past. (Note: *each afternoon* is past in context but it is often used in habitual present contexts, too.)

5. (a) meet (b) appears (c) have been skiing (d) have returned (e) say
Time frame: present. Time signal: nowadays

6. (a) smiles (b) wonder (c) none (*can trace* is verb for the dependent clause) (d) have foreseen (e) lives (f) has spoken (g) is
Time frame: present.

7. (a) had known (b) did not prepare (c) feared (d) feared
Time frame: past. Time signal: before

foreseen his past? (e) He lives in a world of Little League and Pop Warner. (f) He has spoken English all his life. (g) His father is of German descent, a fourth-generation American.

7. (a) I had known a writer's loneliness before, working on my dissertation in the British Museum. (b) But that experience did not prepare me for the task of writing these pages where my own life is the subject. (c) Many days I feared I had stopped living by committing myself to remember the past. (d) I feared that my absorption with events in my past amounted to an immature refusal to live in the present.

EXERCISE 2

Exchange the paragraphs you wrote for the Opening Task with a classmate. After reading the paragraphs, write one or two questions that you have about your classmate's in-groups and ask him or her to respond to them. Then decide whether there is a consistent time frame used for each paragraph. If so, identify the time frames and underline any time indicators. Check with your classmate to see if he or she agrees with your analysis. Discuss any changes you think should be made.

FOCUS **2**

▶ Moment of Focus

Verbs can describe events that happen at a point in time (for example, *last night, three weeks ago*) or an event that lasts a period of time (for example, *all night long, three weeks*). We can call this the **moment of focus**.

Here are examples of **moment of focus** for each of the three time frames: present, past, and future.

Moment of Focus

	POINT OF TIME	PERIOD OF TIME
Present	(a) Her son is four years old **today**.	(b) Her son listens to music **for hours at a time**.
Past	(c) The tornado touched down **just before dawn**.	(d) **During the early nineteenth century**, millions of Italians immigrated to the United States.
Future	(e) **On Saturday morning**, they will leave for their trip.	(f) **In the decades to come**, computer technology will continue to change our lives.

Exercise 2

If you have collected your Ss' paragraphs and will be redistributing them for this exercise, you could pre-assign pairs based on abilities or content. As Ss work in pairs, monitor their progress and assist if needed.

EXPANSION

For more oral practice and opportunity for diagnosing problems, follow this exercise with further class discussion about the in-groups Ss learned about through reading their classmate's paragraphs. Focus on a particular time frame (past, present, future).

FOCUS 2

1. Ask Ss to read the focus box examples for homework. Before they do so, discuss the meanings of *explicit* and *implied*, terms used in the middle section. Use examples (g) and (h) for illustration.
2. In class, review the concepts *point in time* and *period of time*.
3. Put three more time indicators for each concept on the board in random order (e.g., *during the beginning of the semester, at noon*, etc.).
4. Ask Ss to create sentences by adding clauses to the time phrases. (*Lila, what did we study in this class during the beginning of the semester?*) Have them identify the moment of focus—point of time or period of time. The focus examples give simple tenses, but it's fine if Ss use perfect or progressive forms.

SUGGESTION

This would be a good opportunity to review time prepositions. Some typically express a point in time (*on*), others a period of time (*during*). For example (n), ask Ss to identify the changing points and periods of focus.

Workbook Ex. 1, p. 1; Ex. 2, p. 2.
Answers: TE p. 536.

ANSWER KEY

Exercise 2
Answers will vary since Ss are analyzing their classmates' paragraphs.

The time focus may be stated explicitly or it may be implied in the context.

	POINT OF TIME	PERIOD OF TIME
Present	(g) I can't talk **now**; I'm trying to study.	(h) Her son goes to a private school. (Implied: now)
Past	(i) **Until the end of the Cretaceous period**, dinosaurs roamed the earth.	(j) Dinosaurs evolved into two distinct groups. (Implied: During a period of time in the past)
Future	(k) **After you finish that chapter**, I'll give you a ride to school.	(l) The weather will continue to be warm and sunny. (Implied: for a future period of time)

In written and spoken communication, the moment of focus may be the same for a number of sentences or it may change from sentence to sentence:

SAME POINT OF FOCUS	CHANGING POINT/PERIOD OF FOCUS
(m) **When Kay first moved to Chicago** from Bangkok, she had a hard time adjusting to her new life. She didn't like the food at school. Other children seldom talked to her and she had no one to play with.	(n) Kay met Phil **the summer after she graduated from college**. They dated **for two years. When they got married**, it was on the same date, July 15th, that they had first met. **This year** they celebrated their fifteenth anniversary.

EXERCISE 3

The following oral interview passages are from Studs Terkel's book *The Great Divide*, in which Americans talk about their lives and thoughts on changes in America. In small groups, take turns identifying the moment or moments of focus for each passage. (1) Determine whether each moment of focus is (a) a point of time or (b) a period of time. (2) State whether moment of focus is (a) past or (b) present. (3) State whether the moment of focus is (a) explicitly stated or (b) implied.

1. (a) Right now, he's working the night shift at a twenty-four hour service station, with ten or twelve pumps. (b) He pumps the cash register. (c) His goals are very short-term, to get through the day

Verb Tenses in Written and Spoken Communication | **5**

Exercise 3

S U G G E S T I O N S

1. Because this exercise also draws from authentic materials, it would be helpful to give Ss some background context. You could introduce this exercise by saying that Studs Terkel is a well-known author and radio personality in Chicago, who has been interviewing people in the U.S. for many years about their hopes, dreams, and everyday lives and has published the interviews in books. *Working* is perhaps the best known of his books.

2. To help Ss focus on the verbs in the passages, ask them to highlight or underline the verbs as they work through this exercise. When Ss have completed their group work, ask a volunteer from each group to summarize their analysis of one or more of the passages.

Many English learners are confused about the rules of tense usage in writing. They often mistakenly believe that they cannot change verb tenses within paragraphs.

SUGGESTIONS

1. Begin by asking Ss to tell you what their understanding is of when you can change from one verb tense to another in writing. Most likely, some Ss will repeat the "rule" that one should not shift tense within a paragraph. Explain that this is not true, citing Exercise 1, Passage 2 as an example; it starts with a present perfect verb (*have begun*) and shifts to simple present verbs (*presides, says, busies*).

2. Read the first explanation sentences and ask individual Ss to read examples (a) and (b) aloud. Note that these examples show a tense shift but not a time-frame shift. Ask Ss to look again at Focus 1 on p. 2 and to review briefly the various tenses under each time frame.

3. Ask individual Ss to read aloud examples (c), (d), and (e). Point out how these examples show a time-frame shift. Summarize the explanation for (c)–(e) by asking Ss to point out the time marker in (d) that signals the time shift.

4. To reinforce the concepts illustrated by examples (c)–(e), ask Ss to write three sentences: (a) stating a course they took in the past (e.g., *Last year I took biology.*); (b) stating a course they are taking now (*This semester I am taking chemistry.*); (c) stating something *about* the course they are taking now (*Chemistry has been much harder for me than biology.*). The sentences in parentheses could be used to model this task.

Workbook Ex. 3, p. 3.
Answers: TE p. 536.

---

2. (a) Back in the early eighties when the draft-resistance movement began, many of us who were resisters first appeared in public. (b) We debated representatives of the Selective Service. (c) Frankly, we'd usually make them look pretty silly.

3. (a) In the last five years, there's been much more discussion of ethics on the campuses. (b) Remember, many of the young people of the sixties are the professors of today and they haven't changed their basic beliefs.

4. (a) A friend of mine, who is forty, had been a stock analyst on Wall Street fifteen years ago. (b) She married, had babies, raised her children, and now wanted to go back. (c) They said, "It doesn't matter what you did before."

5. (a) I would like to be chief of police. (b) I'll probably apply for jobs. (c) If nothing happens, I'll go to Cape Cod, build a house, and look at the waves.

6. (a) [My students] have learned how to take college tests. (b) They score high, especially in math. (c) They are quite verbal. (d) They give the impression of being bright. (d) Encouraged by their families, they come with the conviction that education is something they want, something they need. (e) But their definition of education is something else.

FOCUS **3**

Consistency in Tense Usage

Being consistent in tense means keeping verbs in the same time frame.

EXAMPLES	EXPLANATIONS
Present Time Frame (a) Self-help groups **have become** very common all over America. (b) These groups **assist** people with everything from weight problems to developing confidence.	The tense may change within a time frame. For example, the tense may change from present perfect to simple present, as in sentences (a) and (b), but the time frame remains in the present.

6   UNIT 1

| Past Time Frame

(c) Vera **graduated** from college last June.

Present Time Frame

(d) She now **works** for a law firm.

(e) She **has worked** there for a month.

Past Time Frame

(f) NOT: She **had worked** there for a month. | Sometimes, however, it is necessary to change from one time frame to another, for example from past to present. A time-frame shift is usually signaled by a time marker (for example, *last week, currently, next year.*)

In example (d) *now* signals a shift from past to present time. Example (e) shifts to the present perfect, but remains in the present time frame.

If (e) had a past-time reference, as in (f), the verb would be ungrammatical because there is no explicit time marker to signal a time-frame shift. Nor is there any reason to depart from the present time frame, which has been established in (d). |

EXERCISE 4

Each of the following passages has one sentence with an inappropriate verb tense. (1) Identify the time frame of the passage. (2) Identify the sentence that has the error and correct it. You may want to consult the time frame chart in Focus 1 for reference. Correction may involve changing the verb tense or using an explicit time marker to signal the shift in time frame. More than one verb tense can be correct in some cases.

▶ **EXAMPLE:** (a) I am taking this coat back to the store. (b) Someone had burned a hole in it. (c) One button is missing too.

Time Frame: *Present*
Error: (b)
Possible Corrections: *Someone **has burned** a hole in it.*
OR *Someone **had burned** a hole in it **before I bought it**.*

1. (a) My music class is really interesting. (b) We have been studying the history of American jazz and blues. (c) I will have been taking this course for six weeks.

2. (a) Sula's in-groups include her softball team. (b) She had belonged to this team for three years. (c) Last year she played second base, but this year she is playing first base.

3. (a) Japanese researchers had demonstrated that a human virus can cause rheumatoid arthritis in mice. (b) The virus, HTLV-1, is capable of inserting its own genetic information into the genes of its host. (c) It causes leukemia and two rare nerve disorders.

4. (a) Although Elvis Presley has been dead for decades, his legacy lives on. (b) For example, there was a computer game "In Search of the King." (c) And the Jockey Club registry lists the following thoroughbred horses: Elvis Pelvis, Triple Elvis, Elvis' Double, Jailhouse Rock, Blue Suede Shoes, and Love Me Tender.

Verb Tenses in Written and Spoken Communication | **7**

Exercise 4

This exercise could be done either as classwork or homework.

A N S W E R K E Y

Exercise 4

1. Error: (c) will have been taking   Correction: change to <u>have taken</u> or add a time reference such as <u>as of next week</u>

2. Error: (b) had belonged   Correction: change to <u>has belonged</u>

3. Error: (a) <u>had demonstrated</u>   Correction: change to <u>have demonstrated</u>

4. Error: (b) was   Correction: change to <u>is</u>

This focus box gives Ss specific reasons for time-frame shifts in writing and speaking.

SUGGESTION

Since authentic texts provide numerous examples of this kind of shifting, you could bring in a current newspaper or magazine article of high interest, duplicated in a handout or put on an overhead projector transparency.

1. Ask Ss to mark the time-frame shifts in several paragraphs.
2. Go over the focus examples and explanations.
3. Ask Ss which of the reasons for shifts apply to the article you looked at.

Workbook Ex. 4, pp. 3–4.
Answers: TE p. 536.

FOCUS **4**

Time-Frame Shifts in Written and Spoken Communication

USE

In written and spoken communication, time-frame shifts sometimes occur, such as from present to past. These shifts will often be necessary when you move from statements that introduce a topic to ones that provide further information about the topic. There may or may not be explicit markers to signal time shifts.

Below are some reasons why you might change from one time frame to another, with examples given for each.

EXAMPLES	TYPE OF TIME-FRAME SHIFT	REASON FOR SHIFT
(a) The city of Wichita Falls **has** an interesting history. It *became* a town over a hundred years ago when the railroad started a route through that area. The land that was to become Wichita Falls *was* a prize in a poker game.	Present → Past	To explain or support a general statement with past description or elaboration on a topic.
(b) Our school **is helping** to conserve natural resources. We *recycled* tons of aluminum last year. We *started* using paper cups instead of styrofoam ones.	Present → Past	To support a claim about the present with examples from the past.
(c) The social connections of Americans **have changed** during the last century. In the past, individuals *depended* on their extended families and neighborhoods for social activities. Today many Americans live far from their extended families and often do not know many of their neighbors.	Present → Past	To support a general statement about change by comparing present and past situations.
(d) Last year our city **witnessed** an increase in the number of people who volunteered time for organizations helping those in need. Donations to these organizations also **increased**. We *need* to continue this assistance to others less fortunate than we are.	Past → Present	To express a comment or an opinion about a topic.

NOTE: The simple present and present perfect tenses often "frame" topics. We frequently use them to introduce topics, to make topic shifts, and to end discussion of a topic. These tenses often express general statements that the speaker believes to be true at the present time.

8 UNIT 1

EXERCISE 5

Here are more passages from Studs Terkel's interviews in *The Great Divide*. Discuss the reasons for the verb tense shifts in each passage. Which passages change tenses within a time frame? Which passages change time frames? Which verb tenses are used to introduce topics in these passages?

▶ **EXAMPLES:** (a) Nothing is forever. (b) You always have to stay flexible, so you can change. (c) Five years ago, we were in the commodity business. (d) You bought and sold. (e) The customer was a farmer in Iowa. (f) Today he is a major New York Bank.

Reason for verb tense shift: The verb tense shifts from present to past to support a general statement about change by comparing present and past situations. This passage changes time frames. The present tense is used to introduce the topic.

1. (a) This kitchen is part of the old house. (b) My great-grandparents bought the place around 1895 or somewhere in there. (c) I'm fourth generation.

2. (a) I think the American dream for most people today is just survival. (b) When people came here from the old country, it was for a better life, not just survival. (c) I see that people that come over today seem to prosper faster than the ones who were born here. (d) Maybe it's because they know what it is to do without.

3. (a) The marketplace has changed in another way. (b) We have major class shifts in America. (c) The middle class, as traditionally known, is disappearing—being split. (d) You have a growing upper class.

4. (a) The role of the radio personality has changed greatly in the last decade. (b) Back then, we were given a pile of records and a few flip cards to read. (c) Keep the conversation to a minimum. (d) I once worked for a guy who had a stopwatch. (e) If you talked over eight seconds, you'd get in trouble. (f) Today, people want to hear what the individual has to say. (g) In the old days, we could squeeze in eight, ten records an hour. (h) Now I'm lucky if I get in two.

5. (a) I've been arrested five times. (b) I'm considered somewhat of a freak because I'm the police chief's wife. (c) I would march with my placard, hoping that the police wouldn't see me. (d) If I saw a policeman, I would hide behind my sign. (e) But they always saw me and they said, Aha, there she goes, the crazy wife of the police chief. (f) The police all hate my husband, so they think I'm exactly what he deserves.

SUGGESTION

Make a graphic organizer for this exercise. Create a chart with four columns labeled as follows: (1) Passage number; (2) Reason for shift; (3) Tense change? (4) Time-frame change? At the bottom of the chart, write: Verb tenses used to introduce topics: For columns 3 and 4, Ss need only put an X under the appropriate column(s). You could prepare this chart for individual handouts, give one chart to a pair or group of Ss, or put the chart on an overhead transparency to work with the class as a whole.

Graphic organizers have many advantages: (1) They help Ss work on tasks with multiple parts; (2) They provide clear visual summaries for Ss (and for you!) when they are completed; (3) They make it easier for you to check student comprehension of a task; (4) Ss tend to be on task more, both individually and in groups, if they have to write down what they have discussed.

UNIT GOAL REVIEW

Ask Ss to look at the goals on the opening page of the unit again. Help them understand how much they have accomplished in each area.

ANSWER KEY

Exercise 5

1. Time-frame shift: Present (a) to past (b) Reason: to give background information.
2. Time-frame shift: Present (a) to past (b) Reason: to support a statement about change by comparing past and present situations.
3. Tense shift within present time frame: Present perfect (a) to present (b), (c) and (d) Reason: to support a general statement expressing change over time with details about the present situation. (You may also want to note the aspectual shift to progressive in (c), indicating an event in progress.)
4. Time-frame shift: Present (tense = present perfect) (a) to past (b)–(d) Reason: to support a statement about change by comparing past and present situations.
5. Tense shift: Present perfect tense (a) to present (b) Reason: to state a present situation that is the result of recent past events./Time-frame shift: Present (b) to past (c)–(e) Reason: To explain a general statement in the present with elaboration about past events.

Tenses used to introduce topics: Present: 1, 2 / Present perfect: 3, 4, 5

USE YOUR ENGLISH

Note: The activities on these "purple pages" at the end of each unit contain communicative activities designed to apply what Ss have learned and help them practice communication and grammar at the same time. For a more complete discussion of the Use Your English activities, see page xxvi of this Teacher's Edition.

Activity 1

Play textbook audio. The tapescript for this listening appears on p. 563 of this book.

Note: Ss with advanced level English proficiency may vary in their listening comprehension skills. If necessary, play the passage more than twice for Ss to get the content and identify verbs.

If possible, have a copy of the *Grammar Dimensions 4* audiotape on reserve in a media lab for Ss who need additional time and practice with listening.

EXPANSION

Bring in another autobiographical audiotape for Ss to listen to and note time-frame shifts.

Workbook Ex. 5, p. 5; Ex. 6, p. 7; Ex. 7, p. 8. Answers: TE p. 536.

Activity 2

VARIATION

1. Select several comic strips with various verb tenses.
2. Make copies of the originals.
3. White out some of the dialogue bubbles.
4. With Ss in small groups, give each group a comic and ask them to write in missing dialogue.
5. Have them analyze the time frames and tense shifts.
6. If time permits, compare their dialogues with the original ones.

Use Your English

ACTIVITY 1: LISTENING / SPEAKING

You will hear two passages from the autobiography *I, Rigoberta Menchu*. Rigoberta Menchu is a young Guatemalan peasant woman who won the Nobel Peace Prize in 1992 for her work to ensure human rights and justice for Indian communities in Guatemala. These passages describe her peasant life in Guatemala. In each passage, there is one or more sentences that shift to a different time frame from the main time frame of the passage (for example, from the past to the present).

STEP 1 Listen to each passage once for content and note the main time frame: present, past, or future.

STEP 2 Listen to each passage again and write down the verbs that represent time-frame shifts and as much of the sentences they are in as you can recall.

STEP 3 Explain the reason for each time frame shift, with reference to Focus 4. Here is some vocabulary from the passage that will be helpful to know while listening:

finca—a Guatemalan farm or plantation where the Indian peasants are contracted to work by the landowners. Crops such as coffee, cotton and sugar are grown.

lorry—a truck that transports people from their villages to the *finca*

altiplano—the mountains

ACTIVITY 2: READING

Scan some comic strips in the newspaper to find ones that use a variety of verb tenses. In groups, discuss what the time frames are for each, and why tense changes occur. As a variation of this activity, cover up or blacken the verbs in comic strips. Then give another classmate the base forms of the verbs (the verb that comes after *to* in *to* + verb) and see if she or he fills in the same tenses as the original. Discuss any differences in choices.

ACTIVITY 3: READING

Select several paragraphs of something you find interesting from a textbook (for example, history, literature, or psychology) or some other book. Analyze the verb tense use in the paragraphs. What types of verb tense shifts or time-frame shifts occur? Analyze the reasons for tense or time-frame shifts.

ACTIVITY 4: READING

Look at a piece of writing you or a classmate has done recently, such as an essay or other type of paper. Analyze the types of verb tense shifts you see. Do you think verb tenses are used appropriately?

ACTIVITY 5: SPEAKING/WRITING

Prepare a brief talk or write an essay in which you compare one of the in-groups you belonged to when you were young that you no longer belong to with one that you belong to now. For example, you could compare two organizations, two schools, two neighborhoods, or two groups of friends.

Activity 3
VARIATIONS
1. Ss could also choose paragraphs from newspapers, magazines, or other books.
2. Ss could work in pairs with texts they bring to class.

Activity 4
Peer response activities are often most useful with focused and specific tasks like this one.

A worksheet will help guide Ss. This task could be set up with a series of directives and questions:
(1) Find examples of verb tense shifts. Write the verbs here. State what tense each is. [leave space]
(2) Are the time frames the same or different?
(3) What is the reason for the tense shift? If the time frame shifted, why?

Activity 5
Either speaking or writing will provide an opportunity for you to diagnose student progress.

The test for this unit can be found on p. 484. The answers are on p. 485.

Unit 2

UNIT OVERVIEW

Unit 2 reviews the meanings and uses of the simple, progressive and perfect tenses, provides guided practice in selecting appropriate forms in context, and gives students (Ss) opportunities for using verb tenses appropriately in communicative contexts.

UNIT GOALS

Review the goals listed on this page so Ss understand what they should be able to know by the end of the unit.

OPENING TASK

Note: The **Opening Task** allows Ss to use the target structures and allows teachers to notice what kinds of help they may need. For a more complete discussion of the Opening Task, see page xxiii of this Teacher's Edition.

This task theme expands the concept of in-groups from Unit 1 to consider those who feel like outsiders when joining a new group. This task should supplement the writing activity in Unit 1, providing more samples of your Ss' control of verb tenses in communicative contexts.

U N I T 2

VERBS

Aspect and Time Frames

UNIT GOALS:
- To use simple verb tenses correctly
- To use progressive verb forms correctly
- To use perfect verb forms correctly
- To understand verb tense meanings and uses in present, past, and future time frames

▶ O P E N I N G   T A S K
Insiders and Outsiders

In Unit 1, the Opening Task asked you to consider the groups to which you belong. At times the process of joining a new group can be uncomfortable. Most of us have experienced the sense of not belonging, of feeling like an outsider, when first joining a new group.

STEP 1   Read the two passages below on the theme of being an "outsider."

The first passage describes the sense of not belonging and confusion that many students experience when entering college, especially when they find themselves in large lecture classes.

> People are taking notes and you are taking notes. You are taking notes on a lecture you don't understand. You get a phrase, a sentence, then the next loses you. It's as though you're hearing a conversation in a crowd or from another room—out of phase, muted. The man on the stage concludes his lecture and everyone rustles and you close your notebook and prepare to leave. You feel a little strange. Maybe tomorrow this stuff will clear up. Maybe by tomorrow this will be easier. But by the time you're in the hallway, you don't think it will be easier at all.

> From Mike Rose, *Lives on the Boundary*. New York: Penguin Books, 1990.

In the next passage, the fictional character Lindo Jong feels like an outsider when joining a new family through marriage. Upon marrying Tuan-Yu, she has moved in with his family and receives a cool reception from her mother-in-law, Huang Taitai:

> No big celebration was held when I arrived. Huang Taitai didn't have red banners greeting me in the fancy room on the first floor. Tuan-yu was not there to greet me. Instead, Huang Taitai hurried me upstairs to the second floor and into the kitchen, which was a place where family children didn't usually go. This was a place for cooks and servants. So I knew my standing.

> That first day, I stood in my best padded dress at the low wooden table and began to chop vegetables. I could not keep my hands steady. I missed my family and my stomach felt bad, knowing I had finally arrived where my life said I belonged.

STEP 2   For ten minutes, write your reaction to the passages. You could discuss one of the passages, or you might want to describe briefly a situation from your own experience or from something you have read that related to the theme of being an outsider. In small groups, take turns reading your reactions aloud.

SETTING UP THE TASK

Have Ss discuss situations in which people might feel like outsiders.

CONDUCTING THE TASK

Step 1

Ss can read the passages silently, out loud, or follow along as you read out loud.

Step 2

As a pre-writing task, have Ss compare their own experiences in school with the first passage. This will help you assess Ss' verb tense use in speech. Your questions could prompt particular verb tense use. For example:
1. Elicit progressive forms by asking Ss what the student in the first passage is describing.
2. Elicit future perfect, a tense not likely to be used in the in-class writing, in questions like "*What do you think will have happened to the student narrating the first passage by the end of the semester? Do you think he or she will have adjusted better to college life?*"

VARIATION

Have Ss discuss only rather than write if your course is more focused on speaking skills.

EXPANSION

The film *The Joy Luck Club* has a number of scenes in which someone is an "outsider" in a group (e.g., one in which an Anglo-American boyfriend goes to his Chinese-American girlfriend's home for dinner). Show a brief segment from *The Joy Luck Club* that reflects the "insider and outsider" theme for Ss to discuss. Note their uses of verb tenses in discussion.

FOCUS 1

S U G G E S T I O N S

1. Ask Ss to read the uses and example sentences for homework. Since this will be a review for advanced Ss, they should be familiar with most of the uses.

2. Explain that the last category, establishing the time frame and the moment of focus, simply means that the speaker or writer uses a particular verb tense to tell a listener or reader whether an event is past, present or future and whether it happened at a point of time (*Jean went to church on Sunday*) or a period of time (*Jean lived in Atlanta for many years.*); see p. 3 and pp. 4–5 of Unit 1 for a review of time frames and moment of focus.

3. Review simple tense uses in context by showing Ss a current newspaper or magazine article on a transparency or handout with selected sentences underlined.

▶ **Review of Simple Tenses**

Simple tenses include the simple present, simple past, and simple future. They have the following uses:

TIME FRAME	EXAMPLES	USE
Present	(a) Our in-groups **help** to define our values.	To express general ideas, relationships, and truths
Past	(b) Immigrants to America in the mid-nineteenth century **included** large numbers of Chinese.	
Future	(c) Families **will** always **be** important to most of us.	
Present	(d) Our family **visits** my grandparents after church every Sunday.	To describe habitual actions
Past	(e) Almost every year we **celebrated** my great aunt's birthday with a family picnic.	
Future	(f) The club **will collect** dues once a month.	
Present	(g) Kay **thinks** she has chosen the right profession.	To describe mental perceptions or emotions
Past	(h) People once **believed** the earth was flat.	
Future	(i) You **will love** our new puppy.	
Present	(j) Phil **has** three brothers.	To express possession or personal relationships
Past	(k) We **owned** a station wagon, but we traded it in for a compact car.	
Future	(l) By next month, Andrea **will have** a complete set of encyclopedias.	
Present	(m) The media **reports** that new evidence has been presented in the trial.	To establish the time frame and the moment of focus
Past	(n) When the United States **passed** the Chinese Exclusion Act in 1882, 100,000 Chinese were living in the United States.	
Future	(o) Phyllis **will call** you Thursday morning; I hope you will not have left for Omaha by then.	

EXERCISE 1

The following statements are from an Internet file called "Frequently Asked Questions" (FAQ). Each statement describes a contemporary myth or strange story. The news group that maintains the FAQ site tries to determine whether the statement is true or false.

For each statement: (1) identify the tense of the verbs in italics; (2) then state what use or uses each verb expresses; (3) discuss whether you think the statements are true or not. (Answers are given on page A-16.)

▶ **EXAMPLE:** The bubbles in plastic wrap *contain* a cheap but toxic gas.

        Tense: *present*   Use: *To describe a general truth*
                                         To express possession

        (Not true)

1. It *is* acceptable to send coconuts through the mail without wrapping them.
2. A mime *had* a heart attack during his performance. People *thought* it was part of his act. He *died*.
3. A penny falling from the top of the Empire State Building *will embed* itself in the pavement.
4. Fast-food shakes that aren't marked "dairy" *have* no milk in them.
5. Albert Einstein *did* poorly in school.
6. Green M & M candies *are* an aphrodisiac.*
7. Contact lenses *will stick* to your eyeballs if you weld something while wearing them.
8. If mold grows on a Twinkie,** the Twinkie *digests* it.

Excerpted from "The Internet's Believe It or Not," *Harper's Magazine,* October 1994.

EXERCISE 2

Go back to Exercises 1 and 3 on pp. 3 and 5 in Unit 1. Find an example of a verb with each of the following uses. Write down your choices and prepare to discuss them in class.

▶ **EXAMPLE:** Waited (from the Examples, Exercise 1)
             past habitual action.

1. past habitual action
2. present habitual action
3. past perception
4. future possession
5. past moment of focus

*An *aphrodisiac* is a drug or food which increases sexual desire.
**A *Twinkie* is a very sweet pastry; it is often referred to as "junk food."

Exercise 1

Because many of the claims in this exercise are actually not true, remind Ss that "to express a general truth" does *not* mean the statement is necessarily true but rather that the speaker claims or believes it is.

EXPANSION

Have Ss check the FAQ website for more contemporary myths and discuss a few of their findings.

Exercise 2

Exercise 1 in Unit 1 has sentences from Richard Rodriguez's autobiography *Hunger of Memory.* Exercise 3 has sentences from Studs Terkel's interviews in *The Great Divide.* If you think Ss would enjoy other sources, you could give them current events texts or pages from other textbooks you use in class, such as a reader, and ask them to find examples of the uses stated in 1–5.

Workbook Ex. 1, p. 10.
Answers: TE p. 537.

ANSWER KEY

Exercise 1

1. *Tense:* present. *Use:* To express a general idea. 2. *Tense:* past. *Use:* To establish time frame and moment of focus. 3. *Tense:* future. *Use:* To express a general truth.
4. *Tense:* present. *Use:* To express possession. 5. *Tense:* past. *Use:* To express time frame and moment of focus. 6. *Tense:* present. *Use:* To express a relationship (m & m's belong to the class "aphrodisiac"); to express a general truth (see note above). 7. *Tense:* future. *Use:* To express a general truth. 8. *Tense:* present. *Use:* To express a general.

Exercise 2

Answers will vary. Examples:
1. *Past habitual action:* returned, Ex.1, 4a; debated, Ex. 3, 2b 2. *Present habitual action:* meet, Ex. 1, 5a; watch, Ex. 3, 2c 3. *Past perception:* knew, Ex. 1,1a; feared, Ex. 1, 7c; 4. *Future possession:* have, Ex. 1, 3b; have, Ex. 1, 3d 5. *Past moment of focus:* began, Ex. 3, 2a; married, Ex. 3, 4b

Note: In some cases a sentence could express more than one use. For example, Ss might perceive (p) as repeated action. If so, make sure they also understand how it also expresses a use they did not choose.

It is important that Ss become comfortable with multiple uses and meanings of grammatical structures; they need to understand that in many cases more than one answer or analysis is possible. Realizing that meaning and uses overlap will help prevent confusion and frustration for both the Ss and you as you work through the focus boxes and exercises.

V A R I A T I O N

To make Focus 2 more of an activity-based review and diagnostic:

1. Photocopy the focus box, cut the second and third example sentences under each use category into strips [(b) and (c) for the first use, (e) and (f) for the second, etc.]. Distribute the strips evenly among small groups of students.

2. Write the six uses listed in column 2 on the board in horizontal columns. Write and briefly explain one example for each—(a) for the first use, (d) for the second, etc.

3. Have groups decide uses of the verbs in their sentences and write the sentence letters on the board under the appropriate category [e.g., (h) under "to express repeated actions"].

4. When groups finish, have them check answers with the chart on p. 16 and discuss any differences.

▶ **R**eview of Progressive Verbs

Progressive verbs include a form of *be* + a present participle (verb + -*ing*).

EXAMPLES		USES
(a)	When Phil gets home from work, Andrea **is** often **studying.**	To describe actions already in progress at the moment of focus
(b)	**I was driving** to the restaurant when I saw the meteor shower.	
(c)	She **will be working** the night shift when I get home.	
(d)	Eric usually goes out to eat on Fridays. This Friday, however, he **is cooking** at home.	To describe actions at the moment of focus in contrast to habitual actions
(e)	The robins usually took up residence every spring in our old apple trees. One summer, though, they **were building** nests in some of the taller trees.	
(f)	Most winters we spend our Christmas vacation at home. But this year we **will be going** to Vermont.	
(g)	She **is** constantly **reminding** me to water the plants.	To express repeated actions
(h)	As a young boy, my brother **was** always **getting** into trouble.	
(i)	Our math teacher **will be checking** our assignments each morning when class starts.	
(j)	Kendra works in the principal's office, but she **is helping** the new school nurse this week.	To describe temporary situations in contrast to permanent states
(k)	My father lived in Chile most of his life, except for two years when he **was living** in Argentina.	
(l)	We'll live in a new home after the winter. Until then, we**'ll be renting** an apartment in the city.	
(m)	The final paper is due soon. I**'m finishing** it as fast as I can.	To describe periods of time in contrast to points of time
(n)	Yesterday the students discussed the projects they **were working** on this semester.	
(o)	When they finish their projects, they **will be evaluating** each others' work for several days.	
(p)	Sara **is doing** volunteer work for the homeless this summer.	To express uncompleted actions
(q)	When I last saw Ali, he **was** still **planting** his vegetable garden.	
(r)	I bet the baby **will** still be **sleeping** when we get home.	

16 UNIT 2

EXERCISE 3

Underline the progressive verbs in the passage below. State what additional information the progressive aspect expresses for each verb. (Refer to the uses presented in Focus 2.)

▶ **EXAMPLE:** (am sitting)

to describe action in progress at the moment of focus

(a) I am sitting under a sycamore by Tinker Creek. (b) I am really here, alive on the intricate earth under trees . . . (c) What else is going on right this minute while ground water creeps under my feet? (d) The galaxy is careening in a slow, muffled widening. (e) If a million solar systems are born every hour, then surely hundreds burst into being as I shift my weight to the other elbow. (f) The sun's surface is now exploding; other stars implode and vanish, heavy and black, out of sight. (g) Meteorites are arcing to earth invisibly all day long. (h) On the planet the winds are blowing: the polar easterlies, the westerlies, the northeast and southeast trades.

From Annie Dillard, *Pilgrim at Tinker Creek*. New York: Bantam, 1974.

EXERCISE 4

In the following passage, a journalist describes virtual reality (VR) and her experience with it at Cyberthon, a twenty-four-hour marathon computer demonstration. Underline the progressive verbs. Then discuss why the writer uses them in the first paragraph and why she shifts from simple past tense verbs to past progressive verbs in the second and third paragraphs.

(1) Some architects are using VR (also called "cyberspace," a term coined by writer William Gibson, who dreamed up VR in his novel *Neuromance*) to show clients what a structure will look like before it's built. (2) Doctors are using it to practice surgery without making a single cut. (3) And, of course, NASA and the Defense Department (which hope to replace jet pilots with VR screens) have been following—and funding—VR since its inception.

(4) I waited in line impatiently for my turn at the Cyberhood, which focuses your eyes on a computer-generated 3-D image; you manipulate yourself, or "fly," by gripping a ball to the left of the machine. (5) The ball, Sense8* President Eric Gullichsen kept repeating to the users, is like your head; think of it as your head. (6) The trouble with that notion is that most people don't yank, twist, twirl, and push their heads, so most people were having trouble with the image: They were flipping it upside down, pulling their "head" back so far that the image became tiny and distant, hitting the floor with their wide-open eyeballs.

*Sense8 is a virtual reality company.

Verbs: Aspect and Time Frames　**17**

This would make a good homework exercise. You could write answers on a transparency for Ss to check their responses. To check individual progress, have Ss write answers on a separate piece of paper to turn in.

Note items that many Ss had incorrect for later review.

(7) The man in front of me, a shortish, plump guy in a blue shirt and jeans, was muttering to himself as he yanked at his "head." Finally he gave in and straightened up. (8) He turned out to be Robin Williams,** but no one paid much attention in this crowd — the machines were the celebrities.

EXERCISE 5

Decide whether a simple tense or progressive tense is appropriate for each blank and give the correct form of the verb in parentheses. The first one has been done for you.

1. Andre (a) (come) _comes_____ from Brazil and (b) (be) _____ a native speaker of Portuguese. Currently he (c) (study) _____ English at the University of Colorado. He (d) (take) _____ two courses: composition and American culture.

2. One of my most important in-groups (a) (be) _____ my church group. Right now we (b) (provide) _____ lunches for homeless people in the city park. Also, some of us (c) (tutor) _____ junior high students in math and English for the summer. Others in my group (d) (spend) _____ part of the summer doing volunteer work at senior citizen centers. We all (e) (feel) _____ that we (f) (gain) _____ a great deal ourselves by participating in these activities.

3. Next summer our family (a) (have) _____ a reunion during the July 4th holiday weekend. My uncle from Finland (b) (try) _____ to come, but he (c) (start) _____ a new business this year so it (d) (be) _____ difficult for him to get away. Another uncle (e) (spend) _____ the whole summer with us. He (f) (work) _____ at my mother's travel agency from June through August.

4. For many immigrants to the United States, their ethnic associations (a) (remain) _____ important in-groups long after they have left their home countries. Even while they (b) (learn) _____ a new language, many (c) (look to) _____ speakers of their native language as an in-group that (d) ((understand) _____ their struggles to adapt to a new way of life.

**A well-known American comedian and actor.

ANSWER KEY

Exercise 5
More than one answer is possible for some.
1. (a) comes   (b) is   (c) is studying   (d) is taking   2. (a) is   (b) are providing (provide)   (c) are tutoring (tutor)   (d) are spending   (e) feel   (f) are gaining (gain)   3. (a) is having   (b) is trying   (c) is starting   (d) is   (e) is spending   (f) is working   4. (a) remain   (b) are learning   (c) look to   (d) understands

EXERCISE 6

Ask another classmate to tell you five things he or she does now as a result of in-group associations. Write a sentence for each, using present-time reference verbs, and report one or two of the ones you find most interesting to the rest of the class.

▶ **EXAMPLE:** *Martin plays the saxophone with a jazz band.*
As a student at Northwestern, he is majoring in environmental sciences.

Verbs: Aspect and Time Frames **19**

V A R I A T I O N

1. Ask each student to write the five things he or she finds out about a classmate on a piece of paper to turn in.
2. Make a handout listing one or two phrases describing each student without including names of Ss (e.g., "plays the saxophone with a jazz band").
3. Give the handout to Ss during the next class. Write on the board: "Who is it?" Have Ss take turns guessing who matches the descriptions (e.g., "I think Thalia plays the saxophone."). After one wrong guess, ask the person described to reveal his/her identity.

Workbook Ex. 2, pp. 11–12.
Answers: TE p. 537.

ANSWER KEY

Exercise 6
Answers will vary.

The uses of perfect verbs are difficult for ESL learners. Advanced learners will be familiar with perfect verbs, but they will generally still have problems with their use in communicative situations. They may also have trouble remembering to put the -ed on the end of past participles.

To illustrate the contrasts in this focus box:

1. Draw a timeline on which you can write dates:

    _X_____X_____X__
    40 yrs ago   1996   Now

2. Mark event and draw lines with arrows showing a time span:

    ___X_____X_____

    finished the chapter   soccer game
                            started

▶ **R**eview of Perfective Verbs

Perfect verbs are formed by *have (has, have, had, will have)* + a past participle (verb -ed or irregular form).

EXAMPLES		USES
(a) *To date,* Mark **has taken** five days off from work for vacation. **(b)** *When I last spoke to my mother,* she **had sent** me a letter, so she didn't want to repeat her news over the phone. **(c)** *By this time tomorrow,* even more acres of the rain forest **will have been destroyed.**		To describe events that happen before the moment of focus. The time phrases and clauses in italics signal the moment of focus.
Continuing to present Present Perfect **(d)** My parents **have lived** in their house for forty years; this year they are remodeling the kitchen.	**Completed Simple Past** **(e)** My grandparents **lived** in their house on Tower Avenue until 1996.	To describe events that started in the past and continue to be true in the present, in contrast with completed events (which are related to the simple past).
(f) I **have finished** that chapter, so I can help you answer the questions. (My finishing the chapter is relevant to my ability to help now.) **(g)** I **had finished** the chapter before the soccer match started, so I was able to watch the whole match. (My finishing the chapter is relevant to having watched the match.) **(i)** I **will have taken** my last exam on the day you arrive here. (My completion of exams is relevant to your arrival date.)	**Contrast with: Simple Past** **(h)** I **finished** the chapter. Then I played video games. (Finishing the chapter and playing games are related only sequentially.)	To describe events that the speaker believes are relevant to the moment of focus. In (f), the moment of focus is the present; in (g), it is the past. (f) and (g) contrast with (h), which has a simple past verb.

EXERCISE 7

Underline the present perfect and past perfect verbs in the following passages. Explain what information is expressed by the perfective aspect for these verbs. What uses listed in Focus 3 are expressed? (A perfect verb can convey more than one kind of information.) The first has been done as an example.

▶ **EXAMPLE:** 1. (d) had seen, heard, learned—past perfect

Information: *describe events that happen before the moment of focus (Fatt Hing at the age of nineteen) and that are relevant to the moment of focus.*

1. (a) By 1851, in a matter of three years, there were 25,000 Chinese in California. (b) Fatt Hing was one of these 25,000. (c) His story is typical of the pioneer Chinese, many who came with him and many who came after him. (d) As a lad of nineteen, Fatt Hing had already seen and heard and learned more about the world than most of the men in his village, who had seldom set foot beyond the nearest town square. (e) For Fatt Hing was a fish peddler who went frequently from Toishan to Kwanghai on the coast to buy his fish to sell at the market. (f) Down by the wharves, where the fishing boats came in, Fatt Hing had often seen foreign ships with their sails fluttering in the wind. (g) He had seen hairy white men on the decks, and he had often wondered and dreamed about the land they came from.

2. (a) The dog has got more fun out of Man than Man has got out of the dog, for the clearly demonstrable reason that Man is the more laughable of the two animals. (b) The dog has long been bemused by the singular activities and the curious practices of men, cocking his head inquiringly to one side, intently watching and listening to the strangest goings-on in the world. (c) He has seen men sing together and fight one another in the same evening. (d) He has watched them go to bed when it is time to get up, and get up when it is time to go to bed. (e) He has observed them destroying the soil in vast areas, and nurturing it in small patches. (f) He has stood by while men built strong and solid houses for rest and quiet, and then filled them with lights and bells and machinery.

From James Thurber, *Thurber's Dogs, A Collection of the Master's Dogs, Written and Drawn, Real and Imaginary, Living and Long Ago.* New York: Simon and Schuster, 1955.

Exercise 7

To help Ss understand the meaning of events happening before the moment of focus, prepare a graphic organizer with two columns. In the first column, have Ss list the perfect verbs (e.g., had seen, had heard); in the second column have them write the moment of focus. They should see that the moment of focus is the same for all uses in these passages: in (1) it is Fatt Hing at the age of nineteen; in (2) it is the present moment from which Thurber is writing.

SUGGESTION

Because the prose is often challenging in authentic texts, background information can help to engage Ss in the text before they start the exercise. For additional background information on the second passage, tell Ss that James Thurber is a famous American humorist and an artist.

If possible, bring one of his books with illustrations to show the class. Or ask a volunteer to look up information about him on the Internet and report back to the class.

ANSWER KEY

Exercise 7

1. (d) had already seen . . . heard and learned . . . had . . . set foot **(e)** had . . . seen **(f)** had seen **(g)** had . . . wondered . . . dreamed
Past perfect describes events that happened before the moment of focus.

2. (a) has got . . . has got **(b)** has . . . been bemused **(c)** has seen **(d)** has watched **(e)** has observed **(f)** has stood by
Present perfect describes events that happened before the moment of focus.

Exercise 8

As with Exercise 5, this would make a good homework exercise. If your Ss are unfamiliar with the state of Texas and its weather, tell them that many parts of Texas typically have extremely hot weather in the summer and early fall.

Exercise 9

This exercise could be assigned for homework or done in small groups.

EXERCISE 8

Decide whether a simple form (present, past) or present perfect should be used for each verb in parentheses. The first has been done for you.

The Hotter'n Hell Hundred

(1) Near the Texas-Oklahoma border, where the wind never (seem) _____seems_____ to stop, where the sun (broil) _____ the blacktop and (sap) _____ the strength, the cyclists (come) _____ each year. (2) They (come) _____ to Wichita Falls, Texas, by the thousands to ride in what (become) _____ the largest one-hundred-mile bicycle race in the world—the Hotter'n Hell Hundred. (3) The race (take) _____ place on Labor Day weekend at the beginning of September, when temperatures regularly (soar) _____ past 100 degrees.

(4) The oddity of this race is that, with each passing year, it (become) _____ more and more a symbol of Wichita Falls, a city that, until recently, (be, hardly) _____ a cycling bastion. (5) In days past, the sight of a bicyclist (cause) _____ heads to turn in the pickup truck. (6) Tornadoes (be) _____ once more numerous than bicyclists in Wichita Falls.

(7) The Hotter'n Hell Hundred (start) _____ in 1982 when a postal worker (suggest) _____ a one-hundred-mile bike ride in 100-degree heat to celebrate Wichita Falls' one-hundredth birthday. (8) Today, the race (command) _____ the attention of almost the whole city as race weekend (approach) _____ .

Adapted with permission from J. Michael Kennedy, "It's the Hottest Little Ol' Race in Texas," *Los Angeles Times*, September 2, 1991.

EXERCISE 9

Decide whether a simple future or future perfect verb should be used for each verb in parentheses. The first one has been done for you.

(1) Our class has been discussing which in-groups we think (be) _____will_____ or (be, not) _____ important to us ten years from now. (2) Hua says she knows her family (remain) _____ an

22 | UNIT 2

ANSWER KEY

Exercise 8

(1) seems, broils, saps, come **(2)** come, has become **(3)** takes, soar **(4)** has become, has hardly been **(5)** caused **(6)** were **(7)** started, suggested **(8)** commands, approaches

Exercise 9

(1) will; will not be **(2)** will remain **(3)** will have ended **(4)** will have been **(5)** will have (or will have had, if meaning before that time) **(6)** will represent **(7)** will have become; will be

important in-group forever. (3) However, she thinks her associations with some campus groups, such as the French Club, (end) _____ by the time she graduates. (4) Kazuhiko thinks that he (be) _____ married for several years by that time. (5) He hopes he (have) _____ a few children of his own. (6) He believes his family (represent) _____ his most important in-group in the future. (7) Jose predicts that he (become) _____ a famous physicist by that time and that one of his important in-groups (be) _____ other Nobel Prize winners.

EXERCISE 10

With a partner, take the roles of Person A and Person B below. Each person should write five questions to ask the other person in an interview, based on the biodata information given. In your questions, use present, past, and future perfect verb forms. Use them in your responses when appropriate. Here are some patterns that may be useful for your questions:

Have you ever (done X)?
Had you (done X) before (Y)?
Do you think you will have (done X) before (Y)?

▶ **EXAMPLE:** Person A: *So you've taken piano lessons. Have you ever studied any other musical instruments?*

Person B: *Actually, yes. Before I took piano lessons, I had studied the violin for a year, but my playing was terrible!*

Person B: *I see you've lived in two other countries besides the United States. Which one did you live in first, and how long did you live in each one?*

Person A: *Well, I had lived in Peru for fifteen years before I moved to Madrid. I lived in Madrid for a little over three years.*

PERSON A	PERSON B
was on the track team in high school	took piano lessons as a child
lived in Peru	grew up in Korea
lived in Madrid	moved to the United States in 1992
traveled in Egypt and Africa	attended the University of Florida
parents live in New Mexico	attended Penn State
enrolled at the University of Texas	currently lives in New York
belongs to a health club	likes to watch basketball
loves old movies	loves to go to music concerts
is a sophomore	works at a television station
will graduate from college in three years	plans to move to Tokyo
plans to do a bicycle tour of Vietnam	will get a degree in broadcast journalism

Verbs: Aspect and Time Frames | **23**

Exercise 10

This exercise gives Ss an opportunity for communicative practice of perfect verbs.

SUGGESTIONS

1. When Ss have finished, discuss the fact that native speakers of English often substitute simple past forms for present perfect and past perfect ones in informal speech. For example, Person A in the example might say *"I lived in Peru for fifteen years before I moved to Madrid."*

2. Point out that this doesn't mean native English speakers *never* use present or past perfect forms in conversation, or that the perfect forms are too formal for speech, but that there is variation between simple past and perfect forms in some contexts.

3. Explain that there are some contexts where present perfect forms *are* needed and where simple past forms would sound odd to most native English speakers. However, keep in mind that what you tell Ss will depend on their proficiency levels. Too much information at one time may only confuse them!

Workbook Ex. 3, p. 12; Ex. 4, p. 14; Ex. 5, p. 15.
Answers: TE p. 537.

As with previous focus boxes, it would be helpful to draw a timeline to illustrate the contrasts between action completed or uncompleted at a present, past or future moment. See the suggestions for Focus 3 on p. 20.

FOCUS **4**

▶ Review of Perfect Progressive Verbs

USE

Perfect progressive verbs include present perfect progressive, past perfect progressive, and future perfect progressive. They are formed by *have (has, have, had, will have)* + *been* + a past participle (verb + *-ing*).

EXAMPLES		
Incomplete: Progressive	Complete: Nonprogressive	**USE**
(a) The jurors **have been discussing** the evidence. They still haven't reported their verdict.	(b) The jurors **have discussed** the evidence for a week. They are ready to report their verdict.	To express actions that have not been completed at the moment of focus, in contrast to actions that have been completed.
(c) Tam **had been listening** to the news when the explosion occurred.	(d) Tam **had listened** to the news before she left for work.	
(e) Jochen **will have been working** on his Master's degree for two years at the end of this month. He expects to finish in six months.	(f) Jochen **will have worked** at the bank for five years when he leaves for his new job in Quebec.	

Exercise 11

This exercise gives Ss an opportunity to choose appropriate verbs for contexts expressing events that have been completed at a specific time (simple past) and ones with events starting in the past and continuing to the present (perfective aspect).

EXERCISE 11

For each blank below, choose a simple past, present perfect, or present perfect progressive verb. The first one has been done for you.

(1) Alfredo (join) _____joined_____ the Friends of the Theater in his community five years ago and (be) _____ an active participant in this group ever since. (2) It (remain) _____ one of his favorite spare time activities even though he (stop) _____ trying out for roles in the plays last year because he (be) _____ too busy. (3) As a member, he (help) _____ promote the plays. (4) At times, he (look for) _____ costumes for the actors. (5) For last month's play, he (work) _____ with the props crew to get furniture and other props

---

ANSWER KEY

Exercise 11
(1) joined; has been **(2)** has remained; stopped; was **(3)** has been helping

(4) has looked for **(5)** worked **(6)** found; made **(7)** has been trying

for the stage sets. (6) He (find) _____ an antique desk to use for one of the sets, and he also (make) _____ a fireplace facade. (7) Most recently, he (try) _____ to get more businesses to advertise in the playbills.

EXERCISE 12
From Ms. H's choice of verb tense below, would you say that her "vowel affairs" have ended or not? Explain.

THE FAR SIDE   By GARY LARSON

"All right! All right! If you want the truth, off and on I've been seeing *all* the vowels—a, e, i, o, u. ... Oh, yes! And *sometimes* y!"

Verbs: Aspect and Time Frames   **25**

Exercise 12
This cartoon reflects the quirky humor of Gary Larson, which has been imitated by a number of other American cartoonists. Before discussing the answer to the question posed with this cartoon, ask Ss to describe the context, eliciting the information that the two characters in the cartoons are consonants ("R" and "h").

Some students may have learned the explanation of English vowels parodied in this cartoon; either they or you can tell others that the phrase "and sometimes Y" is part of the listing of English vowels, since Y is sometimes a vowel (as in *story*) and sometimes a consonant (as in *yes*).

Workbook Ex. 6, p. 16.
Answers: TE p. 537.

ANSWER KEY

Exercise 12
The progressive form of "see" suggests that Ms. H's "vowel affairs" continue to the present.

FOCUS 5

Focus Boxes 5, 6, and 7 summarize the meanings and uses of the present, past, and future time frames, respectively. These focus boxes can serve as reference charts for work throughout Grammar Dimensions. The information Focus Boxes 5, 6 and 7 are repeated in Appendix 1, pp. 449–452 with different example sentences.

FOCUS **5**

Summary: Present Time Frame

FORMS	EXAMPLES	USES	MEANINGS
SIMPLE PRESENT base form of verb or base form of verb + -s	(a) Children **need** social interaction to develop language. (b) Kay **plays** on a volleyball team once a week. (c) Kay **considers** her Thai heritage an important in-group. (d) Andrea **has** a red bicycle.	timeless truths habitual actions mental perceptions and emotions possession	now
PRESENT PROGRES-SIVE am/is/are + present participle (verb + -ing)	(e) I **am completing** my Bachelor's degree in Spanish. (f) Andrea **is writing** an essay. (g) Someone **is knocking** at the door. (h) Kay's brother **is staying** with her this summer. (i) Phil **is making** dinner.	actions in progress duration repetition temporary activities uncompleted actions	in progress now
PRESENT PERFECT have/has + past participle (verb + -ed or irregular form)	(j) Kay **has belonged** to the Sierra Club for four years. (k) Kay **has applied** to several hospitals for positions; she is waiting to hear from them. (l) Andrea **has** just **finished** junior high school.	situations that began in the past, continue to the present actions completed in the past but related to the present actions recently completed	in the past but related to now in some way
PRESENT PERFECT PROGRES-SIVE have/has + present participle (verb + -ing)	(m) Both Kay and Phil **have been playing** volleyball since they were teenagers. (n) This weekend Phil **has been competing** in a tournament which ends tomorrow.	continuous or repeated actions that are incomplete	up until and including now

EXERCISE 13

Choose simple present, present progressive, present perfect, or present perfect progressive for each blank. More than one answer could be correct; be prepared to explain your choices. The first one has been done for you.

(1) Ines (consider) __considers__ her neighborhood in East Los Angeles to be one of her most important in-groups. (2) She (live) _____ in this neighborhood since birth, and she (know) _____ almost everyone in it. (3) Most of the people in the neighborhood (be) _____ from Mexico, but some (be) _____ from Central American countries. (4) Mr. Hernandez, who (live) _____ next door to Ines, always (insist) _____ that he (live) _____ the longest time in the neighborhood. (5) However, Mrs. Chavez, whom everyone (call) _____ "Tia," usually (tell) _____ him to stop spreading tales. (6) Mrs. Chavez (claim) _____ that *she* (be) _____ around longer than anyone. (7) Ines (watch) _____ many of the children younger than herself grow up, and she often (think) of them as her little brothers and sisters—the ones she (like) _____ , that is. (8) Just as her older neighbors (do) _____ for her, she now (help) _____ her younger neighbors keep out of trouble and (give) _____ them advice.

Exercise 13

Exercises such as this provide opportunities to discuss contexts in which writers and speakers have verb tense options, particularly in the contrasts between simple and progressive aspect. For example (2) could be completed either with present perfect or present perfect progressive. Ask Ss to explain what information the progressive forms offer that the simple form doesn't.

Workbook Ex. 7, p. 17.
Answers: TE p. 537.
Workbook Ex. 8, p. 18.
Answers: TE p. 537.

ANSWER KEY

Exercise 13
(1) considers   (2) has lived; knows
(3) are; are   (4) lives/is living; insists; has lived   (5) calls; tells   (6) claims; has been   (7) has been watching/has watched; thinks/has (often) thought/likes   (8) have done; helps; gives

Call attention to the first form in the chart in which speakers express past events with simple present. Tell Ss that present progressive can also be used for this purpose (*Well, last night I'm sitting in my living room and I'm watching TV when I hear a strange sound.*).

SUGGESTION

You could review these past forms by having Ss watch a film clip or recorded TV program with a lot of action and describe it in writing or speech. Elicit examples to write on the board and discuss uses and meanings with reference to the focus box. Consider forms that allow substitution (e.g., past progressive for simple past).

FOCUS **6**

▶ Summary: Past Time Frame

FORMS	EXAMPLES	USES	MEANINGS
SIMPLE PRESENT	(a) So on Friday, Terry **calls** Lila and **tells** her to be ready for a surprise.	past event in informal narrative	at a certain time in the past
SIMPLE PAST verb + *-ed* or irregular past form	(b) Kay **joined** the Girl Scouts when she **was** eight.	events that took place at a definite time in the past	at a certain time in the past
	(c) Phil **attended** Columbia University for two years as an undergraduate.	events that lasted for a time in the past	
	(d) Kay **went** to Girl Scout camp every summer until she entered high school.	habitual or repeated actions in the past	
	(e) Kay always **knew** that she wanted to be a doctor.	past mental perceptions and emotions	
	(f) Although she **did**n't **have** a car in college, Kay **owned** a motorbike.	past possessions	
PAST PROGRESSIVE was/were + present participle (verb + *-ing*)	(g) At midnight last night, Kay **was** still **making** her rounds.	events in progress at a specific time in the past	in progress at a time in the past
	(h) Kay **was talking** to one of the nurses when Phil called.	interrupted actions	
	(i) Andrea **was acting** in a community theater play for a month last year.	repeated actions and actions over time	
PAST PERFECT *had* + past participle (verb + *-ed* or irregular form)	(j) Before starting medical school, Kay **had taken** a long vacation.	actions or states that took place before another time in the past	before a certain time in the past
PAST PERFECT PROGRESSIVE had + *been* + present participle (verb + *-ing*)	(k) Andrea **had been studying** for two hours when her grandmother arrived to take her to the circus.	incomplete events taking place before other past events	up until a certain time in the past
	(l) Phil **had been working** at his computer when the power went out.	incomplete events interrupted by other past events	

28   UNIT 2

EXERCISE 14

The comic strip below uses the following tenses: simple present, present progressive, simple past, past progressive, and past perfect. Find an example of each of these tenses in the comic strip. Then identify one verb phrase from the strip that expresses each of the following meanings:

1. event in progress
2. present situation
3. event completed in the past before another event
4. action completed at a definite point in the past
5. event in progress at a specific time in the past

Reprinted by permission of U.F.S. Inc.

EXERCISE 15

It is doubtful that any of the groups you belong to include trees; in the ancient Greek myths, however, more than a few family members ended up as flora of one sort or another. The following passage tells the story of the mythological character Dryope. For each blank, choose a simple past, past progressive, past perfect, or past perfect progressive form of the verb in parentheses. More than one choice could be possible. Be prepared to explain your choices. The first one has been done for you.

(1) One day Dryope, with her sister Iole, (go) ___went___ to a pool in the forest. (2) She (carry) _____ her baby son. (3) She (plan) _____ to make flower garlands near the pool for the nymphs, those female goddesses of the woodlands and waters. (4) When Dryope (see) _____ a lotus tree full of beautiful blossoms near

Verbs: Aspect and Time Frames **29**

Exercise 14

Comics are excellent authentic texts for looking at verb tense use since they are brief and most Ss enjoy reading them.

EXPANSION

If time and resources permit, have Ss bring in other comics to analyze.

Exercise 15
EXPANSION

For less-guided practice, have Ss (1) write a myth from their culture or another culture or (2) pair up with a classmate and tell a myth or story; then have them pair up with a different classmate to recount the myth or story they were told.

ANSWER KEY

Exercise 14

Simple present: am, are   Present progressive: is happening   Simple past: were, came, saw, thought   Past progressive: were erupting, were melting   Past perfect: had come
(1) Event in progress: is happening
(2) Present situation: am (awake)   (3) Event completed in the past before another event: had come   (4) Action completed at a definite point in the past: came   (5) Event in progress at a specific time in the past: were melting

Exercise 15

(1) went   (2) was carrying   (3) had planned/planned   (4) saw; plucked
(5) flowed; was   (6) fled; took   (7) tried; found; had been rooted/were rooted (first expresses action; second is descriptive)
(8) watched; grew; covered   (9) came; had reached   (10) rushed; embraced; watered
(11) had; had done   (12) begged
(13) told

the water, she (pluck) _____ some of them for her baby.
(5) To her horror, drops of blood (flow) _____ from the stem;
the tree (be) _____ actually the nymph Lotis. (6) Lotis
(flee) _____ from a pursuer and (take) _____
refuge in the form of a tree. (7) When the terrified Dryope (try)
_____ to run away, she (find) _____ that her feet
would not move; they (root) in the ground. (8) Iole (watch)
_____ helplessly as tree bark (grow) upward and (cover)
_____ Dryope's body. (9) By the time Dryope's husband
(come) _____ to the spot with her father, the bark
(reach) _____ Dryope's face. (10) They
(rush) _____ to the tree, (embrace) _____ it, and
(water) _____ it with their tears. (11) Dryope (have) _____
time only to tell them that she (do) _____ no wrong intentionally. (12) She (beg) _____ them to bring the child often to the
tree to play in its shade. (13) She also (tell) _____ them to
remind her child never to pluck flowers and to consider that every tree and
bush may be a goddess in disguise.

From Edith Hamilton, *Mythology*. Copyright 1942 by Edith Hamilton. Copyright renewed 1969 by Dorian Fielding Reid and Doris Fielding Reid. By permission of Little, Brown and Company.

EXERCISE 16

Retell Dryope's story in Exercise 15 in an informal narrative style. Use present tense verbs instead of past tense verbs.

▶ **EXAMPLE:** *One day this woman named Dryope and her sister Iole* **go** *to a pool in the woods. Dryope's* **carrying** *her baby son with her. . . .*

Exercise 16
V A R I A T I O N

Instead of retelling the Dryope myth, Ss could, in pairs, narrate a myth, legend or other story they know in the informal style.

Workbook Ex. 9, pp. 18–19.
Answers: TE pp. 537–538.

ANSWER KEY

Exercise 16
(1) go (2) is carrying (3) plans
(4) sees; plucks (5) flow; is (6) flees;
takes (7) tries; finds; are rooted

(8) watches; grows (9) comes; has reached
(10) rush; embrace; water (11) has; has
done (12) begs (13) tells

Summary: Future Time Frame

FORMS	EXAMPLES	USES	MEANINGS
SIMPLE PRESENT	(a) Kay **completes** her residency next May.	definite future plans or schedules	already planned or expected in the future
	(b) After Kay **finishes** her residency, she will take a vacation.	events with future time adverbials in dependent clauses	
PRESENT PROGRESSIVE	(c) I **am leaving** at 7:00 a.m. tomorrow.	future intentions	already planned or expected in the future
	(d) The family **is spending** the Christmas holidays in Boston.	scheduled events that last for a period of time	
BE GOING TO FUTURE *am/is/are going to* + base verb	(e) The movie **is going to start** in a few minutes.	probable and immediate future events	at a certain time in the future
	(f) I **am going to finish** this no matter what!	strong intentions	
	(g) When you get older, you're **going to wish** that you had saved more money.	predictions about future situations	
	(h) They **are going to travel** in India next summer.	future plans	
SIMPLE FUTURE *will* + base verb	(i) We **will** most likely **stay** at our beach cottage next summer.	probable future events	
	(j) I **will help** you with your homework this evening.	willingness/ promises	
	(k) She**'ll be** very successful.	predictions about future situations	
FUTURE PROGRESSIVE *will* + *be* + present participle (verb + *-ing*)	(l) Kay's parents **will be driving** from Chicago to Palo Alto next week.	events that will be in progress in the near future	in progress at a certain time in the future
	(m) Kay's family **will be living** in Palo Alto until she finishes her residency.	future events that will last for a period of time	

For additional examples, use the sentences in the Appendix 1 chart to review forms, uses, and meanings of these forms.

1. Write examples from Appendix 1 in random order on the board.
2. Ask Ss to identify the form first (e.g., simple present, present progressive) with reference to the first column in Focus 7. Then ask them to identify which use is expressed (e.g., strong intentions, predictions about a future situation).

So that the review doesn't become tedious, select only sentence examples of forms, meanings or uses that you think pose the greatest challenge to your group(s) of students.

FORMS	EXAMPLES	USES	MEANINGS
FUTURE PERFECT *will + have* + past participle (verb + *-ed*)	**(n)** Kay's parents **will have left** Palo Alto before Andrea starts school.	before a certain time in the future	future events happening before other future events
FUTURE PERFECT PROGRESSIVE *will + have + been* present participle (verb + *-ing*)	**(o)** By the end of the year, Kay **will have been living** in California for four years.	up until a certain time in the future	continuous and/or repeated actions continuing into the future

EXERCISE 17

Choose an appropriate future-reference verb tense—simple present, present progressive, be going to, simple future, future progressive, or future perfect—to complete the dialogue below between Justin and his friend Patty. More than one verb tense might be appropriate for some blanks. Read the dialogue with a classmate. Discuss any differences in the choices you made.

Justin: My brother (1) (leave) ___is leaving___ tomorrow for his third trip to Europe this year!

Patty: What time (2) ___does he go/is he going___ (he, go)?

Justin: His plane (3) _____ (take off) really early—at 6 A.M., I think—so he (4) _____ (need) to get out of here by 4 A.M. or so. I (5) _____ (drive) him to the airport.

Patty: So why (6) _____ (he, go) to Europe again?

Justin: It's for his job. He (7) _____ (meet) his company's executives in Germany and then he (8) _____ (spend) a few days in Denmark. You know something? When I (9) _____ (finish) school and (10) _____ (get) a job, I (11) _____ (have) an exciting lifestyle too!

Patty: Oh, really? And what (12) _____ (you, do), if you don't mind my asking.

Justin: Not at all. Next summer, of course, after I (13) _____ (graduate), I (14) _____ (look) for a job for a while. With a

Exercise 17

Ss can complete this exercise as homework and then read aloud their answers for the dialogue in pairs. After they have had a chance to identify and discuss any differences in answers (if the exercise has been done for homework), put the answer key on a transparency for them to check or give each pair a handout with the key.

ANSWER KEY

Exercise 17
(Answers may vary for some.)
(1) is leaving/leaves **(2)** is he going/does he go **(3)** takes off/will take off/is taking off **(4)** needs/will need **(5)** am driving/will drive **(6)** is he going **(7)** is meeting/will meet **(8)** is spending/will spend **(9)** finish **(10)** get **(11)** am going to have/will have **(12)** will you do/will you be doing **(13)** graduate **(14)** will be looking **(15)** will find **(16)** will have saved **(17)** will have made **(18)** will have put **(19)** will be living **(20)** will have **(21)** will do **(22)** am not going to get/won't get **(23)** am going to take/will take **(24)** buy/will buy/am going to buy **(25)** am going to quit/will quit; sail

little effort, I'm sure I (15) _____ (find) a very challenging and lucrative position in my field. Five years or so from now I (16) _____ (save) enough money to put a down payment on a penthouse condominium. By that time, I (17) _____ (make) enough to buy a flashy little sports car. I (18) _____ (put) away enough money by then to rent a beach vacation home every summer.,

Patty: It sounds as if you (19) _____ (live) the good life!

Justin: Well, I just said I (20) _____ (have) enough money to live like that. That doesn't mean I (21) _____ (do) it. Actually, now that I think about it, I (22) _____ (not, get) any of those things. At the end of the five years I (23) _____ (take) all that money I saved and (24) _____ (buy) the largest sailboat I can afford. I (25) _____ (quit) my job and (sail) around the world! Care to join the crew?

Verbs: Aspect and Time Frames | **33**

UNIT GOAL REVIEW

Ask Ss to look at the goals on the opening page of the unit again. Help them understand how much they have accomplished in each area.

USE YOUR ENGLISH

Note: The activities on these "purple pages" at the end of each unit contain communicative activities designed to apply what Ss have learned and help them practice communication and grammar at the same time. For a more complete discussion of the Use Your English activities, see page xxvi of this Teacher's Edition.

Activity 1

Play textbook audio. The tapescript for this listening appears on page 563 of this book.

As a preview to this listening exercise, ask Ss what they speculate about what the title of Oliver Sacks' book (and this passage) could mean.

Workbook Ex. 10, p. 20.
Answers: TE p. 538.

Activity 2
SUGGESTION

Ask Ss to add examples of places in your area that would be interesting for observations.

Use Your English

ACTIVITY 1:
LISTENING/SPEAKING/WRITING

In *The Man Who Mistook His Wife for a Hat*, Dr. Oliver Sacks writes about his experiences treating unusual neurological disorders. You will hear a passage summarizing part of Dr. Sacks' true story of Dr. P., the man he refers to in the title.

STEP 1 Listen to the passage once for overall meaning.

STEP 2 On a separate piece of paper, make a chart like the one below.

STEP 3 Listen to the passage again. In the left-hand column of your chart, write down the past events that occurred before other past events. The first one has been done for you.

Earlier Past Event	Past event
1. *He had been a singer*	1. *Later he became a teacher at the local school of music.*

STEP 4 Listen to the whole passage one more time. In the right-hand column of your chart, write the past event that the earlier past event precedes, as in the example.

STEP 5 Compare your chart with a partner's and discuss the verb forms used in the column.

ACTIVITY 2: WRITING

Find a place that you think would be interesting to observe nature or people: a quiet place outdoors, a school cafeteria, an airport, or a busy restaurant, for example. Spend fifteen or twenty minutes in this place with a notebook to record observations of interesting sights and sounds. You might want to reread Annie Dillard's observations in Exercise 3. Read your observations to the rest of the class or in a small group without telling them where you were. Have your classmates guess the place you are describing.

ANSWER KEY

Activity 1
Earlier Past Event: had been a singer; faces he had known; events had been going on for years; Dr. Sacks had taken off Dr. M's shoes; he had not put his shoe back on; he had forgotten to put the shoe on; he had thought the shoe was his foot; Dr. M had mistaken his wife for a hat.

Past Event: became a teacher at the school of music; did not recognize; when he finally went to Dr. Sacks' office; he was examining Dr. M's reflexes; Dr. Sacks returned to the waiting room (same as above); Dr. Sacks pointed to Dr. M's shoe; Dr. M reached for his wife's head and tried to put it on.

ACTIVITY 3: WRITING/SPEAKING

Choose one person in the class. Describe what you think that person will be doing and how she or he will change in the next ten years or so. Read your descriptions to the class or in a small group to see if your classmates can identify the person.

ACTIVITY 4: WRITING

Reread the passage by James Thurber in Exercise 7. Think of another animal that might have some very different opinions about the human race than humans tend to have about themselves. The animal could be a house pet, such as a canary; another domestic animal, such as a pig; or a wild animal, such as a wolf. Write a description of how this animal has probably regarded the human race.

ACTIVITY 5: SPEAKING/WRITING

Gordon Allport used concepts of in-groups and out-groups to develop a theory about how prejudices are formed. The very nature of in-groups means that other groups are "out-groups." For example, if someone is Catholic, then non-Catholics would be "out-groups." Not all "out-groups" are at odds with each other. However, Allport believed that sometimes people treat certain out-groups as "the enemy" or as inferior to their group. As a result, prejudices towards those of other religions, races, or nationalities may form. Do you see evidence, in your school, community, or a larger context, of "out-groups" who are victims of prejudice? Working in groups, list some of the out-groups you think are discriminated against. Then describe the situation affecting one of these out-groups in an essay. State whether the situation has improved or gotten worse over time and whether you think it will have improved by end of the next decade or so.

Activity 3

VARIATION

Have Ss interview a classmate to discover and report on the classmate's hopes and dreams about his or her future life. This variation is less creative than the activity, but offers more oral communicative practice.

Activity 4

SUGGESTIONS

Elicit or give more examples of animals so that Ss have more possibilities to think about.

Activity 5

VARIATION

For the culminating task, this activity could involve oral group reports or a collaborative essay rather than an individual essay assignment.

The test for this unit can be found on p. 486. The answers are on p. 487.

Unit 3

UNIT OVERVIEW

Unit 3 focuses on an area of the English verb system that is quite challenging for even advanced ESL learners. Contrary to popular belief, identifying subject-verb agreement problems in writing is not always easy. The process requires knowledge of grammar and syntax that not all advanced level learners possess.

This unit offers instruction and practice in identifying the head nouns in subjects with long modifying phrases or clauses, that is, the noun with which a verb must agree in number. It also covers structures that pose the greatest challenges in mastering subject-verb agreement rules in English.

UNIT GOALS

Review the goals listed on this page so Ss understand what they should be able to know by the end of the unit.

OPENING TASK

Note: The **Opening Task** allows Ss to use the target structures and allows teachers to notice what kinds of help they may need. For a more complete discussion of the Opening Task, see page xxiii of this Teacher's Edition.

The purpose of this task is to provide a speaking context that may build upon Ss' knowledge of subject-verb agreement rules for the following kinds of head nouns: quantifiers (*many, most, some*, etc.), percentages, fractions, and gerund phrases (e.g., *watching television*).

SETTING UP THE TASK

In this Task, Ss are asked to: (1) conduct a Gallup reading poll in pairs; (2) pool their responses; (3) tally results; (4) have one person summarize results; and (5) discuss results as a class. Make sure Ss understand the concepts of trends and polls.

U N I T 3

SUBJECT-VERB AGREEMENT

UNIT GOALS:

- To identify the head noun in a subject
- To use correct verb forms for subjects with correlative conjunctions
- To know which kinds of nouns take singular or plural verbs
- To know how subject-verb agreement forms vary in formal and informal English

OPENING TASK
What Are Your Reading Habits?

For over four decades, researchers for the Gallup Poll, which examines national trends, have been surveying Americans' reading habits and attitudes toward reading. They have asked people how often they read, what kinds of reading they do, and how reading compares with watching television as a leisure activity, among other things.

STEP 1   Take a poll of your class's reading habits. In pairs, take turns asking and answering the five questions below, which were used in the Gallup Poll. Write down your partner's responses. The response options are given in parentheses.

STEP 2   Pool the responses of all class members and tally the results. Convert the results for questions 1, 2, 3, and 4a to percentages, as shown in the Gallup results for Question 1.

STEP 3   Have one class member summarize the results. Then discuss them: Were any of the results surprising? For the first question, the Gallup results for three polling periods are shown for you to compare with your class's results. Some of the other results, taken from the 1990 poll, will be presented later in this unit.

Reading Habits

1. Are you reading any books or novels at the present time? (Yes/No)

2. When, as nearly as you can recall, did you last read any kind of book all the way through—either a hardcover book or a paper-bound book? (Within the last week/Within the last month/One to six months ago/Seven to twelve months ago/Over one year ago/Never)

3. During the past year, about how many books, either hardcover or paperback, did you read either all or part of the way through?(None/One to five/Six to ten/Eleven to fifty/More than fifty)

4. (a) Do you have a favorite author? (Yes/No)
   (b) If yes, who is it? (Any choice)

5. Which of these two activities—watching television or reading books—is:
   (a) The most relaxing for you?
   (b) The best way to learn for you?
   (c) The most rewarding for you?
   (d) The most enjoyable way to spend an evening for you?
   Your choices for (a)–(d) : Watching TV/Reading a book/Both/Neither

Gallup Results for Question 1

x	Yes	No
1990 Dec.	37%	63%
1957 March	17%	83%
1949 Jan.	21%	79%
	Yes	No
Class Results		

From *Gallup Poll Monthly,* February 1991.
Reprinted with permission from The Gallup Organization, Inc., Princeton, New Jersey.

CONDUCTING THE TASK

Step 1
Diagnose Ss' accuracy in subject-verb agreement by listening to the student pair surveys.

VARIATION
Since the Gallup Poll is usually done by telephone, student pairs could conduct a telephone survey outside of class. This would provide listening comprehension practice in a context that is often more difficult for ESL Ss than face-to-face conversation. Model how to conduct a survey in class. Choose a student to act as a pollster and interview you. Ss then note your responses. If time permits, model the task even if Ss do the surveys in class.

Step 2
Converting results to percentages is not absolutely necessary, though it allows Ss to compare their results with the actual Gallup Poll.

SUGGESTION
If you do not convert results to percentages, give Ss quantifying vocabulary to discuss results (e.g., *most of our class; the majority of our class; only a few of our class members;* etc.).

Step 3
This step offers more production for diagnosing Ss' language use.

EXPANSION
For an additional diagnostic tool, have Ss write a brief summary of their results, using complete sentences, as a homework assignment.

Note: Focus boxes explain and give examples of each structure. For a more complete discussion of focus boxes, see page xxiv of this Teacher's Edition.

S U G G E S T I O N S

1. Introduce the topic by noting that many Ss may have learned about this grammatical feature of English before, but that it often takes a long time to develop mastery because many languages do not inflect verb for number. Find out how many of your Ss are familiar with the terminology.

2. Have Ss read the top part of the focus box. While they are doing this, write three or four example sentences on the board to illustrate subject-verb agreement, including one with an incorrect verb (e.g., *One student in our class have just completed the reading survey.*). Some sentences can have one-word subjects, but the incorrect sentence should have a subject with modifiers such as a prepositional phrase or adjective clause.
3. Ask Ss to identify the incorrect sentence. Then ask them to find the verb; circle it.
4. Write the phrase *Head Noun* on the board and explain its meaning with reference to the bottom part of the focus box. Ask Ss to find the head noun of the incorrect sentence you have written on the board. Underline the head noun. Correct the sentence by changing the verb.
5. Have Ss look at examples (d)–(h), which illustrate cases of difficulty identifying head nouns. Ask them if the marker differences illustrated in (i) and (j) have ever been a source of confusion for them.

Overview of Subject-Verb Agreement

EXAMPLES	EXPLANATIONS
	In English, certain verbs must show agreement in number (singular/plural) with the subjects of sentences:
(a) I **am** you/we/they **are** he/she/it **is**	• present-tense forms of *be*
	• past-tense forms of *be*
(b) I/he/she/it **was** we/you/they **were**	• present-tense forms of third-person singular verbs
(c) he/she/it **works**	
(d) One of the books that I **am** reading **has** been a bestseller for a year.	If the verb has more than one part, the first part agrees with the subject. Choosing the correct verb form is not always easy, even for native speakers of English. Some reasons for difficulties are the following:
Head Noun **(e)** (The main **reason** we decided to take a trip to the Rocky Mountains) **is** to learn geological history. **(f)** (That **novel** about alien invasions in several South American countries) **has been made** into a TV film.	• subjects with long modifying phrases following the head noun, as in (e) and (f)
(g) The **pair of scissors** you bought **is** really dull now. **(h)** **Every book** in the library **has been entered** in the new computer system.	• nouns and pronoun phrases whose number (singular/plural) may be confusing, as in (g) and (h)
Plural Noun **(i)** Those comic book**s** make me laugh. **Singular Verb** **(j)** That comic book make**s** me laugh.	• the *-s* ending in English as both a plural marker for nouns and a singular marker for third-person present-tense verbs, as in (i) and (j)

EXERCISE 1

To check for subject-verb agreement, (1) identify the subject of the sentence and then (2) find the noun that is the head of the subject. In each of the following sentences, underline the head noun of the subject. Then circle the correct form of the verb in parentheses.

▶ **EXAMPLE:** Many children's <u>parents</u> (begin)/begins) reading to them when the <u>children</u> (is/are) less than three years old.

1. Young people today (is/are) just as likely to read for pleasure as older Americans.

2. The reading survey (finds/find) some good news for those who appreciate reading as a pastime.

3. Today's Americans (is/are) more likely to read to their children than their parents (was/were).

4. Reading to very young children (stimulates/stimulate) them to learn to read sooner.

5. The impact of reading to children at an early age (is/are) dramatic.

6. There (is/are) signs of a coming surge in reading in America.

7. Despite television and its influence, reading (seems/seem) to be coming back into favor.

Adapted from *The Gallup Poll Monthly*, February 1991, with permission of The Gallup Organization, Inc.

Note: The exercises following each focus box provide meaningful practice with the grammar item presented in that particular box. For a more complete discussion of how to use the exercises, see page xxv of this Teacher's Edition.

Exercise 1

Ss practice picking out head nouns that need verb agreement. This exercise can be done individually or in pairs.

Workbook Ex. 1, p. 21.
Answers: TE p. 538.

ANSWER KEY

Exercise 1
Head noun/verb as shown.
1. people/are 2. survey/finds
3. Americans/are; parents/were

4. Reading/stimulates 5. impact/is
6. signs/are (logical subject)
7. reading/seems

FOCUS 2

The biggest problem many Ss have checking subject-verb agreement is that they are not able to identify the word that is the head noun of a long subject.

SUGGESTION

For more practice identifying head nouns:

1. Give Ss additional sentences from a reader, another textbook you use, or a newspaper.
2. Ask them to identify the entire subject first with all its modifiers and then to pick out the head noun for each. They could put brackets [ ] around the subject and use a highlighting pen to mark the head noun.

Identifying Head Nouns in Long Subjects

EXAMPLES	EXPLANATIONS
(a) That **novel** about alien invasions in several southwestern states **has** recently **been made** into a TV movie. **(b)** All of the **characters** in that story written by our teacher **were** very believable.	When the subject head noun and the verb are separated from each other, it is harder to check for agreement. It can be especially troublesome when the head noun is singular but nouns in a modifying phrase are plural or vice versa.
Head Noun Prepositional Phrase **(c)** Another **poll** of Americans' reading and attitudes **was taken** in 1990.	Here are strategies to find the head nouns: • If the subject has a prepositional phrase, locate the head noun to the left of the first preposition (for example, *of*).
Head Noun Compound Preposition **(d)** The **library**, { together with / along with / as well as } bookstores, **provides** reading materials.	• Use the same strategy with subjects followed by compound prepositions, such as *together with, along with,* and *as well as.*
Head Noun with N*ot* **+ Noun Phrase** **(e)** The **child**, not her parents, **was** an avid reader.	• Locate the head noun before *not* + a noun phrase.
Relative Clause **(f)** A **child** who likes to read **books** and whose parents encourage reading **does** better in school.	• Similarly, look to the left of relative clauses (*who, which, that, whose* clauses) to identify the head noun.

EXERCISE 2

The following sentences summarize information about the Gallup Poll's 1990 reading survey. Put brackets [ ] around any modifying phrases following the head noun. Underline the head noun. Circle the appropriate forms in parentheses.

▶ **EXAMPLE:** The <u>library</u>, [along with bookstores], ((provides)/provide) reading materials.

1. The horror story writer Stephen King, together with romance novelist Danielle Steele, (was/were) the most popular of the authors named by the respondents.

2. One of the 1019 respondents to the survey (claims, claim) that (he or she/they) started reading at the age of one!

3. Some respondents, in answer to the question of who their favorite living author is, (gives, give) the name of a writer who has died many years ago.

4. According to Judy Fellman, the President of the International Reading Association, one reason so many parents are reading to their children (is/are) the abundance of children's literature.

5. A father whose own parents read to him when he was young (is/are) more likely to read to (his/their) children.

6. James Michener, as well as V.C. Andrews, (ranks/rank) third in author popularity among those surveyed.

7. A person who belongs to one of the higher income groups (tends/tend) to read more.

8. According to the poll, the college-educated female, not the college-educated male, (is/are) the most prolific (reader/readers), averaging eighteen books a year.

Exercise 2

Ss could complete this exercise in class with a partner or as a homework assignment.

You may want to find out if your Ss have heard of these popular authors or read any of their books.

Workbook Ex. 2, p. 22.
Answers: TE p. 538.

ANSWER KEY

Exercise 2

1. <u>Stephen King</u> [together with romance novelist Danielle Steele] was   2. <u>One</u> [of the 1,019 respondents of the survey] claims he or she   3. <u>respondents</u> [in answer to the question of who their favorite living author is] give   4. <u>reason</u> [that so many parents are reading to their children] is   5. <u>father</u> [whose parents read to him when he was young] is   6. <u>James Michener</u> [as well as V.C. Andrews] ranks   7. <u>person</u> [who belongs to one of the higher income groups] tends   8. <u>female</u> [not the college-educated male] is, reader

FOCUS 3

This focus box summarizes subject-verb agreement rules for correlative conjunctions.

SUGGESTIONS

1. Tell Ss that even native speakers have trouble applying these rules, and that in informal contexts, such as conversation, speakers often do not observe the traditional rules. For example, a native English speaker might say, *"I don't think either my brothers or my sister are going to be able to come to the picnic this afternoon."* Some exceptions to traditional agreement rules are presented in Focus 7 on p. 52.

2. Remind Ss that it is best to use the traditional rules for formal writing and that the focus charts serve as reference tools they should consult to refresh their memories.

FOCUS **3**

Agreement in Sentences with Correlative Conjunctions: *both . . . and*; *either . . . or*; *neither . . . nor*

EXAMPLES	EXPLANATIONS
(a) Both **F. Scott Fitzgerald** and **Charles Dickens were** named as favorite authors in the 1990 reading poll.	**Both . . . and** When two subjects are connected by *both . . . and,* use a plural verb.
(b) Either the library or **bookstores have** current magazines. (c) Either bookstores or the **library has** current magazines. (d) Neither the book nor **the magazines discuss** this issue. (e) Neither the magazines nor **the book discusses** this issue.	**Either . . . or; Neither . . . nor** The traditional rule is that the verb should agree with the head noun after *or* or *nor.*
(f) Either Kay or **I am** going to the library this afternoon. (g) Neither the twins nor **he is** planning to go to the library. (h) Obviously, neither she nor **they are** interested in that topic.	This agreement rule also determines verb form when one or more of the subjects is a pronoun.

EXERCISE 3

Select the appropriate verb form and, in some cases, the correct noun phrase after the verb, for each sentence. In cases of *either . . . or* or *neither . . . nor*, use the rule in Focus 3 to select the verb.

▶ **EXAMPLE:**   Neither the books nor the bookshelf (is/are) mine.

1. Either books or a magazine subscription (makes a nice gift/make nice gifts) for someone.

2. For a less expensive gift, both bookplates and a bookmark (is a good choice/are good choices).

3. Neither the Russian novelist Leo Tolstoy nor the Irish writer James Joyce (was/were) known to more than 50 percent of the 1990 Gallup Reading Poll respondents.

4. She said that either the reserved book librarian or the librarians at the main checkout desk (has/have) the information you need.

5. Both reading and writing (is/are) what we consider literacy skills.

6. Either you or I (am/are) going to present the first report.

7. In my opinion, neither the front page of the newspaper nor the sports pages (is/are) as much fun to read as the comics.

8. (Does/do) either the lifestyle section of the newspaper or the business section interest you?

9. I can see that neither you nor he (is/are) finished with your sections yet.

10. Both my brother and my parents (is/are) reading that new biography of Lyndon Johnson. Neither he nor they (has/have) read more than a few chapters, though.

EXERCISE 4

In groups of three, take turns sharing the responses you gave in the Reading Survey. Make up five statements summarizing the responses of your group using *both . . . and* or *neither . . . nor*. Report your findings to another group.

▶ **EXAMPLES:**   ***Neither*** *Mohammed* **nor** *Juanita has read more than five books this year.*

Both *Tomoyo* **and** *Gregorio have favorite authors. Tomoyo's is Toni Morrison and Gregorio's is Jorge Amado.*

Exercise 3
E X P A N S I O N

Ss could make up "mini-quizzes" with four or five sentences modeled after this exercise to give to a classmate. Ss often enjoy creating quizzes and correcting their classmates' responses, and this type of activity helps reinforce their learning of specific grammatical rules.

Workbook Ex. 3, p. 23.
Answers: TE p. 538.

A N S W E R   K E Y

Exercise 3
1. makes a nice gift   2. are good choices
3. was   4. have   5. are   6. am
7. are   8. does   9. is   10. are, have

Exercise 4
Answers will depend on the Reading Survey responses. (Examples are given in the directions.)

SUGGESTIONS

1. In reviewing material presented in this focus box, pay particular attention to the mass nouns and abstract nouns since these typically cause the most problems for Ss (partly because of their frequency as compared to collective nouns). Ask Ss which of the nouns listed across from (c) and (d) are most problematic for them and if they can expand the lists for either of the two categories.

2. For examples (k) and (l), remind Ss that although these nouns take plural verbs, the nouns themselves cannot have plural markers; that is, we do not use *the youngs, the elderlies, the poors,* etc., to refer to groups of people.

FOCUS **4**

▶ Agreement with Noncount Nouns, Collective Nouns, and Nouns Derived from Adjectives

EXAMPLES	EXPLANATIONS
(a) The new gym **equipment has** just **been delivered**. (b) That **information is** very helpful.	**Noncount Nouns** Noncount nouns in English include mass nouns and abstract nouns. These nouns take a singular verb.
(c) My English **vocabulary has increased**. (d) Your **advice is** always appreciated.	**Mass Nouns** **Abstract Nouns** *equipment* *advice* *furniture* *behavior* *grass* *education* *homework* *information* *machinery* *knowledge* *money* *research* *traffic* *transportation* *vocabulary* *violence*
(e) The **audience is waiting** patiently for the performance to begin. (f) A **flock** of geese **is flying** overhead.	**Collective Nouns** Collective nouns define groups of people or animals: *audience* *group* *class* *herd* *committee* *the public* *family* *swarm* *flock* *team*
(g) The **class is going** on a field trip. (h) The **team has been practicing** all week.	If the group is considered as a whole, use a singular verb. In most cases, collective nouns take singular verbs.
(i) The **class have disagreed** among themselves about where they should go on their field trip. (j) The soccer **team have** differing opinions about strategies for the next game. Some think defense is the key, but others believe a more aggressive strategy is needed.	If the group is considered as individual members, use a plural verb. This usage is less common in American English.

EXAMPLES	EXPLANATIONS
(k) **The young want** to grow up fast and **the old wish** to be younger. (l) Is it true that **the rich are getting** richer and **the poor are getting** poorer?	**Nouns Derived from Adjectives** Noun phrases derived from adjectives that describe people, such as *the young*, *the rich*, and *the homeless*, take plural verbs.

EXERCISE 5

Take turns giving oral responses (between one and five sentences) to the following questions. Use the noun or nouns in bold print as the subject in at least one sentence. The first one is done as an example.

1. What kind of **transportation** do you prefer for getting to school?

▶ **EXAMPLE:** *Well, the **transportation** I prefer **is** driving my own car. But finding a parking space is difficult, so I take the bus most of the time.*

2. What is some good **advice** you've gotten during the past year from a friend, relative, or something you read?

3. What is some useful **information** you've learned in your English class?

4. What home office **equipment** do you think is the most helpful for you as a student?

5. Do you think **violence** is ever justified? Explain your opinion.

6. How would you describe your **knowledge** of sports? (Good? Fair? Poor? Does it vary according to particular sports?)

7. Do you think **the homeless** are being neglected in our society? What evidence do you have for your opinion?

8. Do you believe that **a college education** is necessary for everyone in our society? Who might not need a college education?

EXERCISE 6

The following sentences describe activities of groups. Circle the appropriate verb form for each.

▶ **EXAMPLE:** The group (has/have) just left.

1. The audience for the political rally (was/were) huge.

2. The audience (seems/seem) to have mixed reactions to the President's speech; some people are cheering wildly, while others are walking away, disgusted.

Exercise 5
V A R I A T I O N

To spend less time on this exercise, have Ss choose only one or two questions for responses.

E X P A N S I O N

For homework, ask Ss to write a paragraph summarizing and elaborating their responses to one of the questions.

Exercise 6

Remind Ss to use the focus box charts as reference tools to review rules and examples. The verb agreement rules for collective nouns are difficult for many Ss to remember!

Workbook Ex. 4, p. 24.
Answers: TE p. 538.

---

3. My family (celebrates/celebrate) birthdays with a special dinner.

4. The city government (is/are) ordering a reduction in water usage.

5. A swarm of bees (has/have) built a nest under the eaves of the roof. Look! The swarm (appears/appear) to be flying out in all directions from that spot.

6. The population of Phoenix (is/are) growing every year

7. The population of that country (has/have) disagreed among themselves for years about immigration policies.

8. The disabled (is/are) demanding more attention to their needs.

FOCUS 5

Many Ss, even at the advanced levels, will be unfamiliar with some of these agreement rules, especially the ones governing clause subjects as illustrated in examples (p) through (s).

FOCUS **5**

▶ **Subjects Requiring Singular Verbs**

Some types of subjects always take singular verbs.

EXAMPLES	EXPLANATIONS
	(Some common or proper nouns that end in -s:
(a) **Mathematics is** my favorite subject. Others: *physics, economics*	• courses
(b) **Measles is** no fun to have! Others: *mumps, arthritis*	• diseases
(c) **Leeds is** where my aunt was born.	• place names
(d) **The news** from home **was** very encouraging.	• *news*
(e) *Tracks* **was written** by Louise Erdrich.	• book and film titles
(f) *Dances with Wolves* **was awarded** an Oscar for the best movie.	
	Plural unit words of distance, time, and money:
(g) **Six hundred miles is** too far to drive in one day.	• distance
(h) **Two weeks goes** fast when you're on vacation.	• time
(i) **Fifty dollars is** a good price for that painting.	• money

EXAMPLES	EXPLANATIONS
	Arithmetical operations (addition, subtraction, multiplication, division):
(j) **Three plus seven equals** ten.	• addition
(k) **Four times five equals** twenty.	• multiplication
	Items that have two parts when you use the noun *pair*
(l) My **pair** of scissors **is** lost.	
(m) A **pair** of plaid shorts **was** on the dresser.	
(n) My **scissors are** lost.	
(o) **Those plaid shorts were** on the dresser.	Note, however, that you would use the plural verb if the noun pair is absent.
Subject	**Clause subjects:**
(p) **[What we need] is** more reference books.	The verb is singular even when the nouns referred to are plural.
(q) **[That languages have many differences] is** obvious.	
(r) **[Reading books and magazines] is** one of my favorite ways to spend free time.	Gerund (verb + *-ing*) and infinitive (*to* + verb) clauses also take singular verbs.
(s) **[To pass all my exams] is** my next goal.	

Exercise 7

EXPANSION

As a follow-up to this exercise, ask Ss to contribute more examples for some of the topics here (e.g., cities ending in -s) and then create present tense sentences either as a group or individually for more practice using verbs that agree in number.

Workbook Ex. 5, p. 24.
Answers: TE p. 538.

EXERCISE 7

Imagine that you are competing on a quiz show. For each definition below, you will be given three words, phrases, or numbers. You must choose the correct match and state the answer in a complete sentence.

▶ **EXAMPLE:** a film set in California (*Badlands, Down and Out in Beverly Hills, Star Wars*)

Answer: ***Down and Out in Beverly Hills** is a film set in California.*

1. the number of days in a leap year (364, 365, 366)
2. a disease that makes you look like a chipmunk (shingles, mumps, warts)
3. four (54 divided by 9, 100 divided by 20, 200 divided by 50)
4. a poem written by Geoffrey Chaucer (*The Canterbury Tales, Great Expectations, Guys and Dolls*)
5. a common plumber's tool (a pair of scissors, a pair of pliers, a pair of flamingoes)
6. a city in Venezuela (Buenos Aires, Caracas, Athens)
7. what you most often find on the front page of a newspaper (sports news, national news, entertainment news)
8. the study of moral principles (ethics, physics, stylistics)
9. the number of years in a score (ten, twenty, thirty)
10. a course that would discuss supply and demand (mathematics, economics, physics)

EXERCISE 8

What are your opinions and attitudes about each of the following topics? State at least two things that could complete each of the sentences below. Share some of your answers with the class.

▶ **EXAMPLES:** What this country needs _is health insurance for everyone and better education._

1. What this country needs _____.
2. What I would like to have in five years _____.
3. Having a job while going to school _____.
4. That the rain forests are being destroyed _____.
5. What really irritates me _____.
6. What I find most frustrating about being in school _____.
7. Learning the rules of subject-verb agreement in English _____.

48 | UNIT 3

▶ **Agreement with Fractions, Percentages, and Quantifiers**

With fractions, percentages, and quantifiers *all* (*of*) and *a lot of,* agreement depends on the noun or clause after these phrases.

EXAMPLES	EXPLANATIONS
(a) Fifty percent of the **book is** about poetry. **(b)** Half of **what he says is** not true. **(c)** All (of) our **information is** up-to-date.	Use a singular verb when the subject is: • a singular noun • a noun clause • a noncount noun
(d) One-fourth of the **students have** computers. **(e)** All (of) the **computers need** to be checked.	With plural nouns, use a plural verb.
(f) One-sixth of our **Spanish club has/have** relatives in Mexico. **(g)** A lot of my **family live/lives** in Pennsylvania.	With collective nouns, use either the singular or the plural, depending on your meaning.
(h) Each **book has** a code number. **(i)** Every one of the **students is** on time.	With quantifiers *each, every,* and *every one,* use a singular verb, whether the noun is singular or plural.
(j) A number of **students are** taking the TOEFL exam today.	With *a number of,* use a plural verb since the noun it modifies is always plural.
(k) The number of **students** taking the exam **is** 175.	*The number of,* however, takes a singular verb.
(l) None of the **advice was** very helpful. **(m)** None of the **magazines** I wanted **is** here.	With *none of,* use a singular verb in formal written English.

FOCUS 6

Remembering these agreement rules can be difficult for native and nonnative speakers alike!

Once again, remind Ss that charts such as these are useful for reference when they work on writing assignments. Ss who need to summarize statistical information in academic writing will find the Focus 6 summary chart especially helpful as a reference.

SUGGESTIONS

To help Ss review the rules presented here:
1. Have them identify the entire subjects in sentences (e.g., *fifty percent of the book*).
2. Point out the bolded head noun (word or phrase) that requires agreement.
3. Note that for phrases with fractions, percentages and some quantifiers, the head noun is the object of a preposition (*of the book,* etc.), contrary to other agreement rules in which head nouns are located outside prepositional phrases, as in Focus 2 examples (a) and (c).
4. Pay special attention to example (h) since *each* is a frequently used quantifier, and Ss often use a plural or base form verb (e.g., *have* instead of *has*) with it. On the board or a transparency, write a few verb phrases with base forms expressing facts that would be true of all Ss in the class. Ask them to form sentences using *each student,* supplying the correct singular verb form, for example, *take at least two courses; have a major area of study.* (*Each student takes at least two courses,* etc.)

Summary: Form of the Verb Following Traditional Agreement Rules

	SINGULAR NOUN	NONCOUNT NOUN	PLURAL NOUN	COLLECTIVE NOUN
percentages	singular	singular	plural	singular/plural
fractions	singular	singular	plural	singular/plural
all (of)	singular	singular	plural	singular/plural
a lot of	singular	singular	plural	singular/plural
each, every	singular	singular	singular	
a number of			plural	
the number of			singular	
none of	singular	singular	singular	singular

Exercise 9

E X P A N S I O N

The class might want to respond to this survey question and compare their results with those presented here.

EXERCISE 9

Summarize the information from the Gallup Poll below by writing five sentences about responses of the people surveyed. For subjects, you could use any of the following: *respondents, people surveyed, Americans, those who responded.*

▶ **EXAMPLE:** *Almost three-fourths of the respondents believe they spend too little time reading books for pleasure.*

Survey Question: Thinking about how you spend your nonworking time each day, do you think that you spend too much time or too little time . . .

	Too much	Too little	About right	No opinion
Watching television	49%	18%	31%	2%
Reading newspapers	8%	54%	35%	3%
Reading magazines	6%	65%	24%	5%
Reading books for pleasure, recreation	7%	73%	16%	4%
Reading books for work, school, etc.	9%	62%	19%	10%

Adapted from *Gallup Poll Monthly*, February 1991.

Exercise 9
Answers will vary.
Examples: About half of those who responded feel that they spend too little time reading newspapers./Only nine percent of Americans believe they spend too much time reading books for work or school.

EXERCISE 10

Write three sentences that are true and three that are false about the members of your class, using the words in parentheses as the subjects. Read your sentences aloud to a classmate. Your classmate should decide which are true and which are false and should orally correct each false statement.

▶ **EXAMPLE:** *The number of female students in our class is twelve.*
Response: *False. The number of female students in our class is fourteen.*

1. (The number of) _____ .
2. (Each) _____ .
3. (None) _____ .
4. (All) _____ .
5. (A lot of) _____ .
6. (A number of) _____ .

EXERCISE 11

Fill in each blank of the following radio news report with a *be* verb form that would be appropriate for formal English use.

▶ **EXAMPLE:** A number of reporters from other states _____are_____ in town to cover news about the earthquake.

Here is the latest report on the aftermath of the earthquake. As most of you know, the earthquake has caused a great deal of damage and disruption to our area. A lot of the

houses near the epicenter of the quake (1) _____ badly damaged. A number of trees (2) _____ uprooted in that area also, so be careful if you are driving. All the electricity (3) _____ shut off for the time being. Water (4) _____ turned off also. None of the freeways in the vicinity (5) _____ currently open to traffic. Almost every side street (6) _____ jammed with drivers trying to get back home. The police (7) _____ directing traffic at major intersections. To date, the number of deaths resulting from the earthquake (8) _____ two. All people (9) _____ urged to stay at home if at all possible.

As Ss work on this exercise in pairs, monitor verb forms to make sure they are using the correct forms. Alternatively, have them turn in written sentences after they complete the pairwork.

EXPANSION

After pair practice, each student could choose one sentence to read to the entire class.

Exercise 11

Ss can practice identifying full subjects and head nouns by highlighting or underlining the entire noun phrase and circling the head noun. By asking Ss to do this and checking their answers, you will know whether they are actually finding the correct head noun and not just (a) guessing at the verb form or (b) choosing a word as a head noun that is not the head noun but that has the same number—singular or plural—as the head noun.

In other words, during their work for this unit, make sure Ss learn how to locate head nouns.

Workbook Ex. 6, p. 25; Ex. 7, p. 26.
Answers: TE p. 538.

SUGGESTION

1. Start discussion of this focus box by reading examples (a) and (b) to give Ss a general idea of the types of exceptions dealt with in this chart.
2. Then ask Ss if they have heard native speakers using the less formal forms or come across them in reading. If you have any examples in writing, show them to the class, for example, plural verbs with *none* that occur commonly in media such as newspapers or magazines.

Workbook Ex. 8, p. 27.
Answers: TE p. 438.

► Exceptions to Traditional Agreement Rules

Some of the agreement rules presented in this unit are observed mainly in formal English contexts, especially in formal written English. The following are cases where native speakers of English frequently do not follow the formal (traditional) rules, especially in spoken and less formal written English:

EXAMPLES	EXPLANATIONS
	***Either/Neither of the* + Noun Phrase** Formal rule: use a singular verb with *either* or *neither*.
(a) Either of the outfits **is** ⎫ **(b)** Either of the outfits **are** ⎬ appropriate.	Formal Less formal
(c) Neither of the choices **is** ⎫ **(d)** Neither of the choices **are** ⎬ desirable.	Formal Less Formal
	Either . . . or / Neither . . . nor Formal rule: the verb agrees with the closest subject noun.
(e) Either my parents or John **has** ⎫ the **(f)** Either my parents or John **have** ⎬ car.	Formal Less formal
(g) Neither you nor I **am** ⎫ **(h)** Neither you nor I **are** ⎬ convinced.	Formal Less Formal
	***None* + Prepositional Phrase** Formal rule: use a singular verb.
(i) None of the magazines **is** ⎫ **(j)** None of the magazines **are** ⎬ here.	Formal Less Formal
	***There* + Be (present tense) + Plural Noun** Formal rule: use *are* with plural nouns.
(k) There **are** ⎫ three books here you **(l)** There**'s** ⎬ might like.	Formal Less Formal

Note: Many less formal forms are becoming more common in all but the most formal written English contexts. *There are* is usually used with plural noun phrases in written English, however.

Summary: Form of the Verb with Formal versus Less Formal Usage

	FORMAL	**LESS FORMAL**
Either of the + (plural noun) *Neither of the* + (plural noun) *Either* (noun) *or* (singular noun) *Neither* (noun) *nor* (singular noun) *None of the* + (plural noun)	singular verb	singular or plural verb

EXERCISE 12

Decide which of the underlined verbs would be appropriate for formal written contexts and which would be acceptable in spoken English. Write "formal" or "informal" to indicate the usage.

▶ **EXAMPLES:** *Either of these economics courses <u>are</u> useful for my major.*
Informal

1. Neither of those political surveys <u>are</u> valid because the sample was not random.

2. I am sure that either Professor Tori or Professor Kline <u>have</u> already addressed the issues you mention.

3. As far as we know, none of the experiment's results <u>has</u> been duplicated to date.

4. There<u>'s</u> some results that will surprise you.

5. Neither Dr. Gonzalez nor Dr. Vuong <u>are</u> presenting the findings of their studies until the results are checked again.

6. In conclusion, either of the textbooks I have reviewed <u>is</u> an excellent choice for an introductory chemistry course.

7. We have reviewed the report. None of the figures <u>seem</u> correct; they should be checked again.

8. Either of the reports submitted <u>are</u> useful for further study of this environmental problem.

9. Neither the campus medical center nor the library <u>is</u> safe should a strong earthquake occur.

10. Either you or I <u>are</u> responsible for this month's financial report; please let me know if I should submit it.

11. Neither of the claims Senator Holmes presented <u>is</u> justified.

12. There<u>'s</u> a number of errors in this report.

USE YOUR ENGLISH

Note: The activities on these "purple pages" at the end of each unit contain communicative activities designed to apply what Ss have learned and help them practice communication and grammar at the same time. For a more complete discussion of the Use Your English activities, see page xxvi of this Teacher's Edition.

Activity 1

Play textbook audio. The tapescript for this listening appears on page 564 of this book.

SUGGESTION

If, after previewing this tapescript, you think your Ss will find this a difficult listening exercise, introduce the activity before listening with a brief discussion of the survey's content. Ask Ss their opinions about some of the questions. In doing so, you will introduce orally some of the vocabulary and phrases in the tapescript. This should help them understand the information more easily.

If needed, repeat Step 3.

Activity 2
SUGGESTION

Examples such as these can be found frequently in newspapers and magazines. You may want to start a "data file" of such examples and present them to Ss to review subject-verb agreement rules throughout your course. Ask Ss to contribute to the file if they come across any examples in their reading.

Use Your English

ACTIVITY 1: LISTENING

You will hear a summary of information from another Gallup survey. This one asked people questions about raising children.

STEP 1 As you listen to the summary, take notes on the information you hear.

STEP 2 At the end of the summary, you will hear eight statements based on the information in the survey. Listen to all the statements and decide whether each statement is true or false.

STEP 3 Listen to the statements again, pausing after each one. On a separate piece of paper, write T or F after you hear each statement. If a statement is false, write a correction using a complete sentence.

STEP 4 Listen to the summary again to check your answers and corrections.

ACTIVITY 2: SPEAKING

Below are some examples of spoken and written English that were found in the newspaper. Discuss the traditional rules of subject-verb agreement that have not been observed. How do they illustrate some of the troublesome cases of subject-verb agreement? (Why do you think the speaker or writer used a singular or plural verb in each situation?)

- "I have decided that everyone in these type of stories are rich." (Quoted statement by an actress in reference to a TV movie she appeared in)
- "Her expertise in the water as a lifeguard and her understanding of ocean currents, coupled with the fact that she is a strong swimmer, makes her a strong competitor." (Quoted comment about a champion swimmer)
- "I know there is going to be a major hassle with certain smokers, plus there is going to be a lot of attempts to bypass the regulation." (From a letter to the editor about no-smoking regulations)
- " . . . the chances of him coming back in the next eight years was very unlikely." (Quoted comment about a politician who ran for President)
- "In the Jewelry Center, All That Glitter Sure Is Gold" (Headline for a feature article)

ANSWER KEY

Activity 1

1. False. Most people think the ideal number is two.   2. True.   3. False. In 1996, a greater percentage of Americans (21% vs. 18% in 1990) believe three is the ideal number.

4. True.   5. False. Over half (51%) say that boys are more difficult to raise.   6. True.

7. False. Almost one-third of the respondents feel this way.

ACTIVITY 3: RESEARCH/ SPEAKING/WRITING

Ask another class (or a group of teachers) to respond to the questions in the reading habits survey. Tally the results and write a survey report comparing them to your class's results.

ACTIVITY 4: RESEARCH/ SPEAKING/WRITING

Usage surveys have suggested that native speakers of English often use plural verbs with *either* when *of* plus a plural count noun follows *either,* as in sentences like this: *"Either of those times are okay with me for a meeting."* What do you think native speakers would choose in question forms: *"Are/Is either of those times okay with you?"*

STEP 1 In groups or with a partner, create a set of five questions with *either + of + plural noun* to test what verbs native speakers would choose. Here are some examples:

> **EXAMPLES:** 1. *Do/does either of you boys have a match?*
> 2. *Is/are either of you going to come with us to the movies?*
> 3. *Has/have either of your parents ever worked in a restaurant?*

STEP 2 Conduct a survey by giving your set of questions to at least ten native speakers of English. Ask them to choose the verb they would use.

STEP 3 Write a report of your results or give an oral report to the class.

ACTIVITY 5: WRITING

Write an essay expressing your views about society's treatment of one of the following groups of people: the poor, the disabled, or the elderly. You might want to compare how one of these groups is treated in the United States and in another country.

Subject-Verb Agreement **55**

VARIATION

If Ss have access to the Internet, they could conduct the survey via e-mail.

Activity 4

VARIATIONS

1. If Ss are in a context where there aren't many native English speakers, reduce the number of people they poll.
2. Like Activity 3, this survey could be conducted via the Internet, which might make it easier for Ss to contact native English speakers.

Activity 5

VARIATION

Ss could interview someone about one of these topics and write a report of the interview or interview two people (classmates or others) from different countries for a comparative essay.

EXPANSION

After writing their essays, Ss could give brief reports in small groups for oral practice.

The test for this unit can be found on p. 488. The answers are on p. 489.

TOEFL Test Preparation Exercises for Units 1–3 can be found on pp. 28–31 of the Workbook.
The answers are on p. 539 of this book.

Unit 4

UNIT OVERVIEW

This unit begins with a summary of uses of the passive voice followed by a review of forms in the various tenses. It includes two kinds of passives that many advanced learners will not yet have covered: stative passive and complex passive. This unit also helps Ss understand and practice the use of passive voice to achieve cohesion between ideas across sentences.

UNIT GOALS

Review the goals listed on this page so students (Ss) understand what they should be able to know by the end of the unit.

OPENING TASK

The purpose of this task to provide a writing context—an experiment report—in which writers commonly use passive verbs to describe procedures. The report writing serves as a diagnostic to assess Ss' knowledge of the uses and forms of passive.

UNIT 4

PASSIVE VERBS

UNIT GOALS:

- To know when to use passive verbs rather than active verbs
- To use correct forms of *be* and *get* passives
- To know the correct form and use of passives in descriptions
- To use passives correctly after *that* clauses and infinitive clauses
- To use passives to create connections in discourse

OPENING TASK
A Short-Term Memory Experiment

Short-term memory describes the brain function in which information is retained temporarily, somewhere between thirty seconds and a few minutes. Numerous experiments have been conducted to test the recall of information stored in short-term memory, resulting in various theories about memory. One phenomenon believed to characterize short-term memory is called *the serial position effect*. In this task, you will be testing this effect. (You will find out later exactly what it means.)

STEP 1 With a partner, perform the following experiment to test the serial position effect. One person will take the role of researcher; the other will be the subject. A blank sheet of paper and a pen should be ready for the subject and the subject's book should be closed.

STEP 2 Researcher: Show the list of words on page A-17 to your subject. Ask him or her to study the list of words for one minute. After one minute has passed, close the book.

STEP 3 Subject: Immediately write down on the blank sheet of paper as many of the words as you can recall for one minute. You can write the words in any order. Then give the list to the Researcher. Note: It is important that you start writing immediately after the study time is up.

STEP 4 Read the explanation of the serial position effect on page A-17. Do the results of your experiment support or contradict this belief about short-term memory?

STEP 5 With your partner, write a brief report of the experiment, using the written list of words as your data. Assume that your reader has no previous information about your experiment. In your summary, describe the procedures and summarize the results. Use the model below to start the report.

Memory Experiment

This experiment was conducted to test the serial position effect on recalling information. One subject participated in the experiment. The subject was shown a list of thirty common words. . . .

STEP 6 Share your report with another set of partners. Then save the report for exercises later in this unit.

SETTING UP THE TASK

Ask Ss if they are familiar with other kinds of memory experiments (common topics in introductory psychology courses). Have Ss who do know of other experiments summarize how the experiments were conducted and have the others question them.

CONDUCTING THE TASK

Step 1
V A R I A T I O N

If time does not permit conducting the experiment in class, have Ss get together in pairs to do it outside of class.

Step 2

If the experiment is done in class, monitor Ss during this step to help them observe the time limit.

Step 3

The teacher can serve as time keeper for this step also.

Step 4

You could poll the class for this step to find out the extent to which the hypothesis has been supported by the class experiments.

Step 5
V A R I A T I O N

Have Ss write a summary individually if you want to see how individual Ss use passive verbs in this context.

CLOSING THE TASK

Step 6
S U G G E S T I O N

Collect the reports and redistribute to Ss for later work on exercises in this unit.

REVIEWING THE TASK

To model and elicit passive verb use in an oral context, pose hypothetical questions after the task is completed. For example, ask a student "subject": "*Tam, if you had been shown only 20 words instead of 30, do you think you would have recalled all of them?*"

This unit begins with the uses of passive verbs rather than forms to emphasize the reasons we use passive verbs in speech and writing. Advanced Ss have typically learned and practiced forms of passive verbs; they often have received little instruction on how to use these verbs. Many Ss have also been told in composition classes that they should avoid using passive verbs and use active verbs.

Help Ss become familiar with the terminology in this focus box since it is used throughout this unit. The term *agent* can be defined as the *doer* or *performer* of an action.

SUGGESTIONS

1. If you have collected the written reports from the Opening Task, use sentences from their reports as further examples. You could also use active sentences from the report that could be rewritten in the passive (e.g., *The subject studied the list of words for one minute—The list of words was studied for one minute.*).

2. Supplement the sentences in the focus box with examples from a current newspaper or magazine.

3. Ask Ss if they can think of other contexts in real life in which passive is used to avoid responsibility for behavior (e.g., advertisements in which a company apologizes for having to recall a defective product).

FOCUS **1**

Overview of Passive versus Active Verb Use

EXAMPLES		EXPLANATIONS
ACTIVE VERBS	PASSIVE VERBS	We often use passive instead of active in the following contexts:
(Agent) (a) The brain **retains (Recipient)** information temporarily in short-term memory.	**(Recipient)** (b) Information **is retained (Agent)** temporarily by the brain in short-term memory.	• when we want to focus on the receiver of an action (recipient) rather than the performer (agent) of the action. We do this by making the recipient the grammatical subject. We may express the agent in a *by*-phrase following the verb.
(c) I **asked** the subject to look at the word list for one minute.	(d) The subject **was asked** to look at the word list for one minute.	• when the agent is less important than the recipient of an action. In reporting research procedures, for example, we do not need to refer to the researcher.
(e) The subject wrote down all the words she could remember. She **recalled** a total of thirteen words.	(f) The subject wrote down all the words she could remember. A total of thirteen words **were recalled.**	• when the agent is obvious from the context.
(g) It appears that something **is altering** the rats' brain cells.	(h) It appears that the rats' brain cells **are being altered.**	• when the agent is unknown.
(i) The researchers who did this study **have made** several major errors in analyzing the data.	(j) Several major errors **have been made** in analyzing the data.	• when we want to avoid mentioning the agent. For example, we may not want to say who is responsible for some wrongdoing or mistake.

EXERCISE 1

Provide a likely reason for each of the italicized passive verbs in the sentences below.

▶ **EXAMPLE:** *Two masterpieces of sixteenth century painting were taken from the museum.* The agent is unknown.

1. One method that is *used by* psychologists in research on memory is the relearning method.

2. In the relearning method, people have to relearn information that *was learned* earlier.

3. Sometimes when you *are introduced* to another person, you forget the person's name a few minutes later.

4. It seems that some misleading statements *were made* in advertising your auto repair services.

5. We have just received reports that a bomb *was set off* in the airport terminal shortly before midnight.

6. Construction of the Leaning Tower of Pisa *was begun* by Bonanno Pisano in 1173.

7. Small bits of information *are* often *remembered* by grouping the information into larger units, known as chunks.

8. Short-term memory *has been called* "a leaky bucket."

EXERCISE 2

Reread the paragraph introducing the Opening Task. Identify the sentences that have passive verbs and state why they are used.

EXERCISE 3

With your partner for the Opening Task, look at the report you wrote. If you used any passive verbs, identify the reasons for their use. If you didn't use any, find one or two sentences that you might change from active to passive based on the information in Focus 1. State what use each would reflect.

Exercise 1

Exercises such as this one, which ask Ss to analyze examples based on information in a focus box, are often best done in small groups. In this way, Ss have a chance to discuss the teaching points of the focus box.

Exercise 2

Ss could do this as a homework assignment after doing Exercise 1 in class.

Exercise 3

Collecting this exercise will help you assess Ss' understanding of the teaching points in Focus 1.

Workbook Ex. 1, p. 32.
Answers: TE p. 539.

ANSWER KEY

Exercise 1
Answers may vary.
1. The writer wants to focus on "method."
2. The agent is obvious from the context.
3. The agent is less important than the recipient. 4. The writer may want to avoid directly blaming the agent; also, the actual writer of the ad is unknown. 5. The agent is unknown; the speaker wants to put focus on the bomb. 6. The writer wants to focus on the building, not the builder. 7. The agent is obvious from the context (people in general). 8. The agent is either unknown or considered less important than the recipient.

Exercise 2
Passives in Opening Task (**Note:** This list doesn't include reduced participle clauses such as "believed to characterize.")
1. information is retained (focus on recipient, agent obvious from context). 2. experiments have been conducted (agent less important than recipient). 3. one phenomenon . . . is called (focus on recipient). 4. This experiment was conducted to test . . . (put focus on recipient; agent less important)
5. The subject was shown a list . . . (put focus on recipient; agent less important).

(**Note:** Some Ss may identify "Person B's book should be closed" as a passive statement; however, in this context, "closed" would be an adjective participle as part of a description of the book rather than an action; you might point out the parallel of this pattern to the previous statement "a pen should be ready. . . .").

Exercise 3
Answers will depend on the report Ss wrote in the Opening Task.

▶ Review of Passive Verb Forms

All passive verbs are formed with *be* + or *get* + past participle.

1. Ask Ss to review the forms of passive verbs for homework.
2. Before doing Exercise 4, provide practice in forming the passive with short sentences. Write active forms on the board and prompt forms the tenses your Ss need most practice in. Especially challenging are progressive and perfective forms. Review principles for deleting unnecessary agents (for example: *We are reviewing the passive voice forms today—The passive voice forms are being reviewed today.*).

EXAMPLES	EXPLANATIONS
(a) That movie **is reviewed** in today's newspaper. **(b)** The garbage **gets picked up** once a week.	SIMPLE PRESENT *is/are* (or *get*) + past participle
(c) The possibility of life on Mars **is being explored.** **(d)** We **are getting asked** to do too much!	PRESENT PROGRESSIVE *is/are* + *being* (or *getting*) + past participle
(e) The butterflies **were observed** for five days. **(f)** Many homes **got destroyed** during the fire.	SIMPLE PAST *was/were* (or *got*) + past participle
(g) The Olympics **were being broadcast** worldwide. **(h)** She **was getting beaten** in the final trials.	PAST PROGRESSIVE *was/were* + *being* (or *getting*) + past participle
(i) Short-term memory also holds information that **has been retrieved** from long-term memory. **(j)** Did you hear he**'s gotten fired** from his job?	PRESENT PERFECT *has/have* + *been* (or *gotten*) + past participle
(k) This store **has been being remodeled** for six months now! I wonder if they'll ever finish. **(l)** It looks as though the tires on my car **have been getting worn** by these bad road conditions.	PRESENT PERFECT PROGRESSIVE *has* + *been* + *being* (or *getting*) + past participle
(m) The National Anthem **had** already **been sung** when we entered the baseball stadium. **(n)** He was disappointed to learn that the project **had**n't **gotten completed** in his absence.	PAST PERFECT *had* + *been* (or *gotten*) + past participle

EXAMPLES	EXPLANATIONS
(o) The horse races **will be finished** in an hour. (p) The rest of the corn **will get harvested** this week.	SIMPLE FUTURE *will* + *be* (or *get*) + past participle
(q) I bet most of the food **will have been eaten** by the time we get to the party. (r) The unsold magazines **will have gotten sent back** to the publishers by now.	FUTURE PERFECT *will* + *have* + *been* (or *gotten*) + past participle
(s) The election results **will have been getting tallied** by the time we reach the headquarters	FUTURE PERFECT PROGRESSIVE* *will* + *have* + *been* + *being* (or *getting*) + past participle
(t) A different chemical **could be substituted** in this experiment. (u) Don't stay outside too long. You **may get burned** by the blazing afternoon sun.	MODAL VERBS (Present Time Frame) modal (*can, may, should,* etc.) + *be* (or *get*) + past participle
(v) All of our rock specimens **should have been identified,** since the lab report is due. (w) The file **might have gotten erased** through a computer error.	MODAL VERBS (Past Time Frame) modal (*can, may, should,* etc.) + *have* + *been* (or *gotten*) + past participle

*Note: The *be* form of this passive tense is quite rare. Even the *get* form is not very common.

EXERCISE 4

Rewrite each sentence below to put focus on the recipients of action rather than on the performers (agents) of the action. Delete the agent if you do not think it needs to be mentioned. In some cases, you may want to restate the agent in a prepositional phrase beginning with *in* rather than with *by*.

▶ **EXAMPLE:** The brain stores information.

    Information is stored in the brain.

1. A bundle of millions of fibers connects the brain cells.
2. In visual processing, the right hemisphere of the brain registers unfamiliar faces; the left hemisphere registers familiar ones.
3. The memory does not store an exact replica of experience.
4. The brain alters, organizes, and transfers information into one or more memory stores.

Exercise 4

Before Ss do this exercise, review the reasons for deleting agents (i.e., not including the agent in a *by*-phrase) when transforming a sentence from active to passive.

Exercise 4

1. The brain cells are connected by a bundle of millions of fibers.   2. In visual processing, unfamiliar faces are registered by the right hemisphere of the brain; familiar ones are registered by the left hemisphere.   3. An exact replica of experience is not stored in the memory.   4. Information is altered, organized and transferred into one or more memory stores.   5. Certain facts that the multistore model of memory cannot contain have been discovered (by psychologists). (Agent might be deleted if obvious from the context.)   6. Other ways in which we organize information in long-term memory are now being investigated.   7. The difference between recognition and recall has been demonstrated in numerous experiments.   8. Case studies of stroke victims were used to learn more about information storage.

5. Psychologists have discovered certain facts that the multistore model of memory cannot explain.

6. Researchers are now investigating other ways in which we organize information in long-term memory.

7. Scientists have demonstrated the difference between recognition and recall in numerous experiments.

8. The researchers used case studies of stroke victims to learn more about information storage.

EXERCISE 5

Choose one or more of the following topics to discuss with a partner or in a small group.

1. What advice was given to you by friends or relatives when you did one or more of the following: (a) enrolled in a new school; (b) took up a new sport or hobby; (c) moved to a new place?

2. What is being done today to prevent or cure diseases?

3. What measures have been taken to help disabled people?

4. What improvements have been made recently in your school (facilities, new buildings, courses, etc.)?

5. What changes do you think will have been made in the way we communicate across distances by the middle of the next century?

Exercise 5

E X P A N S I O N S

1. Have members from each group give brief oral summaries of their discussions to the rest of the class or to one other pair or small group.

2. Have Ss write paragraph summaries of one topic as a homework assignment.

FOCUS 3

Most Ss will be familiar with stative passive verbs but may not have learned the distinction between stative and dynamic passives. Stress that stative passives do not have agents, so these forms will not occur with agent *by*-phrases. Ss often forget to put the past participle endings on stative verbs (e.g., they may use *is call* instead of *is called*).

Workbook Ex. 2, p. 33.
Answers: TE p. 539.

FOCUS **3**

Stative Passives in Contrast to Dynamic Passives

EXAMPLES		EXLANATIONS
DYNAMIC PASSIVES	**STATIVE PASSIVES**	Many verbs can be either dynamic or stative depending on their meaning. Dynamic passive verbs describe activities. Stative passive verbs do not report activities; they express states or conditions. Stative passive verbs do not have agents.
(a) The missing library book **was found** in the parking lot by a custodian.	(b) A map of Miami **can be found** on the Internet.	
(c) Our telephone line **is** finally **being connected** tomorrow.	(d) The transmission of a car **is connected** to the gearshift.	
(e) Stella **was called** for a job interview yesterday.	(f) The biological rhythm with a period of about twenty-four hours **is called** a circadian rhythm.	

62 UNIT 4

A N S W E R   K E Y

Exercise 5
Answers will vary.
1. When I moved to Detroit, I was advised to bring a lot of warm clothes because the winters are very cold. 2. A lot of genetic research is being done to determine the role of genes in susceptibility to certain diseases. 3. Ramps have been installed in many buildings for people who are in wheelchairs. 4. Our library was recently expanded. 5. More computer networks will have been established.

EXERCISE 6

Each of the famous monuments or buildings below can be matched to two descriptions in a–j. (1) Match each landmark to the appropriate descriptions. (2) Rewrite each description as a sentence with a passive verb (or verbs) to put focus on the monuments and buildings as the main topics. (3) Delete the agents if they do not add much to the meaning or if they can be inferred from the context. (4) Make any other necessary changes.

EXAMPLE: *The Parthenon is considered to represent the peak of Greek architectural achievement.*

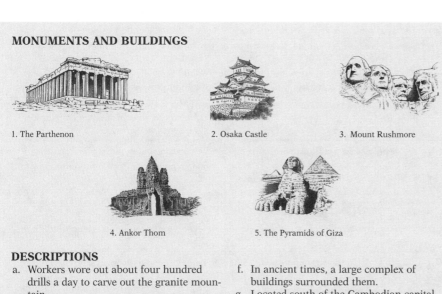

MONUMENTS AND BUILDINGS

1. The Parthenon
2. Osaka Castle
3. Mount Rushmore
4. Ankor Thom
5. The Pyramids of Giza

DESCRIPTIONS

a. Workers wore out about four hundred drills a day to carve out the granite mountain.
b. The Cambodian god-king Suryavarman II intended it to be a funerary monument for himself.
c. Unlike in Europe, where builders used stone for castles, builders made this of wood.
d. People believe that workers constructed them using mounds or ramps to position the stone blocks.
e. Many consider it the peak of Greek architectural achievement.
f. In ancient times, a large complex of buildings surrounded them.
g. Located south of the Cambodian capital of Ankor Thom, people built it in the twelfth century.
h. Pericles had it built to celebrate Athens' victory over the Persians.
i. Guzton Borlum, the sculptor, designed it to symbolize American history and principles.
j. Historians regard it as the most formidable stronghold in Japan before people destroyed it in the early seventeenth century.

Exercise 6

SUGGESTION

Before doing this exercise, ask Ss which monuments and buildings they know and elicit locations. Ss will probably know most of them. If they don't know the countries of any of the monuments or buildings, inform them (1. Greece; 2. Japan; 3. U.S.; 4. Cambodia; 5. Egypt). This will help them match the columns to form sentences.

Workbook Ex. 3, pp. 34–35.
Answers: TE p. 539.

ANSWER KEY

Exercise 6

Note: Answers may vary for some regarding deletion or retention of the agent. Whether or not the agent is deleted would depend in some cases on the broader context in which a statement is made. **1.** e/h **2.** c/j **3.** a/i **4.** b/g **5.** d/f

FOCUS 4

This focus box provides vocabulary associated with various uses of stative passives. Ss should find it helpful as a reference, especially in academic writing.

SUGGESTIONS

1. Use the vocabulary in the chart to create more sentences with stative passives, using information from your local context (e.g., *[your city] is located in [your state/province/region]; [your state/region, etc.] is known for [something famous]).*

2. Textbooks, newspapers, and magazines are good sources for more examples of these uses. Such authentic examples, if readily available, can be more interesting than made-up examples. Bring in examples in which Ss can identify uses, or distribute copies of a school newspaper or other free publication to point out other examples of stative passive uses.

FOCUS **4**

Uses of Stative Passive Verbs

Stative passive verbs have a number of descriptive uses in discourse. Note that many of the stative passives in the examples below are followed by prepositions: *in, with, by, for,* etc.

EXAMPLES	USES
(a) The Amazon River **is located** in Brazil. **(b)** The ratel, a fearless animal, **is found** in Africa and India. **(c)** The Secret Service agents **were positioned** near the President.	• To describe location or position *Located* is often used in geographical description. *Found* typically describes plant and animal habitats. *Positioned* often suggests placement. Other verbs: *placed, situated, bordered (by), surrounded (by)*
(d) *The Daily Scandal* **is filled** with untrue stories. **(e)** The sea horse's body **is covered** with small bony plates.	• To describe characteristics or qualities This type of description is common in science.
(f) Temperature **is measured** in degrees. **(g)** The elements **are listed** according to weight.	• To describe manner or method This use is common in science and mathematics.
(h) France **is divided** into regions. **(i)** Geology **is made up** of many subfields, such as seismology and petrology.	• To describe part-whole relationships Other verbs: *composed (of), organized into*
(j) The Geiger counter **is used** for detecting radiation. **(k)** Greetings such as "How are you?" **are intended** to promote communication, not to get information.	• To describe purpose These verbs may be followed by *for* + gerund (verb + *-ing*) or an infinitive (*to* + verb). Other verbs: *designed, meant*
(l) Do you know the old song that begins: "The knee bone**'s connected** to the thigh bone"? **(m)** The two buildings **are joined** by an elevated walkway.	• To describe connection Other verbs: *attached (to), accompanied (by), separated (by, from)*

EXAMPLES	USES
(n) El Greco **is** best **known** for his religious painting. **(o)** Nagoya Castle **is considered** one of the greatest fortresses in the history of Japan.	• To describe reputation or association Other verbs: *regarded (as), thought to be, viewed (as)*
(p) The ratel **is** also **known** as "the honey badger." **(q)** Pants having legs that flare out at the bottom **are called** bellbottoms.	• To define or name Other verbs: *labeled, named, termed*

EXERCISE 7

Identify the stative passive verbs in each of the following sentences and state the use of each, based on the categories in Focus 4.

▶ **EXAMPLE:** Benin, a small country, *is situated* in West Africa.

Stative passive: *is situated*   Use: *to describe location*

1. As an infant, a person is in his mother's womb; grown up, the person is wrapped in custom; dead, the person is wrapped in earth. (Malay Proverb)
2. Hallucinations are often associated with abnormal mental conditions.
3. In the midwestern United States, soft drinks such as cola drinks or root beer are referred to as "pop."
4. Natural geysers, which are found in Japan, New Zealand, and the United States, are sometimes classified as renewable energy.
5. The Special Olympics is meant to give disabled people an opportunity to compete in athletic contests.

Exercise 7
SUGGESTION
To help Ss acquire active vocabulary for stative passive contexts and to use this vocabulary accurately, call attention to the prepositions or infinitive structures that occur with the passives in this exercise: *situated in, wrapped in, associated with, referred to, found in, classified as, meant to* + verb.

ANSWER KEY

Exercise 7
1. is wrapped; describes characteristics
2. are associated; describes connection
3. are referred to; names
4. are found; describe location
   are classified; defines
5. is meant describes purpose

Exercise 8

Ask student volunteers to write their sentences on the board. Discuss variations that others have created.

Workbook Ex. 4, p. 36.
Answers: TE p. 539.

EXERCISE 8

(1) Match each numbered word or phrase in column A to the appropriate phrase in column B.

(2) Write a sentence for each, using a stative passive.

(3). Add other words or change word forms as necessary.

▶ **EXAMPLES:** 1,d. *Language* **may be defined** *as the spoken or written means by which people express themselves and communicate with others.*

The spoken or written means by which people express themselves and communicate with others **is called** *language.*

A

1. language
2. alcohol thermometers
3. the hand
4. monuments of unknown soldiers
5. human brain
6. Sigrid Undset

B

a. Belgium, Britain, France, Italy, Portugal, and the United States

b. three parts: the hindbrain, the midbrain, and the forebrain

c. the author of *Kristin Lavransdatter,* for which she won the Nobel Prize

d. the spoken or written means by which people express themselves and communicate with others

e. structural specialization at the end of the arm, enabling grip and fine motor tasks that characterize higher primates

f. measure low temperatures

Exercise 8

Forms of some sentences may vary.
1. **d.** may be defined (reverse order: The spoken or written . . . is called language.)
2. **f.** are used   3. **e.** can be defined (**Note:** This sentence would be more difficult to process if the definition were used as the subject of the sentence.)   4. **a.** may be found
5. **b.** is composed   6. **c.** is known (as)

FOCUS **5**

▶ **Complex Passives**

Complex passives are passive constructions followed by *that* clauses or infinitive clauses (*to* + verb).

EXAMPLES	EXPLANATIONS
(a) It **is believed** that primates first appeared on the earth about sixty-nine million years ago. **(b)** It **is said** that the number thirteen is bad luck. **(c)** It **was reported** that a hijacker was arrested this morning.	**Form:** Introductory *it* + passive verb + *that* clause **Use:** This form often serves to introduce a topic, since the new information comes at the end of the sentence.
(d) The topic of today's lecture is early primates. Primates **are believed** to have appeared on the earth about sixty-nine million years ago. **(e)** Many numbers are associated with superstitious beliefs. For example, thirteen **is said** to be an unlucky number. **(f)** A hijacker took over a jumbo jet flying to New York this morning. The hijacker **was reported** to have been demanding that the plane fly to South America.	**Form:** Subject (other than introductory *it*) + passive verb + *to* infinitive **Use:** This form could also be used to introduce topics, but it is especially appropriate after a topic has been introduced because the topic can then be put in the subject position.

EXERCISE 9

For each of the following numbered sentence groups, choose the sentence that best fits the context, using the principles of introducing or continuing topics as discussed in Focus 5. Consider each numbered group to be the beginning of a written article or spoken announcement.

1. Even today, some people believe that opening an umbrella in the house will bring bad luck. In parts of Asia, as early as the eleventh century,
   (a) it was considered to be an insult to open an umbrella inside a building.
   (b) opening an umbrella inside a building was considered to be an insult.

As noted previously, it is likely that your Ss will not have studied complex passives, though they should be familiar with them from their reading or formal speech such as radio or television newscasts.

This focus box explains the different uses of the two complex passive forms depending on whether a topic is newly introduced or has already been mentioned.

SUGGESTION

To familiarize Ss with the forms of complex passives:

1. Write example (a) on the board. Circle *that* to highlight the beginning of the subordinate clause.
2. Have Ss note that the informational fact is expressed in the *that*-clause. What speakers/writers think about the fact is stated in the main clause.
3. Ask Ss to substitute other verbs for *is believed*, giving them base forms (e.g., *know, assume, say*).
4. Write example (d) on the board. Put a slash between *believed* and *to have appeared* to show the structure of the sentence. Circle the two instances of *primates* in the two sentences to highlight the explanatory point about information already introduced to the reader or listener. Note that examples (d), (e), and (f) are variations of the information in (a), (b), and (c).

Exercise 9

SUGGESTION

Have Ss do this exercise in pairs or small groups so that they can discuss the principles explained in Focus 5. Do the first one as a class to clarify the relationship between the different complex passive forms illustrated in Focus 5 and show why writers or speakers would choose one over the other.

---

2. (a) It has been alleged that an employee of the museum is responsible for the theft of dozens of paintings.

(b) An employee of the museum is alleged to be responsible for the theft of dozens of paintings. Police are currently investigating the claim.

3. (a) It was reported this morning that a Pacific blacktip shark gave birth to three healthy pups at Sea World.

(b) A Pacific blacktip shark was reported to have given birth to three healthy pups at Sea World this morning. Officials commented that this marks the first documented birth of the species in captivity.

4. Of the comets that have been recorded, the least frequently returning one is Delavan's Comet, which appeared in 1914.

(a) This comet is not expected to return for twenty-four million years.

(b) It is not expected that this comet will return for twenty-four million years.

EXERCISE 10

The following actions or conditions and their results reflect superstitions in various parts of the world. Express each situation and result in sentences with two complex sentence structures: a *that* clause complex passive and an infinitive.

▶ **EXAMPLE:**

Action/Condition	Result
A picture falls in the house.	Someone will die.

1. *It is said that having a picture fall in the house will result in someone dying.*

   OR *It is said that if a picture falls in the house, someone will die.*

2. *Having a picture fall in the house is believed to cause someone to die.*

Action/Condition	Result
1. You enter a house with the left foot.	It will bring you bad luck.
2. You tie a red string around a finger of your left hand.	It will help your memory.
3. Say the word *abracadabra*.	It will ward off sickness.
4. You have a mole on your neck.	You will get money.
5. Tie knots in an apron.	It will protect you against accidents.

Exercise 10

E X P A N S I O N

1. Ask Ss to work in small groups and create two or three more sentences expressing other superstitions they know.

2. Have groups read their sentences to the rest of the class.

Workbook Ex. 5, p. 37; Ex. 6, p. 38; Ex. 7, p. 39.
Answers: TE p. 539.

▶ **Contexts for the Use of Complex Passives**

Complex passives are often used in journalism, in business, and in academic writing. Although not commonly used in informal spoken English, complex passives are frequent in formal spoken English (for example, news reports, speeches). Some of the most common uses follow.

EXAMPLES	USES
	To achieve an impersonal tone, avoiding the use of *I* or *we:*
(a) It **should be noted** that the results of our experiment cannot be generalized.	• in explanations and observations
(b) This product **is known** to be inferior.	
(c) It **is assumed** that all employees have completed the necessary hiring papers.	• in statements of desired or expected behavior
(d) All homework **is expected** to be turned in on time.	
(e) It **has been ruled** that the prisoner was unfairly convicted.	• in evaluations or judgments
(f) The house **was considered** to be vastly overpriced.	
(g) It **is believed** that baseball was being played in England in the early eighteenth century.	To express information that has not been verified as factual or true
(h) Mr. Blau **is alleged** to have stolen several car stereos.	
(i) In the nineteenth century, it **was thought** that personality traits and mental abilities could be detected by bumps on the head.	To describe past beliefs that are no longer regarded as true
(j) In ancient Greece, lightning bolts **were believed** to be weapons used by Zeus, the king of gods.	
(k) It **is assumed** that more and more species will become extinct if we continue to destroy the world's rain forests.	To express a general expectation about some future event
(l) The weather **is expected** to be warm and sunny all weekend.	

Passive Verbs | **69**

FOCUS 6

This focus box summarizes some of the most common reasons complex passive verbs are used in communicative contexts. Both types of complex passives presented in Focus 5 are shown in the examples.

After you have gone over the uses and examples in this chart, ask Ss if they have been aware of these forms in listening to the news, reading newspapers, etc.

E X P A N S I O N

For further instruction on uses of complex passives:
1. Give Ss sentences illustrating all or some of the uses in the second column. Present them in a random order and do not identify the uses.
2. With Ss working in small groups, have them identify the use for each one.

Exercise 11

EXPANSION

Have Ss research other fascinating facts on the Internet and write sentences with complex passives to express them.

Workbook Ex. 9, p. 41.
Answers: TE p. 540.

EXERCISE 11

EXERCISE 11

The *Guinness Book of World Records* presents hundreds of fascinating facts about the superlatives of the world (and even of the known universe), whether they concern the biggest, the longest, the oldest, or the smallest. Imagine that you are a writer compiling facts for this book; your task is to rewrite the following information in complete sentences. Use the passive form of the verb given in parentheses. Change the phrasing of information and add words as needed. The first has been done as an example. Note that if an activity happened in the past (as in 1b), an infinitive verb expressing it must be perfective: *to* + *have* + past participle.

▶ **EXAMPLE:** **1.** (a) longest living fish: lake sturgeon (think)
The longest living fish is thought to be the lake sturgeon.

OR *It is thought that the longest living fish is the lake sturgeon.*

the lake sturgeon is the longest living fish.

1. (b) life span of one specimen of sturgeon: eighty-two years (report)
It was reported that one specimen lived for eighty-two years.

OR *One specimen was reported to have lived for eighty-two years.*

2. fastest flying insect: the American deer bot-fly (believe)

3. longest prison sentence: 10,000 years, imposed on a convicted murderer in Alabama, 1981 (say)

4. the longest United Nations speech: four hours, twenty-nine minutes, by Cuban President Fidel Castro on September 26, 1960 (know)

5. the smelliest living animal: the African zorilla (consider)

6. total number of active volcanoes: 850 (think)

7. Sirius A, the Dog Star: brightest of the 5776 stars we are able to see (presume)

8. the most baked beans eaten: 2780 by a British woman (allege) (Hint: use *a British woman* as your subject)

70 | UNIT 4

A N S W E R   K E Y

Exercise 11
Some answers will vary.
2. The fastest flying insect is believed to be the . . . 3. It is said that the longest prison sentence was 10,000 years, imposed . . .
4. The longest United Nations speech is known to be four hours, twenty-nine minutes, given by . . . 5. The smelliest living animal is considered to be the . . . 6. It is thought that the total number of active volcanoes is 850. 7. It is presumed that Sirius . . . is the brightest of the 5,776 stars . . . 8. A British woman is alleged to have eaten the most baked beans—2,780.

FOCUS 7

Using the Passive to Create Cohesion in Discourse

EXAMPLES	EXPLANATIONS
(a) For the first time, researchers have found **the remains of a mammal that has been entombed in amber. The remains,** including a backbone and ribs, **are estimated** to be eighteen million to twenty-nine million years old. Discovered in the West Indies, **these remains are believed** to be those of a tiny insect-eating mammal.	As explained in Focus 1, we put focus on a topic in English by making it the grammatical subject. Often a new topic is introduced at the end of a sentence. This topic then becomes the subject of the next sentence. As a result, a passive verb may be needed. Putting the topic in the subject position helps to create cohesion, making it easier for the reader or listener to understand the main ideas.
(b) Biologists have recently determined that **even the tiny brains of bees can recognize and interpret patterns. This feat was** once **thought** possible only through reason. In an experiment, bees learned to look for food only near **certain symmetrical or asymmetrical patterns. These patterns are reflected** in nature, such as blossoms of plants.	Often a synonym for the topic or a shortened form of the topic is used as the subject with a passive verb. (See Unit 6, Focus 2 for more information about these forms of reference.) This also helps to create cohesion. In some cases, it allows the writer or speaker to avoid using a subject with a long modifying phrase.
(c) Most theories of long-term memory **distinguish** skills or habits ("knowing how") from abstract or representational knowledge ("knowing that"). **This distinction is supported** by recent evidence that skill learning and the acquisition of knowledge are handled by different areas of the brain.	The subject of a passive verb may also be derived from the verb of a previous sentence.

The use of passive verbs to achieve cohesion across sentence boundaries is an important principle for advanced learners to be aware of as they develop their academic writing skills. Their writing may sound "nonnative-like" not because grammatical errors exist but because the information structure of sentences fails to focus important information appropriately.

SUGGESTION

To illustrate the ways in which grammatical subjects put focus on topics:

1. Rewrite example (a) with *researchers* as the subject of the last two sentences (e.g., *Researchers estimate the remains. . . . to be. . , etc.*).
2. Ask Ss to tell you what topic the rewritten sentences are focusing on (*researchers*). Note how this differs from the example in the focus box, which focuses on the boldfaced subjects.
3. If necessary, repeat this process with example (b), asking Ss to express the second sentence with a noun that would be the agent of *thought*.

EXPANSION

To help Ss understand the derivation of subjects from verbs as shown in example (c) and develop active vocabulary, give them other verbs and have them come up with the abstract noun forms (e.g., *estimate—estimation; behave—behavior*).

For more communicative practice, have Ss work with a partner. Afterwards, ask for volunteers to explain passive uses to the rest of the class.

EXERCISE 12

Circle the passive verbs in the following passages. Then explain why each passive verb is used.

▶ **EXAMPLE:** One of the world's largest pharmaceutical companies has recently fired its chairperson. The chairman *was suspected* of unethical accounting practices. Explanation: The passive verb *was suspected* is used in the second sentence to put focus on the topic, *the chairman*.

1. Researchers are studying the effects that physical stress and psychological factors have on the immune system. The immune system is designed to do two things: recognize foreign substances (antigens), such as flu viruses and tumors, and destroy or deactivate them.

Adapted from Carole Wade and Carol Tavris, *Psychology*, Harper and Row, 1987.

2. The ability of electric currents to float through certain materials completely untouched, without energy loss, is called superconductivity. This phenomenon was explained in a theory developed in 1972, an accomplishment that won the Nobel Prize. Superconductivity was thought to exist only at extremely cold temperatures, but in 1986, a scientist in Germany discovered a high-temperature superconductor.

3. The repeated eruptions of Mexico's Popocatepetl volcano have resulted in the growth of a lava dome to within fifty feet of the rim of the volcano. The dome is being fed by 20,000 cubic feet of fresh lava daily. If the lava overtops the rim, it could melt glaciers on the side of the mountain and create life-threatening mudflows.

4. In experiments to examine the ways in which infants form attachments to mothers or other caretakers, researchers separated infant chimpanzees from their mothers. Extended separations were found to result in abnormal social development.

5. A team of scientists have decoded the 1700 genes of a microbe living on the ocean floor. This microbe belongs to a class called arachae, a different class from the two most common branches of life—bacteria and eukaryotes, which include plants, animals, and humans. The existence of archaea was first proposed by Carl Woese and Ralph Wolfe at the University of Illinois. Archaea has some characteristics of other life forms but functions differently. About 500 species of archaea have been identified. The life form is thought to produce about 30% of the biomass on earth.

Adapted from "Decoding of Microbe's Genes Sheds Light on Odd Form of Life," *Los Angeles Times*, August 8, 1996.

ANSWER KEY

Exercise 12

Verbs to be circled and explained are in italics:
1. *is designed* Use: to create cohesion and to put focus on "immune system" as the topic of the sentence. 2. *is called* Use: to focus on the topic being defined./*was explained* Use: to create cohesion and to put focus on the topic of superconductivity./*was thought* Use: to create cohesion and to put focus on the topic of superconductivity. 3. *is being fed* Use: to create cohesion and to put focus on the topic of the lava dome. 4. *were found* Use: to create cohesion and to put focus on the topic of the separation of chimpanzees from their mothers. 5. *was proposed* Use: to create cohesion and to put focus on the topic of arachae microbes/*have been identified* Use: to create cohesion and to put focus on the topic of species of arachae./*is thought* Use: to create cohesion and to put focus on the topic of arachae ("the life form").

EXERCISE 13

After each sentence or group of sentences, add a sentence with a passive verb to create cohesion, using the information given in parentheses.

▶ **EXAMPLE:** Any substance that is toxic to insects is known as an insecticide. (We use insecticides to control insects in situations where they cause economic damage or endanger health.)

Insecticides are used to control insects in situations where they cause economic damage or endanger health.

1. The ancient city of Troy was the setting of the legendary Greek siege described in *The Iliad*. (An earthquake destroyed the city around 1300 B.C.)

2. There are three types of muscle in humans and other vertebrates. One type is skeletal muscle. (Under a microscope, we see that this muscle is striped or striated.)

3. Most people associate the phrase "Survival of the fittest" with Darwin's Theory of Evolution. (However, a British philosopher, Herbert Spencer, first used the phrase, and Darwin later adopted it.)

4. The Great Wall of China served as a defensive wall between the old Chinese border with Manchuria and Mongolia. The first section was completed in the third century B.C. (The Chinese later extended it until it was 1400 miles long.)

5. Although the idea of submarines is an old one, the first submarine, made of wood and covered with greased leather, was not built until 1620. David Bushnell invented the first submarine used in warfare in 1776.

Exercise 13
E X P A N S I O N S

If Ss are writing paragraphs or essays for your class, have them check their drafts for places where passive verbs could be used to create cohesion.

1. Select a paragraph from a student essay that could be revised to improve cohesion by using the passive.

2. Put the paragraph on a transparency, a handout, or the board.

3. Have Ss revise the paragraph by making topics the subjects of sentences as in the examples shown in Focus 7 and Exercise 12.

UNIT GOAL REVIEW

Ask Ss to look at the goals on the opening page of the unit again. Help them understand how much they have accomplished in each area.

A N S W E R   K E Y

Exercise 13
Answers will vary.
1. The city was destroyed by . . . 2. Under a microscope, this muscle is seen to be striped or striated 3. However, the phrase was first used by a British philosopher . . . 4. It was later extended until . . . 5. The first submarine used in warfare was invented in 1776 by David Bushnell.

USE YOUR ENGLISH

To give Ss more communicative fluency practice, allow them to work without being immediately corrected. Instead of direct correction, note their errors for later discussion, or use their errors to return to one of the focus boxes to review.

Activity 1

Play textbook audio. The tapescript for this listening appears on page 564 of this book.

SUGGESTION

Ask your Ss if they have heard of these famous experiments and/or similar ones and briefly discuss if so. If you think your Ss need a brief overview of the topic or key vocabulary before listening to the tape, provide them with this information.

Activity 2
VARIATION

Give Ss several pages of a science text or instruction manual with multiple passives to analyze. Try to find one that has both stative and dynamic passives.

Activity 3
VARIATION

To save time, have Ss make up the sentences as homework and then meet with their groups during the next class meeting.

Workbook Ex. 10, p. 42; Ex. 11, p. 43.
Answers: TE p. 540.

Use Your English

ACTIVITY 1: LISTENING/SPEAKING/WRITING

A famous psychology laboratory experiment conducted by Stanley Milgram in 1963 tested subjects' willingness to obey authority even when they believed they would be required to administer painful electric shocks to other subjects. In the taped passage, you will hear a description of the procedures and the results of this experiment. Take notes on the information you hear. With a partner, compare notes to get information you may have missed. Then write a summary of the experiment, using passive verbs where appropriate to put focus on recipients of action and to achieve coherence.

ACTIVITY 2: READING

Find a text that has a number of passive verbs. (Science texts, instruction manuals, and texts that define or classify are good sources). Analyze ten passives that you find. Are they dynamic passives or stative passives? Why did the writer use them?

ACTIVITY 3: WRITING/SPEAKING

In small groups, make up five sentences describing people, places, or things, but don't reveal who/what they are. In each sentence, use a stative passive verb. See if other groups can guess who or what you are describing. Here are some examples. Can you guess the answers?

▶ **EXAMPLES:**
1. *It is divided into nine innings.*
2. *It can be found in tacos, spaghetti sauce, and ceviche.*
3. *This famous British dramatist is known as the Bard of Avon.*
4. *They are also called twisters.*
5. *This country is bordered by Italy, Austria, Germany, and France.*

ACTIVITY 4: WRITING

Draw a diagram or map of one of the following:
- an area (your room, apartment or house, a neighborhood, or commercial district, for example)
- a machine or device
- an invention of your own creation (a machine that writes your papers for you? a device that gets you out of bed in the morning?).

In your diagram/map, label at least four or five objects, parts, buildings, or whatever would be found there. Then write a paragraph describing the locations of objects or the ways in which you have divided your diagram/map into parts. Use stative passives in your descriptions.

ACTIVITY 5: WRITING

As the manager of a large office-supply store, you have observed repeated inappropriate behavior among some of the employees. This behavior includes the following:
- showing up late for work and leaving early
- taking breaks longer than the fifteen minutes allowed
- eating snacks at the service counter
- talking to other employees while customers are waiting for service.

Write a memo to the employees to let them know what kind of behavior is expected of them while they are at work. Since you want to assume an impersonal tone, use complex passives.

ACTIVITY 6: SPEAKING/LISTENING/WRITING

Interview a classmate about family or hometown history. Ask him or her to tell you about some events that are thought to be true but are not documented. The events might concern some long-ago period (for example, "Juan's great-grandfather was believed to have been born in Guatemala. The family is thought to have moved to Mexico in the early 1900s"). They could also include information about your classmate's youth as reported by his or her parents (for example, "Sonia is said to have been very good-natured as a baby.") Take notes during the interview. Then write up a report from your notes, using complex passives where appropriate to express some of the information. If time permits, present your report orally to the class.

Activity 4
VARIATION

1. Have Ss write their paragraph descriptions separate from their diagrams or maps. Tell them not to put their names on the pictures.
2. Post the diagrams/maps (or some of them, depending on the size of your class) on the classroom wall. Label them with numbers or letters (1,2,3; A, B, C, etc.).
3. Have Ss who created the diagrams/maps read their descriptions aloud to the class.
4. Ask Ss to match the description with the diagram or map.

(This variation could also be structured as a small group activity if you collect the diagrams/maps first and redistribute to groups during the next class. If you do this, you could have them put their names on the pictures with removable self-stick notes so that you know who the "artists" are.)

Activity 5
SUGGESTION

Introduce Ss to memo formats by writing a model on the board, distributing a handout from a business writing text, or referring them to templates provided by many word processing programs.

Activity 6
VARIATION

If your Ss live near their family members, they could interview an older relative.

The test for this unit can be found on p. 490. The answers are on p. 491.

Unit 5

UNIT OVERVIEW

Unit 5 assumes that students (Ss) have already studied the article system and generally know when and where to use *a, an, the,* and Ø article. Because many languages do not have an article system, this topic can be especially challenging and cause difficulty through the advanced level. Thus, the unit provides many exercises to help Ss solidify these concepts.

UNIT GOALS

Review the goals listed on this page so Ss understand what they should be able to know by the end of the unit.

OPENING TASK

The purpose of this task is to engage Ss in a discussion about current medical topics. In the course of the discussion, they will talk about nouns associated with medical and research procedures, diseases, body parts, etc., all of which require a fairly sophisticated knowledge of the English article system. With a mixed nationality class, the discussion can become quite lively, as certain practices may be more common in certain countries than others.

UNIT 5

ARTICLE USAGE

UNIT GOALS:

- To distinguish classification from identification meaning in articles
- To use definite, indefinite, and zero articles appropriately
- To distinguish particular from generic reference in articles
- To distinguish abstract generic from concrete generic meaning in articles
- To use the article in definitions of generic nouns
- To use the appropriate articles to correspond to body parts and illnesses

OPENING TASK
Controversial Medical Practices

STEP 1 Read the following list of current or possible practices in the medical profession. Check whether you believe they are ethical or not ethical.

ETHICAL?

Yes	No		
☐	☐	a.	Researchers using animals (mice, cats, cows, etc.) to test the poison level of drugs or the effect of artificial organs that might be implanted into a human being.
☐	☐	b.	Drug companies bribing doctors with vacations and other perquisites ("perks") to prescribe new but less well-known drugs to their patients.
☐	☐	c.	Machines keeping alive severely injured people who are in a vegetative state.
☐	☐	d.	Childless couples using surrogate (substitute) mothers to bear children.
☐	☐	e.	Engineering genetic changes in embryos to prevent birth defects or diseases.
☐	☐	f.	Forcing birth control on a population that for religious or cultural reasons does not desire it.
☐	☐	g.	Parents conceiving a child in order to obtain a matching organ or tissue to save the life of another one of their children.
☐	☐	h.	Poor people selling their own organs in order to make a living.
☐	☐	i.	Requiring doctors to reveal the results if they have a positive AIDS test and to quit their active medical practices.

STEP 2 In small groups, discuss the pros and cons of several of these practices based on information you have heard or read about. Choose one member of your group to take notes on the discussion.

STEP 3 (Recorder) Summarize your group's discussion for the rest of the class. Which topics were the most controversial? Which opinions did your group agree on?

CONDUCTING THE TASK

1. Divide Ss into groups.
2. Assign a notetaker and reporter to each group. The notetaker will take notes on a grid drawn on a lined piece of paper:

Practice	Ethical	Not Ethical
a. Animal Research	Animals were created to serve humankind (Bible)	Animals are living creatures and should not be harmed through research experiments (Bible)
f. Birth Control	Birth control is a positive way to prevent starving populations	Birth control is against God's law (Koran)

Alternatively, give the notetakers large pieces of butcher paper with felt pens and allow them to post their brainstorming results on the walls around the room.

3. Ask the reporter to stand and present the results of his/her group's discussion to the class.

1. Review with Ss that *a* precedes indefinite noun phrases that begin with consonant sounds and *an* precedes indefinite noun phrases that begin with vowel sounds. Emphasize that it is the succeeding sound, not the letter, that determines which indefinite article is required:

a	book, cat, red onion
an	apple, umbrella, an orange plate

BUT:
an hour (following sound is a silent consonant + vowel)
a union (following sound is the semi-vowel y)

2. Classification versus identification may be new concepts for determining correct article usage. State that classification refers to representatives of something or examples of something. Ask Ss what the following items in the classroom are representative of: (Point to posters.) *What are these examples of?* (*They are posters. It's a poster.*) (Point to two female students.) *What are these representatives of?* (*They are women. She's a woman.*) (Point to paper.) *What is this representative of?* (*It's paper. It's a piece of paper. They are papers. They are pieces of paper.*)

3. Now state that identification refers to something particular. (Point to poster.) *What is this?* (*It's <u>a</u> poster.*) *Which particular one is this?* (*It's <u>the</u> library poster.*) (Point to book.) *What is this?* (*It's <u>a</u> book.*) *Which particular one is this?* (*It's <u>the</u> blue book.*)

4. Read the explanations and then ask individuals to take turns reading examples *a* through *g* and *h* through *n*.

Classification versus Identification*
Meaning of Articles

EXAMPLES	EXPLANATIONS
	An indefinite article (*a/an* or Ø) classifies a noun and shows that it represents or reflects a type, group, or a class distinct from some other type, group or class.
(a) What did you see yesterday? I saw **a** horror movie last week.	• singular nouns (*a/an*)
(b) **An** earthquake (a natural disaster) struck at 7:10 A.M.	
(c) **A** gas (a type of gas) that can be deadly is carbon monoxide.	
(d) Ø Stars (celestial bodies) shine brightly.	• plural nouns (Ø)
(e) We expect Ø complications (additional problematic conditions) while she is sick.	
(f) Have you ever seen Ø traffic (passage of vehicles) like this?	• noncount nouns (Ø)
(g) Ø Mango juice (tropical fruit juice) can be made from Ø syrup (thick sweet liquid).	
	The definite article (*the*) can identify a noun and show that it has been singled out in some way. Generally, the speaker or writer knows the listener or reader is aware of the noun because it was previously mentioned or he or she can see it, has heard of it, has experienced it, has read about it, etc.
(h) **The** movie (you heard about it) featured Dracula.	• singular nouns (*the*)
(i) **The** earthquake (you know about it) destroyed many buildings.	
(j) **The** gas (you smell it) can be harmful.	
(k) **The** stars (we read about them) were discovered in 1952.	• plural nouns (*the*)

EXAMPLES	EXPLANATIONS
(l) **The** medical complications (you experienced them) were unexpected.	
(m) **The** traffic (we are riding in it) is dangerous.	• noncount nouns (*the*)
(n) Could you pass **the** maple syrup (you are near it)?	

*Adapted from P. Master, *Systems in English Grammar*. Englewood Cliffs, New Jersey: Prentice-Hall Regents, 1996.

EXERCISE 1

Look at the use of *a, an,* or *the* in each of the following cartoons.

STEP 1 Describe what is happening in each cartoon.

STEP 2 Discuss how the article classifies or identifies its corresponding noun.

▶ **EXAMPLE:** *Two children are pretending to be a doctor and a nurse to a teddy bear mother. The doctor is announcing the gender of a stuffed animal.*

• *"A" is used to classify the newborn as a male.*

It's a boy!

1.

Do you think Bob minds sitting in the back row?

2.

I told you it was an iron.

3.

I beat the eggs. Now what?

Exercise 1

1. Step 1: Three people went to a movie. All the seats were filled except two in the front row and one in the back row. Two found seats in the front row. Bob found a seat in the back row between two attractive women.
Step 2: "The" is used to identify the exact location of the seats (i.e., the very last row in the theatre).

2. Step 1: At an airport security check, a security officer checks a suspicious box that a man brought through. Although the man said the box contained an iron; the security officer insisted on delaying the man and other passengers while he unwrapped the box.
Step 2: "An" is used to classify the type of object in the box (i.e., an iron vs. a gun).

3. Step 1: An inexperienced cook is following a recipe which includes eggs. The humor in the caption is the double meaning of the word "beat"—"beat" can signify hitting an object strongly with a bat or similar weapon or it can mean breaking eggs with a whisk in a bowl.
Step 2: "The" is used to identify the eggs mentioned in the specific recipe at which the man is looking.

Exercise 1

This exercise can be done either individually or as pairwork. Tell Ss to be aware of the use of *a/an* for classification and *the* for identification as they respond.

Exercise 2

Ask Ss to pay attention to the noun following *what* in each question. Remind them that a kind, type, or class of something refers to classification. Something more specific like a feature, aspect, or characteristic in the question calls for identification.

Exercise 3

Some of the answers may be challenging if Ss are not aware that a noun is identifiable if it is a second mention reference or it can be connected to a previous reference by association. For example, once the ambulance has been mentioned, the paramedics can be presumed to be associated with the ambulance and thus are identifiable and referred to with *the—the paramedics* (the paramedics associated with that ambulance).

EXERCISE 2

Answer the following questions with noun phrases. Use *a/an, the,* or Ø to show that the noun is classified (shows kind, type, class, etc.) or identified (shows specific feature, aspect, characteristic, etc.)

▶ **EXAMPLES:**   What part of a holiday dinner do you enjoy the most?
the stuffed turkey (identified)

What kind of meat do you like the most?
beef, a hot dog (classified)

1. What kind of movie is most exciting?
2. What feature of your classroom is unusual?
3. What kind of person is attractive?
4. What type of vegetables do you dislike the most?
5. What aspect of your English class was most interesting this week?
6. What type of clothing is usually made of wool?
7. What characteristic of rap music is unusual?
8. What class of animal gives birth to live young?
9. What part of a chicken do you like eating the most?
10. What aspect of your car or your friend's car is unusual?

EXERCISE 3

Fill in the following blanks with *a/an, the,* or Ø. In which blanks did you use *the* to refer to identifiable nouns?

On (1) ___the___ night of January 11, 1983, Nancy Cruzan,

(2) _____ healthy, twenty-five-year-old woman, lost control of her car

while driving in Jasper County, Missouri. As (3) _____ car overturned,

Nancy was thrown into (4) _____ ditch. When the ambulance reached

(5) _____ ditch, (6) _____ paramedics found her with no

(7) _____ detectable breathing or (8) _____ heartbeat. Today Nancy

lies in (9) _____ Missouri state hospital, in what is described all too

neatly as (10) _____ "persistent vegetative state." In reality, she lies in

(11) _____ bed in (12) _____ hospital, horribly contorted with

(13) _____ irreversible muscular and (14) _____ tendon damage.

She is fed through (15) _____ tube in her side.

ANSWER KEY

Exercise 2
Answers will vary.
1. a detective movie   2. the large orange clock on the wall   3. a person with an enthusiastic personality   4. green vegetables such as broccoli   5. the lesson on adjectives
6. a coat   7. the beat   8. a mammal
9. the thigh   10. the leather seats

Exercise 3
2. a   3. the   4. a   5. the
6. the   7. Ø   8. Ø   9. a   10. a
11. a   12. the   13. Ø   14. Ø   15. a

EXERCISE 4

Fill in the following blanks with *the* or Ø. In which blanks, did you use the Ø to refer to classifiable nouns?

(1) ___The___ students entering our medical schools have

(2) _____ outstanding grade-point averages, and (3) _____

impressive scores on (4) _____ Medical College Admissions Test, and

(5) _____ glowing recommendations. There's no doubt that they have

(6) _____ capability to become (7) _____ good scientists and

(8) _____ good science doctors. But do they have (9) _____ makings

of humanists with (10) _____ commitment to treat everything from

(11) _____ broken bones to (12) _____ broken hearts? It is this

delicate balance between (13) _____ science and (14) _____ wisdom

that makes (15) _____ great physicians—(16) _____ ability to know

what to do with what has been learned.

Article Usage | **81**

Exercise 4

Remind students that classifiable noncount and plural noun phrases are preceded by Ø article. Identifiable noun phrases require **the**.

Workbook Ex. 1, p. 44.
Answers: TE p. 540.

ANSWER KEY

Since Ss have most likely studied uses of the definite article in the past, the focus box should be a review.

SUGGESTIONS

1. Purchase sentence strips and a pocket chart at a teacher's supply store and write the examples (or similar examples) and explanations (preferably in two different colors) on 30 different strips of paper.
2. Pass out one sentence strip per person and ask Ss to wander around the room and try to match their example strip with someone else's explanation strip in the class.
3. If Ss think they have a match, they can place them on the pocket chart until all strips have been arranged.
4. Ask pairs to read their matched sentences aloud for the whole class.

FOCUS **2**

Special Uses of the Definite Article

EXAMPLES	EXPLANATIONS
	Use *the*:
(a) **The sun** is very bright.	• with unique nouns
(b) **The most significant effect** occurred in June.	• before superlatives
(c) **The third component** was missing.	• before ordinals (*first, second, third*, etc.)
(d) **The main operator** was not on duty.	• before modifiers that make the noun that follows specific (*same, sole, chief, only, single, solitary, main*, etc.)
(e) Each of **the experiments** was successful.	• in phrases that refer to a specific part of a whole group
(f) Half of **the population** suffered greatly.	
(g) **The effect** of an earthquake can be felt for miles.	• with identifiable nouns that are followed by a modifying *of*-phrase
(h) We were uncertain about **the cause** of the fire.	
(i) **The beginning** of the movie was frightening.	
(j) A major urban problem is caring for **the poor** (people).	• before adjectives that represent groups of people
(k) "Heartbreak" is a song on **the radio.**	• with certain nouns, such as mechanical inventions and devices, to refer to a general example of something rather than a specific object the speaker/writer has in mind
(l) She got here fast because she took **the train.**	
(m) I went to **the barber** after classes.	• before locations associated with certain typical or habitual activities. The listener/reader may have no idea of the exact location to which the speaker/writer is referring.
(n) Have you been to **the beach** this summer?	
(o) She needs to pick up a few things at **the store.**	

EXERCISE 5

For each of the following sentences, circle the correct article in parentheses. Explain your choices to a partner.

▶ **EXAMPLE:** (A/the) sun is very bright today. I need to buy (a/the) cap at (a/the) store.

The sun is very bright. I need to buy a cap at the store.

Sun *is a unique noun; therefore,* ***the*** *is used.* ***A cap*** *is used because it refers to a type of hat, not to a particular one.* ***The store*** *is used because a location referring to a specific habitual activity (shopping) is being referred to.*

1. All civilizations of (a/the) world are enriched by trade and (a/the) stimulating impact of other cultures.

2. There are two main precursors to skin cancer. (A/the) first indication is spontaneous bleeding on some part of (a/the) skin. (A/the) second is the enlargement of a freckle or mole.

3. I'll be late for (a/the) meeting because I have to make (a/the) deposit at (a/the) bank.

4. (A/the) most significant effect of (an/the) earthquake was (a/the) destruction of many homes.

5. I read (a/the) wonderful story yesterday. (A/the) beginning of the story takes place in Vienna about (a/the) turn of (a/the) century.

6. In (a/the) past, (a/the) most important factor determining world power was (a/the) navy that could navigate (a/the) Mediterranean.

7. There were many reasons for (a/the) success of (a/the) project. (A/the) main reason was that at least half of (a/the) workgroup had Ph.D.s from around (a/the) globe.

8. (A/the) radio described several ways in which (an/the) elderly could obtain (a/the) best medical help.

9. In (a/the) next year, (an/the) exact mechanism by which cell receptors work will be better understood.

10. (A/the) last decade has been marked by (a/the) large increase in violence.

Exercise 5

This activity requires Ss to show their metalinguistic knowledge of the rules studied up to this point in the chapter. Encourage them to refer back to Focus Boxes 1 and 2 to remind themselves of the rules and to verbally describe why a particular article was chosen.

ANSWER KEY

Exercise 5

1. (the) *world* is a unique noun. (the) before identifiable noun followed by modifying *of*-phrase. 2. (the) before ordinal number. (the) phrase which refers to a specific part of a whole. (the) before ordinal number. 3. (the) *meeting* is identifiable to both listener and speaker. (a/the) depends on whether the listener is familiar or unfamiliar with what deposit is being made. (the) is used before locations associated with typical activities. 4. (the) before superlative. (the) refers to a unique experience, at least in recent memory. (the) before identifiable noun followed by *of*-phrase. 5. (a) classifies a type of story. (the) before identifiable nouns followed by modifying *of*-phrase. (the) before identifiable nouns followed by modifying *of*-phrase. (the) identifiable noun—it is assumed the speaker is referring to the turn of the twentieth century. 6. (the) an identifiable time period (the) before superlative. (a) refers to a type of military force. (the) before a unique noun. 7. (the) identifiable noun followed by identifying *of*-phrase. (the) before an identifiable noun. (the) before modifiers that make the noun that follows specific. (the) in phrase which refers to a specific part of a whole. (the) before a unique noun. 8. (the) mechanical invention that is non-specific. (the) before an adjective which represents a group of people. (the) before superlative. 9. (the) before ordinals. (the) before modifiers that make the noun that follows specific. 10. (the) before ordinals. (a) before non-specific nouns.

1. Write the following questions on the blackboard and ask Ss to answer them in complete sentences on a sheet of paper at their desks.
   a. *Where were you at 4:00 a.m. this morning?*
   b. *What time of day was it last night at 12:00?*
   c. *What meal did you eat at about 12:00 today or yesterday?*
   d. *How did you come to school today?*
   e. *In which way did you communicate with your best friend the last time?*
2. Ask Ss to look at the nouns at or near the end of each sentence and tell what they notice about them. For example:
   a. *I was at home.*
   b. *It was midnight.*
   c. *I ate lunch.*
   d. *I came on foot.*
   d. *I communicated by phone.*
   Ss should note that the nouns are not preceded by articles.
3. Review the special uses of Ø in the focus box, which includes some of these familiar topics as well as some idiom uses.

Review and Special Uses of Ø

EXAMPLES	EXPLANATIONS
(a) Ø Flowers should be watered regularly. **(b)** I need to get Ø gas before we start for Seattle.	Ø is used when the following noun is non-specific. Use Ø with: • nouns that have general or generic reference (see Focus 4) • nonspecific nouns that do not refer to a specific quantity or amount
(c) The children ran directly Ø home. **(d)** They went Ø downtown after supper. **(e)** My grandmother walked to Ø school everyday. **(f)** He worked until Ø midnight. **(g)** Ø Spring is a wonderful time of year. **(h)** We had Ø lunch at a very good restaurant. **(i)** The group arrived by Ø car. **(j)** They came on Ø foot from the meeting. **(k)** We were informed by Ø mail that our subscription had been canceled.	Also use Ø with: • certain nouns associated with familiar destinations • certain nouns of time (*night, dusk, noon, midday, midnight,* etc.) • names of seasons (*spring, summer, fall, winter*) • names of meals (*breakfast, brunch, lunch, dinner,* etc.) • means of transportation (*by boat, by plane, on foot,* etc.) • means of communication (*by phone, by mail, by telegram,* etc.)
(l) They walked Ø arm in Ø arm down the aisle. **(m)** The ship was lost at Ø sea. **(n)** He put his heart and Ø soul into the project. **(o)** Peter took Ø care of the details.	Certain idioms use Ø: • phrases joined with *by, in,* or *and* (*day by day, week by week, side by side, arm in arm, neck and neck,* etc.) • participle + preposition + count noun (*wounded in action, lost at sea, missing in action, cash on delivery,* etc.) • phrases joined by *and* (*heart and soul, bread and butter, husband and wife,* etc.) • verb + objects + preposition (*shake hands with, take care of, take advantage of, take part in, take notice of, take pride in,* etc.)

EXERCISE 6

Fill in the following blanks with *a/an, the,* or Ø. More than one answer may be appropriate.

It was (1) ___Ø___ spring and (2) _____ young GI, returning (3) _____ home from (4) _____ war, called his parents from (5) _____ phone booth in (6) _____ bus station. His parents had waited for a message by (7) _____ mail or (8) _____ telegram, but he had not gotten around to writing. On (9) _____ phone, he told his parents that he would be coming by (10) _____ bus and that he would be (11) _____ home by 5:00 that evening. But he hesitated (12) _____ moment and then added that he was bringing (13) _____ home (14) _____ friend, and he hoped that it would be okay with them because his friend was handicapped. He had been wounded in (15) _____ action and had no legs. He asked his parents' permission. They told him that they felt very sorry for (16) _____ friend but they were not really set up to cook (17) _____ breakfast, (18) _____ lunch, and (19) _____ dinner for him—this was not (20) _____ good time for him to come. The mother worked; there were two floors in (21) _____ house; she would have to run up and down; (22) _____ money was tight, etc., etc. As it turned out, (23) _____ young man did not get off (24) _____ bus that night, because he was (25) _____ handicapped soldier. It was their son who had been wounded in (26) _____ action. The parents never saw him again.

1. Tell Ss that the passage is about a soldier returning from war. Ask Ss to fill in the blanks.
2. Have Ss discuss their article choices.
3. If time, ask Ss to express their feelings about the passage without looking at the text. Take note of their use of articles in free speech.

Workbook Exs. 2 & 3, pp. 45–46.
Answers: TE p. 541.

ANSWER KEY

Exercise 6
2. a   3. Ø   4. Ø   5. a   6. The/a   7. Ø
8. Ø/a   9. the   10. Ø   11. Ø   12. a
13. Ø   14. a   15. Ø   16. the   17. Ø
18. Ø   19. Ø   20. a   21. the   22. the/Ø   23. the   24. the   25. the   26. Ø

1. Read the rule stated at the beginning of the box.
2. Ask five different Ss to read the examples in the box.

Workbook Exs. 4 & 5, pp. 46–47.
Answers: TE p. 541.

FOCUS **4**

Particular versus Generic Reference of Articles

Generic reference relates to the general rather than the particular nature of something. Particular reference indicates one member of a class; generic reference indicates all or representative members of a class. Note in the following examples the particular and generalized meanings of *laser* in different contexts.

EXAMPLES	EXPLANATIONS
(a) Her doctor used a **laser** to treat her varicose veins.	• particular reference
(b) The **laser** cured Paul's cataract problem.	• particular reference
(c) The **laser** has been used in medicine since the 1960s.	• generic reference
(d) A **laser** can cut through soft tissue with a searing light.	• generic reference
(e) **Lasers** reduce the recovery period needed for ordinary operations.	• generic reference

EXERCISE 7

For each of the following pairs of sentences, circle the option that makes a general versus a particular reference about the italicized noun phrase. Note that different references are only sometimes marked by different articles.

▶ **EXAMPLE:** (a) An *immunity* is a resistance to infection.

(b) I have an *immunity* to small pox.

1. (a) You should take *the vitamins* on the counter.
   (b) You should take *vitamins* in order to stay healthy.
2. (a) A *cholera epidemic* was started by contaminated food and water.
   (b) *Cholera epidemics* kill many people every year.
3. (a) A *doctor* claimed to have discovered a miracle burn ointment.
   (b) A *doctor* is trained to treat burns.
4. (a) *The motion picture industry* has created many movie idols.
   (b) She is working for *the motion picture industry* in Los Angeles.
5. (a) There is no cure for *a cold*.
   (b) I have had *a cold* for four weeks.

ANSWER KEY

Exercise 7
1. b   2. b   3. b   4. a   5. a   6. b
7. b   8. a   9. b   10. a

6. (a) *The mouse* used in the experiment was injected with morphine.

   (b) *The mouse* is an excellent research animal.

7. (a) The patient will sit in *the wheelchair* until her daughter arrives.

   (b) *The wheelchair* has improved the lives of the handicapped.

8. (a) Angela has been playing *the saxophone* for three years.

   (b) Angela has been playing *the saxophone* that was in the corner.

9. (a) *Some people* have been sitting in the waiting room since 11:00 A.M.

   (b) *People* kept alive only by machines should be allowed to die.

10. (a) *Water* from springs contains minerals.

    (b) *The water* from the spring cured my illness.

FOCUS **5**

The + Plural Nouns for General Reference

EXAMPLES	EXPLANATIONS
	Sometimes, *the* may be combined with plural nouns when referring generally to:
(a) The Sierra Club is intent on saving **the redwoods**.	• plant and animal groups that are the target of special attention
(b) We went to a fund-raising benefit for **the whales**.	
(c) **(The) Neo-Nazis** propagate discrimination and hate.	• social, political, religious, and national groups. (Note that *the* is optional here.) A few nationality words do not allow
(d) **(The) Republicans** have conservative values.	plural endings and require *the*: *the Swedish, the Danish, the Finnish, the*
(e) **(The) Jews** celebrate Passover.	*Polish, the Swiss, the English, the French, the Dutch, the Irish, the Welsh,*
(f) **The Dutch** are very good at learning languages.	*the British, the Chinese, the Japanese,* etc.).

FOCUS 5

S U G G E S T I O N

1. Bring in a National Geographic Magazine or a Sierra Club Magazine that displays pictures of different animals on the endangered wildlife list or presents different groups of people around the world. Flip to one or more pages and ask Ss what they know about some of these—for example, the redwoods, the Tahitians, or the Amish. If you do not have access to such magazines, have Ss brainstorm examples of endangered wildlife or specific social/political/religious/national groups.

2. Ask Ss to read Focus 5 silently.

3. Solicit sentences to write on the board about the groups the students have just seen pictures of. Note examples when *the* is required or is optional.

Exercise 8

Ask Ss to work in pairs and match the associations to particular people. Remind Ss that certain nouns are common nouns that do not correspond to social, political, religious, and national groups (e.g., *criminal*) and, therefore, are not preceded by *the*.

EXERCISE 8

Match up the following associations with the corresponding types of people. (Some associations may apply to more than one group.) Select five statements and write them in complete sentences below.

▶ **EXAMPLE:** *(The) Italians eat a lot of pasta.*
Criminals commit serious crimes.

Association
1. face racial discrimination
2. want equality in marriage
3. know many languages
4. like to dance
5. eat a lot of pasta
6. like to loan money at high interest
7. discriminate against different races
8. must "publish or perish"
9. forget campaign promises
10. pray to Allah
11. want more than the minimum wage
12. commit serious crimes

People
a. Swiss
b. Muslim
c. professor
d. racist
e. politician
f. Brazilian
g. criminal
h. feminist
i. laborer
j. African American
k. Italian
l. banker

1. _____

2. _____

3. _____

4. _____

5. _____

ANSWER KEY

Exercise 8
1. j **2.** h **3.** a **4.** f **5.** k **6.** l **7.** d
8. c **9.** e **10.** b **11.** i **12.** g

Abstract Generic versus Concrete Generic

EXAMPLES	EXPLANATIONS
definite article = the laser indefinite article = a laser zero article = Ø lasers = Ø blood	The most common way to signal general reference in English is: • *the* + singular count nouns • *a/an* + singular count nouns • Ø + plural count nouns • Ø + noncount nouns
(a) **The dermatologist** specializes in skin care. (b) **The platypus** is an unusual creature. (c) The heaviest organ is **the skin**. (d) **The eucalyptus** is native to Australia. (e) What has revolutionized the workplace is **the computer**. (f) It is difficult to play **the harp**. (g) NOT: The towel absorbs water. (h) **An operation** is stressful to one's body. (i) Ø **Carriers** may pass infections on to others. (j) Ø **Ultrasound** can detect the sex of an unborn baby.	There are two types of generic reference:* • <u>Abstract generic reference</u> uses *the* with singular countable nouns and noncount nouns to refer to certain well-defined, entire classes of entities. These entities are humans, animals, organs of the body, plants, complex inventions, and devices that can often serve as agents of change. They are not simple inanimate objects. • <u>Concrete generic reference</u> pertains to each or all of the representatives of a class rather than to the whole class. It uses a greater variety of forms than abstract generic reference does. *a(n)* + singular count noun Ø + plural noun Ø + noncount noun
(k) **A police officer** carries **a gun**. (l) **A laser** directs **a beam of light** to make an incision. (m) **The/A dermatologist** uses a **special solution** to remove warts. (n) **The/A kangaroo** carries **its young** in a pouch. (o) NOT: An elephant is in danger of becoming extinct.	<u>Singular concrete generic nouns</u> with *a(n)* describe generalized instances of something. This means that the noun class is being referred to one member at a time and there may be references to other singular count nouns in the sentence. <u>Abstract generic nouns</u> may be preceded by *a(n)* if they are being referred to one member at a time.

*P Master, "Teaching the English Article System, Part II: Generic versus Specific." *English Teaching Forum*. July 1988.

1. Write the following five words/phrases across the top of a grid on the blackboard: *humans, animals, organs of the body, plants, complex inventions,* and *devices*. Title the list "The Special 5."
2. Ask Ss to volunteer examples of each type of word/phrase, e.g., doctor, bear, liver, fern, tractor, etc.
3. Emphasize that "The Special 5" are the only types of words that can be referred to generically using the definite article *the*.
4. Tell Ss that all other words can be referred to generically with a wider variety of predeterminers: *a, an,* and *Ø*. Read the examples and explanations *a* through *j* in the box.
5. Read examples *k* through *o* and explain that the set of words listed on the board will sometimes be referred to generically with *a, an,* or *Ø* when there is another singular count noun reference in a sentence, e.g., *A politician is a master of deceit* (preferred). *The politician is a master of deceit* (but also acceptable). Both sentences refer to politicians (people) in a general way.

Exercise 9

Remind Ss to refer to the five categories of nouns listed in Focus 6 which favor the use of *the*. Note that the use of an adjective before the noun does not affect the article choice, i.e., The *redwood* is a plant and thus favors the use of *the*. Adding *California* does not change this preference.

Exercise 11

This exercise may be challenging for Ss. Remind them to include words like *its* ____ and *a(n)* ____, in postverbal position, e.g., *A dog is __an__ excellent pet.*

EXERCISE 9

In each set, select one noun phrase that we can refer to with abstract generic *the*. Then, use that noun phrase in a general sentence. Note that descriptive words before and after nouns do not affect the use of generic *the*.

▶ **EXAMPLE:** tattered flag/California redwood/stepbrother
The California redwood is older than other trees.

1. lining of the coat/apartment made of brick/African elephant
2. dust on the moon/illustration of the month/telephone for emergency communication
3. barbecue/artificial heart/Persian rug
4. free love/fin of a fish/French marigold
5. Hungarian embroidery/American automobile/Spanish tile
6. locksmith/key/door

EXERCISE 10

Check the sentences in which *the* could be substituted for *a(n)* to make a generic reference. Then explain why.

▶ **EXAMPLE:** A transistor is used in computers.
*Because the transistor is a complex device, **the** is possible.*

1. An X-ray machine is used in radiotherapy.
2. A solar eclipse lasts about 7.5 minutes.
3. An octopus has eight legs.
4. A sprain is suffered when an ankle is wrenched.
5. A piano has fifty-two white keys.
6. A road is wider than an alley.
7. A human brain is larger than a bird brain.
8. A governor of a state (in the United States) has limited power.

EXERCISE 11

Read the following sentences that use *the* for abstract generic reference of a noun. Replace *the* with *a/an* and add singular noun phrases within a new sentence to show that you are talking about generalized instances of something.

▶ **EXAMPLE:** The dog is man's best friend.
A dog needs its owner's attention every day.

1. The dragon only existed in fairy tales.

_____

2. The store manager needs good organizational skills.

_____

Exercise 9
1. *The African elephant* is a magnificent beast.
2. *The telephone for emergency communication* has become a useful accessory in modern life.   3. *The artificial heart* has allowed many people to live who otherwise would have died.   4. *The French marigold* is a popular variety.   5. *The American automobile* used to be revered all over the world.   6. *The locksmith* can assist people in making keys or unlocking doors.

Exercise 10
1. The X-ray machine (complex device)
3. The octopus (animal)   5. The piano (instrument)   7. The human brain (body part)
8. The governor of a state (human)

Exercise 11
Answers will vary.
1. **b.** A dragon is a mythical beast that breathes fire from its throat.   2. **b.** A store manager knows each of his or her employees.
3. **b.** A plow can ease a farmer's work.

4. **b.** A weeping willow has a special kind of branch that bends towards the ground.
5. **b.** A snail carries its house on its back.
6. **b.** A cactus may display a beautiful type of flower during certain parts of the year.
7. **b.** A piano is often used during a church service.   8. **b.** A stomach is a sac-like organ between the esophagus and the intestines.
9. **b.** An opthamologist uses a special instrument to examine eyes.   10. **b.** A printing press could produce written material much faster than a scribe.

3. The plow is essential to farming.

_____

4. No shade tree is as beautiful as the weeping willow.

_____

5. One of the slowest animals is the snail.

_____

6. The cactus grows in warm climates.

_____

7. The piano is commonly found in American homes.

_____

8. The stomach is essential for digestion.

_____

9. The ophthalmologist examines eyes.

_____

10. The printing press was essential to mass communication.

_____

EXERCISE 12

Describe a usual or general tendency by completing the sentences below.

▶ **EXAMPLE:** A chocolate chip cookie is made of _sugar, flour, butter, and chocolate chips._

1. A good party consists of _____

2. The Internet has changed _____

3. A healthy life includes _____

4. Builders name streets after _____

5. The police are needed for _____

6. Amnesia causes _____

7. Skillful architects create _____

8. A valuable education includes _____

Exercise 12

Encourage Ss to be creative. The longer the sentence, the more opportunity to use multiple count and noncount nouns.

Workbook Exs. 6 & 7, pp. 47–48.
Answers: TE p. 541.

A N S W E R   K E Y

Exercise 12

Answers will vary.

1. A good party consists of good company and a lot of food.   2. The Internet has changed the way people obtain information.   3. A healthy life includes intellectual and social stimulation.   4. Builders name streets after names of trees.   5. The police are needed to execute the law.   6. Amnesia causes someone to forget who and where they are. 7. Skillful architects create magnificent buildings.   8. A valuable education includes instruction in various areas such as language, science, psychology, etc.

This focus box will help Ss to write grammatically correct definitions. Remind Ss not to forget the principles taught in Focus 6 as they create definitions for certain words. Humans, animals, organs of the body, plants, and complex inventions/devices may be preceded by *the*.

FOCUS **7**

▶ **Definitions of Common Nouns**

Standard definitions of generic nouns follow the pattern below. Generic nouns appear in the subject position of these definitions.

GENERIC NOUN	+ BE	+	CLASSIFYING NOUN*	+ RELATIVE PRONOUN	+ VERB PHRASE
(a) **The dinosaur**	is		a prehistoric animal	that	scientists discovered through excavations.
(b) **A dinosaur**	is		a prehistoric animal	that	is now extinct.
(c) **Dinosaurs**	are		prehistoric animals	that	roamed the earth during the Mesozoic Age.

(d) **The chicken** is an animal that lays eggs.	Abstract generic nouns emphasize: • a class Concrete generic nouns emphasize:
(e) **A chicken** is an animal that lays eggs. (f) **Chickens** are animals that lay eggs. (g) **Chicken** is a meat that is very moist.	• an example, any members • a group, all members • all/any of something
(h) **The platypus** is a mammal that lays eggs. (i) **A duck** is a bird that has webbed feet. (j) **Vultures** are birds that are larger than rats.	Definitions can include: • classifications • attributes • comparisons

*See Focus 1.

Exercise 13

E X P A N S I O N

If time, ask Ss to do more exercises with the following words: *taxi driver, naval orange, floppy disk, shoulder blade, cardboard box, old picture,* and *piece of chalk.* (Generally, the latter three are not preceded by *the* for definitions.)

EXERCISE 13

Write incorrect definitions for the words provided below. Then, in pairs, take turns reading and correcting each other's definitions.

▶ **EXAMPLES:** bicycle
  a) *A bicycle is a four-wheeled vehicle that you can sit on.*
  b) *No, a bicycle is a two-wheeled vehicle that you can sit on.*

1. stethoscope	3. liver	5. palm tree	7. nail	9. honey
2. koala bears	4. spatula	6. eye	8. movie stars	10. violin

A N S W E R   K E Y

Exercise 13
Answers will vary. Examples of incorrect definitions:
1. A stethoscope is an instrument which a dentist uses to examine your teeth. **2.** Koala bears are animals which live in the woods of North America. **3.** The liver is a type of flower which blooms at night. **4.** A spatula is an implement which is used to stir oatmeal.

5. A palm tree is a type of tree that grows in frigid zones. **6.** An eye is a part of the body which allows someone to smell. **7.** A nail is a type of song which is popular with teenagers. **8.** Movie stars are marketing executives who sell trips to the moon. **9.** Honey is a substance which gardeners sprinkle on the ground to make flowers grow. **10.** The violin is a tool similar to a hammer.

EXERCISE 14

Find the incorrect article (*a/an*, *the*, *Ø*) in the following definitions. Then, correct the error.

▶ **EXAMPLE:** ~~The~~ Universe is a system of galaxies that was created 10,000 million years ago.

1. The fashion design is a major that requires artistic talent.
2. A radio telescope is telescope that collects long-wavelength radiation.
3. Astronaut is a person who travels in space.
4. A neurosis is mental disorder that is relatively minor.
5. Dirge is a musical piece played at a funeral.
6. In many homes, prayers are said before meal.
7. The somnambulism is a word for a condition called sleepwalking.
8. The mercury is a white metallic element, which is liquid at atmospheric temperature.
9. Vaporization is the conversion of liquid into a vapor.
10. The blackboard is a surface that is used for writing.

FOCUS **8**

Articles with Names of Body Parts

EXAMPLES	EXPLANATIONS
	When generally referring to names of organs, parts of the body, or body fluids, we can use *the*:
(a) **The** heart can be transplanted. (b) Cancer of **the** bladder has been linked to cigarette smoking.	• singular body parts (*the* + noun)
(c) **(The)** blood carries nutrients to body tissues. (d) **(The)** skin is sensitive to ultra-violet rays.	• massive areas or fluids of the body (*the* + noncount noun)
(e) Excessive smoke inhalation damages **the lungs**. (f) Regular exams of **the teeth** will prevent serious dental problems. (g) **The veins** carry blood throughout the body.	• plural or paired body parts (*the* + noun + plural)

Article Usage | **93**

Exercise 14

Remind Ss to look carefully at the noun to determine whether it is one of the "The Special 5" types of nouns that prefer *the* or whether it is another type of count or noncount noun that will require *a*, *an*, or *Ø*.

FOCUS 8

Ss can read this focus box for homework or in class. Note that *the* is generally used with names of body parts, unless the body parts are noncount nouns, in which case *the* is optional.

Workbook Ex. 8, p. 49.
Answers: TE p. 541.

Exercise 15

V A R I A T I O N

Have Ss write false sentences, e.g., *The heart is below the gall bladder,* and then in pairs try to correct each other's sentences.

Workbook Ex. 9, p. 50.
Answers: TE p. 541.

EXERCISE 15

Study the following diagram and write sentences describing the location or function of at least eight of the following body parts.

▶ **EXAMPLES:** a) The diaphragm is below the lungs.
b) The brain controls all muscular movements of the body.

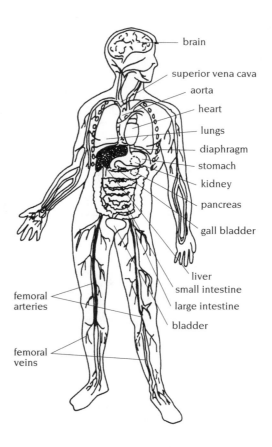

A N S W E R   K E Y

Exercise 15

Answers will vary.
1. The diaphragm is used in the production of speech.   2. The kidney excretes urine.   3. The pancreas is the digestive gland behind the stomach.   4. The femoral arteries carry blood from the heart.   5. The lungs are used to breathe.

Articles with Names of Illnesses

The names of illnesses follow a range of noun patterns:

THE + NOUN	A/AN + NOUN		(THE) + NOUN + PLURAL
the flu	a cold	an ulcer	(the) bends
the gout	a hernia	a stroke	(the) mumps
the plague	a headache	an earache	(the) measles
	a heart attack	a sore throat	(the) hiccups

Ø + NONCOUNT NOUN		Ø + NOUN (WITH FINAL -S)
influenza	leukemia	diabetes
pneumonia	diarrhea	rabies
malaria	mononucleosis	herpes
arthritis	cardiovascular disease	AIDS
cancer	tuberculosis	

EXERCISE 16

Fill in a correct disease/illness that matches the information in the following blanks.

▶ **EXAMPLE:** ___AIDS___ is caused by a blood-borne virus (HIV, Human Immunodeficiency Virus).

1. _____ is a disease that ravaged Europe between 1347–1351.
2. _____ is the bulging out of a part of any of the internal organs through a muscular wall.
3. _____ is a contagious disease that causes red spots to appear on the skin.
4. _____ is caused by a parasite, which is transmitted by a female mosquito.
5. _____ is a form of cancer that is marked by an increase in white blood cells.
6. _____ is an inflammation of the lungs caused by bacteria or viruses.

Article Usage | **95**

ANSWER KEY

Exercise 16
1. the plague 2. a hernia 3. (the) measles 4. malaria 5. leukemia

6. tuberculosis 7. (the) bends 8. herpes 9. a stroke 10. (the)hiccups

---

Note the complex array of articles used with names of illnesses. Answer questions Ss might have about these illnesses.

Exercise 16

This exercise creates a good opportunity for Ss to solidify their knowledge of illnesses.

E X P A N S I O N

1. To help Ss memorize the appropriate articles needed, divide the class into threesomes and have one student create a tic-tac-toe grid with nine of the illnesses listed. For example,

flu	herpes	tuberculosis
sore throat	earache	diarrhea
malaria	mumps	gout

This same student will be the referee for the game.

2. One student will select a square. If he or she correctly supplies the correct article, he or she will write X in the square. If he or she is incorrect, then it is the other student's turn.

3. The game continues until one student gets all Xs or all Os horizontally, vertically, or diagonally.

7. _____ is a decompression sickness experienced in the air or the water.

8. _____ consists of sores on the skin or internal parts of the body and is often caused by stress.

9. _____ is a common name for a cerebral hemor-rhage.

10. _____ is a sound caused by contractions of the di-aphragm.

Exercise 17

Exercises 17–20 provide Ss with several opportunities to practice the articles. Because this is a late acquired structure, Ss will need further practice and review throughout the school term. Additional exercises can easily be created following the models shown here: find the error, fill in the blank, explain the choice, and rewrite full sentences from notes. Almost any text at the Ss' level can be adapted for this purpose.

Exercises 18, 19, and 20

These exercises can be used for diagnostic or testing purposes. They can be done individually or in pairs.

EXERCISE 17

Review all of the rules in Unit 5. Locate ten article errors with *a/an, the,* or Ø in the following paragraph. The first one has been done for you.

(1) The gap between ^the rich and the poor, among countries and within countries, is widening. (2) Most of world's AIDS cases and HIV-infected people are in the developing countries. (3) Yet drug and hospitalization costs mean that "early intervention" is still meaningless concept in these countries. (4) Drug AZT remains too expensive for most of people who need it. (5) The industrialized world's total annual contributions to the AIDS in the developing world is estimated at $200 million or less. (6) The last year, the total expenditure for AIDS prevention and care in New York state alone was five times greater. (7) Total budget of the average national AIDS program in the developing world today is less than medical cost of caring for only fifteen people with AIDS in United States.

Adapted from J. Mann, "Global AIDS: Revolution, Paradigm, Solidarity." In O. Peterson, ed., *Representative American Speeches*, New York: The H.W. Wilson Co., 1991.

EXERCISE 18

Review all of the rules in Unit 5. Locate ten article errors with *a/an, the,* or Ø in each of the following blanks. Explain your choices to a partner.

(1) __Ø__ insulin functions as (2) _____ indispensable middle-man in (3) _____ metabolism. When we eat (4) _____ carbohy-drate foods such as (5) _____ bread, (6) _____ vegetables, or (7) _____ fruit, (8) _____ simple sugar called (9) _____ glu-cose is usually (10) _____ end product of (11) _____ digestion,

and this sugar provides (12) _____ energy to each living cell;

(13) _____ insulin, in its turn, functions as (14) _____ doorman

to these cells, controlling (15) _____ access of (16) _____ glucose

molecules and other food sources such as (17) _____ protein and

(18) _____ fat across (19) _____ cell membrane and into each

cell's interior. With (20) _____ insulin, (21) _____ metabolism is

(22) _____ finely tuned feedback mechanism. Without it, only

(23) _____ trickle of (24) _____ fuel leaks into (25) _____

cells, hardly enough to stoke (26) _____ great human metabolic fur-

nace.

Adapted from S. Hall, *Invisible Frontiers*, New York: The Atlantic Monthly Press, 1987.

EXERCISE 19

Look at the underlined articles in the following paragraph. Explain the choice of
article in each case. Refer to rules in Unit 5.

▶ **EXAMPLE:** Ø carrots

*Carrots are not particular but are a type of vegetable. Therefore, we
use Ø article.*

Some plants, such as (1) Ø carrots, will grow readily from (2) Ø single
cells; others, such as soybeans, will not. No one knows why. This reflects (3)
an ignorance at (4) the fundamental level of the regulation and (5) Ø structure of plant genes and of factors governing (6) the growth of plants. Gaining
such (7) Ø knowledge has the potential of quickening (8) the rate of breeding new plants, raising (9) Ø yields, and extending (10) Ø agriculture to (11)
Ø marginal lands.

From: F. Bloom, "Introduction: Science, Technology, and the National Agenda." In A Report
by the Committee on Science, Engineering and Public Policy of the National Academy of
Sciences, National Academy of Engineering, Institute of Medicine, *Frontiers in Science &
Technology*, New York/San Francisco: W.H. Freeman and Co., 1983.

EXERCISE 20

Imagine that you have just taken notes on a lecture about the medical field.
Rewrite your notes in a paragraph, inserting articles where necessary.

▶ **EXAMPLE:** medical field changed rapidly in lst century
The medical field has changed rapidly in the last century . . .

1. in past, family practitioner responded to all of family's medical
   needs (childbirths, surgeries, diseases, etc.)
2. doctor relied on natural remedies to alleviate pain

ANSWER KEY

Exercise 18
2. an 3. Ø 4. Ø 5. Ø 6. Ø
7. Ø 8. a 9. Ø 10. the 11. Ø
12. Ø 13. Ø/the 14. a 15. Ø/the
16. Ø 17. Ø 18. Ø 19. the 20.
Ø/the 21. Ø 22. a 23. a 24. Ø
25. the 26. the

Exercise 19
(2) generic use (plural noun): *single cells*
refers to all single cells   **(3)** classifiable noun:
refers to ignorance as a type of behavior
(4) before modifier that makes noun specific:
the *fundamental* level   **(5)** generic use
(noncount noun): refers to all of the structure of
plant genes   **(6)** with identifiable nouns that
are followed by a modifying *of*-phrase: the

growth of plants   **(7)** classifiable noun: refers
to a type of knowledge   **(8)** with identifiable
nouns that are followed by a modifying *of*-
phrase: *the rate of breeding new plants*
(9) generic use (plural noun): *yields* refers to
all yields   **(10)** generic use (noncount noun):
agriculture refers to all agriculture
(11) generic use (plural noun): *marginal lands*
refers to all marginal lands

Exercise 20

The medical field has changed rapidly in the
last century. In the past, the family practitioner
responded to all of the family's medical needs
(e.g., childbirths, surgeries, diseases, etc.). The
doctor relied on natural remedies to alleviate

pain. The doctor's role was more of an onlooker
as nature took its course. Today, doctors play a
more active role in healing. With their more
specialized training, they are able to prescribe
wonder drugs and perform surgeries on
patients. Prolonging life has been the ideal
goal. Sometimes lifesaving / enhancing
procedures come in conflict with well-
established social, religious, and moral values.
Thus, there is a need for medical ethics. This is
a field that considers the ethical implications of
medical procedures and argues the reasonable
rights and limits doctors should have in making
decisions about improving, prolonging, or
saving lives.

Workbook Exs. 10,11, & 12, pp. 50–52.
Answers TE p. 541.

UNIT GOAL REVIEW

Ask Ss to look at the goals on the opening page of the unit again. Help them understand how much they have accomplished in each area. At this point, remind them that they have learned many (but perhaps not all) of the most important rules of article usage. Help them to see the importance of paying attention to native speaker speech and writing to see how these rules are applied in practice.

USE YOUR ENGLISH

Activity 1

Play textbook audio. The tapescript for this listening appears on p. 565 of this book. Be sure to play the tape two times, or even three, if Ss are having difficulty catching information about the items.

---

3. doctor's role was more of onlooker as "nature took its course"
4. today, doctors play more active role in healing
5. with their more specialized training, they are able to prescribe wonder drugs and perform surgeries on patients
6. prolonging life has always been ideal goal
7. sometimes lifesaving/enhancing procedures come in conflict with well-established social, religious, and moral values
8. thus, there is need for medical ethics
9. this is field that considers ethical implications of medical procedures and argues reasonable rights and limits doctors should have in making decisions about improving, prolonging, or saving lives

Use Your English

ACTIVITY 1: LISTENING/ WRITING

Listen to the minilecture about computers.

STEP 1 Take notes about the following items in the grid below.

STEP 2 Extend your notes to make as many sentences as you can, using the principles about article selection that you have learned in this unit.

▶ **EXAMPLE** abacus
An abacus was the earliest computing device used by the ancient Greeks and Romans.

1. use of the slide rule	
2. type of machine Gottfried Liebniz built	
3. invention of Charles Babbage	
4. mathematical theory of Alan Turing	
5. CPU	
6. memory	
7. VDU	
8. four ways computers can function	

ANSWER KEY

Activity 1
Answers will vary.
1. The slide rule was used for various kinds of navigational calculation.   2. Gottfried Liebniz built a machine which could perform multiplication.   3. Charles Babbage designed the first mechanical computer.
4. Alan Turing developed the mathematical theory of computation.   5. The CPU is the central processing unit.   6. Memory holds the current program and data.   7. The VDU is a screen used for user input and output.   8. The four ways that a computer can function are: input/output operations, arithmetical operation, logic and comparison operations, and movement of data to, from, and within the central memory of the computer.

ACTIVITY 2: RESEARCH/WRITING

The field of medicine can vary in different cultures. Do research at the library or conduct interviews with other students to learn about the practice of medicine in a place you are not familiar with. What are the medical training, medicine, and techniques associated with synthetic drugs, surgical technology, CAT scans, natural herbal drugs, acupuncture, homeopathy, massage, osteopathy, etc.? From your basic reading or interviewing, select one aspect of medical practice that interests you and write a short paper, incorporating correct use of the generic article.

ACTIVITY 3: READING/SPEAKING

Turn to pages 395–399. This activity presents special advice through runes, or alphabetic characters. Read each rune and accompanying advice. Underline all instances of nouns preceded by *the*. With a partner, discuss why *the* (instead of *a/an* or Ø articles) were chosen.

▶ **EXAMPLE** *You possess genuine power over events and you will find the solution to your problem within yourself.*
The is chosen because it describes an identifiable solution to a particular problem (versus a type of solution, in which case a would be used).

ACTIVITY 4: READING/WRITING

Locate one chapter in an introductory science textbook (physics, chemistry, biology, etc.) that talks about general principles in that field. With a partner, read the first five paragraphs of the chapter. Make a list of abstract generic and concrete generic articles. Which type seems to be more frequent in this type of writing?

ACTIVITY 5: SPEAKING

Discuss which types of political, social, or religious groups would disagree most with each of the medical practices mentioned in the Opening Task. For example, would (the) Catholics be in favor of birth control? Would doctors be in favor of declaring positive AIDS tests results for themselves?

ACTIVITY 6: WRITING

Have you or anyone you've known suffered from any of the illnesses listed in Focus 9? If so, write a paragraph about your own or another's experience.

The test for this unit can be found on p. 492. The answers are on p. 493.

Activity 6
EXPANSION

Obtain permission from Ss with especially good paragraphs to use them in the next class session. Create cloze exercises with the articles removed. Instead of typing *a*, *an*, or *the*, leave a blank. Also leave a blank where Ø article is required. Then, distribute the exercise and ask Ss to fill in the blanks. This should be especially motivating for Ss to see the paragraphs of their classmates.

Activity 2

The research interview option can be especially interesting if you have Ss from eastern and western hemisphere countries.

VARIATION

Step 1: Pair up Ss from different parts of the world. Ask them to share remedies or treatments that may be new or different to their partners for about 10 minutes each.
Step 2: Ask Ss to individually write a paragraph about some of these remedies or treatments. Circulate around the room and select one or two Ss whose paragraphs seem especially interesting and informative.
Step 3: Select Ss to share their paragraphs with the class.
Step 4: Collect the paragraphs from Ss and grade them only for article usage.

Activity 3

This activity will allow Ss to analyze articles in extended text.

Activity 4

Remind Ss to review Focus 6 if they cannot recall the difference between abstract generic and concrete generic articles. Ss should be able to find several examples of abstract generic use, especially in the beginning paragraphs of a chapter.

Activity 5

Some examples of these groups might be: the Moslems, the Christians, the Jews, the Arabs, the Chinese, the Israelis, the feminists, surgeons, nurses, right to life proponents, Planned Parenthood employees, etc.

EXPANSION

If your class enjoys discussing controversial issues and if you are comfortable with disagreement or controversy in the class, have Ss take on the roles of members of these various groups and engage in a debate or "panel discussion."

Unit 6

UNIT OVERVIEW

This unit helps students (Ss) to understand the reference system in English, including personal pronouns, demonstrative pronouns, and determiners, *the* + noun phrase and *such* + noun phrase. Ss should be familiar with all of these forms, but many advanced Ss have difficulty choosing between them in referring to previously stated information. Along with a review of forms, this unit explains the contexts and motivations for choosing reference words and phrases in communicative contexts, both speech and writing.

UNIT GOALS

Review the goals listed on this page so Ss understand what they should be able to know by the end of the unit.

OPENING TASK

The task asks Ss to discuss in groups one of three situations illustrating ways in which men and women in American culture often communicate differently.

Because various reference forms occur in most extended communication, advanced Ss will most likely use some of these forms (e.g., pronouns) in completing the task. As with other Opening Tasks, the explicit focus is on the activity rather than grammatical forms. Focus 1, which follows, will provide example sentences related to the theme of this task.

SETTING UP THE TASK

Have Ss brainstorm generalizations about communication styles of men and women, or, more broadly, generalizations about male or female behavior.

U N I T   6

REFERENCE WORDS AND PHRASES

UNIT GOALS:

- To know the different reference forms in English
- To know the different uses of reference forms for linking ideas
- To use the appropriate reference forms for different contexts
- To avoid unclear reference by using appropriate forms

▶ OPENING TASK
Do Men and Women Communicate Differently?

People often use language differently based on differences in age, education, social status, gender, and so on. In her book *You Just Don't Understand: Women and Men in Conversation*, sociolinguist Deborah Tannen discusses how females and males differ in communication, drawing examples from American English speakers.

STEP 1 Divide into three groups. Each group should be assigned one of the three situations that follow. Using the questions below, discuss in your group what Professor Tannen says are typical female and male responses to the situation.

1. Do you agree that such responses are typical of men and women in the situations described?

2. Have you experienced any exceptions to these generalizations about male-female communication differences?

3. Do you think the gender-based communication differences described are common in cultures other than American culture?

4. Do you think that gender differences alone account for the different responses or could some other variables account for them? What might such variables be?

STEP 2 Have one person in each group present a brief summary of the group's discussion to the rest of the class.

Situation 1
TALKING ABOUT TROUBLES

Someone (male or female) has a personal problem. She or he is very upset and tells a friend about the problem.

If the friend is female: She empathizes by telling the person that she knows how it feels to have the problem. She may provide an example of the same problem or a similar one from her own experience.

If the friend is male: He offers advice about how to solve the problem.

Situation 2
EXPRESSING VIEWS

Someone expresses an opinion about a topic or presents his or her ideas on a topic.

If the listener is female: She expresses agreement with the speaker or, if she disagrees, asks for clarification or further explanation.

If the listener is male: He challenges the speaker's views and explores possible flaws in the argument or idea.

Situation 3
HAVING A CONVERSATION

A group of people at a social event, such as a party, are engaged in conversation.

If the group consists of females: They will tend to view conversation as a way of making connections and sharing experiences among participants. They will seek to use the conversation to establish common bonds among the group members.

If the group consists of males: They will tend to regard the conversation as a way to get attention or to impart information. More so than women, individual men will try to maintain center stage by delivering monologues, telling jokes or lengthy stories, or giving long explanations. They will typically be more concerned with asserting their own status than with establishing common bonds.

CONDUCTING THE TASK
Step 1
V A R I A T I O N

If time permits, groups could discuss more than one situation and compare their responses to those of another group.

Step 2

Note reference forms Ss use (pronouns, demonstrative reference, referential *the*) in summarizing. Put examples on the board as an introduction to the structures of this unit.

E X P A N S I O N S

To provide more information for diagnosing Ss' use of reference forms:

1. Select Ss to role play each of the three situations for the rest of the class before the small group discussions.

2. As either an in-class or homework assignment, have Ss write paragraphs in response to one or more of the questions in Step 1.

3. If Ss have identified cultural differences in communication, ask them to role play one or more of the situations from a different cultural perspective.

Advanced Ss will be familiar with these forms. They may not, however, have learned them as a system associated with English reference. Ask Ss to read the examples and explanations as homework.

Emphasize the importance of reference forms in English to create links between ideas across sentences. To illustrate this:

1. Write two sentences on the board with a noun phrase subject repeated in the second sentence. Underline the repeated noun phrase. Example: *The Opening Task is concerned with communication differences between men and women. The Opening Task describes three communicative situations.* (A nonhuman subject is best since it offers a greater variety of reference forms.)

2. Ask Ss to substitute reference forms for the repeated noun phase. (Elicit forms such as *it, this task, the task.*) Offer others that Ss don't come up with, such as *this activity.* Tell Ss that these substitutions make comprehension easier for listeners and readers than does repeating the noun phrase.

To clarify *such* reference in examples (i) and (j):

1. Write two sentences with ideas that could be summarized by a classifying word on the board. For example, you could write two maxims: *A bird in the hand is worth two in the bush; a stitch in time saves nine.*

2. Write a third sentence using *such* followed by a blank. Ask Ss to supply the classifying word, e.g., *Almost all cultures have such _____.* For this example, Ss might supply *phrases, sayings, proverbs,* etc. Note that *such* reference indicates members of a larger set of items with similar properties.

FOCUS 1

Review of Reference Forms

EXAMPLES	EXPLANATIONS
Referent (a) Ruth enjoys talking about [gender-based language differences]. She finds **the topic** an interesting one.	Words and phrases that refer to information previously stated are called *reference forms*. The information that you are referring to is called a *referent*.
(b) Alma agrees that [men and women communicate differently in our society]. She believes **the observation** is true based on her personal experience.	**Reference Forms** • *the* + noun phrase
(c) Lin: Do you know much about [language variation]? Yumi: Not a lot, but I did read a little about **it** in my introductory linguistics course.	• Pronouns: *it*
(d) [Phonology and semantics] are areas of linguistics. **They** are concerned with language sounds and meanings, respectively. I studied **them** a few years ago.	*they, them*
(e) Our psychology professor says that [men tend to advise friends who come to them with troubles]. My experience supports {**this.** / **this claim.**	• Demonstrative pronouns and determiners: *this; this* + singular/noncount noun
(f) Fred: Do you think [men resist asking for directions]? Yani: I would agree with {**that.** / **that generalization.**	*that; that* + singular/noncount noun
(g) [Two of the gender differences] seem especially true to me. **These** / **These differences** } will be the topic of my paper.	*these; these* + plural noun
(h) George: I know [people who constantly give advice when it's not requested]. Lily: **Those** / **Those people** } are the ones that I avoid!	*those; those* + plural noun
(i) I read several studies about how [young boys are often encouraged to be aggressive and competitive]. I think **such an upbringing** would influence a boy's behavior when he gets older.	• Reference forms with *such such a/an* + singular noun
(j) I've never thought much about how [age, social class, and gender] influence the way we use language. However, I agree that **such factors** probably do affect greatly the ways in which we communicate.	*such* + plural or noncount noun

EXERCISE 1

Underline the reference forms (*the* + noun, *it, this,* etc.) that refer to information in previous sentences. Put brackets around the referents. There may be more than one reference form in a sentence.

▶ **EXAMPLE:**   Our group discussed [the responses to Situation 1].

We didn't always agree that <u>such responses</u> were typical.

1. According to our psychology professor, for women, talk is important for creating connections between people. For men these connections tend to be formed more through activities than talk.

2. Men and women sometimes experience frustration with each other because of their different communication styles. The frustration may be especially great between men and women who spend a great deal of time together.

3. Our professor notes that women have a tendency to make suggestions rather than give commands when they want something done. She thinks this tendency may reflect women's sense that they lack authority in certain situations.

4. Speakers use language differently depending on differences in age, education, social status, and gender. Such differences are of interest to linguists.

5. Pitch and volume are two aspects of speech. The way we use them in speech may affect how we are perceived by others in communication situations.

6. Women have higher pitched voices than men do. This can be a disadvantage when they are trying to assert authority.

7. In some business contexts, women may regard personal questions, such as how a fellow worker spent the weekend, as a way of showing friendliness. Men may consider the questions inappropriate in these contexts.

8. Some studies show that men tend to dominate conversation in groups including males and females. Based on your experience, do you agree with that?

9. I agree with the idea that men and women should try to understand each other's different communication styles. It makes sense to me.

10. We could accept the communication differences we have with the "other gender," or we could try to negotiate different ways of communicating that would be more productive and less frustrating. These are two possible approaches to our differences in communication styles.

This exercise is intended to help Ss become more familiar with the range of reference forms in English and with the kinds of grammatical constructions to which the forms can refer. The most challenging part of the exercise is identifying the referents in the first sentences, especially clause referents.

ANSWER KEY

Exercise 1

1. [connections between people]; these connections . . .   2. [frustration]; the frustration . . .   3. [a tendency to make suggestions rather than give commands when they want something done]; this tendency . . .   4. [differences in age, education, social status, and gender]; such differences . . .   5. [pitch and volume]; them . . .   6. [(the fact that) women have higher pitched voices than men do] or [higher pitched voices]; this . . .   7. [personal questions]; the questions . . .   8. [men tend to dominate conversation in groups including males and females that . . .   9. [the idea that men and women should try to understand each other's different communication styles]; it . . .
10. [We could accept the communication differences we have with the "other gender," or we could try to negotiate different ways of communicating that would be more productive and less frustrating]; these . . .

Exercise 2

EXPANSION

Bring in other short texts with two or three referential forms for Ss to analyze.

EXERCISE 2

The following paragraph describes the common habit of worrying. Discuss what you think the reference is for each underlined reference form. Put brackets around each referent.

Worrying is the most natural and spontaneous of all human functions. It is time to acknowledge <u>this</u>, perhaps even learn to do <u>it</u> better. Man is the Worrying Animal. <u>It</u> is a trait needing further development, awaiting perfection. Most of us tend to neglect <u>the activity</u>, living precariously out on the thin edge of anxiety but never plunging in.

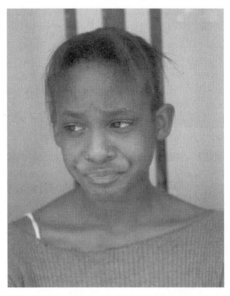

From Lewis Thomas, *The Medusa and the Snail*. New York: Bantam Books, 1979, p. 167.

Exercise 3

VARIATION

If time permits, Ss could write a brief essay instead of just a paragraph. Collecting the assignments afterward will help you to assess Ss' understanding of the structures.

Workbook Ex. 1, p. 53.
Answers: TE p. 541.

EXERCISE 3

Write a paragraph stating your individual opinion in response to one of the questions (1–4) for any of the three situations in the Opening Task. Present evidence or an explanation to support your view. Exchange your paragraph with a classmate. Underline the reference forms and bracket the references in your classmate's paragraph.

Reference Forms with *The* and Demonstrative Determiners

EXAMPLES	EXPLANATIONS
(a) I liked [the novels] very much. I might even reread some of them. I would recommend **the novels** to anyone who wants to know more about Chinese history.	**Complete Repetition** Reference forms may repeat all of the referent. We use this form more often as a later mention than as a second mention.
(b) Oh, look at [this book] in the children's section! My sisters and I must have read **it** a hundred times when we were young.	**Partial Repetition** Some reference forms repeat only part of the referent. We do not usually repeat a demonstrative determiner (*this, that, these, those*) + noun. Instead, we tend to us *it, them* or *the* + (noun phrase.)
(c) I read [two interesting studies about language variation between different age groups]. I have summarized { **the two studies** / **these two studies** } in the introduction of my paper.	We do not usually repeat descriptive modifiers. In (c), only *two* and *studies* have been repeated for both example reference forms.
(d) I read [one study about language differences based on educational levels]. I did not, however, use { **the article** / **that article** } in my paper.	**Synonym** A reference form can be a synonym of the referent. In (d), *article* is used as a synonym for *study* and the modifiers are not repeated.
(e) We went to see [*Hamlet*]. **The play** was performed outdoors at the city center. **(f)** I would like to take [South American literature and the history of jazz] next quarter. Several of my friends recommended **those courses.**	**Classifier** A reference form can also be a classifier of the referent. A classifier word or phrase describes a class or group that could include the referent. In (e), *Hamlet* can be classified as a play. In (f), *courses* classifies the two courses mentioned.

FOCUS 2

This focus box explains the different ways that referential *the* and demonstrative determiners are used.

SUGGESTIONS

1. If Ss can write in their textbooks, ask them to mark the bracketed referents in the first sentences with a highlighter.

2. As you work through the examples with Ss, make sure they understand the following terminology: *synonym* (a word with a similar meaning); *classifier* (a general word that describes members of a set or group); *paraphrase* (writing or saying something in your own words rather than repeating what you have read or heard).

3. Ask Ss to pay attention in their reading to the ways in which native speakers use these forms. Conscious attention to forms in reading is an excellent way for advanced Ss to gain mastery over grammatical systems, whether verbs, article usage, reference forms or other structures. As they read they should ask themselves why writers use particular forms in the contexts in which they occur.

EXAMPLES	EXPLANATIONS
(g) Over the weekend [you should revise your essay and type it]. **The revised paper** should be turned in on Monday. (h) [The aerosol is sprayed into the chamber where the water vaporizes.] **This vaporization process** is repeated.	**Paraphrase** A reference form can also paraphrase a clause or sentence. We commonly use this form to refer to activities and the results of them: Activity: *You revise an essay* Result: *The revised paper* Paraphrases also refer to processes, as in (h). The reference form may repeat part of the referent as in (g) (*revise*), or it may use a classifying or describing word such as *process*, *effects*, or *results* as in (h).

Exercise 4

S U G G E S T I O N

This is a very challenging exercise. If you assign this for homework, do the first one or two items as a class to make sure that Ss understand what they need to do.

EXERCISE 4

Underline reference forms with *the* and demonstrative adjectives in the second sentence of each sentence pair. Bracket the referents in the first sentence. To familiarize yourself with the different forms of reference, state what type of reference is used: (1) complete repetition of the referent, (2) partial repetition, (3) synonym, (4) classifier or (5) paraphrase. As a class, you may want to discuss why the various forms are used.

▶ **EXAMPLE:** Psychologists have distinguished [three dimensions of emotions]. These dimensions can be used to characterize differences in the ways cultures recognize and express emotions.

partial repetition: *It is not necessary to repeat the entire referent. We do not usually use complete repetition when there are modifiers.*

1. One dimension distinguishes between what are called the primary emotions and what are termed the secondary emotions. The primary emotions are considered universal by some psychologists.

2. The primary emotions are also considered to be biologically based. These feelings include anger, grief, joy, and disgust.

3. The secondary emotions are blends of the primary emotions. These emotions, such as contempt (a blend of anger and disgust), are not universal.

ANSWER KEY

Exercise 4

Answers may vary for some.

1. [the primary emotions] <u>The primary emotions</u> (repetition of entire referent)
2. [The primary emotions] <u>These feelings</u> (synonym)
3. [The secondary emotions] <u>These blended emotions</u> (synonym) (partial repetition could also be acceptable)

4. [pleasant emotions] <u>The positive emotions</u> (synonym) (partial repetition could also be acceptable) [unpleasant ones] <u>the negative emotions</u> (synonym)
5. [The last dimension classifies emotions based on intensity.] <u>This classification of feelings</u> (paraphrase)
6. [display rules] <u>These rules</u> (partial repetition)
7. [grief] <u>this emotion</u> (classifier)

4. Another dimension of emotions distinguishes pleasant feelings from unpleasant ones. The positive emotions are ones such as love and joy, whereas the negative emotions are ones such as sorrow and shame.

5. The last dimension classifies emotions based on intensity. This classification of feelings can distinguish worry from terror and sadness from depression.

6. All societies have what are called display rules regarding emotions. These rules dictate how and when people may express certain emotions.

7. For example, in some cultures, people would express grief by crying. In other cultures, this emotion might be expressed by silence.

EXERCISE 5

Make up a sentence with a *the* reference or demonstrative reference to elaborate on ideas in each of the sentences below. The referent is underlined. Try to use a variety of the reference types discussed in Focus 2.

▶ **EXAMPLE:** *Anger* is a primary emotion.

This emotion is biologically based.

1. Everyone has <u>negative feelings</u>.
2. Psychologists note that <u>the smile</u> does not have universal meaning.
3. <u>Facial expressions</u> are important signals of emotion.
4. <u>Fury</u> is a very intense emotion.
5. <u>Nonverbal signals such as posture, gestures, and eye contact</u> also express emotions.

Exercise 5

A follow-up to the work in Exercise 4, this exercise gives Ss guided practice in creating their own sentences that refer to previous text.

A N S W E R   K E Y

Exercise 5
Answers will vary. Examples:
1. <u>negative feelings</u>; However, in some cultures, it is considered polite not to express **these emotions**.   2. <u>the smile</u>; In other words, **this facial expression** does not always mean a person is happy.   3. <u>Facial expressions</u>; We should be aware of **such displays of feeling** if we want to be effective **communicators**.
4. <u>Fury</u>; **This feeling** can sometimes cause people to do things they wouldn't normally do.
5. <u>Nonverbal signals such as posture, gestures and eye contact</u>; **Such expressions** are just as important as words in communicating feelings.

Here the focus is on contexts in which we use personal pronouns and those in which *the +* noun phrase is needed for clarity.

SUGGESTIONS

To help Ss relate the explanations to the examples and get more familiar with terminology:

1. Ask them to read the first section of the chart and tell you what the "one possible referent" is for examples (a) and (b).

2. Ask for volunteers to read the dialogues in (c) and (d). Ask Ss what the "clause referent" is in (c). Ask what the sentence referent is in (d). The responses should the bracketed items.

3. To clarify the explanation in the last chart section:

   Step 1: Replace *the* reference forms with *it* in examples (e) and (f) and with *they* in example (h).

   Step 2: Ask Ss to explain why these pronoun referents might be confusing to a listener or reader. That is, elicit the facts that other nouns are possible referents such as *the movie* in (e), that the referent is far away as in (f), or that pronoun reference would be unclear as in (h).

Workbook Ex. 2 , p. 54; Ex. 3, p. 55.
Answers: TE pp. 541–542.

FOCUS **3**

▶ Using Personal Pronouns versus *The* Noun Phrases

EXAMPLES	EXPLANATIONS
(a) I like [that book] a lot. I read **it** last year. **(b)** Kip is taking [math and English]. **They** are his most challenging subjects, and he has homework for both of **them** almost every day.	Use the personal pronouns *it, they, them* when there is only one possible referent.
(c) Toni: There is evidence that [women tend to add more details to stories they tell than men do.] Ricardo: I believe **it**. **(d)** Tom: [Song's chances of winning a gold medal at the summer Olympics are getting better every day.] Lee: I don't doubt **it**.	Use *it*: • when the one possible referent is a clause • when the one possible referent is a sentence.
(e) I read [the book] before I saw the movie. **The book** was very interesting. **(f)** To Whom It May Concern: I am returning [the enclosed cassette recorder]. The volume control is jammed. Also, the sound quality does not seem very good. **The recorder** came with a one-year guarantee. **(g)** [Violence] is increasing in our society. **The problem** cannot be ignored. **(h)** This medicine should not be taken when you are driving because [it can make you sleepy or it may affect your vision]. **The adverse effects** are only temporary, but nevertheless, you need to be cautious.	Use *the +* noun phrase: • when there is more than one possible referent. In (e), *the book* and *the movie* would be possible referents if you used it. • when the referent might not be clear unless a noun phrase rather than a pronoun is used. In written English, this is often the case when the referent is several sentences before the reference form. • when you want to replace the referent with a classifier, a synonym, or a paraphrase. Sometimes you may want to replace a referent with a paraphrase because you cannot repeat the whole referent and a pronoun reference would not be clear. In (h), the referent is an entire clause. Using *they* for reference would be too vague.

EXERCISE 6

Decide whether *it, they, them,* or *the* + noun phrase is appropriate for each item below. (1) Identify the referent and bracket it. (2) If *the* + noun phrase should be used, choose a noun phrase that fits the context.

▶ **EXAMPLE:** Have you read [the book *Men Are from Mars, Women Are from Venus*]? ___It___ also discusses communication differences between men and women.

(Only one possible referent, so *it* is appropriate.).

1. I have to write a paper for my class about the 1960s. I can't decide whether to write my paper about the Civil Rights marches in the early 60s or about the hippie movement in the late 60s. (a) _____ appeals to me because I'd like to find out more about the history of segregation in the South. (b) _____ are both interesting topics, however.

2. Sandro: Do you think it's true that men tend to be more direct about what they want than women do?
Alicia: Oh yes, I'm convinced of _____.

3. I tried your suggestion to move the second paragraph of my essay to the beginning of the introduction. _____ is a good one; my teacher liked the revision also.

4. Plants break up water into hydrogen and oxygen with the help of sunlight. Sunlight that is caught by grains of chlorophyll in the plant splits the water molecules into hydrogen and oxygen. Most of the oxygen eventually passes out of _____.

5. Scientists believe that there are more than five senses. The organ for the sense of hearing is, of course, the ear. However, in addition, _____ has receptors that help us to create a sense of balance.

Exercise 6
SUGGESTION

Whether Ss complete this exercise in or out of class, spend some time afterwards discussing the reasons for referential choices.

Workbook Ex. 4, p. 56.
Answers: TE p. 542.

ANSWER KEY

Exercise 6
1. **(a)** The Civil Rights marches **(b)** they are
2. it   3. It (or the suggestion) was   4. the plant.   5. it

Advanced Ss should be familiar with space and time meaning contrasts, but they may be less familiar with the contrasts associated with discourse distance and psychological distance.

Emphasize that the meaning contrasts "near" and "far" are determined by speakers and writers—that is, it is a matter of how speakers and writers view a thing, an event, or a situation. Consequently, different speakers/writers could choose different meanings for the same context, expressing different perspectives. For example, it is possible to replace *that* in example (m) with *this*. Remind Ss that the explanations reflect general principles, not absolute rules, which may be especially helpful in revising written prose.

In summary, it is important to help Ss understand that there are indeed principles governing the choice of these forms; on the other hand, they shouldn't get frustrated if they find exceptions to these principles in the language use they encounter in communicative situations.

FOCUS **4**

Demonstrative Determiners and Pronouns

The forms of demonstrative pronouns and determiners *this, that, these,* and *those* tell the reader/listener whether a referent is singular or plural and whether the speaker/writer regards the referent as near or far.

	Singular	Plural
Near	this	these
Far	that	those

EXAMPLES	EXPLANATIONS
	The concept of distance (near or far) may involve the following:
	Space
(a) Take **this chair** right here.	• Near: The speaker regards something as physically nearby.
(b) I'll get two of **these**, please. And one melon.	
(c) Can you see **that** tall **tower** in the distance?	• Far: The speaker regards something as physically distant.
(d) **Those buildings** next to the tower are part of the new arts center.	
	Time
(e) Let's finish watching **this movie**. It's almost over.	• Near: There is a link to present time.
(f) **These** are difficult times because of the economy.	
(g) I'd like to see **that** again. It was one of my favorite musicals.	• Far: Reference is to a time in the past not regarded as close to the present.
(h) **Those** were called the golden years because prosperity was widespread.	
	Discourse Distance
(i) [Age] is another factor affecting language use. **This influence** can be seen in the use of slang.	• Near: The referent is close to the reference form in the text.
(j) [The introduction to my thesis] provided background on my topic. It offered several hypotheses about language differences. **That section** also presented an outline of my thesis.	• Far: The speaker or writer views the referent as distant. In (j), the writer regards the introduction as distant from the part being written.

EXAMPLES	EXPLANATION
(k) I believe [gun control laws are needed]. I feel very strongly about **this**.	**Psychological Distance** • Near: The referent is mentioned by the speaker herself or himself; and is something she believes.
(l) Hal: I think [gun control laws are needed]. Tori: I don't agree with **that**.	• Far: The referent is mentioned by another speaker. Tori disagrees with Hal's position.
(m) When Wilhelm Roentgen discovered the X-ray in 1895, he did not completely understand the nature of these new rays. He called them X-rays because the letter x stands for an unknown quantity in mathematics. **That** is how the X-ray came to be named.	Finally, we often use the demonstrative pronoun *that* in concluding statements to refer to an explanation or description we have given.

EXERCISE 7

Put an appropriate demonstrative form (*this*, *that*, *these*, or *those*) in each blank. If you think more than one might be appropriate, discuss the contexts (including speaker attitude) in which each might be used.

▶ **EXAMPLE:** In the middle of the nineteenth century, many American adventurers headed West to seek their fortunes. At _____that_____ time, gold had been discovered in California and other states. (In referring to the middle of the nineteenth century, *that* indicates distance in terms of time.)

1. I spent my vacation last summer in Costa Rica and had a wonderful time. The people were really friendly, the scenery was beautiful and the weather was perfect. I also loved the food. You should visit _____ country sometime; you'd love it there, too.

2. Have you seen the entertainment section of the newspaper yet? There are a couple new movies at the theaters. (a) _____ movie based on one of Jane Austen's novels looks good. I think I'll pass on the new James Bond film, though. I've never really liked (b) _____ movies.

3. Erin: Did you know that the Pope will be in town (a) _____ weekend?
Victor: No, I hadn't heard (b) _____ .

Reference Words and Phrases | **111**

Exercise 7

Ss will probably come up with different answers for at least some of the items in this exercise. Therefore, it is important to discuss speaker/writer attitudes that would influence different choices.

SUGGESTIONS

1. Some Ss may be uncomfortable with answers that are not clearcut, but advanced learners do need to be aware of factors that affect speakers' and writers' language choices in authentic communicative situations. For example, in sentence (4) a writer might choose *this* for (c) to reflect discourse nearness: The referent *closing the beach to swimming* occurs right before the reference form. On the other hand, a writer could choose *that* for (c) because expressing psychological distance is important: *Closing the beach* is a suggestion made by others and is a solution the writer disagrees with.

2. While Ss should be aware of these differences in speakers' attitudes, they should also be reminded that in some cases only one reference form is appropriate. In other words, that different speaker/writer attitudes exist doesn't mean that "anything goes" in terms of choosing referential forms.

Workbook Ex. 5, p. 57.
Answers: TE p. 542.

4. Dear Senator Rotrosen: I am writing (a) _____ letter to urge you to do something about cleaning up our polluted lake. (b) _____ situation is disgraceful; people are afraid even to go swimming. I know that some officials have suggested closing the beach to swimming, but (c) _____ is certainly not the answer to (d) _____ problem.

5. Have you ever wondered how and why fireflies produce their twinkling lights? (a) _____ lights are created by special glands. At night female fireflies sit on stems of grass while the males fly around flashing their lights. The females flash back and, after signals are exchanged a few times, the male finds the female. (b) _____ is how fireflies mate.

6. Enrique: I'm going to see some all-star wrestling matches tonight. Care to come along?
Soo: No thanks! You really like (a) _____ silly matches? I'd rather stay home and watch a video. Take a look at (b) _____ movies I just picked up. Maybe you'll change your mind.

FOCUS **5**

Using Demonstrative Determiner + Noun Phrase for Clear Reference

FOCUS 5

SUGGESTION
Supplement the examples in this chart with some examples of actual student writing that needs to be revised for clearer reference.

EXAMPLES	EXPLANATIONS
(a) When you do strenuous exercise, you should wear proper clothing and [you should warm up first]. **This warm-up** will help prevent injuries.	Sometimes we need to use a demonstrative determiner + a noun phrase for clear reference.
(b) NOT: **This** will help prevent injuries.	In (b), *this* does not clearly signal the referent. *This* could be interpreted as both wearing proper clothing and warming up.
(c) Before writing your essay, you should try to [brainstorm some ideas and then put your ideas into categories]. **These prewriting techniques** can help you get started on your paper.	Like *the* + noun phrase reference, demonstrative determiner + noun phrase reference can help to describe or classify the referent.

EXERCISE 8

For the following contexts, use a demonstrative determiner and a classifying or descriptive noun to refer to the previous information that is in brackets.

▶ **EXAMPLES:** [Before making gravy, put the flour in a baking pan and bake it for about five minutes.] __This process__ will add to your preparation time, but it will keep your gravy from having a floury taste.

1. [Exciting. Suspenseful. Amusing.] _____ best describe the latest novel by Michael Rozinski.

2. If you spend too much time in the sun, you may get end up with [skin damage and dehydration]. _____ are not worth a sun tan.

3. We'll be hearing a lot from our elected officials about [whether or not taxes should be raised]. _____ continues to be a widely debated one.

If you think your Ss will have problems generating the classifier words for this exercise, give them a list of words from which to choose vocabulary for the blanks. For example, choices for sentence 1 might include *descriptions, phrases, adjectives*; choices for sentence 2 could be *results, physical problems, negative effects*. Ss would choose an appropriate noun or noun phrase and add the correct demonstrative form. In your list, you could include vocabulary that would not be appropriate for any sentences to make the exercise more challenging.

Workbook Ex. 6, p. 58.
Answers: TE p. 542.

ANSWER KEY

Exercise 8
Answers will vary.
1. These words (adjectives) 2. These results (effects) 3. This issue (topic) 4. These expressions (gestures) 5. This reaction (interpretation)

4. [Smiles, frowns, raised eyebrows, and shrugs of the shoulder] all convey emotions. _____ may have different meanings in different cultures, though.

5. [Women] sometimes [think men are being unsympathetic] when they give advice about a problem rather than share troubles._____ stems from a difference between men and women in what they think is an appropriate reaction to such a situation.

Demonstrative Forms versus *The* and *It/Them* References

EXAMPLES	EXPLANATIONS
(a) Oh, I've heard { **that joke** / **the joke** before. / **it**	In many contexts, you can use demonstrative, *the*, or *pronoun* reference forms. All would be acceptable.
(b) Moya told us { **the jokes.** / **those jokes.** / **them.**	The choice often depends on (1) the speaker's or writer's intentions, or (2) what the speaker/writer thinks the listener/reader knows.
(c) I heard [a speaker] on campus this afternoon.	**Emphasizing the Referent** Use demonstrative determiners or pronouns when you want to emphasize the referent.
(d) Less emphasis: **The speaker** was talking about the dangers of nuclear power.	Example (d) emphasizes the topic of nuclear power, not the referent.
(e) More emphasis: **This speaker** was the best I've heard regarding the nuclear power issue.	Example (e) emphasizes the referent more.
(f) I'm not sure if I'll [type my paper myself].	In example (g), *it* puts less emphasis on the referent, focusing on new information (the result of having to type without help). In example (h) placing *that* at the end of the sentence puts more emphasis on the referent *type my paper*.
(g) Less emphasis: If I do, **it** will probably take me all day!	
(h) More emphasis: I have more important things to do than **that**!	
(i) I asked my instructor if I needed [to include a bibliography with my draft]. She told me **that** would not be necessary.	**Avoiding Unnecessary Repetition** Use a demonstrative pronoun to avoid unnecessary repetition.
(j) Repetitious: She told me **[including the bibliography]** would not be necessary.	In example (j), the paraphrase with *the* + noun phrase gives too much information. We often use demonstrative pronouns when the referent is a clause or a sentence.
(k) [This paper] is one of the best I've written. I'm sure my classmates will enjoy **it.**	As mentioned in Focus 2, we do not usually repeat demonstrative phrases in second mention. We use some other reference form such as *it* or *the*.
(l) NOT: I'm sure my classmates will enjoy **this paper.**	

This focus box points out motivations for choosing between demonstrative determiners/pronouns and referential *the* or personal pronouns. The first section of this chart emphasizes speaker/writer intentions in choosing forms.

S U G G E S T I O N S

1. Read aloud the examples (c) through (e). Ask Ss to state what "the referent" is (*a speaker*) and note the difference in the two forms in (d) and (e). Repeat this process for examples (f) through (h), in which the referent is *type my paper myself*.

2. For the teaching points in the last chart section, having volunteers read examples (i) through (l) aloud may help Ss to hear the inelegance of the unnecessary repetition in (j) and (l).

Exercise 9

As with previous exercises, be sure to discuss motivations for different choices so that Ss understand why more than one answer is possible. Refer to the kinds of distinctions summarized in Focus 6 on p. 115 and, if relevant, those in Focus 4 on p. 110.

Workbook Ex. 7, p. 59; Ex. 8, p. 60.
Answers: TE p. 542.

EXERCISE 9

Put an appropriate reference form in each blank. The referent is in brackets. Use one of the following forms: (1) *it*, (2) *the* + noun phrase, (3) demonstrative determiner (*this, that, these,* or *those*) + noun phrase, (4) demonstrative pronoun (*this, that, these,* or *those*). Use the notes in parentheses to guide your choice. For some blanks, more than one choice might be possible.

▶ **EXAMPLE:** An article I read claims that [hot water freezes faster than cold water]. Were you aware of _____*that*_____ ? (Also possible: *that fact*)

1. I've just finished [a really good novel]. _____ was about an American woman who goes to live in India. (Put focus on the theme of the novel.)

2. I also read [a biography] last month. _____ was the most interesting one I have ever read. (Put focus on the subject of the sentence.)

3. I just found out that [Chinese, English, Spanish, Hindi, and Arabic are the most widely spoken languages]. I didn't know _____ before.

4. The Danish linguist Otto Jespersen described several theories on the origins of language. One is called the "ding-dong" theory. [The theory] proposes that speech arose as a result of people reacting to stimuli in their environment and making sounds to reflect it. _____ is not one that is believed by most linguists.

5. Another theory of the origins of language was termed [the "pooh-pooh" theory]. _____ maintains that speech started when people made instinctive sounds caused by emotions.

6. You can eat most vegetables either raw or cooked. [If you cook them], _____ may reduce the nutrients you get. (Emphasize the result.)

7. Nicholas is making sure that the spare tire for his car is well-inflated before he leaves for his business trip. During his most recent trip, [he got a flat tire and was stranded in the desert for hours]. _____ was the last thing he needed after a busy and exhausting week. (Emphasize the referent.)

---

8. We consulted the forest ranger as to whether we could [take our dog with us on our camping trip in the national park]. He said _____ would not be allowed.

9. [Five students] were singled out for awards at our end-of-the-year banquet. _____ had outstanding academic records and had participated in a number of community projects. (Emphasize the referent.)

FOCUS 7

Focus 7 gives more information about meaning contrasts, involving the distinction between *such* reference and demonstrative reference.

Reference forms with *such* are often used in writing and formal speech; however, advanced Ss often have not had much instruction about these forms in their study of English. Your Ss will most likely need practice with the forms, remembering to use articles *a* or *an* with singular nouns after *such* and *-s* plural endings on count nouns after *such*.

Call Ss' attention to the ways in which the same *such* reference phrase can refer to different grammatical structures, as shown in examples (j) through (m), where *such an attitude* refers to several different constructions.

▶ Reference Forms with *Such*

EXAMPLES	EXPLANATIONS
(a) We need [a strong and honest leader]. **Such a person** is Mario Baretta. **(b)** Men and women often have [different responses to the same situations]. **Such responses** may result from the ways they have been brought up. **(c)** You should try to eat more [fruits, vegetables, and whole grains]. **Such foods** are important for good health.	The meaning of *such*, when referring to previous information, is similar to "like that" or "of that type of thing." In (a) *such a person* refers to a person belonging to the type "a strong and honest leader." In (b), *such responses* refer to responses that can be classified as "different for the same situation." With plural nouns, such phrases often follow a list or series of things as in (c).

(d) The police thoroughly investigated [the burglary]. They concluded that only experienced thieves could have accomplished **such a crime**.
 	
(e) Did you hear [what he said]? I've never heard of **such an idea** before.
 	
(f) [Impatiens and fuchsia plants] need little sun. **Such plants** are good for shady areas of your garden.
 	
(g) I can't believe [the things] they told us about their neighbors. In my opinion, they shouldn't repeat **such personal information**.
 	
(h) [Several students] have demonstrated superior performance in the field of mathematics. **One such student** is Ruby Pereda.
 	
(i) Now more than ever we need reform-minded candidates for our city council. **Two such candidates** are Ben Ho and Ulla Teppo.
	Structure forms with *such*:
	• *Such* + singular noun
	  Use *a* or *an* after *such*
	
	• *Such* + Plural Noun
	
	• *Such* + Noncount Noun
	  No article is used after *such* before a noncount noun.
	• (Number) + *Such* + Singular or Plural Noun
	  Note that no article is used with *before student* in (h).

(j) I admire **your attitude**. Such an attitude shows great respect for others. **(k)** They said that **women should stay at home**. Such an attitude does not reflect the feelings of most Americans.	**Referents of *Such* Phrases** The information that references with *such* refer to may be: • a phrase • a clause

118   UNIT 6

EXAMPLES	EXPLANATIONS
(l) **"The world owes me a living."** Such an attitude will not get you very far, my father always tells me.	• a sentence
(m) **Girls should do all the housework. Women should serve the men in the family.** Such an attitude about the role of women is common in my culture, but it seems to be changing.	• more than one sentence

EXERCISE 10

Underline the *such* reference in each of the following groups of sentences or dialogues. Then state what the referent is. If you wish, you may paraphrase the referent.

▶ **EXAMPLE:** Men tend to view conversation as a way to assert status and to impart information. <u>Such attitudes</u> are not as common with women.

Referent: <u>Men's attitudes that conversation is for asserting status and imparting information</u> .

1. The Italian composer Guiseppe Verdi wrote one of his greatest operas, *Falstaff*, when he was eighty. To have created this brilliant musical work at such an advanced age is truly remarkable.

   Referent: _____

2. In the early decades of American film making, Asians were often portrayed as servants, launderers, cooks, gardeners, and waiters. Such stereotypes denied the many achievements of Asian Americans at that time.

   Referent: _____

3. Lightning never strikes in the same place twice. Rattlesnakes intentionally give warnings to their victims by rattling their tails. The sap of a tree rises in the spring. Such beliefs, although common, are not supported by scientific evidence.

   Referent: _____

Exercise 10
SUGGESTION

The directions for this exercise suggest that Ss may want to paraphrase the referent. Helping Ss to create paraphrases by transforming sentences into complex noun phrases, as shown in the example, can help to develop their academic writing skills. You could do this after Ss have completed the exercise if they have used exact words in their answers.

Workbook Ex. 9, pp. 60–61.
Answers: TE p. 542.

ANSWER KEY

Exercise 10
1. <u>such an advanced age</u>; referent: eighty.
2. <u>such stereotypes</u>; referent: Asian servants, launderers, cooks, gardeners and waiters.
3. <u>such beliefs</u>; referent: The first three sentences.   4. <u>such equipment</u>: stationary bicycles, rowing machines, stair climbers (new exercise machines)   5. <u>One such problem</u>; referent: a number of serious problems in our metropolitan areas.   6. <u>Such questions</u>; referent: asking how old a woman is, how much money she makes or how much she weighs.

4. Some people who pursue physical fitness with a passion fill up their homes with stationary bicycles, rowing machines, and stair climbers. Each time a new exercise machine appears on the market, they rush to their local sporting goods stores. However, such equipment is not needed to become physically fit.

   Referent: _____

5. We are now faced with a number of serious problems in our metropolitan areas. One such problem is how to best help the thousands of homeless people.

   Referent: _____

6. When you have just met someone, what types of personal questions should you avoid asking? The answer depends on what culture you are in. For example, in some cultures it might be acceptable to ask a woman how old she is, how much money she makes, or even how much she weighs, but in many cultures such questions are considered impolite.

   Referent: _____

FOCUS **8**

▶ *Such* versus Demonstrative Determiners

EXAMPLES	EXPLANATIONS
(a) When Mr. Clark came to our restaurant, he complained about the location of his table, criticized the menu, insulted the waiter, and failed to leave a tip. We hope we never again have to deal with . . .	*Such* refers to a class or type of thing. Consequently, reference phrases with *such* have a more general meaning than *this, that, these,* or *those* before nouns.
Specific **Type** **(a.1) this** person. **(a.2) such** a person	(a.1) refers to Mr. Clark. (a.2) refers to any person who would act the way Mr. Clark did.
(b) Two types of dinosaurs with bird-like hips were stegosaurs and ankylosaurs. **Specific** **Type** **(b.1) These** dinosaurs . . . **(b.2) Such** dinosaurs . . . were herbivorous.	(b.1) refers to stegosaurs and ankylosaurs. (b.2) refers to all dinosaurs with bird-like hips.
(c) In the United States, it has become common for the media to report every medical problem that the President suffers and every medical treatment, however minor, he receives. Does the public really need . . . **Specific** **Type** **(c.1) this** information? **(c.2) such** information?	(c.1) refers to information about medical problems and medical treatment. (c.2) refers more generally to information that is personal and unimportant in the context.

EXERCISE 11
Answer the following questions based on the examples in Focus 8.

1. Which words after *such* (*a/an*) (person, dinosaurs, information) repeat a word in the preceding sentence? Which do not? How can you explain this difference?

SUGGESTION
To further explain the distinction here, use examples with names of your Ss.
Step 1. Write two sentences on the board with *such* reference in the second sentence, e.g., *Rosa spends three hours doing her homework every night. Such behavior characterizes a conscientious student.* (If you think your Ss would enjoy a more lighthearted example, describe a "party girl.")
Step 2. Elicit other examples that could be represented by the *such* phrase. In this example, you could ask, "*What other types of behavior characterize a conscientious student?*"
Step 3. Replace *such behavior* with the demonstrative phrase *this behavior*. Ask Ss to explain the difference in meaning between *such behavior* and *this behavior*.

EXPANSION
If appropriate for your context (e.g., a composition class), provide classifier vocabulary that would be helpful to your Ss for their academic work. Abstract words such as *concepts, ideas, notions, issues, problems, theories,* etc., can be useful vocabulary for both demonstrative and *such* reference in academic writing and formal speech.

Exercise 11
Because so many of the reference forms in English include lexical items (nouns and noun phrases) and not just grammatical items like pronouns, vocabulary is an important part of developing competence in using reference forms effectively.

Like other exercises in this unit, this exercise and the following one encourage Ss to develop active vocabulary as they work on ways of using reference forms.

This is a good exercise for small group work. Ss can comprae their responses with other groups.

2. Can you think of words that might be substituted for those occurring after *such (a/an)* in the examples? Are they more general or more specific than the words in the examples? How do they change the meaning?

▶ **EXAMPLE:** *such a person—such a grouch*

(more specific; describes Mr. Clark negatively)

3. Often a modifier can be used to make a "class" word more specific. For example, *advanced* in "at such an advanced age" makes it clear that reference is to those ages late in life. In the examples in Focus 8, what modifiers could be added to define more specifically the words following *such (a)*?

EXERCISE 12

STEP 1 For each of the word pairs below, think of one or more categories that could be used to classify or characterize them.

▶ **EXAMPLE:** Word pair: football, hockey

Categories: *sports, spectator sports, violent sports, popular sports*

Word Pair	Categories
(a) love, anger	_____
(b) drug trafficking, murder	_____
(c) earthquakes, hurricanes	_____
(d) backgammon, chess	_____
(e) your choice (list-related words): _____	_____

STEP 2 Now select one of your categories for each word pair. Add to each pair other words or phrases that could be classified by this term.

▶ **EXAMPLE:** *Violent sports: soccer, boxing*

STEP 3 Write a statement (one or two sentences) for each topic above. Use *such* plus the category you selected. (The items could be the word pairs given or the words you added.)

▶ **EXAMPLE:** *I know many people who love to go to football and hockey games. However, I don t enjoy watching **such violent sports**.*

ANSWER KEY

Exercise 12

Answers will vary for all parts.

Step 1 (a) emotions, feelings **(b)** crimes, felonies **(c)** natural disasters, catastrophes **(d)** games, pastimes **(e)** (student's choice)
Step 2 (a) hate, fear, joy **(b)** burglary, rape **(c)** tornadoes, floods **(d)** checkers, Go
Step 3 (a) Everyone is familiar with the emotions of love, hate anger, fear, and joy. Such emotions are, however, expressed differently in different cultures. **(b)** Murder, burglary, and drug trafficking are common urban problems. We need to reduce the frequency of such crimes. **(c)** Every year, earthquakes, hurricanes, and floods cause enormous damage. Unfortunately, we seldom have much time to prepare for such natural disasters.
Step 4 For all statements, replacing <u>such</u> with a demonstrative would refer only to the words previously expressed (e.g., love, hate; murder, burglary) and not to the class they represent.

STEP 4 Discuss the difference in meaning that would result if you replaced *such* in each statement with a demonstrative determiner (this, that, these, those).

▶ **EXAMPLE:** *However, I don't enjoy **those** violent sports.*

"**Such** violent sports" refers to any sports that are especially violent; "**those** violent sports" refers only to football and hockey.

EXERCISE 13

Identify and correct the errors or inappropriate reference forms in each of the following sentences. There may be more than one way to correct errors.

▶ **EXAMPLES:** My friend suggested that I drop out of school and work for a while. I'm not sure what I think about such an advice.

Correction: *I'm not sure what I think about **such advice**.* (*Advice* is a noncount noun, so no article is used.)

1. What did you think about this research? I disagreed with this research.

2. Our math teacher gave us a surprise quiz. Can you believe he would be this unkind man?

3. Many modern cities have both buses and subways. Traffic congestion is certainly reduced by those public transportation.

4. This year I took both an English course and a Spanish course. It was quite easy for me because French is my native language and the two languages are similar.

5. I have a friend who likes to wear only two colors of clothing: blue and purple. She dresses in such colors every day.

6. One study says that male children do not pay as much attention to female children as they do to other males. What do you think about it?

7. Some people insist on giving advice even when it's not requested. Such an advice is generally not appreciated.

8. I am keeping the blue shirt I ordered from you. This shirt fits fine. However, I am returning the striped shirt because this was much too small.

9. In this paper, I plan to discuss two emotions that all cultures share. The two emotions that all cultures share are joy and grief.

10. Did you hear her boast that she never has to study for her courses? The student misses the point of what an education means.

Reference Words and Phrases | **123**

Exercise 13

Before Ss do this exercise, let them know that some of the "errors" are not, strictly speaking, ungrammatical, but rather are inappropriate because speakers and writers don't use them (e.g., repeating the exact words for a second mention when it occurs in an immediately following sentence, as in sentence pair (1) of this exercise).

Workbook Ex. 10, p. 62.
Answers: TE p. 542.

UNIT GOAL REVIEW

Ask Ss to look at the goals on the opening page of the unit again. Help them understand how much they have accomplished in each area.

A N S W E R   K E Y

Exercise 13

1. it (Repetition is stylistically inappropriate.)
2. such an   3. this (or these forms of public transportation)   4. it is similar to Spanish (Error: no referent for the second language in the *two languages*.)   5. these (such suggests other colors in the same class as blue and purple)   6. that/this (depending on speaker attitude toward the referent)   7. such advice
8. it (that one)   9. They (these emotions)
10. That student (or this student, depending on the discourse context.)

USE YOUR ENGLISH

The activities on these "purple pages" at the end of the unit contain situations that should naturally elicit the unit's structures in a more communicative framework. While Ss are doing these activities in class, you can circulate and listen to determine if they have actually achieved the goals on the opening page of the unit.

Activity 1

Play textbook audio. The tapescript for this listening appears on pp. 565–566 of this book.

EXPANSION

Show a movie video clip that illustrates a difference in communication styles. The difference could be based on gender, age, or ethnic background. Have Ss discuss or write about it afterwards.

Activity 2
VARIATION

The Internet could be another source of information for this activity.

Activity 3
VARIATION

Have Ss work in pairs discussing one of the variables mentioned in the activity. Each pair would consider only one variable, but one pair might be concerned with occupational differences, another with age differences, etc. Ask Ss to take notes and then write a paragraph collaboratively.

Use Your English

ACTIVITY 1: LISTENING

You will hear two dialogues. Each dialogue illustrates a difference between male and female communication styles, according to Professor Deborah Tannen. After you have heard the dialogues, either discuss the following questions with a partner or write complete answers.

1. What communication differences do these dialogues illustrate?
2. Have you observed such differences in your own experience?
3. Can you think of exceptions to the generalizations that these dialogues illustrate?

ACTIVITY 2: WRITING/ SPEAKING/LISTENING

In teams, make up lists of statements that include both amazing facts and "untruths." Good sources for hard-to-believe facts are reference books such as *The Guiness Book of World Records* or *Ripley's Believe It or Not* as well as almanacs. Mix in with the amazing facts some of your own statements that are **not** true. Each team should then read their list of statements to another group. The listeners must agree on which ones they believe and which they don't believe. Score a point for each correct judgment as to whether a statement is true or not.

▶ **EXAMPLE:** Team A: *The largest watermelon on record weighed 260 pounds.*
Team B: *We don't believe it.*
The statement is true. Team A gets the point.

ACTIVITY 3: SPEAKING/WRITING

Write a paragraph comparing the language use of different groups based on a variable other than gender. For example, consider differences you are aware of based on age, social status, occupation, geographical location, or education. When you have finished, identify the reference forms you used.

ANSWER KEY

Activity 1
Dialogue 1 shows the supposed difference between men and women in asking directions. (Women tend to readily ask for directions if lost; men often do not want to admit they need help and tend to ask only as a last resort. These, of course, are generalizations.)

Dialogue 2 illustrates the supposed difference between men and women regarding what they consider to be significant information to relate in conversation and the tendency for women to want to relate details about their experiences.

ACTIVITY 4: WRITING

Write a letter to either (a) a business to complain about unsatisfactory merchandise or (b) one of your political representatives (for example, a senator or the President) to voice your opinions about an issue that is important to you. Exchange your letter with another classmate. The classmate should check your use of reference forms to see if they are appropriate and then write a response to your letter, playing the role of the company or person to whom you addressed it.

ACTIVITY 5: WRITING

Choose one of the sentences below to develop a paragraph. Then write the rest of the paragraph, creating a context appropriate for including the sentence. (The sentence could occur anywhere in the paragraph after the first sentence.)

- Those subjects just aren't worth studying.
- Those TV programs should be taken off the air.
- Such advice should be helpful to anyone visiting _____.
  (Choose a city or country to fill in the blank.)
- Such a person is to be avoided whenever possible.
- Such bad luck shouldn't happen to anyone.

ACTIVITY 6: READING

As you do reading for other courses or for your own interests, write down examples of *such* reference forms that you find in a notebook. Include the *such* phrase and the phrase(s) or sentence(s) to which each refers. Make a note of the context (for example, an explanation of a chemical process, a comment on people's behavior, a description of a product in an advertisement). At some point you may want to compare your findings with your classmates' to see the ways in which reference forms with *such* references are used in written texts.

Activity 4
VARIATION

Ss could write letters that would actually be sent to a business or political representative. Ss who don't want to write a complaint letter could write a letter of appreciation for good service to a business, hotel, restaurant, etc. Classmates could serve as peer editors and you could assist with any needed revisions of draft letters. Have each student turn in to you a copy of the revised letter. Ss then report back to the class on responses.

Activity 5

As with Activity 4, Ss could exchange papers with classmates for peer editing and response.

Activity 6

This activity serves either as a suggestion for self-study or could represent a long-term assignment during the course. If the latter, you could ask Ss to turn in the examples they found and then compile a master list of some or all of the examples (depending on the number and your time constraints) to give Ss as a handout.

The test for this unit can be found on p. 494. The answers are on p. 495.

TOEFL Practice Test Exercises for Units 4–6 can be found on pp. 63–65 of the workbook. The answers are on p. 452 of this book.

Unit 7

UNIT OVERVIEW

Unit 7 reviews the different types of relative clauses and then focuses on a less frequent type—relative clauses that modify subjects. Besides providing multiple opportunities for practice, this unit also reviews how to reduce relative clauses.

UNIT GOALS

Review the goals listed on this page so students (Ss) understand what they should be able to know by the end of the unit.

OPENING TASK

This task resembles the old TV program, "What's My Line?" in that individuals try to bluff members of the opposite team. In this case, one person possesses knowledge about four definitions, which are (hopefully) unknown to his or her opponent. As in the TV game, Ss should be encouraged to give no facial or intonation cues that would give away the correct answer. In fact, a student might be encouraged to say a wrong option very confidently and say the correct answer with an incredulous look on his or her face. The whole point is to have a lot of fun while promoting student production of relative clauses modifying subjects.

SETTING UP THE TASK

Make sure Ss understand the word "trivia" and the nature of this game.

CONDUCTING THE TASK

Step 1

Remind Ss to keep their books shut as they are guided through an example.

Step 2

Model definitions that have relative clauses modifying subjects. Give an easy example such as "*A person who teaches adult students at a university is called a (a) student, (b) professor, or (c) assistant?*" *Students should say "a professor."*

UNIT 7

RELATIVE CLAUSES MODIFYING SUBJECTS

UNIT GOALS:

- To use restrictive relative clauses to modify subjects
- To use restrictive relative clauses to make nouns more specific
- To know how to reduce restrictive relative clauses

▶ OPENING TASK
Trivia Challenge

STEP 1 The object of this game is to get the most answers right in a trivia game. Student A looks at page 127. Student B looks at page A-17.

STEP 2 To begin, Student A will create definitions of a person or thing, offering three options. Student B will listen and repeat the definition, completing the sentence with the correct word or phrase. If correct, he or she will receive one point.

STEP 3 Student B will now create definitions in the same way. The partner with the most points wins the game.

▶ **EXAMPLE:**   a person
explores and studies caves
Options: (a) transducer, *(b) spelunker,
(c) coanchor

Student A creates a definition:
*A person who explores and studies caves is called a (a) transducer, *(b) spelunker, or (c) coanchor*
(The correct answer is asterisked (*).)

Student B makes a guess:
A person who explores and studies caves is called a spelunker.
Congratulations to Student B.
He or she will be awarded one point for the correct answer.

Step 3

Read through the example with Ss before permitting Student A to turn to the next page and Student B to turn to the back of the textbook.

Circulate around the room, making sure that Student A is looking at one page and Student B is looking at another.

Student A
Trivia Challenge

Create a Definition:

1. an animal
   It mates for life.
   (a) seahorse, (b) boa constrictor, *(c) Canada goose

2. a book
   Its original title was changed six times.
   (a) *War and Peace* by Leo Tolstoy, *(b) *The Great Gatsby* by F. Scott Fitzgerald,
   (c) *Pride and Prejudice* by Jane Austen

3. an inventor
   Teachers gave him poor report cards.
   *(a) Thomas Edison, (b) Alexander Graham Bell, (c) Robert Fulton

4. a person
   He or she fits the interior parts of pianos.
   (a) mucker, (b) hooker inspector, *(c) belly builder

Guess the Correct Answer:

5. (a) dragonfly, (b) flycatcher, (c) firefly

6. (a) cornball, (b) impostor, (c) daytripper

7. (a) amphora, (b) amulet, (c) aspartame

8. (a) bodice, (b) causerie, (c) bloomers

ANSWER KEY

Student A
1. An animal that mates for life is a Canadian goose.   2. A book whose original title was changed six times was *The Great Gatsby*.
3. A famous person to whom teachers gave poor report cards was Thomas Edison.   4. A person who/that fits the interior parts of pianos is a belly builder.

Student B
5. A fly which is actually classified as a beetle is a firefly.   6. A person who/that behaves in an unsophisticated manner is a cornball.
7. A jar which ancient Greeks and Romans used to carry wine was an amphora.   8. A piece of clothing which is composed of loose trousers gathered about the ankles is bloomers.

FOCUS **1**

SUGGESTION

1. Write the main clause and the full embedded clause with the same subject on different colored strips of paper for examples *a* through *d* (e.g., *The contract is now valid. The contract was signed yesterday.*). Demonstrate how the embedded clause is placed near a noun phrase in the main clause and how *that* substitutes for the repeated noun phrase.

2. Note the word order of relative pronouns that function as objects in the relative clause, i.e., they do not follow regular statement word order. Also note the use of *whose* in *k* and *l,* which substitutes for words such as *his, her,* and *its* in the embedded clause.

Overview of Restrictive Relative Clauses

- A restrictive relative clause modifies a noun phrase in a main clause. It is placed as close to the noun phrase as possible and is used to identify the noun.

Noun Phrase   **Relative Clause**

that

The contract (~~the contract~~ was signed yesterday) is now valid.

Main Clause

- There are four general types of restrictive relative clauses. They may modify main clause subjects or objects. Relative pronouns may be subjects or objects in their own clauses.

TYPES OF RELATIVE CLAUSES	NOUN PHRASE IN MAIN CLAUSE	RELATIVE PRONOUN IN RELATIVE CLAUSE
(a) *The contract* **that was signed yesterday** is now valid. (S S)	Subject	Subject
(b) *The contract* **that he signed yesterday** is now valid. (S O)	Subject	Object
(c) I have not read *the contract* **that was signed** yesterday. (O S)	Object	Subject
(d) I have not read *the contract* **that he signed** yesterday. (O S)	Object	Object

- This unit will focus on restrictive relative clauses that modify subjects in main clauses (like a and b). These clauses can have various relative pronouns, and the relative pronouns can fulfill various grammatical functions. *Whose* can function as a relative determiner.

EXAMPLES	SUBJECT BEING MODIFIED	RELATIVE PRONOUN	FUNCTION OF RELATIVE PRONOUN/ DETERMINER
(e) A person **who/that** sells houses is a realtor.	person	*who/that*	subject
(f) The secretary **whom/that** she hired is very experienced.		*whom/that*	direct object
(g) The employees **to whom** she denied a pay raise have gone on strike.		*whom*	indirect object
(h) The mansions **that/which** were sold last week were expensive.	thing or animal	*that/which*	subject
(i) The computer **that/which** they purchased operated very efficiently.		*that/which*	direct object
(j) The place **that/which** you spoke about is Denver.		*that/which*	object of a preposition
(k) Clerks **whose** paychecks were withheld are in trouble.	person, thing, or animal	*whose*	possessive determiner
(l) The division **whose** sales have reached a million-dollars will go to Hawaii.		*whose*	possessive determiner

Exercise 1

1. Because of the complexity of the diagram, Ss will need time to study it. Tell them that each letter stands for a particular stage in a process. Discuss what is happening in the picture as a class. For example, *"A lamp seems to be burning brightly. Why do you think water is coming through the window? That's right, to put the flame out. Then what happens?"*

2. Ask Ss to read the passage that corresponds to the diagram. This activity is best done in pairs.

3. Ask Ss to describe the picture to each other using as many relative clauses as they can.

EXPANSION

Ss can individually write a summary of the process.

Workbook Exs. 1 & 2, pp. 66–68.
Answers: TE p. 542.

EXERCISE 1

STEP 1 Here is a picture of a rather complex invention created by the artist Rube Goldberg. What do you think this device is used for?

From Charles Keller, *The Best of Rube Goldberg*, 1979. RUBE GOLDBERG™ and © of Rube Goldberg Inc. Distributed by United Media.

STEP 2 Reread the passage and underline all of the relative pronouns/determiners. Then, with your partner, identify and write down the function of the relative pronouns/determiners in each relative clause (subject, direct object, etc.). There may be more than one relative clause in a sentence.

▶ **EXAMPLE:** Sentence (1) *that* —*subject function in relative clause*

(1) A kerosene lamp that is set near the window has a high flame that catches on to the curtain. (2) A fire officer whom a neighbor calls puts out the flame with a stream of water that the officer shoots from outside the window. (3) The water hits a short man who is seated below the window. (4) He thinks it is raining and reaches for an umbrella which is attached to a string above him. (5) The upward pull of the string on one side of the platform causes an iron ball that is resting on the other side of the platform to fall down. (6) The ball is attached to a second string that wraps around a pulley and connects to a hammer. (7) The downward pull of the ball on the second string causes a hammer to hit a plate of glass. (8) The crashing sound of the glass causes a baby pup that is in a cradle to wake up. (9) In order to soothe the pup, its mother rocks the cradle in which the pup is sleeping. (10) The cradle, to which a wooden hand is attached, is on a high shelf above a stool. (11) A man who is sitting on the stool below the shelf and whose back is positioned in front of the wooden hand smiles as the wooden hand moves up and down his back.

STEP 3 Without looking at the sample passage, summarize the process shown in the picture.

EXERCISE 2

For each of the phrases below, write two sentences. Use a *who* relative clause for one and a *whose* relative clause for another.

▶ **EXAMPLE:** will not get a job

A person who is not skilled will not get a job.

A person whose interview skills are poor will not get a job.

1. will not pass the course
2. will be a good leader
3. will make a lot of friends
4. can never take a vacation
5. is prepared to take a test
6. should not drive a car

FOCUS **2**

Making Noun Phrases More Specific with Relative Clauses

LESS SPECIFIC	MORE SPECIFIC	EXPLANATION
(a) A man walked into the office.	(b) A man **who was wearing a pinstriped suit** walked into the office.	A relative clause makes the meaning of the noun it modifies more specific.
(c) The secretary can type seventy words per minute.	(d) The secretary **whom Dolores hired yesterday** can type seventy words per minute.	
(e) A computer is a useful invention.	(f) A computer **that has a CD-rom** is a useful invention.	

FOCUS 2

SUGGESTION

If you have time, provide a little oral work presenting this concept before asking Ss to read the examples.

1. Ask how Ss came to school today. Some might say "on foot" but others will probably say "by bicycle, by car, by bus, etc."
2. Ask them to imagine that they each have left something in or on their vehicle and they want a friend to retrieve it. Ask Ss what they might have left. Some might say, "a scarf, a wallet, a book, etc."
3. Now tell them that you need to know the specific item when they report it missing. Ask them to describe the item. Some may say, *The jacket is blue. Its collar is torn.* Prompt them to restate this in one sentence: "A blue jacket whose collar is torn was left on the bus." Do a few more examples before reading sentences *a* through *d*.

ANSWER KEY

Exercise 2

Answers will vary.

1. A person who does not study will not . . ./ A person whose grades are poor will not . . .
2. A person who knows how to delegate . . ./ A person whose public speaking skills are good . . . 3. A person who is kind and generous . . ./A person whose personality is extremely generous will . . . 4. A person who works all of the time can . . ./A person whose bank account is empty can . . .
5. A person who does not procrastinate studying will . . ./A person whose study habits are good . . . 6. A person who does not have a license should . . ./A person whose eyesight is poor should not . . .

Exercise 3

This is an information gap activity. Before Ss begin, be sure that each member of the pair has a different column covered.

Workbook Exs. 3 & 4, pp. 68–71.
Answers: TE p. 543.

EXERCISE 3

Information Gap: Imagine that you are a new employee for a company. One of your co-workers has agreed to orient you to the new office. Ask a question about the objects or persons in each of the pictures in the left column while covering up the right column. Have your partner distinguish these objects or persons, explaining what he or she knows by looking at the pictures in the right column.

▶ **EXAMPLE:**

New Employee: Ask about what you see (cover up the right column)	Experienced Employee: Tell about what you know (cover up the left column)

box/contains file folders

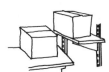

New Employee: *Which box has the file folders?*
Experienced Employee: *The box that is sitting on the shelf has the file folders.*

1. project/I should work on first

2. door/leads to the restroom

ANSWER KEY

Exercise 3

1. Which project should I work on first this morning?/The one which is face down on the desk 2. Which door leads to the restroom?/The first door which is open on the left . . . 3. Which telephone number belongs to the Moesler Corporation?/The number which is second on the list is their number. 4. Which computer has the Internet connection?/The one which is on the left is the one that . . . 5. Which light switch illuminates the front of the conference room?/The switch which is on the right is the one you should turn on. 6. Which is the book that our boss, Mr. Blake, wrote?/The book which Mr. Blake wrote is the second one from the left.

3. telephone number/belongs to the Moesler Corporation

Now switch roles with your partner

4. computer/has the Internet connection

5. light switch/illuminates the front of the conference room

6. book/our boss, Mr. Blake, wrote

Relative Clauses Modifying Subjects | **133**

Because this chart is fairly complex, it might be best to present it using an "uncover technique." Copy the chart onto an overhead transparency. Discuss the examples and explanations for one set of sentences in the grid (i.e., *a* through *c*) and then continue with the next set. If you do not have access to an overhead projector, have Ss cover and uncover the sets in their books as you go along.

FOCUS **3**

▶ Review of Reduced Relative Clauses

EXAMPLES	EXPLANATIONS
(a) The letter (**that**) he sent was never received. **(b)** The accountant (**whom**) he corresponded with was well qualified. **(c)** **NOT:** The accountant with (~~whom~~) he corresponded was well qualified.	We can delete relative pronouns if they function as objects in relative clauses. In examples (a) and (b), *that* and *whom* can be deleted. Relative pronouns cannot be deleted if they follow prepositions such as *with* or *to*.
(d) The conference room (**that is**) situated at the end of the hall is closed. **(e)** The water (**that was**) left in the pitcher evaporated. **(f)** The customer (**who is**) complaining to the manager is my aunt. **(g)** A child (**who had been**) playing on the equipment was asked to leave.	We can delete relative pronouns in relative clauses with auxiliary *be* in progressive or passive constructions. Both the relative pronoun and *be* are deleted.
(h) Chairs (**that are**) in the conference room cannot be moved. **(i)** A board member (**who was**) at the meeting decided to resign.	We can delete relative pronouns in relative clauses with *be* + preposition phrases. Both the relative pronoun and *be* are deleted.
(j) Clients **who are** interested will always return. **(k)** Interested clients will always return. **(l)** **NOT:** Clients interested will always return. **(m)** A girl **who was** beautiful stepped into the room. **(n)** A beautiful girl stepped into the room. **(o)** **NOT:** A girl beautiful stepped into the room	In relative clauses with *be* + adjective, we can delete the relative pronoun and *be*, but the adjective is usually moved before the noun in the main clause.
with **(p)** People (~~who have~~) credentials can be hired. **without** **(q)** The workers (~~who did not have~~) identification were asked to leave.	In relative clauses with *have* or *have not* (= possession or lack of possession), we can delete the relative pronoun and replace *have* or *have not* with *with* or *without*.

EXERCISE 4

Look again at the diagram in Exercise 1 and analyze the operation of the back scratcher. Look particularly at how the objects were affected during the process. Then, write a sentence containing a relative clause with an object relative pronoun. Put parentheses around the words that can be deleted.

▶ **EXAMPLE:** (B) The curtain _(that) the flame touched caught on fire._

  1. (C) The water _____
  2. (E) The umbrella _____
  3. (J) The hammer _____
  4. (K) The plate of glass _____
  5. (N) The cradle _____
  6. (O) The wooden hand _____

EXERCISE 5

Read the following sentences. Identify relative clauses that can be reduced. Mark your suggested revisions directly on the text. Then explain your revisions to your classmates.

> An assertive person
▶ **EXAMPLE:** (a) A person who is assertive can develop great self-confidence.

> with
(b) A person who has self-confidence can do anything.

I changed (a) to "An assertive person can develop great self-confidence" because the relative clause contains "be" + adjective. I changed (b) to "A person with self-confidence can do anything" because the relative clause contains "have."

  1. (a) It is easy to spot the person who is the decision maker in an American business meeting. (b) The decision maker is usually a person who is leaning toward the other members of the group and who is giving direct eye contact.

  2. (a) Body language that is composed of many gestures can communicate 80% of a message. (b) A voice that is friendly, a posture that is relaxed, and a handshake that is firm all convey assertiveness.

  3. (a) Anyone who has been working in the same position for a while will receive criticism at one time or another. (b) Criticism that is unfair needs to be countered. (c) Criticism that is constructive needs to be acknowledged.

  4. (a) A person who is dressing for success in an American business setting should worry about the material, color, and style of his or

---

Exercise 4

This exercise will be simpler if Exercise 1 has already been done.

Exercise 5

This activity is excellent preparation for editing practice that Ss should later be able to do on their own extended compositions.

ANSWER KEY

Exercise 4
Answers will vary.
1. . . . (that) the fire officer used to put out the fire hit a short man (who was) seated below the window. **2.** . . . (which) the short man grabbed was attached to a string (which was) attached to a wooden platform. **3.** . . . that hit a plate of glass was connected to a pulley and a string. **4.** . . . (that) the hammer broke made a crashing sound that woke up a baby pup. **5.** The mother rocked the cradle in which her pup was sleeping./The mother rocked

the cradle (that) her pup was sleeping in.
6. . . . (that was) attached to the cradle scratched the back of the man (who was) sitting on a stool.

Exercise 5
1. The decision maker is usually a person leaning toward the other members of the group and giving direct (be + *-ing* participle)
2. Body language composed of many gestures . . . A friendly voice, a relaxed posture, and a firm handshake all . . . (be + *-ed* participle,

be + adjective) **3.** Anyone working in the same... Unfair criticism needs . . . Constructive criticism needs . . . (be + *-ing* participle, be + adjective) **4.** A person dressing for success in an . . . Generally, a coordinated suit made of an expensive wool appears. . . . Dark colors transmit . . . (be + *-ing* participle, be + adjective, be + *-ed* participle, be + adjective) **5.** . . . Anyone with the determination to keep this image . . .

her clothing. (b) Generally, a suit that is coordinated and that is made of an expensive wool appears most authoritative. (c) Colors which are dark transmit more authority.

5. (a) If you are someone who feels unsatisfied with your personality, do not be discouraged. (b) Anyone who can develop a mental picture of what he or she wants to be can change. (c) Anyone who has the determination to keep this image in his or her mind on a day-to-day basis will see his or her new personality become a reality.

EXERCISE 6
Look at the pictures in Exercise 3 and write six sentences with reduced relative clauses that distinguish the objects. Share your sentences with your classmates.

▶ **EXAMPLE:** *The box with folders is sitting on the shelf.*

EXERCISE 7
Below you will find information about four homes that celebrities sold for various reasons. Write sentences about this information using as many relative clauses modifying subjects as you can. Put parentheses around words that can be deleted.

▶ **EXAMPLE:** *The mansion (that) the oil tycoon sold for $2,000,000 has three fireplaces.*

The penthouse whose owner was a world-renowned physician sold for $4,000,000.

VILLA
Owner: country western singer
Reason for sale: divorce
Price: $3,000,000

Enter through walled gates and find sophisticated hacienda. 2-acre home with horse corral. 6 bedrooms/8 baths. Pool, tennis, jacuzzi, spa.

PENTHOUSE
Owner: world-renowned physician
Reason for sale: death
Price: $4,000,000
Towering 20 stories above downtown. 3 bedrooms/4 bathrooms. Close to Music and Performing Arts Center. Modern design. 20 minutes from beach.

MANSION
Owner: oil tycoon
Reason for sale: bankruptcy
Price: $2,000,000

European chateau with hardwood floors. 50 miles from the coast. 4 bedrooms/ 4 bathrooms. 3 fireplaces. View of lake. Very private acre far from crowds.

BEACHHOUSE
Owner: corporate executive
Reason for sale: job move
Price: $5,000,000
On the beach. 3 acres + private 120 ft. of beachfront. Bright and spacious. Pool room. 3 stories. State-of-the-art sound/video system. 5 bedrooms/ 4 bathrooms. Greenhouse.

Exercise 7
This exercise can be done individually or in pairs.

EXPANSION
Most major U.S. newspaper sections have a real estate section in the Sunday paper. Photocopy and distribute other home descriptions to Ss for further practice describing homes, using relative clauses.

Workbook Exs. 5,6, & 7, pp. 71–73.
Answers: TE p. 543.

UNIT GOAL REVIEW
Ask Ss to look at the goals on the opening page of the unit again. Help them understand how much they have accomplished in each area.

ANSWER KEY

Exercise 6
Answers will vary.
1. The project in the middle of the stack
2. The door leading to . . . 3. The second telephone number is the one which belongs . . . 4. The computer on the left . . .
5. The light switch located on the right . . .
6. The book our boss, Mr. Blake, wrote . . .

Exercise 7
Answers will vary.
1. The house which has a $3,000,000 selling price is owned by a country western singer.
2. The physician whose accomplishments are world-renowned died last month. 6. The house which the oil tycoon is selling for $2,000,000 is on a very private acre of land.
4. The executive whose business has moved to another city must sell her beachfront house as soon as possible.

Use Your English

USE YOUR ENGLISH

The activities on these "purple pages" at the end of the unit contain sitations that should naturally elicit the unit's structures in a more communicative framework. While Ss are doing these activities in class, you can circulate and listen to determine if they have actually achieved the goals in the opening page of the Unit.

ACTIVITY 1 : LISTENING

STEP 1 Listen to the taped segment of a lecture that explains various important business terms. On a separate piece of paper take notes about the terms introduced.

STEP 2 Use your notes to fill in the blanks of the following quiz.

1. The process in which someone decides how their property will be distributed after their death is called _____ .

2. A term which means to substitute an inoffensive term for an offensive one is a/an _____ .

3. A person who has died is referred to as a/an _____ .

4. A term which means to die leaving a will is _____ .

5. The action which describes someone dying without a will is _____ .

6. The land and property which someone owns is called _____ .

7. _____ is called "personal property."

8. _____ is called "a gift."

ACTIVITY 2 : WRITING

Write a letter of complaint to a store or company about a defective item that you bought recently. Try to include at least two sentences with relative clauses modifying main clause subjects.

▶ **EXAMPLE:** *Dear Sir:*

The toaster that I bought in your store last week is defective. The selector lever that determines how dark the toast will be is stuck . . .

Activity 1

Play textbook audio. The tapescript for this listening can be found on p. 566 of this book.

Ss may need to hear the lecture a second or third time in order to obtain the necessary information.

Activity 2
VARIATION

If Ss have difficulty thinking of defective items, suggest one or more of the following problems:

a. a computer—the Internet connection doesn't work
b. a pantsuit—the zipper is broken
c. a lamp—the switch doesn't turn the light on
d. a pair of shoes—they squeak
e. a car—you hear a strange sound
f. a couch—the hide-a-bed mattress was missing

ANSWER KEY

Activity 1
1. estate planning   2. euphemism
3. decedent   4. testate   5. intestate
6. realty property   7. Every kind of property you own (such as stocks, cash, furniture, wedding rings, pets, old magazines, etc.)
8. Property you transfer freely not by stock or trade.

Activity 3

Ss need not be great artists; you can encourage them to draw stick figures and simple geometric shapes to create a "Rube Goldberg-type" invention. Select one or two Ss to describe their invention in front of the class.

EXPANSION

Have pairs exchange diagrams with other pairs and try to describe—orally or in writing—the process in the picture.

Activity 4

This activity allows Ss to creatively use English to describe a chart or diagram of their own choice.

Activity 5

EXPANSION

Pair up Ss from different majors or with different fields of study and ask them to create a list of eight commonly used words or terms in their fields. Then, have each person try to make a definition using the following frame: __(Definition)__ is called _____. If the partner cannot guess the term, then the so-called expert can supply it.

ACTIVITY 3: SPEAKING

Exercise 1 described an unusual invention—a back scratcher. Working with a partner, try to draw a similar diagram for another device. Then describe the various features of the device, following the format of Exercise 1. Choose one of the following ideas or one of your own. Explain to the class how your invention works.

fly swatter	cheese cutter
door opener	window washer
pencil sharpener	adjustable chair

ACTIVITY 4: WRITING

Find an outline, chart, or flow diagram that has various levels or interdependent steps in one of your textbooks or a magazine or newspaper. Describe the diagram using at least three sentences with relative clauses.

▶ **EXAMPLE:**

Unemployment

functional   cyclical   seasonal   structural

There are several types of unemployment. A person who is functionally unemployed has lost his or her job and is looking for another. A person who is a victim of a temporary downswing in the trade cycle is cyclically unemployed. A person who is seasonally unemployed means that he or she is not working during a particular season, e.g., the holiday season or the harvesting season. Someone who is permanently unemployed, and this is probably the most tragic, is a victim of a structural change in society which has made his particular field or skill obsolete.

After you have written your description, reduce all of the relative clauses that can be reduced according to the rules discussed in this unit.

ACTIVITY 5: SPEAKING/WRITING

Discuss the following business-related terms with a partner. Then write a definition for each term. Be sure to use a relative clause in each of your definitions.

▶ **EXAMPLE:** per capita income

The average annual income that a particular population earns is called "per capita income."

bankruptcy	gross national product	exchange rate
sales commission	prime rate	mortgage

ACTIVITY 6: WRITING/SPEAKING

Create your own "Trivia Challenge" game, like the one you played in the Opening Task.

▶ **EXAMPLE:**   an animal

It doesn't carry its young in a pouch.

(a) seahorse, (b) kangaroo, *(c) ostrich

STEP 1   Work with a partner. Think of five items and definitions (you may use your dictionary for ideas).

STEP 2   Get together with another pair. See if they can guess the correct option. The team with the most correct guesses wins the game.

Activity 6

Sometimes an activity like this is best done in a two-day sequence. Create the game on the first day and then play it on the second. Make sure you have some treats or prizes for the winner!

The test for this unit can be found on p. 496. The answers are on p. 497.

Unit 8

UNIT OVERVIEW

Unit 8 follows logically from Unit 7 and focuses on a different relative clause type—relative clauses that modify objects. It shows how to delete relative pronouns in certain relative clauses for greater conciseness in writing.

UNIT GOALS

Review the goals listed on this page so students (Ss) understand what they should be able to know by the end of the unit.

OPENING TASK

The task in this unit is an information gap type similar to the one in Unit 7.

SETTING UP THE TASK

Have a brief class discussion about inventions. Ss might discuss what they feel are the most important inventions in the last century or recent years.

CONDUCTING THE TASK

Step 1:
Ask Ss to refer to designated pages in different parts of the book and be careful not to glance at their partners' pages, where the answers are contained.

Step 2:
Select four Ss to read the two examples aloud.

Move around the room to help with any problems. Make sure the first student is using a phrase such as *"I'm thinking of/imagining something/an object/a useful item that/which . . ."* in order to produce the target structure—a relative clause modifing an object.

VARIATION

To increase the complexity of the task, Ss could think of other inventions or famous personalities and get their partners to guess the answer from the original clues they devise.

UNIT 8

RELATIVE CLAUSES MODIFYING OBJECTS

UNIT GOALS:

- To use restrictive relative clauses to modify objects
- To use multiple restrictive relative clauses in a sentence
- To reduce relative clauses by deleting relative pronouns
- To choose appropriate relative clause forms for formal and informal communication

▶ OPENING TASK
Describing Inventions

You and a partner will work on this task together. Student A should look at the inventions and the invention dates on page 141, and B should look at the pictures and dates on page A-18. Take turns describing one of the inventions on your page without actually naming it. Your partner will guess what you have described.

▶ **EXAMPLE:**   Student A: *I'm thinking of something that was invented in 1593 and that you use to measure the temperature.*
Student B: *Is it a thermometer?*
Student A: *Good guess!*

Thermometer
1593

▶ **EXAMPLE:**   Student B: *I'm thinking of something that was invented about 1590 and that you can look through.*
Student A: *Is it glasses?*
Student B: *No, but it has a lens that you can look through to make small substances appear large.*
Student A: *Oh, it's a microscope.*
Student B: *That's right!*

Compound Microscope
About 1590

Student A

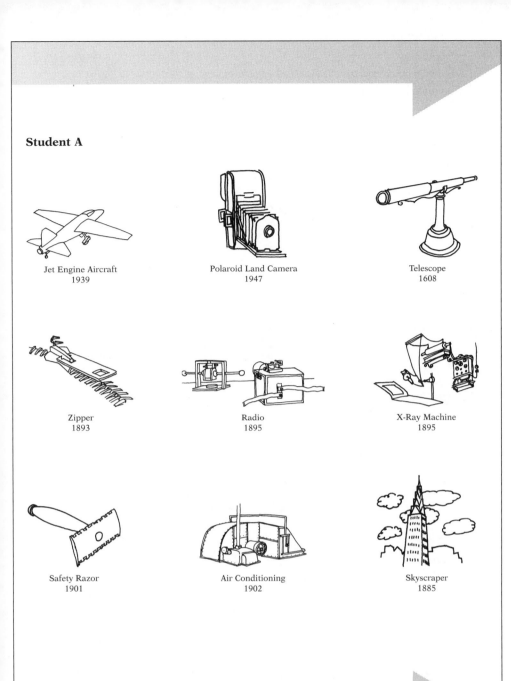

Jet Engine Aircraft
1939

Polaroid Land Camera
1947

Telescope
1608

Zipper
1893

Radio
1895

X-Ray Machine
1895

Safety Razor
1901

Air Conditioning
1902

Skyscraper
1885

If Ss have already done Unit 7, this unit will be much easier. They should be familiar with the different functions a relative pronoun can have when modifying a subject. In this focus box, Ss will expand their knowledge by seeing the variety of functions a relative pronoun can have when modifying an object.

Because this chart is fairly complex, it might be best to present it using an "uncover technique." Copy the chart onto an overhead transparency, if possible. Discuss the examples and explanations for one set of sentences in the grid (i.e., *a* through *d*) and then continue on with the next set. If you do not have access to an OHP, have Ss cover and uncover the sets in their books as you go along.

FOCUS **1**

FORM

Types of Relative Clauses Modifying Objects

Relative clauses that modify objects can have various relative pronouns/determiners and different functions:

EXAMPLES	OBJECT BEING MODIFIED	RELATIVE PRONOUN	FUNCTION OF RELATIVE PRONOUN
(a) She knows a girl **who/that** can dance very well.	person	*who/that*	subject
(b) He looked for the banker **whom/that** he had met at the party.		*whom/that*	direct object
(c) He was angry at the person **whom/that** he had written a letter to.		*whom/that*	indirect object
(d) She talked to the students **whom/that** she was best acquainted with.		*whom/that*	object of a preposition
(e) **OR:** She talked to the students with **whom** she was best acquainted.		*whom*	object of a preposition (directly following preposition)
(f) I have noticed the trash **that/which** is piled on the street.	thing or animal	*that/which*	subject
(g) Did you see the apartment **that/which** he furnished himself?		*that/which*	direct object
(h) He patted the dog **that/which** he had given a bone to.		*that/which*	indirect object
(i) Toronto has a tall tower **that/which** you can get a great view from.		*that/which*	object of a preposition
(j) Toronto has a tall tower from **which** you can get a great view.		*which*	object of a preposition (directly following preposition)

142 UNIT 8

EXAMPLES	OBJECT BEING MODIFIED	RELATIVE DETERMINER	FUNCTION OF RELATIVE DETERMINER
(k) I need to find the man **whose** credit card has expired.	person	*whose*	possessive determiner
(l) I was impressed by the trees **whose** branches seemed to touch the sky.	thing or animal	*whose*	possessive determiner

EXERCISE 1

Read the following story. Underline all relative clauses that modify objects. Circle the noun that is modified by each relative clause.

1) When my mother and I came to the United States, I experienced (a move) from which I felt that I would never recover. 2) My mother and I never got along very well. 3) She was a glamorous fashion model, but I looked like "a plain Jane" who was clumsy and overweight.

4) I was often left alone as my mother left for fancy parties at which she mingled with famous actors, artists, and musicians. 5) I desperately wanted to return to the country from which we had fled in Eastern Europe.

6) My mother was fortunate when she first arrived, for she got her first job through friends of a fellow countryperson who had married an American millionaire. 7) These friends immediately introduced her to everyone that they knew. 8) However, most of these friends were childless, and I had no one with whom I could share my loneliness and misery.

9) Not knowing where I could find happiness, I decided to begin copying the standards of style for which my mother was famous. 10) It had worked for her; perhaps it could work for me. 11) I followed numerous diets that would help me resemble a starved model. 12) Nothing delighted my mother more than the attempts that I made to become more like her. 13) I did not really believe in my new preoccupation with fashion. 14) It actually sent me into deep depressions which lasted weeks.

15) As the years went by, I went away to a prestigious college which provided me with many opportunities to travel abroad and meet famous people. 16) I always seemed to be looking for something that I had not obtained in my youth. 17) Finally, I met someone who could liberate me from all of the fashion nonsense. 18) The love of my life turned out to be a scientist who liked to climb mountains and build things. 19) In fact, he built the first home that we lived in. 20) Believe it or not, this country cottage made possible the quiet life that I had always dreamed of as a teenager.

Exercise 1

Once Ss have done the exercise, ask individual Ss to name the objects they have circled and the relative clauses they have underlined for the whole class.

ANSWER KEY

Exercise 1

The nouns that the students should circle are shown in italics.

3) *"a plain Jane"* who was clumsy and overweight 4) *parties* at which she mingled with famous actors, artists, and musicians 5) *country* from which we had fled in Eastern Europe 6) *countryperson* who had married an American millionaire 7) *everyone* that they knew 8) *no one* with whom I could share my loneliness and misery 9) *standards of style* for which my mother was famous 11) *diets* that would help me resemble a starved model 12) *attempts* that I made 14) *depressions* which lasted weeks 15) *college* which provided me with many opportunities to travel abroad and meet famous people 16) *something* that I had not obtained in my youth 17) *someone* who could liberate me from all of the fashion nonsense 18) *scientist* who liked to climb mountains and build things 19) *home* that we lived in 20) *life* that I had always dreamed of as a teenager

Exercise 2

Model the question and answer process with a student first; you can use the questions in the example. Answers will vary.

Workbook Exs. 1 & 2, pp. 74–75.
Answers: TE p. 543.

FOCUS 2

Use what you know about the personalities and background of your Ss.

1. Before introducing the chart, say: *"I know a student who is from Brazil/plays the guitar/ is the youngest in her family, etc."* Select several different Ss and have the class guess whom you are talking about.
2. Now read the explanation, emphasizing that relative clauses are used to specify who or what is being described.

Exercise 3

SUGGESTION

This exercise may be a little difficult for Ss to do on their own. To demonstrate it:

1. Ask two Ss to come to the front of the room. Assign one student to be the witness and the other to be the criminal investigator.
2. Do the example and the first two or three items to get the class started. The witness will need to be reminded to give a complete response that includes a relative clause. Be patient as Ss struggle to produce this difficult structure.

Workbook Ex. 3, p. 76.
Answers: TE p. 543.

EXERCISE 2

Take turns asking and answering questions about the story in Exercise 1. In each response, use a relative clause that modifies an object.

▶ **EXAMPLES:** Student A: *What kind of move did the author experience?*

Student B: *She experienced a move from which she felt that she would never recover.*

Student A: *How did the young girl look?*

Student B: *She looked like "a plain Jane" who was clumsy and overweight.*

FOCUS **2**

Using Relative Clauses to Modify Nouns

EXAMPLES	EXPLANATION
(a) The police caught a criminal **who had robbed three banks.**	A relative clause provides information that is necessary to identify or limit the noun it modifies. The clause specifies what type of thing(s) or person(s) is being described.
(b) He applied for work at companies **which his father recommended.**	

EXERCISE 3

STEP 1 A crime was committed at the Royal Restaurant.

In pairs, take the roles of a criminal investigator and a witness. The investigator demands that the witness give certain information from the left column below. The witness provides a response with a relative clause modifying an object using events, people, conditions, etc. in the right column below.

▶ **EXAMPLE:** Investigator: *Tell me the name of the man whom you saw at the Royal Restaurant.*

Witness: *I don't remember the name of the man whom I saw at the Royal Restaurant.*

ANSWER KEY

Exercise 2
Answers will vary.

Exercise 3
2. Tell me the name of the woman whom the man was with/I believe the name of the woman was Jones or Johnson.   3. Tell me the type of car that you saw parked near the Billings Bank./I saw a compact car that had a scratch on the right side.
4. Tell me about the tip that the suspect left at the last meal./He left a large tip which I found under the salt and pepper shakers.   5. Tell me the name of the company whose truck was seen across from the Royal Restaurant./I forgot the name of the company whose truck was seen

there.   6. Tell me about the type of sound that you heard near the restaurant./I heard a scream which startled me   7. Tell me about the type of button you picked up at the scene of the crime./I picked up a gold button that I think fell from the robber's jacket.   8. Tell me about the sequence of events that followed the murder./I saw a man who ran down the stairs to a car whose license plate was XXX 123.   9. Tell me about the type of dog that twas in the car./he owned a small, black dog that had one blue eye and one brown eye.
10. Tell me the name of a relative who is close to the female suspect./I know that she had a son whose name was Biffo.

Investigator Information Required	Witness Experiences/Observations
1. Name of the man the witness saw at the Royal Restaurant.	You don't remember the name.
2. Name of a woman the man was with.	Nobody told you the name, but you think the name is Jones or Johnson.
3. Type of car the witness saw parked near the Billings Bank.	You saw a compact car. It had a scratch on the right side.
4. Type of tip the suspect left at the last meal.	He left a large tip. You found it under the salt and pepper shakers.
5. Name of the company. Its truck was seen across the street from the Royal Restaurant.	You forgot the name of the company.
6. Type of sound the witness heard near the restaurant.	You heard a scream. The scream startled you.
7. Type of button the witness picked up at the scene of the crime.	You picked up a gold button. You think it fell from the robber's jacket.
8. Sequence of events following the robbery.	You saw the man run down the stairs to a car. Its license plate was XXX 123.
9. Type of dog in the car.	You saw a small, black dog. It had one blue eye and one brown eye.
10. Name of a relative close to the female suspect.	You know she had a son. His name was Biffo.

STEP 2 Using some of the information obtained at the interview, write one paragraph about the Royal Restaurant crime. Include at least five relative clauses in your narrative.

Relative Clauses Modifying Objects **145**

FOCUS 3

This focus box covers important information for writing: using multiple relative clauses is a way that Ss can make their writing more concise.

SUGGESTION

Provide some extra examples related to your class. Describe individual Ss or their belongings in separate sentences, then show how sentences can combine to form multiple relative clauses. For example: Original Sentences: *Angelica has a backpack. The backpack contains her books. She uses the books for her English classes.* Combined: *Angelica has a backpack that contains the books which she uses for her English classes.*

Exercise 4

SUGGESTION

1. To get Ss thinking, ask if they have ever invented something or known someone who has. You can mention that little inventions like the self-stick note have made their inventors rich.
2. Then, ask Ss to work in pairs and guess for whom the inventions were invented.

▶ Multiple Relative Clauses

USE

EXAMPLES	EXPLANATIONS
(a) Do you need a sleeping bag **which resists rain** and **which you can stuff into a pouch?**	It is possible to use more than one relative clause in a sentence. These relative clauses may modify the same or different nouns.
(b) She was wearing a hat **that my friend designed for a woman who had a funeral to attend.**	
(c) **AWKWARD:** Marissa wrote a letter. The letter complained about cosmetics. She had ordered cosmetics last week.	Multiple relative clauses are used in formal writing to be specific and concise.
(d) **BETTER:** Marissa wrote a letter **which complained about cosmetics that she had ordered last week.**	With multiple relative clauses, we can communicate more information using fewer words and/or sentences.

EXERCISE 4

The following patented inventions were never sold on a wide-scale basis. With a partner, describe for whom the inventions were probably made. Use two relative clauses modifying objects in each sentence.

▶ **EXAMPLE:** carry-all hat
The carry-all hat was probably invented for someone who does not want to carry a purse and who always needs her cosmetics nearby.

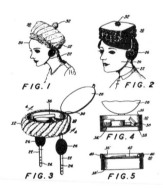

ANSWER KEY

Exercise 4

Answers will vary.

1. The combination deer carcass sled and chaise lounge was probably made for someone who likes to hunt and who wants to take a rest after the excitement of the day. **2.** The eyeglass frame with adjustable rearview mirrors was probably made for someone who had poor eyesight and who was also a little paranoid.

3. The power-operated pool cue stick was probably invented for someone who liked to play pool and who also had a slow stroke.

4. The toilet lid lock was probably invented for people who had a child or who had a pet that they did not want to get into the toilet. **5.** The baby-patting machine was probably made for someone who had a very fussy baby and who got tired of patting the baby all by herself.

---

1. combination deer carcass sled and chaise lounge

2. eyeglass frame with adjustable rearview mirrors

3. power-operated pool cue stick

4. toilet-lid lock

5. baby-patting machine

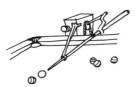

Exercise 5

Remind Ss to look for similar nouns in the sentences in order to determine where and how to embed the sentences together.

Workbook Ex. 4, pp. 77–79.
Answers: TE p. 543.

EXERCISE 5

Combine the following groups of sentences into one sentence that contains two relative clauses modifying objects.

▶ **EXAMPLE:** Molly purchased a house. The house's former owner had made movies. The movies were box-office successes.

Molly purchased a house whose former owner had made movies which were box-office successes.

1. Students should be given scholarships. Scholarships cover all college expenses. College expenses include tuition and living expenses.

2. I am amazed at the invention. The man created the invention for some people. These people are disabled.

3. Most people did not buy chocolates. The youth were selling chocolates at a booth. The booth was located outside a supermarket.

4. Salespeople require an official contract. Clients have provided their signatures on the official contract. Their signatures are legible.

5. She admires one teacher. The teacher knew her subject area. The teacher was fair in grading.

6. A man was kidnapped by thugs. Their main interest was obtaining drugs. The drugs could be sold for thousands of dollars on the black market.

7. The women applauded the policy. The company instituted the policy for pregnant employees. The pregnant employees needed a three-month leave after their children were born.

8. The woman tightly clasped a locket. Her son had given her the locket before he left for an assignment. The assignment was in Saudi Arabia.

▶ **D**eleting Relative Pronouns

EXAMPLES	EXPLANATIONS
(a) I sent a letter **(which)** he never received.	You can delete relative pronouns with the following functions: • direct object
(b) The faculty admired the student **(whom)** they gave the award to.	• indirect object
(c) Tom saw the movie **(which)** Sahib talked about.	• object of preposition
(d) They hope to find an apartment **(that)** is in a quiet area of town. **(e)** **NOT:** They hope to find an apartment is in a quiet area of town.	You can also delete relative pronouns that serve as subjects when the subject is followed by the *be*-verb. When you delete the relative pronoun, the *be*-verb must be deleted as well. The resulting sentences can have:
(f) I met the athlete (who was) **chosen** as "Player of the Year."	• passive and progressive participles
(g) The child is delighted with the puppy (that is) **licking** her face.	
(h) The realtor sold the home (which is) located **on Elm Street.**	• prepositional phrases
(i) She doesn't know anyone (that is) **smart enough** to pass the test.	• adjective phrases
(j) I do not want to be around a person **who has** the flu. **(k)** I do not want to be around a person **with** the flu. **(l)** Have you ever considered a job **that doesn't have** benefits? **(m)** Have you ever considered a job **without** benefits?	When the subject is followed by *have (not)* to indicate possession, you can substitute *with (without)* for the relative pronoun + *have (not)*.
(n) Could you recommend a book that appeals to all ages? **(o)** **NOT:** Could you recommend a book appeals to all ages?	You cannot delete relative pronouns if they are subjects of a relative clause that uses a verb other than *be* or *have*.

This box is similar to Focus 3 in Unit 7, but additionally describes how relative pronouns can be deleted when they function as objects.

Again, because the box is complex, you could use the "uncover" technique—presenting one set of the grid at a time (i.e., *a–c*) and covering the rest. You can do this on an OHP (overhead projector) if possible, or have Ss do this in their books.

Exercise 6

1. Ask Ss to compose a sentence or two about each picture at their desks.
2. Write numbers 1 through 4 across the board.
3. Ask one member of each pair to transfer one of the sentence(s) to the board. Depending upon the size of your class, several sentences should be written under each number.
4. Ask Ss to compare sentences and note similarities and differences.
5. Ask Ss to vote for the most concise sentence under each number.

EXPANSION

Distribute magazine advertisements, postcards, photos, or other pictures that contain some type of activity that Ss can describe. Or have Ss bring in pictures for other Ss to describe.

Workbook Exs. 5 & 6, pp. 80–81.
Answers: TE p. 544.

EXERCISE 6

With a partner, write descriptions of one or more sentences for the following pictures. Use at least one relative clause in each description. Then revise each description, deleting as many relative pronouns as possible. (Follow the rules in Focus 4.)

▶ **EXAMPLE:** A man brought flowers to a woman whom he admires.

Revision: *A man brought flowers to a woman he admires.*

1. _____

3. _____

2. _____

4. _____

ANSWER KEY

Exercise 6

Answers will vary.
1. A man who is wearing a hat is sitting on a boat (which is) in the middle of a lake.   2. A woman who is sitting on a stool which is in a garage is showing a girl who is wearing a striped shirt how to adjust a bicycle wheel.
3. A woman is giving a snack to a dog (that is) sitting in a field which is near a forest.
4. An older woman who is wearing a white blouse is exchanging money with a younger woman who has long hair.

FOCUS 5

Relative Clauses in Formal and Informal Communication

USE

EXAMPLES	EXPLANATIONS
Formal (a) I know the person **whom** he hired. (b) I know the person **who** he hired. (c) I know the person **that** he hired. (d) I know the person he hired. *Informal*	The use or omission of object relative pronouns may vary according to formality. *Whom* is used in formal writing but is often reduced to *who* or *that* in speaking. It can be omitted altogether in informal speech.
Formal (e) He saw the person **at whom** she laughed. (f) He saw the person **whom** she laughed **at**. (g) He saw the person **who** she laughed **at**. (h) He saw the person she laughed **at**. *Informal*	In formal written English, the preposition should always precede the object relative pronoun.

EXERCISE 7
Reread the story in Exercise 1. Mark word order changes and cross out relative pronouns that will make the story less formal.

▶ **EXAMPLE:** When my mother and I came to the United States, I experienced a move ~~from which~~ I felt that I would never recover. from

I was often left alone as my mother left for fancy parties ~~at~~
which she mingled with famous actors, artists, and musicians. at

SUGGESTION
1. Distribute sentence strips to four Ss with sentences *a* through *d* written on them.
2. Write *informal* on the far left side and *formal* on the far right side of the board.
3. Ask the four Ss with strips to stand up and order themselves according to formality across the room. The Ss with sentences *a* and *b* should be on the left and the students with *c* and *d* should be on the right.
3. Read through the focus box as a class.

Exercise 8

EXPANSION

Ask Ss to write a conversation that corresponds to picture 4 in Exercise 6. Ask them to write four or five lines for each person in an informal style. Then, have them modify the dialogue so that it has a more formal style.

Workbook Exs. 7 & 8, pp. 82–83.
Answers: TE p. 544.

UNIT GOAL REVIEW

Ask Ss to look at the goals on the opening page of the unit again. Help them understand how much they have accomplished in each area.

EXERCISE 8

In pairs, read the following dialogue aloud. Then, edit the dialogue to create a less formal style. (Be sure to focus on relative clauses modifying objects and contractions.) Finally, reread the dialogue aloud, including the revisions that you have made.

▶ **EXAMPLE:** **Luca:** Did you hear from the accountant to whom we talked last month?

Luca: Did you hear from the accountant ~~to whom~~ we talked last $_{to}$ month?

Maya: No, I did not. Is he concerned about the bank account which we closed in January?

Luca: No, he is calling about personal taxes that *you* have not paid yet.

Maya: That makes another item that I do not need now—a reminder that I owe money.

Luca: I know what you mean. The accountant with whom I deal is always asking me if I have any earnings that I neglected to mention.

Maya: Well, this year has been especially bad for me. I bought a car for one of my daughters who has very expensive tastes. I came up short at the end of the year, and I still owe taxes on the book royalties that I earned in April and the horse race that I won in September.

Luca: Sometimes I wish the United States collected a tax which is a strict percentage of a person's salary. A lot of other countries collect this type of "flat" tax.

Maya: Well, until that happens, I guess I will have to deal with the accountant after all. Let me know if he calls again.

Use Your English

USE YOUR ENGLISH

The activities on these "purple pages" at the end of the unit contain situations that should naturally elicit the unit's structures in a more communicative framework. While Ss are doing these activities in class, you can circulate and listen to determine if they have actually achieved the goals on the opening page of the unit.

ACTIVITY 1: LISTENING/ WRITING

STEP 1 Listen to the tape and take notes on descriptive information about the following items. You may want to listen a second time to check your notes.

▶ **EXAMPLE:** an apartment building _____ near the downtown _____

1. braids _____
2. a joke _____
3. excuses _____
4. a ring _____
5. a model car _____
6. a writer _____
7. an engineer _____
8. colleges _____
9. a nurse _____
10. an artist _____
11. the hotel _____
12. a carnation _____
13. an unattractive man _____
14. a phone booth _____

STEP 2 Now describe how each item fits into the story. Create sentences using relative clauses modifying objects.

▶ **EXAMPLE:** *Kimi and Fred lived in the same apartment building which was located near the downtown of Los Angeles.*

STEP 3 What do you think will happen next? Write a short paragraph that describes your thoughts. Use at least one relative clause modifying an object in your paragraph.

Relative Clauses Modifying Objects | **153**

Activity 1

Play textbook audio. The tapescript for this listening appears on p. 566 of this book. Play the tape a third time if Ss have difficulty catching all of the information.

ANSWER KEY

Activity 1
Step 1: Answers will vary.
Step 2: 1. Fred tied Kimi's braids which were long and beautiful around the back of her chair. **2.** The whole class laughed at Fred's joke which the teacher did not think was funny at all. **3.** Fred kept thinking of excuses that he could use when he knocked at her door. **4.** Fred gave Kimi a ring which had the engraving "My true love forever." **5.** Kimi gave Fred a model car on which she had painted the words "My heart races for you." **6.** Kimi wanted to be a writer who would write the "Great American Novel." **7.** Fred wanted to be an engineer who would design a famous bridge. **8.** Fred and Kimi went to different colleges which were on different coasts. **9.** Fred married a nurse whom he had met at college. **10.** Kimi married an artist whom she had met at church. **11.** Fred asked Kimi if he could meet her in the lobby of the hotel in which they had had their high school prom. **12.** They both agreed to bring a red carnation which they would wear in their coat lapels. **13.** Kimi saw an unattractive man who was smoking a cigar and whose clothes looked filthy. **14.** Kimi dialed someone from a phone booth which was in the lobby of the hotel.

Activity 2

Step 1: Ask Ss to count off to form pairs (e.g., if there are 30 students, they should number off to 15 twice). Ss with the same number will be paired.

Step 2: Ss should be seated a good distance away from each other as they draw. Remind Ss that they do not have to be perfect artists—a simple sketched diagram with geometric shapes will do.

Step 3: Have Ss find a seat near their partners. Encourage them to use relative clauses. They may say something like: "*My diagram has a circle. There is an X in the circle.*" Instead, ask Ss to combine sentences—"*My diagram has a circle that has an X in it.*"

Activities 3 and 4

VARIATIONS

These activities could also be used as diagnostic writing and speaking exercises at the end or beginning of the unit.

ACTIVITY 2 : SPEAKING

STEP 1 Find a partner

STEP 2 Each partner should draw a simple diagram without letting the other person see it.

STEP 3 Each partner should describe his or her diagram while the other partner tries to draw it on a piece of paper.

STEP 4 Each partner should compare his or her drawing with the original and note any differences between the two.

▶ **EXAMPLE:** *Draw a rectangle which is about 7 inches by 2 inches. Draw a diagonal line which extends from the upper left-hand corner to the lower right-hand corner. Draw an X with a circle around it in the top half. In the bottom half, draw a heart which has an arrow through it.*

ACTIVITY 3 : WRITING

Imagine that you are applying to a university that requires a formal letter of introduction about yourself. In your letter, describe academic and extracurricular activities that have shaped your life. Try to use a number of relative clauses modifying objects. You may want to describe some of the following ideas in your writing:

- a class that you especially enjoyed
- a talent that distinguishes you
- a book whose ideas inspired you
- a sport in which you excel
- a person whom you respect

▶ **EXAMPLE:** *My name is Nikita Korsu. There are many experiences about which I could write that have developed my character. My interest in academics appeared at a young age. In grade school, I had a teacher who inspired me to excel in mathematics . . .*

ACTIVITY 4: SPEAKING/WRITING

STEP 1 In pairs, look at the following picture and describe what you see.

STEP 2 Write a paragraph using at least five relative clauses modifying objects.

▶ **EXAMPLE:** *This picture depicts the dangers of pollution on the environment. Animals are standing in line on a beach which is littered with boxes and cans . . .*

Relative Clauses Modifying Objects   **155**

The test for this unit can be found on p. 498.
The answers are on p. 499.

Unit 9

UNIT OVERVIEW

Unit 9 assumes that students (Ss) have already studied relative clauses but may still have some difficulty distinguishing restrictive from nonrestrictive relative clauses and using nonrestrictive relative clauses appropriately in writing and speaking.

UNIT GOALS

Review the goals listed on this page so Ss understand what they should be able to know by the end of the unit.

OPENING TASK

This task engages Ss in a simulated class reunion. Ss often enjoy the opportunity to practice conversing in a social situation. They could be encouraged to stand up, walk around the room, and "mingle," as in a real party.

SETTING UP THE TASK

You may want to share your own experiences of reunions in the target language culture. Discuss family or high school/college reunions in which those attending are interested in learning how everyone's physical appearances, careers, families, etc., have changed over the years. Point out how some people are even tempted to stretch the truth a bit to impress everyone.

U N I T 9

NONRESTRICTIVE RELATIVE CLAUSES

UNIT GOALS:

- To distinguish restrictive from nonrestrictive relative clauses
- To use nonrestrictive relative clauses in definitions
- To use relative clauses to comment upon an entire idea
- To use nonrestrictive relative clauses with quantifying expressions

OPENING TASK
The Class Reunion

Imagine that you and your classmates are attending your English class reunion ten years from today. As is the case at many class reunions, each of you will want to impress the others with your accomplishments and achievements over the past few years.

STEP 1 Jot down ideas in each of the following categories about what you have done and why it is so good. Be as creative as possible. Then, exchange your list of ideas with a classmate.

STEP 2 In groups of four, take turns bragging about your partner's accomplishments in the following categories, with each person in the group trying to outdo the others.

Category	What?	Why so good?
Your occupation		
Your family		
Your best vacation		
Your home		
Your _____		

▶ **EXAMPLES:** Occupation

    A: *Now Chang is working for Rothwell International, which is one of the biggest engineering companies in the world.*

    B: *Oh, really? Well, Carla works for Unifeat Studios, which is one of the most important motion picture studios in her home city.*

    Family

    A: *Mary's son, who is a tournament chess player, just won a competition.*

    B: *Well, Barry's daughter, who just wrote a play about her hometown, also just received an award.*

CONDUCTING THE TASK
Step 1

Ask Ss to brainstorm individually their likely accomplishments over the next ten years. Since some Ss may feel a little uncomfortable bragging about themselves on an occasion like this (because it is not acceptable in their native cultures), they are asked to exchange their lists of ideas with a classmate.

Step 2

Have Ss form groups of four (two pairs of partners in each) and act out the class reunion. Read the two examples. Encourage Ss to tell exactly what their partners have done and why it is so good. Encourage use of proper nouns, since these often require nonrestrictive relative clauses for elaboration. Remind Ss that in speech, nonrestrictive relative clauses are often preceded by a pause (e.g., "*Guess what? I married a man named Gunther,* (pause) *who is from Germany.*") Ss should have fun producing multiple examples of nonrestrictive relative clauses.

CLOSING THE TASK

As a class, discuss whose accomplishments were the most interesting or astonishing.

EXPANSION

For another diagnostic tool, have Ss write up the accomplishments of the other Ss, or write a brief report on the class reunion. You can save these writing samples and return to them at the end of the unit to help Ss see what they have learned.

1. Write the following two fill-in-the-blank sentences on the board. *I admire teachers_____.*
   I admire my English teacher, _____.
   Ask Ss to comment on the two sentences. What is similar? What is different? (They should note that the first sentence is speaking about teachers in general, but the second one is speaking about their particular English teacher.)

2. Brainstorm on the board some characteristics of all teachers. Ss may say: *well organized, fair, trustworthy, knowledgeable*, etc.

3. Brainstorm some characteristics of you, their teacher (or another teacher in the school). In this case, the qualities may be more specific: *red hair, knowledgeable about pronunciation, New Yorker*, etc.

4. Review Units 7 and 8 that showed how English allows embedding of one sentence into another. Write: *I admire teachers who are fair.* Ask Ss what this means. Clarify that they do not admire all teachers but fair teachers. State that this relative clause is needed to clarify <u>which kind</u> of teachers are admired.

5. Write this sentence on the board: *I admire my English teacher, who is knowledgeable about pronunciation.* Ask Ss whether the information in the relative clause is needed for them to identify their English teacher. They should say *no* because they are all familiar with this talent of their teacher and this is extra or incidental information, stated almost as an afterthought. State that this is the purpose of a nonrestrictive relative clause, to add additional information but not necessary information for identifying the related noun.

6. Ask Ss to silently read Focus 1 or use the "uncover technique" to reveal the rules one by one on an overhead transparency (or in books) for the whole class.

▶ **R**elative versus Nonrestrictive Relative Clauses

EXAMPLES	EXPLANATIONS	
MEANING	A restrictive clause . . .	A nonrestrictive clause . . .
(a) I admire professors **who lecture well.**	• is necessary to identify the noun it describes (not all professors are admired, only the ones who lecture well).	
(b) I admire my professor, **who lectures well.**		• adds additional information; it does not help identify the professor in (b).
FORM		
(c) I prefer to fly on airlines **that have direct routes to major cities.**	• is not set off by commas.	
(d) When I return home to Chicago, I will telephone my mother, **who lives in Joliet.**		• is set off by one or more commas.
(e) Joliet, **which is a suburb of Chicago,** was a wonderful place to grow up.		
(f) My mother will pick me up at O'Hare (**which is the international airport near Chicago**).		• is sometimes set off by parentheses.
(g) She usually meets me at the baggage claim, **which exits onto the street,** rather than at the gate inside the building.		• uses *which* (not *that*) to describe places or things.
(h) **NOT:** She usually meets me at the baggage claim, that exits onto the street, rather than at the gate inside the building.		
(i) I always take the midnight flight, **(pause)** **which is never crowded.**		• is set off by a pause and a drop in intonation in speech.

EXERCISE 1

In the following pairs of sentences, add commas to the sentence that contains the nonrestrictive relative clause. Then explain to a partner why the clause is nonrestrictive.

▶ **EXAMPLE:** (a) The smog that covers Mexico City is very unhealthy.

(b) Smog, which is a fog that has become polluted with smoke, is a pervasive problem in many large cities.

((b) is nonrestrictive because it adds additional information to a general statement about all smog.)

1. (a) The teacher who got married last year will not be returning this year.
   (b) Your English teacher who has a thorough knowledge of English grammar can help you with your grammar problems.

2. (a) People who drink should not drive.
   (b) People who require water to survive may someday run out of pure water.

3. (a) When I get to New York, I'm going shopping at a store which I heard about from a friend.
   (b) When I get to New York, I'm going shopping at Saks Fifth Avenue which is located in downtown Manhattan.

4. (a) The world which is actually pear-shaped was once thought to be flat.
   (b) The world which we live in today is very different from the world a century ago.

5. (a) Samuel Clemens who was a famous American author wrote *Tom Sawyer*.
   (b) Samuel Clemens was the famous American author who wrote *Tom Sawyer*.

6. (a) Yesterday we went to "The City" which is how northern Californians refer to San Francisco.
   (b) Yesterday we went to the city which is directly south of San Francisco.

Exercise 1

Once pairs have made their selections, conduct a whole class discussion about their choices. Emphasize that the understanding and perception of the audience (the listener or reader) must be considered in order to determine whether or not the information in the relative clause is essential in identifying the referent.

ANSWER KEY

Exercise 1

1. **(b)** Your teacher, who has a thorough knowledge of English grammar, can . . . (*Your* in *your teacher* makes this a unique, identifiable noun.) **2. (b)** People, who require water to survive, may . . . (*People* refers to everyone or an entire group and is identifiable.) **3. (b)** . . . New York, I'm going shopping at Saks Fifth Avenue, which . . . (*Saks Fifth Avenue* is a store identifiable by name.) **4. (a)** The world, which is actually pear-shaped, was . . . (*The world* is a one of a kind noun.) **5. (a)** Samuel Clemens, who was a famous American author, wrote . . . (*Samuel Clemens* is a proper noun.) **6. (a)** . . . to "The City," which is how . . . (*The City* is considered a proper noun.)

Exercise 3

EXPANSION

If possible, borrow *The Specialty Travel Index* from the library or a travel agency. Read through the table of contents and scan the pages to give Ss an idea about what is contained in the book. Or photocopy the table of contents and have Ss explain what else is in the book.

EXERCISE 2

Reread your notes from the Opening Task on page 156. Write sentences from your notes with restrictive and nonrestrictive relative clauses. Write N next to the nonrestrictive relative clauses and R next to the restrictive relative clauses. Then, read your sentences aloud, inserting pauses with your nonrestrictive clauses.

▶ **EXAMPLE:** *I now live in Cartagena, which is the most beautiful resort city in Colombia.* N

EXERCISE 3

Put brackets around all of the nonrestrictive relative clauses and circle the noun phrases they modify.

(1) The Specialty Travel Index, [which is well known to travel agents], should be consulted more often by the layman as well. (2) Anyone who is interested in traveling to rare or exotic places will enjoy thumbing through this volume. (3) Four hundred thirty-six tour operators advertise in this index. (4) Entries are organized by subject matter and geographical emphasis and are cross-indexed for your convenience. (5) For example, if you want to visit Mauritius, which is an island in the Indian Ocean, you only need to look under "M" in the geographical index, which is alphabetically organized. (6) If you would like a tour which specializes in "soccer," "solar energy," "space travel," or "spectator sports," you only need to look under "S" in the subject index. (7) "Chocolate tours," "whale-watching tours," "holistic health tours," and "military history tours" are just a few more of the some 176 special-interest tours that are listed in this index.

(8) Irma Turtle, who is one of the advertisers in *The Specialty Travel Index*, began her career in an interesting way. (9) Bored with her job in business, she decided to start a tour-guiding service. (10) Travelers on her first tour explored Algerian rock paintings, which had been discovered in the Central Sahara. (11) Today she leads other exciting tours. (12) For example, the tour of "Pantanal" of Brazil, which contains the world's largest wetlands, offers views of 600 species of tropical birds. (13) Another tour utilizes Berber guides to take travelers through the Atlas Mountains, which are in Morocco. (14) Finally, Jivaro Indians (whose ancestors were headshrinkers) now lead adventuresome tourists through the Ecuadorian Amazon.

(15) The next time you are planning a trip, don't forget to consult *The Specialty Travel Index*, which describes the unusual tours of Irma Turtle and other one-person travel operators.

Adapted from Arthur Frommer, *Arthur Frommer's New World of Travel*, 1988. Used by permission of the publisher: Frommer Books/Prentice Hall Press/A Division of Simon & Schuster, New York.

ANSWER KEY

Exercise 2
Answers will vary.

Exercise 3
(5) Mauritius, [which is an island in the Indian Ocean] (5) the geographical index, [which is alphabetically organized] (8) Irma Turtle, [who is one of the advertisers in *The Specialty Travel Index*] (10) Algerian rock paintings, [which had been discovered in the Central Sahara] (12) the tour of "Pantanal" of Brazil, [which contains the world's largest wetlands] (13) the Atlas Mountains, [which are in Morocco] (14) Jivaro Indians, [whose ancestors were headshrinkers] (15) *The Specialty Travel Index*, [which describes the unusual tours of Irma Turtle and other one-person travel operators]

EXERCISE 4

Imagine you are a tourist visiting Vancouver, British Columbia, on your own. To entertain yourself, you took several tours of the city, which are listed below. Describe three tours you took in a letter to a friend. Use at least one nonrestrictive relative clause in each tour description.

▶ **EXAMPLE:** *Dear Owen,*

I've really been enjoying myself in Vancouver. I've already spent a lot of money on tours, but it has been worth it. First, I took the City of Vancouver Tour, which was a five-hour tour of important sights around the city . . .

Regards,
Your Name

Name: City of Vancouver Tour
Price: $35.00
Description: five-hour bus tour of important points of interest: Stanley Park, Queen Elizabeth Park, Capilano Suspension Bridge

Name: Dinner Theatre Evening
Price: $70.00
Description: bus transportation, six-course dinner, tip, and ticket to theatre "A Streetcar Named Desire"

Name: Victoria City Tour
Price: $75.00
Description: 12-hour bus ride to the capital of British Columbia, ferry toll included, world famous Butchart Gardens

Name: Whistler Resort
Price: $100.00
Description: one day of skiing at world-class resort, lunch, ski rentals not included

Name: Fishing Trip
Price: $175.00
Description: half-day of fishing on Pacific Coast, private boat, guide, tackle, bait, license, lunch

Nonrestrictive Relative Clauses | **161**

Exercise 4

If Ss are having difficulty using nonrestrictive relative clauses, remind them that proper nouns are considered "identifiable" and can be followed by nonrestrictive relative clauses, which require the comma.

Workbook Ex. 1, pp. 84–85.
Answers: TE p. 544.

ANSWER KEY

Exercise 4

Answers will vary.

Dear Owen,

I just got back from my trip to Vancouver. What a wonderful time I had! To orient myself, I took the City of Vancouver Tour, which was a five-hour bus ride to important points of interest. Then, that first evening, I paid $70 for the Dinner Theatre Evening, which consisted of a six-course dinner and the play *A Streetcar Named Desire*.

On the next full tour day, I took the Victoria City Tour, which was a twelve-hour bus ride to the capital of British Columbia. I especially loved seeing the Butchart Gardens, which are world famous.

The next day I decided to go skiing at the Whistler Resort, but I did not realize how expensive it would be. I paid $100 for the ski tows and my lunch, which was a gourmet feast.

On my last full day I took the Fishing Trip, which cost $175. Although the weather wasn't very good, I enjoyed the boat ride and the lunch on the Pacific Coast.

Well, I'll fill you in on more of the details when I return.

Regards,
Teresa

FOCUS 2

1. After reading the focus box examples together, ask Ss to brainstorm computer-related terms, for example: *floppy disk, CD-Rom, hard drive, word processing, byte, DVD drive,* etc.

2. Ask them to include these words and phrases in sentences in which they are also defined, for example: *My computer reads CD-Roms, which are round disks that hold large amounts of information.*

Exercise 5

E X P A N S I O N

Ask Ss to pair up and share common terms from their fields of study, e.g., business, economics, math, child development, etc. Then, ask them to define these words for each other, using nonrestrictive relative clauses.

FOCUS **2**

▶ **Nonrestrictive Relative Clauses in Definitions**

EXAMPLES	EXPLANATION
(a) Pink eye, **which is an eye inflammation,** is contagious. (b) In order to join components of an electronic circuit, you need to solder, **which involves applying a soft metal that melts.**	Nonrestrictive relative clauses are often used for defining terms in sentences.

EXERCISE 5

Imagine you are a world traveler who is getting ready for a long trip. Write sentences describing the items you always take with you. Look at the list below, and add two more of your own. Use a nonrestrictive relative clause to define each one.

▶ **EXAMPLE:** lap-top

> *I always bring a lap-top, which is a portable computer.*

1. luggage cart	**6.** Swiss army knife
2. money belt	**7.** book light
3. travel iron	**8.** _____
4. adapter	**9.** _____
5. travel calculator	

A N S W E R   K E Y

Exercise 5

Answers may vary.

1. I never forget a luggage cart, which allows me to carry very heavy loads.   2. I always wear a money belt, which has a zippered enclosure for my cash and passport.   3. A travel iron, which collapses into a compact position, is handy for touch-up ironing.   4. I always carry an adapter, which allows me to transfer from one type of electrical current to another.   5. I don't leave home without a travel calculator, which has a special ability to translate amounts in one type of currency to another.   6. It is important to carry a Swiss army knife, which contains several knives, a fork, a spoon, a nail file, and even a small pair of scissors.   7. I take a book light, which can be clipped onto the hard cover of a book for late-night reading on a train or plane.   8. Detergent, which comes in small disposable envelopes, is a must for washing clothes.

Using a Relative Clause to Comment on an Entire Idea

EXAMPLES	EXPLANATION
(a) Last week I returned from a three-week cruise, **which was a relief.** (b) I had eaten too much food, **which was a big mistake.**	Some nonrestrictive relative clauses comment on a whole idea in the main clause. These are used most often in informal conversation and always begin with *which*.

EXERCISE 6

STEP 1 Below are excerpts from letters you have written to friends and family about your travel mishaps. How would you explain these mishaps to your next-door neighbor in conversation? Use one of the following adjectives in your comments or one of your own:

disappointing	frightening	painful
exasperating	tiring	embarrassing
expensive	stressful	upsetting

▶ **EXAMPLE:** My brother and I were traveling in Mexico City. We got stuck in a horrible traffic jam in our taxi.

When my brother and I were traveling in Mexico City, we got stuck in a horrible traffic jam, which was very exasperating.

1. My friend and I wanted to save money in Venice. We walked from the train station all the way to our hotel.

2. I went hiking in the Sierra Nevada Mountains. I almost fell off a mountain trail.

3. I went on a bike tour of Canada. I fell down and broke my leg.

4. I left my traveler's checks in my hotel room. I did not have any way to pay my bill at an expensive Tokyo restaurant.

5. Last year I flew to Paris. I had to wait three extra hours to catch my return flight home.

Nonrestrictive Relative Clauses | **163**

1. Try to solicit four volunteers to tell you something *scary, entertaining, painful,* and *humorous* that happened to them. (Each volunteer relates a story in a different emotion.)
2. Once a student has related the experience, summarize what he or she said with a comment using a nonrestrictive relative clause. For example: *Last year Yuko was almost attacked by a bear while she was camping, which was really scary.*
3. Write the four sample sentences on the blackboard.
4. Ask Ss what they think the function of the nonrestrictive relative clause is. They should mention that it is used to comment on the whole idea in the main clause.
5. Note that this structure is usually used in casual conversation.

Workbook Ex. 2, pp. 85–86.
Answers: TE p. 544.
Workbook Ex. 3, pp. 86–87.
Answers: TE p. 545.

A N S W E R   K E Y

Exercise 6
Answers will vary.
Step 1 **1.** . . . which was tiring
2. . . . which was very frightening.
3. . . . which was very painful.

4. . . . which was embarrassing.
5. . . . which was disappointing.   **6.** . . . . which was very expensive.   **7.** . . . which was stressful.   **8.** . . . which was upsetting.

6. I went on a ski trip and broke my wrist. I did not have health insurance so I had to pay for the X-ray myself.

7. I almost missed my flight to London. I had to run to the check-in counter with my suitcase and only had two minutes to spare.

8. I ate something in a restaurant that I had never tasted before. I got sick and could not sleep the entire night.

STEP 2 In groups of three, do the following:
First person: Tell about a travel mishap similar to the ones in Step 1.
Second person: Comment on the first person's travel mishap.
Third person: Summarize the mishap and comment on it using a relative clause.

▶ **EXAMPLE:** First person: *When I was in San Francisco, I took the wrong bus to Fisherman's Wharf.*

Second person: *That must have been frustrating.*

Third person: *When Kathy (first person) was in San Francisco, she or he took the wrong bus to Fisherman's Wharf, which was really frustrating.*

Quantifying Expressions with Nonrestrictive Relative Clauses

EXAMPLES	EXPLANATION
(a) I have five phone calls to make, **all of which** should be done immediately. (b) I need three volunteers, **one of whom** must be strong.	Some nonrestrictive relative clauses comment on all of or some portion of a group of persons or things. To form this type of clause, combine a quantifier (such as *all of, most of, none of, many of, each of, two of*) with a relative pronoun.

EXERCISE 7

You are packing to go away to school. Comment on the items you intend to bring, filling in relevant information, using quantifiers, and providing a comma in each nonrestrictive relative clause.

▶ **EXAMPLE:** I have ___two___ pairs of shoes, _one pair of which must be repaired._

1. I'll need _____ shirts _____.
2. I want to take _____ sweaters _____.
3. I have to have _____ notebooks _____.
4. I'll bring _____ pens _____.
5. I must have _____ CD-roms _____.

Nonrestrictive Relative Clauses | **165**

SUGGESTION

1. Draw two stick figures and label them your two friends Jack and Jill (or any other names you would like). Say: "*I have many friends, two of whom are Jack and Jill.*" Write this on the board.
2. Underneath each name, write what is in each of their lunch bags today:

Jack	Jill
2 sandwiches (peanut butter & jam and cheese) 2 desserts (cookie and piece of cake)	2 pieces of fruit (orange and apple) 2 drinks (water and juice)

3. Ask who has the healthier lunch and explain why. In the response, try to elicit sentences that use quantifying expressions and nonrestrictive relative clauses. For example: *Jack has two sandwiches, one of which is peanut butter and jam and the other of which is cheese. On the other hand, Jill has two pieces of fruit, one of which is an orange and the other of which is an apple.* Write these examples on the board.
4. Ask one student to read the examples and another student to read the explanation in the focus box.

Exercise 7

EXPANSION

Have pairs describe different sets of items to each other. To elicit sentences with *whom*, have them describe their families, their best friends, or their teachers. To elicit sentences with *which*, have them describe the clothes in their closet, the food in their home, or their sports equipment.

ANSWER KEY

Exercise 7
Answers will vary.
1. five / two of which
2. three / two of which
3. four / one of which
4. ten/ three of which
5. six / one of which

Exercise 8

E X P A N S I O N

If you have Ss from large families or who know other people in large families, have them describe the family and their daily routine. For example: *My sister has five children, all of whom are under age 16. At 5:00 a.m. she gets up and makes breakfast for the family, all of whom arise at 5:30 a.m. Her family likes to eat eggs, all of which are either scrambled or fried. They also like to drink milk or orange juice, both of which are served chilled. At 6:00 she drives the children to two different schools, one of which is one mile away and the other of which is two miles away . . .*

Workbook Exs. 4, 5, & 6, pp. 88–89. Answers: TE p. 545.

UNIT GOAL REVIEW

Ask Ss to look at the goals on the opening page of the unit again. Help them understand how much they have accomplished in each area.

EXERCISE 8

A group of teachers are traveling to Vietnam this summer; however, because of different travel interests, they will be arriving and departing at different times from the same three cities: Ho Chi Minh City (HCMC), Hue, and Hanoi.

Study the following schedule with the dates and times (morning or afternoon) of arrival. Then, fax a letter to a travel service in Vietnam that will arrange to pick up the teachers from the airport and deliver them to their hotels. The beginning of the letter appears below.

Name	City	Arrive	Depart	City	Arrive	Depart	City	Arrive	Depart
Peterson	HCMC	6/15 A.M.	6/20 A.M.	Hue	6/20 A.M.	6/21 P.M.	Hanoi	6/21 P.M.	7/30 P.M.
McGill	HCMC	6/18 A.M.	6/20 A.M.	Hue	6/20 A.M.	6/27 A.M.	Hanoi	6/27 A.M.	7/30 P.M.
Orselli	HCMC	6/15 P.M.	6/20 A.M.	Hue	6/20 A.M.	6/27 A.M.	Hanoi	6/27 A.M.	7/30 A.M.
Hopf	HCMC	6/18 P.M.	6/22 A.M.	Hue	6/22 A.M.	6/27 A.M.	Hanoi	6/27 A.M.	7/30 P.M.
Nguyen	HCMC	6/18 P.M.	6/22 A.M.	Hue	6/22 A.M.	6/27 P.M.	Hanoi	6/27 A.M.	7/30 P.M.

Date: _____   Time: _____

To: Vietnam Travel Service   Phone: _____   Fax: _____

From: _____   Phone: _____   Fax: _____

Number of Pages: __1__

Comments: _____

To Whom It May Concern:

A group of teachers will be coming to Vietnam for a visit. I would very much appreciate it if you could arrange airport transportation for the teachers, all of whom have slightly different schedules. Peterson and Orselli, both of whom will arrive at Ho Chi Minh City on June 15, must be picked up in the morning . . .

A N S W E R   K E Y

Exercise 8

Answers will vary.

To Whom It May Concern:

A group of teachers will be coming to Vietnam for a visit. I would very much appreciate it if you could arrange airport transportation for the teachers, all of whom have slightly different schedules. Peterson and Orselli, both of whom will arrive at Ho Chi Minh City on June 15, must be picked up in the morning. The rest of the group will be arriving on June 18, which is after final exams. The whole group, all of whom are scheduled for a morning flight, will depart for Hue on June 20. All will stay for an entire week except Peterson, who will leave for Hanoi on the 21st. The group, all of whom have return tickets to the U.S. on July 30, will need to be taken to the airport at 4:00 p.m.

Thank you for making all of the arrangements!

Sincerely,

(your name)

Use Your English

USE YOUR ENGLISH

ACTIVITY 1: LISTENING / WRITING

Listen to the following excerpts from tour guides of three different places. Take notes about the famous sights. Afterwards, summarize the tour or portions of the tour using nonrestrictive relative clauses.

Sights	Characteristics
▶ **EXAMPLE:** Lafayette Park	one of the best groomed parks in Washington, D.C.
The White House	construction began in 1792
Treasury Building	Andrew Jackson wanted to keep his eye on people handling cash.

First, they saw Lafayette Park, which is one of the best-groomed parks in Washington, D.C. Then, they saw the White House, whose construction began in 1792. Finally, they saw the Treasury Building, which Andrew Jackson wanted to watch carefully because it housed the money.

Nonrestrictive Relative Clauses | **167**

USE YOUR ENGLISH

The activities on these "purple pages" at the end of the unit contain situations that should naturally elicit the unit's structures in a more communicative framework. While Ss are doing these activities in class, you can circulate and listen to determine if they have actually achieved the goals on the opening page of the unit.

Activity 1

Play textbook audio. The tapescript for this listening appears on p. 567 of this book. Ss may hear some new words with difficult spellings. Either tell them they do not have to worry about spelling or put these key words on the blackboard: *Flagstaff House, Cotton Tree Drive, Victoria Peak Tram Terminus, Botanical and Zoological Gardens, Monastery of San Lorenzo de El Escorial, parallelogram, slate columns, dome of the temple, cloister, Propylaea, Acropolis. Propylon, Propylaea, Pericles, Athena Nike, Artemis.*

ANSWER KEY

Activity 1

Answers will vary.

1. The tour took us to Flagstaff House, which contains the Museum of Tea Drinking. Then we went along Cotton Tree Drive, which is a major motorway. Up Cotton Tree Drive, we saw the Victoria Peak Tram Terminus. The Peak Tram, which was built by a Scottish railway engineer, goes up a 45 degree incline to the top. The Botanical and Zoological Gardens contain many tropical plants, some of which are more than a hundred years old. **2.** Today we visited the Monastery of San Lorenzo de El Escorial, which is shaped like a giant parallelogram. It is covered by slate columns, on top of which are large metal globes. In the center of the eastern side of the building is the place in which the upper part of the temple protrudes. Twin bell towers and the magnificent dome of the temple, which reaches 92 meters, projects above the building. Seeing the cloister, patios, fountains, staircases, doors, and windows was an experience we will never forget. **3.** We took a lovely excursion to the Getty Center, which is lodged in the Santa Monica Mountains. The center was designed by Richard Meier, who is associated with architectural modernism. The tram, which took us to the top of the hill, made us feel elevated out of our everyday experience. We walked on traverfire, which came from Italy. We looked at varied displays, which were in the museum. We also saw the Museum Courtyard, which had a beautiful fountain and a Central Garden, which circled around to a pool. At the end of the tour we stopped at the View South, which featured a panoramic view of Los Angeles.

Activity 2

Ask Ss to focus on a tour of only about a two-mile perimeter so that they can be more detailed in their descriptions. Encourage them to use the structures from the entire unit. They should define new words, use quantifying expressions, and give overall comments when appropriate.

Activities 3, 4, and 5

These three activities allow Ss to interact and share information about famous people and interesting places.

ACTIVITY 2: WRITING

You are preparing to be a tour guide of your hometown or the city you are presently living in. Think of five sights that are in a two-mile radius and write the script you would use, incorporating as many details as possible about the sight, such as historical origin, age, and unique aspects.

▶ **EXAMPLE:** *At the beginning of the tour, we will start with the most important place in my town, which is the Plaza Leon. The Plaza Leon, which is more than one hundred years old, is the gathering place for young people on Friday and Saturday nights and for parents and children on Sunday afternoons. Four streets extend out from the Plaza, which have wide sidewalks and are tree-lined. Hernandez Street, which was named after the first mayor of the city, contains all of the food stores—bakeries, fish markets, vegetable stands, etc. Fernando Street, which the first mayor named after his only son, is where all of the professional offices are housed. Via del Mar Street, whose pavement is made of cobblestone, is the only street which still has its original surface. Finally, two universities, one of which is the most famous university in my home country, are located on Horatio Street, which is my favorite street of all!*

ACTIVITY 3: WRITING/SPEAKING

STEP 1 In groups of three, name two facts that are common knowledge about the following people. Then, create one or more sentences that contain relative clauses about these individuals.

John Lennon   Princess Diana   Winston Churchill   Mother Teresa
Abraham Lincoln   Joan of Arc   Mahatma Gandhi   Fidel Castro

▶ **EXAMPLE:** John Lennon (*lead singer of the Beatles, born in Liverpool, England, was killed in New York*) John Lennon, who was the lead singer of the Beatles, was born in Liverpool, England.

STEP 2 Now think of another famous person you are familiar with. Present facts about this person to your classmates.

ACTIVITY 4: SPEAKING/WRITING

Interview several members of your class about various aspects of their native countries. Record that information below. Then, write several sentences, summarizing what you have learned using nonrestrictive relative clauses.

▶ **EXAMPLE:** *María, who is from Mexico, likes mariachi music. She also likes horchata, which is a popular milky white drink.*

Name	Native Country	National Foods, Sports, Dances, etc.
1.		
2.		
3.		

ACTIVITY 5: RESEARCH/SPEAKING

Visit a travel agency and bring in various travel brochures for places you would like to visit. In small groups, compare different destinations and places to stay.

▶ **EXAMPLE:** *I want to go to Hong Kong, which has many four-star hotels.*

ACTIVITY 6: WRITING

In one paragraph, describe the location, dates, people, and activities associated with a reunion you have attended. Use as many nonrestrictive relative clauses as possible.

▶ **EXAMPLE:** *Last summer I attended my family reunion, which was held on a ranch in Montana . . .*

Nonrestrictive Relative Clauses | **169**

Activity 6

This activity could be used as a diagnostic activity or a testing activity in which Ss demonstrate their ability to use nonrestrictive relative clauses.

The test for this unit can be found on p. 500. The answers are on p. 501.

TOEFL Test Preparation Exercises for Units 7–9 can be found on Workbook pp. 90–92. The answers are on p. 545 of this book.

Unit 10

UNIT OVERVIEW

This unit shows students (Ss) how relative adverbs *where, when, why,* and *how* are used in sentences to replace preposition + relative pronouns. It provides instruction and practice with a variety of relative adverb clause forms: those with head nouns + relative adverbs, those with relative adverbs only, and those with head nouns only. The unit ends with a focus on when to use the three patterns based on such variables as how specific the head noun's meaning is and how formal the communicative situation is.

UNIT GOALS

Review the goals listed on this page so Ss understand what they should be able to know by the end of the unit.

OPENING TASK

In this task, Ss work in groups compiling information in responses to questions about their city/region. They report some of their findings to the rest of the class. The task description presents examples of relative adverb structures in all ten of the listed categories, so Ss will be exposed to the forms through reading. They may also use these structures in their responses.

UNIT 10

RELATIVE ADVERB CLAUSES

UNIT GOALS:

- To know when relative adverbs can be used in place of relative pronouns
- To know the different patterns for using relative adverb clauses and use them correctly
- To know when to use the different patterns in speaking versus writing

OPENING TASK
What Do You Know about Where You Live?

STEP 1 Divide into small groups. Consult with your group members to see who can provide any of the following information about the city where you attend classes and the surrounding area.

History:

1. the year or decade when the city was founded (or century if the city is very old)
2. the reasons why people settled in the area, both in its earliest stages as a community and later during its development

Now:

3. the places where you think visitors would most like to go
4. the reasons why you think visitors would enjoy spending time in this city or area
5. the times when "rush hour" begins and ends if you live in a city with a lot of traffic
6. how most people get to work in the area (public transportation, car, bicycle, etc.)
7. the places where it's fun to go shopping
8. the places where you can go to hear live music or dance
9. the places where you can find peace and quiet outdoors
10. the restaurants where you can get the best food

STEP 2 Have one member of each group present some of the most interesting information the group discussed to the rest of the class.

SETTING UP THE TASK

If possible, bring maps of the city you are currently in, postcards, or other visual aids to stimulate discussion about where Ss live now. Have a brief class discussion about notable places and favorite places, or what they might recommend to visitors.

COMPLETING THE TASK
Step 1
V A R I A T I O N

Assign just a few of the topics to different groups, giving each a variety of *when, where, why,* and *how* statements.

Step 2

As group members present their information, write some of the examples on the board. Note ones that use relative adverb clauses. Save others for possible transformation into relative adverb clauses after you have gone over the points in Focus 1.

CLOSING THE TASK
S U G G E S T I O N S

1. To elicit more oral use of relative adverb clauses, ask Ss what other kinds of information about the city or region would be of interest to visitors or tourists.
2. As a homework assignment, ask Ss to write a paragraph for statement 3 and give reasons why.

This focus box introduces the relative adverbs *where*, *when*, *why*, and *how* and explains their meanings in relation to the preposition + *which* clauses they may replace in sentences.

SUGGESTIONS

1. Prompt more examples for the first two types of relative adverb clause by writing on the board words or phrases to expand into sentence definitions. For example: *a river* (a place where), *December* (a time when), etc.

2. You could do the same as described above for *why* clauses (e.g., to cool off, to have a good time, etc.), but it is a bit more difficult to elicit answers spontaneously. For *why* clauses you could give a relative adverb clause (e.g., *a reason why people go to the beach*) and ask Ss to complete it with an infinitive clause (e.g., *to cool off, to swim, to sail*, etc.).

3. To prompt additional examples of *how* clauses, write phrases with I + verb + *how* for Ss to expand, e.g., *I wonder how; I am amazed at how; I can't figure out how.*

Relative Adverbs versus Relative Pronouns

Relative adverbs *where, when, why* and *how* can replace prepositions + the relative pronoun which when these prepositions refer to place, time, reason, or manner.

Relative Adverb	Meaning
where	place
when	time
why	reason
how	manner

RELATIVE ADVERB	REPLACES PREPOSITION + *WHICH*
(to which) **(a)** A spa is a place **where** you go either to exercise or relax.	*to* *at* } *which* *from* *in*
(during which) **(b)** Summer is the time **when** many people take vacations.	*during* *at* } *which* *in* *on*
(for which) **(c)** A reason **why** some people move to large cities from small towns is to find jobs.	*for which*
(the way in which) **(d)** I don't understand **how** you solved this equation.	*(the way) in which*
(e) I like **how** you wrote your paper.	
(f) **NOT:** I like the way how you wrote your paper.	Note that when *how* replaces *in which* you must also delete the noun phrase *the way* before it.

EXERCISE 1

Substitute relative adverbs for preposition + *which* whenever possible. Make necessary deletions. In one sentence you cannot replace *which* with a relative adverb; explain why.

▶ **EXAMPLE:** The beginning of a new year is a time ~~during which~~ ^{when} many
Americans decide to make changes in their lifestyles.

1. On January 1, the day on which resolutions for the new year are often made, we hear people vowing to lose weight, quit smoking, or perhaps change the way in which they behave toward family or friends.

2. Those who want to shed pounds may go to weight loss centers; these are places which offer counseling and diet plans.

3. Others may join a health club at which they can lose weight by exercising.

4. Still others choose a less expensive way to lose weight: They just avoid situations in which they might snack or overeat.

5. People who want to quit smoking may contact organizations that can help them to analyze the times at which they have the greatest urge to smoke and to develop strategies to break the habit.

6. Those who decide to change their behavior toward others may also seek professional help, to find out the reasons for which they act in certain ways.

7. Most people are sincere about their promises on the day on which they are made; however, by February, many New Year's resolutions are just a memory!

JANUARY						
Sun.	Mon.	Tue.	Wed.	Thur.	Fri.	Sat.
			①1	2	3	4
5	6	7	8	9	10	11
12	13	14	15	16	17	18
19	20	21	22	23	24	25
26	27	28	29	30	31	

Exercise 1

V A R I A T I O N

If Ss have worked previously on the relative clause unit, you could give them more practice with the preposition + *which* forms that are synonymous with relative adverbs.

Give them sentences with relative adverb clauses and have them transform them to preposition + *which* clauses. This transformation will reinforce the meanings of the relative adverbs as replacements for these structures and give Ss additional practice with structures that are often difficult for Ss.

Workbook Ex. 1, p. 93; Ex. 2, pp. 94–95.
Answers: TE p. 545.

A N S W E R   K E Y

Exercise 1

1. . . . day <u>when</u> resolutions   2. (Cannot replace <u>which</u> here; not the object of preposition.)   3. . . . club <u>where</u> they

4. . . . situations <u>where</u> they (Could use <u>when</u> here too if situation is perceived as a time.)
5. . . . times <u>when</u> they   6. reasons <u>why</u> they   7. . . . time <u>when</u> they

This chart introduces one pattern of relative adverb clauses. Each of the following two focus boxes shows one other pattern. The three patterns of relative adverb clauses in this unit are:

1. Head noun + relative adverb + clause (Focus 2)
2. No head noun + relative adverb + clause (Focus 3)
3. Head noun + no relative adverb + clause (Focus 4)

Reasons for using these patterns are explained in the last focus box of this unit, Focus 5.

SUGGESTIONS

1. Remind Ss that the term "head noun" refers to the noun that is modified by a clause. Ss will have encountered the concept of head nouns if they worked on subject-verb agreement in Unit 3.
2. Note that the head nouns shown in the first boxed area represent the general concepts of place, time, and reason. The examples (a) through (d) illustrate more specific place and time head nouns.
3. The second boxed area shows how both definite and indefinite nouns can precede relative adverbs.

   Take special note of the ungrammatical form in example (f). This is a common error.

▶ Pattern 1: Relative Adverb Clauses that Modify Nouns

EXAMPLES	EXPLANATIONS
<table><tr><td>Head Noun +</td><td>Relative Adverb +</td><td>Clause</td></tr><tr><td>a place</td><td>where</td><td>you can relax</td></tr><tr><td>a time</td><td>when</td><td>I can call you</td></tr><tr><td>a reason</td><td>why</td><td>you should attend</td></tr></table> **Place** (a) A store **where** we can get cassettes is just around the corner. **Place** (b) Elba is the island **where** Napoleon was exiled. **Time** (c) I'll always remember the day **when** Neil Armstrong first landed on the moon: July 20, 1969. It was my birthday! **Time** (d) We read about the period **when** plagues spread throughout Europe.	Relative adverb clauses often modify nouns. The noun is called a head noun because it is the head of the clause that follows. The head noun is often a general word such as *place, time, or reason*, but it can also be a more specific word, especially for places and times.
<table><tr><td>**Definite Noun**</td><td>**Indefinite Noun**</td></tr><tr><td>**the day** when **the reason** why **the place** where</td><td>**a day** when **one reason** why **some reasons** why **places** where</td></tr></table> (e) Citizens of a country should learn **the way** / **how** } their government functions. (f) NOT: Citizens of a country should learn **the way how** their government functions.	The head noun can be definite (*the* + noun) or indefinite (*a, an, one, some,* or Ø modifier + noun). The head noun can also be singular or plural. When you use *how*, you must delete the head noun. *How* adverb clauses have only two patterns: (1) *the way*; (2) *how*.

EXERCISE 2

Identify each of the head nouns in Focus 1. What other phrases could you substitute for these head nouns? Are your substitutions more general or more specific in meaning than the original ones?

▶ **EXAMPLE:** A spa is a place where . . .
Head noun: a place

Substitution:
A spa is *a kind of health club* where . . .
More specific than *place*

EXERCISE 3

STEP 1 Match each of the time periods in the first column with an event in the second column. Then make sentences using an appropriate head noun + a relative adverb.

▶ **EXAMPLE:** 1887   Sir Arthur Conan Doyle wrote the first Sherlock Holmes story

1887 was <u>the year when</u> Sir Arthur Conan Doyle wrote the first Sherlock Holmes story.

1.	1961	**a.**	Whitcombe L. Judson invented the zipper
2.	August 10	**b.**	most people are fast asleep
3.	3 A.M.	**c.**	many couples get married in the United States
4.	Mesozoic Era	**d.**	Russian cosmonaut Yuri Gagarin orbited the earth
5.	1891	**e.**	Ecuadorians celebrate Independence Day
6.	June	**f.**	dinosaurs roamed the earth

Exercise 2

S U G G E S T I O N

If you think your Ss have limited vocabulary to complete this exercise, it may be best to do this as a whole class activity.

V A R I A T I O N

Give Ss three choices to pick an appropriate substitution for each head noun (e.g., for time: *month, season, period;* for reason: *aspect, purpose, factor*).

Exercise 3

This exercise has four parts, each dealing with a different relative adverb (*where, when, why, how*). Like many of the exercises in this book, this one is content-based, so that Ss can learn information about a variety of topics while they are working with grammatical structures. Ss do not need to have prior knowledge of any of the facts.

A N S W E R   K E Y

Exercise 2
Answers will vary for the second part of each.
1. a place/A spa is <u>a kind of health club</u> (more specific)   2. the time/Summer is <u>the season</u> (more specific)   3. a reason/<u>An explanation</u> why (more general)   4. the way/<u>the manner in which</u> (synonym for way)

Exercise 3
Step 1
1. 1961 was the year when Russian . . .
2. August 10 is the day when Ecuadorians . . .
3. 3 a.m. is a time when most people . . .
4. The Mesozoic Era is a period when dinosaurs . . .   5. 1891 was the year when Whitcombe . . .   6. June is a month when many . . .

Now match places with events. Again, make sentences using an adverb clause with an appropriate head noun. Try to use nouns other than *place* if possible.

▶ **EXAMPLE:** Florida, Missouri   Mark Twain was born here

Florida, Missouri is <u>the city where</u> Mark Twain was born. (Note that *here* is deleted.)

1.	Ankara	**a.**	you can get a pastrami sandwich here
2.	the kidneys	**b.**	bats can often be found here
3.	New Zealand	**c.**	Turkey moved its capital here from Constantinople
4.	basement	**d.**	Maori is spoken here
5.	deli	**e.**	junk is often stored here
6.	caves	**f.**	the water in your body gets regulated here

STEP 3 Match the following reasons to the statements in the second column. Again, give a sentence for each match.

▶ **EXAMPLE:** crime   many people move away from large cities because of this

Crime *is one reason why* many people move away from large cities.

1.	aerobic exercise	**a.**	people look forward to the New Year for this reason
2.	surprise endings	**b.**	some people avoid shellfish because of this
3.	the chance to "turn over a new leaf"	**c.**	many love autumn for this reason
4.	computer malfunctions	**d.**	people enjoy the stories of Guy de Maupassant because of this
5.	beautiful foliage	**e.**	people take up jogging or bicycling to get this
6.	allergic reactions	**f.**	students sometimes don't get papers in on time for this reason

---

ANSWER KEY

Step 2
1. Ankara is the city where Turkey . . .
2. The kidneys are the organs where water . . .
3. New Zealand is a country where Maori . . .
4. The basement is the part of the house where junk . . .   5. A deli is a restaurant where you can . . .   6. Caves are places where bats . . .

Step 3
1. To get aerobic exercise is a reason why people take up . . .   2. Surprise endings are one reason why people enjoy . . .   3. The chance to "turn over a new leaf" is one reason why people look . . .   4. Computer malfunctions are a reason why students . . .   5. Beautiful foliage is one reason why many . . .   6. Allergic reactions are one reason why some people . . .

STEP 4 Finally, match processes or methods in the first column to statements in the second. Make sentences for your matches using either the head noun *way* or the relative adverb *how*.

▶ **EXAMPLE:** Adding *-ed* you do this to form the regular past tense in English

Adding *-ed* is <u>the way</u> you do this to form the regular past tense in English.

OR: Adding *-ed* is <u>how</u> you form the regular past tense in English.

1. studying history	**a.** you do this to teach a dog to lie down
2. journeying by covered wagon	**b.** you can do this to help prevent heart wagon disease
3. conducting an opinion poll	**c.** most early American pioneers traveled West by this method of transportation
4. repeating commands and giving rewards	**d.** the Greek orator Demosthenes did this to learn to speak clearly
5. eating healthy food and not smoking	**e.** people do this to survey the attitudes of large populations
6. talking with stones in his mouth	**f.** you can do this to prepare for a career as a lawyer

EXERCISE 4

Complete each of the blanks with appropriate words or phrases about yourself.

▶ **EXAMPLE:** <u>The shoreline</u> is a place where I <u>go to watch the birds.</u>

<u>Starting with my conclusion</u> is the way I <u>often begin to write a draft for a paper.</u>

1. _____ was the year when I _____ .
2. _____ is the place where I _____ .
3. The reason why I don't like _____ is _____ .
4. The way I get to school/work is _____ .
5. _____ is a/the day when I _____ .
6. _____ is a reason why I _____ .
7. A _____ where I _____ is _____ .
8. _____ is how I _____ .

Relative Adverb Clauses | **177**

ANSWER KEY

Step 4
1. Studying history is one way you can prepare . . . 2. Journeying by covered wagon was the way most early . . . 3. Conducting an opinion poll is one way people survey . . . 4. Repeating commands and giving rewards is how you teach . . . 5. Eating healthy food and not smoking are two ways you can help to prevent . . . 6. Talking with stones in his mouth was how the Greek orator . . .

Exercise 4
Answers will vary.
1. 1990; moved to the United States
2. Griffith Park; go to bicycle 3. the subway; that it is so noisy 4. on the bus
5. Sunday; try to do something fun 6. To get money for tuition; work 7. store; like to shop; The Metropolitan Museum Store 8. Studying late at night; get my homework done

The pattern shown here has no head noun. Advanced Ss should be familiar with this pattern even though they may not be aware of it as one pattern of relative adverb clauses.

SUGGESTION

To relate this pattern to that shown in Focus 2, ask Ss to supply head nouns before the boldfaced relative adverbs so that they can see where there is a "Ø-head noun." Model one or two examples and ask for substitutions, e.g.: *"This is the corner where we will meet tomorrow;" "That was the week when I decided to go to work."*

Workbook Ex. 3, pp. 96–98.
Answers: TE p. 545.

Exercise 5

Ss could take turns restating the sentences in small groups.

Exercise 6

EXPANSION

Have Ss, in small groups, make up two or three more sentences modeled after this exercise. They could use the Internet to get factual information.

Workbook Exs. 4 & 5, p. 99.
Answers: TE p. 546.

FOCUS **3**

▶ Pattern 2: Relative Adverbs without Head Nouns

EXAMPLES	EXPLANATIONS
Relative Adverb + Clause where — he lives when — the term starts why — I called how — she knows	A second pattern with relative adverbs has no head noun. As with Pattern 1, this pattern can express: • place • time • reason • manner

(a) This is **where** we will meet tomorrow.
(b) That was **when** I decided to go to work.
(c) **Why** she left is a mystery.
(d) She explained **how** to change a tire.

EXERCISE 5

Restate each of the sentences you made in Exercise 3 without the head nouns (except for the ones in Step 4 for which you used *how*).

▶ **EXAMPLE:** *1887 was when Sir Arthur Conan Doyle wrote the first Sherlock Holmes story.*

EXERCISE 6

Working with a partner or in a small group, decide whether each statement is true or false. If a statement is false, replace the phrase in italics with something that will make the statement true.

▶ **EXAMPLE:** *Spring* is when birds in the northern hemisphere begin their migration south.

Answer: *False. **Autumn** is when they migrate south.*

1. *New York* is where you can see the Lincoln Memorial.
2. *Late November* is when we celebrate the winter solstice.
3. *Religious persecution* is why many Europeans first settled in what became the United States of America.
4. *Majoring in mathematics* is how most undergraduate students prepare for a career in medicine.
5. *The 1970s* was the decade when Ronald Reagan was president.

ANSWER KEY

Exercise 5
Step 1
1. 1961 was when . . . 2. August 10 is when . . . 3. 3 a.m. is when . . . 4. The Mesozoic Era is when . . . 5. 1891 was when . . . 6. June is when . . .
Step 2
1. Ankara is where . . . 2. The kidneys are where . . . 3. New Zealand is where . . . 4. The basement is where . . . 4. A deli is where . . . 5. Caves are where . . .
Step 3
1. To get aerobic exercise is why . . .

2. Surprise endings are why . . . 3. The chance to "turn over a new leaf" is why . . . 4. Computer malfunctions are why . . . 5. Beautiful foliage is why . . . 6. Allergic reactions are why . . .
Step 4
1. Studying history is how . . . 2. Journeying by covered wagon was how . . . 3. An opinion poll is how . . . 4. Repeating commands and giving rewards is how . . . 5. Eating healthy food and not smoking are how . . . 6. Talking with stones in his mouth was how . . .

Ss should note that meaning changes if a head noun with indefinite article "a" or quantifiers (e.g., "one") are used rather than *the*. The meaning changes from indicating one time/place/reason/way and implies the <u>only</u> time/place, etc.

Exercise 6
1. False—Washington, D.C. is where . . . 2. False—Late December is when . . . 3. True 4. False—Majoring in biology is how . . . 5. False—The 1980's was the decade when . . . 6. False—The bookstore is where . . . 7. True 8. False—Using a meat thermometer is how . . .

6. *The drugstore* is where a bibliophile would go to add to her collection.

7. *Either July or August* is when a person born under the zodiac sign of Leo will celebrate his or her birthday.

8. *Using a meat barometer* is how you check to make sure meat is cooked well enough in the oven.

Pattern 3: Head Nouns without Relative Adverbs

EXAMPLES	EXPLANATIONS
<table><tr><td colspan="3">**Head Noun** + **Clause**</td></tr><tr><td>the place</td><td>we moved to</td></tr><tr><td>the time</td><td>I start school</td></tr><tr><td>the reason</td><td>they left</td></tr><tr><td>the way</td><td>you do this</td></tr></table> **(a)** Cook's is **a store** I go to for kitchen supplies. **(b)** November first is **the day** Catholics celebrate All Saint's Day. **(c)** **The reason** spiders can spin perfect webs is based on their instincts, not learned behavior. **(d)** Public transportation is **the way** many city dwellers get to work.	A third pattern uses only the head noun and its modifying clause. This pattern can also express: • place • time • reason • manner
(e) Dominic's is the restaurant I go **to** for pizza. **(f)** **NOT:** Dominic's is the restaurant I go for pizza. **(g)** Denver is the city I live **in**. **(h)** **NOT:** Denver is the city I live.	With specific head nouns that express place, you must often include a preposition of direction or position.
(i) Dominic's is the place I {**go** / **go to**} for pizza.	The preposition is often optional in informal English when *place* is the head noun.

FOCUS 4

In the third pattern shown here, the relative adverb does not appear after the head noun.

SUGGESTIONS

1. Again, to review the "slots" where grammatical structures do not appear but could, ask Ss to state which relative adverbs could follow the head nouns in examples (a) through (d).

2. Note that the relative adverbs could *not* be inserted in (e) or (g) unless the prepositions *to* (in e) and *in* (in g) were deleted first. Give Ss practice with the different patterns by using your own city, state, or region as an example, modeled after example (h).

Exercise 7

VARIATION

Like Exercise 4, Ss could do this exercise with a partner, eliciting the classmate's information and writing down the answers to turn in or report to the class.

EXERCISE 7

Make sentences using Pattern 3 (head nouns without relative adverbs) to provide information about yourself.

▶ **EXAMPLE:**   where you live

   Winnipeg, Canada is the city I live in.

1. where you were born
2. the date (month, day) when you were born
3. the way you make a certain food you like
4. the reason you are taking a specific course
5. the time of day (for example, morning, afternoon) best for you to get work done
6. a place you like to go to relax or have fun
7. a reason you like or dislike a course you are taking
8. the way people say "good luck" in your native language

ANSWER KEY

Exercise 7

Answers will vary.
1. Bogotá, Colombia is the city I was born in.
2. July 20 is the day I was born.   3. Sautéing with olive oil and onions is the way I like to cook zucchini.   4. To improve my speaking skills in public is the reason I am taking a speech course.   5. The morning is the time I can get the most work done.   6. The gym is where I go to have fun.   7. Its relevance to my career plans is the reason I like my business English course.   8. "Bon chance" is the way people say good luck in my native language.

Contexts for Relative Adverb Patterns

Here are some general guidelines for using the three patterns.

EXAMPLES	EXPLANATIONS
	Pattern 1: Head Noun + Relative Adverb + Clause We tend to use this pattern:
(a) Today is **a day when** all nations will want to join in prayers for peace in the world.	• to focus on or emphasize the time, place, reason, or manner.
(b) This is **the place where** most of my family lived at one time or another.	
(c) I know **a nursery where** you can get beautiful orchids.	• when the meaning of the head noun is specific.
(d) Barton's is **a store where** one can find expensive cameras discounted. (Less formal: Barton's is **where** you can get a fantastic deal!)	• when the context is more formal (such as written versus spoken English).
(e) **A place where** you can buy film is at the corner of Hammond and Belknap.	• when the head noun is the subject of a sentence rather than the predicate. In example (e), **a place** helps to introduce new information.
(f) The corner of Hammond and **Predicate** Belknap is **where** we usually meet.	
	Pattern 2: Relative Adverb + Clause We often omit the head noun:
(g) I know **where** you can find tomato sauce in this market.	• when the head noun has a general meaning (the time, the place) rather than a specific one.
(h) She told us **when** to show up.	
(i) Greece is **where** the Olympics started. (inferred: the country)	• when you can infer the head noun from the context or from general knowledge.
(j) 551 B.C. is **when** Confucius was born. (inferred: the year)	
Less formal	
(k) **Why** she did that is a mystery to me!	• when the context of speech or writing is informal.
	continued on next page

The last focus box in this unit explains when the different patterns are likely to be used.

Note that these are tendencies, not hard and fast rules. In fact, it is difficult to determine which pattern should be used in many contexts because there may be more competing factors. For example, the context may be formal but the head noun may be easily inferred, resulting in omission of the head noun.

Nevertheless, these guidelines can help Ss who wonder how to decide among the various patterns.

Workbook Ex. 6, p. 100.
Answers: TE p. 546.

EXAMPLES	EXPLANATIONS
	Pattern 3: Head Noun + Clause This pattern tends to be used in contexts similar to ones for Pattern 1:
(l) Let us know **the day** you will arrive.	• when the head noun has a more specific meaning.
(m) Please state **the reason** you are seeking this position.	• when the context is more formal.

Exercise 8

As the notes for Focus 5 mentioned, there could be more than one motivation for a choice, so answers are not absolute. However, Ss should be able to explain why they chose a form with reference to the guidelines in Focus 5.

UNIT GOAL REVIEW

Ask Ss to look at athe goals on the opening page of the unit again. Help them understand how much they have accomplished in each area.

EXERCISE 8

Decide whether the form given in (a) or (b) would be more typical or appropriate for each context. Use the guidelines given in Focus 5. Explain your choices.

1. Ethel: Max! What did you just turn off that light for?
   Max: Dear, if you'll wait just a minute, you'll find out . . .
   (a) the reason why I did it.
   (b) why I did it.

2. (a) The day I got married
   (b) When I got married
   . . . was one of the happiest days of my life.

3. (a) A place where you can get a great cup of coffee
   (b) Where you get a great cup of coffee
   . . . is right across the street.

4. Oh no! Can you believe it? I forgot . . .
   (a) the place where I put my keys again.
   (b) where I put my keys again.

5. (a) One reason many people feel stress
   (b) Why many people feel stress
   . . . is that they don't have enough spare time.

6. I would now like all of you in this audience to consider . . .
   (a) the many times your families offered you emotional support.
   (b) when your families offered you emotional support. It's hard to count them all, isn't it?

7. Let me show you . . .
   (a) the way this CD player works.
   (b) how this CD player works.

8. Ms. Cordero just told us . . .
   (a) the time when we should turn in our papers.
   (b) when we should turn in our papers.

9. Last year my family took a trip to see . . .
   (a) the house where my great-grandfather grew up.
   (b) where my great-grandfather grew up.

ANSWER KEY

Exercise 8
Reasons for answers may vary.
1. **(b)** informal, head noun is direct object, general noun   2. **(a)** head noun is subject
3. **(a)** head noun is subject   4. **(b)** informal, head noun is direct object, general
5. **(a)** head noun is specific (one reason), subject   6. **(a)** head noun is specific the (many times); emphasizes the head noun
7. **(b)** informal context, head noun is direct object, general   8. **(b)** head noun is general (can be assumed), direct object
9. **(a)** specific noun, makes clear the place is a house and not a city, area, neighborhood, etc.

Use Your English

ACTIVITY 1: LISTENING

Form groups of three or four and compete in teams. The tape you'll hear will consist of twenty phrases that need to be identified with a place, time, reason, or manner. The phrases will use preposition + *which* clauses. Taking turns, each team needs to identify the phrase by using a sentence with a relative adverb clause. You may use any of the patterns discussed in this unit. If a team gives the wrong answer, the next team will have a chance to correct it. Award points for each correct answer.

▶ **EXAMPLES:** Tape: The continent on which the country of Rwanda is located.
Answer: *Africa is the continent where Rwanda is located.*

Tape: The month in which we celebrate both Lincoln's and Washington's birthdays.
Answer: *February is the month when we celebrate both birthdays.*

Tape: The way in which you say "Thank you" in French.
Answer: *"Merci" is how you say "Thank you."*

ACTIVITY 2: WRITING/SPEAKING

How would you complete statements that begin as follows?
• I'd like to know the date (day, year, century, etc.) when . . .
• I'd like to find out the place (country, city, etc.) where . . .
• I wish I knew the reason(s) why . . .
• I am interested in finding out how . . .
Write a list of statements using each of the relative adverbs above (with or without head nouns) to express things you'd like to know. Use the patterns given to begin your sentences. Share your statements with others in your class to see if anyone can provide the answers.

The activities on these "purple pages" at the end of the unit contain situations that should naturally elicit the unit's structures in a more communicative framework. While Ss are doing these activities in class, you can circulate and listen to determine if they have actually achieved the goals on the opening page of the unit.

Activity 1

Play textbook audio. The tapescript for this listening appears on pp. 567–568 of this book.

Adjust the "rules" of this team game to fit your class size and needs.

Workbook Ex. 7, pp. 100–101.
Answers: TE p. 546.

Activity 2
VARIATION

Set up this activity as a television program role play, in which a panel of participants respond, to the best of their ability, to statements read by other class members representing the television studio audience. Ss could designate a particular panel member to respond to a statement or let any panel member respond. Class members could rotate to change participants on the panel after a certain number of questions.

ANSWER KEY

Activity 1
Possible answers:
1. Wyoming is the state where I would go . . .
2. February 14 is when sweethearts . . .
3. San Francisco is the city where the Golden . . . 4. January is one of the months when Capricorns . . . 5. To honor Americans who died in wars is one reason why Americans . . . 6. W-a-s-h-i-n-g-t-o-n is how you spell . . . 7. To fix a flat tire is why you would buy . . . 8. Illinois is the way you pronounce . . . (The "s" should not be pronounced to get the point for this one.)
9. A drug store is where you . . . 10. To get advice about medical concerns is one reason you . . . 11. The 19th Century is the century when . . . 12. Australia is a country where there . . . 13. Pennsylvania is the state where you would find . . . 14. To let drivers know that it is unsafe to pass is why some roads . . . 15. Halloween is when American . . . 16. Dialing "0" is how you would get help . . . 17. Egypt is the country you would go to . . . 18. June is when most U.S. schools . . . 19. To get the area of the triangle is why you . . . 20. N.O.W. is how you spell . . .

Activity 3

VARIATION

Ss could do this activity orally rather than writing a paragraph.

Activity 4

SUGGESTIONS

To save time in class, have students create lists as homework.

Award points only if you are able to check the Ss' lists first to make sure that they are not too difficult for others to come up with possible responses.

ACTIVITY 3: WRITING

Did you know that some parts of your tongue can be more sensitive to certain tastes than other parts? The picture at the right shows sensitive areas for the four basic tastes: salty, bitter, sweet and sour. In a paragraph, describe the sensitivity location for each taste; use at least two relative adverb clauses.

▶ **EXAMPLE:** *Near the back of the tongue is where we have a sensitivity toward bitter tastes.*

(a)

x Salty   ★ Bitter
• Sweet   ● Sour

ACTIVITY 4: WRITING/SPEAKING

Make lists of places and times/dates as are shown in Exercise 3, either individually or in teams. Then present the items on your list one by one to others who must define or identify the word or phrase in some way with a relative adverb clause. (If you prefer to do this as a competitive game, you could set time limits for responses and award points.) The following are a few examples of items and responses.

Place/date/time	Possible response
February 14	That's a day when people exchange valentines.
Switzerland	It's a country in Europe where skiers like to go because of the Alps
trattoria	It's a restaurant where you can get Italian food.

ACTIVITY 5: SPEAKING/WRITING

With a classmate, take turns telling each other about dates and places that have been important or memorable in your lives. These could be times and locations of milestone events such as birth and graduation, but they could also include a few humorous incidents or dates/places that may not seem so important now but were when you were younger. (Examples: *1990 was the year when I broke my leg playing Frisbee; I'll never forget a trip to Florida, the place where I first saw the ocean.*) Take notes on your partner's events. Then report some of them orally to the class, using relative adverb clauses in some sentences. (In addition to *when* and *where*, you might also use the relative adverb *why* in giving reasons why a date or place was important.)

ACTIVITY 6: WRITING

Create a booklet providing information for tourists or new students about the city where you now live. Use some of the categories provided in the Opening Task as headings for your guide (for example: "Places Where You Can Go for Entertainment") and/or make up others you think would be useful (for example: "Places Where You Can Get the Best Pizza"). You could divide the project so that individuals or small groups would each be responsible for a section or two of the guide.

Activity 5

VARIATION

Ss could interview a friend or relative outside of class instead of a classmate.

Activity 6

VARIATION

Ss could create a website instead of a booklet.

The test for this unit can be found on p. 502. The answers are on p. 503.

Unit 11

UNIT OVERVIEW

Unit 11 assumes that students (Ss) have already studied the correlative conjunctions but may still be having difficulty joining phrases and clauses appropriately, especially in writing.

UNIT GOALS

Review the goals listed on this page so Ss understand what they should be able to know by the end of the unit.

OPENING TASK

This task requires Ss to perform a task that many advanced level Ss will do at one time or another—plan a college schedule.

SETTING UP THE TASK

As an introduction, distinguish the difference between Associate's and Bachelor's degrees and the special types of offerings and limitations of offerings that may appear in an alternative college catalog compared to a regular college one. Ss may also need to know the distinction between required and elective courses.

UNIT 11

CORRELATIVE CONJUNCTIONS

UNIT GOALS:
- To use correlative conjunctions for emphasis
- To join phrases and clauses with correlative conjunctions
- To write sentences with parallel correlative constructions

OPENING TASK
Planning a Course Schedule

Imagine that you would like to enter the New World Alternative College in order to earn an Associate's degree. The following list contains the classes that are offered and the number of required courses and electives in each category to obtain a degree.

NEW WORLD ALTERNATIVE COLLEGE
Course Offerings, Requirements, and Electives

English Course (1 course)
Expository Writing
Technical Writing

Humanities (2 courses)
Linguistics
Philosophy
Religious Studies

Social Sciences (2 courses)
Anthropology
Communication Studies
Economics
Geography

Physical Sciences (2 courses)
Geology
Astronomy
Physics

Mathematics (1 course)
General Mathematics
Computer Science

Life Sciences (2 courses)
Psychology
Biology
Microbiology

Environmental Studies (4 courses)
The Greenhouse Effect
Air Pollution
Garbage Disposal
Hazardous Waste
Acid Rain
Endangered Wildlife

History (1 elective)
U.S. History
World History

Foreign Language (1 elective)
Chinese
French

STEP 1 In the following table, write in two courses from each category that you would be interested in taking. In some cases, there are only two courses to choose from. These are written in for you.

COURSES I WOULD LIKE TO TAKE	#1	#2
English Composition	Expository Writing or Technical Writing	X
Humanities		
Social Sciences		
Physical Sciences		
Mathematics	General Mathematics or Computer Science	X
Life Sciences		
Environmental Sciences		
History	U.S. History or World	X
Foreign Language	Chinese or French	

STEP 2 Discuss your choices in groups of four.

STEP 3 Summarize the results of your discussion.

▶ **EXAMPLES:** *All of us must take either expository writing or technical writing.*
Maria is interested not only in Geology but also in Astronomy.
Neither Tom nor Gustaf would like to take Garbage Disposal.

Step 1: Ask Ss to fill in the table with their course choices from the chart.

Step 2: Ask Ss to compare and contrast their choices. Encourage Ss to use the full range of conjunctions during the discussion (both/and, either/or, not only . . . but also, neither/nor). Write these cues on the blackboard to increase the variety of structures the Ss will try.

Step 3: Encourage a secretary to summarize the results of the group's efforts in writing; this will allow you to see whether or not Ss are aware of how the rules of parallelism apply to correlative conjunctions.

Ss should already be familiar with the coordinating conjunctions and find it interesting to compare these with the correlative conjunction pairs. Ask pairs of Ss to read the dialogue lines in items *a* through *d* to the whole class. Note the accompanying explanations.

FOCUS **1**

▶ # Correlative Conjunctions for Emphasis

EXAMPLES		EXPLANATIONS
Coordinating Conjunctions	**Correlative Conjunctions**	Coordinating conjunctions and correlative conjunctions can be used to show different types of relationships:
and	*both . . . and not only . . . but also*	• additive
or	*either . . . or*	• alternative
nor	*neither . . . nor*	• negative
		In general, the correlative conjunctions are more emphatic.
(a) A: I hope Pablo **and** Karl come to the party next Saturday.		**Additive Relationships** • less emphasis
B: You're in luck! **Both** Karl **and** Pablo are coming.		• more emphasis
(b) C: I hope Pablo is coming to the party next Saturday.		• even greater emphasis (*not only* usually comes before already known information, and *but* introduces new or surprising information)
D: Guess what? **Not only** is Pablo coming, **but** Karl is **also**.		
(c) A: Can you come on Wednesday **or** Thursday?		**Alternative Relationships** • less emphasis
B: Yes, I can come on **either** Wednesday **or** Thursday.		• more emphasis
(d) A: Milly doesn't eat candy, **nor** do I.		**Negative Additive Relationships** • less emphasis • more emphasis
B: You mean **neither** you **nor** Milly has a sweet tooth?		

188 UNIT 11

EXERCISE 1

Answer the following questions with correlative conjunctions for emphasis. Write your answers below.

▶ **EXAMPLE:** Spain doesn't border on Portugal or France, does it?

Yes, it borders on both Portugal and France.

1. President's Day and Valentine's Day aren't in February, are they?
2. Cameroon and Algeria are in South America, aren't they?
3. Honey or sugar can be used to sweeten lemonade, can't it?
4. Whales and dolphins are members of the fish family, aren't they?
5. Niagara Falls is situated in Brazil and Uruguay, isn't it?
6. Martin Luther King, Jr. and Jesse Jackson were prominent black lawyers, weren't they?
7. You can travel from California to Hawaii by boat or airplane, can't you?
8. Ho Chi Minh City and Saigon refer to different places in Vietnam, don't they?

EXERCISE 2

Using the information in parentheses, respond to the following statements with *not only . . . but also.*

▶ **EXAMPLE:** I heard that Samuel has to work on Saturdays. (Sundays)

*Samuel has to work **not only** on Saturdays **but also** on Sundays.*

1. Shirley Temple could dance very well. (sing)
2. The language laboratory is great for improving pronunciation. (listening comprehension)
3. Nola should exercise twice a week. (go on a diet)
4. Becky has to take a test on Friday. (finish a project)
5. Thomas Jefferson was a great politician. (inventor)
6. The dictionary shows the pronunciation of a word. (part of speech)
7. The International Student Office will help you to locate an apartment. (get a part-time job)
8. It rained all day last Tuesday. (last Wednesday)

Correlative Conjunctions **189**

Exercise 1

Remind Ss to use all of the structures. They may be tempted to use *both . . . and* more than *not only . . . but also* and *either . . . or* more than *neither . . . nor* in this practice. Encourage them to practice alternate forms.

Exercise 2

Divide the class into pairs and have Ss take turns reading a sentence and responding to it so that both have the chance to create a response.

Workbook Exs. 1 & 2, pp. 103–106.
Answers: TE p. 547.

FOCUS 2

1. Tell Ss that correlative conjunctions can join different types of phrases. Ask them to identify the types in items *a* through *d*: noun phrases, verb phrases, adjectives, prepositional phrases.

2. Note that *both . . . and* and *neither . . . nor* can join clauses. Read items *e* and *f*.

3. Read items *g* and *h*. Provide two more examples of inversion by showing *do* and *have* insertion: *Not only did he miss work on Wednesday but he also missed work on Monday and Tuesday. Not only has he ridden in a hot air balloon but he has also parachuted from an airplane.*

Exercise 3
E X P A N S I O N

If Ss are enrolled at a school or college, they could also share ideas about what they plan to take during their next term. For example: *I may take either ESL 5 or English 100 next semester.*

Exercise 4

Brainstorm with the class what additional categories they could include. Ideas: hobbies, family backgrounds, organizational affiliations.

Joining Phrases and Clauses with Correlative Conjunctions

EXAMPLES	EXPLANATIONS
(a) **Neither** the pedestrian **nor** the bicyclist saw the car approaching. **(b)** Mary will **not only** complete her coursework **but also** write her Master's thesis by June. **(c)** Mrs. Thomas was **both** surprised **and** jubilant that her daughter was awarded a scholarship. **(d)** Mark usually eats **either** at home **or** on campus.	All four correlative conjunction pairs can join phrases.
(e) **Either** the teacher has to slow down the lecture pace **or** the students need to take notes faster. **(f)** **Not only** was Mr. Jones strict **but** he was **also** unfair.	Only two of the correlative conjunction pairs can join clauses.
(g) **Not only is she** taking physics **but** she is **also** taking biology. **(h)** **NOT:** Not only she is taking physics but she is also taking biology.	In combinations with *not only . . . but also*, the position of the subject following *not only* is inverted with the first auxiliary verb, *be*, or *do*.

EXERCISE 3

Using the information you obtained in the Opening Task on page 186, write sentences about your classmates' preferences.

▶ **EXAMPLES:** *Natasha may take either U.S. History or World History.*
She wants to enroll in microbiology and either psychology or biology.

EXERCISE 4

Think of a couple you know who have lived together for a long time. Fill out the grid with information about the couple. Then, with a partner, discuss the couple's appearance, preferences, habits, or other features of their lives together. Use as many correlative conjunctions as you can.

A N S W E R   K E Y

Exercise 3
Answers will vary.

Exercise 4
Answers will vary.

▶ **EXAMPLES:** Appearance: *Both Chau and George have black hair.*

Preferences: *On weekends Chau and George like to go either out to eat or to the movies.*

Habits: *Chau and George neither smoke nor drink.*

	Name #1:	**Name #2:**
Appearance		
Preferences		
Habits		

FOCUS **3**

Parallelism; Being Concise

NOT PARALLEL	**PARALLEL**	**USES**
clause/noun phrase (a) Not only **was he an honors student** but also **a scholarship recipient.**	**noun phrase/noun phrase** (b) He was not only **an honors student** but also **a scholarship recipient.**	In formal usage, the two phrases that correlative conjunctions join must have the same grammatical structures. If they do not, the sentence will not be parallel and should be rephrased.
gerund/infinitive (c) Both **gaining work experience** and **to earn academic credit** are important benefits of an internship.	**gerund/gerund** (d) Both **gaining work experience** and **earning academic credit** are important benefits of an internship.	*continued on next page*

Correlative Conjunctions | **191**

FOCUS 3

SUGGESTION

Sometimes this principle can be best demonstrated by using colored chalk.

1. Write the following three sentences on the board, with the correlatives in colored chalk and the other words in white chalk: *Moises was not only tired but he was also hungry. Neither the boys heard the shouts nor the girls from their tents. We will talk either at the coffee shop or chat in the bookstore.*

2. Ask Ss what they think is stylistically incorrect about the sentences. Help them induce that the phrases or clauses following the correlatives are not of the same type.

3. Ask Ss to read the focus box silently. Then answer any questions they might have.

Workbook Ex. 3, pp. 106–107.
Answers: TE p. 547.

NOT CONCISE	CONCISE	USES
(e) She knew either **that she needed an A** or **that she needed a B** to pass the course.	**(f)** She knew that she needed **an A** or **a B** to pass the course.	In addition, parallel structures should be concise, without unnecessary repetition.
(g) Not only was **John disqualified because of poor attendance** but **Betty was also disqualified for poor attendance.**	**(h)** Not only **John** but also **Betty** was disqualified because of poor attendance.	

Exercise 5

SUGGESTION

Pair up Ss and ask each pair to be responsible for correcting one item. Once they have done their assigned item, they can begin working on the other items in the exercise. Have one member of the pair write the answer to their assigned item on the board. All of the answers can then be discussed by the Ss and the teacher.

Workbook Exs. 4 & 5, pp. 108–110.
Answers: TE p. 547.

EXERCISE 5

Read each sentence. Write OK next to sentences that are well-formed, parallel, and not repetitious. Rephrase the rest for concise, formal style. The first two have been done as examples.

1. I cannot stand to eat either liver or raw fish. OK
2. Not only is Maria tired but also sick. *Maria is not only tired but also sick.*
3. Not only *The New York Times* carried but also *The Los Angeles Times* carried the story of the train disaster in Algeria.
4. Juanita will both major in English and in sociology.
5. The Boston Red Sox either made the finals in the baseball competition or the Detroit Tigers did.
6. Suzuki neither found her watch nor her wallet where she had left them.
7. The Smith family loves both cats and dogs.
8. Mr. Humphrey thinks either that I should cancel or postpone the meeting with my advisor.
9. Not only am I going to the dentist but also the barber tomorrow.
10. Mary is going to either quit her job or is rearranging her work schedule to take astronomy.
11. I hope that the musicians are both well-rehearsed and that they are calm before the concert.
12. Todd neither saw or talked to his roommate, Bill.
13. Both bringing a bank card and cash is necessary for any trip.
14. Nor my two daughters nor my son wants to take an aisle seat on the airplane.

EXERCISE 6

The following paragraphs have some nonparallel, inconcise structures with correlative conjunctions. Identify and rephrase them for formal usage.

(1) In the last forty years, family life trends have changed dramatically in the United States. (2) In the past, it was expected that everyone would get married in their early twenties. (3) Now having to choose either between a family or a career, many are opting for the career and remaining single. (4) Others are postponing first marriages until their thirties or forties.

(5) If and when couples decide to marry, many are deciding to limit their family size. (6) Not only couples are having fewer children but they are also deciding to have no children at all. (7) On the other hand, some singles are either deciding to raise their own or adopt children by themselves. (8) In addition, many same-sex partners are not only choosing to form binding relationships but also to become parents.

(9) In the past, women worked either for personal satisfaction or to earn extra money for luxuries. (10) Today both husband and the wife must work in order to survive. (11) Because of this, husbands and wives do not always adhere to traditional sex roles. (12) Now either the husband might do the cooking and cleaning or the wife might do the cooking and cleaning.

(13) Both because of the greater stress of modern life and the greater freedom that each partner feels, divorce is becoming more and more common. (14) Neither the rich are immune nor the poor. (15) In some states, the divorce rate approaches fifty percent. (16) Marriage cannot be all bad, though. (17) Not only many people get divorced but these same people also get remarried one or more times throughout their lifetimes.

Correlative Conjunctions | **193**

If Ss are maintaining a portfolio of writing samples in conjunction with this class or in another class they are taking, ask them to look at their previous work and examine their use of correlatives. Have them make corrections according to the rules they have learned in this unit.

UNIT GOAL REVIEW

Ask Ss to look at the goals on the opening page of the unit again. Help them understand how much they have accomplished in each area.

ANSWER KEY

Exercise 6

3. Now having to choose between either a family   6. Not only are couples having fewer children, but they are also   7. are deciding to either raise their own or adopt   8. choosing not only to form binding relationships but also   9. either to achieve personal satisfaction or to   10. Today both the husband and   12. Now either the husband or the wife might do the cooking and cleaning.   13. Because of both the greater stress of modern life and the   14. Neither the rich nor the   17. Not only do many people get divorced but these

USE YOUR ENGLISH

The activities on these "purple pages" at the end of the unit contain situations that should naturally elicit the unit's structures in a more communicative framework. While Ss are doing these activities in class, you can circulate and listen to determine if they have actually achieved the goals in the opening page of the unit.

Activity 1

Play textbook audio. The tapescript for this listening appears on pp. 568–569 of this book. If Ss have difficulty with this listening, play the tape more than once.

Use Your English

ACTIVITY 1: LISTENING

You will listen to a dialog between a college advisor and a student. Listen to the taped conversation, and fill in the grid as the student responds to the advisor's questions.

NEW WORLD ATERNATIVE COLLEGE STUDY PLAN		
	Fall	**Spring**
Year 1		
Year 2		

ACTIVITY 2: WRITING

Imagine that you are a supervisor for a company that allows fairly flexible hours for its part-time employees. Your boss recently called you to find out which day and time would be most convenient for each employee's evaluation conference. In order to help you in your decision, you asked the four workers you are supervising to indicate on the following blank schedule forms which hours they are available. An "A" indicates that a worker is available during a particular hour.

Conference Availability Charts

Pepita

	M	T	W	Th	F
9–10	A		A		A
10–11	A	A			
11–12		A	A	A	
12–1					
1–2			A		A

Tuan

	M	T	W	Th	F
9–10					
10–11					
11–12		A	A	A	
12–1	A	A	A	A	A
1–2			A		A

Tom

	M	T	W	Th	F
9–10					
10–11	A	A			
11–12			A		
12–1	A	A	A	A	A
1–2			A		A

Laleh

	M	T	W	Th	F
9–10	A		A		A
10–11					
11–12			A		
12–1					
1–2		A		A	

Now write a memo to your boss, detailing who is and who is not available at various times for their evaluation conferences. Try to use the words *both*, *either*, or *neither* in your writing.

▶ **EXAMPLE:**

Memo

Dear Mr. Masters,
Both Pepita and Laleh are available from 9 to 10:00 on Monday, but neither Tuan nor Tom can come at that time.

Activity 3

Step 1

Ss should fill out the grid individually.

Step 2

Ss should discuss their responses in pairs.

Step 3

One member of the pair should report the results of the discussion to the whole class. For example: *Tony thinks that both he and his partner should cook meals because they are both working.*

Activity 4

This activity might best be assigned at the beginning of the unit and then reviewed at the end so as to give Ss sufficient time to watch enough TV where these structures might be used.

ACTIVITY 3: SPEAKING

Imagine that you have two children and both you and your spouse have to work outside the home, which leaves little time for running a household. In the chart below, choose which chores you would like to do and which chores you would like your spouse to do by marking an "X" under the appropriate column. If you feel that any of the tasks should be shared, write "B" (for both) under each column. Discuss your choice of respective duties with a classmate, using as many of the expressions you have learned in this unit as possible.

▶ **EXAMPLE:** *Both my spouse and I should share cooking meals because we both work.*

	My Chore	My Spouse's Chore
cook meals	B	B
wash dishes		
vacuum floors		
dust furniture		
decorate the house for holidays		
care for the yard		
bring in the mail		
shop for food		
shop for clothes		
get the car repaired		
pay bills		
clean toilets and fixtures		
do laundry		
take out garbage		
get the children dressed		
give the dog a bath		
take care of a child who is sick		

ACTIVITY 4: LISTENING/ WRITING/SPEAKING

Listen carefully to a television program (for example, a cooking program or a sports program) and jot down the statements you hear that contain *both/and, not only/but also, either/or,* or *neither/nor.* Bring your notes to class and discuss which types of correlatives were used more often and whether they were used to show emphasis or not.

▶ **EXAMPLES:** *You can use either butter or margarine in the recipe.*
Not only did he strike out but he also got hit by a flying bat.

ACTIVITY 5: WRITING/SPEAKING

THE CORRELATIVE GAME

Preparation for the Game

STEP 1 Divide into two teams. Each team should create a set of eighteen cards that contain difficult True/False statements, which will hopefully stump the other team. You should pattern these statements after the structures you have learned in this lesson. For example:

▶ **EXAMPLE:** *Neither South Africa nor Argentina has a northern seaport. (T)*

STEP 2 On a second set of cards, each team will write the names of team members on the opposite team, using the following constructions:

Either *Mary* or *Sam* (six cards with other names)
Both *Tony* and *Maria* (six cards with other names)
Neither *Thanh* nor *Vivian* (six cards with other names)

Rules of the Game

STEP 1 Teams should exchange sets of cards. Each team will have eighteen True/False Cards and eighteen Name Cards.

STEP 2 One member of the first team reads the name card first, for example:

"Either Mary or Sam" This means that only one of these two students can answer the question.

"Both Tony and Maria" This means that both Tony and Maria can help each other answer.

"Neither Thanh nor Sam" This means that Thanh or Sam cannot answer the question, but the rest of the members of the team can.

If the first card is chosen, Mary or Sam decides who will take a guess. For the sake of example, presume Mary decides to try.

STEP 3 The member of the first team reads the True/False statement. If Mary can answer it correctly, she gets one point and the game continues. If she answers it incorrectly, it is the other team's turn.

STEP 4 The team with the most points at the end of the stack of True/False cards wins the game.

Activity 5

Use this as a "change of pace" game. It can be prepared during one period and then played the next.

The test for this unit can be found on p. 504. The answers are on p. 505.

Unit 12

UNIT OVERVIEW

Knowledge and appropriate use of logical connectors are important parts of grammatical competence for advanced level students (Ss). This unit starts with a review of connector types and then focuses on sentence adverbs, or sentence connectors. We have called them sentence connectors so that Ss will be more aware of how they differ from subordinating conjunctions that join clauses within a sentence.

The sentence connectors in this unit are presented in semantic sets, i.e., grouped by the types of logical meanings they represent. Within these sets, distinctions are made among the various connector words and phrases in meanings and in use related to levels of formality.

UNIT GOALS

Review the goals listed on this page so Ss understand what they should be able to know by the end of the unit.

OPENING TASK

For this task, have Ss read and then write a comparison of two creation myths, one from Finland and one from Nauru, Micronesia. The two readings contain several types of sentence connectors. The paragraph writing task is designed to elicit comparison and contrast connectors, but Ss may also use other types of connectors in summarizing various parts of the two stories.

SETTING UP THE TASK

To establish the context for the task, have Ss engage in a brief class discussion about creation myths. What myths do they know from different cultures?

SENTENCE CONNECTORS

UNIT GOALS:

- To understand the differences between conjunctions and sentence connectors
- To use appropriate sentence connectors to express various logical meanings
- To choose appropriate sentence connectors for formal and informal contexts
- To use correct punctuation for sentence connectors in writing

OPENING TASK
How Things Came to Be

Cultures all over the world have creation myths, which explain how life on earth came to be.

STEP 1 Read the two creation myths from Finland and Micronesia that are summarized below. They describe how the earth, the sky, and the first people on earth came to exist.

STEP 2 Write a paragraph describing the similarities and differences between the two creation myths. In comparing the stories, consider the following questions:

1. What existed at the beginning of creation?
2. In what order were things created?
3. How were the earth and sky created?
4. Who was responsible for creating the first people and how were they created?

From Finland:

In the beginning there was only Water, Air, and Air's daughter, Ilamatar. Ilamatar spent her time wandering around the world. One day Ilamatar sank down to rest upon the ocean's face as she was very tired. When she lay down, the seas rolled over her, the waves tossed her and the wind blew over her. For seven hundred years, Ilamatar swam and floated in the sea. Then one day while she lay floating with one knee up out of the water, a beautiful duck swooped down and landed on her knee. There it laid seven eggs. As the days went by, the eggs grew hotter and hotter until Ilamatar could no longer endure the heat and pulled her knee into the water. Because of this, the eggs rolled into the ocean and sank to its bottom. Eventually, one of the eggs cracked. From the lower half of its shell, the earth was formed. From the egg's upper shell, the sky formed over the land and sea. From the yolk of the egg, the sun rose into the sky. From the white of the egg, the moon and stars were created and took their place in the heavens. Later, Ilamatar gave birth to the sea's child, whom she called Vainamoinen. For seven years Vainamoinen swam the seas. Then he went ashore and became the first person on earth.

From Nauru, Micronesia:

In the beginning there was only water and the creator, Areop-Enap, who lived in a mussel shell in the sea. It was very dark in the sea and also in the shell; as a result, Areop-Enap couldn't see very well. He could, however, feel around in the dark. Thus it was that he discovered a large snail and a small snail who were occupying the shell with him. Areop-Enap used his power to change the small snail into the moon and put it at the top of the shell. Then, by the light of the moon, Areop-Enap spotted a worm in the shell. He got the worm to separate the upper and lower parts of the shell. The lower part became the earth, while the upper part became the sky. Because of all this work, the poor worm died of exhaustion. His sweat, dripping into the lower shell, became the salty sea. After the sky and the earth had been created, Areop-Enap placed the big snail into the sky to be the sun. Finally, from stones he made the first people to hold up the sky.

(Adapted from Maria Leach, *The Beginning: Creation Myths around the World*, New York: Funk & Wagnalls, 1956.)

CONDUCTING THE TASK
Step 1
SUGGESTIONS

1. Have Ss read the stories aloud. They could do this in small groups, with each student reading several sentences.

2. For more oral practice, divide Ss into two groups, with half reading the first creation myth and the other half the second. Then each student would work with a partner from the other group. Partners would take turns orally summarizing the myth they read.

Step 2
After you collect the paragraphs, you could use sentences from them for later work on sentence connector types, such as adding connectors to sentence pairs or changing sentences with subordinating conjunctions to two sentences joined by a connector (or to two main clauses joined by a semicolon and connector). You may be able to use some sentences for error analysis and correction.

VARIATION
If Ss worked with a partner on Step 1, they could write a paragraph collaboratively.

CLOSING THE TASK
Have Ss form small groups after the writing activity and compare the paragraphs they have written.

FOCUS 1

This focus box gives an overview of logical connectors and summarizes the three types of structures that signal logical relationships between ideas: coordinating conjunctions, subordinating conjunctions, and sentence connectors. Sentence connectors, the focus of this unit, are also called "sentence adverbs."

Advanced Ss will be familiar with these meanings and with some of the connectors but may not have studied some of them.

If your Ss didn't do the Opening Task, they should at least read the two creation myth stories before studying the chart here. Otherwise, the sentence examples, many of which refer to the stories, may be harder to comprehend.

Begin with a focus on meanings (relationships between ideas) rather than on the three grammatical categories of connectors. Make sure Ss understand that the connector examples in the third column are rewrites of the examples in the first column.

SUGGESTIONS

Step 1: Have Ss read through the chart examples, either in class or as homework.
Step 2: Write the categories of relationships listed in column two on the board. Ask Ss for other connector words or phrases of each type. At this point, don't be concerned with the grammatical categories of their responses (i.e., whether it is a coordinating conjunction, subordinating conjunction, etc.).
Step 3: Review the three types of connectors on this page. Check off words and phrases you listed on the board as you progress through the three sections. Ss will probably be most familiar with the first two types, though often they do not know all the members of the sets and they may not have learned or remember the grammatical labels. Remind Ss that subordinating conjunctions are sometimes called *subordinators*.
Step 4: Let Ss know that sentence connectors are generally the most formal of the connectors; they occur most frequently in academic writing and formal speech. As an example, ask Ss to tell you what sounds odd about these sentences (given orally).
I was really hungry this morning after my first class. Thus, I got a snack at the cafeteria.
Most Ss will know that *thus* sounds too formal in this context. Ask them to state the relationship less formally. Responses could include joining the ideas by *so* or using a reason subordinator like *because* with the first clause.

Connectors

There are many types of meaning relationships that can exist between two ideas. Words or phrases that express these relationships are called connectors. The chart below shows some of these relationships.

EXAMPLES	TYPES OF RELATIONSHIPS	EXAMPLES WITH CONNECTORS
(a) Areop-Enap created the moon. He put it at the top of the shell.	time sequence	**After** Areop-Enap created the moon, he put it at the top of the shell.
(b) Areop-Enap lived in a mussel shell. Two snails lived there.	added idea	Areop-Enap lived in a mussel shell. Two snails lived there **as well.**
(c) In the Finnish myth, the heavens were created from an egg. The sun was formed from the yolk of the egg.	example	In the Finnish myth, the heavens were created from an egg. The sun, **for example**, was formed from the yolk of the egg.
(d) In the Finnish myth, the earth did not exist in the beginning. In the Micronesian myth, at first there was only the sea.	similarity	In the Finnish myth, the earth did not exist in the beginning. **Similarly,** in the Micronesian myth, at first there was only the sea.
(e) In the Micronesian myth, the sun was a snail. In the Finnish myth, the sun came from an egg yolk.	contrast	In the Micronesian myth, the sun was a snail, **whereas** in the Finnish myth the sun came from an egg yolk.
(f) Ilamatar was very tired. She lay down on the ocean's face.	result	Ilamatar was very tired, **so** she lay down on the ocean's face.
(g) Creation myths are universal. They are found throughout the world.	clarification	Creation myths are universal. **That is**, they are found throughout the world.

Types of Connectors

EXAMPLES	EXPLANATIONS
(h) **Independent Clause** Ilamatar kept the eggs on her knee, **Independent Clause** **but** eventually they got too hot.	There are three main types of connectors: coordinating conjunctions, subordinating conjunctions, and sentence connectors. • **Coordinating conjunctions** connect the ideas in two independent clauses. The coordinating conjunctions are *and, but, for, or nor, so,* and *yet.* In written English, we usually write these clauses as one sentence, separated by a comma.
(i) **Dependent Clause** **After** Areop-Enap put the snail in **Independent Clause** the sky, he made people. **(j)** **Independent Clause** Areop-Enap put the snail in the sky **Dependent Clause** **before** he made people.	• **Subordinating conjunctions** connect ideas within sentences. They show the relationship between an idea in a dependent clause and an idea in an independent clause. Common subordinating conjunctions include: **Time** *after, before, once, since, until, when, whenever, while* **Reason** *as, because, since* **Result** *in order that, so that, that* **Contrast** *although, even though, though, whereas* **Condition** *if, even if, provided that, unless* **Location** *where, wherever*
(k) **Independent Clause** Areop-Enap discovered two snails living in the shell with him. **Independent Clause** **In addition,** a worm inhabited the shell, as he later found out. **(l)** **Independent Clause** Ilamatar could not endure the heat from the eggs; **consequently,** **Independent Clause** she put her knee back into the water.	• **Sentence connectors** usually express relationships between two or more independent clauses. The independent clauses may be separate sentences, as in (k). They may also be in the same sentence, separated by a semicolon, as in (l). The remainder of this unit is concerned with the third type of logical connector, sentence connectors.

Exercise 1

This exercise requires analysis of the underlying logical relationships between ideas across sentence boundaries. This is an important academic skill for Ss to develop for reading as well as writing. Obviously, they need to understand these relationships in order to choose appropriate connectors.

Ss tend to have the most difficulty with (5), a clarification relationship. The second sentence in (5) paraphrases the statement *cosmogony is a major theme in myths* and could be related to the first sentence by *in other words* if a connector were added. Another difficult one is (7), which shows contrast. If your Ss don't grasp this relationship, ask them to identify or draw boxes around the contrasting terms: village/order; bush (jungle)/mystery and destructive forces.

Workbook Ex. 1, p. 111; Ex. 2, p. 112.
Answers: TE p. 547.

EXERCISE 1

For each of the sentence pairs below, state what the relationship of the second sentence is to the first: time sequence, added idea, example, similarity, contrast, result, or clarification.

▶ **EXAMPLE:** Ilamatar's child swam the seas for seven years. He went ashore.

Relationship: *time sequence*

1. The myths of many cultures include a god of thunder. The Mayan god of thunder was Chac.

2. In Greek mythology, Ares, the god of war, was often violent and belligerent. The goddess Athena was a peacemaker.

3. Myths entertain us. They help us to understand human behavior.

4. Ancient civilizations did not know the scientific explanations for natural phenomena such as storms. They made up stories to explain these events.

5. In North American Indian cultures, cosmogony is a major theme in myths. These myths explain how the world was created.

6. In a Chinese creation myth, a man named Pan Gu lived in an egg for eighteen thousand years. He woke up and chopped the egg in two with an ax.

7. In many African folktales, the village represents a place of order. The bush, or jungle, represents a place of mystery and destructive forces.

8. Jason, the leader of the Argonauts in Greek mythology, went on a long sea voyage to get the Golden Fleece. The Greek hero Odysseus embarked on a long voyage.

9. In an Indonesian myth, the first woman in the world cursed a great flood that washed away her garden. She was punished with a malformed child who had only one eye, one arm, and one leg.

10. A common animal in many myths and folktales is the trickster. In Asia, the trickster is often a rabbit or a monkey.

ANSWER KEY

Exercise 1
1. example 2. contrast 3. added idea
4. result 5. clarification 6. time sequence
7. contrast 8. similarity 9. result
10. example

Addition Connectors

Simple Addition

CONNECTORS	EXAMPLES	MEANINGS
also	**(a)** You can pay your fees by credit card. You can **also** write a check.	These connectors express simple addition. They have the meaning of *too* or *also*.
in addition	**(b)** Ming has to register for classes today. **In addition,** he has to pay his course fees.	
furthermore	**(c)** This plant requires sun all day. **Furthermore,** it needs rich soil.	
moreover	**(d)** As your mayor, I promise to make this city safe for all. **Moreover,** I will create new jobs.	

Emphatic Addition

CONNECTORS	EXAMPLES	MEANINGS
what is more (informal: *what's more*)	**(e)** We have succeeded in cleaning up the river. **What is more,** we have made it the cleanest in the entire state.	Emphatic connectors signal an idea that stresses some aspect of what has been previously stated. Their meaning is similar to: "Not only *that* (what I just said), but also *this* (what I am saying now)."
as well	**(f)** Ricardo won the award for athletic achievement. He received academic honors **as well.**	
besides (**THIS**)*	**(g)** My brother goes to school full-time. **Besides this,** he manages to work twenty hours a week.	

*In this example and others in the unit, THIS means what has been previously mentioned. THIS will often be a demonstrative pronoun (*this, that, these,* or *those*) or a demonstrative determiner + noun phrase (for example: as well as *this fact*).

Advanced Ss should be familiar with the simple addition connectors. They may be less familiar with those expressing emphatic or intensifying addition. Most of the vocabulary should be familiar to them, but they may not have learned these connectors as a semantic set.

SUGGESTIONS

1. Point out the various placements of connectors within sentences: initially, medially and, in the case of *as well*, finally. Tell Ss that although they may have used many of the connectors, they may tend to put them always at the beginning of a sentence and that they should consider other places in the sentence to focus more sharply on a logical connection. For example, in (a) placement of *also* focuses on *writing a check* as well as *paying by credit card*.

2. Encourage Ss to use forms they haven't used before, or have used very little, and to make those forms part of their active vocabulary. In other words, some Ss may be using only one form (e.g., *also*) as a simplification strategy and may need to be encouraged to expand their repertoire. This will be true for many of the focus box charts in this unit.

3. Note that in spoken and informal written English, *what is more* is often expressed with a contraction: *what's more*.

The first section of the chart on this page explains the difference between simple addition and emphatic addition connectors, which Ss read about on the previous page. The second section explains and exemplifies intensifying connectors, and the third section distinguishes these intensifying connectors from emphatic ones.

For another example to clarify the teaching point of the last section:

Step 1: Write on the board *This summer, I have a lot of plans for spending my time. One of them is to do a lot of traveling.*
Besides that.. (leave space for several sentences).
In fact . . . (leave space for a sentence).

Step 2: Ask Ss what other things they might like to do besides travel throughout Europe. Write responses in full sentences after *besides that.* Then ask them what places they would like to travel to and write a number of them in a list fashion after *in fact.*

Step 3: Ask Ss to explain in their own words the difference between the two additions (prompting a paraphrase of the explanation in the third section).

Simple Addition versus Emphatic Addition

EXAMPLES	MEANINGS
(h) I think I would be an excellent person for this job. My background in computers is extensive. **Simple Addition** **(i)** I **also** have excellent writing skills. **Emphatic Addition** **(j)** I have excellent writing skills **as well.**	We often use simple addition and emphatic addition in the same contexts. The emphatic connector simply stresses the added information more than the simple connector does.

Intensifying Addition

CONNECTORS	EXAMPLES	MEANINGS
in fact	**(k)** Spokane has a lot of rain lately. **In fact,** it has been raining all week.	Intensifying connectors show that an idea will strongly support another one.
as a matter of fact	**(l)** You can take the rest of the pie with you. **As a matter of fact,** I wish you would since I'm on a diet.	
actually	**(m)** Gretchen has never cared for the color magenta. **Actually,** it's one of her least favorite colors.	

Intensifying Addition versus Emphatic Addition

EXAMPLES	EXPLANATIONS
(n) This weekend is going to be very busy. I have a lot of schoolwork to do. **Emphatic addition** **(o)** **Besides that,** I have to finish moving to my new apartment. **Intensifying addition** **(p)** **In fact,** I have to write three papers.	We use emphatic connectors when we add a related idea. (o) adds another activity that will be accomplished. We use intensifying connectors to elaborate an idea. (p) supports the idea of having a lot of schoolwork.

204 UNIT 12

EXERCISE 2

Use an appropriate sentence connector from the list below to show the kind of addition relationship expressed in the last sentence of each pair or group of sentences. More than one connector could be appropriate for most contexts. Try to use each connector in the list once.

also	*moreover*	*besides*
in addition	*what is more*	*in fact*
furthermore	*as well*	*as a matter of fact*
		actually

▶ **EXAMPLE:** Leonardo Da Vinci was a painter and sculptor. He was an architect and a naturalist.

He was an architect and a naturalist as well.

(Other possible connectors: all simple and emphatic addition connectors)

1. The poinsettia is a beautiful plant, but be careful with it around animals. It is poisonous.
2. Jerry has plenty of sunscreen if you'd like to use some when we go to the beach. He has four different kinds.
3. I can't go skating because I have to work on Saturday. I need to get a new pair of skates.
4. The Aztec deity Quetazlcoatl was the god of the sun and the air. He was the god of wisdom and a teacher of the arts of peace.
5. Ladies and gentlemen of the jury: I will show you that the defendant could not possibly have committed this crime. This is an innocent man before you! I will reveal who really should be on trial today.
6. Our teacher asked us if we had ever read *El Cid*. I hadn't. I had never even heard of it.
7. Gina is very talented musically. She plays the flute with the symphony orchestra. She occasionally plays bass violin with a jazz group.
8. Potassium maintains fluid balance in body cells. It controls nerves and muscles.
9. You have an error in article usage in the third paragraph of your report. You need to correct a spelling error in that paragraph.
10. Well, I admit I ate a lot of the cookies that were in the kitchen. I probably had about a dozen.

Encourage Ss to use connectors less familiar to them where appropriate and to try putting the connectors in positions other than the beginning of the sentence. (*As well*, of course, has to be placed at the end of the sentence). Remind them that *also* is the most general of the connectors and can fit many contexts but that some of the other connectors offer more precise meanings for particular contexts.

ANSWER KEY

Exercise 2
Answers will vary.
1. Actually, it is poisonous.   2. As a matter of fact, he has four . . .   3. Moreover, I need to get . . .   4. In addition, he was the god of . . .   5. Furthermore, I will reveal . . .
6. What is more, I had never even . . .
7. She occasionally plays . . . group besides.
8. It also controls . . .   9. You need to correct . . . paragraph as well.   10. In fact, I probably . . .

Exercise 3

EXPANSION

1. For homework, ask Ss to make up two more sentences modeled after the ones here.
2. During the next class, pair Ss and have them take turns asking their partner for information and responding. Monitor the pair work production.
3. This could also be done as a whole class activity, with individual Ss calling on others in the class to respond, e.g., *Katya, state two courses that you like and explain why*. (Note: As with any activity in which you are not able to "screen" in advance Ss' requests for information from classmates, it may be best to give Ss the option to "pass" if they are asked something personal to which they don't want to respond.) Share some of the responses with the class.

Workbook Ex. 3, p. 113.
Answers: TE p. 547.

EXERCISE 3

Make up two sentences for each of the following instructions. Use an addition connector to link ideas between sentences. An example has been given for the first one.

1. Give two reasons why you enjoy something you often do in your spare time.

▶ **EXAMPLE:** *I enjoy volunteer work with children at the hospital because I like children. Besides that, it gives me work experience for my future career in medicine.*

2. Give two reasons why you like one movie or television show you've seen better than another.
3. State two advantages of flying over driving when a person goes on a long trip.
4. State two uses for computers.
5. Give two reasons why people tell stories about themselves.
6. Give two reasons why you would want to improve your English grammar skills.
7. State two differences between English and your native language.
8. Give two reasons why someone should visit a particular city or country.
9. Give two reasons why someone should get to know you.
10. State two things that you are very good at doing.

ANSWER KEY

Exercise 3
Answers will vary. (Examples are given in the directions.)

Alternative Connectors

CONNECTORS	EXAMPLES	MEANINGS
on the other hand *alternatively*	**(a)** I may work this summer. **On the other hand,** I may take a long vacation. **(b)** You could take the history course you eventually need this semester. **Alternatively,** you could complete your schedule with a science course.	These connectors indicate a possibility in addition to the one just mentioned. *On the other hand* and *alternatively* have similar meanings. *Alternatively* is a more formal connector. It is used mainly in written English.
	(c) Washington, D.C., might be fun to visit this summer. <table><tr><td>Other Possibility</td><td>Part Changed in (c)</td></tr><tr><td>**(d)** **On the other hand,** it might be too crowded.</td><td>fun</td></tr><tr><td>**(e)** **On the other hand,** Minneapolis might be a better city to visit in the summer.</td><td>Washington, D.C.</td></tr><tr><td>**(f)** **On the other hand,** it might be better to go there in the fall.</td><td>this summer</td></tr></table>	The "other possibility" could be various parts of a previously mentioned idea. Here are some alternative statements that might follow example (c).

EXERCISE 4

Add a statement after each sentence below that would express another possibility. Use *on the other hand* or *alternatively* to signal the connection.

▶ **EXAMPLE:** I could get a job this summer.

On the other hand, I could take a few courses in summer school.

1. I could stay home this weekend.
2. You might want to get a cat for a pet.
3. The theory of the Big Bang, explaining the origins of the universe, could be correct.

FOCUS 3

The first part of this chart gives Ss two common alternative connectors. *On the other hand* will probably be the most familiar one. Remind Ss that the preposition for this connector is *on* and never *in* and that the article *the* cannot be left out; to do so would produce an unidiomatic version.

The second section of the chart shows how alternative connectors can focus on different parts of a sentence. Exercise 5 will provide practice for this teaching point.

SUGGESTION

Step 1: To help Ss understand the second part of this chart, write this example on the board: *I could buy a cake for dessert tonight. On the other hand . . .*

Step 2: Draw a box around *I*. Ask Ss to substitute a name for *I*. Write a new sentence after *on the other hand*, using a shortened form rather than repeating the entire original sentence (e.g., *On the other hand, Kevin could buy one.*). Have Ss practice the alternative stress put on the substituted name.

Step 3: Repeat the procedure in Step 2 with other parts of the sentence, boxing *make*, then *cake*, then *tonight* and writing each new sentence with substitutions under the previous one. For each, vary some of the words and phrasing of the original (e.g., *On the other hand, I might wait to get one until tomorrow.*) to avoid making your additions sound unnatural.

Step 4: If time permits, and if Ss easily grasped the concept of different possibilities, ask them to tell you one place where they could position *on the other hand* instead of at the beginning of the sentence. (The most natural place would be after *could*.)

ANSWER KEY

Exercise 4
Answers will vary.
1. On the other hand, I could go to a movie.
2. Alternatively, a goldfish would require less care.   3. On the other hand, perhaps there really was an Almighty Creator.   4. Alternatively, you could visit a car dealer and see if they have any good used cars on the lot.   5. On the other hand, it could increase the number of drug users in this country.   6. Alternately, they could limit the kinds of television shows they allow their children to watch.

4. If you're looking for a used car to buy, you could check the classified ads in the newspaper.

5. Legalizing heroin in the United States could help decrease crime.

6. Parents who are upset with the violence that their children see every day on television could write letters to the television stations.

Exercise 5

SUGGESTION

After Ss have completed this exercise, call on groups to tell the class the completions they came up with for one of the numbered statements, with each group reporting a different item.

Workbook Ex. 4, p. 114.
Answers: TE p. 548.

EXERCISE 5

Form small groups. Read each of the statements below. Then take turns forming alternative statements for each one. Each person must focus on a different part of the statement. Use *on the other hand* or *alternatively*.

▶ **EXAMPLE:** It could be fun to get a job making pizzas this summer.

On the other hand,

it could get boring after awhile.
(focus: fun)

it might be more interesting to get work at a television studio.
(focus: a job making pizzas)

it would probably be more fun to eat the pizzas!
(focus: making)

1. Hong Kong might be a good place to go for our winter vacation.

2. Advanced Composition could be a good course for me to take next quarter.

3. It might be fun to go shopping on Saturday.

4. We might want to explore this cave tonight.

5. You could call your family this weekend.

208 UNIT 12

Exemplifying, Identifying, and Clarifying Connectors

EXEMPLIFYING CONNECTORS	EXAMPLES	MEANINGS
for example	**(a)** Reactions to bee stings can be severe. **For example,** a person could experience breathing difficulty.	These connectors introduce examples of what has been mentioned.
for instance	**(b)** Some sports involve considerable body contact. Take, **for instance,** football.	*For example* and *for instance* introduce a typical member of a group or a typical instance.
especially	**(c)** Violence in movies seems to be increasing. Action films **especially** appear to be getting more violent.	*Especially* and *in particular* introduce an important member of a group or an important instance.
in particular	**(d)** Learning the rules for article usage in English can be difficult. **In particular,** the use of articles with generic nouns may be confusing.	
to illustrate	**(e)** The steps for saving your computer file are quite simple. **To illustrate,** we will save the file you have just created.	*To illustrate* and *as an example* often introduce a lengthy example such as a process or narrative.
as an example	**(f)** Many great composers have had their share of misery. **As an example,** consider the life of Mozart.	

IDENTIFYING CONNECTORS	EXAMPLES	MEANINGS
namely	**(g)** There is a very important issue before us; **namely,** we need to decide how to reduce the budget by one-fourth.	These connectors identify something either previously mentioned or implied. They introduce a more specific or detailed elaboration.
specifically	**(h)** I have a question about connectors. **Specifically,** when do you use *in fact?*	

This chart shows connectors that are frequently used in academic writing. Ss will of course be familiar with *for example* and *for instance* and probably with *that is* and *in other words*. As with many of the connectors in this unit, the challenge for Ss will typically be not with forms but meaning distinctions, such as that between *for example* and *as an example*.

SUGGESTIONS

1. Have Ss read through the examples and meanings for homework. Ask them to check the connectors they are familiar with and have used and to put a question mark next to those with which they are less familiar.
2. Note that most of the connectors in this chart are used in formal contexts with the exception of *I mean*.
3. Assign Exercise 6 along with the reading of Focus 4. This will give Ss a chance to select appropriate connectors for specific contexts and provide motivation for reviewing the explanations in this focus box.

CLARIFYING CONNECTORS	EXAMPLES	MEANINGS
that is	**(i)** The garlic should be minced; **that is,** you should chop it into very small pieces.	These connectors signal that something will be rephrased or clarified.
in other words	**(j)** You can't go on with this hectic lifestyle. **In other words,** you need to learn to relax.	We use *that is* and *in other words* in both spoken and written English. *I mean* is less formal; we generally do not use it in formal academic English to clarify a statement.
I mean	**(k)** I can't go to that play. **I mean,** seventy dollars is just too much for me to spend in one evening.	

EXERCISE 6

Use an exemplifying, identifying, or clarifying connector from the list below that would be appropriate for each blank. The first has been done as an example.

for example	*especially*	*to illustrate*	*that is*
for instance	*in particular*	*as an example*	*in other words*

1. Many words in English have origins in Greek myths. *Chaos,* ____for example____, is a word the Greeks used to describe the un-ordered matter that existed before creation.

2. Some natural objects have English names that derive from Roman words for mythological characters. Planets, _____ , have been given such names. _____ , here are a few of them. Jupiter is named after the god of he sky. Neptune, in Roman mythology, was the god of springs and rivers. And Saturn was one of the gods of agriculture.

3. Some names for metals in English also derive from myths. The metal uranium, _____ , comes from the Latin *Uranus* (the god of the sky). The metal tellurium comes from the Latin *Tellus* (the goddess of the earth).

210 | UNIT 12

A N S W E R   K E Y

Exercise 6
Answers may vary.
2. in particular; to illustrate 3. for instance

4. in other words 5. especially; as an example 6. that is

Exercise 6

This would make a good homework assignment so that all Ss have time to think about the underlying relationships of the sentences in this exercise. Some Ss will need more time than others to understand some of the less familiar relationships expressed by connectors such as *in particular*, *especially*, *that is*, and *in other words*. Remind Ss that some statements define or explain words or phrases in a previous statement. This constitutes a clarification (*that is*, *in other words*) relationship. Thus, they may need dictionaries to check words they don't know (e.g., *plutocracy* in 6).

210   Grammar Dimensions, Platinum Edition

4. Sometimes we may refer to an idea as *chimerical;* _____ , it is un-realistic or fanciful. This word comes from the name for a Greek monster, the Chimeaera, which had a lion's head, a goat's body, and a dragon's tail.

5. Some English names for bodies of water also derive from Greek words. This is true _____ in the case of oceans. The name for the Arctic Ocean, _____ , comes from the Greek word for *bear: arkto.* The name for the Atlantic Ocean derives from *Atlantides,* who were sea nymphs. And the word ocean itself comes from *Oceanus,* the oldest member of the mythological race, the Titans.

6. Some governments are known as *plutocracies;* _____ , they are governments run by the wealthy. The word *plutocracy* comes from *Plutus,* the god of wealth.

EXERCISE 7

Add an identification statement after each of the following sentences to further specify information conveyed. Use *namely* or *specifically* to indicate its relationship to the sentence before it.

▶ **EXAMPLE:** There is one thing I really like about you.
Namely, you never blame other people when something is your fault.

1. I'd like to know a few things about you.
2. I have one bad habit I wish I could break.
3. There are several things you might do to improve your financial situation.
4. There are two movies I'd like to see.
5. There are a few things about my future I often wonder about.
6. There is one thing I would like to have accomplished by this time next year.

EXERCISE 8

Following is a list of words along with their definitions. Make up one sentence using each word. Then for each, add an independent clause that explains the word. Use *in other words, that is,* or *I mean* to signal the relationship between the clauses. Use a semicolon to punctuate them.

▶ **EXAMPLE:** intractable   difficult to manage or get to behave
Our new labrador puppy is intractable; in other words, it is hard to make him behave.

1. ichthyologist   (noun)   someone who specializes in the study of fishes
2. polychromatic   (adj.)   having many colors

Sentence Connectors | **211**

Exercise 7

Unlike some of the other sentence connectors in this unit, *namely* and *specifically* are ones many Ss will not be very familiar with and may not have used productively.

This would make a good pairwork or groupwork activity, with Ss reporting some of their statements afterwards to the class.

Exercise 8

E X P A N S I O N

Give groups three or four other words and definitions in strips, with the word on one strip and the definition on another. Ask Ss to match the words to their definitions and create sentences modeled after the example in this exercise.

A variation of this expansion would be to have Ss create the strips, using their dictionaries to find words, which they would give to another group to match and create sentences from.

Workbook Ex. 5, p. 115.
Answers: TE p. 548.

FOCUS 5

There is a fairly small set of connectors expressing similarity. Your Ss will probably be familiar with *similarly* and *likewise*. *In the same way* is perhaps less common.

    The second half of the focus box should be especially useful for Ss in showing how to paraphrase rather than repeat information in sentences joined by similarity connectors.

    The second section also explains the nature of comparisons made using these connectors, the shades of meaning difference among the connectors, and the placement of connectors other than at the beginning of the sentence. Although advanced learners may have seen similarity connectors as part of a list during previous grammar study, they may be uncertain about how to use them in communicative situations.

SUGGESTION

To help Ss focus on the elements of paraphrase shown in the example, identify words and phrases in the first sentences of sentence pairs and ask Ss to tell you what the synonym or paraphrase is. For example, in (d), *collect stamps—>hobby*; in (g), *some new clothes —>a few new outfits*; in (h), *camouflage —>hide*. For some parts of sentences, the paraphrase includes the connector. For example, in (i), *get disturbed during an electrical storm* is paraphrased as *react in the same way*.

3. terriculous	(adj.)	living in the ground	
4. carnivore	(noun)	meat-eating animal	
5. digress	(verb)	to stray from the main topic in speech or writing	
6. captious	(adj.)	tending to find fault with things and to make petty criticisms	
7. xenophobic	(adj.)	having a fear or dislike of strangers or foreigners	
8. equivocate	(verb)	to avoid making a direct statement about something	

FOCUS **5**

▶ Similarity Connectors

CONNECTORS	EXAMPLES		MEANING
similarly	**(a)**	The lungs of vertebrates absorb oxygen from the air. **Similarly,** gills, the respiratory organs of many aquatic animals, take in oxygen from water.	These connectors signal that two or more ideas or situations are alike.
likewise	**(b)**	If you study, you will probably do well on the exam. **Likewise,** if you write in a journal every day, you will probably become a better writer.	
in the same way	**(c)**	Learning to play a musical instrument well requires practice. **In the same way,** learning to speak a second language fluently cannot be accomplished without practice.	

Using Similarity Connectors

EXAMPLES	EXPLANATIONS
(d) Blake likes to collect stamps. **Likewise,** this has been one of Karen's favorite hobbies for years. **(e)** NOT: Blake likes to collect stamps. **Likewise,** Karen likes to collect stamps.	Paraphrase the information after the connector. Don't just repeat the previous information word for word.
(f) Football players try to carry a football across their goal line. **Similarly,** soccer players try to kick a soccer ball into a goal.	The comparison often involves several different terms: FOOTBALL SOCCER *players* ⟷ *players* *carry* ⟷ *kick* *football* ⟷ *soccer ball*
(g) Patrice bought some new clothes when we went shopping. **Likewise,** Mira bought a few new outfits. **(h)** The spots on leopards help to camouflage them in the jungle. **Similarly,** spots on fawns help to hide them in the woods.	*Likewise* and *in the same way* often suggest greater similarity, or sameness, than *similarly* does.
(i) Dogs may get disturbed during an electrical storm. Cats may react **in the same way.** **(j)** A man in the audience started to heckle the speaker. Others behaved **similarly.**	You can use similarity connectors at the end of sentences when you are expressing the point of similarity in a verb phrase.

Exercise 9

This exercise could be done individually, in pairs, or in small groups. You could also conduct the exercise orally with the class as a whole, writing responses on the board.

Workbook Ex. 6, p. 116; Ex. 7, p. 117.
Answers: TE p. 548.

EXERCISE 9

The chart below gives information about myth and folklore spirits in western Europe. Imagine that you are a folklorist, and that you have been asked to write a summary of the ways in which these spirits are similar. As preparation for your summary, use the information in the chart to make at least five pairs of sentences expressing similarity. Use a similarity connector with the second sentence of each pair.

▶ **EXAMPLE:** *Pixies enjoy playing tricks on humans; elves, **likewise,** enjoy fooling people.*

Name of Spirit	fairy	pixie	brownie	elf
Where found	Ireland, England, Scotland	England	Scotland	Scandinavian countries
Typical residence	forests, underground	forests, under a rock	humans' houses, farms	forests
Appearance	fair, attractive, varied size	handsome, small	brown or tawny, small, wrinkled faces	varied: some fair and some dark
Visibility to humans	usually invisible; visible by use of a magic ointment	usually invisible	usually invisible	usually invisible; visible at midnight within their dancing circle
Clothing color	green, brown, yellow favorite: green	always green	brown	varied
Favorite pastime(s)	dancing at night	dancing at night; playing tricks on humans	playing tricks on humans	dancing at night; playing tricks on humans
Rulers	fairy king and queen	pixie king	none	elf-king

ANSWER KEY

Exercise 9
Answers will vary.
- Elves live in forests. Similarly, fairies live in forests but underground./ • Elves are invisible, except at midnight when they are dancing. In the same way, fairies are invisible except when they put on a special ointment./ • Pixies are green. Likewise, fairies can wear green./ • Pixies like to dance at night and play tricks on humans. In the same way, elves entertain themselves by dancing and playing tricks./ • Elves are ruled by kings. Similarly, fairies are ruled by kings and queens.

▶ **C**ontrast and
Concession Connectors

CONTRAST CONNECTORS	EXAMPLES	MEANINGS
however	**(a)** In some creation myths, the sun exists before people do. In others, **however,** people create the sun.	These connectors show that two ideas contrast.
in contrast	**(b)** The characters in legends may be based on people who actually lived. **In contrast,** the characters in fables, often animals, are fictional.	
on the other hand	**(c)** The proposed new hotel complex will benefit our city. **On the other hand,** it will create serious problems with increased traffic.	
though	**(d)** This lake is not very good for fishing. It's great for swimming and water skiing, **though.**	
in fact	**(e)** Early civilizations thought *the earth was the center of the universe.* **In fact,** *the earth revolves around the sun.*	These connectors signal that the following statement is contrary to something previously stated. The contrary parts are shown in italics.
however	**(f)** Some people think that *whales are fish.* **However,** *these animals are actually mammals.*	

FOCUS 6

Advanced Ss should be familiar with most of these connectors, but, as with others in this unit, they may limit their use to only a few of them in actual communication.

SUGGESTIONS

1. Have Ss read through the column of connectors and identify any they are not familiar with or unsure about using.

2. To help Ss understand the difference between the contrast and concessive relationships, write *however* examples (a), (f), and (h) on the board. Using capital letters in schematic formulas, express what is true and not true according to these statements. Example (a) can be expressed as: *In A, B is true in C, D is true.* Example (f) can be described this way: *Some people think A; however, A is not true, B is true.* Example (h) can be expressed: *Although A is true; B is true also.* You could model example (a) with a formula and then elicit formulas from the Ss for the other two examples. If needed, use additional examples.

CONCESSION CONNECTORS	EXAMPLES	MEANINGS
even so	**(g)** New York has many urban problems. **Even so,** it is still a great city.	These connectors signal a reservation about something. The first statement is true, but the second statement is also true or needs to be considered.
however	**(h)** Most of my meal was excellent. The vegetables, **however,** were slightly overcooked.	
nevertheless	**(i)** Native Americans have often had difficulty preserving their traditions. **Nevertheless,** they have been able to pass down old stories about their culture to the new generations.	The second statement may also express surprising or unexpected information.
nonetheless	**(j)** I know mountain climbing can be dangerous. I'd like to try it **nonetheless.**	
despite (THIS)	**(k)** Chifumi has to get up at 5 A.M. to get to school on time. **Despite this,** she has never missed a class.	
in spite of (THIS)	**(l)** The day was cold and rainy. **In spite of the inclement weather,** we decided to take a hike.	
on the other hand	**(m)** Learning a new language can be fun. **On the other hand,** it can be frustrating.	

EXERCISE 10

Use the information in the chart from Exercise 9 to make up five sentence pairs expressing differences between the various European folklore spirits.

▶ **EXAMPLE:** *The favorite pastime of fairies is dancing at night. Brownies, in contrast, enjoy playing tricks.*

ANSWER KEY

Exercise 10
Answers will vary.
• Fairies live in Ireland, England, or Scotland. However, pixies live in England only./ • All fairies are fair. On the other hand, some elves are fair and some are dark./ • Fairies, pixies, and elves have rulers. Brownies have no formal rulers, though./ • Fairies are usually invisible. However, they can be made visible by use of a magic ointment./ • Elves live outside. On the other hand, brownies live in houses and farms.

EXERCISE 11

The chart below gives information about people who have made remarkable achievements in the face of adversity. Use the information to make up sentence pairs linked by a concession connector.

▶ **EXAMPLE:** *Helen Keller was deaf and blind. In spite of these difficulties, she became an eloquent communicator.*

Person	Difficulty	Achievement
Helen Keller	was deaf and blind	became an eloquent communicator
Martin Luther King, Jr.	encountered racial prejudice	preached nonviolence toward adversaries
Beethoven	became deaf	continued to write symphonies
Charles Dickens	grew up in poverty	became a famous novelist
Stephen Hawking	is confined to a wheelchair by Lou Gehrig's disease	became an internationally acclaimed physicist
Jim Abbott	had only one arm	played professional baseball as a pitcher

Exercise 11

This would be a good time to review two connectors Ss often confuse: *despite (THIS)* and *in spite of (THIS)*. Remind them that *despite* is never followed by preposition *of*.

ANSWER KEY

Exercise 11

Answers may vary.

• Despite the fact that Helen Keller was deaf and blind, she was able to become an eloquent communicator./ • Martin Luther King, Jr., encountered much racial prejudice. Nonetheless, he preached nonviolence toward adversaries./ • Charles Dickens grew up in poverty. Nevertheless, he became a famous novelist./ • In spite of being confined to a wheelchair by Lou Gehrig's disease, Stephen Hawking has become an internationally acclaimed physicist./ • Jim Abbott had only one arm. Even so, he played professional baseball as a pitcher./ • Beethoven became deaf; even so, he continued to write symphonies.

Exercise 12

This is another exercise that might be best done as a homework assignment to give individuals time to think about the relationships expressed in the sentence pairs. If Ss write their responses, you will be able to assess their understanding of the differences in meaning relationships.

Workbook Ex. 8, p. 119.
Answers: TE p. 548.

EXERCISE 12

As you have seen in this unit, some sentence connectors may signal more than one meaning relationship. These include *on the other hand* (alternative, contrast, concession), *in fact* (intensifying addition, contrast), and *however* (contrast, concession). Review these connector meanings in Focus 2, Focus 3, and Focus 6. Then write down which relationship each signals in the sentences below.

▶ **EXAMPLE:** You could drive to Denver if you have time. On the other hand, you could consider flying there.

Relationship: *alternative*

1. The mechanic told me the fuel pump needed to be replaced. In fact, the fuel pump was fine.
   Relationship:

2. Your essay is very good. It could use some more variety in vocabulary, however.
   Relationship:

3. I might take biology next quarter. On the other hand, I may take geology.
   Relationship:

4. In the distance, the next city looked fairly close. However, as it turned out, it wasn't very close at all.
   Relationship:

5. That television set is expensive. In fact, it costs triple what my old one cost.
   Relationship:

6. The weather forecast predicted heavy rain all weekend. On Saturday, however, there was not a cloud to be seen anywhere.
   Relationship:

7. This soup has a good flavor. On the other hand, it could use a little salt.
   Relationship:

8. Nylon is a very light material. It is, however, very strong.
   Relationship:

9. I'm having a hard time following these directions. In fact, it seems impossible to figure them out.
   Relationship:

ANSWER KEY

Exercise 12
1. contrast   2. concession   3. alternative
4. contrast   5. intensifying addition
6. contrast   7. concession   8. concession
9. intensifying addition

Connectors Expressing Effects/Results and Purposes

EFFECT/RESULT CONNECTORS	EXAMPLES	MEANINGS
accordingly	**(a)** Rain is an important theme in many African religions. **Accordingly,** their rituals often focus on rain-making and rain-stopping.	These connectors signal that a statement is an effect or result of something. They differ mainly in their degrees of formality. We use *as a result (of)*, *because of*, and *due to* in both spoken and written English. We use *therefore, consequently, thus*, and *hence* more in written English. *Thus* and *hence* are the most formal connectors.
as a result	**(b)** English spelling rules can be confusing. **As a result,** some have proposed simplified spelling.	
as a result of (THIS)	**(c)** Some people suffer from acrophobia. **As a result of this phobia,** they avoid heights.	
because of (THIS)	**(d)** Canvas is strong material. **Because of its strength,** it is used for tents.	
due to (THIS)	**(e)** A megaphone is a hollow cone. **Due to its shape,** it can amplify sound.	To express cause-effect or reason-result relationships in conversation, speakers tend to use subordinating conjunctions like *because* and *since* as in **(j)**, more than sentence connectors.
consequently	**(f)** John couldn't get to the library. **Consequently,** he wasn't able to finish his research.	
therefore	**(g)** The plot of this book is not very original. The ending, **therefore,** is easy to predict.	
thus	**(h)** Spring water is filtered through permeable rocks. **Thus,** it is usually fairly clean.	
hence	**(i)** Fluorocarbons have stable carbon-fluorine bonds; **hence,** they are inert and heat resistant.	
	(j) The ending of this book is very easy to predict **because** the plot isn't very original.	

FOCUS 7

A key point for the first part of this chart concerns use: many of these connectors are found only in more formal contexts.

SUGGESTIONS

1. If you didn't use the *thus* example suggested for Focus 1, you could use it here. Or try another one.

Step 1: Write on the board: *The television show I was watching last night was really boring.____ I turned it off and read my grammar book instead.* Write *hence* in the blank.

Step 2: Ask Ss how they think the second sentence sounds (they should think it sounds strange or funny) and what kind of connector would sound more natural (of the list here *therefore*, but more likely in conversational English the coordinating conjunction *so*).

2. Note that the purpose connectors are usually used only in formal contexts. Speakers tend to use coordinating conjunctions to express purpose. (*We'll test your cholesterol tomorrow, so don't eat anything. Catherine needed to go to the market after work so she took her grocery list with her.*).

PURPOSE CONNECTORS	EXAMPLES		MEANINGS
in order to (DO THIS)	**(k)**	We'll test your cholesterol to-morrow. **In order to check it,** we must ask you not to eat any-thing for four hours.	Purpose connectors also express causal relation-ships.
with this in mind	**(l)**	Catherine needed to go to the market after work. **With this in mind,** she took her grocery list with her.	
for this purpose	**(m)**	The candidate for mayor needed to increase her campaign funds. **For this purpose,** her manager scheduled several fund-raising dinners.	Of the connectors shown here, *for this purpose* is the most formal.

Exercise 13

As with other exercises in this unit, encourage Ss to use connectors that are less familiar to them and to vary their choices.

SUGGESTION

Before Ss do this exercise, ask them which mythological characters they have read or heard about.

Workbook Ex. 9, p. 119; Ex. 10, p. 120; Ex. 11, p. 121.
Answers: TE pp. 548–549.

EXERCISE 13

The two charts below give information about various characters from myths and legends. Use the information from Chart A to make sentence pairs ex-pressing reason-result relationships. Use Chart B to make sentence pairs ex-pressing purpose relationships. For all sentence pairs, use an appropriate sentence connector.

▶ **EXAMPLES:** *The Norse Gods believed nothing could harm Balder, the sun god. Consequently, they thought it fun to hurl weapons at him.*

Robin Hood wanted to help the poor. For this purpose, he robbed the rich.

Con

Chart A

Character(s)	Event/Situation	Result
1. Norse gods	believed nothing could harm Balder, the sun god	thought it fun to hurl weapons at him
2. Con, relative of Pachacamac, Incan god of fertility	was defeated in battle by Pachacamac	left Peru and took the rain with him
3. Gonggong, Chinese god of the waters	had his army destroyed by Zhurong, god of fire	fled in disgrace to the west and smashed into a mountain pillar holding up the sky
4. Paris, Trojan hero	wanted the beautiful Helen of Troy for his wife	gave the goddess Aphrodite a golden apple to win her favor

Chart B

Character(s)	Action/Event	Purpose
1. Robin Hood	robbed the rich	help the poor
2. Haokah, Sioux god of thunder	used the wind as a drumstick	create thunder
3. The Pied Piper of Hamlin	played his musical pipe so the rats would follow him out of town	rid Hamlin Town of rats
4. Momotaro	left his Japanese village and made the dangerous journey to Oni Island	conquer the horrible Oni ogres and bring back the priceless treasures they had stolen

The punctuation rule to highlight is that shown in example (b). Explain to Ss that putting a comma between two main clauses joined by a sentence connector results in an error that some refer to as a comma splice and some as a kind of run-on sentence.

SUGGESTION

Review the sentence connectors Ss will probably use most frequently in their writing, e.g., *also, furthermore, for example, however, on the other hand, therefore, consequently, nevertheless.* Start a list with a few of these and ask Ss which ones they tend to use a lot. Suggest that they pay special attention when editing their writing to sentences that have these words.

Exercise 14

EXPANSION

If Ss are working on other writing assignments in your class, ask them to revise drafts by adding sentence connectors where appropriate and checking for correct punctuation.

Workbook Ex. 12, p. 122.
Answers: TE p. 549.

UNIT GOAL REVIEW

Ask Ss to look at the goals on the opening page of the unit again. Help them understand how much they have accomplished in each area.

▶ ## Punctuation of Sentence Connectors

Many sentence connectors can be used at the beginning, the middle, or the end of a sentence or independent clause. The punctuation surrounding a sentence connector depends on where it appears in a sentence.

EXAMPLES	EXPLANATIONS
(a) Apollo is the god of the sun in Greek mythology. **Similarly,** Balder is the sun god in Norse myths.	If the connector begins a sentence, use a period before it (ending the previous sentence) and a comma after it.
(b) Balder was much loved by the other gods; **however,** he was accidentally killed with a mistletoe dart by one of them.	If the connector begins an independent clause after another independent clause in the same sentence, use a semicolon before it and a comma after it.
(c) Many mythological characters have more than one name. Some, **in fact,** have several name variations.	If the connector is in the middle of a sentence or an independent clause, we usually separate it from the rest of the clause with commas.
(d) Aphrodite is the Greek goddess of love. She is **also** the goddess of beauty.	We do not usually use commas with *also* when it is in the middle of a sentence.
(e) Balder died from his dart wound. His wife Nanna died **as well,** having suffered a broken heart.	We do not use commas before *as well* when it follows a verb.
(f) The gods were grief-stricken when Balder died. The mortals reacted **in the same way.**	If the connector comes at the end of the sentence, punctuation is usually not necessary except for two connectors: *however* and *though.*
(g) Tu, known in Polynesian myths as the angry god, was quite belligerent. He could sometimes be very kind, **however.**	

EXERCISE 14

As a review of the connectors in this unit, go back to Exercise 1. Rewrite the second sentence in each numbered pair, adding an appropriate sentence connector and punctuation where needed.

ANSWER KEY

Exercise 14
Answers will vary. Examples:
1. For example, the Mayan god . . .   2. In contrast, the goddess Athena . . .   3. In addition, they help us . . .   4. As a result, they made up . . .   5. That is, they explain . . .
6. Then he woke up . . .   7. On the other hand, the bush . . .   8. Similarly, the Greek hero . . .   9. Consequently, she was . . .
10. For instance, in Asia . . .

Use Your English

USE YOUR ENGLISH

The activities on these "purple pages" at the end of the unit contain situations that should naturally elicit the unit's structures in a more communicative framework. While Ss are doing these activities in class, you can circulate and listen to determine if they have actually achieved the goals in the opening page of the unit.

ACTIVITY 1: LISTENING/ WRITING

There are a number of Greek myths that explain how certain flowers came to be. Like many myths, different versions exist of these stories; they usually have common elements but vary in some details of the story. You will hear two versions of the Greek myth of Echo and Narcissus, which tells how the Narcissus flower came to be. Listen once to both versions to get a general idea of how they are similar and how they differ. Listen a second time and take notes on each version. When you have finished, briefly collaborate with two or three classmates to fill in any details you might have missed. From your notes, write a description of the similarities and differences of the two versions. Use a variety of contrast and similarity sentence connectors.

ACTIVITY 2: WRITING

In groups, create a list of ten facts or opinions on different topics. Below each fact, leave several spaces. Then pass the list to another group. The members of that group have to add another fact to each statement, using an addition sentence connector to signal the relationship. When they are finished, they should pass the list to another group who will do the same thing until several groups have added sentences to each list.

▶ **EXAMPLES:**   Group 1: *Tomatoes are very good for you.*
Group 2: *In fact, they are a good source of vitamins.*
Group 3: *In addition, they taste good.*
Group 4: *Furthermore, you can use them in a lot of different ways, such as in making sauces or salads.*
Group 1: *San Francisco is a beautiful city.*
Group 2: *It also has great restaurants.*
Group 3: *It's a book lover's city as well.*
Group 4: *What's more, you can go sailing in the bay.*

Sentence Connectors   **223**

Activity 1

Play textbook audio. The tapescript for this listening appears on p. 569 of this book.

SUGGESTION

Before Ss listen to the stories, bring in a picture of Echo and Narcissus from a mythology book. This myth is included in most collections of Greek myths.
The children's section of a library is a good source for mythology books with attractive pictures.
    You could also bring in a picture of a Narcissus flower.

Activity 2

SUGGESTION

Ss could use the Internet as a source for information on topics.

VARIATION

If time constraints prohibit Ss' creating the lists, or if you think your Ss need a somewhat more guided activity, create the lists yourself to distribute to the groups.

ANSWER KEY

Activity 1
Activity 1 involves a summary writing exercise, so the responses will vary.

Activity 3
VARIATION

For a collaborative writing activity, Ss could work in small groups and exchange their lists with another group.

Activity 4
EXPANSIONS

1. Ss could give brief oral reports on their "turning point" or read their essays to a small group.
2. Ask for a few volunteers to read their essays to the rest of the class.

ACTIVITY 3: WRITING/RESEARCH

STEP 1 Make a list of five words that you think others in the class might not be very familiar with. Use a dictionary if necessary. Try to find words that could be useful additions to someone's vocabulary.

STEP 2 Exchange lists with one of your classmates. Each of you should look up the words you have been given in the dictionary to see its range of meanings. Then write one sentence using the word in a context and add a statement defining the word, using one of the clarification sentence connectors (*that is* or *in other words*) as was done in Exercise 8. If you wish, you can connect the sentences with a semi-colon to show their close relationship.

▶ **EXAMPLE:** *Some folktales are moralistic; in other words, these stories instruct people on how to behave.*

STEP 3 Give your sentences to your partner; check each other's sentences for correctness.

ACTIVITY 4: WRITING

"Turning point" is a term we sometimes use to describe an event that has changed or influenced someone in an important way. Consider three turning points in your life. Write an essay in which you explain how each turning point has changed your life. Use reason-result sentence connectors in your explanations.

▶ **EXAMPLE:** *One of the major turning points in my life was when my family left Laos for the United States. Because of this, we had to start a new life and adjust to an entirely different culture. . . .*

ACTIVITY 5: SPEAKING / LISTENING / WRITING

STEP 1 Pair up with another classmate. Your task is to find out six things that you have in common and six things that are different about you. The similarities and differences should not be things that are apparent (for example, not similarities or differences in physical appearance, the similarity of both being in the same class). Consider topics such as goals, hobbies, travels, language learning, families, and various likes and dislikes (foods, sports, courses, books, movies, etc.).

STEP 2 As you discover the similarities and differences, make a list of them. Then, each of you should write six sentence pairs expressing your discoveries, using similarity and contrast connectors. Divide the task equally so that each of you states three similarities and three differences. Share some of your findings with your classmates.

▶ **EXAMPLES:** *Sven started learning English when he was twelve.* **Similarly,** *I first started taking English courses when I was thirteen.*

Wenxia loves to read science fiction. **In contrast,** *I read mostly nonfiction books.*

I love math. Tina, **on the other hand,** *hopes she never has to take another math course in her life.*

ACTIVITY 6: RESEARCH / WRITING

Creation myths from around the world often have similarities; for example, in many myths, the earth and sky are formed by dividing an egg. Find two more creation myths from different cultures. Write an essay in which you summarize each myth and describe similarities and differences between the two myths.

Activity 5
Collecting the sentences will help you assess what Ss have learned in this unit and target any areas that may need review.

Activity 6
VARIATION
If done as a small group collaborative activity, members of each group could present brief oral reports on their research.

The test for this unit can be found on p. 506. The answers are on p. 507.

TOEFL Test Preparation exercises can be found in the workbook on pp. 124–126. The answers are on p. 549 of this book.

Unit 13

UNIT OVERVIEW

The greatest challenge for students (Ss) in mastering the modal system involves the complex system of meaning and use. Therefore, this unit focuses on perfect modal meanings and uses, with a review of form at the beginning.

UNIT GOALS

Review the goals listed on this page so Ss understand what they should be able to know by the end of the unit.

OPENING TASK

The task in this unit asks Ss to write a response to a request for advice about a past situation. This task is modeled in Step 1. Modal perfect verbs are used in all three letters as well as in Mr. Retrospect's reply. The requests in the letters prompt Ss to use modal perfect verbs in their replies.

SETTING UP THE TASK

To help Ss appreciate the humor in this task, before they start Step 1, ask if they are familiar with the word *retrospect* and the idiom *in retrospect*. You could elicit a definition by asking if they know the prefix *retro-* (back) and the root *spect* (look), both of which are parts of many other English words. Ss generally have a high interest in learning new vocabulary and idioms! Give them a few contextual examples of the idiom *in retrospect* using modal perfect verbs. (Example: *Last year, I spent all of my savings to buy a new car. In retrospect, I should have bought a used car; I should have kept some of my savings for emergencies.*)

CONDUCTING THE TASK

Step 1

SUGGESTIONS

1. Have Ss work with a partner, with one student reading the letter aloud and the other the response.
2. Ask Ss if they would have given different advice to Henry.

UNIT 13

MODAL PERFECT VERBS

UNIT GOALS:

- To use the correct forms of modal perfect verbs
- To choose correct modals to express judgments, obligations, and expectations
- To choose correct modals to make deductions and guesses
- To choose correct modals to express results of past conditions and to make predictions

OPENING TASK
Mr. Retrospect's Hindsight and Advice

Mr. Retrospect is an advice columnist who specializes in telling people what they should have done after the fact.

STEP 1 Read the following letter sent to Mr. Retrospect and his reply.

> Dear Mr. Retrospect:
>
>   A few weeks ago I asked a woman out to dinner. She seemed pleased with the invitation, but when my mother and I arrived at her house to pick her up she looked dismayed and said that she suddenly felt ill and couldn't go with us. She didn't look sick to me. She must have changed her mind. What could the reason have been? I must say, I'm a rather handsome guy, so I don't think it was my appearance.
>
>   Henry

Dear Henry:

From what you have described, I'd guess that this woman must have had a different idea of your plans for the evening. Frankly, it's rather unusual for mothers to accompany their sons on dates. You could have taken your mother out to dinner on another night.

Mr. Retrospect

STEP 2 Write a response to one of the following letters.

Dear Mr. Retrospect:

On a recent trip, I visited a relative I don't know very well, one of my great aunts. She lives in a very rural area; the nearest large city is three hundred miles away. I'm her only nephew, so she was really looking forward to my visit. Everything was fine until we sat down to eat. When I asked her what was in the stew she had just served, she announced, "Possum and squirrel," I was so shocked that I refused to eat anything and had to leave the table. I'm afraid that I hurt my great aunt's feelings even though later I said I was sorry. Now I am wondering what I could have said to be more polite.

Wild animal lover (well, squirrels anyway)

Dear Mr. Retrospect:

My hairdresser recently talked me into a new hairstyle that makes me look like a porcupine. I hated it! Unfortunately, he thought it was the perfect style for me. After he finished styling my hair he proclaimed "It's you!" I didn't know what to say. How do you think I should have responded?

Sally

STEP 3 In small groups, share the response you wrote.

Step 2

V A R I A T I O N

If time permits and you want more writing for diagnostic purposes, ask Ss to write responses to both letters. (One response could be written in class, the other as homework.)

CLOSING THE TASK

As a class, discuss the different kinds of suggestions Ss came up with. Was one of the situations more challenging to respond to than the others? Why?

E X P A N S I O N

Step 1: As a homework assignment, ask Ss to compose a letter seeking advice about a situation that the student or someone they know experienced in the past (or make up a situation).
Step 2: During the next class, ask Ss to exchange letters with a partner, who will write a response (either in-class or for homework).

Of the eight focus boxes in this unit, this is the only one that focuses solely on perfect modal forms.

S U G G E S T I O N

To practice active, passive, and progressive forms of modal perfects:

Step 1: Prepare a list of modal forms, main verbs and names of forms
(e.g., 1. *may/watch/progressive*;
2. *must/write/passive*). Include a number of irregular verbs so that Ss will get practice with the past participles.
Step 2: Divide the class into teams of four or five Ss.

Step 3: Write on the board one of the items from your list; abbreviate the forms with A for active, PS for passive, or PR for progressive. The first team must give you the correct form. If they do not, the next team gets to respond. Rotate among the teams until you have finished the list.

FOCUS **1**

Review of Modal Perfect Verbs

Although modal perfect verbs have a number of meanings, the forms are fairly simple.

EXAMPLES	EXPLANATIONS
(a) You **should have seen** that film. (b) They **must have come** from miles away.	**Active voice:** modal + *have* + past participle
(c) That concerto **should have been played** slowly. (d) His house **must have been built** during the last century.	**Passive voice:** modal + *have* + *been* + past participle
(e) I **must have been dreaming!** (f) We **could have been playing** tennis instead of having to clean up after the rainstorm.	**Progressive:** modal + *have* + *been* + present (*-ing*) participle
(g) The game **might** not **have ended** yet. (h) You **may** not **have read** that carefully enough.	**Negative:** In negative forms, *not* comes after the modal.

Summary of Modal Perfect Forms

	subject + modal (not) + have	been	past participle	present participle
ACTIVE	He could (not) have +	—	gone.	
PASSIVE		been	gone.	
PROGRESSIVE		been	—	going.

NOTE: There is also a passive progressive form for perfect modals: modal + *have* + *been* + *being* + past participle: *The old school building* **must have been being demolished** *the week that we were gone.* This verb form, however, is not very common in either spoken or written English.

EXERCISE 1

Complete each blank with a modal perfect verb using the cues in parentheses. The first one has been done as an example.

(1) My friends and I discussed the letters Mr. Retrospect received and the responses we would make to them. (2) Josef thought that Henry (must/be born) <u>must have been born</u> on another planet. (3) Inna agreed and added that his mother (not/could/know) _____ much about dating etiquette either. (4) Takiko thought Henry's date (might/call) _____ him later and (tell) _____ him what the problem was. (5) For a response to his letter, we (would/inform) _____ Henry that his date (may/be) _____ a bit surprised to find out that Mom was chaperoning and that next time Mom should stay home. (6) As for the Wild Animal Lover's dining experience, we all agreed that we (not/could/eat) _____ that dinner either, but we (not/would/want) _____ to hurt the great-aunt's feelings. (7) I suggested that he (might/say) _____ he was allergic to squirrel or possum. (8) That excuse (not/would/stray + -ing) _____ too far from the truth since he probably (would/get) _____ sick from eating it. (9) Finally, concerning the last letter, we disagreed about how Sally (should/respond) _____ to her hairdresser. (10) Rosa thought Sally (could/ask) _____ the hairdresser to restyle her hair. (11) Marty said she (might/suggest) _____ to him that her spiked hair could hurt someone. (12) We all concurred that Sally (should/find out) _____ what her hairdresser planned to do before he styled her hair. (13) We also agreed that the hairdresser (must/think + -ing) _____ only of his own preferences at the time and that Sally should look for a new stylist.

Exercise 1

If Ss do this exercise as homework, they could check their answers in small groups in class and report any differences in their completions.

Workbook Ex. 1, p. 127.
Answers: TE p. 549.

ANSWER KEY

Exercise 1

(3) couldn't have known   (4) might have called/told   (5) would have informed; may have been   (6) couldn't have eaten; might not have wanted   (7) might have said   (8) wouldn't have been straying; would have gotten   (9) should have responded   (10) could have asked   (11) might have suggested   (12) should have found out   (13) must have been thinking

Note that in (4) *might* governs both lexical verbs, *called* and *told*

FOCUS 2

SUGGESTIONS

1. Ask Ss questions that elicit modal perfect answers. *Lisa, what should you have done this past week that you didn't do? What could I have explained better in class this week? Bernard, what might you have done to prepare for your classes better?*

2. Ask Ss to explain a past situation in which someone behaved inappropriately (inconsiderately, rudely, etc.). The situation could be from real life or fiction; it could be from their personal lives or from a movie. Ask questions as needed to prompt use of modal perfects expressing judgments (e.g., *Well, what do you think he might have done instead?*)

FOCUS **2**

▶ # Expressing Judgments about Past Situations: *Should Have, Could Have, Might Have*

EXAMPLES	EXPLANATIONS
(a) You **should have gone** to bed earlier. (But you didn't.) (b) They **shouldn't have spent** so much money. (But they did.) (c) The teacher **could have warned** us that we would have to know all the math formulas for the test. (But she didn't.) (d) Robert **might have written** us that he was coming. (But he didn't.)	The modal forms *should have* (and negative *should not have*), *could have*, and *might have* express judgments about something that did not happen.
(e) You **shouldn't have taken** the day off from work. It created a burden for everyone else. (f) Carmelita **should have treated** her sister better. It created a burden for everybody else. (g) I **shouldn't have taken** the day off from work. Now I'm even more behind. (h) We **should have treated** our sister better. Now she won't even talk to us, and it's all our fault. (i) You **could** / **might** **have called** us when you were in town. We didn't even know you were here. (j) You **might have asked** me if I wanted some dessert before you told the waiter to bring the bill. (k) Ian **could have offered** to contribute to the cab fare. He certainly had the money to do so.	These modals can express a variety of attitudes: • *Should have* and *should not have* with second- or third-person subjects often imply criticism. • With *I* or *we* as the subject, *should have* and *should not have* may express regret. • *Should have*, *could have*, and *might have* can all express irritation, anger, or reproach. In certain contexts, they may express the speaker's judgment that someone has shown a lack of thoughtfulness or courtesy. • *Could have* also expresses capability more directly than *should have* and *might have* do.

EXERCISE 2

Make a statement expressing a judgment about each of the following situations. Use *should have, could have,* or *might have* + verb in your response. Examples are given for the first one.

▶ **EXAMPLES:** A friend failed a test yesterday.

　　　　*She **could have spent** more time studying.*
　　　　*She **might have asked** her teacher for help before the test.*

1. One of your classmates returned a paperback book to you with the cover torn. When you gave it to him, the book was new.
2. A manufacturing company was charged with pouring chemicals into the river.
3. You were stopped by the police while driving your car. Your license plates had expired.
4. A neighbor locked herself out of her apartment and didn't know what to do. So she just sat down on the front steps and waited for someone to notice her.
5. A friend wanted to get a pet but her roommates didn't like cats or dogs. So she moved out of the house she shared with them.

EXERCISE 3

The following story describes the unfortunate experiences of the Park family—Seung, Eun Joo, and their daughter Anna—at a hotel where they recently spent a vacation. For each situation, state what you think the hotel staff or the Parks should have, could have, or might have done.

▶ **EXAMPLES:** When the Parks arrived at the hotel, the front desk clerk was talking on the phone to her boyfriend and ignored them.

　　　　The clerk could have at least acknowledged their presence.
　　　　The Parks should have looked for another hotel!

1. When the clerk got off the phone, she told the Parks that their rooms had been given to someone else. However, other rooms would be available in four hours.
2. The Parks decided to have lunch in the hotel restaurant. Their waiter, who had a bad cold, kept coughing on their table as he took their orders.
3. When the food arrived, Eun Joo's soup was so salty she could feel her blood pressure rising by the second. Seung's pork chop was about as edible as a leather glove. Anna's spaghetti looked like last week's leftovers and it tasted worse.
4. When the Parks were finally able to check into their rooms, the bellhop forgot one of their bags in the lobby. Instead of getting it, he rushed off, explaining that he had to catch a train. Mr. Park ended up bringing the bag up by himself, which made him quite angry.

Modal Perfect Verbs **231**

Exercise 2
EXPANSION

As a homework assignment, ask Ss to write down one more situation modeled after the ones in this exercise. During the next class, Ss read their situations to the class or in small groups for responses.

Exercise 3
Answers could be discussed orally.

Workbook Ex. 2, p. 128.
Answers: TE p. 549.

FOCUS 3

As this focus box explains, the phrasal modal *be to have* is used in formal English. It is not common in conversational English.

SUGGESTION

Tell Ss that native speakers often use nonperfective infinitive forms in informal English (e.g., a speaker might say *We were supposed to take our exam on Friday . . .)* Speakers may also contract these phrasal modals in informal English, e.g., *We were supposedt've bought our tickets yesterday.*

Exercise 4

VARIATION

For an oral exercise, have Ss complete these statements with a partner. Monitor production and note any errors to review as a class.

Exercise 5

VARIATION

For a homework assignment, Ss could interview a friend, dormmate or relative instead of a classmate.

Workbook Ex. 3, p. 129.
Answers: TE p. 549.

FOCUS **3**

▶ # Expressing Obligations and Expectations: *Be Supposed to Have, Be to Have*

Be supposed to have and *be to have* are perfect forms of phrasal modal verbs. Their meanings depend somewhat on the tense of the *be* verb.

EXAMPLES	EXPLANATIONS
(a) We **were supposed to have taken** our exam on Friday, but our teacher was sick.	We use the past tense of *be supposed to have* + past participle to refer to something that was planned or intended but that did not happen.
(b) We **are supposed to have made up** the exam by next week.	We use a present tense form of *be supposed to have* when we expect something to be completed in the future.
(c) I **was to have graduated** in June, but I need to take two more courses for my degree.	*Be to have* expresses similar meanings as *be supposed to have*. *Be to have* is more common in formal English. Like *be supposed to have*, *be to have* refers to a past event that did not occur when *be* is past tense. It refers to a future expectation when *be* is present tense.
(d) Governor Carroll **is to have submitted** his resignation by next Friday.	

EXERCISE 4

Complete the sentences to make statements about yourself.

▶ **EXAMPLE:** I was supposed to have <u>transferred to another college</u> this year, but <u>I needed more financial aid than I was offered</u>.

1. I was supposed to have _____ this year, but _____.
2. In my _____ class, I was supposed to have _____ by (put in a day or date here) _____, but _____.
3. I was to have _____ last (insert time phrase: weekend/ month, etc.) _____, but _____.

EXERCISE 5

Interview a classmate to find out three things that she or he was supposed to have done during the last few months but didn't do. Report at least one of them to the class.

▶ **EXAMPLE:** *Fan was supposed to have gone to the mountains last weekend but her car broke down before she even got out of town.*

232 | UNIT 13

ANSWER KEY

Exercise 4
Answers will vary. Examples:
1. graduated/gone to Paris; I wasn't able to/went to London instead
2. English/chemistry; finished a paper/written a lab report by/Monday/November 12
3. finished my paper/gone to a movie; Monday/weekend; I got sick/but I was too tired to go

Exercise 5
Answers will vary. Examples:
Rudy was supposed to have bought his new motorcycle last week, but he didn't have enough money.   Amy was supposed to have visited her cousins, but they had to go back to Tokyo for a month.

Inferring/Making Deductions from Past Evidence: *Must (Not) Have, Can't Have, Should (Not) Have, Would (Not) Have*

Modal perfect verbs can express two kinds of past inference: We may infer that something (1) almost certainly did or did not happen or (2) probably did or did not happen.

EXAMPLES	EXPLANATIONS
(a) Myla: Our chemistry experiment failed. We **must have followed** the procedures incorrectly. (We **must not have done** it the right way.)	**Inferring Near Certainty** We use *must have* when we infer that something almost certainly happened.
(b) Alberto: We **can't have performed** the procedures incorrectly! I read every step carefully before the experiment and checked each one afterwards, too.	*Can't have* is the opposite of *must have*. We use it to express a belief that something is almost impossible or unbelievable. These examples express strong inferences, not facts. Since both (a) and (b) refer to the same event, one of them must be wrong.
(c) If the test tubes aren't here, Brian **must have taken** them.	Unlike *must have*, *should have* does not express an inference that something almost certainly happened.
(d) **NOT:** If the test tubes aren't here, Brian **should have taken** them.	
(e) Let's check on our second experiment. The powder **should have dissolved** by now.	**Inferring Probability** We use *should have* to express an expectation about a past event. We may infer that something happened, but we don't know for sure.
(f) We **should have gotten** a chemical reaction when we heated the solution, but nothing happened. I wonder what went wrong.	Sometimes we use *should have* to express an expectation about a past event that we know did not occur.
(g) If our observations are correct, the burglary **would have occurred** shortly after midnight.	*Would have* may also express an inference that something probably happened. We use it to speculate about what happened if we accept a certain theory or if we assume certain conditions. Sometimes the condition is stated in an *if*-clause as in (g).
(h) About one hundred seconds after the big bang, the temperatures **would have fallen** to one thousand million degrees.	The condition may be implied rather than directly stated. In (h), the implied condition is: if we accept the big bang theory as a model of how the universe began. The writer uses *would have fallen* instead of *fell* because the big bang theory is hypothetical.

Modal Perfect Verbs **233**

SUGGESTIONS

To elicit statements of near certainty:
Step 1: Before class starts, remove or hide something from the classroom that is usually there (e.g., blackboard erasers, chalk).
Step 2: After the Ss have come in, ask them if they notice anything missing. Give clues if needed.
Step 3: When they have identified the missing item(s), ask them what they think must have happened to it/them or who must have done something to it/them.

To elicit statements of probability: Note the time of day and ask Ss what should have happened in some setting (at their home, in some other part of the world) or what someone they know should have done by that time. Model an example: *Let's see, it's three o'clock; that means the mail carrier should have delivered my mail by now and my daughter should have finished her last class.*

Exercise 6

SUGGESTION

Introduce this exercise by asking if anyone knows of Stephen Hawking. Hawking is a famous physicist and the subject of a documentary film. He has made remarkable achievements despite a severe disability.

Exercise 7

SUGGESTION

This would make a good homework assignment since the concepts underlying the sentences are fairly challenging, and some Ss may need more time to think about the appropriate answers.

Workbook Ex. 4, p. 130.
Answers: TE p. 549.

EXERCISE 6

According to one model of how the universe began, between ten and twenty thousand million years ago the density of the universe and the curvature of space-time became infinite; this point in space-time was termed the "big bang." The following passage describes what some physicists believe probably happened after the big bang. Underline or write down the modal perfect verbs that express probability. Why does the author use these forms instead of simple past tense?

(1) Within only a few hours of the big bang, the production of helium and other elements would have stopped. (2) And after that, for the next million years or so, the universe would have just continued expanding, without anything much happening. (3) Eventually, once the temperature had dropped to a few thousand degrees, and electrons and nuclei no longer had enough energy to overcome the electromagnetic attraction between them, they would have started combining to form atoms. (4) The universe as a whole would have continued expanding and cooling, but in regions that were slightly denser than average, the expansion would have been slowed down by the extra gravitational attraction. (5) This would eventually stop expansion in some regions and cause them to start to recollapse.

From: Stephen Hawking, *A Brief History of Time: From the Big Bang to Black Holes*, Bantam, 1990.

EXERCISE 7

The following sentences express some hypothetical statements about how native languages are learned. Fill in the blanks, using *must have, can't have,* or *should have* and the correct form of the verb in parentheses.

▶ **EXAMPLE:** *Researchers believe children <u>can't have</u> learned their first languages just by memorizing words.*

1. Since the number of possible sentences in any language is infinite, we (learn) _____ our native languages by simply storing all the sentences we heard in a "mental dictionary."

2. Children (develop) _____ their ability to speak their native languages by learning rules from adults because adults are not conscious of all grammar, pronunciation, and meaning rules either.

3. A child (acquire) _____ his or her native language by the age of five; if not, we suspect that something is physically or psychologically wrong.

4. When a native English-speaking child says words like *ringed* and *doed*, this shows that she or he (apply) _____ a familiar rule for the past tense.

5. Similarly, if a child says words like tooths and childs, we speculate that she or he (overgeneralize) _____ the rule for regular plurals.

234 UNIT 13

ANSWER KEY

Exercise 6

(1) would have stopped   (2) would have continued   (3) would have started   (4) would have continued; would have been slowed down

Would have is used here to express inferred probability if the big bang theory is accepted.

Exercise 7

1. must have learned   2. can't have developed   3. should have acquired   4. must have applied   5. must have overgeneralized

Expressing Guesses about Past Situations: *May Have, Might Have, Could Have, Can Have*

We use certain modal perfects to make statements about the past when the speaker is not sure what happened.

EXAMPLES	EXPLANATIONS
(a) The movie **may have** already **started**. There are only a few people in the lobby. **(b)** I **might have gotten** an A on the test. I think I knew most of the answers.	*May have* and *might have* indicate that the speaker doesn't know if an event has occurred but has reason to believe that it has.
(c) I **may have met** him a long time ago. Both his name and face are very familiar. **(d)** I **might have met** him a long time ago, but I doubt it. He doesn't look at all familiar.	From the speaker's viewpoint, *might have* sometimes expresses less possibility of a past event having occurred than *may have* does.
(e) I don't think insects killed our strawberry plants. We **could have used** the wrong kind of soil. Or maybe we didn't fertilize them enough.	*Could have* often expresses one possible explanation among others. The speaker may imply that other explanations are possible.
(f) **Might** Carol **have been** the one who told you that? **(g)** **Could** too much water **have killed** the plants? **(h)** **Can** that **have been** Tomás on the phone? I didn't expect him to call back so soon.	*Might have, could have, can have* (but not *may have*) are also used in questions. *Might have* and *could have* in questions express guesses about a past event. We use *can have* only in questions. Usually a form of *be* is the main verb. The first sentence of (h) can be paraphrased: *Is it possible that Tomás was on the phone?*

SUGGESTION

Step 1: Have Ss read the examples and explanations for homework.

Step 2: During the next class, tell Ss about a few fictional or real-life events that retain an element of mystery (e.g., an unsolved crime, a cat or dog that found its way home from many miles away, an unexplained accident or disaster such as a ship sinking, something you mysteriously lost). Ask them to speculate on what happened. You could even bring in a tabloid magazine and discuss headlines about mysterious events.

Prompt several modals with questions: *What do you think may/might/could have happened?*

Step 3: Write the guesses (or at least the modal perfect verbs in their responses) on the board. If Ss don't use perfect modals, help them transform responses into examples with perfect modals.

SUGGESTION

If done orally, to maximize student participation, have Ss work with a partner or in a small group.

Exercise 9

EXPANSION

Bring in an advice column letter (e.g., from *Dear Abby* or *Ann Landers*) for which Ss can give advice about what someone should have or could have done.

Workbook Ex. 5, p. 131.
Answers: TE p. 549.

EXERCISE 8

Each numbered group of statements below expresses certainty about the cause of a situation. For each, give an alternate explanation, using a perfective modal that expresses possibility. Can you think of any others?

▶ **EXAMPLE:** Look! The trunk of my car is open! Someone must have broken into it!

Alternate explanation: *You may have forgotten to shut it hard and it just popped open.*

1. Rebecca made a lot of mistakes on her economics assignment. She must not have studied the material very carefully.
2. Our English teacher didn't give us back our papers today. She must have been watching TV last night instead of reading them.
3. We invited Nora and Jack to our party but they didn't come. They must have found something better to do.
4. Carlos usually gets off of work at five and is home by six. It's now eight and he's still not home. He can't have left work at five.
5. Christopher Columbus went looking for India and ended up in North America. He must have had a poor sense of direction.

EXERCISE 9

To review the uses of perfect modals so far, return to the letters at the beginning of this chapter. Which of the letters in the Opening Task on pages 226 and 227 has a modal expressing advisability? Which has an inference modal? Which one includes a modal expressing possibility? Identify the perfective modals the letter writers used. Did you use these same modals in your answers? If you did, share some of your answers with the class. If not, give a one sentence answer to each now using these modals in perfective forms.

ANSWER KEY

Exercise 8

Answers will vary. Examples:
1. She may have been nervous during the test./She could have forgotten the material.
2. She could have been grading papers for another class./She may not have been feeling well. 3. They could have gone out of town. / They might have had a previous invitation.
4. He might have had an accident. / He may have stopped to visit someone 5. He could have had poor navigating aids. / He might have gotten some bad advice from his crew.

Exercise 9

Note: Advisability modals are those in Focus 2 that express judgments about past situations. *Modals expressing advisability:* should have responded (Sally); could have taken (Mr. Retrospect) *Inference modal:* must have changed (Henry); must have had (Mr. Retrospect) *Modal expressing possibility:* could have said (Wild animal lover) *Perfect modals used:* Henry: must have changed; could have been; Mr. Retrospect: must have had; could have taken; Wild animal lover: could have said; Sally: should have responded.

▶ Expressing Results of Unreal Conditions: *Would Have, Could Have, Might Have*

EXAMPLES		EXPLANATIONS

	Unreal Condition **Hypothetical Result**
	 (a) If Jung had arrived he **would have seen** us.
	      before noon,
	      Actual Condition **Actual Result**
	 (b) Jung arrived after noon, so he missed seeing us.
		Would have, could have, and *might have* express hypothetical results of conditions that did not happen (unreal conditions).

(c) If I had been at that intersection ten minutes earlier, I **would have seen** the accident. (d) If the car had stopped for the light, the accident **could have been avoided.** (e) If Dorothea had been wearing her seat belt, she **might have escaped** injury.		The following modals express different degrees of probability of the results: • high probability • capable of happening • a chance of happening

We also use these modals in statements that only imply the condition rather than state it directly. These statements may express a missed opportunity or a rejection of one option for another.

EXAMPLES	IMPLIED UNREAL CONDITION	IMPLIED FACT
(f) Tim **would have been** a great father.	if he had been a father.	He is not a father.
(g) I **could have gone** to medical school.	if I had wanted to go to medical school	I did not go to medical school.
(h) Hannah **might have made** the debate team.	if she had tried out for the debate team	She did not try out for the debate team.

SUGGESTIONS:

1. To practice forming unreal conditions and hypothetical result statements:
   Step 1: Prepare a list of three or four "actual conditions" and "actual results" similar to the example in (b) on a transparency or to write on the board.
   Step 2: Show Ss the first condition and result. As a class, transform it into a sentence with an unreal condition and a hypothetical result as in (a).
   Step 3: Ask Ss to work with a partner to transform the other two or three actual conditions and actual results. Have volunteers write their sentences on the board.

2. To review degrees of probability, orally give Ss other examples with *would, could,* and *might* perfect modals as in (c)–(e). Ask them to state the degree of probability with reference to the explanations given for examples (c)–(e).

3. To help Ss understand implied conditions, give them statements about yourself similar to (f)–(h) and ask them to tell you the implied conditions and implied facts: Examples: *I could have been* a concert pianist. *I would have made* a terrific rocket scientist.

Exercise 10

VARIATION

Substitute some of these sentences with ones that reflect current events or local issues.

EXERCISE 10

For each sentence, give two result modals (would have, could have, or might have) that would be appropriate, using the verb in parentheses as the main verb. For each, explain the difference in meaning and/or use between the two modals you choose.

▶ **EXAMPLES:** If the weather had been nicer, they (stay) _____ longer at the beach.

(1) *would have stayed*
(*They definitely wouldn't have left so early; they had intended to be there longer.*)

(2) *could have stayed*
(*It would have been possible to stay longer; this form might be used if cold or rainy weather forced them to leave.*)

1. If Sam had been prepared for the interview, he (get) _____ the job.

2. If you had let me know you needed transportation, I (drive) _____ you to your appointment.

3. If we had been more careful about our environment, we (prevent) _____ damage to the ozone layer.

4. The chairperson (call off) _____ the meeting if she had known so many committee members would not be here today.

Exercise 11

EXPANSION

Ask Ss to make up one more condition modeled after the ones in this exercise to complete for homework or to give to a partner to complete.

EXERCISE 11

Make up three hypothetical results to follow each condition. Use *would have, could have,* and *might have.* Explain your choices of modal based on the degree of probability of each result.

▶ **EXAMPLE:** If I had lived in the nineteenth century, *I would have owned a horse instead of a car. I could have learned how to make ice cream instead of buying it from the supermarket. I might have wanted to be a farmer instead of going into business.*

Explanation: *It is quite likely that I would have owned a horse rather than a car. It is somewhat probable that I would have learned to make ice cream. It's possible, but not very likely, that I would have wanted to be a farmer.*

1. If I could have picked any city to grow up in,

2. If I had been the ruler of my country during the last decade,

3. If I could have been present at one historical event before I was born,

4. If I had been born in another country,

5. If I had been able to solve one world problem of this past century,

238 UNIT 13

ANSWER KEY

Exercise 10
Answers will vary. Examples:
1. might have/would have got(ten)
2. could have/would have driven   3. could have/might have prevented   4. would have/might have called off

Exercise 11
Answers will vary. Examples:
1. I might have chosen Madrid/would have chosen my hometown.   2. I would have worked for racial equality/could have raised taxes.   3. I would have participated in the French Revolution/would have witnessed the first Olympics.   4. I might not have had as many opportunities as I do now/might have spoken another language as my native language.   5. I would have put end to world hunger/would have found a cure for AIDS.

EXERCISE 12

What might be an implied condition for each of the following hypothetical statements? Write down a few of your answers for each sentence.

▶ **EXAMPLE:** I could have won the race.
Possible implied conditions:
If I had just run a little faster at the beginning . . .
If I had trained harder . . .

1. Rob could have been a fluent Spanish speaker.
2. Xavier might have been the class valedictorian.
3. You could have come with us to the planetarium.
4. Kenneth Chen would have been the best candidate for that office.
5. I might have considered being a (*state a career or profession here*).

EXERCISE 13

Seven of the modal perfect verbs in the sentences that follow express unreal conditions. The others do not. Write down the modals expressing unreal conditionals. Then write which meaning each of these modals has: (a) expectation or obligation, (b) result of a stated condition, or (c) result of an implied condition. (See the summary in Focus 8, p. 241.)

1. This essay you wrote is rather brief. You could have developed your ideas more.
2. Would you see if the mail is here? It should have come by now.
3. Anita should have gone to law school. She would have been a good lawyer.
4. Seth could have turned in your assignment for you yesterday if you had let him know you wouldn't be able to attend class.
5. The conference was supposed to have started on Friday, but it was postponed until next month.
6. Elena might have asked me before she took my dictionary. I needed it to write my English paper.
7. I could have told you that the swimming pool would be closed today. You should have asked me before you drove over there.
8. Scientists believe that life on earth could have begun more than 3.4 billion years ago.
9. If that lecture had gone on any longer, I would have fallen asleep.
10. We could have gone out of town for our vacation, but we decided to stay home and remodel the kitchen instead.

Exercise 13
SUGGESTION
Have Ss complete this exercise individually to turn in so that you can assess their understanding of perfect modal meanings.

Workbook Ex. 6, p. 132.
Answers: TE p. 550.

ANSWER KEY

Exercise 12
Answers will vary. Examples:
1. If he had been born in Mexico / Central America . . . If he had interacted more with Spanish speakers . . . 2. If he had done better in physics . . . If Sonia had not gotten better grades . . . 3. If you had called us . . . If you hadn't been so busy . . . 4. If he had run . . . If he had been elected . . . 5. If I had been a more talented violinist, I might have considered being a professional musician.

Exercise 13
1. *could have developed*—result of implied condition (if you had tried to develop your ideas . . .) 2. Not an unreal condition but a probability inference. 3. The first modal does not express an unreal condition but a past judgment; *would have been*—result of implied condition (if she had become a lawyer) 4. *could have turned*—result of stated condition (if you had let him know . . .) 5. *was supposed to have* started—expectation

6. Not an unreal condition but a judgment of past event. 7. *could have told*—result of implied condition (if you asked me . . .) Second modal is not an unreal condition but a judgment of past event. 8. Not an unreal condition but a guess about a past situation. 9. *would have fallen*—result of stated condition (if that lecture had gone on . . .) 10. *could have gone*—result of implied condition (if we had wanted to go . . .)

Although native English speakers do use *will have* future perfect modal forms in speech and informal writing, they often use simple future forms instead. This may require changing the lexical verb. For example, (a) could be restated as: *By the time you get this postcard, I won't be in Portugal any longer (or I'll be back home).* Consequently, some Ss may not have heard these forms much in spoken English and may think they sound "strange." They may also have heard contracted forms and not have been aware that *'ll* represented *will*.

SUGGESTION

Step 1: Draw a timeline on the board with two or three future dates (weeks, months, or years from now, depending on what you want to describe).

Example:

now	Dec.	July	Oct.

Step 2: Under the timeline, write the beginnings of sentences for your timeline: *By December, I will have . . .*
Step 3: Give an example of a completion for your first sentence (e.g., *I will have bought a new computer*). Ask Ss to tell you what they will have done/ seen/ written/bought/tried, etc., by that date.

Exercise 14
SUGGESTION

For more oral practice, have Ss work on this exercise in pairs.

Workbook Ex. 8, p. 133.
Answers: TE p. 550.

Predicting the Completion of a Future Event: *Will Have, Shall Have*

Will have and *shall have* are future perfect modal forms. They express the completion of a future event before another future time.

EXAMPLES	EXPLANATIONS
(a) By the time you get this postcard, I **will have left** Portugal.	Possible meaning: You will get this postcard in a week or so. I'm leaving Portugal tomorrow.
(b) At the end of this week, **I'll have been** in Athens for four months.	In spoken English, *will* is often contracted.
(c) By this date next year, we **shall have reduced** our air pollution by thirty percent.	*Shall have* has the same meaning as *will have*. American English speakers rarely use this form in everyday English. Some types of formal English, such as speeches or legal documents, use *shall have*.

EXERCISE 14
Use the information in the first and second columns of the chart below to express what will have most likely happened by the time period in the third column. You may want to add an *if* or *unless* clause to your sentence if you think it is needed. The first has been done as an example.

▶ **EXAMPLE:** *By July, the Changs' store **will have been** open for seven months.*

Time Period 1	Event of Time Period 1	Time Period 2
1. December	the Changs will open their computer software store	July
2. 2000	Larry will complete all the requirements for his college degree	2001
3. May 1995	Patty Schwartz and Roger Peterson got married	May 2045
4. July	Brina will visit Alaska, the only U.S. state that she's never been to before	August
5. September 1	Winnie has vowed to learn ten new words every day	October 1
6. 1964	laser first used for eye surgery	2014

ANSWER KEY

Exercise 14
Word order of responses may vary.
2. By 2000, Larry will have completed all the requirements . . . **3.** By May 2045, Patty Schwartz and Roger Peterson will have been married for fifty years unless they get divorced or one or both die before that date. **4.** By August, Brina will have visited all of the United States. **5.** By October 1, if she sticks to her vow, Winnie will have learned 300 new words. **6.** By 2014, lasers will have been used for eye surgery for a half century.

Summary of Modal Perfect Verbs

EXAMPLES	MODAL PERFECT VERBS	IMPLIED FACT	MEANING/ USE
(a) You **should have** told me.	*should have* *could have* *might have*	You didn't tell me.	Judgment of past situation
(b) We **were supposed to have left** before Thursday.	*be supposed to have* *be to have*	We didn't leave.	Expectation, obligation
(c) Our professor **must have cancelled** class today.	*must have* *can't have*	—	Inferring near certainty about past situations
(d) The film I dropped off **should have been developed** yesterday.	*should have* *would have*	—	Inferring probability about past situations
(e) She **may have missed** the bus. I don't see her anywhere.	*may have* *might have* *could have* *can have*	—	Expressing guesses about past situations
(f) He **would have written** if he had known you wanted him to.	*would have* *could have* *might have*	He didn't write.	Result of stated unreal condition
(g) You **could have stayed** with us.	*would have* *could have* *might have*	You didn't stay with us.	Result of implied real condition
(h) By next month, they **will have finished** the first stage of the project.	*will have* *shall have*	—	Predicting completion of a future event

Modal Perfect Verbs | **241**

FOCUS 8

Remind Ss that this summary is a good reference chart for their future work and study. They may want to keep a page list in the front of their books or in a separate notebook of *Grammar Dimensions* focus boxes that provide summary information in addition to charts in the appendix.

Workbook Ex. 9, p. 134.
Answers: TE p. 550.

UNIT GOAL REVIEW

Ask Ss to look at the goals on the opening page of the unit again. Help them understand how much they have accomplished in each area.

USE YOUR ENGLISH

The activities on these "purple pages" at the end of the unit contain situations that should naturally elicit the unit's structures in a more communicative framework. While Ss are doing these activities in class, you can circulate and listen to determine if they have actually achieved the goals in the opening page of the unit.

Activity 1

Play textbook audio. The tapescript for this listening appears on p. 570 of this book.

Check to make sure Ss have used a perfect modal verb in each of their responses.

Activity 2

V A R I A T I O N

Ss could work in small groups instead of individually to create the scenarios and exchange them with another group.

Activity 3

Encourage Ss to continue using a variety of modals in their paragraphs.

Use Your English

A C T I V I T Y   1 :   L I S T E N I N G / S P E A K I N G

You will hear two telephone conversations. The first is between friends; the second is a business conversation. Each conversation elicits some type of advice or judgment from one of the speakers.

STEP 1 Listen to the two conversations once to get the meaning.

STEP 2 You will hear each conversation a second time. At the end of each one, take the role of the person who offers advice or makes a judgment. Provide an appropriate response to the person asking for your advice or opinion. Use a perfect modal verb. Write down your responses; then compare them with those of some of your classmates.

A C T I V I T Y   2 :   W R I T I N G

Write three brief scenarios that describe thoughtless, rude, or somehow inappropriate behavior. Exchange scenarios with a classmate and write at least one judgment about each of the situations your classmate has written, using *could have*, *might have*, or *should have*. Use a variety of modals in responding. Afterwards, if time permits, share a few of your situations and responses with the class.

▶ **EXAMPLE:** *You were riding a subway train to school. You were standing up because it was very crowded, and suddenly the train stopped. A woman next to you spilled her diet soda all over your new jacket.*

Judgments:
She shouldn't have been drinking a soda on the train.
She could at least have offered to pay for dry cleaning the jacket.

A C T I V I T Y   3 :   W R I T I N G

Write five sentences stating things that you would (could, might) have done or not done, or situations that would (could, might) have happened in the past if circumstances had been different. Choose one of your sentences to explain in more detail. Write one or two paragraphs based on the sentence you selected.

▶ **EXAMPLE:** *If my family had not moved to the United States, I might not have learned English.*
If my parents had not helped me so much, I couldn't have gone to college.

242 UNIT 13

A N S W E R   K E Y

Activity 1

Because this activity is a role play in which students make up their own responses in a communicative context, there are no set answers to the two parts of this task.

ACTIVITY 4: READING/SPEAKING

Find an article in a book, newspaper, or magazine that describes an unsolved or unexplained situation: a crime, an unusual occurrence, strange weather patterns, etc. Have a class discussion in which students take turns summarizing the unexplained events to the rest of the class and classmates offer probable or possible explanations using *must have, can't have, may have, might have,* and *could have.*

ACTIVITY 5: RESEARCH/WRITING/SPEAKING

Be an amateur detective! The next time you are in a supermarket, observe the items that the person checking out in front of you has in his or her cart or basket. (This is one time when you might want to get behind someone who has a lot of groceries!) Try to note as many items as you can, but don't let the person know that you are doing it. Afterwards, in a classroom oral presentation, briefly describe the person and then state deductions and guesses about him or her based on the items, using perfective modals expressing inference and possibility.

▶ **EXAMPLE:** *He had a case of soda and lots of chips and dip in his cart; he might have been getting ready for a Super Bowl party.*

ACTIVITY 6: WRITING

Imagine what the person in this photograph was like. What do you think his life might have been like? Write a paragraph describing your impressions. Include deductions and guesses using perfect modal verbs.

Activity 4

EXPANSION

Bring in more old photographs for Ss to speculate about. You could use photos from newspapers, magazines, books, or old family photos.

VARIATION

Have Ss work in small groups, with each group discussing a different unexplained situation and then reporting their discussion to the rest of the class.

Activity 5

VARIATION

Ss could do their "sleuthing" in a store other than a supermarket—e.g., a campus store.

Activity 6

SUGGESTION:

Have Ss peer edit each other's paragraphs, checking for correct use of perfect modal verbs in particular.

The test for this unit can be found on p. 508. The answers are on p. 509.

Unit 14

UNIT OVERVIEW

This unit covers structures in English that serve to introduce, connect, and focus topics in discourse. These organizers are especially important in academic and business writing and in formal speaking contexts.

UNIT GOALS

Review the goals listed on this page so students (Ss) understand what they should be able to know by the end of the unit.

OPENING TASK

For this task, Ss work with a partner to brainstorm ideas about a topic and then write a paragraph about it. Only a very long writing task could be expected to produce the full range of discourse organizers in this unit. However, it is likely that Ss will use at least some organizers. In addition, they will be able to review the products of this task in later exercises and to add organizers where appropriate.

SETTING UP THE TASK

Have Ss brainstorm issues at the global, national, and local levels. They can brainstorm individually, on paper, and then share their ideas, or they can brainstorm as a class, with you writing on the board. Emphasize that "issues" tend to be topics about which people can agree or disagree.

UNIT 14

DISCOURSE ORGANIZERS

UNIT GOALS:

- To know how discourse organizers help listeners and readers understand information
- To use appropriate connectors to introduce, organize, and summarize topics
- To use *there* + *be* appropriately to introduce topics that are classified
- To use rhetorical questions to introduce and change topics and to focus on main points

▶ OPENING TASK
Analyzing Issues

What global, national, or local issues interest you most?

STEP 1 With a partner, choose one of the following topics. Each of you will be writing a paragraph about some aspect of the topic.

- pollution
- the problems of the homeless
- teenage pregnancy
- AIDS awareness
- the right to end one's own life if terminally ill
- censorship on the Internet
- crime prevention
- immigration policies
- drug abuse
- safety from terrorism on airplanes
- the English-only movement in the United States
- a social or political problem in the area where you live
- something that needs to be changed at your school or campus (course requirements, needed facilities, etc.)

STEP 2 With your partner, explore the topic by writing five questions about it. Here is an example for the topic of overpopulation:

1. Is overpopulation becoming a more serious problem?
2. How should the problem of overpopulation be dealt with in developing countries?
3. Does anyone have the right to tell others how many children they should have?
4. What are the religious, cultural, and individual factors we need to consider in addressing the population problem?
5. Can we ever solve the problem of overpopulation?

STEP 3 After you and your partner have written the questions, select one question for the issue you chose and write a paragraph answering the question to the best of your knowledge.

STEP 4 When you have finished, exchange paragraphs. Each of you should try to guess the question the other has answered. Save the questions and the paragraphs you wrote for exercises later in this unit.

CONDUCTING THE TASK

Step 1

SUGGESTIONS

1. If the topics listed here do not appeal to you or your Ss, modify or expand them to fit your context and interests. You could use topics from the previous brainstorming activity.
2. Give Ss five minutes or so to read through the topics and to choose one.

Step 2

Give Ss a ten-minute time limit for their exploration of the topic.

Step 3

This step should also have a time limit, perhaps fifteen to twenty minutes

Step 4

You might collect these paragraphs for additional diagnostic purposes or return to them at the end of the unit.

VARIATIONS

1. Have Ss discuss a sequence of factors, issues, causes, effects, problems, or solutions for one of the topics. Such a task would presumably elicit sequential connectors.
2. Ss could do Steps 1, 2, and 3 as homework and bring paragraphs to class for Step 4. This procedure might, however, have the undesired effect of Ss' "cramming" their paragraphs with discourse organizers if they look ahead into the unit and assume they are supposed to use all of the organizers!

CLOSING THE TASK

As a class, discuss some of the topics and ideas Ss wrote about. Which problems are the most difficult to solve? What were some of the most interesting solutions?

This focus box introduces all of the organizers covered in this unit. The chart is organized according to uses, with several organizer forms corresponding to some of the uses (i.e., those for introducing topics and signaling topic shifts). Most of the forms will be familiar to advanced learners; however, they probably will need practice using all of them in communicative contexts. For example, they may be familiar with all of the sequential connectors but may not know which ones are appropriate for chronological and which are appropriate for logical connection (a distinction made in Focus 2).

SUGGESTION

Have Ss read through the examples and explanations for homework. Then assign Exercise 1 as a review and comprehension check of the kinds of organizers that are explained.

FOCUS **1**

▶ Overview of Discourse Organizers

This unit presents structures that speakers and writers use to signal or emphasize the organization of discourse. These structures help the listener or reader follow the discourse, focus on main points, and understand how parts are related. The following are uses of the discourse organizers covered in this unit.

EXAMPLES	EXPLANATIONS
(a) **First,** we need to examine the root causes of crime in our city, such as lack of education. (b) **After that,** the existing laws and programs should be evaluated. (c) **Finally,** we need to determine who will pay for new programs.	**Use:** to show the sequence of topics or main points **Form:** sequential connectors
(d) **There are** many reasons why crime is increasing in our cities. (e) **Is crime really increasing as much as everyone thinks it is?** The answer to this question may surprise you.	**Use:** to introduce topics **Forms:** *there + be*, rhetorical questions
(f) So far, we have considered the positive side of general education requirements. **Next,** let's look at some of their drawbacks. (g) Lack of education may be one cause of crime. **But what about parental responsibilities in cases of juvenile crime?**	**Use:** to signal topic shifts **Forms:** sequential connectors, rhetorical questions
(h) **To summarize,** the statistics just presented indicate that air quality has been steadily improving during the last decade. (i) This paper examines the contributions of recent immigrants to the state economy. **Overall,** my research will show that immigrants have played a significant role in economic development.	**Use:** to introduce a summary of what has been or will be discussed **Form:** summary connectors
(j) **Should we be paying more tuition when we cannot even get the courses we need to graduate on time?**	**Use:** to emphasize key points, especially in argumentative discourse **Form:** rhetorical questions

EXERCISE 1

Match each of the sentences containing discourse organizers in the first column with topics in the second column. Then identify the form of discourse organizer in each and its apparent use. More than one use might be possible. The first has been done as an example.

▶ **EXAMPLE:** 1. i. (kinship systems); Form: *there + be*; Use: *to introduce a topic*

1. There are two types of family relatives I will discuss today: those involving blood relations and those resulting from marriage.

2. What does your clothing reveal about your identity?

3. To summarize, I have described several types of behavior that are typically regarded as masculine.

4. So far I have discussed the benefits of regular exercise. But what about people who become obsessed with workouts and spend half their lives at the sports club?

5. Lastly, I will talk about adrenaline, which is produced by the adrenal gland and raises blood pressure in stress situations.

6. Is there any reason why women and minorities should earn less than white males in comparable jobs?

7. To start with, we will describe one of the most widely used services, known as e-mail. After that, we will discuss news bulletin boards.

8. Thirdly, let's consider programs that feature real-life police on patrols dealing with violent criminals.

9. There are two main types of theories that can categorize most of modern cosmology: evolutionary theories and continuous creation theories.

10. In summary, my presentation today will provide several compelling reasons why our campus needs more space for cars.

a. How the universe was created and evolved

b. Basics of the internet

c. Violence on television

d. Parking problems on campus

e. Gender roles

f. How people express themselves through their style of dress

g. Major hormones in the human body

h. Starting a physical fitness program

i. Kinship systems in anthropology

j. job equality

Discourse Organizers   **247**

Exercise 1

As mentioned previously, Ss should use Focus 1 as a reference to identify the types of discourse organizers.

Workbook Ex. 1, p. 136.
Answers: TE p. 550.

A N S W E R   K E Y

Exercise 1

2. f *form:* rhetorical question/use: to introduce a topic   3. e *form:* summary connector/use: to introduce a summary of what has been discussed   4. h *form:* rhetorical question/ use: to signal topic shift   5. g *form:* sequential connector/use: to show sequence of topics   6. j *form:* rhetorical question/use: to emphasize a key point   7. b *form:* sequential connectors/use: to show sequence of topics 8. c *form:* sequential connectors/use: to introduce a topic   9. a *form:* there + be/use: to introduce a topic   10. d *form:* summary connector/use: to introduce a summary of what will be discussed

As mentioned earlier, Ss sometimes confuse logical and chronological sequence connectors. For example, they may use *at first*, a chronological connector, to introduce the first point of an argument in an essay.

SUGGESTION

Rather than have Ss plod through all of the examples in this chart section by section, try this approach:

Step 1: Explain the distinction between chronological and logical connectors by pointing out a few examples in the focus box or providing a few of your own.

Step 2: Orient Ss to the organization of this chart, with chronological connectors listed first, followed by connectors that could be used for both types of sequence, and concluding with examples of logical connectors.

Step 3: Ask Ss to skim the chart and check any boldfaced connectors that are unfamiliar to them. Instruct them to pay special attention to these.

Step 4: Tell Ss to use the chart for reference and review as they work through the practices in Exercises 2, 3, and 4.

Note that *chronological* can include narratives and procedures.

FOCUS **2**

▶ Sequential Connectors: Chronological and Logical

EXAMPLES	EXPLANATIONS
	Sequential connectors may be chronological, logical, or both:
(a) **At first,** the lake seemed very cold. **Later,** after we had been swimming for a while, it seemed warmer.	Chronological connectors signal the sequence of events in time, such as the events of a story or the steps of a procedure.
(b) I have several items of business to share with you at this meeting. **First,** I will report on our latest expenditures. **Then,** I will present a proposal for our next ad campaign. **Lastly,** I will tell you about holiday party plans.	Logical connectors organize the sequence of events in a text, such as the parts of a speech or an essay. They are especially common in formal, spoken English contexts, such as presentations and academic lectures.

Chronological

EXAMPLES		CONNECTORS	USES
(c)	**At first,** Frederick didn't like his new neighbor.	*at first*	Beginning
(d)	Eva was running slowly in the race at first. **Eventually** she pulled ahead, though.	*eventually*	Continuation
(e)	Our first destination was Seoul, Korea. **Subsequently** we went to Bangkok, Thailand.	*subsequently*	
(f)	**At last** they reached Vancouver, where they planned to spend the night.	*at last*	Conclusion
(g)	**In the end,** both our hero and his adversary die.	*in the end*	

Chronological or Logical

CHRONOLOGICAL	LOGICAL	CONNECTORS	USES
(h) **First,** turn on the ignition.	**(i)** **First,** let's consider the main issues.	*first*	Beginning
(j) **First of all,** check the gas level.	**(k)** **First of all,** I will discuss the arguments against building the new subdivision.	*first of all*	
(l) **To start with,** open a new file and save it.	**(m)** **To start with,** the developers have not done an environmental impact study.	*to start with*	Beginning
(n) **To begin with,** Matt went to Costa Rica.	**(o)** **To begin with,** let's look at the effects of air pollution in the valley.	*to begin with*	
(p) **Next,** he flew to Venezuela.	**(q)** **Next,** I will explain my opponent's stand on this issue.	*next*	Continuation
(r) **Then,** he traveled to Brazil.	**(s)** **Then,** I will summarize the main points of the debate.	*then*	
(t) **After that,** he visited a friend in Argentina.	**(u)** **After that,** I will evaluate the various arguments.	*after that*	
(v) **Finally,** he spent a few weeks in Chile.	**(w)** **Finally,** I will present the implications of my position.	*finally*	Conclusion
(x) **Lastly,** check the oil level.	**(y)** **Lastly,** new jobs are needed.	*lastly*	

Logical

EXAMPLES	CONNECTORS	USES
(z) **The first type of pollution** I'd like to discuss is that caused by automobiles.	*the first* + noun	Beginning
(aa) **One cause of prejudice** is ignorance.	*one* + noun	
(bb) **In the first place,** we need to get more legislation to help the disabled.	*in the first place*	
(cc) **Secondly,** we also have a problem with noise pollution.	*secondly*	Continuation
(dd) **The second point** concerns the issue of whether. . . .	*the/a second (third, fourth,* etc.*)* + noun	
(ee) **A second question we might ask** is who should take responsibility for the homeless?		
(ff) **In the second place,** we need to change our attitudes.	*in the second place*	
(gg) **The last reason** is one I am sure everyone is aware of.	*the last* + noun	Conclusion
(hh) **A final question** might be how we will fund our project.	*a final* + noun	
(ii) **To conclude,** pollution is obviously getting worse in our city.	*to conclude*	
(jj) **In conclusion,** parents must take a more active role in schools.	*in conclusion*	

Exercise 2

E X P A N S I O N

After they complete the exercise, have Ss choose one numbered statement as the topic to write a paragraph. Have them write the paragraph for homework.

EXERCISE 2

Make up a sentence with a beginning sequential connector that could follow each of the sentences below. Try to use a variety of connectors.

▶ **EXAMPLE:** *My family is very special.* **In the first place,** *my father and mother have worked very hard to provide all of us an education.*

1. My family is very special.
2. Learning to do word processing is simple.
3. I appreciate many of the things my friends do for me.
4. Smoking can cause a lot of health problems.
5. We need to start taking major steps to save our planet.
6. When I started learning English, I encountered many difficulties.
7. A person who has really had an influence on my life is (*put person's name here*).

A N S W E R   K E Y

Exercise 2

Answers will vary. Examples:
2. The first thing you need to do is familiarize yourself with program commands. 3. One thing I appreciate is their helping me out with transportation. 4. One problem is that it can lead to heart disease. 5. One thing we need to do is stop the destruction of the ozone layer. 6. To begin with, the word order of sentences in English is different from that of my native language. 7. . . . is my aunt. First of all, she was the one who encouraged me to go to college.

EXERCISE 3

For five of the sentences below, write a list of ideas that could follow, using beginning, continuation, and concluding sequential connectors in your list. Try to use a variety of connectors.

▶ **EXAMPLE:** I can think of several things I don't have that I'd like to have. *To start with, I'd like to have a really good camera. Next, I wouldn't mind having a new car. Lastly, I'd love to have my own house.*

1. There are several things I'd like to do on my next vacation.
2. Our school could use a few improvements.
3. I have a few gripes about _____ . (You pick the topic.)
4. I think I have made progress in several areas during the past few years.
5. My home (apartment/room) is a comfortable place for several reasons.
6. Several world problems seem especially critical to me.
7. I have several goals for my future.

EXERCISE 4

Exchange the paragraph you wrote for the Opening Task with either your partner for that task or another classmate. Did your classmate use any sequential connectors in the paragraph? If so, which ones? If not, would any of the connectors in Focus 2 be appropriate to organize ideas in the paragraph? Discuss your analysis with your classmate.

Exercise 3
EXPANSION

To work further on writing skills, Ss could choose one item and elaborate on each of the sentences in their list with an additional sentence that describes, gives reasons, or in some other way explains further each sentence.

Workbook Ex. 2, p. 137; Exs. 3, Ex. 4, p. 138. Answers: TE p. 550.

ANSWER KEY

Exercise 3

Answers will vary. Example:
2. First of all, more courses could be offered. Secondly, there could be more sections of each course. Finally, the classrooms could be remodeled to be more comfortable.

Exercise 4

This exercise is based on paragraphs Ss wrote. Responses will be based on paragraph analysis.

There + Be is a very common introducing phrase in classification texts.
This chart includes a list of quantifiers and abstract nouns following *there are* in (d), which should provide useful vocabulary to Ss in formal writing and speech contexts.

SUGGESTIONS

1. Remind Ss that subject-verb agreement is needed between the *Be* verb and the noun phrase that follows the verb. Note that all the examples here requiring subject-verb agreement (i.e., all except modal verbs) have plural forms of *Be*.

2. Call attention to the sequential connectors in the boxed chart. Note that the chart offers parallel forms of sequential connectors, as illustrated in horizontal rows. Although some are interchangeable (e.g., *first, secondly*), others are not, so Ss need to be careful with their choices. Remind Ss that they do not use *firstly* as a connector preceding *secondly*, etc.

FOCUS **3**

There + Be as a Topic Introducer

There + be often introduces a topic that the speaker or writer has classified into different parts.

EXAMPLES	EXPLANATIONS
(a) **There are** three ways to get to the freeway from campus. (b) **There were** four principal causes for the recession. (c) **There could be** several explanations for this child's behavior.	The *be* verb can be any tense and can follow a modal verb such as *can, could,* or *may*.
(d) There are { three / a few / several / many / a number of } { aspects / causes / effects / factors / methods / principles / reasons / rules / stages / steps / strengths / theories / ways } to consider.	Noun phrases that come after the *be* verb often include a number or a quantifier (for example, *four, several*) and an abstract general noun (for example, *aspects, reasons*).
(e) There are **three kinds of** rhetorical questions. (f) There are **several types of** students.	Classifying phrases such as *kinds of* or *types of* often follow *there + be*.
(g) There are many driving rules to keep in mind when you get behind the wheel. **The first** rule of the road is to be courteous to other drivers. (h) There are five stages in this process. **In the first stage**, water is drawn through a tube.	You may use sequential connectors, as shown in Focus 2, to organize topics that follow an introduction with *there + be*.

Beginning	Continuing	Ending
first	*second, third,* etc.	*last*
first of all	*secondly*	*finally*
to start with	*next*	*lastly*
the first + noun	*the second, the third,* etc. + noun	*the last* + noun
one	*a second, a third,* etc.	*the last*
one + noun	*a second* + noun, etc.	*a final* + noun
in the first place	*in the second place*	*finally*

The sequential connectors in this chart are most often used for subtopics after *there + be* introducers.

Composition books often caution writers against overusing *there + be*. This is good advice to avoid wordiness; keep in mind that this is not the only way to introduce a topic.

EXERCISE 5

Fill in the blanks with appropriate words or phrases from Focus 3. Use different forms of connectors for each passage. Add commas where needed.

▶ **EXAMPLE:** <u>There are</u> two <u>kinds</u> of twins. <u>The first</u> is called identical. <u>The second</u> is called fraternal.

1. (a) _____ three (b) _____ of extrasensory perception, or ESP, that I will be discussing in today's lecture. (c) _____ I will talk about telepathy, perhaps the best known and most researched area. (d) _____ I will explain telekinesis, which concerns the ability to move a distant object through will power alone. (e) _____ I will describe the phenomenon of precognition, which involves knowing ahead of time about an event.

2. If you have pollen allergies, (a) _____ a number of (b) _____ that you might try to avoid pollen. (c) _____ stay in an air-conditioned room. (d) _____ when you drive, keep your windows up and your air conditioning on. (e) _____ shower as soon as you go inside after being exposed to a lot of pollen. (f) _____ get an air-filter system in your home. (g) _____ if you live in the United States, move to Europe! That continent does not have the ragweed pollen that plagues people in the United States.

3. (a) _____ three main (b) _____ in the process of making rayon, a fabric produced from soft woods and other vegetable materials. (c) _____ the material is pulped. (d) _____ it is treated with caustic soda, nitric acid, and other substances until it turns into a liquid. (e) _____ it is forced through tiny holes in metal, forming liquid filaments which solidify into threads.

4. (a) _____ of pasta, with a great variety of shapes. (b) _____ is macaroni, which is a curved tube. (c) _____ is fettuccine, which looks like a thin ribbon.

Exercise 5

Encourage Ss to vary the connectors they use to complete this exercise.

A N S W E R   K E Y

Exercise 5
Answers will vary. Examples:
1. **(a)** There are **(b)** types/kinds **(c)** To begin **(d)** Then **(e)** Last 2. **(a)** There are **(b)** things **(c)** First of all **(d)** Secondly **(e)** Next **(f)** Then **(g)** Finally 3. **(a)** There are **(b)** steps **(c)** To start with **(d)** Next **(e)** Next 4. **(a)** There are many types **(b)** One is **(c)** A second **(d)** another **(e)** A fourth type **(f)** A fifth type is

Capelletti is (d) _____ ; it is shaped like a hat.
(e) _____ is ravioli; it is square-shaped and stuffed with
cheese or meat. (f) _____ is rotelle, which has a
corkscrew shape. And these are only a few of them!

EXERCISE 6

Write a sentence with *there + be* to introduce a classification for each topic below. Then write at least two or three sentences that could develop the topic.

▶ **EXAMPLE:** *There are three grammar points we will cover this week. One is rel-*
ative clauses. A second is generic articles. The last is the condi-
tional form of verbs.

1. Types of books you like the best
2. Things that you think make a good movie or TV program
3. Topics that you are covering in a particular class for a specific
   amount of time (a week, a quarter, a semester)
4. Steps for performing a procedure that you know how to do (replacing a printer cartridge, solving a math problem, studying for an
   exam, parallel parking)
5. Professions or careers that would be good for someone who likes
   people
6. A topic of your choice

EXERCISE 7

Look again at the paragraph you wrote for the Opening Task on page 245. Did
you use a *there + be* introductory phrase? If so, read your sentence to the class.
If not, make up a sentence that might be used to develop one of your questions,
using *there + be* as an introducer.

Exercise 6
EXPANSION

Like many of the exercises in this unit, this
one could be expanded into a paragraph or
short essay assignment, with Ss choosing
one of the topics.

Workbook Ex. 5, p. 139.
Answers: TE p. 550.

Exercise 6
Answers will vary. Examples:
1. There are two types of books I like the best.
One is science fiction. The second is mysteries.
2. There are four things that I think make a
good movie. First of all, it has to have a good
story. Secondly, the characters need to be
believable. Thirdly, at least some of the
characters have to be likable. Finally, the
technical aspects have to be done well.

Exercise 7
Answers will vary. Responses depend on
paragraphs written for the opening task.

▶ Summary Connectors

Summary connectors also help to organize discourse. Some of these connectors signal that the ideas expressed summarize what has been said before.

EXAMPLES		CONNECTORS	USE
(a)	**In summary,** drug abuse is a major problem today.	*in summary*	General summary
(b)	**To summarize,** we should all exercise our right to vote.	*to summarize*	
(c)	**As has been previously stated,** many people did not consider AIDS a serious problem at first.	*as (has been) previously stated/ mentioned*	Review of main idea

Some summary connectors can be used either for introductions—summarizing what is to be presented—or for conclusions, summarizing what has already been stated.

LINK TO FOLLOWING DISCOURSE (INTRODUCTION)		LINK TO PRECEDING DISCOURSE (CONCLUSION)		CONNECTORS	USE
(d)	I have been asked to report on our recent experiments. **All in all,** they have been very successful.	(e)	From the presentation I have just given, I hope you will agree that, **all in all,** our experiments have been successful.	*all in all*	Summary of points
(f)	**Overall,** the quality of television appears to be declining. For example, the news is becoming more and more like entertainment.	(g)	From the evidence I have presented in this essay, it appears, **overall,** the quality of television is declining.	*overall*	
(h)	**Briefly,** the arguments for gun control can be summed up in the following way.	(i)	**Briefly,** so far I have discussed three of the arguments for gun control.	*briefly*	Condensation of points
(j)	**In short,** the arguments against euthanasia, which I will discuss next, are mostly religious ones.	(k)	**In short,** as I have shown, the arguments against euthanasia are mostly religious ones.	*in short*	

Most of your Ss will probably be familiar with the most common summary connectors (*in summary, to summarize*). However, the second part of this chart, which shows connectors that link to both following and preceding discourse, may be new information to many.

SUGGESTION

Ask Ss to indicate their knowledge of the connectors in the second half of the chart by stating whether connectors are (a) unfamiliar, (b) part of passive vocabulary (discourse connectors) they have encountered but haven't used, or (c) part of their active vocabulary (connectors they use in their own writing or speech). *All in all* and *in short* are expressions that advanced Ss may have heard but may not ever have used.

Exercise 8

SUGGESTION

After group work, have Ss turn in their summary statements so that you can check their understanding of how these connectors are used.

Workbook Ex. 6, p. 141.
Answers: TE p. 551.

EXERCISE 8

Choose three of the sentences or brief passages below. Write a summary statement for each. Use the summary connector indicated in parentheses. In small groups, compare the summary statements you wrote with those of your classmates.

▶ **EXAMPLE:** My paper will discuss the problem of overpopulation. (briefly)
    Summary statement: *Briefly, overpopulation is a serious threat to the survival of all life on earth.*

1. Today, I'd like to talk about something I know every one of you is concerned about. (briefly)

2. By hooking a computer into a national electronic system, you can communicate and get information in a number of ways. For example, you can send and receive messages from others who have subscribed to the system or get the weather report for the day. You can take courses or play computer games. You can make travel reservations or look up information in an encyclopedia. (all in all)

3. Without iron, the body wouldn't have hemoglobin, which is an essential protein. Hemoglobin, found in red blood cells, carries oxygen to the rest of the body. A deficiency of iron can cause headaches and fatigue. (in short)

4. Good friendships do not develop easily; they require effort. You need to make time for your friends. You should be prepared to work out problems as they arise, since things will not always go smoothly. You shouldn't expect perfection from your friends. (in summary)

5. So far I have discussed several of the causes and effects of divorce. (as has been previously mentioned)

6. There are several things to keep in mind if you want to train a dog to obey you. First, you need a lot of patience. Secondly, you should not punish your dog for misbehaving but rather correct the inappropriate behavior. You should never hit a dog unless it is threatening to bite someone. Finally, remember to praise your dog for behaving properly. (all in all)

7. Fellow classmates: We have finally reached this proud moment, when we will receive our diplomas as testimony of our many achievements. In my speech to you this afternoon, I would like to stress what I believe is one of the most important purposes of education. (briefly)

8. In many American cities, it's difficult to get much real news from the local television news programs. For example, the local news on a typical hot summer day might feature interviews with people who are complaining about the weather and perhaps a look at this season's swimwear fashions. You may find out how much money a blockbuster movie made at the box office over the weekend. Another "news" segment might tell you about some new product that you can buy. (overall)

256 | UNIT 14

ANSWER KEY

Exercise 8

Answers will vary. Examples:
1. Briefly, we have a serious problem with homelessness in our city.   2. All in all, there are numerous benefits in connecting to one of these systems.   3. In short, we can't do without iron.   4. In summary, you need to work at being a good friend.   5. As has been previously mentioned, children are sometimes better off in single-parent families, especially if there has been violence in the home prior to divorce.   6. All in all, positive reinforcement is the best way to get your dog to behave properly.   7. Briefly, I think our education should prepare us to contribute to society.   8. Overall, some news shows seem more like commercials than news.

Rhetorical Questions to Introduce and Shift Topics

Rhetorical questions, unlike other questions, are not used to ask for information. Two uses of rhetorical questions are to introduce a topic and to shift from one topic to a new one.

EXAMPLES	EXPLANATIONS
(a) How does nitrogen circulate? **(b)** What are the most common causes of fatigue? **(c)** Is aggression a part of human nature? **(d)** Can Congress save the budget?	The form of a rhetorical question may be either a *Wh*-question (*who, what, when, where, why*) or a *yes/no* question.
(e) "What Is a University?" by John Henry Newman **(f)** "Are Women Human?" by Dorothy Sayers **(g)** "Were Dinosaurs Dumb?" by Stephen Jay Gould	Titles of books, articles, and speeches also use rhetorical questions to introduce topics.
(h) Remember the great health care debate?* **(i)** So far, we have looked at some of the causes of teenage gangs. But what are the effects on the communities in which they live?	Rhetorical questions may introduce background information about a topic. We also use rhetorical questions to signal a shift from one subtopic to another.

*Note that this question leaves off the first two words, *"Do you,"* of the full question form for an informal, conversational tone.

EXERCISE 9

The excerpts below are from the beginning paragraphs of books, articles, or essays. For each, predict what the rest of the text might be about.

1. What do we know about the universe, and how do we know it? Where did the universe come from, and where is it going? Did the universe have a beginning, and if so, what happened before then? What is the nature of time? Will it ever come to an end?

2. Are you as white knuckled as I am when traveling as an air passenger? What's it worth to save a buck?

3. Do you believe that the more you diet, the harder it is to lose weight because your body adapts and turns down your rate of burning calories—your metabolism?

4. Why is it that when newspapers are confronted with a story that has anything to do with sex, they often screw it up?

Discourse Organizers | **257**

This is the first of two charts that explain the forms and uses of rhetorical questions in organizing texts. In this focus box, the rhetorical question examples introduce or shift topics. In both cases, then, they introduce new topics. Most of the examples are taken from real texts.

Writer and speakers use rhetorical questions to engage their readers and listeners, i.e., to make them active participants in the reading or listening activity. They also show the writer's/speaker's awareness of audience, since the rhetorical questions suggest a dialogue between writer/reader or speaker/listener.

SUGGESTION

Discuss the reasons writers and speakers use rhetorical questions for topic introductions and shifts. Why not use declarative phrases or sentences instead (e.g., How Nitrogen Circulates, The Most Common Causes for Fatigue) ?
Use the examples in the focus box to raise questions about usage. Ask Ss how they feel about rhetorical questions they encounter in reading. Do they usually seem more effective than a statement?

Exercise 9
SUGGESTION

Since this exercise is brief and has some difficult vocabulary, it may work best as a whole class discussion. In this way, you can explain idiomatic usage such as *white knuckled* (nervous) in 2, *screw it up* (do it the wrong way) in 4.

Workbook Ex. 7, p. 142.
Answers: TE p. 551.

The rhetorical questions explained here are those used to emphasize rather than introduce points.

SUGGESTION

Step 1: Create a transparency or handout of a current newspaper editorial or magazine essay that uses a number of rhetorical questions so Ss can see questions in context. The "Turning Point" essays in *Newsweek Magazine* are often good sources for rhetorical questions as are syndicated columns on editorial pages of newspapers. Underline the questions.

Step 2: Have Ss analyze the functions of the rhetorical questions.

FOCUS **6**

▶ Rhetorical Questions to Focus on Main Points

Another kind of rhetorical question focuses the listener/reader on the main points of a topic and emphasizes the speaker/writer's viewpoint. It is sometimes called a "leading question."

EXAMPLES	SPEAKER/WRITER VIEWPOINT	EXPLANATIONS
(a) Haven't we had enough wars?	We have.	Leading rhetorical questions seek agreement from the listener or reader. They imply a *yes* answer. In other words, from the writer's or speaker's viewpoint, a negative answer is not possible.
(b) Don't divorced fathers as well as mothers have rights?	They do.	
(c) Isn't English hard enough to learn without all those different article usage rules?	It is.	
(d) We've had enough wars, haven't we?	We have.	Leading questions have the same meaning as negative tag questions that seek agreement (falling tone in spoken English).
(e) What kind of solution is that to our problem?	It is a bad solution.	Another type of rhetorical question that focuses on main points implies a response in the negative. In other words, the speaker/writer will not take *yes* for an answer.
(f) How much longer can we ignore the signs of global warming?	We can't ignore them any longer.	
(g) Who was more committed to nonviolence than Gandhi?	No one was more committed.	

EXERCISE 10

Write a leading rhetorical question to express each of the following opinions. More than one form is possible, and some ideas need to be rephrased, not just transformed into a question. State the positive implication of each in parentheses.

▶ **EXAMPLE:** Opinion: We've gone far enough in the space race.
Possible questions and implications:
Isn't it time to stop the space race? (It is.)
Haven't we gone far enough in the space race? (We have.)
Shouldn't we consider stopping the space race? (We should.)

1. Our senior citizens deserve more respect.
2. We need to start thinking more globally.
3. Our school already has too many required courses.
4. Women deserve the same job opportunities as men.
5. All people should have a place to live.

EXERCISE 11

State the writer's viewpoint for each of the following rhetorical questions. Then state what you think is the thesis (the main point) of each text that follows. Discuss which of the questions you find most effective in making their points.

▶ **EXAMPLE:** How many Americans can afford a $45,000 Mercedes-Benz? Should auto safety be reserved only for the wealthy?
Writer's viewpoint: *Not many Americans can afford a Mercedes and auto safety should not be reserved for only the wealthy.*
Thesis: *Auto safety devices should be put on all cars, not just expensive cars.*

1. Fair-minded people have to be against bigotry. How, then, can fair-minded people ignore, condone, or promote discrimination against divorced fathers—100 percent of whom are men—and make believe it isn't discrimination?
2. I am, I hope, a reasonably intelligent and sensitive man who tries to think clearly about what he does. And what I do is hunt, and sometimes kill . . . Does the power that orchestrates the universe give a deer more importance than a fly quivering in a strip of sticky tape?
3. One of the more popular [comic book] characters is Wolverine, a psychopath with retractable metal claws embedded in his hands and a set of killer instincts that makes him a threat to friend and foe alike. This is a proper role model for children?

Exercise 10
VARIATION

Replace or add items that you think are more timely or interesting for your Ss.

Exercise 11
SUGGESTION

These authentic texts have sophisticated vocabulary. Provide or elicit synonyms for some of the words before Ss work on this exercise:
1. bigotry: prejudice
   condone: approve of
   promote: encourage
2. the power that orchestrates the universe: the creator of the universe
   quivering: shaking
3. psychopath: criminally insane person
   retractable: able to bring inside
4. fatal: deadly
   overbite: a person's upper teeth overlap the lower teeth

ANSWER KEY

Exercise 10
Answers will vary. Examples:
1. Don't our senior citizens deserve more respect? (Implication: They do). 2. Shouldn't we start thinking more globally? (Implication: we should). 3. Aren't there too many required courses in our school already? (Implication: There are). 4. Isn't it time to give women the same job opportunities as men? (Implication: It is). 5. All people should have a place to live, shouldn't they? (Implication: They should.)

Exercise 11
1. Fair-minded people cannot ignore, condone, or promote such discrimination against divorced fathers. Nor can they make believe it isn't discrimination. 2. The power that orchestrates the universe does not give a deer more importance than a fly quivering in a strip of sticky tape. 3. This is not a proper model for children. 4. No murders are accounted for by these dental problems. 5. Everyone needs a moisturizer!

Exercise 12

S U G G E S T I O N S

1. Find out if any of your Ss are familiar with the work of Isaac Asimov.
2. If time permits, call on Ss to read paragraphs aloud. After each paragraph, identify any rhetorical questions and analyze what functions they serve to develop the essay.

Note: Some Ss have challenged the logic of Asimov's argument. Your Ss may want to comment on the validity of his claims.

UNIT GOAL REVIEW

Ask Ss to look at the goals on the opening page of the unit again. Help them understand how much they have accomplished in each area.

---

4. In 1977 the federal government spent twice as much on dental research as it did on alcoholism research. How many murders and fatal accidents are accounted for by impacted wisdom teeth or unsightly overbite?

5.

EXERCISE 12

The following excerpts from an essay by Isaac Asimov use six rhetorical questions to develop an argument about the need for population control. Identify the rhetorical questions. Then discuss how the author uses them to develop his ideas. What is the overall effect of the questions? Discuss which ones you think are most effective in emphasizing key points and introducing subtopics.

LET'S SUPPOSE . . .

Suppose the whole world became industrialized and that industry and science worked very carefully and very well. How many people could such a world support? Different limits have been suggested, but the highest figure I have seen is twenty billion. How long will it take before the world contains so many people?

For the sake of argument, and to keep things simple, let's suppose the demographic growth rate will stay as it is, at two per cent per annum. . . . At the present growth rate our planet will contain all the people that an industrialized world may be able to support by about 2060 A.D. . . .

Suppose we decide to hope for the best. Let us suppose that a change *will* take place in the next seventy years and that there will be a new age in which population can continue rising to a far higher level than we think it can now. . . . Let's suppose that this sort of thing can just keep on going forever.

Is there any way of setting a limit past which nothing can raise the human population no matter how many changes take place?

Suppose we try to invent a real limit; something so huge that no one can imagine a population rising past it. Suppose we imagine that there are so many men and women and children in the world, that altogether they

---

A N S W E R   K E Y

Exercise 12

Rhetorical Questions

Paragraph 1: How many people could such a world support? How long will it take before the world contains so many people?

Paragraph 4: Is there any way of setting a limit past which nothing can raise the human population no matter how many changes take place?

Paragraph 7: How long, then, will it take for the world's population to weigh as much as the entire planet?

Paragraph 9: Do you suppose that perhaps in the course of the next 1,600 years, it will be possible to colonize the Moon and Mars, and

the other planets of the Solar System? Do you think that we might get many millions of people into the other world in the next 1,600 years and thus lower the population of the Earth itself?

Discussion:

In this excerpt, Asimov uses all of these questions to introduce the topics that follow by providing answers to the questions. These questions help to organize Asimov's hypothetical situation and to involve the reader in wondering about the answers to the questions. (If X happened, what would Y be like? What could we do about X?) They also anticipate possible reader responses as in paragraph 9.

weigh as much as the whole planet does. Surely you can't expect there can be more people than that.

Let us suppose that the average human being weighs sixty kilogrammes. If that's the case then 100,000,000,000,000,000,000 people would weigh as much as the whole Earth does. That number of people is 30,000,000,000,000 times as many people as there are living now.

. . . Let us suppose that the population growth-rate stays at 2.0 percent so that the number of people in the world continues to double every thirty-five years. How long, then, will it take for the world's population to weigh as much as the entire planet?

The answer is—not quite 1600 years. This means that by 3550 A.D., the human population would weigh as much as the entire Earth. Nor is 1600 years a long time. It is considerably less time than has passed since the days of Julius Caesar.

Do you suppose that perhaps in the course of the next 1600 years, it will be possible to colonize the moon and Mars, and the other planets of the solar system? Do you think that we might get many millions of people into the other world in the next 1600 years and thus lower the population of the Earth itself?

Even if that were possible, it wouldn't give us much time. If the growth-rate stays at 2.0 percent, then in a little over 2200 years—say by 4220 A.D.—the human population would weigh as much as the entire Solar system, including the Sun.

From Isaac Asimov, *Earth: Our Crowded Spaceship,* Fawcett, Greenwich, CT, 1974.

USE YOUR ENGLISH

The activities on these "purple pages" at the end of the unit contain situations that should naturally elicit the unit's structures in a more communicative framework. While Ss are doing these activities in class, you can circulate and listen to determine if they have actually achieved the goals in the opening page of the unit.

Activity 1

Play textbook audio. The tapescript for this listening appears on p. 570 of this book.

Ss may need to hear the tape two or three times in order to get both the main ideas and the discourse organizers.

Activity 2
EXPANSION

Have Ss bring in a scrambled description of a common procedure, using the apple pie recipe as a model, and have a partner put the steps in order.

Workbook Ex. 8, p. 143; Ex. 9, p. 144.
Answers: TE p. 551.

Use Your English

ACTIVITY 1: LISTENING/ WRITING/SPEAKING

You may at times have wished you had a photographic memory—that is, one that remembers everything it receives as input—especially when you need to study for an exam. However, not being able to forget anything can be detrimental, as case histories in abnormal psychology have shown. You will hear a brief psychology lecture on the benefits of forgetting. Listen for the discourse organizers (sequential connectors, *there + be*, summary connectors, rhetorical questions) that the speaker uses as cues to introduce topics and focus on the main points. Take notes on the main ideas of the lecture on a separate sheet of paper. Then, listen to the tape one more time and write down the discourse organizers the speaker used to organize the lecture. Compare your notes and the list of discourse organizers with several classmates.

ACTIVITY 2: READING/WRITING

Are you familiar with the saying "It's as American as baseball, motherhood, and apple pie"? The apple pie reference probably means eating it rather than making it, but here's a chance to test your knowledge of American cooking. The recipe below explains how to make an apple pie. The directions, however, are not in the proper sequence. In small groups or with a partner, rewrite the steps of the recipe. Add sequential connectors to some of the sentences to help organize the text.

APPLE PIE

- Stir the mixed ingredients with the apples until the apples are well coated.
- Dot the top of the pie with ½ tablespoon of butter before putting on the top crust.
- Line a 9-inch pie pan with a pie crust; put aside while you prepare the apple filling.
- Cover the pie with a top crust and bake it in a 450-degree oven for 30 minutes.
- Peel, core, and cut 5 to 6 cups of apples into very thin pieces.
- Place the coated apples in layers in the pie shell.
- When the pie comes out of the oven, sprinkle 1 cup of grated cheese on top and put it under a broiler to melt the cheese.
- Combine and sift over the apple slices ½ cup of brown sugar, ⅛ teaspoon of salt, 1 tablespoon of cornstarch, and ¼ teaspoon of cinnamon.

262 UNIT 14

ANSWER KEY

Activity 1

Discourse Organizers Used: Who has not wished for a photographic memory? All in all; at first; later; finally; first of all; secondly; a third problem; in short

Activity 2

Order in directions: Line 9-in. pie pan. . . ; peel, core, and cut. . . ; combine and sift. . . ; stir mixed ingredients. . . ; place coated apples. . . ; dot top of the pie. . . ; cover the pie. . . ; when the pie comes out of the oven . . .

ACTIVITY 3: WRITING/READING/SPEAKING

Think of a topic that can be classified into parts or aspects (kinds of things, steps in a process, etc.), choosing something that your classmates would know something about. Write a sentence for the topic using *there are*.

▶ **EXAMPLES:** *There are lots of things you need to be aware of when you're driving.*
There are several ways to get from campus to the airport.
There are many kinds of students at this school.

Exchange papers with another classmate and write one thing/way/kind etc. that could develop the topic. When you are through, exchange again with a different student and add something to another paper. Use appropriate connectors. Continue exchanging papers until each has at least three or four sentences that develop the topic. Read some of the results aloud.

ACTIVITY 4: SPEAKING OR WRITING

Expand one of the following topics into a short talk, using discourse organizers. Present your talk to the class or in small groups.
- *There are a number of things a new student to this campus should be told when he or she gets here.*
- *There are several (or many) goals I have for the future.*
- Choose one of the topics mentioned in the Opening Task, focus boxes, or exercises in this unit.

ACTIVITY 5: READING/WRITING/SPEAKING

Look through magazines and newspapers for evidence of rhetorical questions in advertisements. Discuss the kinds of questions that are used to sell products. Then create your own ad for a product, either a written one that might be used in a magazine or a script that could be used for a TV or radio commercial. Share your creations with the class; if possible, perform the commercials.

ACTIVITY 6: WRITING

Choose one of the topics from the Opening Task on page 245 or another issue that interests you. Write a persuasive essay in which you express an opinion on the topic. Try to convince your readers of the validity of your viewpoint. Use appropriate discourse organizers in developing your essay.

Activity 3

If some Ss find it difficult to develop any of their classmates' ideas, encourage them to be creative. For example, a student developing the second topic in the example could write about travel routes or modes of transportation.

Activity 4
VARIATIONS

1. Have Ss write a paragraph or essay rather than create an oral report.
2. Have Ss brainstorm new topics for this activity focusing on campus or local issues. They can brainstorm individually, in small gropus, or as a class with you writing their ideas on the board.

Activity 5
VARIATION

Another option for an ad would be to create a website for a product.

Activity 6
VARIATION

The class could hold a debate on one of the topics, with teams collaborating on a presentation using discourse organizers.

The test for this unit can be found on pp. 510–511.
The answers are on p. 512.

Unit 15

UNIT OVERVIEW

This unit begins with a review of conditional forms and then covers conditional forms that are especially challenging even for advanced students (Ss).

UNIT GOALS

Review the goals listed on this page so Ss understand what they should be able to know by the end of the unit.

OPENING TASK

Like other Opening Tasks, this one strongly prompts but does not force use of the structure being focused on since the task is fairly open-ended and interactive. Examples of the conditionals *only if* and *unless* are presented in the opening quoted statements.

The task asks Ss to discuss the rules, regulations, and hardships experienced by older family members when those members were young.

SETTING UP THE TASK

To engage Ss in the topic, tell them a story about what your own older relatives have described regarding the restrictions or hardships they encountered, or some of the ones you experienced when you were growing up. Use some examples of this unit's conditional structures in your story.

UNIT 15

CONDITIONALS

Only, If, Unless, Even Though, Even If

UNIT GOALS:

- To know the different kinds of conditional sentences in English
- To use *only if, unless, not unless,* and *if not* correctly to express conditions
- To know the difference between *even though* and *even if* and use them correctly
- To use conditional forms to give advice

▶ OPENING TASK
When They Were Young

"When I was young, we went out to eat only if it was a special occasion."

"When I was a child, we were lucky if we went to the movies a few times a year!"

"When I was your age, we couldn't leave the table unless we asked permission."

Do these comments sound familiar? Part of the process of growing up is listening to your parents, grandparents, or other older relatives tell you how things were different "back then" or "when we were your age."

STEP 1   In many societies, life in the past was more difficult than it is now, and children had less freedom than they do today. Consider what your older relatives (parents, grandparents, etc.) have told you about the way life was for them when they were younger. List some of the rules, restrictions, and hardships they have described.

STEP 2   In small groups, write down some of the things your older relatives could not do as a result of the rules, restrictions, and hardships. Here are some examples:

▶ **EXAMPLES:**   *Bertha's mother couldn't drive a car even after she got her license unless one of her parents went with her.*

     Antonio's great aunt could go out on dates only if one of her older brothers went along.

     To support his family, Hyung's grandfather took a job as a grocery store clerk in the United States even though he had owned his own business in Korea.

STEP 3   Report some of your group's most interesting descriptions to the rest of the class. Discuss whether you think your older relatives would enjoy being young now. Explain why or why not. Give some examples of things that they would probably like or things they would dislike.

CONDUCTING THE TASK

Step 1

Ss should brainstorm ideas individually first.

Step 2

The examples here are intended to encourage Ss' use of conditional forms.

Step 3

The Ss' oral reports of their discussion may provide opportunities for you to transform some of their findings into conditional statements. You may be able to raise additional questions using conditional forms: *So, Pietro, you say that your grandfather had to work seven days a week. Did he have to work even if there was a special holiday?* Encourage Ss to ask questions also.

VARIATION

If time does not permit doing the entire activity, cut the last parts of this step and just have Ss report the group findings.

The chart in this focus box provides an overview of conditional forms. The four exercises that follow help Ss review their previous study of conditional tenses before focusing on the special forms in this unit.

For homework, ask Ss to review the three types of conditionals (and their subclassifications) on the first page of this chart. The second part of the chart on p. 267 serves as a reference guide for Ss to return to when they need it. The focus of classwork in reviewing these forms should be on examples (a)–(i).

S U G G E S T I O N

To review the various conditional tenses, ask Ss questions that prompt the various forms: *If you miss the registration deadline for classes, what happens? Midori, if you have free time on the weekends, what do you usually do? When you were younger, how did your parents usually act if they didn't want you to do something or go somewhere with your friends?* Write responses on the board, label the types (e.g., general truth, etc.) and note the corresponding examples in the focus box.

FOCUS **1**

▶ Review of Conditional Sentences with *If*

EXAMPLES	EXPLANATIONS
General Truth (a) If you **are** sixty-five or older, you **qualify** for senior citizen discounts.	**Factual Conditionals** One common type of factual conditional describes general truths. This type of conditional is often used in the sciences to describe physical laws.
Habitual Present (b) If my great-grandmother **comes** over, we usually **go** to the park.	Another common type of factual conditional refers to habitual events. The event may be present or past.
Habitual Past (c) When my mother was young, if relatives **visited** on Sunday, they **stayed** all day.	
Inference: Explicit (d) If that **was** grandmother on the phone, she **must have missed** the train.	A third type of factual conditional infers something. The inference may be explicit or implicit. In explicit inference, the main-clause verb includes the modal *must* or *should*.
Inference: Implicit (e) If that **is** grandmother on the phone, she **is** still in Connecticut.	
(f) If my great-grandmother **comes** tomorrow, we **may go** to the park.	**Future Conditionals** These conditionals describe future events.
Present Hypothetical (g) If we **lived** closer to our grandparents, we **would see** them more often. (We don't live close to our grandparents; we don't see them as often as we would like to.)	**Hypothetical Conditionals** The present hypothetical conditional describes conditions that are untrue or hypothetical.
(h) If my great-grandmother **were** alive today, she **might** not **approve** of the tattoos that many young people have.	
Past Hypothetical (i) If my great-aunt **had been born** about fifty years later, she **might have been** a doctor instead of a nurse.	Past hypothetical conditionals describe conditions and results that were unreal or untrue in the past.

Summary of Verb Tenses Used With Conditional Sentences

TYPE OF CONDITIONAL	IF-CLAUSE	MAIN CLAUSE
Factual: general truth Factual: habitual	simple present simple present simple past	simple present simple present simple past
Factual: inferential	simple present simple past *will* *be going to* } + base verb	various tenses
Future	simple present	*will* *could* *may* } + base verb *might* *be going to*
Hypothetical: Present	simple past or subjunctive *were*	*would* *could* } + base verb *might*
Hypothetical: Past	past perfect (*had* + past participle)	*would have* *could have* } + past participle *might have*

EXERCISE 1

To review verb tenses for conditional tenses, complete each of the blanks by writing the appropriate form of the verb in parentheses. The first has been done as an example.

1. If my aunts and uncles (go) _____*go*_____ out for dinner, they always (eat) _____*eat*_____ at the same Italian restaurant.

2. My mother has two older sisters. She told me that if she (be) _____ the oldest in the family, her parents (expect) _____ her to do much of the housework, so she was glad that she was the youngest child.

Exercise 1
S U G G E S T I O N

Assign this as a follow-up homework exercise to the oral review conducted using the Focus 1 conditional tenses. Use this to diagnose Ss' knowledge of tenses in conditional forms. Review tenses as needed.

A N S W E R   K E Y

Exercise 1
2. had been; would have expected
3. comes; will bring   4. will telephone; am staying/stay   5. had; would make   6. is;
must be   7. disagree; should remember
8. will spend; finishes   9. is; will have/has
10. went; would miss

3. If my brother (come) _____ for a visit from Ecuador next summer, he (bring) _____ his entire family, including two dogs and a parrot.

4. I (telephone) _____ my family this weekend if I (stay) _____ in town.

5. If my family and I (have) _____ the time, we (make) _____ videotapes of all of our older relatives to create a family history. We never seem to have much free time, though.

6. If that package we just got (be) _____ from Uncle Carlos, it (must, be) _____ my birthday present.

7. If family members (disagree) _____ about values, they (should, remember) _____ that it is natural for different generations to think differently.

8. Gretchen (spend) _____ the whole year with her grandfather in Berlin if she (finish) _____ her senior project before June.

9. Could you see who's at the door? If that (be) _____ my sister, she (have) _____ the charcoal for the barbecue.

10. We're not going on vacation until next month. If we (go) _____ now, we (miss) _____ seeing my cousins, who are touring the east coast this summer.

EXERCISE 2

With a partner, take turns asking and answering the following questions about the school or schools you have attended. Answer each question with a complete conditional statement. If necessary, think of a particular class in a school you attended.

▶ **EXAMPLES:** What happened if a student got into a fight at your school?
Possible answers:
In my elementary school, if a student got into a fight, the principal called up the parents.
If a student got into a fight in my high school, he or she was suspended for a few days.
In junior high school, if a student got into a fight, he or she had to meet with the school counselor.

Exercise 2

E X P A N S I O N

Choose one or two of the topics from the list and conduct a brief class discussion in which you encourage Ss to use conditional forms. Ask further questions related to the topic: *Hilda, if a student assigned to detention after school didn't show up, what happened then?* If relevant, identify cultural differences in the ways Ss were treated for a particular type of behavior.

What happened in one of your classes in elementary, junior high, or high school if:

1. a student walked in twenty minutes late to class?
2. a student didn't turn in the homework assignment?
3. a student cheated on an exam?
4. a student constantly interrupted the teacher?
5. a student broke a rule such as not chewing gum in class, not talking out of turn, etc.?
6. a student gave the wrong answer?
7. the students strongly disliked a teacher?

EXERCISE 3

Complete each of the following past conditional statements. First complete the conditional statement with any other information you want to add; then express a hypothetical past result.

▶ **EXAMPLES:** If my elementary school had. . . .
If my elementary school had offered English classes, I would have learned English more easily.
If my elementary school had been less strict, I would have enjoyed it more.

1. If I had had a chance to . . .
2. If my parents (or mother or father) had lived . . .
3. If my grandparents had been able . . .
4. If my family had been . . .
5. If my English teacher had given . . .

EXERCISE 4

Add a condition to each of these past hypothetical statements.

▶ **EXAMPLE:** I would have studied more
If I had known I was going to get a C in my biology course last quarter, I would have studied more.

1. I would have worked harder
2. I would have been happier
3. my last year in school would have been easier
4. my parents would have been upset with me
5. my life would have been less complicated

Exercise 3

EXPANSION

Have each student write down one past conditional statement on a small piece of paper and pass it to the person next to him or her to complete. Remind them not to write anything that might embarrass another student. Share some of the responses.

Exercise 4

Have Ss do this as a chain exercise in groups of three or four, with group members taking turns responding orally to each hypothetical statement. Share a few responses with the class as a whole.

Workbook Ex. 1, p. 146.
Answers: TE p. 551.

Conditionals: Only If, Unless, Even Though, Even If   **269**

ANSWER KEY

Exercise 2
Answers will vary. Examples:
1. In my high school, if. . . , the student would have been marked absent the whole period.   2. In my English class, if. . . , the student would have received a zero.   3. If. . . , the student would have been sent to the principal's office.   4. If. . . , the student might be suspended from class.   5. If. . . , the student might be asked to stay after school.   6. If. . . in my math class, the teacher would have helped the student get the correct answer.   7. If. . . , they might not pay attention at all in class.

Exercise 3
Answers will vary. Examples:
1. . . . take guitar lessons, I could have been in a band.   2. . . . during the past century, they might not have come to the U.S.   3. . . . to move here, they would probably have done so.   4. . . . less adventurous, we might not have moved so much.   5. . . . us less homework, I would have been able to go dancing last night.

Exercise 4
Answers will vary. Examples:
1. . . . on my essay if I had known some of my classmates would be reading it.   2. . . . if I could have gone back to Athens for the summer.   3. . . . if I hadn't had to take so many courses each quarter.   4. . . . if I had dropped out of school.   5. . . . if my parents hadn't gotten sick last fall.

Ss often find the logical concepts underlying these conditionals confusing. Give Ss ample practice converting *only if* to *unless* statements and vice versa so that they understand the reverse relationship between these two subordinating conjunctions. (This is the focus of Exercise 6 also.)

S U G G E S T I O N S

1. As you review the points in this chart, use *only if* and *unless* sentences from the introduction to the Opening Task and from Step 2 of the task for examples to Ss to transform (e.g., from the Opening Task introductory sentences: *When I was a child, we didn't go out to eat unless it was a special occasion; When I was your age, we could leave the table only if we asked permission.*)

2. Using examples related to your Ss' lives, write sentences on the board with blanks to complete: *You can take English 2 _____ you have completed English 1. You can't take English 2 _____ you have completed English 1.*

FOCUS **2**

MEANING

▶ **Exclusive Conditions:** *Only If and Unless*

We use both *only if* and *unless* to express the only condition under which an event will or should take place.

EXAMPLES	EXPLANATIONS
(a) **Main Clause: Affirmative** As a girl, my grandmother went shopping **Condition** **only if** she had finished her assigned chores.*	Use *only if* when the main clause is affirmative. It means "only on the condition that."
(b) **Main Clause: Negative** As a girl, my grandmother didn't go shopping **Condition** **unless** she had finished her assigned chores.	Use *unless* when the main clause is negative. It means "except on the condition that."
(c) **Main Clause: Affirmative** As a girl, my grandmother stayed home **Condition** on Saturday **unless** she had finished her homework.	You can also use *unless* when the main clause is affirmative. The implication, however, is negative. In (c), the implication is that Grandmother didn't go anywhere on Saturday if she hadn't finished her homework.
(d) Nowadays, my grandmother would spend the day shopping **only if** she **were** bored.	For hypothetical present, use the subjunctive form *were* in formal written English, just as with other hypothetical conditionals.

*In spoken English, native speakers often separate *only if,* placing *only* before the main verb and *if* after it. As a girl, my grandmother *only* went shopping *if* she had finished her chores, she would *only* spend the day shopping now *if* she were bored.

EXERCISE 5

Decide whether *if*, *only if*, or *unless* should be used in each blank. The first one has been done for you.

In the Old Days . . .

As each generation matures, it tends to judge the younger generations as somehow not quite measuring up to those of the past: the new generation may be regarded as a bit lazier, less disciplined or less imaginative. My family was no exception.

"Drive to school!" my father would exclaim to my siblings and me. "Why, when we were your age, we walked everywhere (1) _____unless_____ there was a severe snowstorm. And if we couldn't walk, we went by car (2) _____ the buses weren't running." The meal options were generally fewer for my parents' generation also: (3) "_____ we didn't like what was served for dinner," my mother would remind us, "we had to eat it anyway." According to my parents, entertainment was more active before television watching became the main leisure pursuit, and obligations more strictly followed. As children, they usually played games outside (4) _____ the weather was dreadful. And that, of course, was allowed (5) _____ all homework had been completed. Later, dating in high school wasn't permitted (6) _____ grades were acceptable, and then (7) _____ the parents had met the potential date.

Perhaps people shouldn't talk about the past (8) _____ they promise not to make the present sound so much worse than the past. Or they could make comparisons (9) _____ they admit that some aspects of the past weren't so great. On the other hand, glorifying the past and complaining about the present may be an inalienable right of the older generations.

ANSWER KEY

Exercise 5
(1) unless   (2) only if   (3) if   (4) unless
(5) only if   (6) unless   (7) only if   (8) unless   (9) only if

Exercise 6

This transformation exercise is intended to reinforce understanding of the inverse relationship between *only if* and *unless* and to practice using the appropriate negative or affirmative verb forms.

EXERCISE 6

Make each of the following a negative condition by using *unless* instead of *only if* and making other changes as necessary.*

▶ **EXAMPLE:** When I was your age, we went to the movies only if it was a holiday.

When I was your age, we *didn't go* to the movies *unless* it was a holiday.

1. Back in the old days, we locked our houses only if we were going on a vacation.
2. We could have ice cream for dessert only if it was a special occasion.
3. We could go out after dinner only if we had cleaned up the kitchen.
4. In high school, we were permitted to stay overnight at our friends' houses only if all the parents had met each other.
5. We were allowed to go to house parties only if they were chaperoned by adults.

*In spoken English, native speakers often separate *only if*, placing *only* before the main verb and *if* at the end of the verb phrase.

ANSWER KEY

Exercise 6
1. . . . we didn't lock our houses unless we . . . 2. We couldn't have ice cream for dessert unless it . . . 3. We couldn't go out after dinner unless we . . . 4. . . . we weren't permitted to stay overnight at our friend's house unless the parents . . . 5. We weren't allowed to go to house parties unless they . . .

FOCUS 3

Fronted *Only If* and *Not Unless* Clauses

EXAMPLES	EXPLANATIONS

(a) **Only if** our parents approved
   Verb   Subject   Verb
   could we   **go** out on a date.
	You can use *only if* or *not unless* at the beginning of a sentence to emphasize a condition. Invert the subject and the first verb in the main clause. The first verb may be an auxiliary (*be, have, do*), a modal verb (*will, could, may,* etc.), or main verb *be*.

(b) **Not unless** a party was chaperoned
   Verb Subject   Verb
   did my parents **allow** me to attend.	

(c) **Unless** he finishes his chemistry project,
   Subject Verb
   he   **is** not **going** on the weekend trip.
	Do not invert the subject and first verb when you begin a sentence with *unless*. Separate the condition from the main clause with a comma.

EXERCISE 7

Add an *only if* or *not unless* conditional clause to the beginning of each of the following statements to emphasize a condition. Make other changes as needed.

▶ **EXAMPLE:** It's fun to do calculus problems.
      Only if you love mathematics is it fun to do calculus problems.

  1. Most snakes will try to bite a person.
  2. Going bungee jumping is fun.
  3. Learning the conditional forms in English is easy.
  4. Spiders make great pets.
  5. It is worth spending ten years to get a Ph.D.
  6. Watching MTV is the best way to spend your free time
  7. I will get up at 4 A.M. tomorrow.

FOCUS 3

This focus box shows the special emphatic forms of these conditionals, which require subject-verb inversion.

SUGGESTION

Write the noninverted forms of examples (a) and (b) on the board (or elicit forms from the class) so Ss can see how the parts of the sentence change when we use fronted emphatic forms. (Fronted forms for focus and emphasis are the topic of Unit 24.)

    Noninverted forms: (a) *We could go out on a date only if our parents approved.* (b) *My parents allowed me to attend a party only if it was chaperoned.*

    Note in the case of (b) that the noun phrase *a party* and its referent *it* are reversed so that in both conditional forms the noun phrase occurs first.

Exercise 7

Since this is a creative task with potential for humor, Ss may enjoy working with a partner or in a small group. For example, some students may want to argue that MTV is a great way to spend free time, in which case they would begin with an *unless* clause!

Workbook Ex. 2, p. 147; Ex. 3, p. 148.
Answers: TE p. 551.

ANSWER KEY

FOCUS 4

These grammatical concepts are difficult, so your Ss shouldn't be discouraged if they don't grasp them immediately!

SUGGESTION

1. Don't try to cover the entire focus box all at once. Go over one section at a time.
2. To teach the first section:
   Step 1: Ask Ss to read the first section silently.
   Step 2: Put a visual representation of (a) on the board, creating a work schedule for Juana (e.g., Mon.–Thurs., 10–2). List a time for the math course, one that doesn't conflict (e.g., Tues., Thurs., 3–4). Discuss example (a) with reference to the schedule.
   Step 3: Say that the math class time has changed; write a time that conflicts. Ask if Juana will take a math course based on this information.
   Step 4: Go over (b), which should be easier for Ss to process after discussing (a).
3. To supplement the past condition examples, try: (a) An example about yourself that expresses something you wouldn't have been able to do without a lot of help, (b) An example relevant to your Ss or your context (e.g., *The basketball team couldn't have won the game if Natasha hadn't scored so many points*). Remind Ss that the most probable meaning of the condition for both (c) and (d) is contrary to fact. Ss shouldn't be too concerned if they don't understand the possible (second) interpretation of *unless*.
4. Present the points for section three in two steps: (1) the points represented by (e) and (f); (2) the expressions exemplified in (g) and (h) followed by the note about *unless* as shown in (i) and (j).

FOCUS **4**

▶ *If ... Not versus Unless*

EXAMPLES	EXPLANATIONS
(a) **Future Main Clause** Juana will take a math course . . . **Future Conditional Clause** . . . if it does not conflict with her work schedule. . . . unless it conflicts with her work schedule. **(b)** **Future Main Clause** She won't take a science course . . . **Future Conditional Clause** . . . if it does **not** satisfy a requirement. . . . **unless** it satisfies a requirement.	**Future or Hypothetical Conditions** In statements that express future or hypothetical events, subordinators *if . . . not* and *unless* have roughly the same meaning. They describe the negative conditions under which something will or may happen.
(c) **Main Clause: Contrary to Fact** Violeta couldn't have passed her Latin exam . . . **Condition: Contrary to Fact** . . . if she had**n't** had a tutor. **(d)** **Main Clause** Violeta couldn't have passed her Latin exam . . . **Condition** . . . **unless** she'd had a tutor.	**Past Conditions** In statements that express past conditions, use *if . . . not* to express a condition that is contrary to fact when the main clause is also contrary to fact. The meaning of (c) is that Violeta **did** pass the exam and she **did** have a tutor. Two meanings are possible when we use *unless* to state the condition. In (d) the most probable meaning is the same as example (c): Violeta **did** have a tutor; she **did** pass the exam. However, another possible meaning is that Violeta **did not** pass the exam and that only tutoring might have kept her from failing.
(e) Wen and Temu wouldn't have so much homework **if** they were **not** taking calculus. **(f)** **NOT:** Wen and Temu wouldn't have so much homework **unless** they were taking calculus. **(g)** Thanks for helping me get my new job. **If it weren't for** you, I would still be working at that horrible place. **(h)** **If it hadn't been for** the encouragement of her English-speaking friends, Pham wouldn't be so fluent in English. **(i)** **NOT: Unless** it were for you . . . **(j)** **NOT: Unless** it had been for the encouragement of her English-speaking friends . . .	**Present: Contrary to Fact Main Clause** To express a statement that is contrary to present fact, use *if . . . not* to state the condition. In (e), Wen and Temu **are** taking calculus; they **do** have a lot of homework. We do not use *unless* for this meaning. We also use the expressions *if it weren't for* + noun and *if it hadn't been for* + noun to express conditions with main clauses that are contrary to present fact. In (g), the speaker is not working at the horrible place; in (h), Pham is fluent in English. The conditions have made these present facts possible. We do not use *unless* as shown in (i) and (j).

EXERCISE 8

Complete each of the blanks by forming a negative conditional statement with the cues in parentheses. The cues describe conditions that are contrary to fact. Use *if . . . not* or *unless* as appropriate. In cases where both are possible without a change in meaning, give both. Add any words or phrases you think are needed.

▶ **EXAMPLE:** Sandy needs two more courses in chemistry to graduate. He's glad now that he took a chemistry course last year. <u>If he hadn't completed</u>

<u>Chemistry I, he wouldn't have been able to enroll in Advanced Chemistry</u>

<u>this term.</u>

<u>Unless he had completed Chemistry 1, he wouldn't have been able to enroll</u>

<u>in Advanced Chemistry this term.</u>

(not complete Chemistry I/not be able to enroll in Advanced Chemistry this term)

1. Roberto's advisor was concerned that Roberto had decided not to take a typing class. Roberto explained that _____ _____ . (not drop the typing class/not be able to work at the pharmacy last month)

2. Earl has been complaining all term about the amount of reading he has to do for his courses. He says that the history class is the worst. In fact, _____ _____ . (not take a history course/have only light reading right now for his classes)

3. Leila is glad that she tape-recorded her grandfather talking about his child-hood. _____ . (not record his reminiscences/not know about this part of her family history.)

4. Natasha took a TOEFL preparation course. She told me that _____ _____ . (not take the course/be much more worried about the exam)

EXERCISE 9

Complete the following sentences with a statement about yourself.

▶ **EXAMPLE:** If it hadn't been for my parents, I *might not have gone to college.*

1. If it hadn't been for my parents,
2. If it weren't for my friends' support,
3. If it weren't for (name)_____ 's good advice,
4. If it hadn't been for my knowledge of _____ ,

Conditionals: Only If, Unless, Even Though, Even If **275**

Exercise 8

The distinctions between forms here are difficult. Give Ss ample time to work on this exercise.

Exercise 9

E X P A N S I O N

Have Ss make up their own conditional statement to complete and develop the topic in a paragraph. They can write the paragraph for homework.

Workbook Ex. 4, p. 149.
Answers: TE p. 551.

A N S W E R   K E Y

Exercise 8

1. . . . if he had not dropped the typing class, he wouldn't have been able to work at the pharmacy last month.   2. . . . if he had not taken a history course, he would have only light reading now for his classes.   3. Unless she had recorded his reminiscences, she would not have known about this part of her family history.   4. . . . unless she had taken the course, she would be much more worried about the exam.

Exercise 9

Answers will vary. Examples:
1. . . . I would have considered a different profession instead of joining the family business.   2. . . . I might not have tried out for the soccer team.   3. . . . I might not have decided to further my education.
4. . . . computers, I wouldn't have been offered that job.

SUGGESTIONS

1. To help Ss understand or review the meaning of *even though*, write one or two things on the board you have accomplished that were difficult for some reason (e.g., *I learned how to ski*) and then ask Ss to state difficult things they have accomplished. Write a list of the responses. Next to your response, write a condition that made your accomplishment difficult (e.g., *even though I am not very coordinated*). Then ask individual Ss to add *even though* clauses alongside the accomplishments written on the board.

2. To clarify the meaning of *even if*, tell Ss that you are determined to do something in the future even though it may be difficult or unpleasant (e.g., *My house is really a mess. I am determined to clean my entire house from top to bottom this weekend.*) Have Ss ask you questions to judge your determination using the formula "*Will you do X if Y?*" with "X" being the activity you named. For example, "*Will you clean your house if friends drop over?*" If possible, respond to each question in the affirmative (with tongue in cheek if Ss try to ask questions they think will make you lose your determination!) : "*Yes, I'll clean my house even if my friends drop over;*" "*Oh yes, I'll probably stay home and clean my house even if someone offers me free tickets to the Miami Dolphins game on Saturday afternoon.*"

3. Make sure Ss take note of (g). This is a very common error.

▶ *Even Though* and *Even if*

Both even though and even if emphasize conditions. However, their meanings are different.

EXAMPLES	EXPLANATIONS
(a) My uncle walked to work **even though Actual Condition** his job was five miles away. (His job was five miles away; nevertheless, he walked to work.)	*Even though* is an emphatic form of *although*. It means "despite the fact that." The condition after *even though* expresses a reality.
(b) My uncle will walk to work **even if Real or Not Real Condition** it is raining. (He walks when it rains as well as when it doesn't rain.)	*Even if* is an emphatic form of *if*. It means "whether or not." The condition after *even if* may or may not be a reality.
(c) My uncle {walks / used to walk} to work **even if it** {rains. / was raining.}	*Even if* can mean "even when" with habitual present conditions and past tense conditions. We can paraphrase (c): He walks to work even when it rains; he used to walk to work when it was raining.
(d) **Even if** I have to stay up all night, I will finish this paper. **(e)** **NOT: Even** I have to stay up all night, I'll finish this paper. **(f)** **Even though** it was late, we stayed up to find out who had won the election. **(g)** **NOT: Even** it was late, we stayed up to find out who had won the election.	*Even* versus *Even If* and *Even Though* *Even* cannot be used as a substitute for *even though* or *even if*. *Even* is not a subordinator. In your writing, you should check any uses of *even* to make sure that you don't mean *even if* or *even though*.

EXERCISE 10

Choose the correct form, *even though* or *even if*, for each blank.

▶ **EXAMPLE:** The children bought their mother a special gift last Mother's
Day ___even though___ they didn't have much money.

1. Fran's mother was never without a car. However, she would often
walk three miles to the market _____ she could have
driven if she had wanted to.

2. _____ Duane's grandfather had a daytime job, he also
worked every evening for many years.

3. Our family had a rule for dinner: We had to eat at least a few bites
of each kind of food. _____ the food was something we
had tried before and didn't like, we still had to eat a mouthful.

4. Last Christmas Eve, _____ the temperature dropped to
below zero, my father insisted we take our traditional stroll through
the neighborhood singing Christmas carols.

5. We'd love for you to spend the holidays with us. It would be
wonderful if you could stay at least a week. But _____
it's only for a day or so, we hope you'll plan to come.

EXERCISE 11

Complete each of the blanks below with information about your efforts to
achieve current goals and your dreams for the future. Share your responses with
your classmates.

1. Even though I don't like to _____,
I do it anyway because _____.

2. I try to _____
even if _____.

3. Even though _____,
I hope I can _____.

4. Even if I never _____,
I still _____.

5. I would like to _____
even though _____.

Exercise 10

This exercise can be a follow-up diagnostic
after oral work described above.

Exercise 11
V A R I A T I O N

Ss could interview someone outside of class
to get responses. They could read some of
them during the next class and the class
could assess the interviewees' knowledge of
these structures.

Workbook Ex. 7, p. 152.
Answers: TE p. 552.

A N S W E R   K E Y

Exercise 10

1. even though   2. Even though   3. Even if
(*Even though* is possible; however, this choice
would be more appropriate with verbs *may have
been* and *would have*, expressing habitual past
events.)   4. even though   5. even if

Exercise 11

Answers will vary. Examples:
1. get up early . . . I have a class that begins
at 8:00.   2. do some kind of exercise every
day . . . I'm tired   3. my biology grades are
not too great . . . enter medical school.
4. get to Italy . . . like to study Italian.
5. visit Tokyo . . . I hear entertainment is quite
expensive there.

FOCUS 6

This focus box offers one common context of usage—advice—for the structures covered in this unit.

Go over examples (e) and (f) so that Ss understand the irony. In most classes, someone will be able to offer a paraphrase other than the implication given in parentheses.

SUGGESTION

Ask Ss to what extent ironic language like that in (e) and (f) exists in their native languages and if these examples seem humorous to them. Discuss the importance of understanding humor in different cultures to develop communicative competence. (Advanced Ss often comment that the most difficult part of comprehending classroom discourse is understanding their classmates' and teachers' jokes!)

Exercise 12

SUGGESTION

Have Ss work on this exercise with a partner in class.

▶ Giving Advice

EXAMPLES	EXPLANATIONS
(a) Don't make reservations at the Four Seasons restaurant **unless** you're prepared to spend a lot of money. **(b)** Take a foreign language course **only if** you're willing to do homework faithfully every day. **(c)** You should pay your taxes on time **even if** you have to borrow the money. **(d)** Be sure to take a trip to the waterfall **even though** it's a long drive on a dirt road. It's well worth the trouble!	We often use connectors such as *unless, only if, even if,* and *even though* in statements that offer advice.
(e) Don't go to see the movie *Last Alien in Orlando* **unless** you need a nap. (Implication: The movie is really boring!) **(f)** Take English 4 **only if** you have nothing to do on the weekends. (Implication: The class is difficult; you'll have a lot of homework.)	We sometimes use humorous conditions with advice statements to make a point indirectly. The advice in (e) and (f) has an ironic tone; the conditions are not meant to be taken literally.

EXERCISE 12

Make advice statements by combining information in the Condition and Advice columns. First match each condition with an appropriate piece of advice. Then make a full statement, using an appropriate conjunction: *if, only if, unless, even if, even though*. Make any changes necessary. The Conditions statements can either begin or end your sentences.

Condition	**Advice**
you have plenty of water	take a hike in Death Valley

Unless you have plenty of water, don't take a hike in Death Valley.
Take a hike in Death Valley only if you have plenty of water.

Condition	**Advice**
1. you don't have a wetsuit to keep you warm	**a.** order the Kung Pao chicken
2. you are in Cody, Wyoming	**b.** take a riverboat cruise on the Mississippi River
3. you have exact change for the busfare	**c.** walk to the top of the cathedral in Seville, Spain
4. you love spicy food	**d.** get on a bus in New York City
5. the doorman at your hotel calls a cab for you	**e.** treat yourself to a good meal in Paris
6. you like slow-moving leisurely trips	**f.** don't go swimming off the Oregon Coast in winter
7. you don't mind climbing a lot of stairs	**g.** be sure to visit the Buffalo Bill Museum of the Wild West
8. your budget is limited	**h.** don't forget to tip him

Conditionals: Only If, Unless, Even Though, Even If **279**

A N S W E R   K E Y

Exercise 12
(Forms of answers will vary)
1. **f** . . . unless you have a wet . . .   2. **g** If you are in Cody . . .   3. **d** . . . only if you . . .
4. **a** If you love . . . order . . *or* only if . . .

5. **h** If the doorman . . .   6. **b** . . . only if you like . . . *or* if you like   7. **c** . . . only if you don't mind climbing   8. **e** Unless your budget . . .

Exercise 13
E X P A N S I O N

All of these topics could be developed as a paragraph or essay. Ss might enjoy reading paragraphs or short essays aloud in small groups afterwards.

Workbook Ex. 3, p. 148.
Answers: TE p. 551.

Exercise 14

This error analysis exercise includes errors that we have often seen in Ss' writing.

Workbook Ex. 8, p. 153; Ex. 9, p. 154.
Answers: TE p. 552.

UNIT GOAL REVIEW

Ask Ss to look at the goals on the opening page of the unit again. Help them understand how much they have accomplished in each area.

EXERCISE 13
Working with a partner, make up sentences that offer advice for at least five of the following situations using an *only if* or a *not unless* clause.

▶ **EXAMPLE:**   What to do or not to do in the city where you live
   Don't plan to go out for dinner at a restaurant in my hometown unless you can get there before 10 P.M.

1. How not to get lost at a particular place (your campus, a shopping mall, a city)
2. What to wear or what not to wear for a night on the town where you live
3. When *not* to do something where you live
4. A place someone shouldn't shop at because of high prices or poor quality
5. A course or subject not to take at your school
6. A movie someone should not waste their time to see
7. A book someone should not bother to read

EXERCISE 14
The paragraph below has five errors involving the conditionals focused on in this unit. Identify and correct them.

HOW TO EVALUATE HEALTH NEWS

(1) These days we are constantly hearing and reading about biomedical studies concerned with factors that affect our health. (2) Even these studies often present results as general "facts," the conclusions are not always true. (3) Only if multiple studies have been done it is wise to generalize results to a larger population. (4) Furthermore, you shouldn't be too quick to believe a study unless the number of subjects involved isn't large, because generalizations cannot be made from a small sample size. (5) Even the sample size is big enough, the results may not be statistically significant. (6) In other words, a statistical difference between two factors may be important only the difference could not happen by chance.

Exercise 13
Answers will vary. Examples:
1. Don't attempt to get around the University of Michigan campus without a map.   2. If you are male, don't go to The Palace Restaurant unless you are wearing a jacket and tie.
3. Don't go to the downtown post office at noon unless you want to spend your whole lunch hour there.   4. Shop at Mimi's Boutique only if you don't mind spending $200 for a blouse.   5. You should take Introduction to Computers only if you have never seen or turned on a computer.   6. Don't bother to see "Dumber Than Ever" unless you like stupid jokes.   7. Don't read that biography of Bob Marley unless you don't mind terrible writing.

Exercise 14
(2) Even **though** these studies   (3) have been done **is it** wise   (4) involved **is** large
(5) Even **if**   (6) important only **if**

Use Your English

ACTIVITY 1: LISTENING

You will hear two brief passages providing advice about health and safety issues. After each one you will hear three statements. Only one is a correct paraphrase of an idea in the passage. Choose the correct paraphrase. Compare your answers with those of your classmates.

   1. a b c   2. a b c

ACTIVITY 2: WRITING/SPEAKING

Consider some of the family or school rules that you, your siblings, and your friends had to follow when you were younger. Create a list of rules that could be expressed with *if, unless,* or *only if* conditions. Use the categories below for ideas. In small groups, compare your lists. If possible, form groups that include different cultural backgrounds and discuss some of the cultural similarities and differences revealed by your lists.

- Mealtime etiquette
- Eating snacks
- Watching television or playing computer games
- Having friends over or staying at friends' houses

- Dating
- Going out with friends at night
- Making long distance phone calls
- Classroom rules
- School cafeteria rules

▶ **EXAMPLES:** *In my elementary school in Taiwan, we were allowed to speak in class only if we raised our hand and the teacher gave us permission.*

When I was in high school, I couldn't have any of my friends over to visit unless one of my parents was home.

USE YOUR ENGLISH

The activities on these "purple pages" at the end of the unit contain situations that should naturally elicit the unit's structures in a more communicative framework. While Ss are doing these activities in class, you can circulate and listen to determine if they have actually achieved the goals on the opening page of the unit.

Activity 1

Play textbook audio. The tapescript for this listening appears on pp. 570–571 of this book. You may need to play the tape two or three times.

Activity 2
VARIATION

Divide Ss into groups and assign one of the topics to each group. Have Ss use comparison and contrast connectors (*similarly, in contrast, etc.*) in writing statements related to the group members. Direct them to Unit 12, Focuses 5 (p. 212) and 6 (p. 215) for a review of these connectors. Have groups give brief oral presentations afterwards.

ANSWER KEY

Activity 1
1. a **2.** b

Activity 3

VARIATION

Eliminate Step 2. Collect the lists that individual Ss have written either in class or as homework. Choose one or more items from each Ss' list to put on a handout or transparency and present for the next class. Have Ss assist in making any needed corrections.

Activity 4

SUGGESTION

Some Ss might also want to contribute artwork (drawings, cartoons) for the guides, either their own or from a published source (the Internet, magazines, etc.).

ACTIVITY 3: WRITING/SPEAKING

Most of us have some strong opinions or beliefs about things that we would never do or that we would be very unlikely to do. For example, a person might believe that she would never accept a job that she hated or would never live in a very cold climate.

STEP 1 Make a list of five things that you believe you would be very unlikely to do. For each item on your list, imagine a circumstance under which you might change your mind or be forced to behave differently and write it down as a possible exception. Use either *unless* or *only if.*

▶ **EXAMPLE:** *I wouldn't live in a very large city.*

Exception: *I would do it only if I could be chauffeured wherever I wanted to go.*

STEP 2 Compare your responses with those of your classmates.

ACTIVITY 4: WRITING

Here's a chance to share your knowledge. Either individually or as a collaborative project with some of your classmates, create a brief guide for one of the following topics. Your guide could be intended as a Web page for the Internet or a poster.

• A guide that informs students which courses at your school to avoid or which to take only under certain conditions
• Advice about what to do or not to do in your hometown or country
• A travel guide to some place you've been that you like
• A guide explaining the basics of how to use the Internet or some specific aspect of it
• A guide for women on understanding men
• A guide for men on understanding women
• A guide of your choice

For as many items as possible, use condition statements with *only if, unless, even if,* or *even though.* Your conditions could be humorous or serious.

A C T I V I T Y 5 : W R I T I N G

Imagine that you could be in charge of your school or city for a year. You could make any rules or laws you wish, and everyone would have to obey them. Make a list of the regulations you would enforce, using conditional statements where they might be needed.

▶ **EXAMPLE:** Rules for School:
The teachers cannot assign homework unless it truly promotes learning.

Students can arrive late to class only if they have a written excuse or a small gift for me.

A C T I V I T Y 6 : S P E A K I N G / W R I T I N G

Write an essay describing the life of one of your older relatives or friends from information you have heard about him or her. If possible, interview the person. Use at least a few conditional statements in your description.

Activity 5

S U G G E S T I O N

Have Ss create lists in groups and then transfer their rules to large poster paper on the classroom walls for discussion and evaluation.

V A R I A T I O N

Have Ss present their laws orally, as a kind of campaign speech. The class—or another class—can vote on the future leader.

Activity 6

This activity returns to the central theme of this unit, describing "the way things were" in the past for older family members (or friends).

S U G G E S T I O N

If it is not possible for Ss to interview an older relative, see if Ss can visit a retirement home to interview people.

The test for this unit can be found on p. 513. The answers are on p. 514.

TOEFL Test Preparation Exercises for Units 13–15 can be found on pp. 156–158. The answers are on p. 552 of this book.

Unit 16

UNIT OVERVIEW

Unit 16 assumes that students (Ss) have a good understanding of complex sentence structures in which subordinate clauses of time and cause are joined to main clauses in a sentence. Building on this foundation, the focus boxes provide instruction on how to reduce and punctuate these clauses as well as how to avoid dangling participles, a recurring problem in developing writers.

UNIT GOALS

Review the goals listed on this page so Ss understand what they should be able to know by the end of the unit.

OPENING TASK

The purpose of this task is to report the route of a traveler presumably living in the 1800s somewhere in North America.

SETTING UP THE TASK

Prior to class, wrap up several coins in a square of red cloth or felt and tie a string around it. Tell Ss they will be reading a story in which a red bag plays a part. To increase interest, ask Ss to guess the answers to the following questions: (1) *What is in the bag?* (2) *Who owned it?*, and (3) *Why is it important?* Then ask Ss to open their books and read the diary.

U N I T 16

R E D U C I N G A D V E R B C L A U S E S

UNIT GOALS:

- To know how to reduce adverb clauses of time and cause
- To position and punctuate reduced adverb clauses
- To reduce adverb clauses with emotive verbs
- To avoid dangling participles in writing

▶ O P E N I N G T A S K
The Lone Traveler

On one of your hiking trips to Mills Landing, you found an old diary with a few notes scrawled in it. Apparently, a lone traveler had kept a record of his travels about one hundred years ago.

Jan. 30: Discouraged by poor crops. No cash. Left Springton by wagon in search of work.

Feb 4: Today searched for job in Powtown. No luck. All jobs require skills I don't have.

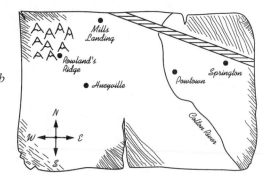

March 15: Crossed the Colton River but raft turned over. Lost everything except diary and watch. Walked to Hueyville.

March 18: No work in Hueyville. Met kind woman there. Told me about vacant house abandoned by miners near Rowland's Ridge.

March 21: Sold my watch for supplies. Hiked to Rowland's Ridge. Found shack and moved in.

March 27: Days and days of rainy weather. Decided to fix up place. Borrowed tools to fix roof, walls, and floors.

March 29: Hammering floorboards. Saw red bag. Opened it. Eureka! A bag full of money. I am rich.

April 8: Guilty conscience. Worry about possible owner. Hiked to Mills Landing and asked Sheriff what to do. Says the money is mine because money left long ago. No one will ever claim.

STEP 1 Using your map (provided on previous page), trace the traveler's steps with a partner.

STEP 2 With your partner, write a brief article for the local newspaper about the lone traveler's story. Describe the traveler's route and what occurred along the way.

▶ **EXAMPLE:**

100-Year-Old Diary of Traveler Found

Yesterday a diary was found which tells the story of a former resident of the area. Apparently, one hundred years ago, a lone traveler, discouraged by poor crops and having no cash, had left Springton in order to find work. Searching for a job in Powtown, the traveler . . .

CONDUCTING THE TASK

Step 1

Ask Ss to work in pairs and trace the traveler's route using lines and arrows. The route should be as follows: Springton→Powtown→Hueyville→ Rowland's Ridge→Mills Landing.

Step 2

With the same partner, ask Ss to take out a piece of paper to write a short newspaper article about the traveler. They may copy the first few sentences of the example. Remind Ss to include as much detail as they can, or create a new article of their own. Prompt reduced clauses by telling Ss that they may want to begin one or more of their sentences using the following verbs: *crossing, selling, hiking, terrified, disheartened,* or *worried*.

SUGGESTION

1. To emphasize that reduced adverb clauses are derived from full clauses with the same subject as a main clause, write sentence *a* on the blackboard using white chalk for all words except *we*, which you should write in a different color. Underline the identical subjects. State that this condition of same subject is necessary in order to consider reducing the clause to the phrase (*while*) *hiking*.

2. Ask individuals to take turns reading examples *c* through *h*, noting the time meaning for each.

3. Write example *i* on the board and ask Ss to identify the two separate subjects (*Sam* and *we*) in the sentence. Ask if it is possible to reduce the first clause. Ss should acknowledge that it is <u>not</u> since *Sam* and *we* are not the same.

▶ **R**educing Adverb Clauses of Time

We can reduce adverb clauses of time that contain the words *before, after, while, when,* and *since*. To do this, the subject of the main clause and the adverb clause must be the same. These reduced clauses are called participle phrases and use verb + *-ing*.

FULL ADVERB CLAUSE	REDUCED ADVERB CLAUSE*	TIME MEANING
(a) **While we are hiking/were hiking/hiked,** we admire/admired the scenery around us. *are/were* V + *-ing* ⟶ V + *-ing*	(b) **(While) hiking,** we admire/admired the scenery around us.	A time happening at the same time as the time expressed in the main clause
(c) **Since he has/had been living in Paris,** he has/had learned to speak French quite well. *has/had been* V + *-ing* ⟶ V + *-ing*	(d) **(Since) living in Paris,** he has/had learned to speak French quite well.	A time occurring before and up to the point of the time expressed in the main clause
(e) **After we have/had hiked around the canyon,** we are/were exhausted. *have/had* V + *-ed* ⟶ *having* + V + *-ed*	(f) **(After) having hiked around the canyon,** we are/were exhausted.	A time occurring before the time expressed in the main clause
(g) **When they are/were being searched,** they feel/felt nervous. *are/were* + *being* + V + *-ed* ⟶ *being* + V + *-ed*	(h) **(When) being searched,** they feel/felt nervous.	A time occurring at the same time or immediately after the time expressed in the main clause
(i) **When Sam gets tired,** we will leave.	(j) **NOT:** Getting tired, we will leave.	The subject of the main clause and the subject of the adverb clause are not the same. The adverb clause cannot be reduced.

*For some of these reduced adverb clauses, you can either keep or leave out the adverb, as in (b), (d), (f), and (h) above.

EXERCISE 1

Complete the following sentences about the out-of-doors. Give advice, using *should* or *shouldn't*.

▶ **EXAMPLE:** After getting lost in the woods, <u>you should look for familiar landmarks such as hills or trees</u>.

1. While walking along a narrow ridge, _____.
2. When hiking in an area with poisonous snakes, _____.
3. After having fallen into icy water,_____.
4. Before entering a meadow filled with deer, _____.
5. When washing dishes in the wilderness, _____.
6. Before lighting a fire in the woods, _____.
7. Before being attacked by mosquitoes, _____.
8. After having spotted a bear, _____.

EXERCISE 2

Read the following story. Reduce the full adverb clauses of time where possible.

(1) Since ~~he graduated~~ ^{graduating} from high school, Juan has been working and studying very hard. (2) While he attends classes at a community college, he works part-time at a bank. (3) After he graduates from the community college, he would like to attend a four-year university in order to become an architect. (4) Some day Juan would like to get married and have a family. (5) However, before he gets married, he is planning to take a trip to Europe. (6) When he is traveling through Europe, he hopes to see the great architecture of France and Spain.

EXERCISE 3

Reflect on your last month of activities and write at least five sentences containing reduced adverb clauses of time like those shown in Focus 1.

▶ **EXAMPLE:** *After having taken my biology exam, I had to take a nap.*

This exercise can be done either individually or as pairwork. Tell Ss to be aware of time frames as they create their responses.

Exercise 2

This is good editing practice for Ss learning to make their writing more concise. Remind them to search for subordinate clauses that contain the same subject as the main clause in order to identify a place to make a reduction.

Workbook Exs. 1 & 2, pp. 159–160.
Answers: TE p. 552.

ANSWER KEY

Exercise 1
Answers will vary.
1. . . . you should stay close to the ridge wall.
2. . . . you should always look where you are going.   3. . . . you should change into dry clothes as quickly as possible.   4. . . . you should be still and try to take a photo or two.
5. . . . you shouldn't use detergent that will pollute a fresh-water stream.   6. . . . you should make sure you are not under a tree with dry limbs and leaves.   7. . . . you should put on some mosquito repellent.   8. . . . you shouldn't make a noise.

Exercise 2
(2) While attending classes . . .   (3) After graduating from . . .   (5) Before getting married, . . .   (6) When traveling through Europe, . . .

Exercise 3
Answers will vary.

1. Draw two columns on the board and label them *cause* and *effect*. Under *causes* write the following examples: *standing on your head, pinching your nose, not tying your shoes*, etc.
2. Ask Ss to think of effects that will occur with each activity. You should begin each sentence and allow individuals to finish it. For example: *standing on your head, . . . you might turn blue. Pinching your nose, . . . you might stop breathing. Not tying your shoes, . . . you might trip on your laces.*
3. Ask Ss to silently read examples *a* through *h*. After they have finished reading, highlight the fact that the participle phrase can refer to different time frames and can also be made negative by adding the words *not* and *never*.

FOCUS **2**

Reducing Adverb Clauses That Show Cause

We can also reduce adverb clauses containing *because, since,* and *as* to *-ing* phrases. Again the subject in the main clause must be the same as the subject in the adverb clause.

FULL ADVERB CLAUSE	REDUCED ADVERB CLAUSE*	CASUAL MEANING
(a) **Because we take/ took/are taking/were taking the bus,** we save/saved a lot of money.	(b) **Taking the bus,** we save/saved a lot of money.	The participle phrase contains the cause or reason. The main clause contains the result. The participle phrase can re-
(c) **Since I have/had been rehearsing every day,** I am/was ready to per- form.	(d) **Rehearsing every day,** I am/was ready to per- form.	fer to present and past time as was shown in Focus 1.
(e) **As I have/had never gone skiing,** I want/wanted to take lessons.	(f) **Never having gone ski- ing,** I want/wanted to take lessons.	In the reduced form, a negative word like *never* or *not* can precede the auxiliary verb. This
(g) **Because he is/was not being watched by the police,** he is/was free to move.	(h) **Not being watched by the police,** he is/was free to move.	means that the action did not occur.

*These reduced clauses do not include the adverb. That is, it is not possible to say "Because taking the bus, we saved a lot of money."

288 UNIT 16

EXERCISE 4

Tony and Maria have had several mishaps on their camping trip. Suggest a cause for each mishap by adding a reduced adverb clause to each sentence below. Compare your completed sentences with a partner.

▶ **EXAMPLE:** They got lost on their hike.
Not having brought a map, they got lost on their hike.

1. Tony was bitten by mosquitoes.
2. They were very thirsty.
3. They were very hungry.
4. Maria jumped in fright.
5. Maria was shivering.
6. Tony developed a blister.

EXERCISE 5

Imagine that you have received a letter from a friend who is having a difficult time adjusting to life at a university in the United States. She is making excuses for several of her actions. Write a piece of advice for each problem, using a reduced causal adverb clause.

▶ **EXAMPLE:** Because I arrived at my first class late, I waited outside the room and missed the entire lecture.
Having arrived to the class late, you should have quietly entered the room and sat down.

1. Because I have no computer, I do not type my papers.
2. Since I watched a lot of TV, I did not do my homework.
3. As I have not understood my instructor, I have stopped going to class.
4. Because I do not know anyone, I sit alone in my room for hours.
5. Since I hate the food on campus, I go out for dinner every night and now I'm almost broke.
6. As I am embarrassed by my accent, I do not speak to many people.
7. As I am very shy, I do not ask questions about my assignments in class.
8. As I got a D on my last test, I am planning to drop my class.
9. Because I made expensive long distance calls to my family every other night, I ran up a huge phone bill.
10. Since I did not have enough time to write my research paper, I copied most of the information from an encyclopedia.
11. Because I was put on academic probation, I have felt very depressed.
12. Since I do not speak English very well, I speak my native language with friends from my native country.

Reducing Adverb Clauses | **289**

Exercise 5

V A R I A T I O N

Ask one student to read the problem and the other student to give him or her oral advice to solve it using reduced adverb clauses. Then, ask Ss to write out the exercise on a sheet of paper for homework.

Workbook Exs. 3 & 4, pp. 161–163.
Answers: TE p. 553.

A N S W E R   K E Y

Exercise 4
Answers will vary.
1. Not having remembered the insect repellent . . . 2. Having forgotten their water bottle . . . 3. Not having eaten all day . . . 4. Seeing a wolf . . . 5. Not having put on her down parka . . . 6. Having walked too long in boots that were too small . . .

Exercise 5
Answers will vary.
1. Not having a computer, you should go to the school computer lab. 2. Having watched too much TV, you should have turned it off so that you could concentrate on your homework. 3. Not having understood your professor, you should ask for clarification during the lecture or visit him or her during office hours. 4. Not knowing anyone, you should make a greater effort to get involved in clubs or extracurricular activities. 5. Hating the food on campus, you should learn to cook. 6. Being embarrassed by your accent, you should take an accent improvement class. 7. Being very shy, you should ask about your assignments during your professor's office hours. 8. Having gotten a "D" on your last test, you should study a little harder to do better on the next test. 9. Having made too many long distance calls to your family, you should think about e-mailing or faxing messages to your family. 10. Not having had enough time for your research paper, you should not have plagiarized, no matter how short on time you were. 11. Having been put on academic probation, you should go visit with your advisor. 12. Not speaking English very well, you should try to practice English with some new English-speaking friends.

Workbook Exs. 5–7, pp. 163–165.
Answers: TE p. 553.

FOCUS **3**

▶ Position and Punctuation of Reduced Adverb Clauses

EXAMPLES	EXPLANATIONS
(a) **Hiking alone in the mountains,** Diane always carries water and a compass.	Reduced adverb clauses (participle phrases) may appear at the beginning, middle, or end of a sentence.
(b) The doe, **having been frightened by the noise,** disappeared from the clearing.	
(c) The trackers waded across the river, **holding tightly to the reins of their horses.**	
(d) The trackers waded across the river **while holding tightly to the reins of their horses.**	Commas are needed in all positions, except the sentence-final position with the adverb included, as in (d).

EXERCISE 6

Insert commas where needed in the following story.

(1) Tiffany was a very lucky girl. (2) Being born into a very wealthy family she always got everything she wanted. (3) She was given a pony before celebrating her eighth birthday. (4) After turning ten years old she had a tutor to teach her anything she wanted to learn. (5) Enjoying sports she learned how to sail, ski, and scuba dive. (6) Turning twelve her interests changed to travel. (7) Enjoying traveling she decided to have her sixteenth birthday on a ship. (8) For a whole weekend, she and her friends were eating, playing games and dancing while cruising to Mexico.

(9) Tiffany's luck began to change, however, on her eighteenth birthday. (10) Her parents promised her a shiny red sports car, but they told her that she would have to pay for the insurance herself. (11) Not having a well-paying job she avoided buying insurance and drove her car anyway. (12) One night, speeding along a winding road she saw another car coming towards her. (13) She beeped loudly, but the car did not move over. (14) She swerved her car to the right barely missing the other car as it drove by. (15) Her car hit a tree, but she was not hurt. (16) Arriving on the scene a police officer asked to see her driver's license and her insurance identification. (17) Lucky Tiffany's luck ran out when she told him that she had no insurance. (18) Unfortunately, she had to pay for the damages to the car out of her own pocket not having followed her parents' advice.

EXERCISE 7

Match the following main clauses and participle phrases. Try placing the participle phrases in different positions, using commas as necessary.

▶ **EXAMPLE:** *Praising its taste, Marco Polo drank tea during his visit to China.*
(7-f)

Participle Phrases	Main Clauses
1. Having healed numerous individuals from malaria	a. agriculture and industry have ruined tropical lands.
2. Conquering American tropical lands	b. bananas are available in every season.
3. Sold either as fresh fruit or made into juice	c. the natives sucked on the tender green shoots.
4. Upsetting the natural order of climate and ecology	d. pineapple has been an important cash crop.
5. Prompting explorers to leave on long voyages	e. pepper was a prize commodity in the Middle Ages.
6. Grown almost year-round	f. Marco Polo drank tea during his visit to China.
7. Praising its taste	g. the Spaniards were introduced to cocoa and chocolate.
8. Extracting the sweet juice from the sugar cane	h. quinine is a very useful medicinal plant.
9. Dried	i. cinnamon rolls up into small sandy-brown cigarette shapes.

Exercise 7
Ordering may vary.
1. h **2.** g **3.** d **4.** a **5.** e **6.** b
7. f **8.** c **9.** i

1. Write the word *amuse* on the blackboard. Ask if anyone knows what type of verb this is. (Ss should say "emotive verb".)
2. Ask one student to read aloud the list of emotive verbs in the focus box.
3. Ask Ss to give you sentences using the verb *amuse* that involve at least two different people. Make sure that some examples are in the passive voice. For example: *The uncle amused the children with a funny face. The mother was amused by her baby's smile.*
4. Ask Ss to identify which of the preceding sentences focuses on the person experiencing an emotion and which one focuses on a person causing an emotion.
5. Write the following incomplete sentences on the board:
   CAUSE: Amusing_____
   EXPERIENCER: Amused _____ by
   Then, ask Ss to complete the sentences using reduced adverb clauses. They should provide sentences with the following structures: *Amusing the children, the uncle made a funny face* and *Amused by her baby's smile, the mother laughed.*
6. Have Ss take turns reading aloud examples in the focus box.

Workbook Ex. 8, pp. 165–166.
Answers: TE p. 553.

▶ Reduced Adverb Clauses with Emotive Verbs

EXAMPLES	EXPLANATIONS
Emotive Verbs: amuse confuse frustrate please annoy embarrass interest puzzle bewilder excite intrigue shock bore frighten irritate surprise captivate	Reduced adverb clauses often contain emotive verbs (verbs that express feelings or emotions).
(a) **Amused** by the movie, Tony laughed out loud. **(b)** **Frightened** by the noise, Donna left to investigate.	If we use the *-ed* participle, the focus is on the person experiencing the emotion.
(c) The clown stood on his head, **amusing** the spectators. **(d)** Two students whispered in the back of the room, **annoying** the teacher.	If we use the *-ing* participle, the focus is on the person or thing causing the emotion.

EXERCISE 8

Circle the correct option.

▶ **EXAMPLE:** Nick jumped, _____ by the lightning.
     (a) frightened   (b) frightening

1. The hikers, _____, gazed at the lovely waterfall.
   (a) surprised and bewildered   (b) surprising and bewildering
2. _____ by mosquitoes, Miko could not sleep.
   (a) Bothered   (b) Bothering
3. The movie, while _____ and sensational, was inappropriate for children.
   (a) intrigued   (b) intriguing
4. _____ that the bears had invaded the camp, the family left.
   (a) Irritated   (b) Irritating
5. _____ by the lecture, many students fell asleep.
   (a) Bored   (b) Boring

292 | UNIT 16

A N S W E R   K E Y

Exercise 8
1. a 2. a 3. b 4. a 5. a 6. a
7. b 8. b 9. a 10. b

6. _____ in Indian artifacts, Martin collected arrowheads.
   (a) Interested   (b) Interesting

7. They walked north instead of east, _____ their directions.
   (a) confused   (b) confusing

8. The play, while _____ and funny, did not keep us awake.
   (a) amused   (b) amusing

9. The children walked away with their heads down, _____.
   (a) embarrassed   (b) embarrassing

10. The trapeze artist did a double flip in the air, _____ the audience with her performance.
   (a) excited   (b) exciting

FOCUS **5**

Avoiding Dangling Participles

A dangling participle occurs if the subject of the main verb is not the same as the implied subject of the participle phrase. To avoid this error, both participle and main verb should relate to the same subject in a sentence.

DANGLING PARTICIPLES	MEANING AS WORDED
(a) The path was more visible **carrying a flashlight.**	The path was carrying a flashlight. **Reword:** Carrying a flashlight, I could see the path.
(b) **Using binoculars,** the pond was clearly defined.	The pond was using binoculars. **Reword:** Using binoculars, I could see the pond clearly.
(c) **Enclosed in a waterproof can,** the hikers kept the matches safe.	The hikers were enclosed in a waterproof can. **Reword:** Enclosed in a waterproof can, the matches were kept safe by the hikers.

FOCUS 5

Note: Even for native English speakers, dangling participles are a common writing error. Once Ss understand why dangling participles are ungrammatical structures in standard written English, they usually enjoy the unintended humor often created by such structures. For example, in the Focus 5 sentences we have paths carrying flashlights, ponds using binoculars, and hikers enclosed in waterproof cans! The identification and/or correction of dangling participles is often part of advanced-level standardized English examinations.

1. Tell the Ss a story about something that recently happened to you or someone else. For example, tell them that you were driving on a freeway Friday night when all of a sudden one of your tires went flat.
2. Write a sentence with a dangling participle summarizing your experience: *While driving on the highway, one of my tires suddenly went flat.*
3. Tell Ss you need to edit this sentence because it doesn't accurately express your meaning. Ask them who was driving. When they say it was you, ask them to identify what you have written instead as the "doer" of the action. When they identify *one of my tires*, erase the entire clause after the adverb clause and write *I*. Then ask Ss to complete the sentence to express what happened.

Exercise 9

Note: For this exercise Ss can also rewrite the participle clause. In some cases, this may mean changing a participle clause to a subordinate clause with a subject and verb.

SUGGESTIONS

1. Give Ss some practice with this before they do the exercise by reading aloud the example.
2. For more practice changing participle clauses to subordinate adverb clauses, use sentences in Exercise 9. For example, the participle clauses in (1) could be rewritten as *After Jane was sprayed by a skunk*; the participle clause in (5) could be rewritten as *After we soaked her clothing for thirty minutes*.
3. If time permits, discuss sentences in Exercise 10 that could *not* easily be rewritten with a subordinate clause before or after doing Exercise 10. Also note that there may be several ways to improve a sentence.

Workbook Ex. 9, pp. 167–168.
Answers: TE p. 553.

UNIT GOAL REVIEW

Ask Ss to look at the goals on the opening page of the unit again. Help them understand how much they have accomplished in each area.

EXERCISE 9

While hiking in the woods in some parts of the world, a person may encounter a skunk and be unexpectedly sprayed. The following sentences relate to Jane's experience with this, but some of them contain dangling participles. Identify which sentences are incorrect, explain why they are humorous as they are presently stated, and reword the main clause to make each sentence correct.

▶ **EXAMPLE:** Hiking in the woods, a skunk crossed Jane's path.
This sentence is humorous because it suggests that the skunk, not Jane, was hiking in the woods. The appropriate form would be "While Jane was hiking in the woods, a skunk crossed her path."

1. Having been sprayed by a skunk, she screamed loudly.
2. Frightened and humiliated, we walked Jane back to the campground.
3. Having returned to the campground, we looked for some catsup.
4. Applying a thick coat of catsup all over her body, the skunk smell was neutralized.
5. Soaking her clothing for thirty minutes in vinegar and water, the smell diminished.
6. Having been victimized by a skunk, we were informed by Jane that she will think twice about hiking in the woods again.

ANSWER KEY

Exercise 9

1. O.K.   2. It sounds as if the friends were frightened and humiliated, not Jane. *Correct:* Frightened and humiliated, Jane walked back to the campground.   3. O.K.   4. It sounds as if the skunk smell applied the thick coat of catsup. *Correct:* Applying a thick coat of catsup all over her body, Jane was able to neutralize the skunk smell.   5. It sounds as if the smell was soaking her clothing. *Correct:* Soaking her clothing for thirty minutes in vinegar and water, Jane was able to diminish the smell.   6. It sounds as if her friends were victimized by the skunk. *Correct:* Having been victimized by a skunk, Jane will think twice about hiking in the woods again.

EXERCISE 10

Rewrite these sentences to correct the participle errors. There may be several ways to correct a sentence.

▶ **EXAMPLE:** After having been bitten by mosquitoes, the ointment felt soothing to her skin.
After having been bitten by mosquitoes, she rubbed a soothing ointment onto her skin.

1. James pet the dog, while barking.
2. While having a bath, water leaked over the sides of the tub.
3. The hurricane terrified people, being driven from their homes.
4. Slithering along the path, I spied a snake.
5. Nearly suffocated by the heat, the room was packed with people.
6. The canned fruits and jams helped the family survive, having prepared for the winter.
7. Sobbing and wailing, the search party was able to locate many survivors.
8. Sitting on the beach, the waves seemed huge to Martin.
9. After spending two hours in the waiting room, the nurse finally called his name.
10. Convicted of the murder of her two sons, the judge sentenced the woman to death.
11. Having achieved so much in so little time, Cecelia's award was well deserved.
12. Since being relocated in Philadelphia, his homesickness grew stronger.

ANSWER KEY

Exercise 10

Answers will vary.

1. The dog, while barking, allowed James to pet him. 2. While I was having a bath, I allowed the water to leak . . . 3. Terrified, people were driven from their homes by the hurricane. 4. I spied a snake, slithering along the path./Slithering along the path, a snake appeared before me. 5. Packed with people, the room felt suffocating. 6. Having prepared for the winter by canning fruits and vegetables, the family was able to survive.

7. Sobbing and wailing, the survivors attracted the search party to the scene of the accident. 8. Sitting on the beach, Martin gazed at the huge waves 9. After spending two hours in the waiting room, he was finally called by the nurse. 10. . . . the woman was sentenced to death by the judge. 11. Having achieved so much in so little time, Cecelia deserved the award. 12. Since being relocated in Philadelphia, he became more and more homesick.

USE YOUR ENGLISH

The activities on these "purple pages" at the end of the unit contain situations that should naturally elicit the unit's structures in a more communicative framework. While Ss are doing these activities in class, you can circulate and listen to determine if they have actually achieved the goals in the opening page of the unit.

Activity 1

Play textbook audio. The tapescript for this listening appears on p. 571 of this book.

EXPANSION

Since every student response will be different, you may allow volunteers to read their paragraph completions aloud to show Ss the variation.

Activity 2

VARIATION

1. If you are familiar with a particular talent of one of your Ss, ask him or her to demonstrate a procedure or process for the class (for example, how to make origami animals, how to prepare a simple dish, or how to draw cartoons).

2. Ask Ss to summarize the procedure in a paragraph, using at least two reduced adverb clauses.

Use Your English

ACTIVITY 1: LISTENING/ WRITING

STEP 1 Relax, close your eyes, and listen attentively to five taped descriptions. Each one is unfinished. Use your imagination to create a visual image that completes each piece. Listen to each description a second time. Stop the tape after each one. What do you see? Write your ideas in complete sentences below. Try to use as many participle phrases as you can.

▶ **EXAMPLE:** *Looking ahead, I see high jagged peaks. Each one is covered with snow. Dotting the landscape below, hundreds of lakes are nestled among groves of trees.*

STEP 2 Now listen again and write down any *-ed* or *-ing* participle phrases that you hear.

▶ **EXAMPLES:** *The propeller turning and the engine roaring, the plane is ready for takeoff.*
Ascending higher and higher, you see nothing but white fog in every direction.

ACTIVITY 2: WRITING

We often use reduced adverb clauses to give directions for carrying out some procedure. Consider something you know how to do very well that requires several motions (for example, making beef jerky, changing a tire, operating a video camera). Then, write the directions to do this activity, using at least two reduced adverb clauses.

▶ **EXAMPLE:** *Before making beef jerky, purchase three pounds of lean beef. Cut strips of the beef about one-half-inch thick. Then, hang these strips on a wood framework about four to six feet off the ground. After building a smoke fire, allow the meat to dry in the sun and wind.*

ACTIVITY 3: READING/LISTENING/WRITING

The Old West has been a popular theme of many books, movies, and television programs. Action-packed scenes show men and women of the frontier fighting against excessive temperatures, hunger, wild animals, and outlaws. Read a western story or watch a western show on TV or at a theater and try to summarize an impressive scene. Use at least four reduced adverb clauses in your summary.

▶ **EXAMPLE:** *Hearing that fifty head of cattle had disappeared from the Parker Ranch, the sheriff organized a tracking party to try to recover the animals. Twelve men, chosen for their riding skill and speed, were assembled. Rising early in the morning, the tracking party began their search. Following the tracks of the cattle, the men located all fifty head at the base of a ravine before noon. They also located the three rustlers who had stolen them. Riding back to the Parker Ranch, the trackers were relieved that the outlaws had been captured.*

ACTIVITY 4: LISTENING/WRITING

Imagine you are a sports announcer for a local TV station. Watch five minutes of a sports event, e.g., basketball, baseball, or football, and take notes on what happened. Write a paragraph describing the players' activities.

▶ **EXAMPLE:** *Crossing second base, Tony Evans was tapped by another player. Running to third, he tripped and fell . . .*

ACTIVITY 5: LISTENING/SPEAKING

Check out a "Books on Tape" novel (for example, Charles Dickens' *A Tale of Two Cities*, Mark Twain's *Huckleberry Finn*, Willa Cather's *O, Pioneers*) from your local library or video store. Play the tape and identify one or two descriptive passages. Within these passages, listen for examples of reduced adverb clauses. Share these examples with your classmates.

Reducing Adverb Clauses **297**

Activity 3
VARIATION

If time permits, for a more guided activity, and one that would permit more student collaboration, show twenty minutes or so from a classic western film (e.g., *High Noon, Stagecoach, McCabe and Mrs. Miller*) or give Ss an excerpt from a western novel (e.g., one by Louie Lamour) for them to summarize. A film clip might be best since Ss would then need to rely on their notes rather than a written text. Since all Ss would be working from the same source, they could work in pairs to write the summaries.

Activity 4
EXPANSION

In addition to writing a paragraph, Ss could present their texts orally to the rest of the class or in small groups.

VARIATION

Give Ss other contexts to describe. For example, Ss could chronicle their own or someone else's odyssey in outer space or a journey by time machine travel into the past or the future.

Activity 5

This activity assumes a rather high level of proficiency in listening comprehension.

VARIATION

As with the suggestion for Activity 3, make this a classroom activity:

1. Find a taped novel or short story at your campus or public library and locate an appropriate excerpt. (Consider a novel or story you have previously read.)
2. Ask Ss to summarize part of the text using reduced adverb clauses. Or identify reduced adverb clauses in advance, give Ss written examples, and ask them to listen for the examples.

The test for this unit can be found on p. 515. The answers are on p. 516.

Unit 17

UNIT OVERVIEW

Prepositions can be one of the most difficult language structures to master in English. Unit 17 assumes that students (Ss) have already learned how to locate objects in space (e.g., *The pencil is on the desk*) and have learned various peculiarities of prepositions (viz., that they are deleted in sentences such as *She went home*). Focus will instead be on the co-occurrence of prepositions with verbs, adjectives, and nouns in speech and writing.

UNIT GOALS

Review the goals listed on this page so Ss understand what they should be able to know by the end of the unit.

OPENING TASK

This task encourages Ss to make observations and draw conclusions about groups of people who move from one country to another.

SETTING UP THE TASK

As a class or in small groups, Ss can discuss their impressions of the photographs.

CONDUCTING THE TASK
Step 1

Bring in additional photos from magazines or books. Encourage Ss to tell their classmates what they know about these different groups.

UNIT 17

PREPOSITION CLUSTERS

UNIT GOALS:

- To use verbs with the correct preposition clusters
- To use adjectives with the correct preposition clusters
- To use common multiword preposition clusters
- To use preposition clusters to introduce a topic or identify a source

OPENING TASK
New Arrivals

STEP 1 Look at the following pictures and captions describing immigrants and refugees from around the world.

Somalian refugees in a refugee camp.

Italian immigrants deplaning in Australia.

STEP 2 Now think about one group of refugees or immigrants that has recently settled in your native country or in a country you are familiar with. Think about the circumstances surrounding the group's departure from their homeland and present living conditions in the new country. Jot down notes about these circumstances in the chart below.

Immigrant or Refugee Group = _____	
1. Why they departed from their country	
2. What they hope for in their new country	
3. What group (if any) they are at odds with in the new country	
4. What aspects of life they are unaccustomed to in the new country	
5. Who they associate with in the new country	
6. What jobs they are good at in the new country	
7. How their contributions result in a richer cultural heritage for the new country	

STEP 3 Discuss the results of your brainstorming with your classmates.

Step 2

Ask Ss to complete the chart individually. You might give examples of recent immigration movements particular to the region in which they are living.

Step 3

Listen to the way Ss use prepositions as they share their knowledge of immigration in small groups. Be aware that this topic may be sensitive for certain students, especially those who are from war-torn areas. Also be aware that certain stereotypes may be stated, which you and other Ss do not agree with. Use this discussion as an opportunity for greater communication and understanding among Ss as you and the class discuss certain immigration reasons, expectations, experiences, and contributions.

FOCUS **1**

SUGGESTION

1. Ask student pairs to brainstorm any verbs that they know that must be followed by a preposition. Ss might mention verbs in the focus box as well as some of their own.
2. Call on one reporter from each pair to provide examples.
3. Ask Ss to read the focus box silently.
4. Note that some of the verbs by themselves are transitive (e.g., *plan, count*) and others are intransitive (e.g., *differ, consist*).

Exercise 2

Ask Ss to complete this exercise individually and then share answers with a partner.

Workbook Exs. 1 & 2, pp. 169–170.
Answers: TE p. 553.

▶ **Verb + Preposition Clusters**

EXAMPLES	EXPLANATION
(a) Refugees **differ from** immigrants in that they have not chosen to leave their homeland.	Verb + preposition clusters must be followed by noun phrases or gerunds.
(b) Refugees usually **plan on** returning to their homeland as soon as the hostilities are over.	

> **Other examples of verb + preposition clusters are:**
> consist of   count on
> hope for   deal with

EXERCISE 1

There are four verb + preposition clusters in the chart prompts in the Opening Task. Can you identify them? Now, use your notes from the chart and write four sentences about the immigrant or refugee group you described, using verb and preposition clusters.

▶ **EXAMPLE:** *The Vietnamese departed from Vietnam in order to find better economic and political conditions.*

EXERCISE 2

The following incomplete sentences contain verb + preposition clusters. Complete them in two ways, with a noun phrase and with a gerund.

▶ **EXAMPLE:** The new parents marveled at ⎰ *the beauty of their child.* ___ (noun phrase)
⎱ *seeing their son for the first time* . (gerund)

1. A healthy diet consists of ⎰ _____ .
⎱ _____ .

2. The plan called for ⎰ _____ .
⎱ _____ .

3. Does anyone object to ⎰ _____ ?
⎱ _____ ?

ANSWER KEY

Exercise 1

The verb + preposition clusters are:
(1) depart from, **(2)** hope for,
(5) associate with, **(7)** result in.
Answers will vary.
They *hoped for* an opportunity to live freely.
They *associate* mostly *with* themselves.
Their refined aesthetic sense *has resulted in* many contributions to the arts.

Exercise 2

Answers will vary.
1. a carefully monitored diet/eating lots of fruits and vegetables. 2. billions of funds/entering the country from the north
3. a drink on the way home?/leaving the party early? 4. your love and support/becoming a doctor 5. the introductions/unloading the

cargo from the van 6. his friends/playing sports 7. the fight against drugs?/winning the election? 8. the war/opening the new nuclear plant. 9. the two girls?/helping her friends and smothering her friends?
10. the amendment/banning citizens' possession of weapons

4. Ever since I was a child, I have counted on _____ .
_____ .

5. As it is very late, you can dispense with _____ .
_____ .

6. After the accident, Jaime withdrew from _____ .
_____ .

7. Will the president succeed in _____ ?
_____ ?

8. The protesters were demonstrating against _____ .
_____ .

9. Why can't she distinguish between _____ ?
_____ ?

10. I don't agree with the politician who believes in _____ .
_____ .

Ask one student to read aloud the examples and the explanation for the class. If needed, provide additional examples, perhaps related to your class/context or an academic context in general: *The teachers united with the students on protecting the new graduation requirements.*

Exercise 3

Model this exercise with a student first so that Ss understand how the questions and answers should proceed.

EXPANSION

Ask Ss to use the 7 verb + preposition clusters to create 7 more original sentences.

▶ Verb + *With* Clusters

EXAMPLES	EXPLANATION
(a) The laborers **consulted with** their union. (b) They decided not to **cooperate with** management.	Verb + *with* clusters show association between or among people.

Other examples of verb + *with* clusters are:

associate with	join with	unite with
deal with	side with	

EXERCISE 3

Ask and answer *should* questions with a partner. Use the words from the three columns below for ideas.

▶ **EXAMPLE:** *Should homeowners deal with realtors to sell their homes?*
No, they shouldn't deal with realtors; they should try to sell the houses themselves.

	Subject	Verb + Preposition	Object
1.	homeowners	associate with	their children
2.	criminals	cooperate with	students
3.	the rich	consult with	ophthamologists
4.	parents	deal with	the police
5.	patients	join with	realtors
6.	young people	side with	gangs
7.	teachers	unite with	the poor

ANSWER KEY

Exercise 3
Answers will vary.
2. Should criminals cooperate with the police to reduce their jail terms?   3. Shouldn't the rich unite with the poor in the fight against AIDS?   4. Should parents side with their children under any circumstances?

5. Should patients consult with ophthalmologists about their eyes?
6. Should young people join with gangs who are breaking rules of law and order?
7. Should teachers associate with students outside of class?

FOCUS 3

▶ Verb + *From* Clusters

EXAMPLES	EXPLANATION
(a) The garage was **detached from** the house.	Verb + *from* clusters imply separation.
(b) Rice pudding **differs from** bread pudding.	

Other examples of verb + *from* clusters are:

abstain desist detach deviate	*from*	differ dissent emerge escape	*from*	flee recede recoil retire	*from*	separate shrink withdraw	*from*

EXERCISE 4

Fill in one of the verbs + *from* from Focus 3 in each blank below. You may need to change the verb form in some examples.

1. Certain groups follow restrictive dietary laws. For example, Orthodox Jews
   (a) _____ pork and shellfish. Sometimes these and other groups
   who (b) _____ the status quo or (c) _____ the norm
   are considered strange by outsiders but extremely religious by those from
   within the same community.

2. Refugees come to a foreign country to live for many different reasons. They
   want to (a) _____ persecution, war, disaster, or epidemics.
   Certain Southeast Asians have (b) _____ tragic conditions in their
   native lands but have become successful in their new homes around the
   world.

3. Some newcomers to a country go through culture shock. This
   phenomenon makes some people (a) _____ social relationships.
   Because of depression, they also sometimes (b) _____ responsibilities. They may even (c) _____ psychological help because they
   are not used to dealing with doctors for psychological problems.

4. Mr. Johnson is getting older. His hair (a) _____ his forehead. Next
   year he plans to (b) _____ his job.

Preposition Clusters **303**

FOCUS 3

Ask one student to read examples *a* and *b* and the explanation for the class. Then ask Ss to provide synonyms for the phrases in the box, e.g., *abstain from = refrain from, desist from = discontinue, detach from = separate from, deviate from = diverge from,* etc.

As with Focus 2, you could give (or elicit) additional examples related to your class or to an academic context: *The student's ideas <u>differed from</u> the teacher's.*

Exercise 4

Encourage Ss to use past, present and infinitive verb forms to fill in the blanks.

ANSWER KEY

Exercise 4
Answers will vary.
1. **(a)** abstain from **(b)** deviate from
(c) differ from **2. (a)** escape from **(b)** emerged from **3. (a)** shrink from **(b)** recoil from **(c)** withdraw from **4. (a)** is receding from **(b)** to retire from

Teacher's Edition: Unit 17 **303**

FOCUS 4

Ask Ss to silently read the focus box. Point out that in each of these examples, *for* could be replaced by the expressions *to get* or *to have.* For example, *I yearn to have a cigarette every morning. I wish to get a new job.* As with Focuses 2 and 3, you could provide additional examples related to your class or to an academic context: *After two hours, the students <u>long for</u> a break.*

Workbook Ex. 2, p. 170.
Answers: TE p. 553.

Exercise 5

One of the best ways to teach preposition clusters is by grouping verbs that take the same preposition together. This exercise contains several common verb + preposition combinations. Ask Ss if they can determine the general meanings of *at, of, to, on,* and *at* in each item group. They should induce meanings such as: *of +concerning, to + towards, on + entering on, in + within some type of limits, at + toward or in the direction of.*

Exercise 6

1. Ask Ss to take turns making sentences.

2. Ask the class to brainstorm other groups coming to the U.S. today. Write these names on the board, e.g., Russians, Tibetans, Kosovics, etc.
3. Collaboratively write a paragraph about what these groups *yearn for, pray for, ask for, thirst for, hope for, wish for,* or *long for* in leaving their native countries.

FOCUS **4**

▶ Verb + *For* Clusters

EXAMPLES	EXPLANATION
(a) I **yearn for** a cigarette every morning. (b) I **pray for** the strength to stop smoking.	Several verb + *for* clusters relate to desire or need.

Other examples of verb + *for* clusters are:				
ask for	*thirst for*	*hope for*	*wish for*	*long for*

EXERCISE 5

Select one or two of the sets of preposition clusters below. Create short paragraph(s) with the verb + preposition clusters and then share the results with your class.

▶ **EXAMPLE:** rebel at, shudder at, jeer at

*The people held up their fists and **jeered at** the tanks as they moved into the city. They had been **rebelling at** following the central government for the past twenty-five years. They **shuddered at** the thought of military rule in their own quiet neighborhoods.*

1. talk of, think of, disapprove of
2. listen to, object to, reply to
3. plan on, embark on, live on
4. believe in, persist in, result in
5. look at, laugh at, point at

EXERCISE 6

Study the chart on the next page about immigration movements to the United States. Use different verbs + *for* to describe why the different groups came to the United States.

▶ **EXAMPLE:** Cubans   *The Cubans longed for freedom in a non-Communist country.*

1. Irish
2. Germans
3. Norwegians
4. Poles
5. Jews
6. Austrians
7. Italians
8. Mexicans
9. Haitians
10. Vietnamese

What other immigrant groups are coming to the United States today? Why?

ANSWER KEY

Exercise 5

Answers will vary.
1. The group <u>talked of</u> forming a committee to help the homeless. They <u>thought of</u> several projects they could pursue. Most <u>disapproved of</u> distributing "free handouts." 2. She <u>listened to</u> all of the arguments against the new shopping mall. She <u>objected to</u> many of them. That is why she decided to <u>reply to</u> the most offensive ones with a series of letters to the mayor. 3. We are <u>planning on</u> a South Seas trip which we will <u>embark on</u> in the middle of February. We will <u>live on</u> our boat for the next

few months, only getting off at major ports.
4. I <u>believe in</u> equal rights for women. I will <u>persist in</u> supporting the Equal Rights Amendment until it is passed. This will hopefully <u>result in</u> better living and working conditions for future generations of women. 5. We <u>looked at</u> the funny antics of the clown. My daughter <u>laughed at</u> his big, red nose. My son <u>pointed at</u> his very large black shoes.

Exercise 6

Answers will vary.
1. The Irish <u>longed for</u> a land where they could raise good crops. 2. The Germans <u>wished for</u>

better economic times. 3. The Norwegians <u>yearned for</u> good farmland. 4. The Poles <u>thirsted for</u> a place with no political repression. 5. The Jews <u>prayed for</u> a place where they would have religious freedom. 6. The Austrians <u>hoped for</u> a less populated land. 7. The Italians <u>thirsted for</u> economic opportunity. 8. The Mexicans <u>longed for</u> a peaceful existence. 9. The Haitians <u>yearned for</u> a more prosperous life. 10. The Vietnamese <u>wished for</u> a noncommunist government.

---

304 Grammar Dimensions, Platinum Edition

Major Immigration Movements to the United States

Group	When	Number	Why
Irish	1840s and 1850s	About 1½ million	Famine resulting from potato crop failure
Germans	1840s to 1880s	About 4 million	Severe economic depression and unemployment, political unrest, and failure of liberal revolutionary movement
Danes, Norwegians, Swedes	1870s to 1900s	About 1½ million	Poverty; shortage of farmland
Poles	1880s to 1920s	About 1 million	Poverty; political repression; cholera epidemics
Jews from Eastern Europe	1880s to 1920s	About 2½ million	Religious persecution
Austrians, Czechs, Hungarians, Slovaks	1880s to 1920s	About 4 million	Poverty; overpopulation
Italians	1880s to 1920s	About 4½ million	Poverty; overpopulation
Mexicans	1910 to 1920s	About 700,000	Mexican Revolution of 1920; low wages and unemployment
	1950s to 1990s	About 2 million	Poverty; unemployment
Cubans	1960s to 1990s	About 700,000	Communist takeover in 1959
Dominicans, Haitians, Jamaicans	1970s and 1990s	About 900,000	Poverty; unemployment
Vietnamese	1970s and 1990s	About 500,000	Vietnam War 1957 to 1975; Communist takeover

Source: U.S. Immigration and Naturalization Service

Workbook Exs. 3 & 4, pp. 171–172.
Answers: TE p. 553.

1. Write the following 5 statements on the board and conduct a short survey with the class. Ask Ss to raise their hands for the answers *usually, sometimes,* or *rarely* as you tally the results in a little chart. For example:

	Usually	Sometimes	Rarely
a	////	//	/
b	/	////	//
c	///	/	///
d	////	///	
e	/	///	///

   a. I am homesick for my birthplace.
   b. I am confident in my research skills.
   c. I am close to my parents.
   d. I am interested in reading fiction.
   e. I am satisfied with my English ability.

2. Ask volunteers to summarize the results: *Our class is usually homesick for our birthplaces, Our class is only sometimes confident in our research skills,* etc.

3. Ask Ss to look at the 5 sentences and notice what follows the verb. They should note that there are two types of adjectives—common ones like *close* and others derived from participles like *interested.*

4. Ask volunteers to read examples *a* through *d* aloud.

5. Ask the class to read the other examples silently.

Exercise 7

EXPANSION

Ask Ss to create a few more questions with these additional adjective + preposition combinations: *capable of, certain of, different from, famous for, faithful to, fond of, guilty of, jealous of, popular with, ready for, superior to,* and *useful to.*

▶ Adjective + Preposition Clusters

EXAMPLES	EXPLANATION
(a) The house stands **adjacent to** the river. (b) The town is **dependent on** fishing.	Adjective + preposition clusters
(c) We are **burdened with** high taxes. (d) Miwa **is accustomed to** eating three meals a day.	*Be* + adjective (*-ed*) + preposition clusters

Other examples of adjective + preposition clusters are:

free immune } *from* safe	eager homesick } *for* sorry	compatible unfamiliar } *with* content
expert good } *at* swift	proficient rich } *in* successful	careless happy } *about* enthusiastic
ignorant afraid } *of* proud		

EXERCISE 7

Create your own questions for the following answers, using two different adjective + preposition phrases from Focus 5.

▶ **EXAMPLES:** A healthy mathematician
   *Who is **free from** disease and **good at** math?*

   A sloppy executive
   *Who is **careless about** his appearance and **successful in** his job?*

1. A calm athlete
2. A claustrophobic politician
3. An anxious addict
4. A clean mechanic
5. A weary worrier
6. A joyful seamstress
7. A repentant runner
8. Your suggestion

ANSWER KEY

Exercise 7
Answers will vary.
1. Who is content with a quiet disposition and good at sports?   2. Who is afraid of closed spaces and successful in politics?   3. Who is concerned about too many things and addicted to drugs?   4. Who is free from dirt and expert at fixing cars?   5. Who is tired of work and concerned about everything?   6. Who is happy about life and good at sewing?   7. Who is sorry for what she did wrong and swift at running?   8. Answers will vary.

EXERCISE 8

Discuss what the following organizations are *interested in, concerned about, accustomed to, committed to, dedicated to,* and/or *preoccupied with.*

▶ **EXAMPLE:** The World Bank
The World Bank is interested in aiding the world's poor.

1. Greenpeace
2. European Community
3. The Peace Corps
4. The United Nations
5. The Red Cross
6. UNICEF
7. The Fulbright Program
8. Amnesty International
9. Your suggestion
10. Your suggestion

FOCUS **6**

Multiword Preposition Clusters

Some preposition clusters consist of three or more words.

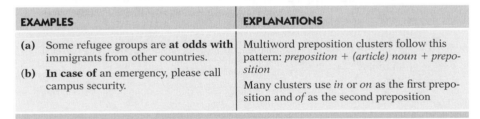

EXAMPLES	EXPLANATIONS
(a) Some refugee groups are **at odds with** immigrants from other countries. **(b)** **In case of** an emergency, please call campus security.	Multiword preposition clusters follow this pattern: *preposition + (article) noun + preposition* Many clusters use *in* or *on* as the first preposition and *of* as the second preposition

Exercise 8

SUGGESTION

If Ss are unfamiliar with these organizations, give them a few hints. Write, in random order, the following nouns and phrases on the board and ask Ss to match the noun with the appropriate organization and create a sentence describing the organization's main purpose: *stopping inhumane activities, curing sick children, working for world peace, regulating finances, protecting the environment, providing medical help, helping underdeveloped nations, funding opportunities for scholars.* (Example: environment + Greenpeace, *Greenpeace is interested in saving the environment.*)

Workbook Exs. 5 & 6, pp. 172–173.
Answers: TE p. 554.

FOCUS 6

1. Dictate the following sentences to your Ss.
   a. *In case of emergency, leave the building through the rear exit.*
   b. *On behalf of John, we want to thank you for being here.*
   c. *In the event of an earthquake, do not use the elevator.*
   d. *On the advice of Dr. Smith, you should take your pills.*
2. Ask Ss to underline the multiword preposition clusters that they have heard.
3. Ask them to describe how they are similar and different.
4. Ask them to read the focus box silently for more examples.

ANSWER KEY

Exercise 8
Answers will vary.
1. Greenpeace is interested in saving the environment.   2. The European Community is dedicated to regulating the finances of the European nations.   3. The Peace Corps is committed to helping underdeveloped nations.   4. The United Nations is concerned about world peace.   5. The Red Cross is accustomed to providing medical help during times of war or famine.   6. UNICEF is dedicated to curing children's diseases.   7. The Fulbright Program is preoccupied with giving opportunities for scholars to share their knowledge in other parts of the world.   8. Amnesty International is dedicated to exposing and stopping inhumane activities throughout the world.

Common multiword clusters:			
in + noun + *of*	*on* + noun + *of*	*in* + *the* + noun + *of*	*on* + *the* + noun + *of*
in case of	*on account of*	*in the course of*	*on the advice of*
in charge of	*on behalf of*	*in the event of*	*on the basis of*
in place of	*on top of*	*in the habit of*	*on the part of*
in lieu of	*on grounds of*	*in the name of*	*on the strength of*
in favor of		*in the process of*	*on the face of*

Less regular combinations:			
by means of	*in return for*	*at odds with*	*with the exception of*
with respect to	*in addition to*	*for the sake of*	

EXERCISE 9

Write *in* (*the*) or *on* (*the*) in the following blanks.

▶ **EXAMPLE:** ___*On the*___ basis of the evidence, the defendant was ac-
quitted.

1. _____ case of an emergency, duck under your desks
   and cover your heads.
2. _____ account of his great skill, he completed the task
   with ease.
3. _____ advice of my physician, I must take these pills
   and get plenty of rest.
4. I have decided to buy the warehouse _____ strength of
   expert opinion.
5. _____ event of an earthquake, do not panic.
6. She wants a divorce _____ grounds of mental
   cruelty.
7. He will pay the bail _____ lieu of staying in jail.
8. She is _____ habit of joking when she should be serious.
9. _____ behalf of the committee, I would like to thank
   you for all of your work.
10. _____ course of the evening, everyone laughed and had a
    good time.

ANSWER KEY

Exercise 9
1. In 2. On 3. On the 4. on the 5. In
the 6. on 7. in 8. in the 9. On
10. In the

EXERCISE 10

Working with a partner, fill in the following blanks with the expressions below. Compare your answers with those of your classmates.

in the habit of	with reference to	for the sake of
as a consequence of	with the purpose of	in lieu of
for lack of	with an eye to	
on account of	in addition to	

▶ **EXAMPLE:** <u>With reference to</u> your question, many Afghans are living in Pakistan and Iran.

1. The United States is _____ turning back many Mexicans from its southern border.
2. Bulgarians of Turkish descent are emigrating from Bulgaria _____ reuniting with their families in Turkey.
3. European Jews and North American Jews have inhabited Israel _____ recreating a Jewish homeland.
4. _____ the bloodshed in Sri Lanka, many Tamils have left Sri Lanka and gone to England.
5. One reason some Vietnamese have been turned back to Vietnam from Hong Kong is _____ space.
6. Nicaraguans have fled to the United States _____ escaping war.
7. After 1975 many Cambodians escaped into Thailand _____ humane treatment.
8. _____ Moroccans and Tunisians, Senegalese have immigrated to Italy to find work.
9. _____ starvation, Nigerians, Ugandans, Sudanese, and Chadeans have fled to other African countries.
10. _____ staying in Romania, many Romanians of Hungarian descent are moving to Hungary.

Exercise 10

E X P A N S I O N

Ask Ss to work alone and create at least 5 original sentences using the expressions in the box.

Workbook Exs. 7 & 8, pp. 174–175.
Answers: TE p. 554.

A N S W E R   K E Y

Exercise 10
1. in the habit of   2. with the purpose of/with an eye to   3. for the sake of/with the purpose of/with an eye to   4. As a consequence of   5. for lack of   6. for the sake of/with an eye to   7. for lack of   8. In addition to   9. On account of/as a consequence of   10. In lieu of

1. Explain to Ss the purpose of *speaking about/of* for introducing a topic.
2. Explain that you will play a simple game with them in which you will talk about a particular topic and you will have them interrupt you using one of the expressions just mentioned followed by a question. For example, you will say: *"The weather has been very hot today."* And a student will reply *"Speaking of/about the weather, hasn't this been a hot autumn in general?"*
3. Practice with a few more examples:
   a. *I plan to assign a lot of homework tonight.*
   b. *I very much enjoy going to the movies.*
   c. *I hope that there won't be much traffic on the way home tonight.*
   d. *I need to buy some new clothes.*
4. Ask Ss to read the focus box for other ways to introduce a topic with preposition clusters as well as how to identify a source.
5 Give Ss a little oral practice with identifying a source by having them report one piece of advice that their mother or father gave to them in the past. For example: *According to my mother, it is not advisable to swim after eating a big meal.*

Exercise 11

Ask Ss to complete the sentences in pairs. Randomly ask one member of a pair to read one sentence to the rest of the class.

FOCUS **7**

▶ # Preposition Clusters: Introducing a Topic/ Identifying a Source

EXAMPLES	EXPLANATIONS
(a) **Pertaining/Relating to** immigrant quotas, the United States has tightened its restrictions in recent years.	Some preposition clusters can introduce a topic.
(b) **Speaking about/of** persecution, certain immigrant groups have endured more than others.	
(c) **With respect/reference to** culture shock, most immigrant groups experience it in one form or another.	
(d) **Based on/upon** immigration statistics, more men than women emigrate from their native countries.	Other preposition clusters can identify a source.
(e) **According to** Professor Herbert, many immigrants decide to return to their native countries after a few years.	

EXERCISE 11

Complete the following sentences.

▶ **EXAMPLE:** Based on the weather report, _____it will rain tomorrow_____.

1. According to scientists, _____.
2. With respect to our solar system, _____.
3. With reference to recent political events, _____.
4. Speaking about discrimination, _____.
5. Relating to my last conversation with my family, _____.
6. Based upon my own observations, _____.
7. According to the dictionary, _____.
8. Pertaining to the death penalty, _____.
9. With respect to the students in this class, _____.
10. Speaking of good movies, _____.

ANSWER KEY

Exercise 11
Answers will vary.
1. the ozone layer is fast depleting 2. it seems to be expanding 3. something needs to be done about settling racial tensions 4. laws should be passed to protect all citizens from this practice 5. I have decided to spend the summer in Paris 6. he will never make a good baseball player 7. the word advisor has two spellings—*a-d-v-i-s-o-r* or *a-d-v-i-s-e-r* 8. I do not think it is ever justified 9. we are all very good at taking tests 10. did you see on video yet?

EXERCISE 12

Supply the appropriate prepositions for the blanks in the following passage adapted from John Crewdson's *The Tarnished Door* (New York: Times Books, Inc., 1983, pp. 96–97).

The reforms of the McCarran Act of 1952 limited annual immigration to the United States to 290,000, with 120,000 of the immigrants coming (1) _____from_____ Western Hemisphere countries and the other 170,000 coming (2) _____ Eastern Hemisphere countries. Preference was given (3) _____ the reunification of families by reserving three-quarters of each year's visas for relatives of resident aliens and citizens of the United States. Thus, most immigrants over the 290,000 were family members who were exempted (4) _____ the numerical limits of the preference system. Because one-fifth of the visas were reserved (5) _____ persons with needed talents or skills, many of those who did get visas were unsuited (6) _____ all but the most menial work. The year the law was passed, the United States admitted 113,000 immigrants from Europe and only 71,300 from Asia, Mexico, Africa, and Latin America. By 1977 the number of European immigrants had fallen (7) _____ 70,000 while the number of Asians, Africans, Mexicans, and Latin Americans had risen (8) _____ 231,000.

In 1976, in an effort to increase the equitability of visa distribution still further, the 20,000 annual ceiling on immigrants from each Eastern Hemisphere nation was also imposed (9) _____ all Western Hemisphere countries, including Mexico, which until then had by itself accounted (10) _____ about half the Western Hemisphere's quota of 120,000 visas a year.

Preposition Clusters | **311**

Exercise 12
EXPANSION
Assign Ss to look for paragraphs in the newspaper that illustrate various preposition clusters described in this chapter. Ask them to share their results with the class.

Workbook Ex. 9, p. 175.
Answers: TE p. 554.

UNIT GOAL REVIEW

Ask Ss to look at the goals on the opening page of the unit again. Help them understand how much they have accomplished in each area.

ANSWER KEY

Exercise 12
(1) from (2) from (3) to (4) from
(5) for (6) for (7) to (8) to (9) on
(10) for

USE YOUR ENGLISH

The activities on these "purple pages" at the end of the unit contain situations that should naturally elicit the unit's structures in a more communicative framework. While Ss are doing these activities in class, you can circulate and listen to determine if they have actually achieved the goals on the opening page of the unit.

Activity 1

Play textbook audio. The tapescript for this listening appears on p. 572 of this book.

EXPANSION

Ask Ss to write a short paragraph about John F. Kennedy's administration based on the tape excerpt. Ask them to include at least 3 preposition clusters in their paragraph.

Use Your English

ACTIVITY 1: LISTENING / WRITING

Listen to the following tape and take notes about President John F. Kennedy's administration. After listening to the tape, answer the following questions, using preposition clusters in each response.

▶ **EXAMPLE:** What is one positive cause that JFK contributed to?
He contributed to the establishment of the Peace Corps.

1. What was Kennedy's administration known for?
2. How did he unite with Americans of all colors and religions?
3. What were the elderly happy about?
4. Speaking about school segregation, what did Kennedy do?
5. Who cooperated with local technicians to build roads in Tanganyika, Africa?
6. Who did the United States join with to form the Organization for Economic Cooperation and Development?
7. What were the Latin Americans enthusiastic about in 1962?
8. Why did the United States and Russia consult with each other?

ACTIVITY 2: RESEARCH/WRITING

The following terms relate to intercultural contact or movement from, to, or within a country. Find definitions of the following terms from dictionaries, encyclopedias, textbooks, classmates, your teacher, etc. Give definitions of these terms while citing your sources, using the expression *according to*.

▶ **EXAMPLE:** ***According to*** the World Book Encyclopedia, a refugee is any uprooted person who has a well-founded fear of persecution for reasons of race, religion, nationality, membership in a particular social group, or political opinion.

1. refugee
2. emigrant
3. guest worker
4. brain drain

5. multiculturalism
6. political correctness
7. melting pot
8. xenophobia

ACTIVITY 3: WRITING

The Statue of Liberty in New York Harbor has a plaque at its base that states the following:

> Give me your tired, your poor
> Your huddled masses yearning to breathe free,
> The wretched refuse of your teeming shore.
> Send them, the homeless, tempest-tossed to me,
> I lift my lamp beside the golden door!

Do you believe it is possible for countries such as the United States to have an open-door policy? Should all people who desire it be allowed to freely immigrate and settle in the United States? What, if any, limits should be put on immigration? Should there be quotas? What obligation would the new country have to support the immigrants? Write a short composition on this topic, incorporating at least five preposition clusters you have learned in this unit.

Activity 2

1. Divide the class into 5 to 6 groups and ask them to seek definitions of the 8 terms for homework. Each group will be assigned a different source, e.g., dictionary, encyclopedia, classmates, textbooks on immigration, the teacher (you will need to make yourself available during an office hour for this), or family members.

2. On the next day, ask Ss to form groups and orally share the information they obtained from different sources. As much as possible, assure that Ss who consulted different sources are seated together.

3. Ask Ss to collaboratively write a paragraph that incorporates the meanings derived from various sources. Also ask them to use the words and phrases in Focus 7 for variety in their citations.

Activity 3

SUGGESTION

When grading the compositions, be selective in your grading by ignoring all grammar errors except the preposition clusters. In this way, Ss will know that they should focus on mastering this structure at this time.

Activity 4

VARIATION

This game could be extended by asking the two teams to create a second set of eight cards with other preposition prompts. This time they could exchange the cards and produce questions (instead of statements) in order to win. Bring some candy or small prizes to reward the winning team.

Activity 5

This activity is best done as a homework assignment. It is difficult to predict how prevalent these structures will be in random TV show or video excerpts. However, if the entire class has the same assignment and Ss are only required to listen for 15 minutes, it should not be too burdensome. Generally, there will be 3 or 4 Ss who listened to an excerpt that contained multiple examples of this structure. Even a few good examples when shared with the class will allow Ss to realize that these structures do indeed occur in authentic oral discourse.

ACTIVITY 4: WRITING/SPEAKING

Form two teams. Have each team create a set of eight cards that contain various types of preposition clusters with one or more prepositions missing. For example:

| hint _____ | _____ reference _____ |
| elegible _____ | _____ favor _____ |

Exchange cards with another team. See which team is most accurate at producing sentences with *because* clauses and the preposition cluster on the card.

▶ **EXAMPLES:**
1. *I like to* **hint at** *what I want for my birthday because my family never knows what to buy.*
2. *I was* **eligible for** *the grand prize because I had entered the contest.*
3. *In* **reference to** *his request, I do not feel that we should grant it because he is very irresponsible.*

ACTIVITY 5: LISTENING/WRITING

Watch fifteen minutes of a nature TV show or video that describes the life cycles, migration patterns, communication habits, etc. of an animal (for example, polar bear, bumblebee, salmon, jack rabbit, Canada goose). Jot down examples of preposition clusters that you hear.

▶ **EXAMPLE:** *Canada geese depart from their homes in the north and fly south for the winter.*

ACTIVITY 6: WRITING/SPEAKING

The suffix -ism refers to a doctrine, practice, system, quality, or theory. For example, "terrorism" is a practice of using terror to accomplish a particular end. Below you will find an explanation of terrorism that utilizes adjective + preposition phrases. Create more sentences that explain other "isms," using the same adjective + preposition phrases or others of your choice. Then present these explanations to a small group or the class.

▶ **EXAMPLE:** *Terrorism is often **associated with** hijacking. It is usually **accompanied by** violence. It is based on/upon perceived injustices among groups. It is dependent on people willing to risk their own lives. It is harmful to innocent bystanders.*

- commercialism?
- internationalism?
- capitalism?

- racism?
- socialism?
- feminism?

- communism?
- nationalism?
- _____

ACTIVITY 7: LISTENING/ WRITING/SPEAKING

As a class, brainstorm several controversial topics. These can be social issues, legal problems, or political debates. Then, form groups of three. Assign a different role to each group member: Interviewer, Respondent, and Notetaker. Have the Interviewer ask the Respondent his or her opinion about one of the social, legal, or political issues suggested. (The Interviewer should ask the Respondent to be specific about what aspect of the issue he or she agrees or disagrees with and what source or evidence he or she has used to support this position.) The Notetaker will jot down examples of preposition clusters that are heard in the conversation and later share these notes with the other two group members.

▶ **EXAMPLE:** affirmative action

Interviewer: How do you *feel about* affirmative action?
Respondent: In general, I am *in favor of* it.
Interviewer: How about in the university setting?
Respondent: There I feel that it is essential.
Interviewer: Why do you say that? Could you give me an example? . . .

Activity 6
EXPANSION
Ask Ss to contrast the following pairs of terms using the same adjective + preposition phrases: *negativism vs. positivism, conservatism vs. liberalism, creationism vs. evolutionism, monotheism vs. polytheism.*

Activity 7
The organization of this activity frees up the teacher to circulate around the room and provide supportive encouragement and prompting to all groups. It also allows the two Ss having the conversation in each group to concentrate on their ideas, not the grammar point. The notetaker, however, has a chance to do focused listening for preposition clusters. If time, the roles should be rotated so that each individual has a chance to perform each role.

The test for this unit can be found on p. 517. The answers are on p. 518.

Unit 18

UNIT OVERVIEW

Unit 18 provides an overview of gerunds and infinitives in their perfective, progressive, and passive forms. It also contrasts the two types of structures and provides numerous exercises to help students (Ss) select and use the appropriate verb form.

UNIT GOALS

Review the goals listed on this page so Ss understand what they should be able to know by the end of the unit.

OPENING TASK

This task encourages Ss to evaluate candidates for an experimental space station.

SETTING UP THE TASK

Some of the characteristics of this living situation are similar to those present in the Biosphere experiment in the southwestern United States. You may want to draw this to the Ss' attention for a more authentic discussion. Encourage Ss to discuss what they know about Biosphere.

CONDUCTING THE TASK

Step 1: Divide the class into pairs. Ask each pair to review the characteristics of the space station and then consider the qualifications of each of the 10 candidates.

UNIT 18

GERUNDS AND INFINITIVES

UNIT GOALS:

- To identify the functions of gerunds and infinitives in a sentence
- To use a variety of gerund and infinitive structures correctly
- To distinguish gerunds from infinitives
- To use *for* with infinitives and *'s* with gerunds
- To use gerunds as objects of prepositions and phrasal verbs

▶ OPENING TASK
Skills and Qualifications

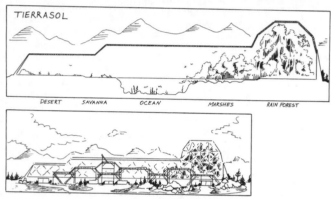

STEP 1 You and a partner have been asked to consider the strengths and weaknesses of the following ten applicants for "Tierrasol," an experimental space station in the Arizona desert. This glass-and-steel station will test on Earth how well human beings could survive in a space station on Mars. Those selected will enter the structure and not leave for two years. The station is airtight and has:

- a greenhouse-like structure
- miniature deserts, marshes, oceans, savannas, and rain forests
- plants typical of various regions
- insects, fish, fowl, and small mammals
- individual apartments and laboratories for each Tierrasolian
- a library, a computer center, and communications facilities for all Tierrasolians
- the capability to receive newspapers, mail, and television broadcasts

STEP 2 In pairs, jot down ideas about why you think each person in the chart that follows might like to be a candidate. Think about why he or she would want to be part of the experiment and what positive skills or characteristics he or she could bring to the project.

Step 2: Encourage pairs to jot down at least two ideas per candidate.

Candidate	Rationale
Computer Engineer female, 25 years old	She probably wants to participate because her husband might participate. Having good computer skills could help the team communicate from Mars to Earth.
Microbiologist husband of computer engineer, 35 years old	
Police Officer male, 45 years old	
Waste Management Specialist wife of police officer pregnant, 41 years old	
Former Peace Corps Health Worker female, 52 years old, single	
Medical Intern female, 24 years old, single	
Farmer male, 43 years old, widowed	
Ecologist male, 23 years old, single	
Astronaut female, 36 years old, married	
Politician male, 58 years old, divorced with three children	

STEP 3 Share the results of your brainstorming with your classmates.

Step 3: Have each pair share a few of their ideas with the class. This can be done orally or in writing on the board.

CONCLUDING THE TASK

Discuss as a class what the most important skills or characteristics would be for a candidate. You can also discuss whether or not the Ss might like to participate in such a project themselves. What skills or characteristics might they have as candidates for this project? What would be exciting or difficult about being a part of this project?

1. Explain that English has several *clause within a clause* constructions. Relative clauses are one type that Ss may be familiar with. Write this example on the board: *A lawyer who passes the Bar Exam may practice in this state.* Ask one student to put brackets around the embedded clause.

2. Explain that they may also be familiar with full clausal *that-* complements with tensed verbs. Write these examples on the board: *They hope that she is better. They said that she speaks French.*

    Ask one student to come to the board and bracket the embedded clauses (*that she is better; that she speaks French*).

3. Add that Ss will also encounter subjunctive complements. Write the following example on the board: *The woman insisted that we be ready by 5:00 a.m.* Ask Ss to identify the embedded clause. (If they notice the untensed *be* verb, explain that this will be discussed in more detail in Unit 22.) Once identified, bracket the embedded clause (*that we be ready*) on the board.

4. State that the gerunds and infinitives represented in the focus box are actually tenseless clauses in which the subject is understood to be the same subject as the one in the tensed clause, as in *j* where the person seeing the play is "Paco." Write: *Paco hopes [Paco sees the play]* on the board. Also explain that the subject may be easily inferred from the context as in *a.* Write this sentence on the board: *[For people] to travel to Mars would take months.*

5. By this level Ss generally have had most experience with gerunds and infinitives as direct objects and need to expand their knowledge of the other functions. Ask individuals to read the examples and explanations for the different functions of gerunds and infinitives while the rest of the class listens.

Overview of Gerunds and Infinitives

EXAMPLES	EXPLANATIONS
(a) **Speaking English** is fun. (b) **To travel to Mars** would take months. (c) It would take months **to travel to Mars.**	Infinitives (*to* + verb) or gerunds (verb + *-ing*) can have various functions in a sentence: **Subject:** Gerunds and infinitives can function as subjects. However, it is more common for infinitives that are subjects to move to the end of the sentence with *it* as the new subject.
(d) His dream was **to sail around the world.** (e) Her hobby is **weaving baskets.**	**Subject Complement:** A subject complement follows *be* and refers back to the subject of the sentence.
(f) I don't understand the need **to take a ten-minute break.** (g) The instruction **to wear safety goggles** has saved many people's eyes.	**Noun Complement:** Noun complements explain the nouns that they refer to. The infinitive can be a complement to certain abstract nouns (for example, *advice, decision, desire, fact, opportunity, order, plan, possibility, proposal, request, refusal, requirement, suggestion, way, wish*). (See Unit 21, Focus 1 for a more extensive list of abstract nouns.)
(h) I am sorry **to inform you of the delay.** (i) They were pleased **to meet you.**	**Adjective Complement:** Certain adjectives can be followed by infinitives. These include: *afraid* *disappointed* *pleased* *amazed* *eager* *proud* *anxious* *eligible* *ready* *apt* *(un)fit* *reluctant* *ashamed* *fortunate* *sad* *bound* *glad* *shocked* *careful* *happy* *sorry* *certain* *hesitant* *sure* *content* *liable* *surprised* *delighted* *likely* *upset* *determined*
(j) Paco hopes **to see the play.** (k) Carol remembered **mailing the package.**	**Direct Object:** A direct object follows a verb. Depending upon the verb and accompanying meaning, the object may be an infinitive or a gerund.
(l) **By studying hard,** you can enter a good school. (m) Thank you **for helping me.** (n) **NOT:** He lost the deal because of wait too long.	**Object of Preposition:** Gerunds, not infinitives, are objects of prepositions.

EXERCISE 1

Read the following text and underline all gerunds and infinitives. Then identify the function of each one.

(1) Alan Loy McGinnis in his book *Bringing Out the Best in People* (Augsbur Publishing House, Minneapolis, 1985) describes twelve important principles or rules for helping people to perform to the best of their ability. (2) The first rule is to expect the best from the people you lead. (3) A true leader needs to drop the role of "watchdog" and to display a positive attitude toward everyone who works under him or her. (4) The second principle is to make a thorough study of the other person's needs. (5) Walking a mile in another person's shoes will allow a leader to truly understand someone he or she is working with. (6) The third rule is to establish high standards of excellence. (7) Many people have never learned the pleasure of setting high standards and living up to them. (8) The fourth rule is to create an environment where failure is not fatal. (9) People who expect to succeed all of the time often cannot rise from a failure. (10) An effective motivator needs to know how to help people deal with their failure.

(11) "Climbing on other people's bandwagons" is the fifth principle that McGinnis suggests. (12) A good leader needs to identify the beliefs and causes of the people that he or she works with. (13) By using these good ideas, he or she can encourage them to pursue as many of these goals as possible. (14) Employing models to encourage success is the sixth rule. (15) Everyone loves hearing about true success stories of others to build confidence and motivation. Recognizing and applauding achievement is the seventh rule. (16) A good leader tries to look for strengths in people and catch them "doing something right" so that he or she can compliment them.

(17) The eighth rule is to employ a mixture of positive and negative reinforcement. (18) Using praise is only one of many methods used to motivate. (19) Sometimes a person does his or her best because he or she is afraid to be punished. (20) The ninth and tenth rules relate to appealing sparingly to the competitive urge and placing a premium on collaboration. (21) Some competition is good; however, the decision to work with other people creates good morale and allows the job to be completed more efficiently.

(22) The eleventh principle is to learn how to deal with troublemakers in a group. (23) A leader who does not learn how to handle a problematic person will never learn how to stay in difficult situations and solve them. (24) Finally, the twelfth rule is to find ways to keep the motivation of the leader, himself or herself, high. (25) Renewing oneself through sports, reading, going to a restful spot, etc. are all necessary for the good leader to become energized and to successfully perform the other eleven principles.

Which functions of gerunds and infinitives are most common in this selection? Is the "*to*-verb" structure always a complement? What other meaning can it have? (Hint: review sentences 15 and 18.)

Gerunds and Infinitives | **319**

Exercise 1

1. Pair up Ss and have one student read the text aloud while the other student underlines the gerunds and infinitives.
2. Ask Ss to identify the function of each gerund or infinitive referring to Focus 1.

Workbook Ex. 1, p. 177.
Answers: TE p. 554.

ANSWER KEY

Exercise 1
(1) bringing (object of prep.) (2) to expect (subj. comp.) (3) to drop (object); to display (object) (4) to make (subj. comp.)
(5) Walking (subject); to . . . understand (object) (6) to establish (subj. comp.) (7) setting (obj. of prep.); living up (obj. of prep.)
(8) to create (subj. comp) (9) to succeed (object) (10) to know (object) (11) Climbing (subject) (12) to identify (object)

(13) using (obj. of prep.); to pursue (object)
(14) Employing (subject) (15) hearing (object); Recognizing (subject); applauding (subject) (16) to look (object); catch (object) (17) to employ (subj. comp.)
(18) Using (subject) (19) to be punished (adj. comp.) (20) appealing (obj. of prep.); placing (obj. of prep.) (21) to work (noun comp.) to be completed (object) (22) to learn (subj. comp.) (23) to handle (object);

to stay (object) (24) to find (subj. comp.)
(25) Renewing (subject); reading (subject); going (subject); to become energized (adj. comp.); to . . . perform (adj. comp.)

Question: Most frequent functions are: object, subject, subject complement, object of preposition, adjective complement, and noun complement. The *to*- verb structure in 15 and 18 means "in order to."

FOCUS 2

Ss are most likely familiar with the different verb tenses (if they have completed Units 1 and 2). This focus box will allow them to see how tense is incorporated with gerund and infinitive forms.

S U G G E S T I O N

1. Copy the examples and explanations on two different colors of sentence strips.
2. Pass out the 20 strips to individuals or pairs in the class (depending upon class size).
3. Ask Ss to stand up and try to match the examples with the explanations. Once all Ss have found their matches, ask them to put the sentence strips in a pocket chart. It should resemble Focus Box 2.

FOCUS **2**

▶ Infinitives and Gerunds in Perfective, Progressive, and Passive

EXAMPLES	EXPLANATIONS
(a) Eva's plan has always been **to return** to her homeland.	simple infinitive (*to* + verb)
(b) She hoped **to have earned** an Olympic gold medal by the time she was twenty.	perfective infinitive (*to* + *have* + past participle)
(c) Their goal is **to be working** by March.	progressive infinitive (*to* + *be* + present participle)
(d) We wanted **to have been swimming** by now.	perfective progressive infinitive (*to* + *have* + *been* + present participle)
(e) The suggestion **to be seen** by a surgeon was never followed.	passive infinitive (*to* + *be* + past participle)
(f) They were happy **to have been chosen** for the award.	perfective passive infinitive (*to* + *have* + *been* + past participle)
(g) Part of the problem is not **knowing** enough.	simple gerund (verb + -*ing*)
(h) She was excited about **having watched** the race from start to finish.	perfective gerund (*having* + past participle)
(i) **Being appointed** to the board of directors is a great responsibility.	passive gerund (*being* + past participle)
(j) **Having been selected** for the experiment gave her career a boost.	perfective passive gerund (*having been* + past participle)

EXERCISE 2

With a partner, discuss the following topics using infinitives and gerunds in simple, perfective, progressive, and passive forms. Give reasons for your responses.

▶ **EXAMPLE:** A movie you enjoyed seeing

> *I enjoyed seeing "Star Wars I" because I like science fiction.*

Exercise 2

E X P A N S I O N

Ask Ss to look at the examples in the focus box and write original sentences illustrating each verb form. For example: Simple infinitive: *To become a doctor has always been Maria's plan.*

---

1. a holiday food you like to eat
2. a present you would like to be surprised with
3. a sport you enjoy playing
4. a place you are excited about having seen
5. another name you would like to have been named
6. a job you would like to be doing right now
7. a famous person in history you would like to have met
8. a topic you would like to have been studying by now
9. a story you liked being told as a child
10. a feeling you had after having been recognized for something

EXERCISE 3

A woman received a $1000 prize for winning a short-story writing contest. Her acceptance speech appears below. Fill in the appropriate gerund or infinitive. In some cases, more than one answer may be correct.

It is a great honor (award) __to be awarded__ this generous prize tonight. (1) _____ (present) an award for something that I enjoy doing anyway thrills me. (2) _____ (say) that I am indebted to my parents would be an understatement. (3) _____ (have) parents who were trained as teachers gave me an important start. From the time I was very young, (4) _____ (study) four hours every day after school was required. It was a frequent sight (5) _____ (see) my siblings discussing main points and rehearsing the answers to problems. (6) _____ (scold) by our parents for not paying enough attention to our work would have been the greatest shame.

Besides doing my homework for school, (7) _____ (read) fiction and nonfiction books took up much of my leisure time. (8) _____ (read) so many types of books by the time I got to college proved to be a marvelous advantage. (9) _____ (see) so many good written models allowed me to creatively and effortlessly produce my own work for my university English classes.

Today, it requires more discipline for me (10) _____ (be) a good writer. (11) _____ (marry) with three children leaves less time to write. It requires initiative (12) _____

Gerunds and Infinitives **321**

Exercise 3

1. Ask student pairs to fill in the blanks with the appropriate gerund or infinitive form.
2. Ask 3 different students to read the three different paragraphs aloud.
3. Discuss any incorrect answers.

(arise) every day at 5:00 A.M. to write. (13) _____ (write) in this manner is the only way that I have been able to produce several short stories and a few poems. (14) _____ (not receive) very good marks on my essay pieces in college, I have left essay writing to some other writer! Well, I can see that my time is up. It has been an honor (15) _____ (select) as the winner of this contest and I thank my parents, family, and all of you for your recognition today.

EXERCISE 4
Fill in the following blanks with appropriate infinitives. More than one answer may be possible.

▶ **EXAMPLE:** The requirement _____ *to wear* _____ a spacesuit is essential protection for the astronaut.

1. Few people have made the decision _____ an astronaut.
2. The proposal _____ expendable rockets with rockets that could return to Earth saved a great deal of money for the taxpayer.
3. The space program strictly heeded the advice _____ the astronauts for eighteen days after their flight to the Moon in order to assure their good health.
4. The suggestion _____ a "moon base" would allow much useful scientific research.
5. A precaution _____ after every spaceflight includes isolating lunar samples until the scientific team is satisfied that no risk of contamination remains.
6. The decision _____ space-walks occurred in 1964 with Project Mercury.
7. The first words _____ by Neil Armstrong as he stepped on to the surface of the moon were "That's one small step for a man; a giant leap for mankind."
8. The next challenge _____ is a mission to Mars.

EXERCISE 5
With a partner, take turns asking and answering the following questions. Use an adjective complement in each of your responses.

▶ **EXAMPLE:** What are you bound to do after you finish your schooling?
I am bound to get a job as a computer technician.

Remind Ss that these are examples of noun complements followed by infinitives. For extra practice, ask Ss to share their opinions about the following ideas:
a. your friend's advice to go to a movie instead of finish your homework (*I think my friend's advice to go to a movie instead of finish my homework will get me in trouble*).
b. your grandfather's suggestion "to be seen and not heard."
c. your friend's refusal to speak to you in English.
d. your friend's suggestion to eat with chopsticks instead of metal utensils.

Exercise 5

Once pairs have completed this exercise, ask for volunteers to share their best answers for each item with the whole class.

Workbook Ex. 2, p. 178.
Answers: TE p. 554.

A N S W E R   K E Y

Exercise 4
Answers will vary.
1. to become 2. to replace 3. to isolate
4. to create 5. to take 6. to do 7. to be stated 8. to be pursued

1. What type of food are you hesitant to eat?
2. What are you apt to do in the next few weeks?
3. Which clubs here or in your native country are you eligible to join?
4. What sport are you reluctant to try?
5. What movie are you likely to see in the next few weeks?
6. Which country would you be delighted to visit?
7. Which student in your class is most liable to be successful?
8. What are you sure to do after your class today?
9. Which friend are you most happy to know?
10. What movie star or musical star would you be ready to meet?

FOCUS **3**

Gerunds versus Infinitives

Certain types of verbs (verbs of emotion, verbs of completion/incompletion, and verbs of remembering) can be affected by the choice of infinitive or gerund.

EXAMPLES	EXPLANATIONS
(a) **To eat** too much sugar is not healthy. (b) **Eating** too much sugar is not healthy.	Infinitive and gerunds as objects and sub-jects sometimes have equivalent meanings.
(c) **ACTUAL:** For the time being, I **pre-fer** *being* a housewife. (d) **POTENTIAL:** When my children are grown, I would **prefer** *to get* a job outside the home. (e) **ACTUAL: Playing** golf every day is boring. (f) **POTENTIAL: To play** golf every day would be my idea of a happy retire-ment.	In other cases, we choose an infinitive or gerund by the meaning of an action. We of-ten use gerunds to describe an actual, vivid, or fulfilled action. We often use infinitives to describe potential, hypothetical, or fu-ture events.

1. Write the following pairs of sentences on the blackboard: *I forgot to feed the fish. I forgot feeding the fish.*
2. Draw a timeline that shows the different times of forgetting and discuss the differences in meaning.

NOW

___/_____/_____/___

forget   feed

I forgot to feed the fish

Explain that, in this case, you forgot that you needed to feed the fish and you didn't feed them at all.

NOW

___/_____/_____/___

feed   forget

I forgot feeding the fish.

In this case, you did feed the fish, but you forget that you fed them later.

3. Emphasize that this is a dramatic example of the difference in meaning that the choice of gerund or infinitive can make. The verb *remember* can also have a distinct meaning when followed by the gerund versus the infinitive.
4. Other types of *emotion* and *completion/incompletion* verbs (refer to Appendix 4B) may also take gerunds or infinitives depending upon whether one is referring to an actual or potential event. Ask Ss to tell you whether the infinitive or the gerund form of the verb *study* would be most suitable in the following blanks:
   a. I will begin _____ my homework after school gets out today.
   b. I will begin _____ right now.
   Ask Ss to identify which sentence suggests something that has not yet happened and which one suggests an event that is ongoing. Ss should supply to *study* in the first blank and *studying* in the second.
5. Ask Ss to silently read the rest of the focus box to learn of other verbs that behave in this way.

Workbook Ex. 3, p. 179.
Answers: TE p. 554.

Verbs of Emotion

ACTUAL EVENT	POTENTIAL EVENT
(g) Did you **like** *dancing* that night? You seemed to be having a good time.	**(h)** Do you **like** *to dance*? I know a good nightclub.
(i) Tim **hates** *quarreling* with his wife over every little thing.	**(j)** Tim **hates** *to quarrel* with his wife. It would be the last thing he would want to do.
(k) I **preferred** *studying* astronomy over physics.	**(l)** I **prefer** *to study* physics next year.

Verbs of Completion/Incompletion

ACTUAL EVENT	POTENTIAL EVENT
(m) I **started** *doing* my homework. Question #1 is especially hard.	**(n)** Did you **start** *to do* your homework?
(o) Did you **continue** *watching* the program yesterday after I left?	**(p)** Will you **continue** *to watch* the program after I leave?
(q) He **began** *speaking* with a hoarse voice that no one could understand.	**(r)** He **began** *to speak,* but was interrupted by the lawyer.
(s) She **stopped** *listening* whenever she was bored.	**(t)** She **stopped** *to listen* to the bird that was singing. (Note: *to* means "in order to".)
(u) They **finished** *reading* the book.	**(v)** I will **finish** *reading* this book before I go shopping. (Note: *Finish* always requires a gerund.)
	(w) **NOT:** I will finish to read the book.

Verbs of Remembering

EXAMPLES	TIME SEQUENCE	EXPLANATION
(x) Tom **remembered** *closing* the door.	First: Tom closed the door. Then: Tom remembered that he did so.	Besides the real event and potential event meanings, *remember, forget,* and *regret* signal different time sequence meanings when we use a gerund or an infinitive.
(y) Tom **remembered** *to close* the door.	First: Tom remembered that he needed to close the door. Then: Tom closed the door.	

EXERCISE 6

In the Opening Task on pages 316 and 317, you and your classmates considered the candidates for Tierrasol. At the last minute, the media released new information about the candidates based on several confidential interviews. Read and select the correct verb in each of the quotes that follow. In some cases, both verbs may be correct. If so, explain why.

▶ **EXAMPLE:** Microbiologist: I would like (<u>to go</u>/going) only if my wife could go.
*(**To go** is preferred because the situation is hypothetical.)*

1. Microbiologist: (To live/living) in Tierrasol without my wife would be dreadful.

2. Computer engineer: I love (to smoke/smoking). As a matter of fact, I smoke three packs of cigarettes a day.

3. Police officer: (To carry/carrying) a gun is a necessity. In fact, I don't go anywhere without it.

4. Waste management specialist: I mean (to stay/staying) in Tierrasol only until the baby is born.

5. Former Peace Corps health worker: I hated (to work/working) under stressful conditions. That's why I returned early from my assignment.

6. Medical intern: (To pass/passing) the Medical Boards Exam this fall is my intention. Unfortunately, I have already failed it twice.

7. Farmer: I loathe (to live/living) in closed spaces. I have claustrophobia.

8. Ecologist: I regret (to inform/informing) the committee in my application that I was a water quality expert because I actually have limited knowledge of this area.

9. Astronaut: I will continue (to benefit/benefiting) from this experience in future space missions, even after Tierrasol.

10. Politician: Did I remember (to tell/telling) you that funding for future Tierrasol projects will be one of my major campaign issues once this project is finished?

A N S W E R   K E Y

Exercise 6

1. to live/living (represents a future thought or emphasizes real action) 2. smoking (is a habitual, real action) 3. carrying (is a statement of fact) 4. to stay (represents a future intention) 5. working (is a real, past action) 6. to pass (refers to a future action) 7. living (refers to a habitual action) 8. informing (refers to someone getting information right now) 9. to benefit (refers to a future action) 10. to tell (question implies that this is not a completed action)

1. Write the following three patterns on the blackboard:
   a. Subject + _____ to + sit.
   b. Subject + _____ object + to + sit.
   c. Subject + _____ + sitting.

2. Ask Ss to insert verbs in the blanks that can make grammatical sentences. They can select any subject or object that they wish. They might supply verbs such as *desire, choose,* or *manage* in the first blank; verbs such as *tell, allow,* or *help* in the second blank; and verbs such as *avoid, admit,* and *stop* in the third blank.

3. Ask Ss to turn to Appendix 4B and look at the different types of verbs comprising Lists A through C. Encourage them to associate the groups of verbs with their general meanings, e.g., emotion, mental activity, communication, causation, etc. Note that certain verbs in List A can optionally include *for,* e.g., *I expect (for) him to come early. They will desire (for) us to bring gifts. The man would love (for) them to help.*

4. Ask Ss to read the box for more information about gerunds and infinitives.

Exercise 7

V A R I A T I O N

1. After doing Exercise 7, ask pairs to close their books and try to reconstruct Einstein's life history. Encourage them to write a short paragraph summarizing his childhood, his youth, and his adulthood.

2. Ask them to use Appendix 4B to check their use of infinitives and gerunds.

3. Have volunteers from different pairs read their summary to the class.

▶ # Gerunds and Infinitives as Direct Object

EXAMPLES	EXPLANATIONS
	Another way to predict the form of a direct object complement (either gerund or infinitive) is by the choice of verb in the base sentence.
(a) Scientists **appear** to be getting close to an explanation. (b) **NOT:** Scientists appear being getting close to an explanation.	• An infinitive must follow *want, need, hope, promise,* and *appear* (and other verbs in List A on pages A-8). Notice here that many of these verbs (although not all) signal potential events, a meaning of infinitives discussed in Focus 3.
(c) Juan **hates** (for) **Isabel** to worry.	• Some verbs from List A (*desire, hate, like, love* and *prefer*) may optionally include *for* with the infinitive complement when the infinitive has an explicit subject.
(d) Einstein **convinced other scientists** to reject Newtonian physics. (e) **NOT:** Einstein convinced to reject Newtonian physics. (f) **NOT:** Einstein convinced other scientists rejecting Newtonian physics.	• *Advise, convince, invite* and *warn* (and other verbs in List B on page A-9) are followed by infinitive complements with explicit subjects.
(g) Einstein **risked** introducing a new theory to the world. (h) **NOT:** Einstein risked to introduce a new theory to the world.	• *Appreciate, enjoy, postpone, risk,* and *quit* (and other verbs in List C on pages A-9 and A-10) take only gerunds. Notice that many of these verbs (although not all) signal actual events, a meaning of gerunds discussed in Focus 3.

EXERCISE 7

Read the following text. Underline all direct object infinitives, and circle all direct object gerunds. (Not every sentence may have one.)

Then, make a list of the verb + infinitive or gerund combinations that you find.

▶ **EXAMPLE:** **Verb** + **Infinitive** **Verb** + **Gerund**
  learn *to speak* *prefer* *saying*

A N S W E R   K E Y

Exercise 7

The gerunds that the students should circle are shown in italics.
(4) to attend **(7)** to distrust and become
(8) *teaching* **(9)** to prosper **(10)** *feeling*
(11) to leave **(12)** to matriculate **(13)** to enter, to apply **(16)** *studying*; to teach
(17) to matriculate **(21)** to obtain **(22)** to reward **(25)** to take hold; to destroy The "to-verb" in #15 and #20 means *in order to.*

(4) begin + attend **(7)** force + Einstein + to distrust/to become **(8)** begin + teaching/feeling **(9)** fail + to prosper **(10)** begin + feeling **(11)** ask + him + to leave **(12)** to be not able + to matriculate **(13)** decide + to apply **(16)** enjoy + studying; want + to teach **(17)** permit + to matriculate **(21)** fail + to obtain **(22)** intend + to reward **(25)** begin + to take hold; threaten + to destroy

EINSTEIN'S EARLY EDUCATION

(1) Albert Einstein was born in Ulm, Germany, in 1879. (2) Because he learned <u>to speak</u> at a late age, his parents feared that he was retarded. (3) Modern observers prefer (saying) that he was a daydreamer. (4) When he was five years old, Einstein began to attend a Catholic school. (5) One instructor was especially critical of his abilities and told his parents that it did not matter what field young Albert chose because he would not succeed in it. (6) In 1889, Einstein transferred to a very strict German school called the Luitpold Gymnasium. (7) The rigid structure forced Einstein to distrust authority and become skeptical.

(8) At age twelve, Einstein picked up a mathematics textbook and began teaching himself geometry. (9) By 1894, Einstein's father's business had failed to prosper, and the family moved to Italy. (10) Einstein, however, remained behind and began feeling lonely and unhappy. (11) Consequently, he paid less attention to his studies and was finally asked by one of the teachers to leave. (12) He joined his family in Italy but was not able to matriculate at a university because he did not have a diploma. (13) When he heard that a diploma was not necessary to enter at the Swiss Polytechnique Institute in Zurich, he decided to apply.

(14) Einstein traveled to Switzerland but did not pass the entrance examination. (15) He was not prepared well enough in biology and languages, so he enrolled in the Gymnasium at Aarau to prepare himself in his weaker subjects. (16) Albert enjoyed studying in Aarau more than at the Lietpold Gymnasium because the teachers wanted to teach students how to think. (17) He took the exam again and was finally permitted to matriculate into a four-year program. (18) Einstein did not excel during these years at the Institute. (19) In fact, he rarely attended the lectures. (20) He read his books at home and borrowed his classmates' notes to pass tests.

(21) When Einstein graduated in 1900, he failed to obtain a position at the Institute. (22) His professors did not intend to reward Einstein's lackadaisical attitude toward classes with a position. (23) Because he did not get an academic appointment, he worked at the Swiss Patent Office. (24) He worked there for several years until he was offered an appointment as Associate Professor of Physics at the University of Zurich. (25) It was there that Einstein's revolutionary theories of space-time began to take hold and threatened to destroy the reputations of other colleagues who had built their careers on Newton's ideas of a clockwork universe.

What meaning does the "*to*-verb" structure have in sentences 15 and 20?

EXERCISE 8
Complete the following sentences based on the passage in Exercise 7. Use an infinitive or gerund. The first one has been done for you.

▶ **EXAMPLE:** As a baby, Einstein appeared _____*to be*_____ retarded.

1. As a young child, he failed _____ his teachers.

2. At age twelve, Einstein decided _____ himself geometry.

---

3. Einstein neglected _____ his homework.

4. When Einstein's family left for Italy, he quit _____ .

5. Because of this, one teacher advised him _____ school.

6. Without his family, he couldn't help _____ lonely.

7. He didn't mind _____ his family in Italy.

8. Unfortunately, he couldn't begin _____ at a university without a diploma.

9. He tried _____ the Swiss Polytechnique but could not pass the entrance exam.

10. He regretted _____ the entrance exam the first time.

11. Professors at the Polytechnique declined _____ Einstein a position because of his lackadaisical academic performance.

12. As a clerk at the Swiss Patent Office, he continued _____ about physics.

13. The University of Zurich invited Einstein _____ a faculty member.

14. Many professors couldn't help _____ Einstein's unusual ideas.

15. Soon he began _____ well-established professors with his revolutionary theories.

EXERCISE 9

Look back at the notes you made for the Opening Task on page 317 and additional information you learned in Exercise 16. Assume that only five of the applicants can be chosen for the two-year experiment in the Tierrasol structure.

STEP 1 In pairs, rank order the applicants from 1 (= most desirable) to 10 (= least desirable). Consider what might be the appropriate mix of males and females, whether married couples or singles are preferable, what skills and abilities are most essential, what compatibility factors should be considered, etc.

STEP 2 As a whole class, come to a consensus about which five applicants would be most desirable.

STEP 3 After this discussion, answer the following questions.

1. Who has the class chosen to be the top five finalists?

2. Was there any candidate that you personally regretted eliminating?

3. Did any of your classmates persuade you to select someone that you had not originally selected?

Exercise 9

If Ss completed the Opening Task and extended their knowledge of Tierrasol applicants in Exercise 6, they should be ready to do this exercise. Note that Step 3 asks three questions that will require Ss to answer using verbs from Lists A (e.g., *choose*), B (e.g., *persuade*), and C (e.g., *regret*) from Appendix 4B.

Workbook Exs. 4–9, pp. 180–186.
Answers: TE p. 554–555.

ANSWER KEY

Exercise 9
Answers will vary.

For with Infinitives and *'s* with Gerunds

EXAMPLES	EXPLANATIONS
(a) **(For people)** to see is a wonderful gift. (b) **(Your)** neglecting your teeth will cause an earlier return to your dentist.	The subject of an infinitive or a gerund is often not stated but can be implied from context. It will either have a general reference or a specific one that can be determined from other references in the sentence or paragraph.
(c) **For a Russian** to be the first man in space was commendable. (d) Her desire was **for them** to take a trip around the world.	When an infinitive functions as a subject or a subject complement, any stated subject of the infinitive should be preceded by *for*. If a pronoun follows *for*, it must be in object form.
(e) They hoped **for her** to be able to attend the concert. (f) I expected **(for) him** to be there when I finished. (g) We advised **the couple** to postpone their marriage.	When the infinitive functions as a direct object, its stated subject should take object form if it is a pronoun and may or may not be preceded by *for*. Three options are possible depending upon the verb. (See Focus 4.)
(h) **Their denying the allegation** was understandable. (i) I didn't like **the dog's barking** all night.	When the subject of a gerund is stated, it takes the possessive form.

EXERCISE 10

Read the descriptions of problem situations. Following each description is a statement about the problem. Fill in the blank with *for + noun/pronoun* or a possessive construction to complete each sentence.

▶ **EXAMPLE:** Sue went to a party. Ralph did not speak to her all evening. Sue
disliked ____Ralph's____ ignoring her at the party.

1. Burt did not get enough sleep last night. He ended up yelling at
Mrs. Gonzalez, his boss. _____ yelling at his boss was
a big mistake.

---

1. Write on the board the following examples: *We hoped [they would come to the graduation].* ⇒ *We hoped for them to come to the graduation. John postponed [his son will travel to Hawaii].* ⇒ *John postponed his son's traveling to Hawaii.* Emphasize that when a subject of an infinitive or gerund is stated, it is necessary to change the subject of the embedded clause to either an object pronoun or the possessive form, respectively.
2. Inform Ss that a less formal variant of the possessive gerund complement substitutes a noun phrase or object pronoun in place of the possessive form. Thus, in conversation, many native speakers will say: *John postponed his son traveling to Hawaii.* OR *John postponed him traveling to Hawaii.*

Exercise 10

Have each pair take turns reading the first sentence and filling in the correct word or phrase in the second. This procedure will prevent Ss from simply searching for infinitives or gerunds after the blank and not reading the content of the item to select the correct choice of words.

---

2. Mrs. Sutherland warned students to do their own work during the test. Sue got caught cheating. _____ to get caught cheating was shameful.

3. Tony did not watch where he was going and ran into the rear end of the car in front of him. The driver of the car resented

_____ hitting her car.

4. Nina always goes to bed at 9:00 P.M. Her friend, Nathan, forgot and called her house at 11:00 P.M. Nina was very angry. Nina expected

_____ to call at an earlier hour the next time.

5. Bill's grandmother mailed him a birthday package, which arrived a week before his birthday. Bill couldn't wait and opened the package early. Bill's mother was upset about _____ opening the present before his birthday.

6. Ursula left the house when it was still dark. When she got to school, she noticed that she was wearing one black shoe and one brown shoe. _____ to leave the house without checking her shoes was very silly.

7. Mrs. Lu has several children who make a lot of noise everywhere they go. All of her neighbors are very upset. _____ to let her children run wild angers the neighbors.

8. Michelle has asked Than to go to the movies several times. Than always tells her that he can't because he has to watch a TV show, do his homework, call his mother, etc. Michelle is tired of

_____ making excuses.

EXERCISE 11

Read the following sentences. Write C beside correct sentences and I beside the incorrect sentences and make all necessary corrections. Be sure to refer to Focuses 3, 4, and 5 to review the rules.

▶ **EXAMPLE:** _____I_____ He agrees ^to^ speak at the convention.

1. _____ I expected him to see me from the balcony, but he didn't.

---

2. _____ They intended interviewing the ambassador the last week in November.

3. _____ I regretted to tell her that she had not been sent an invitation to the party.

4. _____ Patty has chosen attending the University of Michigan in the fall.

5. _____ Have you forgotten to fasten your seat belt again?

6. _____ Terry getting married surprises me.

7. _____ Would you please stop to talk? I cannot hear the presenter.

8. _____ Did he suggest us go to a Japanese restaurant?

9. _____ She can't stand to do her homework with the radio turned on.

10. _____ Mr. and Mrs. Hunter forced their daughter's joining the social club against her will.

11. _____ For they to be traveling in Sweden is a great pleasure.

12. _____ Please remember working harder.

13. _____ Mary tends to exaggerate when she tells a story.

14. _____ I don't mind Tai to arrive a little late to the meeting.

15. _____ Would you care have a drink before we eat dinner?

16. _____ John avoided go to the dentist for three years.

17. _____ They can't afford taking a trip to the Caribbean this year.

18. _____ She coming late to the appointment was a disappointment.

The rules in this box are fairly straightforward. Ss need to remember that a gerund (not an infinitive) is an object of a preposition or a phrasal verb, except when the preposition is *for*, (e.g., *She asked for Tom to go with her*. NOT: *She asked for Tom going with her*).

FOCUS **6**

Gerunds as Object of Prepositions and Phrasal Verbs

EXAMPLES	EXPLANATIONS
(a) The Tierrasol committee could not **agree to** the farmer's **being** on the list of finalists. **(b)** The members **argued about keeping** the police officer and the Peace Corps worker as well.	Gerunds generally follow verbs + prepositions, such as *agree to, look at, worry about,* etc.
(c) The teacher **asked for the committee to make** a decision within twenty minutes. **(d)** She **hoped for them to make** their announcement by 4:00.	An exception to this is when the preposition is *for* with such prepositional verbs as *ask for, ache for, care for, hope for, long for,* etc. In this case, use an infinitive with a "subject."
(e) The inhabitants will be able to **carry on eating** at regular mealtimes. **(f)** I can't **put up with listening** to so much rap music. **(g)** They will **look forward to returning** to regular eating patterns once the experiment is over.	Phrasal verbs and phrasal verbs followed by prepositions (*put up with, cut down on, stand up for,* etc.) always take the gerund (versus infinitive) form. Note that the first *to* is not an infinitive marker in (g) but is a part of the phrasal verb + preposition *look forward to*.
(h) Church authorities were not **accustomed to thinking** that the sun was the center of the universe. **(i)** These theories made the Catholic Church **suspicious of** Galileo's **being** a loyal Christian.	We also use gerunds following adjective + preposition combinations such as *content with, surprised at, annoyed by*.

Exercise 12

Remind Ss to pay attention to the preposition. If the preposition is *for*, Ss need to use the infinitive form; otherwise, they will use the gerund form.

EXERCISE 12

Since the beginning of time, human beings have tried to understand who they were and where they came from through religious beliefs, theories, and rituals. Write general statements about these ideas, using the prompts below. Include a gerund or infinitive in each response.

▶ **EXAMPLE:** people   believe in   (human beings evolved from apes)
Some people believe in human beings' having evolved from apes.

ANSWER KEY

Exercise 12
1. Some religions insist on God's having created living things.   2. Some cultures call for people to have dietary restrictions.
3. Some cultures think about their ancestors' being pleased or displeased with them.
4. Some people hope for relatives to be reunited in an afterlife.   5. Some members wait for God to return to the chosen people.
6. Some believers complain about other people's not believing   7. Some religions argue about priests' having proper authority.
8. Some members agree to their children being baptized.

1.	religions	insist on	(God has created living things)
2.	cultures	call for	(people have dietary restrictions)
3.	cultures	think about	(their ancestors are pleased or displeased with them)
4.	people	hope for	(relatives are reunited in an afterlife)
5.	members	wait for	(God returns to the chosen people)
6.	believers	complain about	(other people don't believe)
7.	religions	argue about	(priests have proper authority)
8.	members	agree to	(their children are baptized)

EXERCISE 13

Read the following notes about important figures in scientific history. Write sentences about each person, using one of the following expressions: *celebrated for, famous for, good at, proficient in, renowned for, skillful in,* or *successful in.*

▶ **EXAMPLES:** Aristotle, Greek philosopher, laws of motion
Aristotle was a Greek philosopher who was famous for developing theories about motion.

1. Ptolemy, Egyptian philosopher and astronomer, made charts and tables from an observatory near Alexandria, Egypt

2. Descartes, French philosopher, developed a theory of knowledge by doubting, believed intuition was the key to understanding

3. Copernicus, Polish astronomer, concluded that the sun was at the center of the universe

4. Kepler, German astronomer and mathematician, realized that planets travel in ellipses rather than circles

5. Galileo, Italian astronomer and physicist, improved the telescope; wrote *The Starry Messenger*, which refuted the prevailing theory of an earth-centered universe

6. Newton, English mathematician, determined general laws of motion and the laws of gravity

7. Einstein, German physicist, published the Special Theory of Relativity and the General Theory of Relativity, introduced the concepts of gravitational fields and curved space

Exercise 13

EXPANSION

Ask Ss pairs to create 7 more sentences about famous or infamous people they are familiar with using the adjective + preposition combinations provided. For example, *Adolph Hitler was renowned for the atrocities he committed in Europe.*

ANSWER KEY

Exercise 13

Answers will vary.
1. Ptolemy was an Egyptian philosopher and astronomer who was successful in making charts . . .   2. Descartes was a French philosopher who is renowned for developing a theory . . .   3. Copernicus was a Polish astronomer who was famous for concluding that the sun . . .   4. Kepler was a German astronomer and mathematician who was celebrated for realizing . . .   5. Galileo was an Italian astronomer and physicist who was skillful in improving the telescope . . .   6. Newton was an English mathematician who was famous for determining the general laws . . .   7. Einstein was a German physicist who was proficient in developing new concepts such as gravitational fields and curved space . . .

Exercise 14

Ask Ss pairs to fill in the appropriate gerund or infinitive.

EXPANSION

As a review, ask Ss to refer back to Focus Box 1 and identify the function of each of the verb forms—e.g., subject, subject complement, noun complement, adjective complement, direct object, or object of preposition. For example, #1 functions as a direct object. #2 functions as an object of preposition.

Workbook Exs. 11–13, pp. 188–190.
Answers: TE p. 555.

UNIT GOAL REVIEW

Ask Ss to look at the goals on the opening page of the unit again. Help them understand how much they have accomplished in each area.

EXERCISE 14

Fill in the following blanks with a gerund or infinitive.

After taking off on the last Mercury mission, Gordon Cooper settled in for a good night's sleep halfway through his journey. Compared with most of the duties of spaceflight, it seemed (1) _____to be_____ (be) an easy enough undertaking. But Cooper ended up (2) _____ (have to wedge) his hands beneath his safety harness to keep his arms from (3) _____ (float around) and (4) _____ (strike) switches on the instrument panel.

Since Cooper's flight, (5) _____ (sleep) in space has become a routine matter—maybe too routine. When carrying out an especially boring or tiring task, some astronauts have nodded off—only they didn't really nod: they simply closed their eyes and stopped (6) _____ (move). There are none of the waking mechanisms that we would expect (7) _____ (have) on earth—one's head (8) _____ (fall) to one side or a pencil (9) _____ (drop) to the floor.

Space crews have also found that they don't need handholds and ladders to get around; they quickly learn (10) _____ (push off) with one hand and float directly to their destinations. (11) _____ (eat), use a computer, or do some other stationary task, astronauts now slip their stockinged feet into loops or wedges attached to the floor. Similarly, a single Velcro head strap suffices (12) _____ (keep) sleeping astronauts from (13) _____ (drift out) toward the ventilation ducts.

A favorite recreation in space is (14) _____ (play) with one's food. Instead of carrying food all the way to their mouths with a utensil, some experienced astronauts like (15) _____ (catapult) food from spoons. Although (16) _____ (drink) coffee seems like the most natural thing on Earth, in space it won't work. If you tried (17) _____ (tip) the cup back to take a drink, the weightless coffee would not roll out. One astronaut offers the following advisory: "Don't let your curiosity tempt you into (18) _____

334 UNIT 18

(explore) a larger clump of liquid than you're prepared

(19) _____ (drink) later." If you don't start

(20) _____ (drink) your blob with a straw, it eventually attaches itself to the nearest wall or window.

    Although spaceflight has its irritations, these are necessary if astronauts are to soar. The whole idea of airborne testing is to make

(21) _____ (live) and (22) _____ (work) in weightlessness easy and unremarkable for ordinary folk.

Adapted from: D. Stewart. "The Floating World at Xero G." *Air and Space.* August/September 1991, p. 38.

USE YOUR ENGLISH

The activities on these "purple pages" at the end of the unit contain situations that should naturally elicit the unit's structures in a more communicative framework. While Ss are doing these activities in class, you can circulate and listen to determine if they have actually achieved the goals on the opening page of the unit.

Activity 1

Play textbook audio. The tapescript for this listening appears on p. 572 of this book. Ss may need to hear the tape more than once to complete the sentences.

EXPANSION

If Ss are familiar with the O.J. Simpson trial, which took place in Los Angeles and was broadcast throughout the world, ask them to create a paragraph comparing the two famous cases. Encourage them to use at least 5 infinitive and/or gerund structures in their paragraphs and to underline these forms wherever they are used.

Use Your English

ACTIVITY 1: LISTENING

Listen to a story about a famous unsolved mystery. Use information from the tape to complete each sentence below. Use a phrase containing an infinitive or a gerund based on what you have heard.

▶ **EXAMPLE:** Cullen was not good at ___conversing___.

1. _____ describes Priscilla's fashion tastes.
2. Cullen finished _____ .
3. _____ was one indication of Cullen's violence.
4. Priscilla and Cullen decided _____ .
5. Priscilla allowed various characters _____ .
6. Cullen probably resented Priscilla's _____ .
7. Beverly Bass and her friend "Bubba" Gavel tried _____ .
8. Soon after the crime, the police succeeded in _____ .
9. _____ was "Racehorse" Haynes' best talent.
10. "Racehorse" Haynes convinced the jury _____ .
11. The prosecutors failed _____ .
12. The jurors admitted _____ .

ANSWER KEY

Activity 1
Answers will vary.
1. Wearing racy clothing   2. . . . building a $6 million house as a monument of their new life together.   3. Having broken Priscilla's collarbone   4. . . . to separate in July 1974.
5. . . . to be entertained at her home.
6. . . . being allowed an increase in support payments.   7. . . . to come to Priscilla's aid.
8. . . . locating Cullen at his home.
9. Being a very good criminal attorney . . .
10. . . . to discount Priscilla's witness because of her bad reputation.   11. . . . to condemn Cullen.   12. . . . to not being convinced that Cullen was innocent.

ACTIVITY 2: WRITING

Imagine that you are a newspaper journalist and you have just witnessed the takeover of a small island nation by a totalitarian regime. Three weeks of intensive investigation has uncovered a complete story of what happened. Write a short objective article summarizing events and answering the following important questions. Use at least five noun complements in your writing.

▶ **EXAMPLE:** *At 6:00 A.M. Caribbean time, Dimiti Island was peacefully taken over by a military junta who have been struggling for power for the past ten years. On Thursday, President Martin made the appeal to the United Nations* **to help his small island nation;** *however, the request* **to send peace-keeping troops** *was refused.*

1. Who made an appeal to the United Nations to help the country?
2. What happened to the request to send peace-keeping troops?
3. Who made the suggestion to call another meeting for negotiation?
4. Why was the reminder to continue negotiations ignored?
5. Why did the military resist the advice to wait another month?
6. Who gave the order to enter the palace grounds?
7. Who gave permission to enter the gates of the presidential palace?
8. Why can't the President make an appeal for the people to fight against the military?
9. Who has the motivation and ability to stop the intruders?
10. Why is there a tendency for small island governments to be overtaken in this manner?

ACTIVITY 3: WRITING

You are a news reporter called to interview a visitor from another planet. Although this creature looks very much like a human being and speaks English, you find that she has some very different characteristics. Describe what you learned from the alien as a result of your interviews. You might include some information about what the alien is accustomed to, annoyed at, capable of, concerned about, desirous of, incapable of, interested in, suited for, susceptible to, sympathetic toward, and weary of. Use at least five gerund complements in your report.

▶ **EXAMPLE:** *The alien has a very unusual diet. She is used to eating tree bark and grass.*

Activity 2

1. Ask Ss pairs to answer questions 1 through 10. Encourage them to be as creative as possible in their answers.
2. Then have student pairs collaboratively write the article using the answers. Remind them to locate the island in any part of the world and provide interesting details about the location, individuals involved, and negotiation activities.
3. Ask one member of each student pair or selected individuals to read their articles aloud to the class.

Activity 3
EXPANSION

1. Once Ss have described their alien, they can draw a picture of him/her/it as well. Distribute colored pens and paper to each student. Ask them to sketch their alien.
2. Ask Ss to turn in the pictures. Sort through them in random order and then redistribute them to Ss. Give each student a piece of tape and ask them to post someone else's alien picture on the wall.
3. Randomly select individuals to read their reports.
4. Ask the Ss to point to the alien on the wall that they think is being described.

Activity 4

Have pairs discuss time travel answering the five questions provided. Note that different types of gerunds and infinitives will be required in their responses.

Activity 5

Encourage Ss to score the other pair's quizzes.

Activity 6

This activity requires that Ss have done the Opening Task, Exercise 6, and Exercise 9. They should highlight their strengths, such as career, physical condition, age, marital status, special skills, etc. The letter should begin: "Dear Tierrasol Selection Committee:"

ACTIVITY 4: SPEAKING

According to Einstein's special theory of relativity, astronauts who make a round-trip journey to a nearby star at a speed near the speed of light might age only a year or so. However, when they return to earth, they would find everyone else a great deal older. This type of "time travel" to the future is possible. Would you consider volunteering for such a mission? What would be the consequences of doing so? When you returned, would you continue to love your spouse or partner even though you would no longer be the same ages? What would you arrange to do on your first day back? Would you enjoy accepting future space mission assignments? Discuss these questions with your classmates.

ACTIVITY 5: SPEAKING/WRITING/READING

With a partner, write a fifteen-item quiz which you can give to another pair of classmates to test their knowledge of gerunds and infinitives.

▶ **EXAMPLE:** 1. *I am interested in* _____ *(fly) to Tahiti.*
2. *The teacher needs Tom* _____ *(ask) his parents for permission.*

ACTIVITY 6: WRITING

You have decided that you would like to be included in the Tierrasol project. Write a letter to the Tierrasol selection committee, explaining why you feel you are qualified for the project. Try to be as persuasive as you can while using at least two gerund complements and four infinitive complements in your writing.

ACTIVITY 7: LISTENING/SPEAKING

Listen to a video or a taped TV drama or romance. Jot down at least ten examples of infinitives or gerunds that you hear. Share your results with the class.

ACTIVITY 8: WRITING/SPEAKING

STEP 1 Imagine that you have an entire day free and you have limitless energy to enjoy the many activities that your town or city has to offer. Make a list, being fairly specific about where you want to go, what you want to see, what you want to eat, etc.

▶ **EXAMPLE:**
1. Eat an omelet for breakfast at the restaurant "Beach Cafe."
2. Go shopping for three hours at the Silverstone Shopping Center.
3. Eat lunch and watch a noon performance of "Guys and Dolls" at the Searchlight Pavilion.
4. Go swimming at the public pool for two hours.
5. etc.

STEP 2 Share your plans with a partner.

▶ **EXAMPLE:** In the morning, I want to eat an omelet at the Beach Cafe. Then, I'd like to go shopping for two hours at the Silverstone Shopping Center. . . .

STEP 3 Now imagine that you are visiting a town or city for just one day and a travel agent has just given you this same list of ideas as suggestions. Comment on your partner's recommendations using as many structures covered in this unit as possible.

▶ **EXAMPLE:** The plan/recommendation/suggestion to eat an omelet at the Beach Cafe sounds wonderful.

It would be nice/a thrill/interests me to go shopping for three hours at the Silverstone Shopping Center.

I can't stand/detest/don't like seeing musicals, so I'd like to do something else besides watching "Guys and Dolls."

Gerunds and Infinitives **339**

Activity 7

This activity provides good listening practice for gerund and infinitive structures.

1. Ask Ss to create a log sheet with two columns—one for infinitives and one for gerunds.
2. For homework, ask Ss to watch a program for about 30 minutes and jot down as many examples as they can.
3. The next day, put Ss in pairs and ask them to share what they learned.

Activity 8

This activity is a good cumulative activity for the unit. You can use it to assess student learning as well as diagnose continuing areas of weakness.

The test for this unit can be found on p. 519. The answers are on p. 520.

TOEFL Test Preparation Exercises for Units 16–18 can be found on pp. 191–193 of the workbook.
The answers are on p. 556 of this book.

Unit 19

UNIT OVERVIEW

This unit reviews forms of perfective infinitives, explains their meanings, and presents some of the typical communicative contexts in which they are used.

UNIT GOALS

Review the goals listed on this page so students (Ss) understand what they should be able to know by the end of the unit.

OPENING TASK

This task asks Ss to read a series of statements about witnessing or participating in historical events and to rank their appeal in terms of whether they would like to have seen, heard about, or in some way been involved in the event.

All of the statements in the first step of this task include an example of a perfective infinitive. The examples include a mix of regular and irregular past participles. With the ten statements, Ss get repeated exposure to the target form, thereby prompting its use in their responses.

SETTING UP THE TASK

Ask Ss to read through the events and identify unfamiliar historical figures or vocabulary. For example, if Ss know what heavyweight boxing is, they don't need to be familiar with Rocky Marciano as a fighter; on the other hand, if they have never heard of Anna Pavlova, it might help them to know that she was a very famous dancer. If time permits, Ss could share their knowledge about the events or people.

UNIT 19

PERFECTIVE INFINITIVES

UNIT GOALS:

- To use the correct forms of perfective infinitives
- To use perfective infinitives to express ideas and opinions about past events
- To use perfective infinitives to express emotions and attitudes
- To use perfective infinitives to express obligations, intentions, and future plans
- To use perfective infinitives with *enough* and *too*

▶ OPENING TASK
Time Travel to the Past

Have you ever wished you could go back in time and meet famous people from past eras, see things that no longer exist in the world, or participate in exciting historical events?

Napoleon

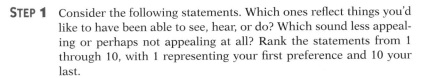

STEP 1 Consider the following statements. Which ones reflect things you'd like to have been able to see, hear, or do? Which sound less appealing or perhaps not appealing at all? Rank the statements from 1 through 10, with 1 representing your first preference and 10 your last.

I would like . . .

- to have seen Michelangelo painting the Sistine chapel.
- to have watched Rocky Marciano win the heavyweight boxing championship in 1952.
- to have attended a performance by the famous blues singer, Billie Holiday.
- to have been at Waterloo when Napoleon surrendered.
- to have observed dinosaurs before they became extinct.
- to have seen Anna Pavlova, the Russian ballerina, dance in Tchaikovsky's *Swan Lake* ballet.
- to have walked through the Hanging Gardens of Babylon.
- to have spoken with Confucius, the great Chinese philosopher.
- to have heard the Greek epic poet Homer recite *The Iliad* or *The Odyssey*.
- to have taken a cruise on the Nile River in Queen Cleopatra's barge as the sun was setting.

STEP 2 Compare your ratings with those of a few of your classmates. Briefly explain the reasons for your top one or two choices.

STEP 3 Write two more statements expressing things that you would like to have seen, heard, or done.

CONDUCTING THE TASK

Step 1
Ss can consider and rank the statements individually.

Step 2
Listen as Ss discuss their rankings to get a sense of their familiarity with perfective infinitives. Ss often omit the *would* before *like*.

Step 3
Collect Ss' responses for further diagnosis. Responses could also be used later for revision.

E X P A N S I O N

For further assessment, follow up the task with additional questions. For example: *What would you like to have done if you were able to live for 200 years? What would you like to have done if you lived in the 19th century?* Both of these questions would prompt a variety of lexical verbs.

FOCUS 1

This focus box shows the formation of perfective infinitives and shows where they can occur in a sentence.

SUGGESTION

To help Ss understand the syntactic roles of perfective infinitives, have them use a highlighter or bracketing techniques to identify the entire perfective infinitive clauses (e.g., *to have seen the first football game ever played, to have been at home all evening,* etc.)

You can show these schematically on the board using X to replace the clause and labeling the kind of clause.

Examples:

		object
(a)	I'd like	X
(b)	She claimed	X
	subject	
(d)	X	was a dream
		come true for her.

Exercise 1

Cultural note: Ask Ss if they know of Ted Turner, who, among other things, started the CNN Broadcasting station, has owned a major league baseball team (the Atlanta Braves) and was married to actor Jane Fonda.

FOCUS **1**

Review of Perfective Infinitive Structures

EXAMPLES	EXPLANATIONS
Perfective Infinitive **(a)** I'd like **to have seen** the first football game ever played. **(b)** She claimed **to have been** at home all evening. **(c)** I expect **to have finished** my term paper by tomorrow night.	**Forming the Perfective Infinitive** Perfective infinitives have the form *to + have* + past participle (*-ed* or irregular verb form).
(d) **To have won** the Boston Marathon was a dream come true for her. **(e)** It is useful **to have reviewed** the chapter before you attend the lecture. **(f)** I would love **to have seen** his face when he opened the present. **(g)** The question **to have been debated** was whether the union should go on strike. **(h)** Research writing is a good course **to have taken.** **(i)** Thanh is too young **to have known better.** **(j)** Those pants were big enough **to have fit** a giant!	**Types of Perfective Infinitive Clauses** Like other infinitives, perfective infinitives occur in a number of clause types in sentences: • subject • postponed subject after introductory *it* • object • adjective • degree complement

EXERCISE 1

In the following passage, Ted Turner, a well-known American businessman, talks with interviewer Studs Terkel about some of the things he would like to have done. Underline the perfective infinitives he uses. The first one has been done as an example.

(1) I would like <u>to have lived</u> a whole bunch of lives. (2) I would like to have gone to West Point or Annapolis and had a military career, I would like to have been a fireman, I would like to have been a state trooper, I would like to have been an explorer, I would like to have been a concert pianist, an Ernest Hemingway, an F. Scott Fitzgerald, a movie star, a big league ballplayer, Joe Namath. (3) I like it all. (4) I would like to have been a fighter pilot, a mountain climber, go to the Olympics and run the marathon, a general on a white horse. (5) A sea captain, back in the days of sailing ships, sailed with Horatio Nelson. (6) I would like to have gone with Captain

---

ANSWER KEY

Exercise 1

(2) to have gone; to have been; to have been; to have been; to have been   **(4)** to have been

(6) to have gone   **(7)** to have been   **(9)** to have gone   **(11)** to have discovered

---

Cook to find the Spice Islands, with Columbus, with Sir Francis Drake. (7) I would like to have been a pilot, a privateer, a knight in shining armor, gone on the Crusades. (8) Wouldn't you? (9) I'd like to have gone looking for Dr. Livingston, right? (10) In the heart of darkest Africa. (11) I would like to have discovered the headwaters of the Nile and the Amazon River.

EXERCISE 2

Write five statements about things you would like to have done, using perfective infinitive clauses. Exchange the five statements you wrote with another classmate. Report one or more of your classmate's statements to the rest of the class or a small group, using a *that*-clause with a past perfect verb.

▶ **EXAMPLE:** Statement: I would like to have heard Jimi Hendrix play the American National Anthem.
Paraphrase: *Olivia wishes that she could have heard Jimi Hendrix play the American National Anthem.*

Note that in the paraphrase, *could* is used as the modal with *wish* as the main clause verb.

EXERCISE 3

Complete the blanks with perfective infinitives. Use the verb in parentheses.

▶ **EXAMPLE:** She was happy (break) __to have broken__ the record for the one-hundred-meter dash.

1. (a) The elderly gentleman next door considers himself (be) _____ quite a romantic fellow in his younger days. (b) He claims (write) _____ passionate love letters to more than a dozen women. (c) Not all of his letters got the responses he had hoped for, but in his opinion, it truly was better (love) _____ and lost than never (love) _____ at all.

2. David: (a) It was really nice of Hector (give) _____ us his car for our trip to the Grand Canyon. We had a great time.
   Alana: (b) Oh, he was happy (be able to) _____ help you out. (c) I'd really like (go) _____ with you on your trip, but my cousins were visiting that weekend.

3. (a) Jeanne is too smart (believe) _____ the story Russ told her the other day. (b) His story was outlandish enough (convince)_____ her that it was far from the truth.

4. (a) Dear Fran: Accepting that job offer was a wise decision for you (make) _____ . (b) We're glad (have) _____ you as our office mate for the past three years. (c) Good luck! With your talent, we expect you (receive) _____ a big promotion before long.

Exercise 2
EXPANSION
Have Ss use one of their statements as the topic sentence for a paragraph in which they further explain it with description or providing reasons.

ANSWER KEY

Exercise 2
Answers will vary. (Examples given in the directions.)

Exercise 3
1. **(a)** to have been   **(b)** to have written   **(c)** to have loved; to have loved   2. **(a)** to have given   **(b)** to have been able to   **(c)** to have gone   3. **(a)** to have believed   **(b)** to have convinced   4. **(a)** to have made   **(b)** to have had   **(c)** to have received

SUGGESTIONS

1. With explanations of the perfect verb tenses (present perfect, past perfect), drawing a timeline can provide a visual representation of relationships between events.

Draw timelines on the board to illustrate when events occurred in relation to later ones.

Example:

```
       report        can go
       finished      to soccer
                     game
(a)_____X_____X_____
       last          today
       night
```

2. Note that with (c) and (d), it is the main verbs that make the event either unfulfilled (d) or doubtful (d). To emphasize this point, substitute *is glad* for *wanted* in (c). This would make the event fulfilled (and of course then would not make sense with the sentence that follows).

3. The teaching points and examples in the last section may be confusing at first to Ss because the sentences are so similar, with only the verb tenses and perfective infinitive forms changing. Explain that native speakers tend to use the forms for (g) and (h) for the same contexts: somebody did something in the past; it was a nice thing. The comment clauses in (i) and (j) refer to different times, a past event for (i) and a present or future event for (j).

4. To further exemplify this last distinction, put a list of past and present events on the board and elicit comments: *My friend sent me some flowers. (It is nice of her to have done that.) The teachers will hold a farewell party for Ss tomorrow night. (It is nice of them to do that.)*

Workbook Ex. 1, p. 194; Ex. 2, p. 195.
Answers: TE p. 556.

Expressing Past Events

Perfective infinitives (*to + have +* past participle) express events that are past in relation to a present, past, or future moment of focus.

EXAMPLES	EXPLANATIONS
(a) Jaime is happy **to have finished** his report last night so he can go to the soccer game with us today. (b) Ben considers Phillipe **to have been** his best friend ever since they started college three years ago. (Ben still considers him to be his best friend.)	**Past in Relation to the Present** Perfective infinitives signal an event or condition in the past. The event or condition may continue to the present.
(c) Dr. Yamada wanted **to have completed** her research before last August. However her funds for the project ran out. (d) The driver claimed **to have stopped** for the traffic light before the accident occurred.	**Past in Relation to the Past** The event expressed by the infinitive clause may be unfulfilled. With verbs that express beliefs or attitudes, such as *claim* or *consider,* the event in the infinitive clause may or may not have actually happened.
(e) Winona expects **to have made** all of her plane reservations by next week. (f) Winona expects **to make** all of her plane reservations by next week.	**Past in Relation to the Future** The event expressed by the infinitive clause may be a future event that takes place before another time in the future. We also commonly use infinitives that are not perfective (*to +* verb) to carry the same meaning for future events.
Perfective: Past (g) It **was** nice of you **to have done** that. **Nonperfective: Past** (h) It **was** nice of you **to do** that. **Perfective: Past** (i) It **is** nice of you **to have done** that. (You did something in the past.) **Nonperfective: Present, Future** (j) It **is** nice of you **to do** that. (You are doing something right now or will do something in the future.)	**Past Tense vs. Present Tense Main Clauses** When the main clause is past tense, speakers often use nonperfective infinitives to express the same meanings as perfective ones. When the main clause is present tense, use: *Infinitive* *To Express* perfective past meaning nonperfective present or future meaning

EXERCISE 4

Complete each blank with a perfective infinitive using the verb in parentheses. Then state which type of meaning each one expresses: past relative to the present, to the past, or to the future.

▶ **EXAMPLE:** I would like (accompany) _to have accompanied_ the Castenada family on their travels across the country.

1. By the end of August, the Castenada family plans (tour) _____ most of the East Coast; they have been traveling in the United States all summer and have only two weeks left.

2. They intended (visit) _____ all of their West Coast relatives before the end of June, but they couldn't because of car trouble.

3. Eight-year-old Ruby Castenada says that she would like (spend) _____ the entire summer at Disneyland.

4. So far, Mr. and Mrs. Castenada consider the highlight of their vacation (be) _____ their camping trip in Michigan.

5. At the beginning of the trip, Tracy, their teenage son, was upset (leave) _____ all his friends for the summer.

6. However, now he admits that he would like (see) _____ even more of the country and hopes to travel again soon.

7. The Castenadas' goal is (visit) _____ all of the continental United States before Tracy goes away to college.

EXERCISE 5

Restate the infinitives in the following quotations as perfective infinitives. If you had to choose one of them for a maxim to live by, which one would you select? Can you think of any other sayings that use perfective infinitives?

▶ **EXAMPLE:** To win one's joy through struggle is better than to yield to melancholy. (Andre Gide, French author)

To have won one's joy through struggle is better than t*o have yielded* to melancholy.

1. What a lovely surprise to finally discover how unlonely being alone can be. (Ellen Burstyn, American actress)

2. To endure what is unendurable is true endurance. (Japanese proverb)

3. I would prefer even to fail with honor than to win by cheating. (Sophocles, Greek dramatist)

4. To teach is to learn twice over. (Joseph Joubert, *Pensees*)

5. It is better to be happy for a moment and burned up with beauty than to live a long time and be bored all the while. (Don Marquis, "the lesson of the moth," *Archy and Mehitabel*)

6. Youth is the time to study wisdom; old age is the time to practice it. (Rousseau, *Reveries of a Solitary Walker*)

Perfective Infinitives **345**

A N S W E R   K E Y

Exercise 4

1. to have toured (future) 2. to have visited (past) 3. to have spent (present) 4. to have been (present) 5. to have left (past) 6. to have seen (present) 7. to have visited (future)

Exercise 5

1. . . . to have discovered . . . 2. To have endured what is unendurable . . .
3. . . . to have failed; to have won 4. to have taught . . . to have learned . . .
5. . . . to have been happy . . . (to have) been burned . . . to have lived . . . (to have) been bored. 6. . . . to have studied wisdom; . . . to have practiced . . .

This chart shows two other forms of perfective infinitive.

To review the progressive and passive forms
1. Write the label "Progressive" on the board.
2. Write several phrases with base form verbs followed by a colon. Have Ss, using the focus chart, give the progressive infinitive forms; write them on the board (e.g., :*I'd like/swim: I'd like to have been swimming*). Show Ss how to expand a few of the phrases: *I'd like to have been swimming last weekend instead of working in the chemistry lab.*
3. Repeat the procedure of Steps 1 and 2 for passive forms. Write the label "Passive" on the board with phrases under for Ss to transform. Example: *I'd like/tell: I'd like to have been told the truth.* Some irregular verbs that would work well for context: *keep, leave, build, hear, make, meet, sleep, speak, win.* *Hope* could be used as a main verb instead of *like* for some of the phrases. Consult the list of common irregular verbs in Appendix 8, p. 463 for other verbs.

Workbook Ex. 3, p. 196.
Answers: TE p. 556.

Exercise 6

Ask Ss to write out and turn in this assignment to assess their use of these forms in a guided context. If assigned for homework, do the first one in class together to ensure that Ss understand the examples.

Wookbook Ex. 5, p. 198.
Answers: TE p. 556.

Progressive and Passive Forms of Perfective Infinitives

EXAMPLES		EXPLANATIONS
(a)	I'd like **to have been watching** when Bart received his award for bravery.	**Progressive Form** *to + have + been +* verb *+ -ing*
(b)	Mr. Park believed the police **to have been guarding** his store when the robbery occurred.	
(c)	Bart would like me **to have been sent** a ticket to the ceremony.	**Passive Form** *to + have + been +* past participle
(d)	Mr. Park believed himself **to have been given** false information by the police.	

EXERCISE 6
Rewrite each of the following clauses as a perfective infinitive clause. The clauses begin with *that*, *ø-that* (*that* has been deleted), or *when*. Make any word changes that are necessary.

▶ **EXAMPLES:**   *ø-that* clause: Josef wishes he could have discovered the Cape of Good Hope with Diaz.

infinitive clause: *Josef would like to have discovered the Cape of Good Hope with Diaz.*

that-clause: Veronica believes that she was shortchanged.

infinitive clause: *Veronica believes herself to have been short-changed.*

1. Our English teacher expects that we will finish our oral reports on our favorite celebrities by the end of next week.
2. Henri would prefer that he be the last one to present, but unfortunately for him, he is scheduled to be first.
3. Isela believes she was greatly misinformed by one of her interview subjects.

A N S W E R   K E Y

Exercise 6
1. Our English teacher expects us to have finished our oral reports . . .   **2.** Henri would prefer to have been the last one to present . . .
3. Isela believes herself to have been greatly misinformed . . .   **4.** We would like to have heard more . .   **5.** Jocelyn hoped to have been given a chance . . .   **6.** Gerard claims

to have been sent an autograph . . .
7. Sandra reported Meryl Streep, her favorite actress, to have been at the symphony . . .
8. Ty considers himself to have gotten . . .
9. Berta would like to have been eating dinner . . .   **10.** I will be relieved to have presented my report . . .

4. We wish we could have heard more about Shaun's talk with Janet Jackson. (Change *wish* to *would like*)

5. Jocelyn hoped she would be given a chance to interview her favorite author, but the interview didn't work out.

6. Gerard claims that he was sent an autograph from a "major motion picture star," whose identity he is keeping a secret.

7. Sandra reported that Meryl Streep, her favorite actress, had been sitting in front of her at a Carnegie Hall concert.

8. Ty thinks that he has gotten the most interesting interview with a celebrity. (Use *consider* for the main verb.)

9. Berta wishes that she had been eating dinner at the Hollywood restaurant last Friday night because someone told her that her favorite basketball player was there.

10. I will be relieved when I have presented my report since getting up in front of others makes me anxious.

FOCUS **4**

Negative Forms of Perfective Infinitives

EXAMPLES	EXPLANATIONS
	Formal English
(a) The three nations were wise **not to have signed** the agreement until they could discuss it further.	In formal written English, put negative forms (*not, never,* etc.) before the infinitive verbs.
(b) **Not to have been contacted** for a job interview greatly disappointed Daniel.	
(c) During his entire term, Representative Bolski appears **never to have voted** in favor of extra funds for child care.	
	Informal English
(d) **To have not been invited** to the party made her upset.	In less formal English, speakers sometimes put negative forms after *have.*
(e) I seem to **have not brought** the book I meant to give you.	
(f) That woman claims **to have never seen** the money that turned up in her purse.	

Perfective Infinitives | **347**

FOCUS 4

This focus box shows the placement of negative forms with perfective infinitives in both formal and informal English. Remind Ss that in informal English, speakers also use the nonperfective forms in some of the contexts shown here (e.g., *The three nations were wise not to sign the agreement . . .*). In other contexts, such as (e), this would not be possible; e.g., a speaker wouldn't say *I seem to not bring the book* but might avoid using a perfective infinitive by saying: *I think I forgot the book I meant to give you.* The point here is not to encourage Ss to avoid complex structures but to help them understand (a) where these structures have meanings similar to others they have heard or seen and (b) how the structures can be used to achieve more precise meaning, especially in formal contexts.

EXERCISE 7

Rewrite each of the following sentences so that it contains a negative perfective infinitive clause. Use the pattern for formal written English.

▶ **EXAMPLE:**   It appeared that Dr. Moreau had not been in Marseilles the last
weekend in April.

*Dr. Moreau appeared <u>not to have been</u> in Marseilles the last week-
end in April.*

1. In reviewing evidence gathered for the murder trial,
Detective Armand believed that the facts had not
supported Dr. Moreau's claims of innocence.

2. It was quite strange, Armand mused, that Dr.
Moreau had not told his housekeeper he would be
away the weekend the murder occurred. (Replace
that with *for* + noun)

3. Furthermore, the doctor did not seem to remember much about the
inn he claimed he had stayed in that weekend. How very odd!

4. Also, the doctor claimed that he had never known the victim,
Horace Bix; yet Bix's name was found in his appointment book.

5. All in all, Detective Armand believed that Dr. Moreau had not given
the police truthful answers to a number of questions.

A N S W E R   K E Y

Exercise 7
1. . . . the facts not to have been
supported . . .   **2.** . . . . mused, for Dr.
Moreau not to have told . . .

3. . . . seemed not to have remembered . .
4. . . . . claimed never to have known . . .
5. . . . believed Dr. Moreau not to have
given . . .

FOCUS 5

Expressing Likes, Preferences, and Dislikes Contrary to Past Fact

	EXAMPLES	EXPLANATIONS
Would + verb *would like*	**(a)** I **would like to have spent** the class period reviewing for the exam. (I would have liked to spend the class period reviewing for the exam.)	Use *would* + verbs with perfective infinitives to express likes, dislikes, and preferences about things that did not happen.
would love	**(b)** My parents **would love to have joined** us for dinner. (My parents would have loved to join us for dinner.)	Alternative forms of these sentences are given in parentheses. The alternative form has a perfective main clause verb and a nonperfective infinitive.
would prefer	**(c)** I **would prefer not to have had** an early morning class. (I would have preferred not to have an early morning class.)	
would hate	**(d)** **Wouldn't you hate to have been** in that crowded room? (Wouldn't you have hated to be in that crowded room?)	
	(e) We **would have liked to have spent** the class period reviewing for the exam.	Native English speakers sometimes use perfective forms for both clauses in speech. Although this pattern would sound fine to many native English speakers, it is not considered standard for written English.

This focus box and the three following explain and illustrate communicative contexts in which perfective infinitives are used. Encourage Ss to learn and practice the structures with the commonly co-occurring *would + verb* phrases.

SUGGESTION

Ask Ss questions eliciting perfective infinitive forms: "*Serina, what would you have preferred to do instead of coming to class this morning? Yoshi, how would you like to have spent last weekend if you could go anywhere?*" If Ss give responses without perfective infinitives, help them transform them by writing their responses on the board and prompting the infinitive forms, e.g., *I wish I could have gone scuba diving —> I'd like to have gone scuba diving.*

Workbook Ex. 4 , p. 197.
Answers: TE p. 556.

Exercise 8
SUGGESTION

This is a good exercise for oral production. You could have Ss practice question forms by using the prompts for oral questions and answers.

Exercise 9

VARIATION

Ss could do a brief in-class writing on one or two topics instead of reporting orally to a classmate.

Workbook Ex.7, p. 200.
Answers: TE p. 556.

EXERCISE 8

Use the cues below to make sentences expressing a past wish that did not materialize or an unpleasant event that was avoided. Use the standard English pattern of *would like, would love, would prefer,* or *would hate* followed by a perfective infinitive. Make any changes that are necessary, including any needed verb tense changes.

▶ **EXAMPLE:** be asked to present my report first
I would like to have been asked to present my report first.

1. take all of my final exams on one day
2. forget the answers to the test questions
3. go to the movies instead of taking the exam
4. be the only one in class without the assignment
5. be given true-false questions for the entire test
6. study geology instead of biochemistry
7. walk into the classroom and find out the teacher was absent
8. be watching music video tapes all afternoon
9. not know that class was canceled
10. present an oral report rather than a written one

EXERCISE 9

Choose any five of the following topics. For each topic, write a statement expressing a past wish. With a classmate, explain the reasons for one or two of your statements.

▶ **EXAMPLE:** An experience while traveling
I would prefer to have flown from England to France instead of going by boat across the channel.
Reason: *The sea was very rough that day and I got seasick.*

1. The way you spent one of your last vacations
2. Your participation in a sports event as an athlete or spectator
3. A course you had to take
4. A paper or report you had to write
5. A meal you had recently
6. An experience you had at a party or other social event
7. (A topic of your choice)

ANSWER KEY

Exercise 8
1. I would like to have taken . . . 2. I would hate to have forgotten . . . 3. I would prefer to have gone . . . 4. I would hate to have been . . . 5. I would like to have been given . . . 6. I would prefer to have studied . . . 7. I would like to have walked . . . found out . . . 8. I'd love to have been watching 9. I'd hate not to have known . . . 10. I'd prefer to have presented

Exercise 9
Answers will vary. Examples:
1. I would like to have spent last summer in Portugal. 2. I would like to have played soccer in high school. 3. I would prefer to have had more emphasis on poetry in my literature class. 4. I would like to have researched my topic more. 5. I would like to have tried the spicy mussels at the Thai restaurant we went to. 6. I would like to have danced a little more at the party last weekend.

▶ **Expressing Other Emotions and Attitudes with Perfective Infinitives**

EXAMPLES	EXPLANATIONS
(a) I **am sorry** to have missed your party.	• *be* + adjective
(b) They **were shocked** to have been treated so rudely.	
(c) **It was generous of you** to have lent us your bicycles.	• *it* + *be* + adjective (+ *of* + noun)
(d) **It is annoying** to have been waiting so long for a ticket.	
(e) **It is a pleasure** to have met you after all these years.	• *it* + *be* + noun phrase
(f) **It was a miracle** to have found the contact lens in the swimming pool.	
(g) **It was fortunate for us** to have discovered the mistake.	• (*it* + *be* + adjective) *for* + noun/ objective pronoun
(h) **For them** to have had three plane delays in one day was very unlucky.	
(i) It **must** be exciting to have lived in so many countries!	You may also use modal verbs before *be* with many of the expressions.
(j) It **would** be a disappointment to have missed the parade. I'm glad we made it on time!	

EXERCISE 10

Make sentences with perfective infinitive clauses, using the cues. Use a variety of structures. If you wish, add descriptive words or phrases to expand the sentences.

▶ **EXAMPLES:** Be foolish . . . think that no one would notice
John must be foolish to have thought that no one would notice he had taken the dangerous chemicals.

It was foolish of us to have thought no one would notice we were missing from class.

1. Be a tragedy . . . lose so many homes in the volcanic eruptions
2. Be unwise . . . build a home so close to the volcano
3. Be kind . . . donate your time to volunteer work

Perfective Infinitives | **351**

FOCUS 6

Note that *it was generous of you* and similar phrases are useful for expressing appreciation and gratitude in formal contexts such as thank-you notes or letters (e.g., *it was generous/kind/nice/ thoughtful of you to do X*). Similarly, *It was a pleasure to have . . .* could be used in follow-up letters after job or college admissions interviews, etc.

SUGGESTION

Tell Ss that while speakers do use other nonperfective as well as perfective forms in some of these contexts, the perfective forms express meaning more precisely. In other cases, nonperfective infinitives indicate a future event. Explain (or elicit an explanation) of the meaning difference between *I am sorry to have missed your party* and *I am sorry to miss your party*.

Exercise 10

Ss could do this exercise orally, as a class or in pairs.

A N S W E R   K E Y

Exercise 10
1. It was a tragedy to have lost . . .   2. It was unwise to have built . . .   3. You were kind to have donated . . .   4. For them to have shown up . . . was astounding.   5. For her to have worn jogging shorts . . . was considered improper./It was considered improper for her to have . . .

Exercise 11

SUGGESTION

Have Ss create responses in small groups. Then ask for volunteers to write one of their responses on the board. Have Ss help you make any needed corrections as you read through the responses.

Workbook Ex. 8, p. 201.
Answers: TE p. 556.

4. Show up at the party together . . . be astounding (Start with *for* + noun)

5. Wear jogging shorts . . . was considered improper

EXERCISE 11

Use an expression from Focus 6, Exercise 10, or a similar one to make up a response for each of the situations below. Use a perfective infinitive in your response.

▶ **EXAMPLE:** You have recently spent three days at the beach house of your parents' friends while they were not there. You are writing them a thank-you note.

It was very generous of you to have let me stay in your beach house during my trip to the coast.

1. You have just remembered that today is the birthday of one of your friends who lives in another city, and you forgot to send her a birth-day card. You buy a card and want to write a note to tell her you're sorry.

2. A friend helped you move from one apartment to another. You want to send him a thank-you note.

3. You are having a conversation at a party with someone you have just met. She has been telling you about her trip to see the Summer Olympics.

4. You recently went shopping in a department store. When you tried to purchase something, the salesman kept you waiting for several minutes while he chatted with a friend on the phone. You are writing a letter of complaint to the manager of the store.

5. You are writing a letter to a friend. You want to tell her how fortunate you were recently. You just heard that you were awarded two scholarships to attend school next year.

6. You call up the mother of a friend to thank her for having given a going away party for you before you move to another city.

7. A friend did not show up for a class three sessions in a row. This strikes you as strange because he has never missed a class before. Another friend asks you if you know where he has been, but you don't.

8. Someone you know has recently bought a very expensive new car. The person doesn't have much money, so you think it was an unwise purchase.

ANSWER KEY

Exercise 11

Answers will vary. Examples:
1. I'm really sorry to have missed your birthday.
2. It was so nice of you to have helped me move. 3. Oh, I'd love to have seen some of the events live, especially the track and field events. 4. I was truly surprised to have received such bad service in your store. 5. I was fortunate to have been awarded two scholarships for next year. 6. It was very kind of you to have given me a party. 7. No, I have no idea. It's really unusual for Minhhuy to have missed so many classes. 8. In my opinion, it was unwise of Megumi to have bought such an expensive car since she may not be able to afford the payments.

FOCUS 7

Expressing Uncertainly about Past Events

EXAMPLES	EXPLANATIONS
(a) I **seem to have forgotten** my home-work assignment. Oh wait, here it is in my notebook!	After the verbs *seem* and *appear*, perfective infinitives express uncertainty about past events based on present evidence.
(b) This assignment **appears to have been written** rather hastily.	Sometimes the "uncertainty" is actually a way to avoid directly accusing or criticizing someone.
(c) Hmmm . . . someone **seems to have eaten** all the ice cream.	

EXERCISE 12

Make up a sentence with *appear* or *seem* followed by a perfective infinitive for each of the following situations.

1. You go for a job interview. The interviewer asks to see your application form. You realize you must have left it at home. Respond to the question.

2. You are a teacher. One of your students looks as if she is on the verge of falling asleep. Make a comment to her.

3. As you are getting ready to leave the classroom, you discover that you no longer have your notebook, which was with you when you entered the room. Make a comment to the class as they are walking out.

4. You have just finished reading a novel that is the worst one you have ever read. Make a comment to a friend about the author of the book.

5. When the teacher starts going over the homework assignment, you realize that you did the wrong one. The teacher calls on you for an answer. Give an appropriate response.

Perfective Infinitives | **353**

S U G G E S T I O N

Since *seem* is the most common verb used with perfective infinitives to express uncertainty about the past, give Ss infinitive verb prompts and help them to create sentences. Examples: *lose —>: I seem to have lost my glasses. break—-> I seem to have broken the chain on my bicycle. leave out —-> I seem to have left out a verb in this sentence.* As with other points for this unit, this one provides an opportunity to review past participles of common irregular verbs.

Exercise 12
E X P A N S I O N

Have Ss write one more situation as a homework assignment. Collect them and select two or three to read each class period during the next three classes, eliciting responses from Ss as a mini-review of this teaching point. You can vary the response mode (e.g., one day have Ss individually write down a response, during the next class have them discuss the situation with the person next to them, etc.).

Workbook Ex. 9, p. 202.
Answers: TE p. 557.

Here the focus is on the main verb vocabulary that precedes perfective infinitives in expressing obligations, etc. You can provide or elicit additional examples related to your class or to an academic context: *Silvia was to have spent the entire weekend studying, but she ended up going to a party. She plans to study next weekend instead.*

Exercise 13

V A R I A T I O N

Have Ss interview a partner to get answers. Call on Ss to report responses to the rest of the class, using indirect speech: *By next week, Ari plans to have. . . . .; Helen said she was supposed to have . . .*

Workbook Ex. 10, p. 203.
Answers: TE p. 557.

FOCUS **8**

▶ ## Expressing Obligations, Intentions, and Future Plans

USE

EXAMPLES	EXPLANATIONS
(a) The engineers **were supposed to have checked** all the controls before the shuttle was launched. **(b)** Caroline **was to have spent** the entire summer sculpting, but she ended up working at a bank for a month.	Perfective infinitives may follow phrasal modals *be supposed to* or *be to*. They express past obligations or plans that were not fulfilled.
(c) Do you **plan to have written** your report before Sunday? **(d)** The weatherman **expects** the rains **to have ended** by next weekend.	With verbs such as *plan, intend, hope,* and *expect,* perfective infinitives express a future time before another future time.

EXERCISE 13

Complete the following sentences with information about yourself; use a perfective infinitive clause in each.

▶ **EXAMPLE:** By tomorrow I intend *to have bought my sister a birthday present*.

1. By next week I plan _____.
2. I intend _____ within the next five years.
3. I was supposed _____ but I didn't because _____.
4. I expect _____ before _____.
5. By _____ I hope _____.

A N S W E R   K E Y

Exercise 13
Answers will vary.
1. to have finished reading that novel
2. to have completed my degree   3. to have
become a senior this year/I was three credits short   4. to have gotten married . . . the end of the decade   5. next year . . . to have visited my grandparents in Indonesia

---

Perfective Infinitives with *Enough* and *Too*

EXAMPLES	EXPLANATIONS
adjective + *enough* **(a)** The earthquake was **powerful enough** to have destroyed a whole city. (The earthquake could have destroyed a whole city.)	***Enough*** Following *enough*, perfective infinitives often express an event that could have happened but did not happen.
***enough* + noun** **(b)** I got **enough homework** on Friday to have kept me busy for a week. (The homework could have kept me busy for a week.)	
***too* + adjective** **(c)** We were **too tired** to have gone anywhere last night. (We didn't go anywhere last night because we were too tired.)	***Too*** Following *too*, perfective infinitives may express events that did not occur. The main clause gives a reason.
***too* + *many/much* + noun** **(d)** She has **too much intelligence** to have done so poorly on the exam. (She did poorly, but I am surprised because she is so intelligent.)	The perfective infinitive after *too* may also express the speaker's disbelief that something did not occur.

EXERCISE 14

Use the phrases below to create sentences about past possibilities using perfective infinitives.

▶ **EXAMPLE:** poison . . . strong enough

The poison that the child accidentally swallowed was strong enough to have killed her, but fortunately she recovered completely.

1. the noise . . . loud enough

2. they ate enough popcorn . . .

3. fireworks . . . bright enough

4. wind . . . strong enough

ANSWER KEY

Exercise 14
Answers will vary. Examples:
1. The noise was loud enough to have broken the sound barrier.   **2.** She ate enough popcorn to have filled her up for a week.
3. The fireworks were bright enough to have been seen for miles.   **4.** The wind was strong enough to have toppled several trees.   **5.** The weather in Moscow was cold enough to have made us all want to find a nice warm room indoors.   **6.** We heard enough bad news to have lasted us a year.

SUGGESTION

1. Write on the board other sentences with *could* + perfective verb to transform into sentences with perfective infinitives. Example: *The food we had for dinner last night could have fed twenty people!* —> *We had enough food for dinner last night to have fed twenty people!*
2. Write sentences similar to the ones in brackets under (c) and (d). Example: *We didn't go swimming in the lake because it was too cold, so we took a boat ride instead.*—> *The lake was too cold to have gone swimming in, so . .*

Exercise 15

SUGGESTION

Assign this exercise as homework and collect to assess progress.

EXERCISE 15

The following sentences express disbelief about an event or explain why something didn't happen. Combine the ideas in each pair of sentences into one sentence, using a perfective infinitive clause.

▶ **EXAMPLE:** She couldn't have done well in the marathon last fall. She had sustained too many minor injuries.

Combined: *She had sustained too many minor injuries to have done well in the marathon last fall.*

1. My brother couldn't have cheated on a test. He is too honest.

2. You couldn't have stopped taking piano lessons! You have too much talent.

3. Stan couldn't have bought that wild tie himself. He is too conservative.

4. Charmaine didn't stay at that low-level job. She has too much ambition.

5. They couldn't have taken on any more debts. They have too many already.

UNIT GOAL REVIEW

Ask Ss to look at the goals on the opening page of the unit again. Help them understand how much they have accomplished in each area.

ANSWER KEY

Exercise 15

1. My brother is too honest to have cheated. . . . 2. You have much too much talent to have stopped . . . 3. Stan is too conservative to have bought . . . 4. Charmaine has too much ambition to have stayed . . . 5. They have too many debts to have taken . . .

Use Your English

ACTIVITY 1: LISTENING/WRITING/SPEAKING

Imagine that you have just returned from a two-week vacation. The dates of your vacation were July 14 through the 28th. You will hear four messages that have been left on your telephone answering machine.

STEP 1 Take notes as you listen to each message.

STEP 2 Use your notes to create responses that you could leave on the answering machines of the people who called. Use at least one perfective infinitive form in each response.

STEP 3 Share your favorite responses with a small group of classmates.

ACTIVITY 2: RESEARCH/SPEAKING/WRITING

Interview ten people about regrets—either their greatest regrets or most recent ones. Then write the results of your survey using statements with perfective infinitives. Share the results with your classmates. Here are some examples of paraphrases:

▶ **EXAMPLES:** Jack's regret: that he stopped dating Shirelle
Paraphrase: Jack is sorry to *have stopped* dating Shirelle.

Risa's regret: that she didn't go to Vienna for her vacation
Paraphrase: Risa is sorry not *to have gone* to Vienna for her vacation.

Blanca's regret: that she never learned Spanish from her mother
Paraphrase: Blanca is sorry never *to have learned* Spanish from her mother.

Perfective Infinitives | **357**

USE YOUR ENGLISH

The activities on these "purple pages" at the end of the unit contain situations that should naturally elicit the unit's structures in a more communicative framework. While Ss are doing these activities in class, you can circulate and listen to determine if they have actually achieved the goals on the opening page of the unit.

Activity 1

Play textbook audio. The tapescript for this listening appears on p. 573 of this book.

Workbook Ex. 11, p. 204; Ex. 12, p. 205.
Answers: TE p. 557.

Activity 2

SUGGESTIONS

1. Find a short essay that deals with the topic of regrets to provide background on this topic. Read it aloud to Ss or give them a copy as a handout.

2. Help Ss to develop a lead-in to their research question if they are interviewing people outside the class.(e.g., *"I'm doing a class research project about the kinds of things that people regret. For example, some people regret not doing certain things, like not studying hard enough, or they're sorry they did something. Could you tell me one or two things that you have regrets about?"*)

VARIATION

Have Ss discuss their own regrets with classmates in small groups and to write down the results using perfective infinitives.

ANSWER KEY

Activity 1
This is a role play activity with Ss creating their own responses, so answers will vary.

Activity 3

VARIATION

As a homework assignment, Ss could interview a friend or friends instead of classmate.

Activity 4

Encourage Ss to be creative and have fun with this one!

ACTIVITY 3: SPEAKING/WRITING

Interview one or more classmates about things that they hope or expect to have done or have seen during the next five years. Here are examples of some categories you might consider. Think of others that might be interesting to find out about. (Trips they hope to have made? Classes they expect to have passed? New foods they hope to have tried?)

- Places you hope to have visited
- Hobbies you hope to have engaged in
- Educational degrees you expect to have received
- Possessions you hope to have obtained
- Books you'd like to have read
- Skills you hope to have learned or developed

Present some of your findings in a brief oral report to the class.

ACTIVITY 4: WRITING/SPEAKING

A "tall tale" is a story that contains a great deal of exaggeration for a humorous effect. Imagine that you are at a Tall Tales Convention in which people compete to make up the funniest exaggerations. You have entered the "Enough is Enough Category"; for this competition you must come up with statements like "The sidewalk was hot enough last weekend to have fried an egg on it" or "We made enough food last night to have invited the state of Texas for dinner." Either individually or in teams, make up entries for the competition. Have others vote on the best ones.

ACTIVITY 5: WRITING/LISTENING

Write an imaginary interview or dialogue between you and a famous person who is no longer living. (It could be someone you mentioned in the Opening Task.) In your dialogue use some perfective infinitive phrases. For example, you could ask the person what she or he might like to have done differently if circumstances had been different or if the person had lived at a different time. Or you might have the person comment on what he or she was happy or sorry to have done or how exciting, frustrating, etc. it was to have experienced certain events. Read your dialogue to class members without telling them who the famous person is; see if they can guess the person's identity.

Activity 5

SUGGESTIONS

1. To get information for their interviews, Ss could research a famous person using the Internet.
2. Give Ss a list of famous people to consider in case some Ss have trouble thinking of a subject for their dialogue.

3. On the board, model the first part of a dialogue that might take place between you and a famous person who is no longer living.
4. Tell Ss they can write a humorous interview/ dialogue if they wish. This could increase some of your Ss' motivation to write.

The test for this unit can be found on p. 521. The answers are on p. 522.

Unit 20

UNIT OVERVIEW

Unit 20 introduces and expands students' (Ss') knowledge of three adjective complement structures: *that* clauses, infinitives, and gerunds. Distinct meaning differences of these three types and adjective complement word order are the two main principles taught.

UNIT GOALS

Review the goals listed on this page so Ss understand what they should be able to know by the end of the unit.

OPENING TASK

In this task, Ss will consider human beings' relationship to animals.

SETTING UP THE TASK

SUGGESTIONS

1. Introduce the task by bringing in photos of some of the items in the grid on the next page (e.g., animal research lab).
2. Bring in realia (e.g., bottle of shampoo displaying a disclaimer that animals have not been used in testing the product). Use the realia and/or photos to spark a brief, general discussion about humans and animals.

UNIT 20

ADJECTIVE COMPLEMENTS IN SUBJECT AND PREDICATE POSITION

UNIT GOALS:

- To use three types of adjective complement structures
- To use adjective complements in subject and predicate position
- To choose among infinitives, gerunds, and *that* clauses

▶ OPENING TASK
Human Beings' Relationship to Animals

STEP 1 As you look over the following list, think about the positive and negative associations each term has.

STEP 2 Jot down your ideas for as many terms as you can with a partner.

Term	Positive	Negative
1. animal research	provides a way to test the safety of drugs and cosmetics	animals dissected, injected, and killed in experiments
2. fur coat		
3. zoo		
4. oil tanker		
5. veal		
6. ivory		
7. pesticide		
8. campground		
9. bullfight		
10. hunting		
11. highway construction		

STEP 3 After your discussion, write down statements about several of the terms, including both positive and negative associations. Here are some sample statements about the first term, animal research:

It is unethical for animals like gorillas and chimpanzees to be used in medical research. That this research tests the safety of drugs and cosmetics is undeniable. But researchers' blindly generalizing the findings from these experiments to human beings does not make sense. In addition, injecting and killing these animals during experiments is inhumane.

CONDUCTING THE TASK

Step 1: Ask Ss to think about the positive and negative aspects of animal research. Some Ss may know that animals have played a role in doctors' finding treatments for polio, cancer, diabetes, etc. They may also know that many animals have been killed as a result of these experiments.

Step 2: Asks pairs to continue brainstorming and filling in the grid.

Step 3: Encourage Ss to write positive and negative associations using a variety of descriptive words (adjectives) like *great, important, disgusting, sad,* etc.

CLOSING THE TASK

Discuss how thoughts about humans and animals may vary in different cultures. Encourage Ss to make comparisons between their home countries, or other countries they know about, and their current country of residence.

Explain that an adjective complement is a type of clause that is embedded into a subject of a sentence and then followed by a predicate that contains a linking verb and an adjective. This structure is most evident with a *that* clause, which contains a subject and a normal verb phrase. However, it is also evident with an infinitive and gerund complement, which contain a subject (even if followed by an apostrophe) and a verb (even if an infinitive form).

Exercise 1

Remind Ss to read the entire item first to obtain clues for filling in the blank with the correct verb.

FOCUS **1**

▶ **Overview of Adjective Complements**

EXAMPLES		EXPLANATIONS
(a)	**adjective complement + adjective** **Killing these animals** is inhumane.	Adjective complements can appear in subject position in front of linking verbs (such as *appear, be, become, look, remain, seem*) followed by adjectives.
(b)	**That the blue whale is becoming extinct** seems sad.	Adjective complements are of three types: • *that*-clause (consisting of *that* + clause)
(c)	**For campers to pollute streams** is irresponsible.	• infinitive (consisting of *for* + noun phrase + *to* + base verb)
(d)	**Bulls' being killed** in bullfights appears brutal.	• gerund (consisting of *'s* + verb + *-ing*)
(e)	Joshua appears ready **for the hunting season** to begin.	The adjectives that precede adjective complements and follow animate subjects generally show positive expectation (e.g., *ready, anxious, happy, eager,* etc.).
(f)	Michelle is eager **for Joshua to shoot a fox.**	
(g)	Michelle is eager to have a fox coat.	If the main subject and the complement subject are alike, we delete the *for* phrase.
(h)	**NOT:** Michelle is eager for herself to have a fox coat.	

EXERCISE 1

In the following short texts, complete the adjective complements with *that*-clauses, *for/to* infinitives, or gerunds.

▶ **EXAMPLE:** Elizabeth Mann Borghese, who was the daughter of the writer Thomas Mann, taught her dog to take dictation on a special typewriter. Her dog's __taking dictation__ is amazing.

1. Once a woman was thrown off a yacht and three dolphins rescued her and led her to a marker in the sea. Another time, several fishermen were lost in a dense fog, and four dolphins nudged their boat to safety. Dolphins' _____ is well-documented.

2. Mrs. Betsy Marcus' dog Benjy was known to sing "Raindrops Keep Fallin' on My Head." For a dog _____ is incredible.

ANSWER KEY

Exercise 1
Answers will vary.
1. helping humans   2. to sing   3. kill these animals   4. speaking to singular and plural groups differently   5. to reappear   6. could communicate with sign language

3. At one time, passenger pigeons were very numerous. Now there are none because of massive hunting and the destruction of their natural forest home. That hunters _____ is sad.

4. Jaco, an African gray parrot, could speak German. When his master left the house alone, he said, "God be with you." When his master left with other people, he said, "God be with you all." Jaco's

    _____ is fascinating.

5. The dwarf lemur and the mountain pygmy possum were considered extinct. However, in recent years, these animals have reappeared.

    For extinct animals _____ is inspiring.

6. Washoe, a female chimpanzee, was taught sign language. She was able to make up words like *drink-fruit* (for watermelon) and *water-bird* (for swan). That Washoe _____ is intriguing.

EXERCISE 2

Imagine that you are an animal instead of a human being. What would make you happy if you were one of the following pets? Write your answers in first person and use one of the adjectives: *anxious, eager, happy,* or *ready.*

▶ **EXAMPLE:** cat
    *I would be **eager** for my owner to feed me a tuna casserole.*
    *I would be **happy** to lie around in the sun.*

1. horse
2. parrot
3. dog
4. mouse
5. goldfish
6. snake

Exercise 2

Note that there are only a small number of adjectives that follow animate subjects like *I, he, the girls,* etc., and are preceded by adjective complements. In other words, it would not be possible to insert an adjective like *vicious* or *impossible* in the example sentences. NOT: *I would be vicious for my owner to feed me a tuna casserole.*

Workbook Exs. 1 & 2, pp. 206–207.
Answers: TE p. 557.

ANSWER KEY

Exercise 2
Answers will vary.
1. I would be happy to gallop around freely.
2. I would be eager to practice new words.
3. I would be ready to take walks with my master.   4. I would be happy to eat food scraps on the floor.   5. I would be anxious to have the lights go out so that everyone wouldn't look at me in my fish tank.   6. I would be happy to slither around on the ground.

This focus summarizes how English speakers manage information in discourse. If a person writes or talks to someone, they normally will refer to what they think their audience understands or refer to what their interlocutor has said before presenting something new that they want to say. This is why we sometimes put an adjective complement in subject position. However, if English speakers are beginning a new topic, they will often reserve the piece of information for the predicate position in the sentence. The reason for this is that the information will be more memorable for the audience listening to or reading it.

Exercise 3

E X P A N S I O N

Ask Ss to add a follow-up sentence to the sentences beginning with *it*. This will reinforce the idea that when the complement structure is in the predicate, it introduces a new idea that begs for further comment. Give an example on the board: *From all of the evidence, it was obvious that the defendant was guilty. No one ever really doubted it.* Ask Ss if they have other ideas for a follow-up sentence. Write these on the board as well. Then continue with items 2, 3, 4, and 7.

FOCUS **2**

▶ **Adjective Complements in Subject and Predicate Position**

EXAMPLES	EXPLANATIONS
(a) I am sorry to say that certain businesses that sell sculptured ivory objects have hired poachers to kill elephants for their tusks. **For poachers to take the tusks from live elephants** is alarming. **That they sell them is** abominable. Worst of all, **elephants' becoming an endangered species because of this** is criminal.	In subject position, adjective complements usually contain a known idea, either previously mentioned or assumed through context.
It **+ linking verb + adjective + adjective complement** **(b)** It is interesting **that medical researchers have made important medical discoveries through animal research.** They need to continue this work. **(c)** It is necessary **for protesters to call for a moratorium on animal testing.** Animals have rights too!	When *that*-clauses and infinitives contain new information, they will more commonly appear in predicate position. We move the *that*-clause or the infinitive to the end of the sentence and add *it* at the beginning.
(d) **NOT:** It is abominable poachers' killing elephants.	Gerunds do not normally occur with *it* constructions.

EXERCISE 3

Fill in the blanks with a variety of appropriate linking verbs and adjectives from the following lists. More than one answer may be correct.

Linking Verbs	Adjectives		
appear	apparent	improper	obvious
be	bad	inappropriate	odd
become	compulsory	irrational	sad
look	depressing	irritating	surprising
remain	disappointing	likely	true
seem	impossible	necessary	unfortunate

▶ **EXAMPLE:** From all of the evidence, it ___was obvious___ that the defendant was guilty.

1. Crime is rampant in many parts of the world. That teenagers commit many of these crimes _____.

2. It _____ for children to attend elementary and secondary school in the United States.

3. It was a long, hard winter. Felicia's being shut inside every day
_____.

4. It _____ that the president will be reelected if the economy continues to recover.

5. The young man stayed out until 3:00 A.M. For him not to listen to his parents _____.

6. All of the other men had been rehired by the company. John's still being unemployed _____.

7. It _____ for two wrongs to make a right.

8. Everyone knew that President Rabin had been shot. That he had been shot by one of his own people _____.

9. The fashion designer's clothes this season are very extreme. For vinyl to be mixed with fur _____.

10. I have stopped going to the theater on Saturday afternoons. Children's whispering and throwing popcorn in the air _____.

EXERCISE 4

What do you think about the following activities or ideas? Use adjective complements in your answer.

▶ **EXAMPLES:** (you) saving a little money every month

It's wise (for me) to save because I might need some extra money some day.

OR

My saving money has become essential to my future.

1. (elderly people) skydiving (= jumping from a plane with a parachute on)
2. (you) studying English grammar
3. (your relative) riding a motorcycle without a helmet
4. (cities) banning smoking in all public places
5. (your friend) copying someone else's paper
6. (the government) making alcohol illegal

Exercise 4
E X P A N S I O N
Do the same expansion as in Exercise 3. Ask Ss to provide follow-up sentences for the options beginning with *it*.

A N S W E R   K E Y

Exercise 4
Answers will vary.
1. It's surprising for elderly people to skydive.
2. My studying English grammar is helpful to my accuracy. 3. It's unwise for your relative to ride a motorcycle without a helmet. 4. For cities to ban smoking in all public places seems extreme. 5. My friend's copying someone else's paper is dishonest. 6. For the government to make alcohol illegal is controversial. 7. Teacher's creating schools for profit rather than for service seems selfish. 8. For a single person to join a singles club seems obvious, yet many people do not do it. 9. A poor person's winning the lottery is encouraging. 10. My forgetting my friend's name was very embarrassing.

Exercise 5

1. Ask Ss if they have ever heard of incidents of animals harming humans in their native countries.
2. Ask them to share these with the class.
3. Assign them to do this exercise in pairs.

Workbook Exs. 3–5, pp. 208–210.
Answers: TE p. 557.

---

7. (teachers) creating schools for profit rather than having public schools
8. (a single person) joining a singles club
9. (a poor person) winning the lottery
10. (you) forgetting someone's name

EXERCISE 5

Comment on the following facts found in the *Book of Lists 2* using a *that*-clause in subject position.

▶ **EXAMPLE:** Tigers do not usually hunt humans unless they are old or injured. However, a tigress, the Champawat man-eater, killed 438 people in the Himalayas in Nepal between 1903 and 1911.
That so many people were killed in Nepal by a tiger is tragic.

1. Black bears do not usually hurt humans unless they are hungry. When the Alaskan blueberry crop was poor in 1963, black bears attacked at least four people, one of whom they killed, because no other food was available.

2. In the central provinces of India, leopards have been known to enter huts and kill humans. One famous leopard, the Panawar man-eater, is reputed to have killed four hundred people.

3. On March 25, 1941, the British ship *Britannia* sank in the Atlantic Ocean. While the twelve survivors sat in a lifeboat, a giant squid reached its arm around the body of one of them and pulled him into the ocean.

4. In South America, people have reported losing fingers, toes, or pieces of flesh while bathing in piranha-infested waters.

5. In 1916, four people were killed as they were swimming along a sixty-mile stretch of the New Jersey coast. The attacker was a great white shark.

EXERCISE 6

Consider your responses during the Opening Task on page 361 and create dialogues with facts about animals, using a *that*-clause and the adjective provided.

▶ **EXAMPLE:** shocking   Q: What's so shocking?
A: ***It is shocking*** *that the oil from the grounded oil tanker killed thousands of innocent animals.*

1. irresponsible
2. encouraging
3. sad
4. important
5. outrageous
6. fortunate

ANSWER KEY

Exercise 5
Answers will vary.
1. That black bears were starving in 1963 was unfortunate. 2. That one leopard killed so many people is terrible. 3. That one survivor was drowned by a squid is paradoxical.
4. That people can lose a finger, toe, or piece of flesh while bathing is devastating. 5. That people were killed while swimming recreationally is tragic.

Exercise 6
Answers will vary.
1. It is irresponsible that highways have destroyed natural animal habitats. 2. It is encouraging that zoos have begun treating their animals more humanely. 3. It is sad that calves are killed to provide veal for diners.
4. It is important that more politicians become aware of the illegal ivory trade. 5. It is outrageous that bulls are killed for sport.
6. It is fortunate that more people are becoming courteous campers.

Infinitives, Gerund, and *That* Clauses

EXAMPLES	EXPLANATIONS
(a) Many zoos have instituted stricter laws regarding the care of their animals. **That zoos protect their animals is important.** (b) **Zoos' protecting their animals** is important.	Infinitive, gerund, and *that*-clauses have different meanings. *That*-clauses and gerunds refer to actual or fulfilled events. In examples (a) and (b) the adjective complements refer to the fact that zoos actually do already protect their animals.
(c) Many zoos have reported higher numbers of animals dying in captivity. **For zoos to protect their animals** is important.	Infinitives refer to future ideas or potential events. In example (c), zoos potentially can protect their animals (but they don't necessarily do so).

EXERCISE 7

What would be unexpected/odd/surprising/unusual/impossible/strange for the following people to do or to have done? Write a sentence that expresses your idea.

▶ **EXAMPLE:** Eskimos   *Eskimos' living in grass huts would be strange.*

1. dictators
2. busybodies
3. bus drivers
4. procrastinators
5. Napoleon
6. Mahatma Gandhi
7. the ancient Greeks
8. your mother
9. your friend's father
10. our class

---

1. Ask Ss to name a few activities that they do in your class on a regular basis. Write these on the board (e.g., *Workbook exercises, pairwork exercises, warm-up activities, composition assignments,* etc.).
2. Next to these words, ask Ss to give you an adjective that describes how it feels to do these activities (e.g., *helpful, fun, useful, hard,* etc.).
3. Give Ss a sample sentence combining these adjectives with an adjective complement. For example, *That we did workbook exercises every night was helpful. Our doing pairwork exercises is fun.*
4. Ask Ss whether or not this structure indicates that the activity took or takes place or has not been completed.
5. Contrast this with another example: *For us to eat ice-cream in every class would be unwise.* Ask Ss whether or not this action has taken place. Point to the *for/to* infinitive and explain that this relates to future or potential events.
6. Ask Ss to read *a, b,* and *c* examples and explanations aloud.

Exercise 7

V A R I A T I O N

Ask Ss to produce original sentences about themselves. For example, *For me to dye my hair would be strange. My making a long distance call during the day would be unusual.*

Workbook Exs. 6 & 7, pp. 211–213.
Answers: TE p. 558.

A N S W E R   K E Y

Exercise 7
Answers will vary.
1. Dictators' allowing people to vote would be surprising. 2. Busybodies' minding their own business would be impossible. 3. Bus drivers' allowing people to smoke on the bus would be impossible. 4. Procrastinators' doing things on time would be odd.
5. Napoleon's having been a benevolent dictator would have been surprising.

6. Mahatma Gandhi's having resorted to violence would have been unexpected.
7. The ancient Greeks' believing in an anthropomorphic god would have been surprising. 8. Your mother's not teaching you good manners would have been odd.
9. Your friend's father remarrying would be impossible. 10. Our class's being dismissed early would be unexpected.

EXERCISE 8

Circle the best option and explain your decision.

▶ **EXAMPLE:** 1. (a) It is heartening that the Beauty Cosmetics Company of London has refused to test its products on animals since its establishment.

(b) It would be heartening for the Beauty Cosmetics Company of London to refuse to test its products on animals.

*(The Beauty Cosmetics Company has actually refused already, so answer **a** with the **that**-clause is correct.)*

1. (a) It is shocking that commercial whalers have almost exterminated the blue whale.

(b) It would be shocking for commercial whalers to almost exterminate the blue whale.

2. (a) It is sad that dolphins catch diseases from humans at dolphin recreational swim centers.

(b) It would be sad for dolphins to catch diseases from humans at dolphin recreational swim centers.

3. (a) After an oil spill, it will be important that animals are rescued.

(b) After an oil spill, it will be important for animals to be rescued.

4. (a) Companies' cutting down the Amazonian rain forests will lead to ecological disaster.

(b) For companies to cut down the Amazonian rain forests would lead to ecological disaster.

5. (a) For the child to whine seemed annoying to all of the crew.

(b) The child's whining seemed annoying to all of the crew.

UNIT GOAL REVIEW

Ask Ss to look at the goals on the opening page of the unit again. Help them understand how much they have accomplished in each area.

ANSWER KEY

Exercise 8

1. **(a)** This is a true fact that whalers have almost exterminated the blue whale. 2. **(a)** It is true that dolphins catch diseases from humans at these centers. 3. **(b)** Focus is on a future event with *After an oil spill.* 4. **(a)** This is a fact that companies are cutting down the Amazonian rain forests. 5. **(b)** The whining occurred in the past, so this is a statement of fact.

Use Your English

ACTIVITY 1: LISTENING

Listen to the following taped excerpts and circle the appropriate comment that would follow from what you have heard.

▶ **EXAMPLE:** Tonya: *Did you hear the good news?*
Francisco: *No, what?*
Tonya: *Rosa's parents just bought her a car for her birthday.*
(a) That Rosa got a new car for her birthday is amazing.
(b) For Rosa to get a new car will be amazing.

1. (a) It's annoying that such a smart aleck like Tom should have such luck!
   (b) For Harvard to give such an expensive scholarship is annoying.
2. (a) It is essential for human beings to revere animals for their intelligence and strength.
   (b) It is true that many human beings have killed animals in order to obtain food and clothing.
3. (a) That citizens care so much about the needy in Los Angeles is encouraging.
   (b) Citizens' neglecting the needy in Los Angeles will lead to serious consequences.
4. (a) Scientists' working in the Gobi Desert is extraordinary.
   (b) That we now know something about dinosaur parental care is astonishing.
5. (a) It's great that she got a new computer.
   (b) It's great for her to get a new computer.

ACTIVITY 2: RESEARCH/WRITING

Research several animals that are in danger of becoming extinct. Find out how they are dying or being killed. Then, write a short paragraph, giving your feelings and opinions about **one** of these animals. Several suggestions are given below.

California condor	orangutan of Borneo
Arabian oryx	blue whale
spotted owl	giant Panda

Adjective Complements in Subject and Predicate Position | **369**

USE YOUR ENGLISH

The activities on these "purple pages" at the end of the unit contain situations that should naturally elicit the unit's structures in a more communicative framework. While Ss are doing these activities in class, you can circulate and listen to determine if they have actually achieved the goals on the opening page of the unit.

Activity 1

Play textbook audio. The listening for this activity appears on p. 573 of this book. Play the tape several times if necessary.

Activity 2

Encourage Ss to use at least two adjective complements in their paragraphs.

ANSWER KEY

Activity 1
1. a 2. b 3. b 4. b 5. a

Activity 3

1. Write the following words on the board: beads, pistol grips, and dice.
2. Ask Ss to brainstorm in pairs what these words have in common. They should determine that all these objects are made of ivory.
3. Ask one student to read the paragraph that follows the question and the answer. *Hunters cut . . .*
4. Ask the pairs to write the letter of complaint.
5. Ask one member of each pair to read the letter of complaint aloud to the class.

Activity 4

1. Make a library assignment for Ss to research one of the diseases. Assign 3 or 4 students per topic.
2. Ask Ss to bring their notes on one of these diseases to the next class period.
3. Have Ss give short oral reports to one another on their results. Encourage them to use at least one adjective complement.

ACTIVITY 3: WRITING

What do rosary beads, pistol grips, and dice have in common? They are all made of ivory, sometimes illegally obtained. Hunters cut the tusks from elephants with chainsaws, sometimes while the animals are still alive. Then they sell the tusks to businesspeople who smuggle them out of the country in gas tankers, cargo trucks, or personal luggage. Often political officials collaborate in the crime by issuing false import permits. Great profits are made all around at the elephant's expense.

Imagine that you have bought an ivory figure for $1000 and later learned that the ivory had been illegally obtained. Write a letter of complaint to the company from which you bought the figure. Use statements such as, "I have just learned that the figure I bought from you was made of illegally obtained ivory. Your selling me such an item is outrageous."

ACTIVITY 4: RESEARCH/SPEAKING

Find out how animals have been used in research of one of the following diseases: polio, diphtheria, mumps, hepatitis, diabetes, arthritis, high blood pressure, AIDS, or cancer. As a result of your research, express your opinions in a short oral report on the use of animals in furthering medical progress. Do you feel that it is important or unnecessary?

▶ **EXAMPLE:** *It is important for researchers to use animals in their research . . .*

ACTIVITY 5: SPEAKING/WRITING

Michael W. Fox in his book *Inhuman Society: The American Way of Exploiting Animals* (New York: St. Martin's Press, 1990, p. 46) has expressed his opinion on modern zoos in the following way:

Today's zoos and wildlife safari parks are radically different from the early iron and concrete zoos. It takes money to run a modern zoo, and zoo directors realize that they must compete with a wide variety of leisure-time activities. Concession stands, miniature railroads, and other carnival amusements, as well as dubious circuslike shows with performing chimps or big cats, lure many visitors to some of our large zoos and wildlife parks. What tricks and obedience the animals display are more a reflection of the power of human control than of the animals' natural behavior. Performing apes, elephants, bears, big cats, dolphins, and "killer" whales especially draw the crowds. Man's mastery over the powerful beast and willful control over its wild instincts is a parody of the repression and sublimation of human nature and personal freedom.

STEP 1 In pairs, discuss the preceding paragraph.

- How do modern zoos differ from zoos in the past?
- Do spectators at modern zoos actually have a chance to see an animal's true nature?
- What does the last sentence mean?

STEP 2 Individually, write a short paragraph explaining whether or not you agree with Fox. What statements do you feel are true? What statements do you feel are questionable? (Use at least three adjective complements in your writing.)

Activity 5
VARIATION

This activity, like the others, focuses on the unit topic of animals. For more variety, ask Ss to bring in or write a paragraph about another controversial topic and follow the same steps: discuss the article and write a reaction to it.

The test for this unit can be found on p. 523. The answers are on p. 524.

Unit 21

UNIT OVERVIEW

Unit 21 contains information about noun complements that can be quite challenging for advanced students (Ss), even though they may have had exposure to complement structures at earlier levels (e.g., *The fact that John was late bothered me*). This unit provides an overview of noun complements, distinguishes the *that* clause from a restrictive relative clause, and introduces the function of the *that* clause noun complement in discourse.

UNIT GOALS

Review the goals listed on this page so Ss understand what they should be able to know by the end of the unit.

OPENING TASK

The purpose of this task is for Ss to explain eight types of natural phenomena.

SETTING UP THE TASK

1. Ask if there are any Ss who are especially knowledgeable about science. Divide the class into small groups, assigning these "science experts" to be the group leaders.
2. Point to the map and ask Ss if they can explain the answer to the question about coastlines. Have Ss cover up the answer, which is given below the map.

UNIT 21

NOUN COMPLEMENTS TAKING *THAT* CLAUSES

UNIT GOALS:

- To use noun complements to explain abstract nouns
- To distinguish *that* clause noun complements from restrictive relative clauses
- To use *that*-clause noun complements in subject position to signal known or implied information
- To use *the fact* + *that* noun complements appropriately
- To use *that* clause noun complements after transitive adjectives and phrasal verbs

OPENING TASK
Explaining Natural Phenomena

How good are you at explaining natural phenomena? Would you be able to explain why the North American and South American eastern coastlines and the Eurasian and African western coastlines appear to be mirror images of each other?

One account for this phenomenon is the theory that all of these continents once formed a single continent and subsequently moved apart.

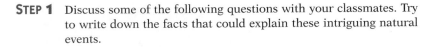

STEP 1 Discuss some of the following questions with your classmates. Try to write down the facts that could explain these intriguing natural events.

1. What explains the observation that in some parts of the world leaves change color and fall from the trees each year?

2. What explains the observation that shooting stars speed across the sky?

3. What explains the fact that there are oases in desert environments?

4. What accounts for the fact that some rainbows are partial and some are full?

5. What could illustrate the idea that physical activity is difficult at high altitudes?

6. What could illustrate the law that heat flows from a warm place to a cooler place?

7. What fact could explain why the sun and moon appear larger near the horizon?

8. What fact could account for a person's reflection appearing upside down in a spoon?

STEP 2 Now add a few questions of your own about other intriguing natural events that you are curious about. Once you have written your questions, see if your classmates know the facts that explain them.

CONDUCTING THE TASK

Step 1: Encourage Ss to guess the explanations even if they do not understand exactly why these phenomena occur. If noun complements do not occur in spoken discourse, you may want to request that Ss use the following words in their explanations: *observation, fact, idea,* or *law*. Possible answers appear in the Exercise 3 answer key. These could be compared against the Ss' explanations.

Step 2: Encourage the small groups to think of other intriguing natural events that other groups in the class might find difficult to explain. Have each group share one more natural event and have the other groups guess the explanation by writing down their responses with a felt tip pen on an overhead transparency. Compare the explanations and give a prize to the group that comes the closest to the real explanation.

CLOSING THE TASK

Discuss which natural events the class is still unsure about, which theories seem the most plausible, and where the students might go to obtain the information. You could also encourage creative possibilities (or myth-making) to account for some of the unknown phenomena.

1. Ask Ss to take turns reading examples and explanations in pairs.
2. To help reinforce the abstract nouns, ask Ss to interact using a short 3-line dialogue:
   Student A: *I heard <u>the request</u>.* (fill in one of the words from the list)
   Student B: *What <u>request</u>?* (repeating the word that Student A has said)
   Student A: *The <u>request that we turn off the lights before leaving the room/to turn off the lights before leaving the room</u>* (fill in a *that* + clause or an infinitive)

FOCUS **1**

Overview of Noun Complements

EXAMPLES	EXPLANATIONS
(a) The theory **that water expands when it is frozen** is testable. **(b)** The requirement **for workers to wear safety glasses** is important.	Noun complements are of two types: *that*-clauses and infinitives. • The *that* clause is a way of explaining the noun. • The *for-to* infinitive also explains the noun. • Both types of complements follow abstract nouns. Many abstract nouns have verb counterparts (*requirement/require, advice/advise, reminder/remind,* etc.).
Abstract Nouns (+ *That* Clause): *answer news request* *appeal notion statement* *axiom possibility suggestion* *fact proposal theory* *hypothesis reminder thesis* *idea reply*	With some abstract nouns, we use a *that*-clause to form noun complements.
Abstract Nouns (+ Infinitives): *advice permission request* *appeal plan requirement* *command preparation suggestion* *instruction proposal tendency* *motivation recommendation* *order reminder*	Another group of abstract nouns takes infinitives.
(c) Most people understand the recommendation **that citizens should pay higher taxes.** **(d)** Most people understand the recommendation **for citizens to pay higher taxes.**	Some nouns, such as *request, recommendation, and suggest* may take either a *that*-clause or an infinitive as a complement.
(e) The fact **that students must pay higher tuition** disappoints us. **(f)** We read about the need **for more volunteers to help the poor.**	Noun complements may appear with nouns in subject or object position.

374 | UNIT 21

---

374 Grammar Dimensions, Platinum Edition

EXERCISE 1

Underline each noun complement. Circle the abstract noun that precedes it.

▶ **EXAMPLE:** Early scientists believe (the notion) that matter could be divided into four basic elements: earth, water, air, and fire.

1. The tendency for liquids to turn into gases is well-known.

2. Moisture in the air provides the catalyst for industrial fumes to react
and form acid rain.

3. Galileo proposed the hypothesis that all falling bodies drop at the
same constant speed.

4. The possibility for a sailor to get lost at sea is low if he or she has a
compass.

5. The idea that people can survive without light is nonsense.

6. The fact that overhead cables sag on a hot day proves that solids expand when heated.

EXERCISE 2

Summarize the information from the text by completing the statements that
follow.

SOLAR RAYS AND OUR SKIN

The increase of hydrofluorocarbons in the atmosphere is dangerously depleting the earth's ozone layer. The effect of this is that people are having greater
exposure to ultraviolet light rays. Can these solar rays increase the chances of
skin cancer? Yes, in fact, they increase the cases of malignant melanoma—the
deadliest type.

According to The American Cancer Society, hundreds of thousands of new
cases of skin cancer will be diagnosed in the United States each year. About
five percent of these will be malignant melanoma. To prevent more cases,
many doctors say that people should stay out of the sun altogether. This is especially true for redheads and blondes with freckled skin. At the very least, a
person should cover up and wear a sunscreen with a high sun-protection factor (15, 25, or 30) during the periods of the day when ultraviolet rays are
strongest.

A good example of an anti-skin-cancer campaign comes from Australia.
Life-guards in the state of Victoria wear T-shirts with the slogan "SLIP! SLOP!
SLAP!" which means slip on a shirt, slop on some sunscreen, and slap on a
hat. Although these hints may not please all sunbathers on beaches around the
world, they might very well save their lives.

Exercise 1

Divide the class into pairs and ask one
student to orally read the items while the
other underlines and circles the appropriate
words.

Exercise 2

This exercise is cognitively challenging. Ss
must keep information from the text clearly in
memory as they place it after an abstract
noun and make a comment about it.

V A R I A T I O N

For a greater challenge, assign Ss to do a
similar task with a text of their own choosing
for homework. Remind them to use the two
types of noun complement structures when
they comment on the text.

A N S W E R   K E Y

Exercise 1
The abstract nouns that the Ss should circle are
italicized.
1. *the tendency*; for liquids to turn into gases
2. *the catalyst*; for industrial fumes to react
and form acid rain   3. *the hypothesis*; that all
falling bodies drop at the same constant speed
4. *the possibility*; for a sailor to get lost at sea
5. *the idea*; that people can survive without
light   6. *The fact*; that overhead cables sag on
a hot day

Exercise 2
1. people are having greater exposure to
ultraviolet rays   2. Fair-headed people have
less natural protection against the sun's rays
3. thousands of people have malignant
melanoma   4. people to stay out of the sun
altogether   5. people to slip on a shirt, slop
on some sunscreen, and slap on a hat

► **EXAMPLE:** The news that <u>hydrofluorocarbons are depleting the earth's ozone layer</u> is alarming.

1. The fact that _____ indicates why there has been an increase in cases of malignant melanoma.

2. The fact that _____ explains why blondes and redheads burn easily.

3. The fact that _____ is evidence that ultraviolet rays can cause skin cancer.

4. The doctors' recommendation for _____ is not very popular.

5. The amusing reminder for _____ has changed the sunbathing habits of people in Australia.

EXERCISE 3

Reread the questions in the Opening Task on page 373 and answer them, using a *that* clause in object position.

► **EXAMPLE:** What explains the observation that "shooting stars" speed across the sky?
The observation that "shooting stars" speed across the sky can be explained by meteorites' burning up as they hit the earth's atmosphere.

Exercise 3

Ss can complete this exercise individually or in pairs.

Workbook Exs. 1 & 2, pp. 214–215.
Answers: TE p. 558.

Exercise 3

1. Leaf pigments (which assist some plants during photosynthesis) becoming visible when the leaf dies in the fall explains the observation that the leaves of some trees change color and fall to the ground during cold weather.
2. Bits of interplanetary matter (meteorites) entering the earth's atmosphere and burning up explains the observation that stars shoot across the sky.   3. A groundwater table near the roots of palms and other plants explains the fact that there are oases.   4. Rainfall not filling the air over a large enough area accounts for the fact that there is only a partial rainbow.   5. Troubled breathing during mild exercise in the mountains illustrates the idea that activity is difficult at high altitudes.   6. An ice cube melting in a glass of water illustrates the law that heat flows from a warm place to a cooler place.   7. The sun and the moon appearing larger than normal is explained by the fact that the eye evaluates the size of the sun and the moon against the size of objects on the earth near the horizon, e.g., trees, hills, buildings, etc.   8. A person's reflection appearing upside down is explained by the fact that the concave parts of a spoon act as a lens. If the spoon were flat, it would reflect like a mirror.

FOCUS **2**

That Clause Noun Complements versus Restrictive Relative Clauses

EXAMPLES	EXPLANATIONS
(a) The story **that she opened a restaurant** is untrue. (b) The requirement **that students do their homework** is necessary.	A *that*-clause noun complement defines an idea. In (a), *opening a restaurant* is "the story." The sentence still makes sense even if *the story* is deleted. In this sentence, *which* cannot replace *that*. Likewise in (b), the main idea of the sentence is kept even if *the requirement* is omitted.
(c) The story **that/which she told** was untrue. (d) The requirement **that/which students must follow** is outdated.	A restrictive relative clause limits an idea. *The story* in (c) relates to a particular story, the one that she told. The sentence will not make sense if *the story* is deleted. In this sentence, *which* can replace *that*. The same is true in (d), where the sentence will not make sense if *the requirement* is deleted.

EXERCISE 4

Which sentence in each of the following pairs contains a noun complement? Circle your choice.

▸ **EXAMPLE:** (a) The idea that they didn't question the witnesses was shocking.
(b) The idea that he had was exciting.

1. (a) Many people dispute the fact that human beings evolved from apes.
   (b) Many people accept the fact that he just mentioned.
2. (a) The suggestion that she included in the letter will never be followed.
   (b) The suggestion that a person should warm up before jogging is important.
3. (a) The reply that she did not need help came as a surprise.
   (b) The reply that contained important information was received too late.
4. (a) I believe the theory that opposites attract.
   (b) I believe the theory that my uncle proposed.
5. (a) The news that was relayed on Thursday was disappointing.
   (b) The news that the war had started depressed everyone.

If possible, make an overhead transparency of this focus box and use the "uncover technique" to explain the difference between a *that* clause noun complement and a restrictive relative clause. (Present one set of the grid, a–b, then c–d, at a time.)

Exercise 4

Remind Ss to try removing the abstract noun to see if the sentence makes sense. If it still does, they have chosen the noun complement.

Workbook Ex. 3, p. 216.
Answers: TE p. 558.

ANSWER KEY

Exercise 4
Answers will vary.
1. a 2. b 3. a 4. a 5. b

FOCUS 3

In other units, Ss have been introduced to the concept of new and old information management within texts. Note that this is another example of new information (the comment) being saved for last and old information placed in subject position. Ask Ss to watch for this as they read for other classes or for pleasure. Assign them to find at least one example to share with the class by the end of the unit.

Exercise 5

E X P A N S I O N

1. Ask Ss to form pairs and think of one fact that may be new or surprising to their partners. For example, *I have a pet snake that I keep in my room.*
2. Then, have partners comment on the fact that they have heard using a noun complement structure. For example, *The fact that you have a pet snake in your room is very surprising.*

Workbook Ex. 4, pp. 216–217.
Answers: TE p. 558.

That Clause Noun Complements in Subject Position

EXAMPLES	EXPLANATIONS
(a) Harry had to write many papers in college. He never learned how to type. **The idea that Harry graduated from college without knowing how to type** astonishes me.	*That* clause noun complements in subject position contain known or implied information. The predicates comment upon the facts or ideas contained in *that* clauses following *the fact/idea/news,* etc.).
(b) When Teresa was diagnosed with cancer, everyone thought that she would not survive. Then, after several months of chemotherapy, the doctor said he could see no trace of the disease. **The fact that she was cured** is a miracle.	

EXERCISE 5

The following paragraphs describe amazing facts about famous people. Make observations about each set of facts using a *that*-clause following the *fact/idea/news,* etc.

▶ **EXAMPLE:** When Beethoven was twenty-eight years old, he became deaf. In spite of this, he was still able to compose music.

The fact that Beethoven composed music while he was deaf is amazing.

---

1. Marie Antoinette and Louis XVI ate very well, while their Parisian subjects could not afford bread. When hearing of this, the unsympathetic queen is reported to have said, "Why, then, let them eat cake."

2. United States President Richard Nixon resigned from office in 1974 after a very serious governmental scandal. His Republican associates who were interested in having him reelected had installed wiretaps at the headquarters of the Democratic National Committee at the Watergate Hotel. Rather than being honest, Nixon tried to cover up the scandal and this led to his downfall.

3. In 1919, Rudolph Valentino, a famous American movie star, married Jean Acker. In his silent films, he played the part of the great lover. But, on the wedding day, Acker ran away and Valentino never consummated his marriage with her.

4. For years, athletes did the high jump by jumping sideways or straddling over the bar. Then, Dick Fosbury discovered that he could break world records by going over head first, flat on his back. The technique is now called the Fosbury Flop.

5. The Japanese had long revered their emperor as divine. However, Emperor Hirohito destroyed this image by announcing to his people in 1946 that it was a false conception that he was descended from God. In fact, even at the early age of fourteen, Hirohito had doubted his own divinity.

ANSWER KEY

Exercise 5
Answers will vary.
1. The fact that Marie Antoinette was very unsympathetic toward her subjects was despicable. 2. The news that Nixon was aware of the wiretaps at the Democratic National Committee headquarters but tried to cover up this knowledge was the beginning of the end of his presidential career. 3. The idea that Rudolph Valentino's marriage with Jean Acker was never consummated contradicts the idea that he was a great lover. 4. The proposal that athletes could break world records by going over the high-jump bar head first came as a big surprise. 5. The theory that Japanese emperors are descended from God was doubted by Emperor Hirohito at the early age of fourteen.

If possible, make an overhead transparency of this focus box and use the "uncover technique" on the overhead projector as you review these rules with Ss. (Present one set of sentences on the grid at a time.)

This information will be especially helpful to Ss who are doing expository writing. Remind Ss to edit their compositions in other classes for these wordy structures.

Workbook Ex. 5, pp. 217–218.
Answers: TE p. 558.

▶ *The Fact That . . .*

EXAMPLES	EXPLANATIONS
(a) **Less formal:** The fact that she refused the money showed her sense of pride. (b) **Formal:** That she refused the money showed her sense of pride. (c) **Less formal:** People generally acknowledge the fact that Japan must find alternate ways to use its space. (d) **Formal:** People generally acknowledge that Japan must find alternate ways to use its space.	*The fact + that* clause noun complements in (a) and (c) are similar in meaning to the *that* clauses in (b) and (d); however, we generally consider them less formal.
(e) **Wordy:** He believed the fact that his daughter had been kidnapped, and he understood the fact that he would need to pay a ransom. (f) **Concise:** He believed that his daughter had been kidnapped, and he understood that he would need to pay a ransom.	In writing, overuse of *that* clauses in object position with *the fact* can lead to wordiness. In most cases, it is better to use the simple *that* clause.
(g) The detectives concealed **the fact that** they had searched the room. (h) The soldiers accepted **the fact that** they had been defeated. (i) The police officers disregarded **the fact that** they needed a search warrant. (j) NOT: The police officers disregarded that they needed a search warrant.	Certain verbs (such as *accept, conceal, discuss, dispute, disregard, hide, overlook, support*) require the use of *the fact that* clauses in object position, however.

EXERCISE 6

The following passage contains too many *the fact that* clauses. Underline instances of *the fact* in the text. Then, cross out those that do not seem necessary or are incorrect.

(1) Citizens may believe ~~the fact~~ that they are safe from hazardous wastes, but they are misled. (2) Hundreds of chemical companies say the fact that they are disposing of toxic wastes, yet they conceal the fact that they are illegally dumping them or improperly disposing of them. (3) The tragic result is the fact that dangerous wastes are seeping into the water supply. (4) Although many man-

ufacturers do not want to accept the fact that they need to find alternate means of disposal, environmental agencies are forcing them to do so. (5) Unfortunately, it has been too late in some cases. (6) The fact that residents who live near toxic wastes sites often have greater chronic respiratory and neurological problems than people who do not supports the fact that toxic waste is a major health issue. (7) Chemical companies can no longer overlook the fact that something must be done. (8) Experts claim the fact that landfills having double liners is one solution. (9) Companies also need to accept the fact that recycling and substituting hazardous chemicals for safer ones in their products will greatly improve the situation for their communities.

FOCUS **5**

That-Clause Noun Complements Following Transitive Adjectives and Phrasal Verbs

EXAMPLES	EXPLANATION
(a) He is tired of **the fact that she refuses to see him.** (b) NOT: He is tired of that she refuses to see him. (c) He played down **the news that his team won.** (d) NOT: He played down that his team won.	When *that*-clause noun complements follow transitive adjectives (adjective taking a preposition + a noun phrase) or phrasal verbs, they must be *the fact/news/idea/theory*, etc. *that*-clauses rather than simple *that*-clauses.

Examples of Transitive Adjectives	Examples of Phrasal Verbs
disappointed in *worried about* *proud of* *sick of* *tired of*	*play down* *long for* *give in* *face up to* *put up with*

Have various Ss read the rules in the focus box aloud. Note that the preposition in the transitive adjective and the phrasal verb dictates the need for a *that* clause noun complement.

SUGGESTION

If necessary, provide more examples with the phrases in the box. For example, *The teacher was worried about the fact that no one had done the homework.*

Exercise 7

1. Assign items ahead of time to pairs or small groups.
2. Because the items in this exercise form a chronological story, have Ss write sentences that could logically follow from each other. Encourage them to be creative. For example: *His mother worried about the fact that he had lost his bubble gum fortune. His negligence accounted for the fact that 10,000 sticks of bubble gum ended up on the factory floor . . .*
3. Ask one member of each pair or group to read the mini-story to the class.

Exercise 8

EXPANSION

Ask each student to write another strange action on a slip of paper. Put these into a hat and ask each student to withdraw one slip (not his or her own), read it, and tell what he/she would do to clear up the confusion. This can be done as a whole class exercise or in pairs.

Exercise 9

This exercise could also be used as a diagnostic or testing exercise.

EXERCISE 7

Imagine that a very wealthy entrepreneur has just lost his fortune. Comment upon the circumstances of his condition using the words below and the fact/idea/news, etc. that clauses.

▶ **EXAMPLES:** businessman (face up to)

The businessman had to face up to the fact that he had lost his millions.

1. his mother (worried about)
2. negligence (account for)
3. his creditors (wary of)
4. his employees (indignant at)
5. his wife (put up with)
6. the lawyers (proud of)

EXERCISE 8

Suppose you saw people doing the following strange actions. What facts would you bring up in order to help clear up their confusion? Write a sentence about what you would say.

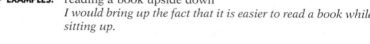

▶ **EXAMPLES:** reading a book upside down
I would bring up the fact that it is easier to read a book while sitting up.

1. washing the dishes with laundry detergent
2. making lasagna without cheese
3. playing soccer with a baseball
4. taking pictures without film in the camera
5. watching a TV with no sound
6. spelling the word *fish* with *ph* before *i* instead of *f*.

EXERCISE 9

The following sentences review the structures learned in this unit. Correct those that contain errors or are too wordy according to formal writing rules. Write **OK** next to those that are correct.

▶ **EXAMPLES:** The teacher overlooked the fact that Hung had not done his homework. *OK*

The fact that she made a confession ~~untrue~~. (*was* ^)

1. Tom believes the fact that light travels faster than sound.
2. The request for her to stop smoking was ignored.
3. The fact that the automobile increased the distance a person could travel made it possible for a person to live and work in different places.
4. She is tired of that she always has to wash the dishes.
5. We are concerned about that there will be no more food.
6. I am grateful for the fact that the doctor assisted me in my decision.
7. Did the glasses help to conceal the fact that he had a scar on his left eyelid?
8. The fact that Mary finished her homework.
9. The fact that twenty million Russians died during World War II is tragic.
10. The request that we ignore the crime was considered unacceptable.

A N S W E R   K E Y

Exercise 7
Answers will vary.
1. His mother was worried about the fact that her son had not eaten for days. 2. His negligence of his business accounted for the fact that his business failed. 3. His creditors were wary of the fact that the man did not repay his debts. 4. His employees were indignant at the news that they would have to find new jobs immediately. 5. His wife could no longer put up with the fact that she rarely saw her husband anymore. 6. The lawyers were proud of the fact that they could recover much of the man's fortune.

Exercise 8
Answers will vary.
I would remind them of/bring up/mention the fact that:
1. the dishes should be washed with dishwashing detergent 2. lasagna requires cheese. 3. to play soccer, a person needs a soccer ball 4. they need to insert film into the camera 5. they need to turn up the sound 6. the f sound is spelled with an f and not *ph*

Exercise 9
1. Tom believes that light travels . . .
2. The request that she stop . . . 3. OK
4. She is tired of the fact that she always . . .
5. We are concerned that there . . .
6. I am grateful that the doctor . . .
7. OK 8. The fact that Mary finished her homework impressed us. 9. That twenty million Russians died . . . 10. OK
11. Do you agree with the statement that blondes . . . 12. OK

11. Do you agree the statement that blondes have more fun?

12. That Jerome passed the bar examination made it possible for him to practice law.

EXERCISE 10

What will the world be like in the third millennium? In a book called *Megatrends* 2000 (New York: Morrow, 1990) John Naisbett and Patricia Aburdene describe what they believe will transform the world, or, in some cases, American culture. Here are some of their predictions:

1. The English language will become the world's first truly universal language.

2. Nations, especially the "superpower" countries, will regard war as an obsolete way of solving problems.

3. Even as peoples of the world communicate more closely, individual cultures will increasingly find their unique qualities important and seek to preserve racial, linguistic, national, and religious traditions.

4. The arts will replace sports as American society's dominant leisure activity; Americans will consider alternatives to attending sports events such as football and baseball.

5. The trend of the future in the global economy is "downsizing": producing and using smaller, lighter, and more sophisticated products (for example, smaller computers, lighter building materials, electronic impulses used for financial transactions instead of paper).

6. In the first decade of the third millennium, we will think it quaint that women in the late twentieth century were excluded from the top levels of business and politics.

7. The world's nations will increasingly cooperate to address global environmental problems.

Which of these hypotheses do you consider almost a certainty by the end of the twenty-first century? Which do you think probable? Which do you find unlikely developments? Fill in the following blanks with your opinions.

▶ **EXAMPLES:** I agree with the idea that _the arts will become popular, but I do not believe that Americans will lose their love of football._

The prediction that _English will be the world's universal language is already true_ .

1. I am skeptical of the notion that _____.

2. The tendency for _____.

3. I believe the statement that _____.

4. The suggestion that _____.

5. I doubt the possibility that _____.

Noun Complements Taking *That* Clauses | **383**

Exercise 10

1. Divide the class into small groups of no more than 5 and ask Ss to discuss the ideas, make connections to other things they have read or heard, and express their opinions about any of the ideas.
2. Have each member of the group fill in one of the blanks, summarizing his or her opinion.
3. Ask the group members to share their completed sentences with each other while you circulate around the room.

Workbook Exs. 6–8, pp. 218–222.
Answers: TE p. 558.

UNIT GOAL REVIEW

Ask Ss to look at the goals on the opening page of the unit again. Help them understand how much they have accomplished in each area.

USE YOUR ENGLISH

The activities on these "purple pages" at the end of the unit contain situations that should naturally elicit the unit's structures in a more communicative framework. While Ss are doing these activities in class, you can circulate and listen to determine if they have actually achieved the goals on the opening page of the unit.

Activity 1

Play textbook audio. The tapescript for this listening appears on pp. 573–574 of this book.

1. Ask Ss if they are familiar with the requirements for entering a university in the United States. Have Ss share personal experiences of themselves or others. Identify 2 or 3 criteria that are important—such as grade point average, test scores, and excellent performance in other activities.
2. Play the tape one or two times, according to Ss' level of comprehension.

3. Ask Ss to create at least 3 sentences beginning with *The fact that . . .* describing what they have learned. Have one member of the pair report the sentences to the class in a whole class feedback session.

Activity 2

V A R I A T I O N

Ask Ss to write down a social, civic, or environmental problem on a slip of paper. Put the papers in a hat and have Ss choose one (not the one that they submitted). Have each student state one reason for the problem they have picked.

Activity 3

1. Ask Ss to research the topics on the Internet or in the library and to take notes on the facts that explain the phenomena.
2. Assign Ss to write a short report. Grade the report for the accurate use of noun complements.

Use Your English

ACTIVITY 1: LISTENING/SPEAKING

STEP 1 Listen to the interview between a university admissions officer and several interested high school seniors. Take note of any interesting facts you hear.

STEP 2 Describe the interesting facts you learned to a classmate. Use as many noun complements as you can.

▶ **EXAMPLE:** *The fact that the admissions officer mainly looks at GPA and college entrance examination scores surprises me.*

ACTIVITY 2: SPEAKING

Discuss the specific reasons behind some of the following environmental problems: pollution of cities, extinction of animals, toxic waste, etc.

▶ **EXAMPLE:** *The fact that people have continued to drive gasoline engines has created the pollution problem in cities.*

ACTIVITY 3: READING/WRITING

In the Opening Task on page 373, you discussed certain natural facts. Investigate one or more issues mentioned there (meteorites, rainbows, oases, lightning, eclipses, etc.) or one of your own and write a short report explaining what facts give them the unusual properties that they have. Use at least three noun complements in your report.

▶ **EXAMPLE:** *Some people say that lightning never strikes the same place twice. However, the fact that we cannot scientifically predict when or where lightning will strike makes it difficult to refute this idea . . .*

ACTIVITY 4: LISTENING/SPEAKING

Watch a mystery or detective program on TV or at the movies with your class-mates. Discuss why the central characters were not able to solve the mystery or crime sooner than they did. What facts were concealed, disregarded, or over-looked? What facts finally led to the solution of the mystery?

▶ **EXAMPLE:** *The mother concealed the fact that Tony had a twin brother. The fact that Tony had a twin brother made the police finally realize that it was Tony's twin, Jimmy, who was guilty.*

ACTIVITY 5: READING/WRITING

Read several editorials or opinion essays. Then write your own view of the ideas in the essays by using noun complements.

▶ **EXAMPLE:** *The idea that people should not be allowed to own weapons makes sense.*

Activity 4

You may ask Ss to all watch the same program on TV (e.g., *The X Files, Unexplained Mysteries, L.A. Law, Perry Mason*), and report back the next day about what facts led to the solution of the mystery. If Ss are allowed to watch a program of their own choice, you might require that they write a short synopsis of the story and then reveal the facts that led to the solution of the mystery.

Activity 5

1. Ask Ss to read an editorial or opinion essay from the newspaper or the Internet.
2. Ask Ss to write their view of the ideas using at least one noun complement.

3. Ask Ss to bring in the editorial to share with another classmate. Have them share with a partner the main points of the essay and the sentences they have created to express their opinion.

The test for this unit can be found on p.525. The answers are on p. 526.

TOEFL Test Preparation Exercises for Units 19–21 can be found on pp. 223–225 of the workbook.
The answers are on p. 559 of this book.

Unit 22

UNIT OVERVIEW

Unit 22 adds the subjunctive complement to those already presented in the previous unit. The subjunctive complement is similar to the other forms, except the verb in the embedded clause is tenseless. These complements occur after verbs of advice or urging or nouns derived from these verbs and when advice adjectives are in the main clause. You might tell students (Ss) that the subjunctive is a formal structure that native speakers sometimes neglect to use in informal speaking and writing.

UNIT GOALS

Review the goals listed on this page so students understand what they should be able to know by the end of the unit.

OPENING TASK

The purpose of this task is to have Ss settle controversial problems using an arbitrator or third-party judge.

SETTING UP THE TASK

As an introduction, you can share experiences in which you have used an arbitrator (e.g., neighborhood dispute, divorce proceedings) or your Ss can share any of their experiences.

UNIT 22

SUBJUNCTIVE VERBS IN *THAT* CLAUSES

UNIT GOALS:

- To use subjunctive verbs in *that* clause complements with verbs of advice and urging
- To use subjunctive verbs in noun complements that refer to nouns of advice or urging
- To use subjunctive verbs in adjective complements

OPENING TASK
Solving Problems

It is not uncommon for two different people or groups of people to disagree about the rightness of an issue or the solution to a problem. Often another person who does not favor either side will be called in to serve as an arbitrator. For this task, one or more classmates should role-play each side of one or more of the following issues. One other person, as the arbitrator, should listen, ask questions, and give recommendations to the two parties (for example, *I suggest that _____; I recommend that _____; I propose that _____*).

Case #1

A young woman would like to attend an all-male college. The president of the college wants to maintain the one-hundred-year tradition of an all-male campus.

Case #2

A girl was in a serious car accident one year ago. She has been in a coma ever since and is not expected to recover. The doctors want to keep her alive. The girl's mother sees that there is no hope for her recovery and would like to remove her from the life-support system.

Case #3

A father keeps his children at home rather than sending them to school because he feels children are being taught ideas against his religion. The school board feels it is unlawful to prevent children from getting a well-rounded education.

Case #4

A supervisor fires a worker because the supervisor believes he is often late, undependable, and disrespectful. The worker denies these charges and claims that he is overworked and called names by his supervisor.

CONDUCTING THE TASK

1. Divide the class into groups of three and ask each group to solve the four problems, switching the following roles with each new case: someone in favor of the issue, someone against the issue, and the arbitrator. The arbitrator will more than likely supply the largest number of target structures in this role play (subjunctive verbs in *that* clauses). Therefore, it is imperative that as many Ss as possible serve as the arbitrator.

2. While Ss are working, you should circulate around the room noting correct and incorrect uses of the target structure.

1. Write the following three words on the board: *demand, recommend,* and *insist.* Ask Ss to order these three words according to how strongly the speaker or writer feels about something. They should indicate that *recommend* is the weakest, *insist* is stronger, and *demand* is the strongest.

2. Give them an example to clarify this meaning: *I recommend that you brush your teeth every day. I insist that you wear your seatbelt. I demand that you stop calling me.* Emphasize that these verbs are used with subjects that are exerting some force or opinion on certain objects. Also indicate these are only three verbs of a longer list that require subjunctive verbs in *that* clauses that follow them.

3. Ask Ss to read the focus box silently.

4. Ask Ss comprehension questions about what Ss have read, for example: *What form of the <u>be</u> verb is used in a past tense sentence?* (be-base form) *What is the difference between <u>The teacher requested that we should do our homework</u>. and The <u>teacher demanded that we do our homework?</u>* (The first one is less formal.)

FOCUS **1**

▶ **Subjunctive Verbs in *That* Clauses**

EXAMPLES	EXPLANATIONS
(a) The arbitrator recommends that Susan not **be** fired. **(b)** It was stipulated that he **abandon** the plans.	*That* clause complements of verbs of advice and urging must contain a present subjunctive verb.
(c) Her father demanded that they **be** back by 12:00. **(d)** The committee stipulated that Mary **follow** all of the instructions.	The subjunctive verb is the base form of the verb: *be, go, take,* etc. We use the base form for all singular and plural subjects.
(e) **Formal:** The president insisted that the meeting **begin** on time. **(f)** **Informal:** Jody suggested that we **should eat** at 6:00.	For a similar yet less formal effect, use *should* + base form instead of the subjunctive.

Verbs of advice and urging that require subjunctive verbs in *that*-clauses:

advise	*insist*	*prefer*	*stipulate*
beg	*move*	*propose*	*suggest*
command	*order*	*recommend*	
demand	*pledge*	*request*	
determine	*pray*	*require*	

EXERCISE 1

During the Opening Task on pages 386 and 387, what were some of the recommendations that the arbitrator made to the conflicting parties?

▶ **EXAMPLE:** *He suggested that the president reconsider the all-male policy.*

A N S W E R   K E Y

Exercise 1
Answers will vary.
2) The arbitrator advised that the doctor consider the quality of life of the patient in her present state.   3) The arbitrator

recommended that the school board review the curriculum proposed by the parent.   4) The arbitrator suggested that the worker bring in tangible evidence to support his case.

EXERCISE 2

Use the following base sentence to make comments about each of the situations in items 1 through 6. Fill in the first blank with the correct form of the verb in parentheses and the second blank with a subjunctive verb or *should* + base form, whichever is more appropriate.

Base sentence: She (or he) ＿＿＿＿＿＿ that he (or she) ＿＿＿＿＿.

▶ **EXAMPLE:** A boss to her employee (recommend)

She ＿*recommends*＿ that he ＿*call her tomorrow*＿.

1. A friend who wants to give another friend some information (insist)
2. An actor to a director who may offer him a part in a play (suggest)
3. A doctor to a patient who might have a deadly disease (require)
4. A neighbor to another neighbor who is too busy to talk (propose)
5. A father to an unsuitable companion for his daughter (forbid)
6. A salesperson to a customer (advise)

FOCUS **2**

Subjunctive Verbs in Noun Complements

EXAMPLES	EXPLANATION
(a) Suggest: **The suggestion that he be fired** was met with resistance. (b) Request: She didn't listen to **his request that she take a sweater.** (c) Advise: **His advice that she be set free** was unwise.	Nouns that come from verbs of advice and urging may also take a *that* clause with a subjunctive verb. Some of these nouns are *advice, command, decision, demand, order, pronouncement, recommendation, request,* and *suggestion.*

EXERCISE 3

Imagine that you live in an apartment complex surrounded by some very disagreeable neighbors in apartments 4A through 4F. Answer the following questions, using the prompts provided and a subjunctive complement.

▶ **EXAMPLE:** What did the man in 4A do when you told him his music was too loud?

ignore/suggestion

He ignored my suggestion that he turn down the stereo.

Subjunctive Verbs in *That* Clauses | **389**

1. What did the person in 4B do when you asked her to return your watering can?

    not heed/proposal

1. What did the person in 4B do when you asked her to return your watering can?

    not heed/proposal

2. What did the man in 4C do when you wanted him to stop being a Peeping Tom?

    laugh at/demand

3. What did the woman in 4D do when you told her to stop stomping around?

    not listen to/demand

4. What did the man in 4E do when you asked him not to come home drunk?

    refuse to pay attention to/request

5. What did the couple in 4F do when you advised them to give their dog away?

    ignore/advice

Exercise 4

Encourage Ss to use a variety of predicate structures—*be* (as in the example) as well other *auxiliary + verb* structures after the noun complement. For example, *His aunt's advice that he <u>work overtime without pay is unwise/will certainly impoverish him/doesn't make sense.</u>*

Workbook Exs. 2 & 3, pp. 227–229.
Answers: TE p. 559.

EXERCISE 4

Imagine that you have a friend Yang, whose family has given him a great deal of advice about how to succeed on his new job as a computer programmer. Which advice of Yang's family do you think was useful and which wasn't? Write a sentence that expresses your opinion of each family member's suggestion.

▶ **EXAMPLE:** Uncle/flirt with the secretaries

    His uncle's advice that he flirt with the secretaries was not appropriate.

Note: Try to use as many advice or urging nouns as you can.

Family Member	Advice
Uncle	flirt with the secretaries
Grandfather	be accurate in your math
Mother	be friendly
Sister	bring your boss coffee every day
Brother	be in good physical condition
Aunt	work overtime without pay
Father	act confident

Exercise 4

Answers will vary.

His grandfather's advice that he be accurate in his math was very important. His mother's recommendation that he be friendly went a long way. His sister's advice that he bring his boss coffee every day was inappropriate. His brother's suggestion that he be in good physical condition was very wise. His aunt's recommendation that he work overtime without pay caused problems with his fellow employees. His father's suggestion that he act confident was great.

FOCUS **3**

Subjunctive Verbs in Adjective Complements

EXAMPLES	EXPLANATION
(a) **That he type** is essential. (b) It is essential **that he type.** (c) **That she be punctual** is important. (d) It is important **that she be punctual.**	Adjective complements can sometimes take subjunctive verbs. This is true when advice adjectives like *advisable, desirable, essential, imperative, important, mandatory, necessary, requisite, urgent,* and *vital* are in the main clause.

EXERCISE 5

STEP 1 Using the information from the following job advertisements, fill in the following statements with *that*-clauses containing subjunctive verbs.

---

236   Employment

Accountant ★
Accounting firm seeks individual w/ min 2 yr exp. Good communication skills & ability to assist clients. Biling Chinese required. Previous exp in CPA firm a plus. Call Mr. Tang 213-627-1409

Accountant Executive
Local firm has a fabulous opportunity for a tax accountant. Two + years tax or accounting experience, a strong client service mentality, and a team oriented approach required. Position can be full time. Send in resume 555 East King. Big City Pa 34543

Chemist ★
Stable, fast-growing company seeks chemist for formulation of industrial products. Must have BS degree chemistry & min. 5 yrs. exp. Nonsmoker preferred. Excellent benefits. Redex Co. 714-773-2221

Customer Service lot of work full-time. Fax resume to 234-345-4567

---

236   Employment

Customer Service
30 Jobs Temp to Perm
WANTED!
People with good Customer Service skills that can work 3:30pm to 12am 5pm-9pm. If you can, we need you ASAP Call! 458-4847-6666

Drivers-Shuttle ★
AIRWAY Shuttle needs outstanding drivers for day and eve shifts. Must be clean-cut, highly ethical, energetic. Great benefits and friendly environment.
AIRWAY 818-775-8156

Education:
Elementary Principal Twelve month postion available on or before January 1, 2001. Elementary teaching experience and elementary certification required. Knowledge certification required.

---

236   Employment

File Clerk
Min. 1 yr exp in law file rm. Knowledge of ofc equipment. Ability to work without supervision. Good command of English for switchboard relief. Mrs. Jacobsen 310-395-6662

Grocery
Fox's market has immediate! openings for part-time or full-time meat cutters. Vacation, Life insurance, Medical insurance, Profit sharing. Call 333-4444

Manager ★
10 new Asst. Managers for marketing & sales needed. No exp. necessary. We will train. Must be 18 & older. Must have car. Work in a wild & crazy office.
Super's 818-774-8234

Nurse ★
Opportunity for career-minded RN. Participate in clinical trials & oversee needs for patients on daily basis. Need good track record of exp. be able to learn fast, self-starter. If interested, call Westside Hospital 213-454-6210

Subjunctive Verbs in *That* Clauses   **391**

FOCUS 3

Review adjective complements from Unit 20. Give Ss additional examples of adjective complements, related to your class or an academic context, and show how they can take subjunctive verbs: *It is necessary that you attend class regularly. That you attend class regularly is necessary.*

Exercise 5
V A R I A T I O N

Ask for 6 volunteers to act out the roles of personnel directors at companies who are recruiting employees. Ask them to make statements such as: *I am looking for an accountant. It is essential that he or she have at least two years of experience . . .* etc.

Workbook Exs. 4 & 5, pp. 229–231.
Answers: TE p. 559.

UNIT GOAL REVIEW

Ask Ss to look at the goals on the opening page of the unit again. Help them understand how much they have accomplished in each area.

▶ **EXAMPLE:** It is important <u>that the accounting applicant be bilingual in Chinese and English</u>. (accountant)

1. _____ is essential. (chemist)
2. It is mandatory _____. (shuttle driver)
3. _____ is desirable. (file clerk)
4. It is imperative _____. (manager)
5. It is necessary _____. (nurse)

STEP 2   Create five more of your own sentences with information from the ads.

Use Your English

ACTIVITY 1: LISTENING / WRITING

Listen to the recording of a radio broadcaster who gives people advice about relationships.

STEP 1   Jot down notes about each of the problems and the advice given.

	Problem	Advice
a. Female Caller:		
b. Male Caller:		

STEP 2   Now write a short paragraph summarizing your opinion of the broadcaster's advice to these two callers. Use at least two subjunctive complements in your writing.

392 UNIT 22

The activities on these "purple pages" at the end of the unit contain situations that should naturally elicit the unit's structures in a more communicative framework. While Ss are doing these activities in class, you can circulate and listen to determine if they have actually achieved the goals in the opening page of the unit.

Activity 1

Play textbook audio. The tapescript for this listening appears on p. 574 of this book.
1. Ask Ss if they have ever listened to talk radio shows in which people get advice about health, finances, and love. Play the tape and have Ss take notes in the grid.
2. Provide a sentence stem if Ss are having difficulty: *the doctor suggested that the woman_____.*

EXPANSION

Encourage Ss to watch the weekly TV sitcom *Frasier* if it is broadcast in their area or listen to Dr. Laura Schlesinger, a syndicated radio talk show host, to summarize the advice given to one or more of the callers.

ACTIVITY 2: READING/WRITING

The owner of a factory has been losing a great deal of money, and he realizes that he must let five of his employees go. You and a partner, the company's personnel manager and assistant personnel manager, must review the performance of the ten most problematic employees.

STEP 1 Read each of the problems of the employees and jot down exactly what the employee did that was inappropriate.

STEP 2 Discuss which employees have the most serious problems.

STEP 3 Make checkmarks in the right columns indicating which five employees you need to fire and which five you wish to retain.

STEP 4 Write a short report to the owner of the factory, explaining your decision.

▶ **EXAMPLE:** *Dear Mr. Johnson,*
Related to your last request, I have determined which five employees should be dismissed. I suggest that Dawn M. be fired because she has missed thirty days of work during the last three months . . .

Name	Problems	Examples	Fire	Retain
Dawn M.	absenteeism	missed 30 days of work		
Homer O.	lack of ambition			
Gunnar F.	criminal background			
Sang S.	incompetence			
Fern M.	laziness			
Sherry B.	alcohol problem			
Maggie W.	clumsiness			
Ly P.	dishonesty			
Mina A.	disagreeableness			
Ann K.	loose morals			

Activity 2

EXPANSION

For Step 4, have each partner copy the paragraph. Then redivide the Ss into new pairs and ask them to share and compare their reports with each other.

Activity 3

SUGGESTION

This exercise is best done as a homework assignment. On the following day, ask Ss to share the most interesting problems and pieces of advice.

Activity 4

1. Bring in a few "defective" items (e.g., broken heel on shoe, snagged sweater, cracked jar, flimsy handle on a pot, etc.) to class.
2. Ask one student to role play as a customer asking the clerk to correct the problem. Ask the clerk to act reluctant at first to exchange or fix the item but later to agree to do it (once a demand has been made).

3. Divide Ss into pairs and ask them to continue the activity with their own examples.
4. Ask Ss to write the results of their role plays on a piece of paper.

Activity 5

This activity is best done as homework. You can use class time for pre-writing/ brainstorming or for pre-editing a draft of the letter.

EXPANSION

Have Ss read a partner's letter and, in class, write a reaction to it taking the opposite position and refuting the points. Encourage continued use of the subjunctive.

ACTIVITY 3: READING/WRITING

Read at least five advice letters and responses in the newspaper from the columns of "Ann Landers," "Dear Abby," and "Miss Manners." Summarize the problems and the advice given to persons requesting the advice.

▶ **EXAMPLE:** *A man had attempted many times to quit smoking. Counseling, nicotine chewing gum, and "cold turkey" were all ineffective. Abby suggested that he try acupuncture.*

ACTIVITY 4: SPEAKING/WRITING

Have you or any of your classmates ever paid for something that was defective or did not work (for example, a piece of clothing, a gadget, a machine)? Or have you ever paid for a service you discovered later had not been performed (for example, had your car fixed, your computer repaired, your watch cleaned)? How did or would you request the salesperson or service provider to correct these mistakes? Summarize your own and your classmate's responses.

▶ **EXAMPLE:** *Jocelyn suggested that the saleswoman replace the sweater because of the unraveling yarn.*

ACTIVITY 5: READING/WRITING

Select a letter to the editor in a newspaper or an editorial that discusses a political, environmental, or civic problem.

STEP 1 Summarize the issue.

STEP 2 State the writer's position.

STEP 3 List any solutions/suggestions made by the writer. Use at least two subjunctive complements in your list.

ACTIVITY 6: READING/SPEAKING

Over a thousand years ago, Anglo-Saxon and Scandinavian wizards and magicians used the power of runes to divine their future. Runes are alphabetic characters used much like tarot cards or I-Ching ideograms to obtain divine guidance on life's questions. You will have a chance to test the power of runes as a guide in the following activity.

STEP 1   Form groups of three or four students. Think of a question you would like answered about some area of your life (such as work, relationships, travel, or money).

▶ **EXAMPLE:** *How will I get home for the holidays?*

STEP 2   Point to one of the runes on the chart on page 399.

▶ **EXAMPLE:** *YR*

STEP 3   Choose a number between 10 and 30 and move your finger clockwise the number of spaces you selected.

▶ **EXAMPLE:** *13*

STEP 4   The rune you land on is your oracle. Read the text about this rune.

▶ **EXAMPLE:** *Hagal*

STEP 5   Share your question with your classmates and paraphrase your rune's "advice."

▶ **EXAMPLE:** *It suggested that I be on my guard because my prospects may change unexpectedly and it urged that I be cautious and patient.*

Activity 6

If Ss enjoy doing horoscopes, they should enjoy this activity as well. Carefully follow the steps for the best results.

The test for this unit can be found on p. 527. The answers are on p. 528.

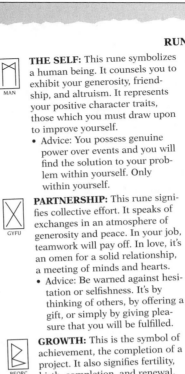

RUNES

THE SELF: This rune symbolizes a human being. It counsels you to exhibit your generosity, friendship, and altruism. It represents your positive character traits, those which you must draw upon to improve yourself.

• Advice: You possess genuine power over events and you will find the solution to your problem within yourself. Only within yourself.

PARTNERSHIP: This rune signifies collective effort. It speaks of exchanges in an atmosphere of generosity and peace. In your job, teamwork will pay off. In love, it's an omen for a solid relationship, a meeting of minds and hearts.

• Advice: Be warned against hesitation or selfishness. It's by thinking of others, by offering a gift, or simply by giving pleasure that you will be fulfilled.

GROWTH: This is the symbol of achievement, the completion of a project. It also signifies fertility, birth, completion, and renewal. An end or a beginning.

• Advice: You are on the brink of a new departure. Have faith.

CONSTRAINT: The rune of the master of us all: time. Now is the moment to free yourself of material things and cultivate the life of the mind. Be patient, careful, and resolute. Thought is preferable to action.

• Advice: The mind rules. Don't be grasping in your pursuit of success. Don't rush things. Wisdom alone will lead you to accomplishment.

FLOW: This is the quintessential female rune. It augurs well for everything that touches on artistic creativity, summoning up your re-serves of intuition and imagination. Talents that are hidden will come to the fore. Work with them!

• Advice: Don't give in to doubt. Let your deepest desires express themselves. Don't question your abilities.

WARRIOR: This is an arrow shot into the air. In your work life, this means you should get a project rolling and have both a competitive spirit and a will to win. In love, it suggests passion, sex, and fertility.

• Advice: Act firmly and positively. Rely only on yourself, your energy, and your desires. It's simple: Motivate yourself.

DISRUPTION: This rune is like a disruptive hailstorm. It represents the random in life—its problems and everyday frustrations.

• Advice: Be on your guard: Your prospects may change unexpectedly. Only caution and patience will lead you to success because the final decision is out of your hands.

THE UNKNOWABLE: This mysterious oracle reserves the right to remain silent and to withhold all advice.

SIGNALS: This rune deals with knowledge and learning. It is telling you that some sort of test awaits, one in which you may need the help of someone who is an expert.

• Advice: Study the situation thoughtfully. Express your wishes but don't decide anything off the top of your head.

FERTILITY: This especially concerns the family. It predicts the birth of a child, a marriage, or the improvement of life in the home. In matters of health, it foresees a healing process.

- Advice: Tenderness and care will bring about growth. You're only just at the beginning, but soon the results will be visible.

 INITIATION: This is an enigmatic sign that speaks of hidden happenings. It stresses the importance of mystery, the revelation of a secret, and the possibility of finding something or someone. It's the rune of second chances.

PEORTH

- Advice: Follow your intuition. The solution to the problem lies not in what you can see but in what you can feel.

 SEPARATION: The rune suggests a change concerning material goods, cultural heritage, legacies, or money in general. Professionally, efforts must be made to stabilize a certain situation.

ODAL

- Advice: Expect some difficulties or delays. Good things come to those who wait. Avoid flighty behavior, doing too many things at once, or spending too much.

 JOURNEY: This signifies a journey or a major move. It can indicate the arrival of good news or an important change. Professionally, your activities are successful—plans may change and any negotiations will end favorably for you.

RAD

- Advice: Be prepared to change course, to travel, to be more open-minded.

 PROTECTION: A very positive rune. It speaks of being protected by an important person, whether at work or in love. You have a lot of self-confidence because this is a splendid time for you.

EOLH

- Advice: Positive change is in the offing. Control your emotions and be ready to meet all challenges.

 OPENING: An optimistic sign, a good omen of beginnings (or renewals). If you are ill, this rune signifies a healing or cure. In affairs of the heart, it indicates the start of an intimate relationship.

KEN

- Advice: The time is for action, not surrender. In love, it promises good times.

 STRENGTH: Growth and rewarding change, especially in your professional life. You should act energetically, for new responsibilities are yours for the taking. Your abilities will be put to the test.

UR

- Advice: Act with determination and do your best. Your work conditions may noticeably improve.

 BREAKTHROUGH: Another positive rune that signifies prosperity and improvement. It represents the light after darkness, and triumph over adversity.

DAEG

- Advice: Take full advantage of opportunities when they arise. Remain serene and upbeat.

 GATEWAY: You will soon receive good news that may change your life. But you will have to make a decision that will require a lot of thought.

THORN

- Advice: Learn to listen to the opinions of others. Seek out help and wait for the right moment to act. If you don't have enough self-confidence, hold off.

 DEFENSE: This rune involves danger that can, and should, be overcome. In fact, the goal you wish to attain is within reach,

YR

but you have to become more flexible and change your way of seeing things.

- Advice: This is just a warning. You can improve the situation by questioning the way you think and changing the way you act.

WHOLENESS: This represents luck, victory, and the fulfillment of your hopes. In all areas of your life (work, love, health, etc.), energy is on the upswing.

- Advice: Take advantage of it.

POSSESSIONS: This is very positive, an omen of increased wealth. New financial opportunities are the order of the day. It's also a symbol of victory, struggle, and an obstacle overcome.

- Advice: Consolidate your gains and persevere along your path. Material reward will soon follow.

HARVEST: This rune symbolizes what has been sown and will soon be reaped. Thus, it speaks of work, perseverance, and patience. The earth has a natural cycle: planting and harvesting.

- Advice: You are on the right path, the one that leads you to a reward. Don't stop halfway. But don't forget, things take time.

STANDSTILL: This involves obstacles, a cooling in your relations with others. At work, it can mean a loss of motivation. Passivity may get the better of you. In love, a relationship may lose passion and ardor.

- Advice: For the moment, put your plans on hold. Before you act, wait for the situation to improve on its own.

MOVEMENT: This motion can involve a change of job, a business trip, a long journey, or a new home. This rune is a source of progress, demanding that you keep an open mind.

- Advice: Be prepared to take control and get ready to adapt. Your horizons are broadening. Get rid of your hang-ups and throw yourself into an adventure.

JOY: You'll get pleasure from your work. Your artistic talents or manual skills will be unleashed. Joy will be found in your love life, through emotional and physical fulfillment. A change is coming, if your enthusiasm doesn't flag.

- Advice: Use your creative gifts and your intuition to achieve your goals. Everything depends on how much fun you get out of accomplishing things.

Thorsons, an imprint of Harper Collins Publishers. Limited Extracts and material from *The Runic Workbook* by Tony Willis.
Layout reprinted with permission from *Elle* Magazine © 1991 ELLE Publishing L. P.

Unit 23

UNIT OVERVIEW

Unit 23 reviews the way that *do, no,* and *not* structures are used for emphasis in discourse. The focus boxes and exercises on *no* and *not* structures may also provide a useful review of standard English rules for certain basic English writers who find double negation acceptable in their dialects.

UNIT GOALS

Review the goals listed on this page so students (Ss) understand what they should be able to know by the end of the unit.

OPENING TASK

The purpose of this task is to consider consumer needs of several different segments of the population.

SETTING UP THE TASK

To introduce the topic, you might ask Ss what they know about the consumer needs of teenagers in the target language culture. The Ss may be young enough themselves to know this information first-hand, or they may be parents or brothers and sisters of teenagers and be able to suggest certain current fads (e.g., rap music, roller blades, hiking boots, etc.).

UNIT 23

EMPHATIC STRUCTURES

Emphatic *Do, No* versus *Not*

UNIT GOALS:

- To use emphatic *do* to add emphasis to a sentence
- To choose *no* versus *not* to emphasize a negative statement

▶ OPENING TASK
Looking at Consumer Needs

Advertising agencies spend a lot of time and money finding out what consumers like and dislike. VALS (Values and Lifestyles) typology* is a system for describing different types of consumers. Imagine that you work for an advertising agency and that you are trying to identify the likes and dislikes of potential consumers. Use the VALS typology to help you make your decision.

*VALS typology was developed by SRI, an important research service.

STEP 1 Read the VALS (for Values and Lifestyles) descriptions. List items or services that you think the nine groups of consumers would and would not want to purchase.

STEP 2 Conduct a mock advertising agency meeting where you convince members of your team of the needs of each type of consumer.

▶ **EXAMPLE:** *Survivors really do need medical care!*

Survivors will have no money for luxuries.

Survivors won't buy any expensive fur coats, but they **will** *buy practical warm woolen ones!*

VALS Typology Consumer Types	Consumer Items or Services that Would and Would Not Appeal to Group
1. Survivors: Old, intensely poor, fearful, depressed, despairing. This group represents about 4 percent of the adult population.	NEED: good medical care DON'T NEED: luxuries (expensive fur coats, etc.)
2. Sustainers: Living on the edge of poverty, often unemployed, angry, resentful, sentimental, family-oriented, intensely patriotic, deeply stable. This group represents about 7 percent of the adult population.	
3. Belongers: Mostly female, traditional, conventional, contented, sentimental, family-oriented, intensely patriotic, deeply stable. This group is the largest in the typology, accounting for about 38 percent of the adult population.	
4. Emulators: Youthful, ambitious, status conscious, clerical or skilled blue collar, want to appear successful, to make it big. A relatively small group, accounting for about 10 percent of the adult population.	
5. Achievers: Middle-aged, more heavily male, most affluent group, leaders, materialistic, self-assured, successful. "Mover and shakers," these people make up over 20 percent of the adult population.	
6. I-Am-Me's: Young, often students, narcissistic, fiercely independent, individualistic, impulsive, dramatic. Next to the smallest group in the typology, accounting for only 3 percent of the adult population.	
7. Experientials: Youthful, artistic, seeking direct experience and inner growth. This group accounts for 5 percent of the adult population.	
8. Societally Conscious: Affluent (second only to Achievers), most highly educated of all VALS types, mature, successful, concerned with social issues, leaders. Account for about 11 percent of the adult population.	
9. Integrateds: Combine the power of the Achievers with the sensitivity of the Societally Conscious, mature, tolerant, understanding. Represent only about 2 percent of the adult population.	

Source: J. Niefeld. *The Making of an Advertising Campaign.* Englewood Cliffs, N.J.: Prentice Hall, 1989.

CONDUCTING THE TASK

Step 1: Divide the class into small groups. Ask each group to read the definitions of each consumer type and brainstorm consumer items or services that would appeal to each group based on the descriptions.

Step 2: Ask Ss to imagine they are at a mock advertising agency meeting in which they must emphasize the actual needs of each group to other members of the agency. Encourage Ss to be persuasive and forceful in their presentations. They should make it very clear when they agree with others' suggestions and when they don't. This culminating "meeting" can be done using whole class, half class, or quarter class groupings. In any case, make note of the ways Ss emphasize their points and how successful they are.

CONCLUDING THE TASK

Discuss the mock ad agency meeting as a class. Which arguments were most convincing? Why?

FOCUS 1

1. For a change of pace, dictate the focus box explanations with the Ss' books closed. First, read all three sentences at normal speed. Then, read the sentences pausing after the following thought groups: 1. We can add emphasis/to a sentence/by stressing the auxiliary or the be verb./ 2. In sentences where there is no auxiliary or be verb/we can add do/and stress it for emphasis./ 3. We often add extra emphasis with an emphatic adverb/like really or certainly/and a strongly stressed do. Now read the sentences a third time at normal speed and ask Ss to proofread their work.

2. Ask Ss to try to provide example sentences for each rule.

3. Ask Ss to check the accuracy of their dictation as well as their sample sentences by reading the focus box.

Workbook Exs. 1 & 2, pp. 232–233.
Answers: TE p. 559.

▶ Emphatic *Do*

EXAMPLES	EXPLANATIONS
(a) I *will* write you a letter as soon as I arrive. (b) He *is* going to Mexico during the winter break. (c) Sally *has* finished her homework. (d) Todd *is* a world-class swimmer.	We can add emphasis to a sentence by stressing the auxiliary or the *be* verb.
(e) I *do* believe in miracles. (f) Professor Dean *did* get her conference paper accepted.	In sentences where there is no auxiliary or *be* verb, we can add *do* and stress it for emphasis.
(g) Juan *really does* know the answer to the question. (h) They *certainly did* see us at the exposition.	We often add extra emphasis with an emphatic adverb like *really* or *certainly* and a strongly stressed *do*.

EXERCISE 1

Read the following script for a radio commercial aloud. Then go over it again silently and underline examples of emphatic *do*.

It is no secret that many famous people, including Napoleon, Catherine the Great, Pope Julius II, and even the Queen of England loved silk clothes. In the thirteenth century Marco Polo traveled the "Silk Road" and brought silk to Venice. You can be sure that Italian royalty did value this precious fabric. Some of the designs embroidered into their clothing were copies of frescoes designed by Leonardo da Vinci.

Today, there are no world-class dress designers who have not used Italian fabrics made of Chinese silk yarn. Oscar de la Renta has said, "What diamonds do for the hand, silk does for the body." Silk does have a luxurious and romantic quality. Silk dresses and suits do add beauty and style to any wardrobe.

You do want to be considered as successful as those who know what quality is, don't you? No one who is anyone should be without this unique fabric. Do buy a silk outfit today!

ANSWER KEY

Exercise 1
royalty <u>did</u> value; silk <u>does</u> have . . .; . . .
suits <u>do</u> add; You <u>do</u> want; <u>Do</u> buy

Some Ways to Use Emphatic *Do*

EXAMPLES	EXPLANATIONS
(a) A: You have a good thesis. B: Really? A: Yes, you really **do** have a good thesis.	Emphatic *do* can: • add emphasis to a whole sentence.
(b) **Do** come in! **(c)** **Do** give him my best regards!	• add emphasis to an imperative. This use of emphatic *do* softens a command and shows polite encouragement.
(d) A: You didn't lock the back door. B: You're wrong. **I did** lock it.	• contradict a negative statement. This use of emphatic *do* is very common in arguments. In such situations, the *do* verb generally refers back to a previous statement.
(e) A: Bob didn't cheat on the test. B: Then, what **did** happen? OR Who **did** cheat? OR What **did** he cheat on?	• be used to ask a clarification question about a previously mentioned negative statement.
(f) It was no surprise to me. He seldom **did** complete his homework. **(g)** To make a long story short, she always **does** get her own way.	• add emphasis to a verb used in connection with an adverb of frequency such as *never, rarely, seldom, often,* or *always.*
(h) I'm relieved that he **does** have his credit card (because I thought he might have forgotten it).	• emphasize a positive result regarding something that had been unknown or in doubt.
(i) Even though I do not usually enjoy fiction, **I did** enjoy John King's latest novel.	• indicate strong concession bordering on contrast.

Emphatic Structures: Emphatic *Do*, *No* versus *Not*   **403**

FOCUS 2

1. Ask four Ss to make four false statements about Ss in the class. For example, *Susan is wearing a red sweater. Tomás hasn't arrived yet. Tomiko will go to lunch at 10:00 a.m. Ahmed and Ali came to school by bus.* Write these sentences on the blackboard. (Try to elicit at least one sentence that will require the emphatic *do.*)

2. Ask four other Ss to refute these statements. Since this box follows Focus 1, in which Ss were shown the different ways to show emphasis, they should be able to produce the correct forms.

3. Note that these forms are used to contradict a statement. Explain that this is just one of several uses of these structures and that they will read about more uses in the focus box.

4. Ask Ss to read the focus box silently.

Exercise 2

This exercise should promote a "party-like" atmosphere as Ss move around the room and compliment each other. Remind Ss that the appropriate response to a compliment is "thank you."

Exercise 3

E X P A N S I O N

Ask pairs to take turns making four more original suggestions to each other.

Exercise 4

Remind Ss to look for instances of the simple verb (without an auxiliary element), for example, *return* in the fourth line and then add a form of *do*. They should also be attentive to the tense of the verb in order to choose the correct form, in this case, *do* not *did*.

Workbook Ex. 3, pp. 233–234.
Answers: TE p. 559.

EXERCISE 2

Circulate around the room and give at least ten compliments to other students using the auxiliary, *be*, or emphatic *do* verbs.

▶ **EXAMPLES:** You **have** done your hair very nicely.
You certainly **are** wearing a beautiful necklace.
That certainly **is** a nice shirt.
I really **do** like your loafers.

EXERCISE 3

Use *do* structures to make the following invitations, requests, or suggestions.

▶ **EXAMPLE:** suggestion to sit down
Do sit down.

1. invitation to put a friend's bags in your room
2. request to come early to the party
3. suggestion to tell the children to quiet down
4. invitation to have some more punch
5. request to put the money in a safe place
6. suggestion to turn off the lights when you leave the conference room
7. invitation to have a bite to eat
8. request to let relatives know you'll be late for your visit

EXERCISE 4

Bruce and Gary are brothers, but they often have arguments. Read the following argument and cross through all the places where you think it is possible to use emphatic *do*. Rewrite those sentences with an appropriate form of the *do* verb. The first one has been done for you.

Bruce: Did you take my flashlight? I can't find it anywhere.

  Gary: Well, I haven't got it. I always return the stuff I borrow.

Bruce: No, you don't.

                  I do return the things I borrow!

  Gary: That's not true! ~~I return the things I borrow~~! It's probably on your desk. I bet you didn't look for it there.

Bruce: No, I looked on my desk, and it's not there.

  Gary: Well, don't blame me. You can't find it because you never clean your room.

Bruce: I clean my room!

  Gary: Oh, no you don't!

A N S W E R   K E Y

Exercise 2
Answers will vary.

Exercise 3
1. Do put your bags . . . 2. Do come early .
. . 3. Do be quiet. 4. Do have some . . .
5. Do put the money . . . 6. Do turn off the
. . . 7. Do have a bite . . . 8. Do let
them know . . .

Exercise 4
Answers will vary.
Gary: . . . I do return . . .
Bruce: I do clean . . .
Bruce: I certainly do clean . . .
Bruce: I really did clean . . .
Bruce: I bet you did put it . . .
Gary: I do return everything . . .
Bruce: I do look after my . . .
Bruce: It does have . . .
Bruce: You really do make me . . .

Bruce: I certainly clean it up! I cleaned it up last night as a matter of fact.

Gary: You didn't.

Bruce: I really cleaned it up last night. Hey, there's my flashlight under your bed.

Gary: Well, I didn't put it here.

Bruce: I bet you put it there. Anyhow, that proves it: You take my stuff and you don't return it.

Gary: I told you before: I return everything I borrow. You just don't look after your things properly.

Bruce: I look after my things. Anyway, from now on, I'm going to lock my door and keep you out.

Gary: You can't. That door doesn't have a key.

Bruce: That's where you're wrong. It has a key and I'm going to lock you out!

Gary: Oh, be quiet!

Bruce: Do you know something? You make me sick. You really make me sick.

Gary: You make me sick too!

Get together with another student and take the parts of Gary and Bruce. Read the dialogue, paying particular attention to the stress patterns of emphatic *do*. If possible, record yourselves and listen to how emphatic you sound.

SUGGESTION

Select one pair of Ss to model how the dialogue might be spoken. Serving as coach, make corrections if the appropriate word or the appropriate stress has not been used.

Emphatic Structures: Emphatic *Do, No* versus *Not*   **405**

Ss should find this explanation very straightforward and will likely have little difficulty with these concepts. If the information appears too easy, feel free to skip this focus box. Note that I is a double negative and is not considered grammatical in standard American English.

FOCUS **3**

▶ **Not versus No**

EXAMPLES	EXPLANATIONS
(a) They do not have any suggestions for the project. They have **no** suggestions for the project. **(b)** Norwegian tourists did not come to Miami this year. **No** Norwegian tourists came to Miami this year.	To emphasize a negative statement, we can use *no* + noun in place of *not/-n't* + verb.
(c) I have **no** fear of flying. **(d)** She is taking the bus because she has **no** car today. **(e)** He has **no** chairs in his apartment.	We use *no* with noncount nouns, singular count nouns, and plural count nouns.
(f) They are indebted to **no one**. **(g)** I saw **nobody** by the river. **(h)** He managed **nothing** well. **(i)** That business decision led him **nowhere**.	We can combine *no* with other words to make compounds. *no* + *one* = *no one* *no* + *body* = *nobody* *no* + *thing* = *nothing* *no* + *where* = *nowhere*
(j) Mike doesn**'t** have **any** money. **(k)** We haven**'t** seen **any** pelicans all day. **(l)** **NOT:** She won't earn no money.	In standard English, a negative sentence (with *not* after the first auxiliary verb or *be*) with a second negative component uses *not . . . any*.

Exercise 5

Ss can do this exercise individually or in pairs.

EXERCISE 5

STEP **1** Match the first part of the sentence in column A with something from column B that makes sense and is grammatical. The first one has been done for you.

Lily went to a party last night.

A

1. She had hoped to make some new friends, but she didn't meet

2. She had to drive home, so she didn't drink

3. She was very hungry, but when she arrived there wasn't

4. She talked to a few people, but she didn't have

5. Some people were dancing, but Lily didn't have

6. She wanted to sit down, but there weren't

7. Finally, she said to herself: "This party isn't

8. So she went home early and decided not to go to

B

a. any food left.

b. anyone to dance with.

c. any more parties.

d. anyone interesting.

e. any fun!"

f. any alcohol.

g. anything to say to them

h. any chairs.

STEP 2 Rewrite each sentence of Step 1 using *no* or an appropriate *no* + compound. Change the verbs as necessary. The first one has been done for you.

1. She had hoped to make some new friends, but she met nobody interesting.

EXERCISE 6

Edit the following speech for errors with negative constructions. When you are finished, read it aloud to a partner and see if there are any more changes you want to make. The first sentence has been edited as an example.

(1) The year 2025 ~~no is~~ *is not* as far away as it might seem. (2) Today we don't have no direction. (3) If we don't get any direction, our dream for our nation is sure to explode. (4) No children will have the things we had. (5) There isn't nobody who cannot benefit from the few principles I will share with you today. (6) Please listen carefully. (7) If you don't listen to anything I say, the consequences will be fatal.

(8) First, it isn't good for nobody to feel that they deserve everything when they don't put any sweat and struggle in getting it. (9) Even more, this nation can't tell nobody nowhere that it is entitled to world leadership just because

Exercise 6

Circulate while Ss are reading the speech aloud. At the end of the exercise, ask for one or two volunteers to read the speech in front of the classroom with good pronunciation, stress, and phrasing.

they had it in the past. (10) You can never take nothing for granted in this country. (11) I hope you will work hard to achieve.

(12) Next, I believe that no people should set goals and then do anything not to achieve them. (13) If you set a goal, work hard and humbly to accomplish it. (14) Even if you don't get no credit, it is important to keep trying because you and your maker know what you accomplished.

(15) Another important piece of advice is not to work just for money. (16) Money alone can't strengthen nobody's family nor help nobody sleep at night. (17) Don't let nobody tell you that wealth or fame is the same as character. (18) It is not O.K. to use drugs even if everyone is doing it. (19) It is not O.K. to cheat or lie even if every public official does.

(20) Finally, no person should be afraid of taking no risks. (21) No anybody should be afraid of failing. (22) It shouldn't matter to nobody anywhere how many times you fall down. (23) What matters is how many times you get up.

(24) Let's not spend no more time talking. We are all responsible for building a decent nation to live in! Let's not let no more minutes pass.

FOCUS **4**

When to Use *No* for Emphasis

EXAMPLES	EXPLANATIONS
(a) I didn't have any friends when I was a child. **(b)** I had **no** friends when I was a child.	Statements using *no* as the negative word instead of *not* emphasize what is missing or lacking. In speaking, we often stress the word *no* for extra emphasis.
(c) NEUTRAL: I didn't meet anybody interesting at the party. **(d)** EMPHATIC: I met **nobody** interesting at the party. **(e)** NEUTRAL: I didn't learn anything new at the conference. **(f)** EMPHATIC: I learned **nothing** new at the conference.	*No* + compound also emphasizes what is missing or lacking. Sentence (c) sounds neutral, a statement of fact. Sentence (d) sounds more emotional, emphasizing the lack of interesting people.

EXERCISE 7

Lily is describing the party (in Exercise 5) to her best friend and is telling her what a miserable time she had. Imagine you are Lily and try describing the party from her point of view, emphasizing all the negative aspects of the evening. If possible, record yourself and listen to see how emphatic you sound.

EXERCISE 8

Emphatic language is very common in public speeches. Read aloud the extracts from speeches below and notice the different ways each speaker uses language to emphasize his message. Underline any examples that you can find of the emphatic language discussed in this unit. Do you notice any other techniques the speakers use to get their points across?

1. Jesse Jackson: Speech to the Democratic National Convention, July 20, 1988

When I was born late one afternoon, October 8, in Greenville, South Carolina, no writers asked my mother her name. Nobody chose to write down our address. My mama was not supposed to make it. You see, I was born to a teenage mother who was born to a teenage mother. I understand. I know abandonment and people being mean to you, and saying you're nothing and nobody, and can never be anything. I understand . . . I understand when nobody knows your name. I understand when you have no name . . . I really do understand.

2. Donald Kagan: Address to the Class of 1994 of Yale College, September 1, 1990

We now have the mechanisms that do permit the storage of data in staggering amounts and their retrieval upon demand. And one of the by-products is the approaching end of the age of specialization. The doom of the specialist draws closer every time someone punches the keys on a word processor. Of course, we will still need doctors, lawyers, plumbers, and electricians. But will there still be a brisk market for all the specialties we have fostered in the economic and social fields? I doubt it. The future will belong to those who know how to handle the combinations of information that come out of the computer, what we used to call the "generalist." The day of the generalist is just over the horizon and we had better be ready for it.

Emphatic Structures: Emphatic *Do*, *No* versus *Not* | **409**

VARIATION

1. Have pairs describe the party to each other.
2. Once everyone has had a chance to practice, ask for a volunteer who is willing to be critiqued for a tape recording. Tape the student.
3. Replay the tape-recording and ask the student to self-critique himself or herself.
4. Ask the other Ss to give positive comments about the student's performance. Then ask Ss to give one or two suggestions for improvement.
5. Encourage others to tape-record themselves at home for extra practice.

Exercise 8

Both excerpts use emphatic language, but the first one also uses the repetition of *I* to emphasize the speaker's identification with someone who is illegitimate by birth and illegitimate in the society.

Workbook Ex. 5, p. 236.
Answers: TE p. 560.

UNIT GOAL REVIEW

Ask Ss to look at the goals on the opening page of the unit again. Help them understand how much they have accomplished in each area.

ANSWER KEY

Exercise 7
Answers will vary.
Lily had a miserable time at the party. She met no friends, had no alcohol, ate no food, had nothing to say to anyone, had no partner to dance with, could find no chairs, had no fun, and decided to go to no more parties.

Exercise 8
1. no writers . . . Nobody chose . . . you're nothing and nobody . . . when nobody knows . . . no name 2. . . . do permit . . . . . .by-products is . . . . . .we will still . . . future will belong . . .

USE YOUR ENGLISH

The activities on these "purple pages" at the end of the unit contain situations that should naturally elicit the unit's structures in a more communicative framework. While Ss are doing these activities in class, you can circulate and listen to determine if they have actually achieved the goals on the opening page of the unit.

Activity 1

Play textbook audio. The tapescript for this listening appears on pp. 574–575 of this book. You may need to play the tape more than once for Ss to note all the advice in the lecture.

Activity 2

To liven up this activity, you might bring in buttons and hats and decorate the room with streamers. You could also invite another class in to hear the campaign speeches and vote for the "best" candidate.

Use Your English

ACTIVITY 1: LISTENING / WRITING / SPEAKING

STEP 1 Listen to the lecture on how to create a good advertisement. Take notes and pay special attention to the suggestions given.

STEP 2 Summarize the speaker's advice in a short paragraph.

▶ **EXAMPLE:** *A good ad should have three main ingredients. The ad should include information about the product and its unique advantage. . . .*

STEP 3 Now revise your paragraph so that it sounds more emphatic. Use some of the techniques you have learned in this chapter.

STEP 4 Now read your paragraph aloud to a classmate, stressing words appropriately.

ACTIVITY 2: WRITING / SPEAKING / LISTENING

STEP 1 Organize a political campaign in class. Divide into groups. Each group represents a new political party. With your group, create a name and draw up a list of all the things you stand for and all the things you will do if you are elected.

STEP 2 Make a poster representing your beliefs and prepare a short speech to persuade people to vote for you. Each member of your group should be prepared to speak on a different aspect of your party's platform.

STEP 3 Give your speeches to the rest of the class and decide who has the most persuasive approach. If possible, record your speech and afterward listen to what you said, taking note of any emphatic structures you used and how you said them.

ACTIVITY 3: SPEAKING/WRITING

STEP 1 Get together with another student. Think of a relationship or a situation in which people often have disagreements (for example, parent/child; brother/sister, boyfriend/girlfriend, spouse/spouse, roommate/roommate, and so on). Choose one such relationship and brainstorm all the possible issues these people might argue about.

STEP 2 Choose one issue and take the role of one of the people in the situation (your partner takes the role of the other). Create the argument these two people might have on this issue. Write your dialogue and prepare to perform it in front of the class. Before you perform, check to see how emphatically you state your point of view.

STEP 3 Perform your dialogue for the class.

ACTIVITY 4: RESEARCH/WRITING/SPEAKING

STEP 1 Think of someone famous whom you truly admire because of his or her ideas. This person could be an important figure in any field, such as:

Communications	Peter Jennings, Connie Chung, Larry King
Politics	Geraldine Ferraro, Keizo Obuchi, Nelson Mandela
Business	Bill Gates, Stephen Covey, Rupert Murdoch
Entertainment	Stephen Spielberg, Celine Dion, Oliver Stone

STEP 2 Go to the library and do some research about the person you have selected by using encyclopedias, *The Reader's Guide*, biographical references, speech references, etc.

STEP 3 Write a short essay describing what traits, activities, or ideas of this person impress you the most.

STEP 4 Give a speech to your classmates convincing them of the admirable traits, activities, and ideas of this person. Use as many emphatic structures from this unit as you can.

▶ **EXAMPLES:** *Even though some people think Barbara Walters is an egotistical newsreporter, she does deliver informative news.*

Steves Covey's simple behavioral principles really do apply as much to the workplace as to the home.

There is no Hollywood producer as political as Oliver Stone.

Activity 3
Encourage Ss not to read their dialogues. Give adequate time to practice so that Ss are comfortable with their dialogues and can communicate more naturally.

Activity 4

V A R I A T I O N

If they prefer, Ss can select a celebrity not on this list. This could be a good opportunity for Ss to raise consciousness about important international figures who may be unfamiliar to other students.

The test for this unit can be found on pp. 529–530.
The answers are on p. 531.

Unit 24

UNIT OVERVIEW

This unit covers a topic many advanced students (Ss) have not encountered in formal grammar study: the structures that may be moved to the beginning of a sentence for emphasis or contrast. In some cases, fronted structures are repeated as a stylistic device to create parallel structures across sentence boundaries.

UNIT GOALS

Review the goals listed on this page so Ss understand what they should be able to know by the end of the unit.

OPENING TASK

This task creates teams of scriptwriters who must complete one scenario and then read it for the rest of the class. The last sentence of each scenario (the one that will need completion) starts with a fronted structure.

SETTING UP THE TASK

SUGGESTION

If time permits, first show video excerpts of one or more film types (science fiction, horror story, etc.) to help set the tone for the task.

UNIT 24

FRONTING STRUCTURES FOR EMPHASIS AND FOCUS

UNIT GOALS:

- To know what kinds of structures can be moved to the front of sentences for emphasis
- To know when to change the subject/verb order for fronted structures
- To use fronted negative forms for emphasis
- To use fronted structures to point out contrasts and focus on unexpected information

OPENING TASK
Film Scenarios

When someone mentions the film industry, we usually think first of actors and directors. When film awards are handed out, however, we are reminded that behind all good movies stand creative scriptwriters.

STEP 1 Form groups with members of your class. Each group will be a team of scriptwriters. Imagine that you are being considered for a film company contract based on your imaginative ideas.

STEP 2 For the scenario or scenarios below that your group chooses or is assigned, think of a completion for the last line of dialogue or description.

STEP 3 When the groups have finished, take turns reading the scenarios along with the completions. As a class, you may want to vote on the ones you think are the most creative.

FILM 1: SCIENCE FICTION

SCENARIO: For weeks the townspeople of Spooner, a small lake resort town, have observed signs that something horrible has invaded their community. Trees, shrubs, and even the flowers have begun to die. Dogs howl at night and cats are afraid to go out. One summer Saturday night, many of the townsfolk are, as usual, celebrating the end of the week at the local dance hall, when they become aware of an eerie green glow outside. They rush out to see what it is. Moving slowly toward them across a field is . . .

FILM 2: HORROR STORY

SCENARIO: Ten people have agreed to spend a week in a large and very old mansion on the edge of town. Strange events have occurred in this house over the past few years, and the people assembled this evening want to find out if there is truth to rumors that the house has been cursed. They are all seated at the dining room table, with their leader, Madame Montague, at the head.

Madame Montague: My friends, you all know why we are here. Before we spend another hour in this house, there is one thing that I must demand of all of you. Under no circumstances should . . .

FILM 3: ROMANCE

SCENARIO: Max and Ramona are a young couple in their twenties who have been dating for a year. Max is passionately in love with Ramona and wants to marry her, but he's not sure if she's as much in love with him as he is with her. Max is trying to find out how Ramona feels about him.

Max: Ramona, you know how much I love you. (Long pause. No response from Ramona.) Tell me honestly, what do you think of me?

Ramona: Max, never have . . .

FILM 4: MYSTERY

SCENARIO: Detective Hendershot has been called to the scene of a crime—a murder, to be exact. He is now in the master bedroom, where the unfortunate victim was discovered. Hendershot opens and searches the dresser drawers one by one, hoping to find the murder weapon or some other clue to the crime. He opens the last drawer, the bottom one, and sifts through its contents. There, buried under a pile of silk scarves, is . . .

FILM 5: ADVENTURE STORY

SCENARIO: After three days of wandering aimlessly in the heart of the Brazilian rain forest, a group of scientists have to admit that they are hopelessly lost. The head of the expedition, Professor Winbigler feels it is time to warn the others of a great danger to them that she has encountered while separated from the group.

Professor Winbigler: My fellow scientists, I didn't want to tell you this, but now that I fear we may not get out of here for a while, I believe you should be alerted. Far more threatening to our survival than the poisonous snakes and spiders are . . .

CONDUCTING THE TASK

Step 1

If possible, divide the class into five groups since there are five scenarios. If that would put too many in a group (i.e., more than four or five), give some groups the same scenario.

VARIATION

If Ss need some direction or motivation, do the first scenario with the class as a whole (without correcting any ungrammatical structures offered for the time being). Brainstorm a list of possible endings. Then distribute the other four scenario assignments to groups.

Step 2

Suggest that each group brainstorm a number of possibilities and then choose the best one. Set a time limit for brainstorming and selection (e.g., ten minutes).

VARIATIONS

1. If you have enough time, assign more than one scenario to each group or ask each group to choose several.
2. Do one round of the activity as described and then have groups or individuals make up additional endings for the scenarios.

Step 3

Because all of the scenarios are meant to be entertaining, encourage the Ss who read them aloud to do so dramatically. Have Ss save their completions to consider after you have covered the material in Focus 1.

FOCUS 1

This focus box introduces fronted structures and explains that for some of these structures, the order of subject and verb or subject and auxiliary of the sentence will need to be reversed.

SUGGESTION

As an introduction to later focus boxes (which will cover the types of fronted structure in detail), discuss here the subject-verb word order of the final sentences Ss completed in the Opening Task scenarios since all of these sentences had inverted order:

1. Elicit examples the Ss used to complete the task.
2. Write one on the board for each film type and label the subject, the verb and, for Film Scenarios 2 and 3, the inverted auxiliaries.

Exercise 1

This purpose of this exercise is to help Ss become more familiar with fronted structures and to note ones that require subject-verb (or auxiliary) inversion.

SUGGESTION

Ask for student volunteers to read the dialogue out loud before Ss work on the identification task.

▶ Fronted Structures

EXAMPLES		EXPLANATIONS
(a) **Not Fronted** The townspeople went outside **because they were curious.**	**(b)** **Fronted Because they were curious,** the townspeople went outside.	In English, you can place special emphasis on some ideas by moving words or phrases from their usual place in a sentence to the front of the sentence. This process is called "fronting," and the resulting structures are known as "fronted structures."
(c) I would **not** leave this town **for anything.**	**(d)** **Not for anything** would I leave this town.	
(e) **The storm was** so terrible that many people lost their homes.	**(f)** So terrible **was the storm** that many people lost their homes.	**Subject-Verb and Subject-Auxiliary Order** When you front some structures, the word order in the rest of the sentence changes. The order of the subject and verb or the subject and the auxiliary is reversed (inverted). The verb or the auxiliary comes before the subject instead of after it. These structures will be shown in Focus 3 and Focus 4.

EXERCISE 1

In the dialogue below, a group of friends who have just been backpacking in the mountains are telling some other friends about their trip. Each numbered sentence contains a fronted structure. For these sentences, underline the subject and circle the main verb and any auxiliaries. If the subject and the verb (or the subject and an auxiliary) have been inverted, write "I" at the end of each sentence.

▶ **EXAMPLE:** Not once (did) we (see) a wild animal. **I**

Karen: Well, to begin with, we had to hike straight uphill for six miles. I couldn't believe how steep it was! (1) Never have I been so tired in my whole life!

Toshi: Really! Listen, next time all the food will be freeze-dried. (2) Not for anything would I carry a twenty-pound pack uphill again!

ANSWER KEY

Exercise 1
Words that should be circled are in italics; subjects are underlined.
1. *have* I *been* **I**   2. *would* I *carry* **I**   3. we *got up*   4. *could* we *see* **I**   5. *had* we
dropped **I**   6. we *unpacked*   7. *did* I *discover* **I**   8. *had* the rest of us **I**   9. we *pounded in*   10. *did* we *get soaked* **I**
11. the most beautiful rainbow *appeared*
12. *do* you *realize* **I**

Phan: (3) At dusk we finally got up to our campsite; it was gorgeous! We were on the shores of a pristine mountain lake, surrounded by pine trees. (4) Nowhere could we see another person.

Kent: (5) However, no sooner had we dropped all our stuff on the ground than the storm clouds rolled in. (6) In a big hurry we unpacked everything we had.

Mario: (7) Yeah, and not until then did I discover that I hadn't packed my rain poncho.

Karen: (8) Neither had the rest of us.

Toshi: We tried to pitch the tents as fast as we could but it wasn't fast enough. (9) With every stake we pounded in, it seemed to rain harder. (10) Not only did we get soaked, but some of our food got wet too.

Phan: But fortunately the storm ended almost as quickly as it had started. (11) And on the other side of the lake the most beautiful rainbow appeared.

Mario: All in all, even though it was a hard climb getting there, it was worth it. (12) You know, seldom do you realize how peaceful life can be until you get away from civilization!

Fronting Structures for Emphasis and Focus | **415**

This focus box divides fronted structures into three types: those that do not require that the subject and verb or auxiliary be inverted, those that do, and those that may be optionally inverted.

SUGGESTION

1. Give Ss an overview of what the three parts of the charts cover. If you have gone over examples of inversion for Focus 1 as suggested, Ss will be familiar with the concept.
2. Ask Ss to read the examples and the descriptions of the types for homework so they have a general idea of the content.

    In class, explain that most of these fronted structures are more common in written and formal spoken English than in informal English. They are often used in literature as stylistic devices to create special emphasis and focus.

FOCUS **2**

Inversion of Subjects and Auxiliaries and Verbs with Fronted Structures

Fronted Structures that Do Not Require Inversion

ADVERBIAL NOT FRONTED		FRONTED ADVERBIAL		TYPE OF ADVERBIAL
(a)	She works on her novel **during the evenings.**	**(b)**	**During the evenings** she works on her novel.	Time
(c)	Detective Wagner sorted the evidence **with great care.**	**(d)**	**With great care,** Detective Wagner sorted the evidence.	Manner
(e)	Something strange must be happening **if the dogs are howling.**	**(f)**	**If the dogs are howling,** something strange must be happening.	Condition
(g)	Max showered Ramona with gifts **in order to win her heart.**	**(h)**	**In order to win her heart,** Max showered Ramona with gifts.	Purpose
(i)	The townspeople left **because they were afraid.**	**(j)**	**Because they were afraid,** the townspeople left.	Reason
(k)	The group would meet in the living room of the old mansion **every night.**	**(l)**	**Every night** the group would meet in the living room of the old mansion.	Frequency (after verbs)

Fronted Structures that Require Inversion

NOT FRONTED	FRONTED WITH INVERSION	STRUCTURE
(m) The townspeople *were* **so afraid** that they hardly ventured out of their neighborhoods.	**(n)** **So afraid** *were* the townspeople that they hardly ventured out of their neighborhoods.	Adverbials of extent or degree (*so* + adjective/ adverb + *that*)
(o) A small boy *was* **in the library.**	**(p)** **In the library** *was* a small boy.	Adverbials of position when the main verb is *be*
(q) We *have* **never** *seen* such generosity.	**(r)** **Never** *have we seen* such generosity.	Negative adverbials of frequency that come before the main verb (*never, rarely, seldom*)
(s) Max *would* **not** leave Ramona **for anything.**	**(t)** **Not for anything** *would* Max *leave* Ramona.	Other negated structures
(u) A beam of light *was* **moving toward them.**	**(v)** **Moving toward them** *was* a beam of light.	Present participles + modifiers
(w) A note *was* **stuck in a branch of the willow tree.**	**(x)** **Stuck in a branch of the willow tree** *was* a note.	Past participles + modifiers
(y) The cinematography of this movie *is* **more interesting than** the plot.	**(z)** **More interesting than** the plot of this movie is the cinematography.*	Comparative structures
(aa) (Paraphrase: The soldiers *did not know* that the enemy was just over the hill.)	**(bb)** **Little** *did* the soldiers *know* that the enemy was just over the hill.	Implied negation Because the negation is implied rather than explicit, there is no non-fronted form with *little*.

*Note in (z) that the phrase *of this movie* has also been moved to the front to give the reader more information at the beginning of the sentence

Optional Inversion with Fronted Structures

ADVERBIAL NOT FRONTED	FRONTED ADVERBIAL	TYPE OF ADVERBIAL
(cc) A leopard appeared **from the western hills.**	**(dd) From the western hills** a leopard *appeared*. (No inversion) **(ee) From the western hills** *appeared* a leopard. (Optional inversion)	Direction
(ff) An old woman sits **on the park bench.**	**(gg) On the park bench** an old woman *sits*. (No inversion) **(hh) On the park bench** *sits* an old woman. (Optional inversion)	Position, when the main verb is not *be*.

Exercise 2

SUGGESTIONS

1. Ss might enjoy working on this exercise with a partner or in a small group.
2. After completing this exercise, ask for volunteers to read some of the sentences aloud or write them on the board.

EXERCISE 2

Use the cues in parentheses to add adverbial phrases or clauses to the end of each sentence. Then to emphasize the description you added, move it to the front of a new sentence. You will need to write two sentences for part a. and two for part b. If you wish, you can add other descriptive words or phrases. Be creative; try to use new vocabulary!

▶ **EXAMPLES:** The odd creatures were standing in front of them. (a. manner)

1. *The odd creatures were standing in front of them with hungry looks on their angular faces.*
2. Fronted: *With hungry looks on their angular faces, the odd creatures were standing boldly in front of them.*

The scientists heard a piercing shriek. (b. time)

1. *The scientists heard a piercing shriek shortly before dawn.*
2. Fronted: *Shortly before dawn, the scientists heard a piercing shriek.*

1. The townspeople were absolutely terrified. (a. time b. frequency)
2. Detective Hendershot will find the murderer. (a. condition b. manner)
3. The group explored the nooks and crannies of the old house. (a. time b. purpose)

A N S W E R   K E Y

Exercise 2
Answers will vary. Examples:
1. At night . . ./Every evening . . .   2. If he remains determined . . ./With his usual cleverness . . .   3. The first day they were there . . ./As they wanted to know if there were really any ghosts . . .   4. Toward what they thought was civilization . . ./To see if they could find a route out of the jungle . . .
5. Sitting in her tent . . ./If she is not too tired . . .

4. The scientists wandered. (a. direction b. purpose)
5. Professor Winbigler faithfully writes in her journal. (a. position b. condition)

EXERCISE 3
Use an appropriate word or phrase from the list below to complete the blanks with fronted structures.

little did I know	peeking out from under
not for anything	a snowdrift
never	stuffed into the toe
sitting at the bottom of the hill	so embarrassed
coming toward me from the right	worse than the beginning of
	my excursion

I'm not sure if I ever want to go skiing again. (1) _____ have I felt so frustrated trying to have fun! First, I had trouble just getting on the boots and skis I had rented. One of the boots wouldn't fit; then I discovered that (2) _____ was an old sock. I was so nervous that I hadn't realized what it was. Next I discovered that getting to the top of the hill on the chair lift was no small feat. (3) _____ that one could fall numerous times before even getting started. Once I made it to the top, I couldn't believe how small everything looked down below. (4) _____ was a tiny building that I recognized as the chalet. My first thought was: (5) _____ am I going to go down this slope. As it turned out, my first thought was probably better than my second, which was to give it a try. (6) _____ was the end of it. As I raced uncontrollably down the slope terrified, I suddenly saw that (7) _____ was another skier. We collided just seconds later. (8) _____ , I muttered an apology. That was it for me for the day. (9) _____ did I feel that I spent the rest of the afternoon finding out how to enroll in a beginning ski class.

Exercise 3
This would be a good follow-up homework assignment.

Workbook Ex. 2, p. 239; Ex. 3, p. 240. Answers: TE p. 560.

A N S W E R   K E Y

Exercise 3
(1) Never   (2) stuffed into the toe
(3) Little did I know   (4) Sitting at the bottom of the hill   (5) Not for anything
(6) Worse than the beginning of my excursion
(7) coming toward me from the right
(8) Peeking out from under a snowdrift
(9) So embarrassed

FOCUS 3

The focus box shows four different patterns of inversion.

SUGGESTIONS

1. For example pairs (e)/(f), (g)/(h), and (m)/(n), ask Ss to identify the auxiliaries and main verbs that follow the subject (*have left*, *stay*, and *been, respectively*). These verbs have not been boldfaced so that the subject-auxiliary inversion in the fronted versions would be more apparent.

2. Take special note of the comparative form in (p), in which both auxiliary and *be* are fronted. *Annoying* here is a participle adjective and not part of a progressive verb. Ss can use the *very* test to identify participle adjectives: *The dust is very annoying* (adjective). NOT: *My little brother is very annoying me constantly* (*annoying* = main verb).

▶ **Patterns of Inversion with Fronted Structures**

EXAMPLES		EXPLANATIONS
Not Fronted	**Fronted**	**Pattern 1: Simple Verbs**
(a) **I** never **said** such a thing!	(b) Never **did I say** such a thing!	When you front a structure requiring inversion and the sentence has only a simple verb, add *do* except when the main verb is a form of *be*.
(c) **She walked** so slowly that it took her an hour to get to school.	(d) So slowly **did she walk** that it took her an hour to get to school.	
(e) **Max could** never have left Ramona.	(f) Never **could Max** have left Ramona.	**Pattern 2: Complex Verbs** Complex verbs have a main verb and one or more auxiliaries.
(g) **They would** not stay in that house for anything.	(h) Not for anything **would they** stay in that house.	In sentences with complex verbs, invert the first auxiliary and the subject.
(i) **The director is** seldom here on time.	(j) Seldom **is the director** here on time.	**Pattern 3: *Be* Verbs** When the verb is *be* with no auxiliaries, invert the subject and *be*.
(k) **The speaker was** so boring that many in the audience fell asleep.	(l) So boring **was the speaker** that many in the audience fell asleep.	
(m) **There has** never been so much excitement in this town.	(n) Never in this town **has there** been so much excitement.	**Pattern 4:** ***Be* + Auxiliary Verbs** In sentences with fronted adverbials, invert the first auxiliary and the subject.
(o) **The dust has been** more annoying than the noise during the remodeling of the library.	(p) More annoying than the noise **has been the dust** during the remodeling of the library.	In sentences with fronted comparatives, put both the auxiliary and *be* before the subject.

EXERCISE 4

After each of the following phrases, add a main clause that expresses your opinions or provides information. If the fronted part is a position adverbial, use a *be* verb to follow it.

▶ **EXAMPLES:** Near the school
Near the school is a small coffee shop.

So puzzling . . . that
So puzzling was the homework assignment that most of us didn't finish it.

1. Seldom during the past few years
2. More fascinating than my English class
3. Rarely during my lifetime
4. In my bedroom
5. More important to me than anything
6. Seldom in the history of the world
7. More of a world problem than air pollution
8. So interesting . . . that
9. Stored in the recesses of my brain, never to be forgotten,
10. Waiting for me in the future
11. In the front of my English textbook
12. Better than ice cream for dessert
13. Loved and respected by many admirers
14. So terrible . . . that

EXERCISE 5

Make up a sentence in response to each of the following. Use a fronted structure for emphasis.

▶ **EXAMPLE:** Describe what is in some area of your classroom.
In the back of our classroom are posters of many countries of the world and a large map of the world.

1. State how exciting something is to you by comparing it in degree to something else. (Start with "More exciting . . .")
2. Tell how infrequently you have done something.
3. Describe how angry you were in a certain circumstance. (Start with "So angry . . .")
4. Describe how happy you were in another circumstance.

Fronting Structures for Emphasis and Focus **421**

Exercise 4
EXPANSION

Have Ss choose one of the sentence completions and write a paragraph developing it.

Workbook Ex. 2, p. 239; Ex. 3, p. 240.
Answers: TE p. 560.

Exercise 5
EXPANSION

Like Exercise 4, this exercise could be followed by a paragraph writing assignment for either in-class writing or homework as the sentence completions suggest topics that could be elaborated by description, explanation, reasons, etc.

Workbook Ex.4, p. 241.
Answers: TE p. 560.

ANSWER KEY

Exercise 4
Answers will vary. Examples:
1. have I left town   2. is my history class
3. has it snowed in my hometown   4. is a portrait of my family   5. is my family
6. have so many governments collapsed at once   7. is overpopulation   8. was the new mystery . . . I bought that I read the whole book in one evening   9. is the memory of the first trip we took to Europe   10. is, I'm sure, a happy life   11. is the table of contents
12. is chocolate mousse   13. is "the Saint of India," Mother Teresa   14. was the storm that it left many houses in ruins

Exercise 5
Answers will vary. Examples:
1. More exciting than taking a short trip would be taking a trip around the world.
2. Seldom have I stayed up all night.   3. So angry was I when I found out I failed the exam that I threw it away.   4. So happy was I when by brother came to visit me that I told everyone I knew.

SUGGESTION

To give practice with subject-auxiliary or verb inversion:

1. Prepare sentence examples with noninverted forms on slips of paper. (Examples: *I have never been so upset about a mistake; I have not missed a day of work this year; You shouldn't drive while drinking under any circumstances; I have not been anywhere that has so many restaurants on one block as this city does.*)

2. Have Ss work with a partner. Give each pair one strip with a sentence to rewrite with a fronted structure. They can use the charts for reference. Have them read the original and the fronted version to the rest of the class (with dramatic emphasis!).

FOCUS **4**

Fronted Negative Forms: Adverbials

For all of these fronted negative adverbials below, you must invert the subject and auxiliary or the subject and the simple verb.

Adverbs and Adverb Phrases

WORD/PHRASE	NOT FRONTED	FRONTED
never	**(a)** I have **never** laughed so hard!	**(b) Never** have I laughed so hard!
not once	**(c)** I have **not** missed my Portuguese class once this semester.	**(d) Not once** have I missed my Portuguese class this semester.
not for + (noun)	**(e)** I would **not** commute four hours a day **for all the money in the world!**	**(f) Not for all the money in the world** would I commute four hours a day!
not until + (noun)	**(g)** She did **not** realize the ring was missing **until the morning.**	**(h) Not until the morning** did she realize the ring was missing.
not since + (noun)	**(i)** We have **not** had so much rain **since April.**	**(j) Not since April** have we had so much rain.
under no circumstances	**(k)** You will **not** be allowed to leave **under any circumstances.**	**(l) Under no circumstances** will you be allowed to leave. (*not any → no*)
in no case	**(m)** We can **not** make an exception **in any case.**	**(n) In no case** can we make an exception.
in no way	**(o)** This will **not** affect your grade **in any way.**	**(p) In no way** will this affect your grade.
no way (informal)	**(q)** I am **not** going to miss that concert **for any reason!**	**(r) No way** am I going to miss that concert.
nowhere	**(s)** I have **not** been **anywhere** that is as peaceful as this place.	**(t) Nowhere** have I been that is as peaceful as this place.

Adverb Time Clauses

CLAUSE	NOT FRONTED	FRONTED
not until + clause	**(u)** I will **not** believe it **until I see it!**	**(v)** **Not until I see it** will I believe it!
not since + clause	**(w)** I have **not** had so much spare time **since I started high school.**	**(x)** **Not since I started high school** have I had so much spare time.

EXERCISE 6

Add the negative fronted structure in parentheses to the following sentences for emphasis. Make any other changes that are necessary.

▶ **EXAMPLE:** I hadn't ever been so upset. (never)
  Never *had I been so upset.*

1. We can't let you retake the examination. (under no circumstances)
2. I haven't missed a class. (not once)
3. Homer won't miss graduation. (not for anything)
4. This didn't change my attitude about you. (in no way)
5. I won't tell you my secret. (not until + a time phrase)
6. She hasn't allowed any misbehavior. (in no case)
7. You may not have access to the files. (under no conditions)
8. I wouldn't trade places with him. (not for a million dollars)

EXERCISE 7

Complete the following with a statement based on your experience or opinions.

1. Not since I was a child . . .
2. Not until I am old and grey . . .
3. Not until years from now . . .
4. Not since I started . . .
5. Nowhere . . .
6. Not for anything . . .

Fronting Structures for Emphasis and Focus | **423**

Exercise 6
E X P A N S I O N

For more practice, ask Ss to create a "warning" that they would put on their bedroom (or dorm room) door using *Under no circumstance should . . .* or *Under no conditions should. . . .* (Another modal verb such as *can* is possible, but include a modal so Ss get practice with inversion rather than writing an imperative statement.)

Exercise 7
S U G G E S T I O N

This would make a good oral activity, but Ss do need time to think of ideas. Give a few responses of your own as a model. If your class/group is small, go around the room for one or two of the items, having each person state the fronted phrase and complete it.

Workbook Ex. 5, p. 242.
Answers: TE p. 560.

A N S W E R   K E Y

Exercise 6
1. Under no circumstances can we let . . .
2. Not once have I missed . . .   3. Not for anything will Homer miss . . .   4. In no way did this change my . . .   5. Not until the end of the week will I tell . . .   6. In no case has she allowed . . .   7. Under no conditions may you have . . .   8. Not for a million dollars would I trade . . .

Exercise 7
Answers will vary.
1. have I played that game   2. will I stop jogging in the park   3. will I be able to graduate   4. learning English have I felt so positive about my progress   5. are there restaurants like they have in Hong Kong
6. would I drop out of school

Two additional grammatical structures that can be fronted are presented here. Have Ss note that both of them require inversion of subject and verb or auxiliary.

SUGGESTIONS

1. Focus on the conjunctions in the second part of the chart since these are more commonly used than fronted noun phrases objects.
2. To practice the form exemplified in (g) and (j):
   Step 1: Give Ss statements orally such as the one in (e) and have them use names of others in the class to respond to. Example: *I don't have time to finish my paper tonight.* (Student A: *Neither does Johan.* Student B: *Nor does Kai.*) Use past as well as present tenses (e.g., *I didn't watch the news last night. Neither did A. Nor did B.*) Tell Ss that the *nor* form is not common in informal American English speech.
   Step 2: If Ss seem to catch on easily, ask them to make up negative statements like the one in (e) for others to respond to.
3. For practice of inversion forms in *not only . . . but also. . .* , write examples on the board for Ss to transform:
   Step 1: Put a topic on the board (e.g., this English class). Ask Ss to give you two reasons, two qualities, two conditions, etc.—whatever would fit the topic (e.g., two reasons this English class is helpful). Write the two phrases or sentences on the board.
   Step 2: Write on the board a sentence modeled after (l). (Note: Example (l) uses emphatic *does*. This sentence could also be expressed without *does,* using *tastes.* For the fronted form, however, *does* + base verb is required.)
   Step 3: Ask Ss to write on scratch paper a "*Not only . . . but also*" sentence modeled after (m). Ask for a volunteer to write the sentence on the board. Discuss any variations.

▶ Fronted Negative Forms: Objects and Conjunctions

As with the negative adverbials in Focus 4, these fronted structures require subject-auxiliary or subject-verb inversion.

Noun Phrase Objects

PHRASE	NOT FRONTED	FRONTED
not + singular noun*	**(a)** The sky was brilliant; he could **not see one cloud** in any direction.	**(b)** The sky was brilliant; **not one cloud** could he see in any direction.
	(c) We will **not** spend **another penny** on your education unless your grades improve.	**(d)** **Not another penny** will we spend on your education unless your grades improve.

*A plural form is possible with *no* (*no clouds could he see*), but the emphasis would not be as strong as with the singular form.

Conjunctions

WORD/ PHRASE	NOT FRONTED	FRONTED
neither, nor	**(e)** I have no idea why the mail didn't come.	
	(f) My mother **doesn't either.**	**(g)** **Neither** does my mother.
	(h) My sister **doesn't either.**	**(i)** **Nor** does my sister.
	(j) **No one** else does **either.**	**(k)** **Neither** does anyone else.
not only (. . . *but also*)	**(l)** Frozen yogurt does **not only** taste good, but it's also good for you.	**(m)** **Not only** does frozen yogurt taste good, but it's also good for you.
no sooner (. . . *than*)	**(n)** The exam had **no sooner** started than we had a fire drill.	**(o)** **No sooner** had the exam started than we had a fire drill.

EXERCISE 8

After each of the following statements, add a sentence using the fronted negative in parentheses.

▶ **EXAMPLE:** The German swimmers did not win any medals at the Olympics. (Nor)
Nor did any swimmers from France or the United States.

1. I tried to do the homework but I couldn't understand the assignment. (neither)

2. I've been working on this math assignment almost the entire night. (not one more minute)

3. The main star of the film could not get along with the director. (nor)

4. I just love to visit large cities. (not only)

5. Look how skinny that model is! (not one ounce of fat)

6. We do not want to buy products from companies who use dishonest advertising. (not another dollar)

7. Leon was sorry he had decided to go sailing. (no sooner)

8. Our art history professor will not accept late papers. (neither)

9. Learning Greek could help you in several ways. (not only)

10. It has been reported that the terrorists will not release their hostages. (nor)

Exercise 8

Assigning this exercise for homework will give you an opportunity to assess individual progress. The forms *neither* and *not only (but also)* are ones Ss may find particularly useful in their writing.

E X P A N S I O N

Have Ss work with a partner in a mock job interview. They can decide what the job is. Ask them to take turns as the interviewee answering the question: *Why should I hire you?* using a fronted negative. Give them an example *(Not only am I responsible but also I am very creative.)*.

Workbook Ex. 6, p. 243.
Answers: TE p. 560.

A N S W E R   K E Y

Exercise 8
Answers will vary. Examples:
1. Neither could any of my friends who are in the class.   2. Not one more minute am I going to spend on it.   3. Nor could some of the other actors.   4. Not only are there lots of things to do but also interesting people to watch.   5. Not one ounce of fat does she have anywhere.   6. Not another dollar will be spent on these products.   7. No sooner had he left the harbor when a storm arose.
8. Neither will he let anyone make up quizzes they miss.   9. Not only would you be able to read Greek classics in the original, but it could help you learn the meanings of English words that have Greek roots, prefixes, and suffixes.
10. Nor will they allow the hostages any to speak to the media.

Tell Ss that the forms here are used mostly in formal English, including literature, to emphasize or show contrasts.

S U G G E S T I O N S

1. Read aloud to hear the rhythms of the sentences.
2. Discuss the differences between examples in the pairs (a) and (b) and (c) and (d) in the use of fronted structures. The first sentences in each pair are identical, but the boldfaced fronted structures have different uses (one emphasis, the other contrast) depending on what information is given in the sentences following them.

FOCUS **6**

▶ Fronted Structures: Emphasizing, Contrasting, and Focusing on Unexpected Information

EXAMPLES	EXPLANATIONS
Emphasis (a) **In the evenings** she writes. It is a time when the house is quiet and peaceful and she can concentrate. **Contrast** (b) **In the evenings** she writes. **The mornings** are devoted to gardening and **the afternoons** to her job at a publishing company. **Emphasis** (c) **On the first floor of the store** are men's clothes. This floor also has luggage. **Contrast** (d) **On the first floor of the store** are men's clothes. **On the second floor** are women's clothes and linens.	**Adverb Phrases** Reasons for fronting: • to emphasize information • to point out contrasts For adverbials of time, place, or frequency, the context determines whether contrast or some other kind of emphasis is intended. The fronting of contrast phrases emphasizes parallel structures. Parallelism of this kind is a stylistic device used to stress ideas and create rhythm.
(e) Who could be at Sara's door at this late hour? Sara squinted through the peephole to see who the mystery caller was. **Participle** **Focus on Subject** **Staring back at her** was her long-lost brother. **Comparative** (f) **More important to me than anything else** **Focus on Subject** is my family.	**Participle Phrases and Comparatives** Reason for fronting: • to emphasize a subject that contains new or unexpected information by moving it to the end of the sentence.

EXAMPLES	EXPLANATIONS
(g) **Never** have I seen such a display of bravery! (h) **Not until the last votes were counted** would the senator admit defeat. (i) **Under no circumstances** may you enter this building after midnight. (j) **Not a single promise** did he make that wasn't eventually broken.	**Negative Structures** Reasons for fronting:* • to emphasize unusual or unexpected actions or events • to stress particular aspects of events or actions • to create strong commands that prohibit actions • to emphasize the "negativeness" of things, events, or actions

*These uses often overlap; a fronted negative may emphasize in several different ways.

EXERCISE 9

State what you think is the main reason for fronting each of the underlined structures. Do you think it is primarily for (1) emphasis of the fronted structure, (2) contrast of the structure, or (3) focus on a delayed subject that contains new or unexpected information?

1. <u>Only when Marta drives</u> does she get nervous. At other times she's quite calm.

2. The phone rang. Howard was sure it was his best friend Miguel calling. Picking up the phone, he shouted, "Yo!" <u>Responding to his greeting</u> was his biology professor.

3. <u>Not since I was in elementary school</u> have I been to the circus. Believe me, that was a long time ago!

4. Welcome to the Little River Inn. We hope you will enjoy your stay here. <u>To your right</u> is a cooler with ice and the soft-drink machines. <u>To your left and around the corner</u> is the swimming pool and jacuzzi.

5. <u>To start this lawnmower,</u> you need to pull the cord very hard and quickly. To keep it going, you should set the lever in the middle.

6. Minh heard a noise coming from underneath his parked car. Getting down on his knees, he looked under the front of it. <u>There, crouched on the right front tire</u> was a tiny kitten.

7. <u>Not until I hear from you</u> will I leave. I promise I'll stay here until then.

8. <u>During the long winters</u> Bonnie does a lot of reading. She loves to lounge by the fire with a good book.

Exercise 9
SUGGESTION

Have Ss discuss reasons in small groups. Afterwards, check to see if the groups agree on reasons and discuss any differences.

ANSWER KEY

Exercise 9
Some answers may vary because uses sometimes overlap.

1. 2   2. 3   3. 1   4. 2   5. 1   6. 3
7. 1   8. 1   9. 3   10. 1

9. The crowd was waiting excitedly to see who would win this year's Boston marathon. <u>A few minutes later, across the finish line</u> came a runner from Kenya.

10. <u>Had I known the movie was so long,</u> I doubt I would have gone to see it. I had no idea that it would last for five hours!

Exercise 10

This exercise has a variety of different error types. Some of them—like (2)—are not ungrammatical but inappropriate because the language use is socially inappropriate.

EXERCISE 10

In each of the students' responses to the teacher's questions below, there is something wrong either with the **form** of the statement or the **use** in context. Identify the problem. Correct errors in form and explain problems with usage.

1. **Teacher:** Meeyung, is it true that you got to see the fireworks during the Statue of Liberty's anniversary celebration?

   Meeyung: Oh yes! Never I have seen such a beautiful display of fireworks!

2. **Teacher:** Alex, the bell rang five minutes ago. Please turn in your exam.

   Alex: Hey, no way am I turning this in.

3. **Teacher:** Wilai, I don't seem to have your homework. Did you turn it in to me?

   Wilai: No, I'm sorry, never have I turned it in.

4. **Teacher:** Javier, did you find that chapter explaining verb tenses helpful?

   Javier: Yes, not only it helped me with present perfect but it also explained conditionals well.

5. **Teacher:** Patrice, I'm really sorry to hear you've been so ill. I hope you're better now.

   Patrice: Thank you. I *was* really sick all month. No sooner I got rid of the flu when I got pneumonia.

6. **Teacher:** Kazuhiko, I could help you after class if you can stay for a while.

   Kazuhiko: I'm sorry. Not for an hour could I stay because I have another class at 4:30.

UNIT GOAL REVIEW

Ask Ss to look at the goals on the opening page of the unit again. Help them understand how much they have accomplished in each area.

ANSWER KEY

Exercise 10
1. *Never have I seen* · · · (Form)   2. *No way* = informal register; inappropriate for context. (Use)   3. Fronted negative not appropriate for this context; *never* shouldn't be emphasized.
4. (Use)   4. *Not only did it help* · · · (Form) · · ·
5. *No sooner did I get rid of the flu* · · · (Form)   6. Fronted negative not appropriate for this use.

Use Your English

USE YOUR ENGLISH

The activities on these "purple pages" at the end of the unit contain situations that should naturally elicit the unit's structures in a more communicative framework. While Ss are doing these activities in class, you can circulate and listen to determine if they have actually achieved the goals on the opening page of the unit.

ACTIVITY 1: LISTENING

In a recent survey, a number of well-known Americans, including authors, media specialists, politicians, and artists, were asked to name movies that they felt defined the American character. You will hear descriptions of two of these films. After you have listened to each description, choose the statement, a or b, which accurately paraphrases an idea in the description.

Pollyanna
  a. Americans have never hated or envied the rich.
  b. Americans have never hated the rich, just envied them.

Mr. Smith Goes to Washington
  a. Political corruption in Washington continues until an innocent man from a small town arrives.
  b. Political corruption in Washington stops before an innocent man from a small town arrives.

Activity 1

Play textbook audio. The tapescript for this listening appears on p. 575 of this book.

SUGGESTIONS

1. Before Ss begin this task, find out if any in the class have seen either of the two films. If so, they could provide brief oral summaries.
2. Discuss briefly the notion of a film defining a country's character.

ACTIVITY 2: WRITING/SPEAKING

Make a list of some things you believe you would **never** do under any circumstances. For emphasis, start your statements with a negative word or phrase. Then share your list with one or more classmates to see if they also would never do the things on your list, and have them discuss their lists with you. Finally, write a summary of your discussion, pointing out your similarities and differences on this topic.

▶ **EXAMPLES:** *Under no circumstances would I take an advanced course in physics.*

No way would I ever eat squid. (informal usage)

Activity 2

To make this activity more interactive, Ss can mingle and try to compare their statements with as many Ss as possible within a given time frame.

Workbook Ex. 7, p. 244 Ex. 8, p. 245.
Answers: TE p. 560.

Fronting Structures for Emphasis and Focus | **429**

ANSWER KEY

Activity 1
Pollyanna: b
Mr. Smith Goes to Washington: a

Activity 3

VARIATION

Ss could rewrite an advertisement from a web page using fronted negatives.

Activity 4

VARIATION

This activity could be constructed as a guessing game:

Step 1: Ss write a brief description of a place (a room, a building, a park, part of the campus, an area of a city, etc.) using fronted adverbials. The place should be one that they think everyone knows. In their description they should not state what the place is. For example, they could start: *As you walk into this building./If you are on this street/When you get to this part of the campus*, etc.

Step 2: Ss read their descriptions to classmates in a small group. The group tries to guess the places.

ACTIVITY 3: WRITING/SPEAKING

Advertisements and commercials often use strong claims to sell products. Imagine that you are a copywriter for an ad agency. Team up with another classmate. With your partner, choose a product (one that already exists or make one up) to sell; write an advertisement for either print media (magazine, newspaper), radio, or television. In your ad, use at least two fronted structures to emphasize something about your product. Present your ad/commercial to the class, and give them a chance to discuss your claims.

ACTIVITY 4: WRITING

Write a paragraph in which you describe one of the following:

• the contents of a room as someone might see the room upon entering it.

• a machine or appliance with a number of parts.

Use some fronted adverbials of position for contrast or emphasis in your description.

▶ **EXAMPLES:** As you come into the living room, there is a large chintz sofa. In front of the sofa is a maple coffee table. To the left of it is an end table that matches the coffee table, and to the right stands a bookcase. On top of the bookcase sits my favorite vase. It's a deep turquoise blue.

The parts of my computer include the monitor, the printer, the computer itself, and the control panel. On the control panel are four switches. To the far left is the switch for the computer. Next to it is the switch for the monitor. To the right of the monitor switch is the one for the printer.

ACTIVITY 5: SPEAKING

With a partner or in a small group, describe an event that affected you strongly; for example, a time when you were especially happy, excited, angry, frightened, surprised, etc. Use a fronted structure, such as a comparative, to emphasize the way you felt.

ACTIVITY 6: WRITING

Write a review or synopsis of a book, television show, or movie that you especially liked or disliked. Use some fronted structures for emphasis, contrast, or focus.

Activity 5
SUGGESTIONS

1. Have Ss think of a topic and what they might say about it as a homework assignment. Many Ss may find it difficult to come up with a fronted structure spontaneously in conversation if they have not used them very often.
2. Give Ss an example or two of phrases that might precede fronted negatives in informal contexts so that they will sound more natural. Some examples: *Listen, I'll tell you, never have I been surprised as when I walked into the house and my all my friends were there for my birthday. Let me tell you, never was I so frightened as when I saw that movie "The Blair Witch Project."*

Activity 6
SUGGESTIONS

1. Create a booklet of the reviews and synopses and give copies to the class to read.
2. If your class has a website, have them post the reviews and synopses on the web so that classmates can respond to them.

The test for this unit can be found on p. 532. Answers are on p. 533.

Unit 25

UNIT OVERVIEW

This unit covers two types of structures that are used to emphasize information in English. The focus boxes for these units begin with a focus on the forms, followed by the contexts for use. *It*-clefts are most often used in writing and formal speech situations, though they also occur in less formal speech. *Wh*-clefts are more common in speech, both informal and formal.

UNIT GOALS

Review the goals listed on this page so students (Ss) understand what they should be able to know by the end of the unit.

OPENING TASK

This task asks Ss to match statements about personality traits with particular birth orders: oldest, middle, youngest, or only child. *It*-cleft structures are prompted in the sample answers, given in Step 2.

SETTING UP THE TASK

To get Ss engaged in the topic of the task, take a quick class poll to find out how the class members fall into the various birth orders.

UNIT 25

FOCUSING AND EMPHASIZING STRUCTURES

It-Clefts and Wh-Clefts

UNIT GOALS:

- To use *it*-cleft sentences to put special emphasis on information
- To know what parts of a sentence can be used for focus in *it*-clefts
- To know how to use other kinds of cleft sentences for questions and statements
- To use *wh*-clefts to put focus on information at the end of sentences

OPENING TASK
How Does Birth Order Influence Personality?

You may have at times judged someone's behavior according to their position in a family as the oldest, youngest, middle, or only child. For example, you might have considered a friend's "take charge" attitude as characteristic of an oldest child or a brother's or sister's "spoiled" behavior the result of being the youngest. If you are an only child, you may have heard the generalization that only children are very confident.

STEP 1 Read the following observations about personality traits associated with particular birth orders that were made by two clinical psychologists.

Personality Traits Associated with Birth Orders

(a) tends to be self-critical and perfectionist

(b) is often the most secretive

(c) is usually very comfortable with older people

(d) tends to be skilled at defending himself or herself

(e) may sometimes try to be all things to all people

(f) as a child, may find others of the same age immature

(g) often feels most obligated to follow the family rules and routines

(h) may be confused about self-image as a result of being simultaneously welcomed, adored, bossed around, and disliked by siblings

(i) tends to be the most conservative

(j) is typically self-sufficient

(k) often subject to self-doubt due to not being taken seriously by family members

(l) may often feel like a "fifth wheel" (a feeling of not belonging or being an "extra")

From: Bradford Wilson and George Edington, *First Child, Second Child* . . . . New York: McGraw-Hill, 1981.

STEP 2 Based on your knowledge of your family members personalities (including yours) and the personalities of friends whose birth order you know, guess which order each trait characterizes: the only child, the oldest child, the middle child, or the youngest child. Here are answers to (a) and (b):

(a) *It's the oldest child who's often the most self-critical and perfectionist.*

(b) *It's the middle child who tends to be secretive.*

STEP 3 After you have guessed a birth order for each trait, briefly discuss your choices in small groups.

STEP 4 As a class, share results of your group discussions: Which ones did you most often agree about? Which resulted in the most differing guesses?

STEP 5 Check the answers to this task on page A-16. Comment on ones that surprised you the most.

▶ **EXAMPLE:** *What surprised me the most is that the middle child is often secretive. My brother's girlfriend is a middle child and she tells everyone about everything!*

Step 1

VARIATION

Have Ss form groups for this step and Step 2 rather than doing them individually.

Step 3 and 4

In this part of the task Ss guess which traits in Step 1 are associated with different birth orders and discuss the reasons for their choices.

SUGGESTION

If you found out your Ss' birth orders before beginning the task, use this information to group Ss for these steps. Having a range of the different birth orders in each group will make discussion more lively.

Step 5

This last step prompts statements using *Wh*-clefts.

SUGGESTION

To prompt *wh*-clefts with other phrases besides the one in the example, start with one of your own observations: *What I thought was the most surprising was.* . . . You could also ask Ss if there were any statements that they wondered about, prompting statements beginning with: *What I wondered about was.* . . . Again, offer an example of your own: *What I wondered about was why the middle child would feel like a "fifth wheel".*

Ss will most likely be familiar with the form of *it*-clefts but may not use them productively or may use them with a limited range of focus elements.

S U G G E S T I O N S

1. To practice the form of *it*-cleft sentences, review the personality traits and birth orders in the task. Tell Ss you are going to make some statements about the traits associated with birth orders and to correct you if you make any statements that are untrue according to the psychologists' observation. Start with a "true" statement (e.g., *The youngest child may be confused about self-image*.)

2. Then give a series of "false" statements and have Ss correct them. Write *it*-cleft sentences on the board expressing "true" statements under the appropriate category.
   Example: *The oldest child tends to be the most secretive.* (Not true.) Correction: *It is the middle child who tends to be the most conservative.*

Exercise 1

This exercise can be done orally or as homework. Ss will use the Opening Task information to complete it.

FOCUS **1**

Structure of *It*-Cleft Sentences

EXAMPLES		EXPLANATION
(a) **No Special Emphasis:** My brother is conservative, not me. (b) **Emphasis: It is my brother** who is conservative, not me!		*It*-cleft sentences put special emphasis on one part of a sentence. The part that is emphasized is introduced by it and a form of *be*.
Focus Element (c) It is the youngest child **Sing. Plural** (d) It **is** oldest children and only children **Future** (e) It **will be** on a Saturday **Past** (f) It **used to be** my mother	**Clause** who is often both a rebel a charmer. who tend to be the most assertive. that we leave, not a Sunday. who did all the cooking, but now we all help.	"Cleft" means to divide. The cleft sentence divides a sentence into two parts: (1) a focus element and (2) a clause beginning with *that, who, when, or where.* The verb is singular even when the focus element is plural. The *be* verb is usually present tense. However, we also use other tenses.
(g) It **must** be red wine (h) It **can't** be the youngest child	that stained this carpet. who is the most conservative.	We can use modal verbs in cleft sentences to express degrees of probability.

EXERCISE 1

Complete each blank below with a word or phrase that fits the context.

1. It couldn't be _____ who are confused about self-image because they don't have any siblings.

2. I think it must be _____ who often has the self-image problem because the older ones might have mixed feelings about the baby of the family.

3. It might be _____ who is generally self-sufficient because as a child he or she might have had to do a lot of things alone.

A N S W E R   K E Y

Exercise 1
1. only children   2. the youngest child   3. the only child   4. it is   5. the youngest child   6. it is only children

4. Psychologists Wilson and Edington claim that, of all birth order positions, _____ the middle child who is apt to be the most popular among other people.

5. The two psychologists say it is _____ who may be fearless and have a strong sense of exploration because that child often feels protected by older siblings.

6. They have also observed that _____ who tend to have difficulty dealing with interruptions from others because they did not have brothers or sisters who interrupted them.

This chart provides an overview of the different parts of a sentence that we can put focus on in *it*-cleft sentences.

SUGGESTION

As a homework assignment, ask Ss to read the examples and note structures.

Ss do not have to remember the grammatical labels for the various structures, but they should get a feeling for the different ways we can focus information by fronting with introductory *it*. They should also be aware that these structures create special focus on information and are not just arbitrary restructurings of sentences to achieve "sentence variety."

Workbook Ex. 1, p. 247; Ex. 2, p. 248.
Answers: TE p. 561.

Focus Elements in Cleft Sentences

We can focus on various parts of a sentence in the focus element of cleft sentences.

CLEFT SENTENCE	FOCUS	ORIGINAL SENTENCE
(a) It is **the President** who appoints the cabinet.	Subject	The President appoints the cabinet.
(b) It is **the cabinet** that the President appoints.	Direct object	
(c) It is **the Speaker of the House** with whom the President often disagrees. (formal)	Object of preposition	The President often disagrees with the Speaker of the House.
(d) It is **the Speaker of the House** that the President often disagrees with. (less formal)		
(e) It was **an awful shade of yellow** that they painted the Oval Office.	Complement (noun)	They painted the Oval Office an awful shade of yellow.
(f) It was **greenish yellow** that they painted it.	Complement (adjective)	They painted it greenish yellow.
(g) It was **due to illness** that the Vice-President resigned.	Prepositional phrase	The Vice-President resigned due to illness.
(h) It was **after World War II ended** that the baby boom began in the United States.	Dependent clause	The baby boom began in the United States after World War II ended.
(i) It was **to ensure the right of women to vote** that the Twelfth Amendment to the Constitution was passed.	Infinitive or Infinitive clause	The Twelfth Amendment to the Constitution was passed to ensure the right of women to vote.

EXERCISE 2

Restate the following sentences about the United States civil rights movement of the 1960s to emphasize the information indicated in parentheses. Change any other wording as necessary.

▶ **EXAMPLE:** Black students staged the first sit-in at a lunch counter in Greensboro, North Carolina, in 1960. (Emphasize the date)

It was in 1960 that black students staged the first sit-in at a lunch counter in Greensboro, North Carolina.

1. White and black civil rights workers sat together in "white only" sections of restaurants and other public places to protest segregation. (Emphasize the purpose.)

2. In 1962, President Kennedy sent United States marshalls to protect James H. Meredith, the first black student at the University of Mississippi. (Emphasize the place.)

3. The civil rights movement reached a climax in 1963 with the march on Washington. (Emphasize the event.)

4. Martin Luther King, Jr., delivered his famous "I Have a Dream" speech during the march on Washington. (Emphasize the speech.)

5. Three young civil rights workers were tragically murdered in Mississippi on June 22, 1964. (Emphasize the date.)

6. Martin Luther King, Jr., led civil rights marches in Selma, Alabama, and Montgomery, Mississippi, in 1965. (Emphasize the places.)

7. King was assassinated by James Earl Ray in Memphis, Tennessee, in 1968. (Emphasize the assassin.)

8. We now celebrate the achievements of this great civil rights leader in January. (Emphasize the month.)

EXERCISE 3

Imagine that each of the situations below is true. Provide an explanation, either serious or humorous, emphasizing the reason.

▶ **EXAMPLE:** You were late to class yesterday.

It was because the bus didn't come that I was late to class.

1. You didn't have an assignment done that was due.

2. You missed a medical appointment.

3. You forgot a relative's birthday. (You choose the relative.)

4. You didn't eat anything for two days.

5. You stumbled and fell crossing the street.

Focusing and Emphasizing Structures: It-Clefts and Wh-Clefts **437**

Exercise 2

Since the content of this exercise can be considered an academic topic, having Ss write the answers will give them practice with academic writing skills.

Exercise 3
S U G G E S T I O N S

1. Provide more models before Ss work on this exercise by asking the class to brainstorm more responses for the example (either serious or humorous).

2. Have Ss do this exercise orally in small groups, with each group brainstorming two or three examples for each item. Ask Ss to share some of their explanations with the class.

Workbook Ex. 3, p. 249.
Answers: TE p. 561.

ANSWER KEY

Exercise 2
1. It was to protest segregation that . . .
2. It was to the University of Mississippi that . . .   3. It was with the march that . . .
4. It was the famous "I Have A Dream" . . .
5. It was on June 22, 1964, that three . . .
6. It was in Selma, Alabama, and Montgomery, Mississippi, that Martin . . .   7. It was James Earl Ray who . . .   8. It is in January that we . . .

Exercise 3
Answers will vary. Examples:
1. It was because someone stole my notebook that I don't have my assignment.   2. It was because I overslept that I missed . . .   3. It was because I was so busy that I forgot . . .
4. It was because I was ill that I didn't . . .
5. It was because the street was icy that I stumbled . . .

FOCUS 3

This focus box shows several uses of *it*-clefts in communicative situations.

SUGGESTIONS

1. To explain further the use of *only* with a focus element, write a few global or local problems on the board, such as *poverty* or *violent crime*. Give an example of a necessary step to address the problem: *It is only education that can make a big difference in the poverty level.* Ask Ss to identify key solutions to other problems.

2. To form *it*-cleft purpose statements, ask Ss to give you reasons for choices they have made: *Leo, why did you decide to major in computer science?* Purpose statements can be expressed with prepositional phrases as in (f) and (g), with infinitive clauses (*It was to prepare myself for a good job that I majored in computer science*) or with *because*-clauses (*It was because I have always loved to work with computers . . .*). Call Ss' attention to the *that*-clause structures after the introductory element.

Exercise 4
SUGGESTIONS

1. Conduct this as a whole class exercise. Ask one student a question for the first item (*Nicholas, which of your family members or friends tends to watch the most TV?*). Write the question on the board if you think Ss need it to model the phrasing of the first part. After the student has responded with a cleft sentence, have him or her call on another student. Repeat the procedure with the second student calling on a third, etc.

2. If you want Ss to focus on skills in paraphrasing information (restating part of the original phrase in their own words), ask them to write answers as homework. Model one or two more items in class, focusing on paraphrase (e.g., *tends to watch the most TV —> usually spends a lot of time watching TV /is the biggest "couch potato"; has the best sense of humor —> is the funniest person I know*).

It-Clefts in Spoken and Written Communication

EXAMPLES	EXPLANATIONS
(a) **It is the middle child** who is most secretive. (The middle child is distinguished from the eldest and youngest children.)	**Distinguish Member of a Group** *It*-cleft sentences can distinguish one member of a group as having certain qualities.
(b) **It is only love** that can bring world peace. (Love is the only thing that can bring world peace.) **(c)** **It is only my best friend** who can cheer me up when I'm down. (My best friend is the only person who can cheer me up.)	In some cases the "group" may include all other things or people. We use *only* before the focus element to convey this meaning.
(d) A: I think the youngest child is the one who tends to be secretive. B: I don't agree. **It's the middle child,** I think, who is most secretive. **(e)** What color paint is this? **It was blue** that I ordered, not green!	**Express Contrast** We sometimes use cleft sentences to point out a contrast or to note something that is commonly believed but not true. In spoken English, the contrasting word or phrase receives extra stress. In (e), *blue* is stressed because it contrasts with *green*.
(f) **It was out of concern** that we called our neighbor to see if she was all right. **(g)** **It was for a general education requirement** that I took art history.	**Emphasize Purpose or Cause** *It*-clefts can also emphasize the purpose or cause of something. These often include prepositional phrases beginning with *out of* or *for*.

EXERCISE 4

Which person in your family or circle of friends best matches the following descriptions? In your response, use a cleft sentence beginning with *it is* (or *it's*). Also, try to paraphrase (put in your own words) the description.

▶ **EXAMPLE:** would be most likely to complain about young people's behavior

It's my grandmother who would be most likely to complain about the way young people act.

1. tends to watch the most TV
2. has the best sense of humor

ANSWER KEY

Exercise 4
Answers will vary. Examples:
1. It's my sister who tends to be a frequent TV watcher   2. It is my friend Juan who is the funniest.   3. It's I (or *me*, informally) who would be most likely to do that.   4. It's my brother Nima who can't get up.   5. It's my mother who is most talented in art.   6. It's my friend Sophia who would help out immediately.   7. It's my cousin who most often makes excuses for not doing housework.   8. It's my aunt who most like talking about other persons.

---

3. would be most likely to park a car and forget where it was

4. has the most trouble getting up in the morning

5. is the most artistic

6. would be most likely to stop and help if he or she saw someone in trouble

7. most often tries to get out of doing housework

8. most enjoys gossiping

EXERCISE 5

Complete each blank by choosing a word from the list below for a focus element and creating a cleft sentence. The first has been done as an example.

anger   music
curiosity   pride
faith   a sense of humor

1. ___It was anger___ that made God banish Adam and Eve from the Garden of Eden, according to the Judeo-Christian Bible.

2. _____ that often keeps us from admitting our mistakes.

3. _____ that caused Pandora's downfall in the Greek myth; she had to find out what was in the box.

4. _____ that has been called the language of the soul.

5. _____ that keeps most of us from taking ourselves too seriously and helps us to deal with the ups and downs of life.

6. _____ that has helped many people withstand religious persecution.

Exercise 6

Imagine you have been asked to edit a reference book for errors. Unfortunately, much of the book turns out to be a collection of misinformation. As you read each "fact" below, identify the incorrect part. Write a sentence indicating what needs to be corrected, using a cleft sentence to highlight that element.

▶ **EXAMPLE:** Mark Twain wrote the classic novel *Huckleberry Flan* in 1884.

Correction: *It is **Huckleberry Finn** that Mark Twain wrote.*

1. The United States Congress first began meeting in Washington State in 1800.

2. New York City has two baseball teams: the Mets and the New York Blue Jays.

Exercise 5

If needed, briefly explain the cultural references in this exercise (Adam and Eve, Garden of Eden, Bible, Pandora).

Exercise 6
SUGGESTION

This content-based exercise requires some cultural knowledge. If you have Ss who may not be familiar with some of the facts, consider: (1) eliminating those items that could be problematic (e.g., 2); (2) highlighting the part that is false as a clue (e.g., *State* in 1); (3) having Ss work in groups; (4) having Ss use reference books or the Internet to research the information.

ANSWER KEY

Exercise 5
2. It is pride **3.** It was curiosity **4.** It is music **5.** It is a sense of humor **6.** It is faith

Exercise 6
1. It was in Washington, DC, that Congress met in 1800. **2.** It is the Yankees and the Mets that are New York City teams. **3.** It is Shakespeare, not Moliere, who wrote *Romeo and Juliet*. **4.** It was America to which Columbus sailed in 1492./It was America that Christopher Columbus sailed to in 1492./It was to America that . . . **5.** It was the moon that the United States astronauts first landed on in 1969./It was on the moon that . . . **6.** It was in China that Kublai Khan founded the Yuan dynasty. **7.** It was the famous *Mona Lisa* that Leonardo da Vinci painted. **8.** It is the body's nervous system that these are parts of. **9.** It was Egypt that Nefertiti ruled.

3. One of the most famous tragedies of all times, *Romeo and Juliet* was written by Moliere in 1595.

4. Christopher Columbus sailed to India in 1492.

5. United States astronauts first landed on Mars in 1969.

6. In 1260 Kublai Khan founded the Yuan dynasty in Japan.

7. Leonardo da Vinci painted the famous *Moaning Lisa* around 1500.

8. The brain, the spinal cord, and the nerves are parts of the body's digestive system.

9. Nefertiti ruled India along with her husband King Akhenaton during the 14th century B.C.

EXERCISE 7

STEP 1 Make lists of your four favorite foods, your four favorite movies (or TV programs), and your four favorite school subjects.

STEP 2 To indicate which item ranks highest in each of the three lists, fill in the blanks of the sentences below. Share one of your responses with classmates.

1. I love to eat _____ , _____ , and _____ . But it is _____ that I would choose if I had to eat only one food for a week.

2. I could watch _____ , _____ , and _____ quite a few times, but it is _____ that _____ .

3. I enjoy _____ , I like to study _____ , and I also like _____. However, if _____ , it is _____ that I would choose.

STEP 3 Make up another list of four favorite things of some other category (e.g., books, sports). Then write a sentence using the pattern in step 2.

Exercise 7

Ask Ss to share some of their responses with a partner or group.

V A R I A T I O N

For Step 3 Ss could create a sentence with blanks modeled after those in Step 2 and give to a classmate to complete.

Workbook Ex. 4, p. 250; Ex. 5. p. 251; Exs. 6 & 7, p. 252–253. Answers: TE p. 561.

It-Clefts: Emphasizing Time, Place, and Characters

EXAMPLES	EXPLANATION
(a) It was **in the early spring** that Sylvia finally felt well enough to make the trip to Budapest. (b) It was **on a cold day in February, 1860,** that Abraham Lincoln delivered his eloquent Cooper Union speech against slavery. (c) It was **in Barbizon** that Rousseau founded the modern school of French landscape painting. (d) It was **Shakespeare** who inspired Beethoven's creation of his String Quartet opus 18, number 1.	In narratives such as stories or historical accounts, we may use cleft sentences to emphasize the time, place, characters (or real people) in the narrative.

The emphases shown here are often used as stylistic devices in writing and formal speech for both fiction and nonfiction.

S U G G E S T I O N

If possible, find some authentic examples of this emphatic use in novels or historical narratives.

Exercise 8

VARIATION

As an oral activity, you could call on Ss to focus on different features of the same item: *Hans, make a statement about Machiavelli, focusing on the date. Jenny, make another statement focusing on the event.*

Workbook Ex. 8, p. 253; Ex. 9, p. 255; Ex. 10, p. 256.
Answers: TE p. 561.

EXERCISE 8

Choose one feature to highlight in the following historical facts and write an introductory sentence for a historical narrative about each.

▶ **EXAMPLES:** ***It was Cheops*** *who started building the pyramids in Egypt around* 2700 B.C. (Emphasizes person)

It was around *2700 B.C.* *that Cheops began building the pyramids in Egypt.* (Emphasizes date)

Person	Date	Place	Event
Cheops (king)	around 2700 B.C.	Egypt	started building the Pyramids
Machiavelli (statesman)	1513	Florence, Italy	accused of conspiracy
John James Audubon (artist)	April 26, 1785	Cayes, Santo Domingo	born
Emily Dickinson (poet) (poet)	1862	Amherst, Massachusetts	began correspondence with Thomas Wentworth Higgins
Joaquium Machado de Assis (writer)	1869	Rio de Janeiro, Brazil	married Portuguese aristocrat, Carolina de Novaes
Jean Sibelius (composer)	1892	Helsinki, Finland	wrote the symphonic poem "Kullervo"
Aung San Suu Kyi	1991	Mynamar	received word that she had won the Nobel Prize

ANSWER KEY

Exercise 8

Answers will vary. Examples:
It was in Florence, Italy, that Machiavelli was accused of conspiracy.   It was on April 26, 1785, that John James Audubon was born in Cayes, Santo Domingo.   It was Thomas Wentworth Higgins with whom Emily Dickinson began to correspond in 1862.   It was Carolina de Novaes whom Joaquium Machado de Assis married in Rio de Janeiro in 1869.   It was in Helsinki, Finland, that Jean Sibelius wrote the symphonic poem "Kullervo" in 1892.   It was in 1991 that Aung San Suu Kyi received word that she had won the Nobel Prize.

FOCUS 5

Other Forms of Cleft Sentences

EXAMPLES	EXPLANATIONS
(a) **Who was it** that gave you that information? (b) **Why was it** (that) they decided to move? (c) **When was it** (that) you left Shanghai?	***Wh*-Cleft Questions** In *Wh*-questions, *it* and *be* are inverted, changing the order to *be* + *it* after the question word (question word + *be* + *it*). In examples (b) and (c), *that* is in parentheses because it is optional.
(d) **Was it out of pity** (that) he let the old man move into his house? (e) **Is it Spanish 3** (that) you're taking this quarter?	***Yes-No* Cleft Questions** We must also invert *it* and *be* in *yes-no* questions.
(f) **What a nice essay it was** (that) you wrote about your father!	***What a* + Noun Phrase** This type of cleft sentence (*What a* + noun phrase + *it* + *be*) expresses wonder, delight, admiration, or surprise.
(g) I told you before (that) **it was Marsha who called you**, not Marianne. (h) The President announced (that) **it was because he was ill that he would not be seeking re-election.**	**That Clauses** As you have seen in some exercises in this unit, focus elements may be that clauses in reported speech.

EXERCISE 9

Make up a cleft sentence for each situation that follows to emphasize some piece of information.

▶ **EXAMPLE:** You told a friend that *Braveheart* was going to be on TV on Monday night. He thought you said Tuesday and missed seeing it. Tell him what you said.

I told you it was on Monday night that it was going to be on, not Tuesday!

1. You're not sure why a customer service representative at a bank wanted to know your place of birth for a checking account application you were filling out. Ask him.

This focus box shows a variety of other emphatic forms.

SUGGESTIONS

1. Elicit the nonemphatic forms for (a), (b), and (c), so Ss can see how these forms differ and how they are constructed. (*Who gave you that information? Why did they decide to move? When did you leave Shanghai?*)
Note that in (c), *that* after *who was it* is not a complementizer *that* like the ones in parentheses in (b) and (c). It is a relative pronoun (substituting for *who*) and serves as the subject of *gave*. Therefore, it is not optional in formal English though speakers might delete it in informal contexts.

2. Ask Ss questions to elicit yes/no answers like those in the second section: *Tanya, is it in 2005 that you'll be finishing your degree?*

Exercise 9
EXPANSION

Ask Ss to role play some of the situations for the rest of the class.

Workbook Ex. 11, pp. 256–257.
Answers: TE p. 562.

ANSWER KEY

Exercise 9
Answers will vary. Examples:
1. I'm not sure why it is that you want to know where I was born.   2. What a great speech it was that you gave the other day!   3. Could you please tell me again when it was that the Manchu Dynasty ended?   4. They said it was because the engine failed that the plane crashed.   5. Who was it that you were on the phone with so long?

2. You want to compliment a classmate on a great speech that she gave in class the day before.

3. You've been listening to a history lecture about China and missed hearing the date when the Chinese revolution ended the Manchu dynasty. Politely ask your instructor to tell you the date again.

4. You and your family are watching the news. The newscaster has just announced the cause of a major plane crash to have been an engine failure. A member of your family was distracted and didn't hear this information. Tell him or her what the newscaster said.

5. You have been trying to call a close friend for three hours, but the line has been busy. You wonder who she could be on the line with. When you finally get through, you ask her.

Wh-Clefts

EXAMPLES	EXPLANATIONS
(a) What the world needs **is peace and justice.** **(b)** What we want **is a woman in the White House.**	Unlike *it*-clefts, *wh*-clefts put focus on information at the end of the sentence.
Assumption **Be** **Focus** **(c)** **Where** he goes **is** a mystery to me. **(d)** **What** Barbara Tomas **is** honesty and compassion. **(e)** What she is **is** a brilliant politician.	The assumption (what we already know or understand) is introduced by a *wh*-word. The focus adds new information. A form of *be* links the two parts of the sentence. When the sentence has two *be* verbs, the second *be* links the two parts. In spoken English, the first *be* verb would be stressed and followed by a pause. (What she *is* is . . .)

EXERCISE 10

Match the phrases in column A with the appropriate word or phrase from column B. Connect them with an appropriate form of *be* and write complete sentences. The first has been done as an example.

▶ **EXAMPLE:** 1. *What a lepidopterist specializes in **is** the study of moths and butterflies.*

A
1. What a lepidopterist specializes in
2. What Florida produces
3. What Alexander Graham Bell invented
4. What Martin Luther King, Jr., believed in
5. Where the United States President lives
6. Where the capital of South Korea is
7. What "mph" means
8. Where the Pyramids are located
9. What Brazilians speak
10. What most Americans eat at Thanksgiving
11. What Jimmy Carter was

B
turkey
Seoul
Portuguese
the study of moths and butterflies
in Egypt
the 39th President
racial equality
in the White House
citrus fruit
the telephone
miles per hour

The important distinction here in comparison to *it*-clefts is that these structures focus on information at the end of sentences. The *it*-cleft constructions did the opposite, moving information to the front of sentences for emphasis.

SUGGESTIONS

1. Write several other non-cleft statements on the board and have Ss transform them into *wh*-clefts: *We want a fair minimum wage for everyone. We need more places for students to study quietly on our campus. We know that global warming may become a serious problem.*
2. Write two categories on the board: *What we want* and *What we need.* Ask Ss to help you make up sentences to express changes that they would like to see or that they think are needed in your program or on your campus.

Note that the *be* verb must agree in number with what follows.

Workbook Ex. 12, p. 258.
Answers: TE p. 562.

ANSWER KEY

Exercise 10
1. is the study of moths and butterflies
2. is citrus fruit **3.** is the telephone
4. is racial equality **5.** is in the White House
6. is Seoul **7.** is miles per hour **8.** is in Egypt **9.** is Portuguese **10.** is turkey
11. was the 39th President

This focus box illustrates the connections that *wh*-clefts often make to something another speaker has said.

SUGGESTIONS

Make up a number of false statements on slips of paper such as the one in example (b) (*Mozart wrote plays*). Make up ones that Ss can easily correct (for example, *We are now learning about gerunds and infinitives.*) Put the slips in a box and have individual Ss or groups draw them one by one and respond with a *wh*-cleft correction modeled after the answer in (b).

Exercise 11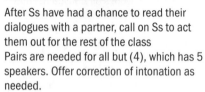

After Ss have had a chance to read their dialogues with a partner, call on Ss to act them out for the rest of the class
Pairs are needed for all but (4), which has 5 speakers. Offer correction of intonation as needed.

Workbook Ex.13, p. 259.
Answers: TE p. 562.

UNIT GOAL REVIEW

Ask Ss to look at the goals on the opening page of the unit again. Help them understand how much they have accomplished in each area

---

Using *Wh*-Clefts for Emphasis

EXAMPLES	EXPLANATION
(a) A: How much money does the director earn? B: **What she earns** is none of your business! **(b)** A: Mozart wrote plays. B: Actually, **what Mozart wrote** was music. Perhaps you mean Moliere.	*Wh*-clefts are more common in spoken English than in written English. The *Wh*-phrase often refers to a statement or idea that has been previously expressed.

EXERCISE 11

Rewrite the underlined words using a *Wh*-cleft. Then act out the conversations with a partner, using appropriate emphasis. The first has been done as an example, with the emphasis in italics.

1. **Matt:** Henry drives a Porsche.
   David: Are you kidding? <u>He drives a Ford.</u>
   Matt: Really? He told me it was a Porsche.

   EXAMPLE: *Wh*-cleft: *What he drives is a* **Ford.**

2. **Frank:** Margo tells me you're a painter.
   Duane: That's right.
   Frank: Do you sell many of your paintings?
   Duane: Well, actually, <u>I paint houses.</u>

3. **Nick:** I'm tired. I think I'm going to take a nap.
   Lisa: Nick, <u>you need some exercise.</u> That will make you feel much better than a nap, I think.

4. **Teacher:** Do you have any suggestions about how we can improve this class?
   Fusako: <u>We'd like less homework.</u>
   Ricardo: <u>And we'd prefer a test every week.</u>
   Soraya: <u>And I need more grammar to pass my writing exam.</u>
   Bernadine: <u>And I'd like a different textbook.</u> This one isn't very challenging.

5. **Howard:** Do you know Barry? He writes novels.
   Tessa: I don't think that's true. <u>He writes instruction manuals for computer programs.</u>

6. **Lia:** What are you getting Carol and Bart for their wedding?
   Shelley: <u>They'd really like a microwave,</u> but I can't afford it, so I'm getting them a coffee grinder.

ANSWER KEY

Exercise 11
2. . . . what I paint is houses 3. Nick, what you need is . . . 4. What we'd like is less... And what we'd prefer is . . . And what I need is . . . And what I'd like is . . . 5. What he writes is . . . 6. What they'd really like . . .

Use Your English

USE YOUR ENGLISH

The activities on these "purple pages" at the end of the unit contain situations that should naturally elicit the unit's structures in a more communicative framework. While Ss are doing these activities in class, you can circulate and listen to determine if they have actually achieved the goals on the opening page of the unit.

ACTIVITY 1: LISTENING/SPEAKING

Divide the class into two or three teams for a quiz show competition. On the tape you will hear questions followed by a choice of three answers. After each question and possible answers, the teacher will stop the tape. Teams will take turns giving answers, which must be in the form of a cleft sentence. For each correct answer, a team will receive two points. Both the answer and the form must be correct to be awarded the points.

▶ **EXAMPLES:** Who was president before Bill Clinton?
(a) Jimmy Carter   (b) George Bush   (c) Ronald Reagan
Correct answer: *It was George Bush who was president before Clinton.*

What does a baseball player get when he or she hits a ball out of the park?
(a) an out   (b) a triple   (c) a home run
Correct answer: *What the player gets is a home run.*

Activity 1

Play textbook audio. The tapescript for this listening appears on pp. 575–576 of this book.

VARIATION

If you prefer not to have a team game, have Ss write answers individually on a separate piece of paper.

ACTIVITY 2: WRITING/SPEAKING

Make up five descriptions that could be used for members of your class. Write your descriptions as verb phrases, similar to Exercise 1. (Be careful not to write any descriptions that would offend anyone or hurt someone's feelings!) Write down who you think best fits the description. Take turns reading your descriptions and have classmates say who they think matches each, using a cleft sentence. Then tell them whether you agree or disagree. Here are a few examples to get you started:

▶ **EXAMPLE:** A: *Tells the funniest stories*
B: *I think it's Josef who does that.*
A: *I agree.*

Activity 2

VARIATION

Ss could write their descriptions with a partner or in a small group.

ANSWER KEY

Activity 1

1. **c** It is green that you get when you mix . . .
2. **c** It is in an ocean that you would . . .
3. **b** It was Beethoven who wrote that symphony.   4. **a** It is Seattle that is most . . .
5. **c** It is the diaphragm that separates . . .
6. **b** It is in hockey that . . .   7. **a** It was Martin Luther King, Jr., who . . .   8. **c** It is osteoporosis that . . .   9. **b** It is acrophobia that . . .   10. **c** It is "mass" that "m" stands for . . .   11. **c** It was Thomas Edison who . . .
12. **b** It is "West Side Story" that . . .   13. **c** It is the heart that the term . . .   14. **a** It is the American National Anthem that . . .   15. **b** It is intelligence quotient that the . . .   16. **a** It is the beginning of the play that you read.
17. **b** It is in the game Monopoly that . . .
18. **a** It is a saxophone that . . .   19. **b** It is geology that you would study . . .   20. **c** It is in South America that . . .

Activity 3

Ask Ss to include a cleft statement in their paragraph other than the one given in the directions.

Activity 4

Explain that the process here is a brainstorming one (making a list and then choosing from the list). This is a helpful procedure for generating ideas for writing assignments.

VARIATION

Have Ss give a brief oral summary using cleft sentences to a small group on their topic either in addition to or instead of writing a paragraph.

Activity 5

Use these paragraphs to assess Ss ability to use cleft sentences productively.

Activity 6

VARIATION

Ss could also write about a good friend instead of a family member.

The test for this unit can be found on p. 534. Answers are on p. 535.

TOEFL Test Preparation Exercises for Units 22–25 can be found on pp. 260–262 of the Workbook.
The answers are on p. 562 of this book.

ACTIVITY 3: WRITING

People who are against the government's controlling the sales of guns often say "It's not guns that kill; it's people who kill." Do you agree with this logic? Write a paragraph or essay giving your opinion about this statement.

ACTIVITY 4: WRITING

Consider some films you have seen or books, poetry, or short stories that you have read. For each, what was one of the main things you admired or that you felt made it good? Write your responses in a list. Then elaborate one of them by writing a paragraph about it. Here are a few examples of the types of comments that might be made:

▶ **EXAMPLE:** *It is the beautiful cinematography and interesting story that* make *Out of Africa* such an enjoyable movie.

ACTIVITY 5: WRITING OR SPEAKING

Write a narrative paragraph describing the place, time, and other significant information about one of the following:

- The circumstances of your birth or someone else's you know
- A historical event
- A current event

To begin your narrative, choose one of the features to highlight in a cleft construction as was shown in Focus 4 on page 441. If time permits, read your paragraph to classmates in small groups.

ACTIVITY 6: WRITING

Which of the personality traits listed in the Opening Task seem to fit you or members of your family? Write a paragraph describing who it is that they fit.

Appendices

Appendix 1A   Present Time Frame

Form	Example	Use	Meaning
SIMPLE PRESENT base form of verb or base form of verb + -s	Many plants **require** a lot of sun to thrive.	timeless truths	now
	Luis **works** every day except Sunday.	habitual actions	
	We **think** you should come with us.	mental perceptions and emotions	
	Veronica **owns** the house she lives in.	possession	
PRESENT PROGRESSIVE *am/is/are* + present participle (verb + -ing)	They **are** just **finishing** the race.	actions in progress	in progress now
	She **is picking** strawberries this morning.	duration	
	Someone **is pounding** nails next door.	repetition	
	My friend **is living** in Nova Scotia for six months.	temporary activities	
	I **am changing** the oil in my car right now.	uncompleted actions	
PRESENT PERFECT *have/has* + past participle (verb + -ed or irregular form)	She **has attended** the university for four years; she will graduate in June.	situations that began in the past, continue to the present	in the past but related to now in some way
	I **have read** that book too. Did you like it?	actions completed in the past but related to the present	
	The movie **has** just **ended.**	actions recently completed	

A-1

Form	Example	Use	Meaning
PRESENT PERFECT PROGRESSIVE *have/has* + present participle (verb + *-ing*)	I **have been dialing** the airline's number for hours it seems. I can't believe it's still busy.	repeated or continuous actions that are incomplete	up until and including now
	This weekend Michelle **has been participating** in a job fair which ends on Sunday afternoon.		

Appendix 1B   Past Time Frame

Form	Example	Use	Meaning
SIMPLE PRESENT	So yesterday he **tells** me he just thought of another way to get rich quick.	past event in informal narrative	at a certain time in the past
SIMPLE PAST verb + *-ed* or irregular past form	We **planted** the vegetable garden last weekend.	events that took place at a definite time in the past	at a certain time in the past
	Pei-Mi **taught** for five years in Costa Rica.	events that lasted for a time in the past	
	I **studied** English every year when I was in high school.	habitual or repeated actions in the past	
	We **thought** we were heading in the wrong direction.	past mental perceptions and emotions	
	Jose **had** a piano when he lived in New York.	past possessions	
PAST PROGRESSIVE *was/were* + present participle (verb + *-ing*)	When I talked with him last night, Sam **was getting** ready for a trip.	events in progress at a specific time in the past	in progress at a time in the past

Form	Example	Use	Meaning
PAST PERFECT *had* + participle (verb + *-ed* or irregular form)	My parents **had lived** in Hungary before they moved to France.	actions or states that took place before another time in the past	before a certain time in the past
PAST PERFECT PROGRESSIVE *had* + *been* + present participle (verb + *-ing*)	We **had been hurrying** to get to the top of the mountain when the rain started.	incomplete events taking place before other past events	up until a certain time in the past
	I **had been working** on the last math problem when the teacher instructed us to turn in our exams.	incomplete events interrupted by other past events	

Appendix 1C   Future Time Frame

Form	Example	Use	Meaning
SIMPLE PRESENT	Takiko **graduates** next week.	definite future plans or schedules	already planned or expected in the future
	When Guangping **completes** her graduate program, she will look for a research job in Taiwan.	events with future time adverbials (*before, after, when*) in dependent clauses	
PRESENT PROGRESSIVE	I **am finishing** my paper tomorrow night.	future intentions	already planned or expected in the future
	Amit **is taking** biochemistry for two quarters next year.	scheduled events that last for a period of time	

Form	Example	Use	Meaning
BE GOING TO FUTURE *am/is/are going to* + base verb	The train **is going to arrive** any minute.	probable and immediate future events	at a certain time in the future
	I **am going to succeed** no matter what it takes!	strong intentions	
	Tomorrow you**'re going to be glad** that you are already packed for your trip.	predictions about future situations	
	We **are going to have** a barbecue on Sunday night.	future plans	
SIMPLE FUTURE *will* + base verb	It **will** probably **snow** tomorrow.	probable future events	
	I **will give** you a hand with that package; it looks heavy.	willingness/promises	
	Tomorrow **will be** a better day.	predictions about future situtations	
FUTURE PROGRESSIVE *will* + *be* + present participle (verb + *-ing*)	I **will be interviewing** for the bank job in the morning.	events that will be in progress at a time in the future	in progress at a certain time in the future
	Mohammed **will be studying** law for the next three years.	future events that will last for a period of time	
FUTURE PERFECT *will* + *have* + past participle (verb + *-ed* or irregular verb)	He **will have finished** his degree before his sister starts hers in 2001.	before a certain time in the future	future events happening before other future events
FUTURE PERFECT PROGRESSIVE *will* + *have* + *been* + present participle (verb + *-ing*)	By the year 2000, my family **will have been living** in the U.S. for ten years.	up until a certain time in the future	continuous and/or repeated actions continuing into the future

All passive verbs are formed with *be* + or *get* + past participle.

SIMPLE PRESENT *am/is/are* (or *get*) + past participle	That movie **is reviewed** in today's newspaper. The garbage **gets picked up** once a week.
PRESENT PROGRESSIVE *am/is/are* + *being* (or *getting*) + past participle	The possibility of life on Mars is being **explored.** We **are getting asked** to do too much!
SIMPLE PAST *was/were* (or *got*) + past participle	The butterflies **were observed** for five days. Many homes **got destroyed** during the fire.
PAST PROGRESSIVE *was/were* + *being* (or *getting*) + past participle	The Olympics **were being broadcast** worldwide. She **was getting beaten** in the final trials.
PRESENT PERFECT *has/have* + *been* (or *gotten*) + past participle	The information **has been sent.** Did you hear he**'s gotten fired** from his job?
PRESENT PERFECT PROGRESSIVE *has* + *been* + *being* (or *getting*) + past participle	This store **has been being remodeled** for six months now! I wonder if they'll ever finish. It looks as though the tires on my car **have been getting worn** by these bad road conditions.
PAST PERFECT *had* + *been* (or *gotten*) + past participle	The National Anthem **had** already **been sung** when we entered the baseball stadium. He was disappointed to learn that the project **had**n't **gotten completed** in his absence.
FUTURE *will* + *be* (or *get*) + past participle *be going to* + past participle	The horse races **will be finished** in an hour. The rest of the corn **will get harvested** this week. The election results **are going to be announced** in a few minutes.

FUTURE PERFECT *will* + *have* + *been* (or *gotten*) + past participle	I bet most of the food **will have been eaten** by the time we get to the party. The unsold magazines **will have gotten sent** back to the publishers by now.
FUTURE PERFECT PROGRESSIVE *will* + *have* + *been* + *being* (or *getting*) + past participle	Our laundry **will have been getting dried** for over an hour by the time we come back. I'm sure it will be ready to take out then. NOTE: The *be* form of this passive tense is quite rare. Even the *get* form is not very common.
PRESENT MODAL VERBS modal (*can, may, should,* etc.) + *be* (or *get*) + past participle	A different chemical **could be substituted** in this experiment. Don't stay outside too long. You **may get burned** by the blazing afternoon sun.
PAST MODAL VERBS modal (*can, may, should,* etc.) + *have* + *been* (or *gotten*) + past participle	All of our rock specimens **should have been identified** since the lab report is due. The file **might have gotten erased** through a computer error.

APPENDIX 3   Sentence Connectors

Meaning	Connectors

Addition
    Simple addition
    Emphatic addition
    Intensifying addition
	also, in addition, furthermore, moreover,
	what is more (what's more), as well, besides
	in fact, as a matter of fact, actually

Alternative	*on the other hand, alternatively*
Exemplifying	*for example, for instance, especially, in particular, to illustrate,* *as an example*
Identifying	*namely, specifically*
Clarifying	*that is, in other words, I mean*

Meaning	Connectors
Similarity	*similarly, likewise, in the same way*
Contrast	*however, in contrast, on the other hand, in fact*
Concession	*even so, however, nevertheless, nonetheless, despite (+ noun phrase), in spite of (+ noun phrase), on the other hand*
Effects/Results	*accordingly, as a result, as a result of (+ noun phrase), because of (+ noun phrase), due to (+ noun phrase), consequently, therefore, thus, hence*
Purpose	*in order to (+ verb), with this in mind, for this purpose*

APPENDIX 4 Gerunds and Infinitives

Appendix 4A Overview of Gerunds and Infinitives

Examples	Explanations
	Infinitives (*to* + verb) or gerunds (verb + *ing*) can have various functions in a sentence:
(a) **To know many languages** would thrill me. **(b)** **Speaking English** is fun.	• subject
(c) His dream was **to sail around the world.** **(d)** Her hobby is **weaving baskets.**	• subject complement
(e) Paco hopes **to see the play**. **(f)** Carol remembered **mailing the package.**	• object
(g) By **studying hard,** you can enter a good school. **(h)** Thank you for **helping me.**	• object of preposition (gerunds)
(i) I don't understand the need **to take a ten-minute break.** **(j)** The instruction **to wear safety goggles** has saved many people's eyes.	• noun complement (infinitives)
(k) I am sorry **to inform you of the delay.** **(l)** They were pleased **to meet you.**	• adjective complement (infinitives following adjectives)

to + verb

EXAMPLE: Julia hates to be late.

List A
As mentioned in Unit 18, Focus 4, some of the verbs in List A may also take gerunds if an actual, vivid or fulfilled action is intended. (Example: Julia hates being late.)

Verbs of Emotion

care	loathe
desire	love
hate	regret
like	yearn

Verbs of Choice or Intention

agree	plan
choose	prefer
decide	prepare
deserve	propose
expect	refuse
hope	want
intend	wish
need	

Verbs of Initiation, Completion, and Incompletion

begin	manage
cease	neglect
commence	start
fail	try
get	undertake
hesitate	

Verbs of Request and Their Responses

demand	swear
offer	threaten
promise	vow

Verbs of Mental Activity

forget	learn
know how	remember

Intransitive Verbs

appear	seem
happen	tend

Other Verbs

afford (can't afford)	continue
arrange	pretend
claim	wait

List B

object + *to* + verb

EXAMPLE: She reminded us to be quiet.

Verbs of Communication

advise	permit
ask*	persuade
beg*	promise*
challenge	remind
command	require
convince	tell
forbid	warn
invite	urge
order	

Verbs of Instruction

encourage	teach
help	train
instruct	

Other Verbs

expect*	prepare*
trust	want*

Verbs of Causation

allow	get
cause	hire
force	

* Can follow pattern A also.

List C

verb + *-ing*

EXAMPLE: Trinh enjoys playing tennis.

Note that when the subject of the gerund is stated, it is in possessive form.

We enjoyed his telling us about his adventures.

Verbs of Initiation, Completion and Incompletion

avoid	give up
begin	postpone
cease	quit
complete	risk
delay	start
finish	stop
get through	try

Verbs of Communication

admit	mention
advise	recommend
deny	suggest
discuss	urge
encourage	

List C (continued)

Verbs of Ongoing Activity

continue	keep
can't help	keep on
practice	

Verbs of Mental Activity

anticipate	recall
consider	remember
forget	see (can't see)
imagine	understand

Verbs of Emotion

appreciate	like	miss	resent
dislike	love	prefer	resist
enjoy	mind (don't mind)	regret	tolerate
hate		can't stand	

APPENDIX 5   Preposition Clusters

in + noun + *of*	*on* + noun + *of*	*in* + *the* + noun + *of*	*on* + *the* + noun + *of*
in case of	on account of	in the course of	on the advice of
in charge of	on behalf of	in the event of	on the basis of
in place of	on top of	in the habit of	on the part of
in lieu of	on grounds of	in the name of	on the strength of
in favor of		in the process of	on the face of

Other Combinations

in by means of	in return for	at odds with	with the exception of
with respect to	in addition to	for the sake of	

Appendix 6A   General Types of Relative Clauses

Example:	Noun Phrase in Main Clause	Relative Pronoun in Relative Clause
S S (a) The contract **that** was signed yesterday is now valid.	Subject	Subject
S O (b) The contract **that** he signed yesterday is now valid.	Subject	Object
O S (c) I have not read the contract **that** was signed yesterday.	Object	Subject
O O (d) I have not read the contract **that** he signed yesterday.	Object	Object

Appendix 4B   Relative Clauses Modifying Subjects

Example:	Types of Noun in Main Clause	Relative Pronouns	Function of Relative Pronoun
(a) A person **who/that** sells houses is a realtor.	person	who/that	subject
(b) The secretary **whom/that** she hired is very experienced.		whom/that	object of verb
(c) The employees **to whom** she denied a pay raise have gone on strike.		whom	object of preposition
(d) Clerks **whose** paychecks were withheld must go to the payroll office.		whose (relative determiner)	possessive determiner
(e) The mansions **that/which** were sold last week were expensive.	thing or animal	that/which	subject
(f) The computer **that/which** they purchased operated very efficiently.		that/which	object of verb
(g) The division **whose** sales reach the million-dollar point will win a bonus.		whose (relative determiner)	possessive determiner

Relative Adverbs with Head Nouns

Head Noun	Relative Adverb	Clause
a place	where	you can relax
a time	when	I can call you
a reason	why	you should attend

Relative Adverbs without Head Nouns

Relative Adverb	Clause
where	he lives
when	the term starts
why	I called
how	she knows

Head Nouns without Relative Adverbs

Head Noun	Clause
the place	we moved to
the time	I start school
the reason	they left
the way	you do this

Appendix 7A   Verb Complements

that	*for-to*	*'s gerund*	*Type*
			SUBJECT basic order
(a) **That** Tom spent the whole day shopping surprised us.	**(b)** **For** Tom **to** spend the whole day shopping would surprise us.	**(c)** Tom**'s spending** the whole day shopping surprised us.	
(d) It surprised us **that** Tom spent the whole day shopping.	**(e)** It would surprise us **for** Tom **to** spend the whole day shopping.	**(f)** It surprised us— Tom**'s spending** the whole day shopping. (When this structure occurs, there is a pause between the main clause and the complement.)	complement after *it* + verb
		OBJECT	
(g) We hope **that** the the children take the bus.	**(h)** We hope **for** the children **to** take the bus.	**(i)** not applicable	indicative form
(j) Ms. Sanchez suggests **that** he wait in the lobby.	**(k)** not applicable	**(l)** not applicable	subjunctive form

Appendix 7B   Adjective Complements

that	*for-to*	*'s gerund*	*Type*
			SUBJECT basic order
(a) **That** Lisa went to the meeting was important.	**(b)** **For** Lisa **to** go to the meeting was important.	**(c)** Lisa**'s going to** the meeting was important.	
(d) It was important **that** Lisa went to the meeting.	**(e)** It was important **for** Lisa **to** go to the meeting.	**(f)** It was important— Lisa**'s going** to the meeting. (When this structure occurs there is a pause between the main clause and the complement.)	complement after *it* + verb

that	*for-to*	*'s gerund*	*Type*
			PREDICATE indicative form
(g) Mr. Walker is happy **that she works** at the company.	**(h)** Mr. Walker is happy **for** her **to** work at the company. (This structure only occurs with a subset of adjectives like *ready, anxious, happy, eager,* etc.)	**(i)** not applicable	
(j) Chong demands **that she be** on time.	**(k)** not applicable	**(l)** not applicable	subjunctive form

Base Form	Simple Past	Past Participle	Base Form	Simple Past	Past Participle
arise	arose	arisen	leave	left	left
awake	awoke	awoken	let	let	let
bet	bet	bet	lie	lay	lain
beat	beat	beaten	lose	lost	lost
become	became	become	make	made	made
begin	began	begun	mean	meant	meant
bite	bit	bitten	meet	met	met
bleed	bled	bled	pay	paid	paid
blow	blew	blown	put	put	put
break	broke	broken	read	read	read
bring	brought	brought	ride	rode	ridden
build	built	built	ring	rang	rung
buy	bought	bought	rise	rose	risen
catch	caught	caught	run	ran	run
choose	chose	chosen	say	said	said
come	came	come	see	saw	seen
cost	cost	cost	sell	sold	sold
cut	cut	cut	send	sent	sent
do	did	done	set	set	set
draw	drew	drawn	shake	shook	shaken
dream	dreamt/dreamed	dreamt/dreamed	shine	shone/shined	shone/shined
drink	drank	drunk	shut	shut	shut
drive	drove	driven	sing	sang	sung
eat	ate	eaten	sink	sank	sunk
fall	fell	fallen	sit	sat	sat
feel	felt	felt	sleep	slept	slept
fight	fought	fought	speak	spoke	spoken
find	found	found	spend	spent	spent
fly	flew	flown	stand	stood	stood
forget	forgot	forgotten	steal	stole	stolen
forgive	forgave	forgiven	strike	struck	struck
freeze	froze	frozen	swing	swung	swung
get	got	gotten	swim	swam	swum
give	gave	given	take	took	taken
go	went	gone	teach	taught	taught
grow	grew	grown	tear	tore	torn
hang	hung	hung	tell	told	told
hear	heard	heard	think	thought	thought
hide	hid	hidden	throw	threw	thrown
hit	hit	hit	understand	understood	understood
hold	held	held	wake	woke	woken
hurt	hurt	hurt	wear	wore	worn
keep	kept	kept	win	won	won
know	knew	known	wind	wound	wound
lay	laid	laid	write	wrote	written
lead	led	led			

A n s w e r   K e y (for puzzles and problems only)

UNIT 2

Answer to Internet Frequently Asked Questions in Exercise 1 (page 15)

1. It *is* acceptable to send coconuts through the mail without wrapping them.
   True
2. A mime *had* a heart attack during his performance. People *thought* it was part of his act. He *died*.
   False
3. A penny falling from the top of the Empire State Building *will embed* itself in the pavement.
   False
4. Fast-food shakes that aren't marked "dairy" *have* no milk in them.
   True
5. Albert Einstein did poorly in school.
   False
6. Green M & M candies *are* an aphrodisiac.
   False
7. Contact lenses *will stick* to your eyeballs if you weld something while wearing them.
   False
8. If mold grows on a Twinkie, the Twinkie *digests* it.
   False

UNIT 25

Answers of Opening Task (page 433)

a) oldest, b) middle, c) only, d) youngest, e) middle, f) only, g) oldest, h) youngest, i) oldest, j) only, k) youngest, l) middle

A-16

Exercises (second parts)

List of Words for Short-Term Memory Experiment (page 57)

book, hand, street, tree, sand, rose, box, face, pencil, nail, pan, dog, door, school, shoe, cloud, watch, lamp, stair, glue, bottle, card, movie, match, hammer, dance, hill, basket, house, river

Definition of the Serial Position Effect (page 57)

If a person is asked to recall a list of words in any order immediately after the list is presented, recall of words at the beginning and end of the list is usually best; words in the middle of a list are not retained as well. This observation is based on a model of learning that assumes the first words are remembered well because they are rehearsed and because short term memory at that point is relatively empty. The last words are remembered well because they are still in the short-term memory if the person tries to recall immediately.

UNIT 7

Opening Task (page 126)

Student B

Guess the Correct Answer:

1. (a) seahorse, (b) boa constrictor, (c) Canadian goose
2. (a) *War and Peace* by Leo Tolstoy, (b) *The Great Gatsby* by F. Scott Fitzgerald, (c) *Pride and Prejudice* by Jane Austen
3. (a) Thomas Edison, (b) Richard Nixon, (c) Henry Thoreau
4. (a) mucker, (b) hooker inspector, (c) belly builder

Create a Definition: (* indicates the correct answer)

5. a fly
   It is actually classified as a beetle.
   (a) dragonfly, (b) flycatcher, *(c) firefly
6. a person
   He or she pretends to be someone else.
   (a) cornball, *(b) imposter, (c) daytripper
7. a jar
   Ancient Greeks and Romans used it to carry wine.
   *(a) amphora, (b) amulet, (c) aspartame

8. a piece of clothing
   It is composed of loose trousers gathered about the ankles.
   (a) bodice, (b) causerie, *(c) bloomers

UNIT 8

Opening Task (page 140)

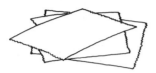

Paper
About A.D. 105

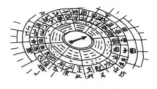

Magnetic Compas
1100s

Television
1920s

Safety Elevator
1853

Typewriter
1867

Laser
1960

Telephone
1876

Gasoline Automobile
1885

Airplane
1903

Credits

Text Credits

Text in Exercise 1 on p. 3 adapted from *The Hunger of Memory* by Richard Rodriguez. Reprinted by permission of David R. Godine, Publisher, Inc. Copyright © 1982 by Richard Rodriguez.

Text in Exercise 3 on p. 5 and Exercise 5 on p. 9 adapted from Studs Terkel, *The Great Divide,* © 1988 by Studs Terkel. Reprinted with permission of Pantheon Books, a division of Random House, Inc.

Text in Exercise 1 on p. 15 from "The Internet's Believe It or Not." Reprinted with permission by Terry Chan.

Text in Exercise 3 on p. 17 from Annie Dillard, *Pilgrim at Tinker Creek,* Copyright © 1974 by Annie Dillard. Reprinted by permission of Harper-Collins Publishers, Inc.

Text in Exercise 4 on p. 17 from "Get a Cyberlife," by Peggy Orenstein, which originally appeared in the May/June 1991 issue of *Mother Jones Magazine,* © 1991, Foundation for National Progress.

Text in Exercise 7 on p. 21 from James Thurber, *Thurber's Dogs, A Collection of the Master's Dogs; Written and Drawn, Real and Imaginary, Living and Long Ago.* Copyright © 1955 by James Thurber. Copyright renewed 1983 by Rosemary A. Thurber. Reprinted by arrangement with Rosemary Thurber and the Barbara Hogenson Agency.

Text in Exercise 8 on p. 22 from J. Michael Kennedy, "It's the Hottest Little Ol' Race in Texas," *Los Angeles Times,* September 2, 1991.

Text in Exercise 15 on p. 29 from Edith Hamilton, *Mythology.* Copyright 1942 by Edith Hamilton. Reprinted with permission by Magad F. Riad Cloriad and Associates.

Text in Exercise 1 on p. 39, and Exercise 9 on p. 50, adapted from *The Gallup Poll Monthly,* February 1991, with permission of The Gallup Organization, Inc.

Text in Exercise 11 on p. 70 adapted from *The Guinness Book of World Records.* Reprinted with permission by Guiness World Records Limited.

Text in Focus 7 on p. 71 from "Busy and Smart Too," *Los Angeles Times,* August 18, 1996.

Text in Exercise 12 on p. 72 adapted from "Decoding of Microbe's Genes Sheds Light on Odd Forms of Life." Reprinted with permission by the Associated Press.

Text in Focus 6 on p. 84 adapted from P. Master, "Teaching the English Article System, Part II: Generic versus Specific," in *English Teaching Forum*. July 1988.

Text in Exercise 18 on p. 96 adapted from S. Hall, *Invisible Frontiers*. New York: The Atlantic Monthly Press, 1987. Reprinted with permission.

Text in Exercise 19 on p. 97 adapted from F. Bloom "Introduction: Science Technology, and the National Agenda: in a report by the Committee on Science, Engineering, and Public Policy of the National Academy of Sciences, National Academy of Engineering, institute of Medicine entitled *Frontiers in Science and Technology: A Selected Outlook*. Reprinted with permission by the National Academy of Sciencies.

Situations 1 through 3 on p. 101 and Exercise 1 on p. 103 adapted from Deborah Tannen, *You Just Don't Understand: Women and Men In Conversation*.

Text in Exercise 2 on p. 104 from Lewis Thomas, *The Medusa and the Snail*. New York: Bantam Books, 1979, p. 167.

Text in Exercise 4 on p. 106, adapted from C. Wade and C. Tavris, *Psychology*. New York: Harper and Row, 1987.

Text in Activity 4 on p. 138 from *Hutchinson Pocket Encyclopedia*. London: Helicon, 1987. Reprinted with permission by Deirdre Luzwick.

Illustration on p. 155 from *Endangered Species: Portraits of a Dying Millennium*. Copyright © 1992 by Deirdre Luzwick. Reprinted by permission of HarperCollins Publishers, Inc

Text in Exercise 3 on p. 160: Reprinted with the permission of Macmillan General Reference, a wholly owned subsidiary of IDG Books Worldwide, Inc., from ARTHUR FROMMER'S NEW WORLD TRAVEL, by Arthur Frommer, Copyright © 1988 by Frommer Books, a division of Macmillan Publishing.

Text in Opening Task on p. 199 adapted from Maria Leach, *The Beginning: Creation Myths around the World*. New York: HarperCollins Publishers, 1956.

Text in Focus 4 on p. 233 and Exercise 6 on p. 234 from *A Brief History of Time: From the Big Bang to Black Holes*. by Stephen Hawking. Copyright © 1990 Stephen Hawking. Reprinted by permission of Bantam Books.

Text in Exercise 12 on pp. 262–263 from Isaac Asimov, *Earth: Our Crowded Spaceship*, Greenwich, Connecticut: Fawcett, 1974.

Text in Exercise 6 on p. 309 from U.S. Immigration and Naturalization Service.

Text in Exercise 12 on p. 315 from John Crewdson, *The Tarnished Door.* New York Times Books, Inc., © 1983 by John Crewdson, pp. 96–97. Reprinted with permission.

Text in Exercise 1 on p. 323 adapted from *Bringing Out the Best in People,* by Alan Loy McGinnis, copyright © 1985 Augsburg Publishing House. Used by permission of Augsburg Fortress.

Text in Exercise 14 on pp. 338–339 adapted from D. Steward, "The Floating World at Xero G." *Air and Space.* August/September 1991, p. 38. Reprinted with permission.

Text in Exercise 5, p. 370 adapted from Wallace et al., *Book of Lists 2.* New York: William Morrow & Co., 1980. © David Wallechirnsky.

Text in Activity 5 on p. 375 Copyright © 1990 by Michael Fox. From INHU-MANE SOCIETY: THE AMERICAN WAY OF EXPLOITING ANIMALS   by Michael Fox. Reprinted by permission of St. Martin's Press, LLC.

Text in Exercise 10 on p. 387 adapted from John Naisbett and Patricia Aburdene, *Megatrends* 2000.

Text in Opening Task on p. 407 from *The Making of an Advertising Campaign* by Niefeld, © 1989. Reprinted by permission of Prentice-Hall, Inc., Upper Saddle River, NJ.

Text in Opening Task on p. 439 from Bradford Wilson and George Edington, *First Child, Second Child . . . .* New York: McGraw-Hill, 1981.

Photo Credits

Page 1, photo by CORBIS/Bob Kristi; photo by CORBIS/Joseph Sohm, ChromoSohm Inc. Page 12, photo by THE STOCK MARKET/Tom Stewart/© 98. Page 13, photo by CORBIS/Tom Nebbia. Page 19, photo by Jonathan Stark for Heinle & Heinle. Page 22, photo by CORBIS/Kelly-Mooney Photography. Page 25, THE FAR SIDE © 1985 FARWORKS, INC. Used by Permission. All rights reserved. Page 29, Reprinted by permission of U.F.S. Inc. Page 36, photo (left) by THE STOCK MARKET/ © Rich Meyer; photo (right) by THE STOCK MARKET/ © 90 Tom Tracy. Page 39, photo by CORBIS/Laura Dwight. Page 51, photo by CORBIS/Grant. Page 56, photo by Jonathan Stark for Heinle & Heinle. Page 76, photo by CORBIS/Paul A. Souders. Page 81, photo by Jonathan Stark for Heinle & Heinle. Page 85, photo by Jonathan Stark for Heinle & Heinle. Page 100, photo by THE STOCK MARKET/ © 1995 Rob Lewine. Page 104, photo by Jonathan Stark for Heinle & Heinle. Page 114, photo by Jonathan Stark for Heinle & Heinle. Page 117, photo by Jonathan Stark for Heinle & Heinle. Page 149, photo (top right) by CORBIS/Steven Chenn; photo (middle left) by THE STOCK MARKET/David Stocklein © 1987; photo (middle right) by THE STOCK MARKET/ © Roy Morsch; photo (bottom left) by THE STOCK MARKET/Copyright, George W. Disario 1993; photo (bottom right) by THE STOCK MARKET/ © 94 David Stoecklein. Page 156, photo by CORBIS/Ric Ergenbright. Page 180, photo by Jonathan Stark for Heinle & Heinle. Page 187, photo by CORBIS/Bob Krist. Page 198, photo by CORBIS/Paul Thompson. Page 243, photo by Jonathan Stark for Heinle & Heinle. Page 244, photo (left) by Jonathan Stark for Heinle & Heinle; photo (right) by Jonathan Stark for Heinle & Heinle. Page 264, photo (left) by CORBIS/Jonathan Blair; photo (middle) by CORBIS/Kevin R. Morris, photo (right) by CORBIS/Charles O'Rear. Page 278, photo by CORBIS/WildCountry. Page 285, photo by CORBIS/Bettmann. Page 298, photo (left) by Jonathan Stark for Heinle & Heinle; photo (right) by CORBIS/Peter Turnley. Page 301, photo by Jonathan Stark for Heinle & Heinle. Page 335, photo by CORBIS. Page 340, photo by CORBIS/Archivo Iconografico, S.A. Page 360, photo (left) by CORBIS/Vince Streano; photo (right) by CORBIS/ © Archivo Iconographico, S.A. Page 386, photo by CORBIS/Laura Dwight. Page 400, photo (left) by CORBIS/Jennie Woodcock; photo (right) by CORBIS. Page 405, photo by Jonathan Stark for Heinle & Heinle. Page 409, photo by CORBIS/AFP. Page 412, photos by Photofest. Page 415, photo by CORBIS/Brain Vikander. Page 432, photo (left) by CORBIS/Laura Dwight; photo (right) by CORBIS/Paul A. Souders.

C-4 | CREDITS

Index

with
    deleting relative pronouns using, 148–149
    in preposition cluster, 300, 302, 308
    reduced relative clauses and, 134–136
    stative passive verbs using, 64
without
    deleting relative pronouns in, 148–149
    reduced relative clauses and, 134–136

would have in modal perfect verbs, 233, 237, 241
would, perfective infinitive used with, 349–350

yes/no questions, rhetorical questions using, 257
yes–no clefts, 443–444
yet, coordinating conjunction use of, 201

TESTS AND ANSWERS

Grammar Dimensions Book 4

Name _____

Unit 1 Verb Tenses in Written and Spoken Communication

Score _____
100

A. **Each of the following passages has one sentence with an incorrect verb tense for the context. Rewrite the incorrect sentences. (5 points each)**

1. **(a)** We're going to the park for a picnic. **(b)** We had decided to leave at 9.

   (c) Everyone's bringing food.

2. **(a)** Betsy is the best student in my math class. **(b)** She's been getting A's all year.

   (c) She will have been the only student with an A average.

3. **(a)** She had already finished lunch. **(b)** She's going to be leaving soon.

   (c) You'll have to hurry if you want to say good-bye.

4. **(a)** My best friend plays the clarinet in our band. **(b)** She has played for two years.

   (c) Last year she had played the flute too.

5. **(a)** Tom has been to visit several times. **(b)** He always brought his dog, Buster.

   (c) Fortunately, now that we have a cat, he'll have to leave Buster home.

B. **Retell this description of past events by changing the verb tense to make it seem more immediate. (4 points each verb)**

Last week I had the strangest experience when I took my poodle, Suzette, for a walk. We had just gotten to the corner when I noticed a man a few houses behind me. He was walking a large Doberman pinscher, so I quickly moved to the other side of the street to let them pass. Suzette had had a fight and been bitten by another large dog and I didn't want her to get into trouble. Well, I was very surprised when the man and his dog crossed the street too. I started walking really fast in order to keep far ahead of them. Suddenly, the man called out and asked me to stop. He said that his dog really liked poodles and he was hoping that our dogs could meet! I told him that I never allowed Suzette to make friends with strangers.

UNIT 1 ANSWERS

A.
1. (b) We have decided to leave at 9.
2. (c) She will be / is the only student with an A average.
3. (a) She has already finished lunch.
4. (c) Last year she played the flute too.
5. (b) He always brings his dog, Buster.

B. The first sentence does not change. All other verbs change as follows:

We <u>have</u> just <u>gotten</u>; I <u>notice</u> a man; He <u>is</u> <u>walking</u>; I quickly <u>move</u>; Suzette <u>has</u> <u>had</u> a fight and <u>been</u> <u>bitten</u>; I <u>don't</u> <u>want</u>; I <u>am</u> very surprised; <u>cross</u> the street; I <u>start</u> walking; the man <u>calls</u> and <u>asks</u>; He <u>says</u>; his dog really <u>likes</u>; he <u>was</u> happy; I <u>tell</u> him; I never <u>allow</u>

Complete the following paragraph, with the simple present, present progressive, present perfect, present perfect progressive, simple future or future perfect. (5 points each)

My daughter's most important in-group (1) _____ (be) her school class. We

(2) _____ (not live) in this town for very long, so she (3) _____

(not have) time to develop a lot of other associations. Many of the children in her

class (4) _____ (live) in our neighborhood. That (5) _____ (make)

it pretty easy for her to make friends. Her best friend (6) _____ (be) Emily,

the girl next door. Emily and Susan (7) _____ (play) together for six

months and they (8) _____ (be) very close. Unfortunately, Emily's family

(9) _____ (get) ready to move to another town. Susan (10) _____

(begin) thinking about her life after Emily (11) _____ (leave). She

(12) _____ (plan) a surprise going away party for Emily. I

(13) _____ (encourage) her to invite the whole neighborhood. I

(14) _____ (think) we should have big party. This July we

(15) _____ (be) here two years and we (16) _____ (not have) a

party. This (17) _____ (be) a good opportunity to repay the kindness that

our neighbors (18) _____ (show) us since we (19) _____ (move)

in. After all, good neighbors (20) _____ (be) hard to find.

UNIT 2 ANSWERS

1. is
2. have not lived
3. has not had
4. live
5. makes/has made
6. is
7. have been playing/have played
8. are
9. is getting
10. has begun
11. leaves
12. is planning
13. am encouraging/have encouraged
14. think
15. will have been
16. have not had
17. will be
18. have shown
19. moved
20. are

Rewrite the sentences. Six are correct. (5 points each)

1. The principal cause of his health problems were his refusal to follow his doctor's advice.

2. Everyone have arrived except the teachers.

3. The magazine articles which I found in her room was all about plastic surgery.

4. My children, not their father, refuses to watch television.

5. All of the people I met on my trip out west were helpful and friendly.

6. A country which does not take care of its poor are destined to fail.

7. Neither he nor Marion have decided where to go.

8. Either the dog or the cat are always sick.

9. Both the audience and the actor starts applauding.

10. The herd of cattle was last seen running across the field.

11. A lot of the information in those books is wrong.

12. Ten dollars are too much money for a child.

13. Making tables and chairs are no work for people with Ph.D.'s

14. What I gave you was fifteen dollars.

15. The homeless in our town have a new shelter near the courthouse.

16. Half of the children is absent today.

17. One tenth of the amount were recovered.

18. The vocabulary in my sociology textbooks are very difficult.

19. Economics was my downfall in college.

20. The government need to listen to the people.

UNIT 3 ANSWERS

1. was
2. has arrived
3. were
4. refuse
5. correct
6. is
7. has
8. is
9. start
10. correct
11. correct
12. is
13. is
14. correct
15. correct
16. are
17. was
18. is
19. correct
20. needs

A. Rewrite the incorrect sentences. One sentence is correct. (6 points each)

1. I have been received many reports of serious problems with our new procedures.
2. We had getting mail from her regularly when suddenly she stopped writing.
3. My new website will have been design by the time you get your computer next month.
4. The prizes are going to be given out next month.
5. The house will clean up before we leave.

B. Rewrite each sentence below to put focus on the recipients of action rather than on the performers. Delete the agent if you do not think it needs to be mentioned. Make any other necessary changes. (7 points each)

6. Computers process most types of information much more quickly than humans can.

7. The "motherboard" is the part of the computer that does the most work.

8. Yesterday, my office computer "crashed" and destroyed most of my files.

9. Luckily, my secretary David had made copies of almost everything.

10. I'm going to ask if the computer store can fix it in their repair shop.

11. You can sometimes find good deals on used computers.

12. Many people no longer believe that a home computer is an extravagance.

C. After each sentence or group of sentences, use the information in parentheses to add a sentence with a passive verb. (10 points each)

13. In the 16th century the Tutsi tribe moved into Rwanda and took over from the Hutu. (We can attribute their current problems to this event.)

14. The Internet is a mass of computer networks that are linked globally. (A group of university professors and the military started it about 20 years ago.)

15. Grade point averages have been rising steadily over the last 20 years. (Professors at elite institutions like Stanford and Princeton rarely give grades below a B.)

UNIT 4 ANSWERS

A.   1. I have received . . .

2. We had been getting mail . . .

3. will have been designed

4. correct

5. The house will be / get cleaned up. . .

B.   6. Most types of information can be processed much more quickly by computers than by humans.

7. Most of the work (of the computer) is done by the "motherboard."

8. . . .and most of my files were destroyed.

9. Luckily, copies of almost everything had been made by my secretary, David.

10. . . .if it can be fixed in the computer store's repair shop

11. Good deals on used computers can sometimes be found.

12. It is no longer believed that the home computer is an extravagance.

    OR: That the home computer is an extravagance is no longer believed.

C. 13. Their current problems can be attributed to this event.

14. It was started by a group of university professors and the military about 20 years ago.

15. Grades below a B are rarely given (by professors) at elite institutions such as Stanford and Princeton.

A. Rewrite the incorrect sentences. Four are correct. (4 points each)

1. They have a lot of new furnitures.
2. A: Have you seen anyone near my office today?
   B: I saw the boy leaving earlier but I don't know who he was.
3. Children need structure in their lives.
4. A: What kind of fruit do you like the most?
   B: The mangos.
5. Did you see the eclipse of the moon?
6. A: I like your haircut.
   B: Thanks. I went to the barber this morning.
7. I saw this interesting show on a television last night.
8. Jenny went by the car.
9. We were standing hand in hand when we met them.
10. Japanese have a very interesting culture.
11. Arms race is finished.
12. A sugar maple is the state tree of Vermont.
13. You should buy yourself the pair of fur-lined boots.
14. He got vaccination against the measles.
15. The bilingualism is the ability to speak two languages equally well.

B. Complete the following paragraph with a/an, the, or Ø (4 points each)

(16) _____ endocrinologist is (17) _____ internist who

diagnoses and treats (18) _____ patients with problems involving

(19) _____ endocrine glands. Over- or under-production of

(20) _____ hormones produced by these glands affects

(21) _____ person's rate of (22) _____ growth, metabolism and

sexual development. At top hospitals, (23) _____ endocrinologists consult

with other specialists on problems from (24) _____ diabetes, to

(25) _____ cancer.

UNIT 5 ANSWERS

A.
1. furniture
2. a boy
3. correct
4. Mangos
5. correct
6. correct
7. on television
8. by car
9. correct
10. The Japanese
11. The arms race
12. The sugar maple
13. a pair of
14. a vaccination
15. Bilingualism is

B.
16. An
17. an
18. Ø
19. the
20. Ø/the
21. a
22. Ø
23. Ø
24. Ø
25. Ø

A. Rewrite the sentences to replace inappropriate references. One is appropriate. (5 points each)

1. A: Where did you get that blouse?
   B: I bought this blouse at Fashion House.
2. My son will only eat hot dogs and pizza. He eats such foods every day.
3. She told everyone my secret. I never thought she would be this disloyal.
4. She's always telling me to lose weight. Such an advice is not helpful.
5. The candidate says that government is too big. Do you agree with it?
6. Tom and Mark are always getting into trouble. The children have never been disciplined at home.
7. I have planned to spend today in the place that I like best and see least. The place that I like best and see least is my own home.
8. They moved almost every year. Such frequent the changes made it difficult for their daughter to make friends.
9. She quoted some interesting research in her paper. It was done on monkeys at Brown University.
10. She plans to visit Thailand and Malaysia. I think her parents recommended Thailand and Malaysia.

B. Complete the sentences with *it, they, them, the* + noun phrase, *this, that, these* or *those*. (5 points each)

11. Coffee may not be as healthy as tea, but _____ gets a relatively clean bill of health from most doctors.

12. A: A 1991 study showed that teenagers who work do poorly in school.

    B: Well, I think the results of _____ were inconclusive.

13. Since hand push lawn mowers don't pollute the air, _____ will be exempt from clean air laws.

14. A: Did you hear that Tom won the lottery?

    B: No, I hadn't heard _____.

15. She is suffering from high blood pressure and heart disease. Today I often see

    patients with problems like _____.

UNIT 6 ANSWERS

A. 1. it
2. eats them/these foods everyday
3. that
4. such advice
5. with that?
6. Those children
7. that place is my own home
8. frequent changes
9. correct
10. recommends those countries

B. 11. it
12. that study
13. they
14. that
15. these

A. Use the relative pronoun in parentheses to write a sentence with each phrase. Make sure the relative clause modifies the subject in each case. (7 points each)

1. is not ready to work (who)

2. are never home (whose)

3. is useless (that)

4. on the table (that)

5. will not succeed (whose)

6. were angry (to whom)

7. were donated by my mother (which)

8. was a Nobel prize winner (whom)

9. stole the money (who)

10. went to the hospital (that)

B. Identify and rewrite the relative clauses that can be reduced. (5 points each)

11. The money that I gave him was never deposited.

12. The children who had completed their homework left early.

13. The coffee that I made was too strong.

14. The woman who my sister met was from India.

15. Characters that are interesting are essential in a good movie.

UNIT 7 ANSWERS

A. Sample Answers:

1. Anyone who is not ready to work should leave.
2. Children whose parents are never home get into trouble.
3. The book that I found is useless.
4. The dishes that are on the table are hers.
5. Teachers whose students do not respect them will not succeed.
6. The women to whom he gave the presents were very appreciative.
7. The cookies which you bought were donated by my mother.
8. The man to whom I spoke was a Nobel prize winner.
9. The boy who stole the money is in jail.
10. The child that went to the hospital is my cousin.

B. 11. The money I gave him
12. Cannot be reduced
13. the coffee I made
14. the woman my sister
15. Interesting characters

A. Combine the following groups of sentences into one sentence which contains two relative clauses which modify objects. (10 points each)

1. Dan sold his car to a man. The man's wife had a job. The job required a car.
2. We met people. Their children attend a special school. The school is only for gifted students.
3. He wrote a computer program. The program allowed people to communicate. The people spoke different languages.
4. I bought my house from a man. The man planned to take a trip. He had dreamed about the trip for his whole life.
5. He invented an instrument. The instrument allowed people to see things. The things were too small to be seen with the naked eye.

B. Edit the sentences to create a less formal style. (5 points each)

6. I went to job interview yesterday and the man with whom I spoke was very kind.

7. She's unhappy about the grade which she received on her last test.

8. The meeting at which I met him was a long time ago.

9. The woman whom you hired is my best friend.

10. You should be careful of whom you make fun.

11. He was involved in the accident about which I told you.

12. The combustion engine is the invention to which we owe a great debt.

13. Martha is the editor for whom I wrote the article on Venice.

14. We met with the people with whom we had spoken before.

15. That is the man to whom I gave the book.

UNIT 8 ANSWERS

A. 1. Dan sold his car to a man whose wife had a job that/which required a car.
2. We met people whose children attend a special school which/that is only for gifted students.
3. He wrote a computer program that/which allowed people who/that spoke different languages to communicate.
4. I bought my house from a man who/that planned to take a trip that he had dreamed about for his whole life.
   OR: . . .to take a trip about which he had dreamed for his whole life.
5. He invented an instrument which/that allowed people to see things that/which were too small to be seen with the naked eye.

B. 6. the man I spoke to
7. the grade she received
8. meeting I met him at
9. woman you hired
10. careful who you make fun of
11. the accident I told you about
12. the invention we owe a great debt to
13. the editor I wrote the article on Venice for
14. the people we had spoken with before
15. the man I gave the book to

A. Read the sentences and add commas where needed. (6 points each)

1. My friend Anna who lives in Iowa is a farmer.

2. Traveling to Costa Rica was an interesting experience which I will never forget.

3. Their car which cost only $1500 is very reliable.

4. His father who is 78 still walks 2 miles a day.

5. I like books which describe travel adventures.

6. Anyone who likes James Bond will like this movie.

7. I went to visit her house which was a mess!

8. She gave me three books two of which I had already read.

9. Someone tried to break into my house last night which was really frightening.

10. The highway which is near my house is I 91.

B. Combine the sentences with a nonrestrictive relative clause. (8 points each)

11. I saw the Thompson girl. I had been very rude to her.

12. She visited her old house. She hadn't been there for 30 years.

13. On New Year's we eat lasagna. Lasagna is an Italian dish.

14. One of my students is going to fail. Her father is a doctor.

15. A caller ID device is useful. It is very inexpensive.

UNIT 9 ANSWERS

A. 1. Anna, Iowa,
    3. car, $1500,
    4. father, 78,
    7. her house,
    8. books,
    9. night,

B. 11. I saw the Thompson girl, whom I had been very rude to.
    12. She visited her old house, which she hadn't been to for 30 years.
    13. On New Year's we eat lasagna, which is an Italian dish.
    14. One of my students, whose father is a doctor, is going to fail.
    15. A caller ID device, which is very inexpensive, is useful.
        (OR: . . . , which is useful, is very inexpensive)

A. Combine the phrases to make sentences using relative adverbials + an appropriate head noun. Make any other necessary changes. (7 points each)

1. 1969   Neil Armstrong stepped on the moon

2. spending many hours in the language lab   I perfected my pronunciation

3. noon   most people eat lunch

4. San Francisco   you can ride on a cable car

5. lack of exercise   so many people have heart problems because of this

6. Christmas   people give each other presents

7. boring highways   many people prefer to fly for this reason

8. the kitchen   we like to sit and talk

9. walking or jogging   you can do this to get healthier

10. the woods   I like to spend time alone here

B. Rewrite the sentences when possible. Substitute relative adverbs *when, where, why* or *how* for preposition + *which* whenever possible. (6 points each)

11. December 2, 1984, is the day on which my daughter was born.

12. She can't explain the reasons for which she had decided to quit.

13. He needs to go to a school at which he can study engineering.

14. You must change the way in which you behave.

15. You must try not to attend parties at which many people will be drinking.

UNIT 10 ANSWERS

A.
1. 1969 is the year when. . .
2. Spending many hours in the language lab is how. . .
3. Noon is when. . .
4. San Francisco is the place/city where. . .
5. Lack of exercise is the reason why. . .
6. Christmas is a time when. . .
7. Boring highways are the reason why. . .
8. The kitchen is the place/room where. . .
9. Walking or jogging are the exercises/things that. . .
10. The woods is the place where I like to. . .
11. the day when
12. the reasons why
13. school where
14. the way you behave
15. parties where

B.
11. when
12. why
13. where
14. cannot substitute *how* unless *the way* is also deleted (give credit for both)
15. where

A. Rewrite the sentences that have incorrect parallelism. (8 points each)

1. Not only we were hungry but also thirsty.

2. Both leaving home and your friends are difficult things to do.

3. The teacher encouraged and praised the students respectively.

4. They neither replaced the money nor gave me an apology.

5. Patricia will both need money and a place to stay.

B. Use the information in parentheses to combine the sentences. (6 points each)

6. Sam speaks French. Sam speaks Italian. (*both*)

7. She has two cars. She has a motorcycle. (*not only/but also*)

8. My mother earns about $60,000 a year. My father earns about $30,000 a year. (*respectively*)

9. He was a Nobel prize winner. He was a wonderful human being. (*not only/but also*)

10. Mike isn't taking Betty to the dance. Mike isn't taking Crista to the dance. (*neither/nor*)

11. I'm going to quit school. I'm going to quit my job. (*either/or*)

12. The politicians are greedy. The politicians are stupid. (*both/and*)

13. Making a mistake is costly. Making a mistake is dangerous. (*both/and*)

14. Dick was arrested for selling state secrets. Margaret was arrested for selling state secrets. (*not only/but also*)

15. Driving a car is one thing you never forget. The ability to swim is one thing you never forget. (*both/and*)

UNIT 11 ANSWERS

A. 1. Not only were we hungry. . .
2. Leaving both your home and . . .
3. The teacher encouraged and praised the students.
4. correct
5. will need both money and. . .

B. 6. Sam speaks both French and Italian.
7. Not only does she have two cars but she also has a motorcycle.
8. My mother and father earn about $60,000 and $30,000 a year, respectively.
9. He was not only a Nobel prize winner but also a wonderful human being.
10. Mike is taking neither Betty nor Crista to the dance.
11. I'm going to quit either school or my job.
12. The politicians are both greedy and stupid.
13. Making a mistake is both costly and dangerous.
14. Not only Dick but also Margaret was arrested for selling state secrets.
15. Both driving a car and swimming are things you never forget.

A. Add a connector from the list below to each sentence. Do not use any connector more than once. (6 points each)

besides   especially   even so   however   in addition   in particular

likewise   nevertheless   on the other hand   similarly   what's more

1. He stole the club's money. _____, he tried to blame it on someone else.

2. She's not a very hard worker. _____, she's very creative.

3. Winter driving can be difficult;_____ driving on snowy roads.

4. Melissa doesn't like visiting her relatives; _____ Betsy would rather do other things.

5. This year has been a difficult one; _____ I still feel as though it's been worth it.

B. Add a sentence that would logically follow each connector. (7 points each)

6. He promised to cut taxes and he didn't. Furthermore _____.

7. We really loved Venice. As a matter of fact, _____.

8. She never explains what she expects us to do. Besides that, _____.

9. Cutting taxes is probably a good thing. On the other hand, _____.

10. You could come with me. Alternatively, _____.

11. He is a very unfair boss. For instance, _____.

12. I have a lot of questions about the project we are supposed to do. Specifically, _____.

13. Your bedroom is in a terrible mess and I can't stand it. In other words, _____.

14. Taking care of your health is your responsibility. Similarly, _____.

15. Tim at least confessed, whereas _____.

UNIT 12 ANSWERS

A. Possible Answers

1. In addition, What's more, Besides
2. On the other hand, However,
3. In particular, Especially
4. similarly, likewise
5. even so, nevertheless, however

B. Possible Answers

6. I don't like his stand on defense.
7. we stayed a week longer than we had planned.
8. she has a very short temper.
9. it may mean reductions in social programs.
10. you could go by yourself on the bus.
11. he once took credit for a suggestion that I gave him.
12. when are we supposed to start?
13. clean up or get out.
14. you are responsible for your own mental stability.
15. Bill would never even admit what he'd done.

A. Rewrite the incorrect modal form in each sentence. (4 points each)

1. You should gone to Pete's party. It was great!
2. Sandy not might go with her if she had seen the note.
3. He must have playing the tuba not the flute!
4. The house should have finished six months ago!

B. Complete the sentences with the perfect modals below. Use each modal at least once. (7 points each)

must (not) have   can't have   could (not) have   might (not) have

should (not) have   be (not) supposed to have   will (not) have

5. I don't believe in ghosts. You _____ seen one.
   You _____ been dreaming.

6. A: Why isn't Tom here?
   B: I'm not sure. His class _____ ended late or his
      car _____ broken down.

7. A: I can't believe that you walked nine miles in the rain!
      You _____ called me.

8. We _____ cheated on the test. Now we're going to get kicked out
   of school.

9. I _____ finished this work last Friday.

10. How can she drive across country next month? She _____ taken
    her driving test by then.

11. If I am correct, the thief _____ hidden in the museum until it
    closed.

12. _____ you _____ finished the painting by the time I
    get back?

13. A: I can't believe that Betty drove by without offering us a ride.
    B: She would never do that on purpose. She _____ seen us.

UNIT 13 ANSWERS

A.
1. should have gone
2. might not have gone
3. must have been playing
4. should have been finished

B.
5. couldn't have/must have
6. could have/might have; could have/might have
7. should have
8. shouldn't have
9. was supposed to have/should have
10. won't have
11. must have
12. Will you have
13. must not have

A. Complete the following sentences with one of the discourse organizers below. (6 points each blank)

all in all   at first   at last   briefly   first   in the first place

next   overall   the last reason   then   to begin with   secondly

in the second place   to summarize   eventually

1. I'd like to begin with a brief history of Afghanistan. _____,
   Afghanistan was formed as a country in 1747.

2. So I hope that you will join with us in creating a new society. _____,
   a vote for Cleary is a vote for the future.

3. First it rained, then the limousine was late and the caterer delivered the food
   to the wrong place. _____, my wedding day was a disaster!

4—5. Well Tom there are several reasons why I have decided to fire you. _____,
   you lied on your employment application. _____, you proceeded to
   start causing trouble in the office.

6—7. _____ I'd like to thank you for inviting me to speak at this
   meeting. _____, I'd like to tell you about a young man I just met.

8. _____, these examples prove that the proposed law will hurt the
   middle class.

9. So, looking at the statistics from this perspective, we can see
   that _____ this has actually been a good year for United Electronics.

10. Pushing the car was very difficult but _____ we were able to get it
    off the highway.

B. Write two sentences that could follow from the sentences below. Use connectors from the list above. Do not use any connector more than once. (8 points each)

11. I think that there are a number of problems with the transportation system in
    our town.

12. There are several reasons why I think I'm qualified for this job.

13. Getting regular exercise is good for you.

C. Write a summary statement for each of the passages below. Use the summary connector in parentheses. (8 points each)

14. Have you ever wondered why there are so many families today with two working parents? Are both parents working because they can or because they must? (in short)

15. Most people today are aware of the health problems that being very overweight can cause. However, many people do not realize the psychological cost of obesity. (in summary)

UNIT 14 ANSWERS

A.
1. To begin with/First
2. Briefly/To conclude/In the end
3. All in all/Overall
4. First of all/First/In the first place/To begin with
5. Then/Next/Secondly
6. First of all
7. Then/Next/Secondly
8. To summarize/In short
9. overall/all in all
10. eventually

B. Sample answers:
11. First of all, we do not have enough buses. Next, they never run on time.
12. To begin with I'm very hard worker. Secondly, I have fifteen years' experience.
13. First it has many obvious health benefits. In the second place, it also improves your mental state.

C.
14. In short, are we sacrificing our children for economic gain?
15. In summary, the overweight may suffer more psychologically than physically.

Grammar Dimensions Book 4

Unit 15 Conditionals *Only If,/Unless,*
           Even Though,/Even If

Name _____

Score _____
            100

A. Complete each of the sentences by writing the appropriate form of the verb in parentheses. (6 points each)

1. Hurry! If you _____ (leave) quickly, you _____ (be able) to catch them.

2. If I _____ (be) older, I _____ (have) a lot more freedom.

3. If you _____ (arrive) on time, you _____ (see) them. But now they're gone.

4. He _____ (study) more unless he _____ (think)
   he _____ (fail).
   Unfortunately he knows he's going to pass.

5. When I was young, my parents never _____ (let) me watch
   television, unless I _____ (finish) my homework.

6. If it _____ (not be) for James, I _____ (still be) in Texas.

7. Even though he _____ (break) his leg, he _____ (not miss) a day of work last year.

B. Complete each sentence with *even though* or *even if*. (6 points each)

8. They wouldn't have won _____ they had practiced more.

9. _____ she had already had three accidents, her father bought her a new car.

10. _____ I leave at 10, I'll never get there on time.

C. Complete the sentences logically and grammatically. (8 points each)

11. _____ unless you're in great physical shape.

12. If you had given me the money, _____.

13. _____ only if he's first in his class.

14. If it hadn't been for his bad advice, _____.

15. Even if _____, I would have gone to Europe with you.

UNIT 15 ANSWERS

A.
1. leave; will be able to
2. were; would have
3. had arrived; would have seen
4. wouldn't study; thought; was going to fail
5. let; finished
6. were not; would still be
7. broke; did not miss

B.
8. even if
9. Even though
10. Even if

C. Sample answers:
11. Don' try mountain climbing
12. I would have spent it already
13. He will get a scholarship
14. I would still have the money in the bank
15. you had made me really angry

A. Rewrite the incorrect sentences. Two sentences are correct. (6 points each)

1. Because leaving late, we missed the plane.

2. Frustrated and embarrassed, the telephone rang and she answered it.

3. The cat ran widly about the room, excited the dog.

4. As I had never met them before, I didn't want to ask for a favor.

5. Walked three times a day, Melissa kept her dog healthy.

6. Using matches, the fire started easily.

7. Chewing her nails in frustration, the exam was difficult for Nora.

8. Having hit the girl, the police arrested him.

9. After waiting for three hours, my mother finally arrived.

10. Not being able to get out of bed, I read a lot of books.

B. Complete each sentence with a reduced adverb clause or a main clause. (8 points each)

11. Confused by the announcements, _____.

12. _____, we quickly extinguished the fire.

13. Not having studied for the exam, _____.

14. Going straight off the cliff, _____.

15. _____, Mexico is a perfect vacation spot.

UNIT 16 ANSWERS

A. There are several possible ways to correct many of the sentences. Sample answers:

1. Because we left late . . . / Leaving late . . .
2. . . . she answered the telephone when it rang.
3. . . . exciting the dog
4. correct
5. . . . Melissa's dog was kept healthy / By walking the dog three times a day . . .
6. . . . the fire was started easily
7. . . . Nora found the exam very difficult
8. . . . he was arrested by the police
9. After being delayed three hours . . .
10. correct

B. Sample Answers:

11. she went to ask for help.
12. Frightened by the flames,
13. I did very poorly
14. the car crashed into the ravine below
15. Possessing many excellent beaches and interesting historical sites,

Grammar Dimensions Book 4

Unit 17 Preposition Clusters

Name _____

Score _____
100

A. Complete the sentences with one of the prepositions in the list below. (5 points each)

at   for   from   in   of   on   to   with

1. The store is adjacent _____ the movie theater.

2. William objects _____ staying late.

3. We were counting _____ your going with us.

4. According _____ the weather report, we should not drive today.

5. They had planned _____ asking everyone.

6. No one's hungry, so we can dispense _____ the snacks.

7. He called _____ a return to family values.

8. Maria will withdraw _____ the race tomorrow.

9. Trifle is an English desert that consists _____ cake, custard and fruit.

10. The students are unfamiliar _____ American traditions.

11. We are going to abstain _____ voting.

12. I'm sure that they will not cooperate _____ each other.

13. We all long _____ peace and quiet.

14. Peg's brothers and sisters are very dependent _____ her.

15. She's very proficient _____ Spanish.

B. Complete the sentences with the multiword preposition clusters below. (5 points each)

in case of   in the process of   on account of
on behalf of   on the advice of

16. I'd like to give you this gift _____ all your employees.

17. _____ trying to shut the door, I broke the window.

18. We went by car _____ our neighbors.

19. I have to leave early _____ my job.

20. Please call 911 _____ emergency.

UNIT 17 ANSWERS

A. 1. to
    2. to
    3. on
    4. to
    5. on
    6. with
    7. for
    8. from
    9. of
    10. with
    11. from
    12. with
    13. for
    14. on
    15. in

B. 16. on behalf of
    17. In the process of
    18. on the advice of
    19. on account of
    20. in case of

Name _____

Score _____
100

A. Rewrite the incorrect sentences using formal style. One sentence is correct. (6 points each)

1. Last Tuesday at work he regretted to tell me of her death.

2. He never minds his wife arriving late.

3. For he to be thrown out of school was a great scandal.

4. You neglected sending me an invitation.

5. She never stops to talk and it's difficult to get away.

6. They suggested me to go with them.

7. You quitting your job pleases him.

8. I remembered calling her but she wasn't home.

9. My grandfather always tended to be late for dinner.

10. It would be amazing for we to win the lottery.

B. Complete the following sentences using the gerunds or infinitives. (8 points each)

11. I am reluctant _____.

12. Try to continue _____.

13. He's sick of _____.

14. _____ would be a great achievement.

15. They convinced _____.

UNIT 18 ANSWERS

A. 1. . . . regretted telling me . . .
2. . . . his wife's arriving late.
3. For him to be . . .
4. . . . neglected to send me. . .
5. . . . stops talking.
6. . . . suggested that I. . .
7. Your quitting . . .
8. . . . remembered to call . . .
9. correct
10. . . . for us . . .

B. Sample answers:
11. to try new things
12. exercising everyday
13. being the only one who works
14. Finishing on time
15. us to leave early

A. Rewrite the incorrect sentences. One sentence is correct. (4 points each)

1. He claims to been told to come here.

2. It must be wonderful have finished knowing that you've done your best.

3. Under the circumstances, it was very kind of him to have let you stay.

4. He appears to leave yesterday without anyone noticing.

5. He wants to have gone at 8 tomorrow.

B. Rewrite each of the following sentences so that it contains a perfective infinitive clause. Sometimes you will have to combine two sentences into one. Make any other word changes that are necessary. (8 points each)

6. We need to leave the house by 6 A.M.

7. Margaret considers that she was cheated by the car dealer.

8. She will be happy when she completes the driving course since she can't stand the instructor.

9. Our teacher claims that she was not given complete autonomy in the classroom.

10. Betsy didn't want to go to the party but she wanted to be invited.

11. You lent me $100. That was very generous.

12. Not visiting the Smithsonian Museum would have been a disappointment. (use *it*)

13. This letter looks as if it was written by a child. (use *appear*)

14. Danny couldn't have gotten a D on the exam. He's too smart.

15. I was supposed to visit Washington last month but the trip was canceled.

UNIT 19 ANSWERS

A.   1. to have been told
   2. . . . to have finished . . .
   3. correct
   4. . . . to have left . . .
   5. . . . wants to go . . .

B.   6. . . . need to have left . . .
   7. Margaret considers herself to have been cheated by . . .
   8. . . . happy to have completed the driving course . . .
   9. . . . claims not to have been given complete. . .
   10. . . . wanted to have been invited.
   11. For you to have lent me $100 was very generous. OR: That was very generous for you to have lent . . .
   12. It would have been a great disappointment not to have visited the Smithsonian Museum.
   13. This letter appears to have been written by a child.
   14. Danny is too smart to have gotten a D on the exam.
   15. I was supposed to have visited Washington last month . . .

Grammar Dimensions Book 4

Name _____

Unit 20 Adjective Complements in Subject and
Predicate Position

Score _____
                                        100

A. Rewrite or combine these sentences to include an adjective complement. (6 points each)

1. School is about to end and the teachers seem very ready for it.

2. He goes 'walking' in the woods in his wheelchair. That's incredible.

3. The community must protest the construction of more apartment houses. It is crucial.

4. Parents should discipline their children. It is imperative.

5. The employees are going to get a raise next month. That will be amazing.

6. In Judaism sacred books cannot be thrown away. They must be buried. This is unusual.

7. He didn't work on his stamp collection. It became impossible.

8. Sandra was killed in a traffic accident. It was tragic.

9. We are going to leave. Michael seems unhappy.

10. A vegetarian may agree to eat meat. It would be unusual.

B. What do you think about the following ideas? Use adjective complements in your answers. Begin your sentences with word in parentheses. (8 points each)

11. your friend/hitchhiking across the U.S.   (My)

12. your mother/coming to visit for six months   (For)

13. your brother/winning the lottery   (His)

14. a teenager/getting married   (It)

15. an immigrant/studying English   (That)

UNIT 20 ANSWERS

A. Sample answers:
1. The teachers seem ready for the school year to end.
2. That he goes "walking" in the woods in his wheelchair is incredible. It is incredible that he goes . . .
3. It is crucial that the community protest the construction of more apartment houses.

   It is crucial for the community to protest the construction of more apartment houses.
4. That parents discipline their children is imperative. It is imperative that parents discipline their children.
5. For the employees to get a raise next month will be amazing.

   That the employees will get a raise next month is amazing.
6. It is unusual that in Judaism sacred texts cannot be thrown away and must be buried.
7. It became impossible for him to work on his stamp collection.
8. Sandra's / Her being killed in a traffic accident was tragic.

   It was tragic for Sandra to be killed in a traffic accident.
9. Michael seems unhappy for us to leave.
10. It would be unusual for a vegetarian to agree to eat meat.

B. Sample answers:
11. My friend's hitchhiking across the United States worries me.
12. For my mother to come to visit for six months would be difficult.
13. His winning the lottery is incredible.
14. It is foolish for a teenager to get married.
15. That an immigrant study English is imperative.

Grammar Dimensions Book 4

Unit 21 Noun Complements Taking *That* Clauses

Name _____

Score _____
100

A. Rewrite the incorrect sentences. Two sentences are correct. (6 points each)

1. I believe the fact that Kennedy was killed by Lee Harvey Oswald.

2. She is worried about that the children will go hungry.

3. The fact that we all need to conserve the environment.

4. You have to face up to you are now bankrupt.

5. The fact that he couldn't go is of no important to me.

6. He was disappointed with the fact that you didn't answer his letter.

7. The theory that stress can sometimes be helpful has already been proven.

8. We agree with that children should be seen and not heard.

9. My boss played down that he was going to be promoted.

10. I'm proud of the fact that I painted the house without help.

B. Complete the following statements with a noun complement. (8 points each)

11. My friend's suggestion that _____ was ridiculous.

12. The possibility that _____ is very remote.

13. I am skeptical of the notion that _____.

14. The tendency for _____ is very dangerous.

15. For _____ is absurd.

UNIT 21 ANSWERS

A.
1. I believe that . . .
2. . . . worried that . . .
3. The fact that we all need . . . (is well accepted.) any logical phrase.
4. face up to the fact that . . .
6. disappointed that you . . .
7. correct
8. . . . agree that children . . .
9. . . . down the fact that . . .
10. . . . proud that . . .

B. Sample answers:
11. we present a play
12. the earth will be hit by a comet
13. wealth equals worth
14. parents to leave young children at home alone
15. you to decide to quit now

A. Rewrite the incorrect sentences. One sentence is correct. (4 points each)

1. She demanded me to leave immediately.

2. He recommends that you stay home for at least three days.

3. I propose that we will vote on the issue.

4. Your advice that he takes five subjects was very unwise.

5. She asked that we went to see her.

B. Write sentences with subjunctive verbs using the verbs in parentheses. (8 points each)

6. A teacher to his student. (request)

_____

7. One friend to another who is going to move away. (propose)

_____

8. A mother to her son. (insist)

_____

9. A married woman to her youngest sister who wants to get married. (suggest)

_____

10. An employer to an employee who is always late. (recommend)

_____

C. Complete the following sentences with subjunctive verbs in noun and adjective complements. (8 points each)

11. The suggestion that _____ was rejected.

12. She paid no attention to the requirement that _____.

13. Your advice that _____ was very helpful.

14. That _____ is crucial.

15. It is mandatory that _____.

UNIT 22 ANSWERS

A. 1. She demanded that I leave . . .
    2. correct
    3. I propose that we vote . . .
    4. Your advice that he take . . .
    5. She asked that we go . . .

B. Sample Answers:
    6. The teacher requested that he rewrite his paper.
    7. I propose that we should plan to talk at least once a month.
    8. I insist that you be home by 11.
    9. I suggest that you wait a while.
    10. I recommend that you buy an alarm clock.

C. Sample Answers:
    11. we all contribute $100 was rejected . . .
    12. . . . only people under 25 could apply.
    13. . . . I put off making a decision . . .
    14. . . . he do this on his own . .
    15. . . . students buy the textbooks.

A. Rewrite parts of the following dialog using *do* or *no* for emphasis where possible and appropriate. There are 10 sentences to change. Write the line number of each change. (6 points each)

1. A: Do you have that money I lent you last month? You said you'd give it back to me by the 15th.

2. B: I gave it back to you. Don't you remember?

3. A: Oh, maybe you're right. Well, in that case, can I borrow $25? I don't have any money right now.

4. B: You don't have any money! You always have money!

5. A: That's not true. I don't always have money. I work on commission and I didn't sell any cars this week. That's why I'm broke.

6. B: You didn't sell any cars?

7. A: Well, that's not completely true. I sold one. But I gave him such a good deal that I hardly made any money.

8. B: Why did you do that? Did he give you a hard luck story?

9. A: He didn't give me a hard luck story but he gave me a good reason to give him a good price.

10. B: What was that?

11. A: He was my brother!

12. B: Well, then you should ask him for a loan.

13. A: I asked him and he said that he didn't have any money because he'd just bought that car.

14. B: Well, I'd like to help you out, but I just lent Mike some money.

15. A: Mike? But he never pays back his debts.

16. B: That's not true. He pays them back. It just takes a while. He promised to give me the money next week.

17. A: Good luck! Well, I guess I'll have to ask my sister.

18. B: Your sister? She's only 15! She doesn't even have a job.

19. A: She doesn't have a regular job but she baby-sits and she makes a lot of money.

B. Complete the sentences logically and grammatically. (9 points each)

20. A: Guess what mom? The dentist said that I didn't have any cavities!

    B: _____.

21. A: Did you get a letter from Sarah?

    B: _____.

22. A: You never wash the dishes.

    B: _____.

23. A: I didn't have any customers today.

    B: _____.

24. A: Do you have your homework?

    B: _____.

UNIT 23 ANSWERS

A. Sentences to change:

    2. I did give it back to you

    3. have no money

    4. You have no money!

    6. You sold no cars?

    7. I did sell one.

    9. but he did give me a good reason. . .

   13. he had no money

   16. He does pay them back.

   19. but she does baby-sit

B. Sample answers:

   20. B: You had no cavities!

   21. B: Well, I did get one.

   22. B: That's not true. I do wash dishes when I have time.

   23. B: You had no customers!

   24. B: No, I don't have my homework, but I do have a great excuse.

A. Rewrite the incorrect sentences. Two are correct. (6 points each)

1. From the woods we suddenly heard a terrifying scream.

2. Not for anything I would go with you.

3. More exciting than the money, the realization was that she was now free.

4. So depressed is Martha that she won't come out of her room.

5. Seldom I have seen such a good performance.

6. So quickly he left that he forgot his coat.

7. Under no circumstances he will be allowed in the class.

8. Not only she walked to school alone but she carried all of her books.

9. No sooner you left than they arrived.

10. Not since was I in San Francisco, I have seen such beautiful views.

B. Add an adverbial phrase or clause to the beginning of each sentence. The word in parentheses tells you which kind of phrase or clause to add. Do not use these words in your new sentences. (8 points each)

11. The customers began running for the door. (manner)

12. My class went exploring in the woods. (time)

13. The police searched the building. (purpose)

14. Tracy and her younger brother sat. (place)

15. The car started rolling down the hill. (manner)

UNIT 24 ANSWERS

A.
1. correct
2. . . . anything would I . . .
3. money, was the realization . . .
4. correct
5. Seldom have I seen . . .
6. So quickly did he leave that . . .
7. circumstances will he be allowed . . .
8. Not only did she walk to school . . .
9. No sooner had you left than . . .
10. Not since I was in . . . have I seen . . .

B. Sample Answers:
11. Screaming in fright, the customers began . . .
12. Long after midnight, my class went . . .
13. In order to catch the thief,
14. On the cliff edge, Tracy and her brother sat. / sat Tracy and her brother.
15. So slowly that no one noticed, the car started . . .

Unit 25 Focusing and Emphasizing Structures:
It-Clefts and *Wh*-Clefts

A. Change each of the following sentences into cleft sentences emphasizing the underlined information. (6 points each)

1. My house <u>is on Maple Street,</u> not Oak Street.

2. We will arrive <u>on a Tuesday,</u> not Monday.

3. <u>Lightning</u> must have started the fire.

4. <u>Bob</u> used to run the family business, but now Dave does.

5. <u>The Security Council</u> makes most of the important decisions in the United Nations.

6. The Korean War started <u>after World War II had ended.</u>

7. The stop sign was installed <u>to make the streets safer for the children.</u>

8. He did <u>a quick and sloppy job.</u>

9. All the striking employees were fired by <u>the plant manager.</u>

10. They were finally married <u>on a lovely day in late spring.</u>

B. Create cleft sentences using the clauses below and the words in parentheses. (8 points each)

11. A: They told me that you met him in the park.

    B: That's not right. _____ was at Jane's wedding. (where)

12. _____ you saw in her office? (who)

13. _____ is a higher minimum wage. (what)

14. A: I hear that you're a writer. Are you famous?

    B: Well actually, _____ are textbooks. (what)

15. A: Thank you for the lovely dishes you gave us for our wedding.

    B: But _____ was a cookbook. (what)

UNIT 25 ANSWERS

A.
1. It is Maple Street my house is on, not Oak.
2. It is Tuesday we will arrive, not Monday.
3. It must have been lightning that started the fire.
4. It was Bob who used to run the family business.
5. It is the Security council . . .
6. It was after World War II had ended that the Korean War started.
7. It was to make the streets safer for children that the stop sign . . .
8. It was a quick and sloppy job that he did.
9. It was the plant manager who fired all the striking employees. / who all the striking employees were fired by . . .
10. It was on a lovely day in late spring that they were finally married.

B.
11. Where I met him
12. Who was it
13. What we need now
14. what I write are textbooks
15. what I gave you was

WORKBOOK ANSWER KEY

Unit 1

Verb Tenses in Written and Spoken Communication

EXERCISE 1

(1) arrived   (2) had never been   (3) is studying   (4) expects; will be working   (5) doesn't work out; 'll go   (6) has been living/has lived   (7) has; closes / is closed; has   (8) have ever been; was; invited   (9) Have you ever thought   (10) 'll go   (11) had spoken; had been trying   (12) has given up   (13) will have known

EXERCISE 2

The explanation for any discrepancy will vary. Discrepancies will probably occur in regard to aspect rather than time frame.

EXERCISE 3

Answers will vary.
1. . . . I thought I could do anything.   2. . . . there will be a colony established on the moon.   3. . . . a fire broke out at the Mayfair restaurant.   4. . . . she has lost a lot of weight.
5. . . . my parents are flying to Brazil.   6. . . . there was peace and prosperity throughout China.   7. . . . the cure for many diseases will be found.   8. . . . I heard a noise outside the door.
9. . . . I'll be taking some time off to travel.   10. . . .the seas rose several inches.   11. . . . our family has been operating a small manufacturing business.   12. . . . the Normans invaded England.   13. . . . I will have left the country.   14. . . . we have studied more than a hundred idioms.   15. . . . I will probably be interviewing someone for my research project.

EXERCISE 4

1. (d) ~~will be~~ is   2. (c) ~~wasn't~~ isn't   3. (c) ~~took~~ takes
4. (c) ~~will take~~ takes   5. (b) ~~have paid~~ pay   6. (a) ~~retained~~ retain   7. (d) ~~tells~~ told   8. (a) ~~see~~ saw

EXERCISE 5

1. (b) haven't been   (a) remember   (c) was   (c) was (a) seems
2. (b) will go   (c) will take   (c) will do   (a) has   (c) will buy (c) was getting   (c) switched   (a) get   (b) has helped   (b) was going
3. (c) looked   (c) looked   (c) felt   (c) wanted   (c) asked (b) give   (b) become   (b) is not
4. (c) have been writing   (c) have probably never read   (b) wrote (c) is   (c) have also learned   (b) have hunted and roamed   (a) do
5. (c) have lived   (b) isn't   (b) gets   (b) covered   (b) know (b) ended   (d) had done   (a) issued   (b) would live
6. (a) has never been painted   (b) knows   (c) was planted (c) wanted   (c) expanded   (c) gelled and formulated   (b) is becoming   (c) felt   (a) am not sitting

EXERCISE 6

A student is taking an exam. . . At the end of the period, the professor announces that time is up and the students have to turn. . . All the students come to the front and put their exams. . . one student who remains. . . . When the student comes to the front. . . professor tells him that his grade will be lowered for. . . student stiffens and indignantly asks. . . professor replies. . . student replies. . . lifts the huge pile of papers and places. . .

EXERCISE 7

Answers will vary.

Unit 2

Verbs: Aspect and Time Frames

EXERCISE 1

1. had 2. will contact 3. makes 4. decorated 5. will own
6. thought / saw 7. reveal 8. will spend 9. gives 10. will believe

EXERCISE 2

1. (a) wonder (b) are looking for (c) have (d) look
(e) ask (f) understand (g) work (h) believes (i) feels
(j) gives (k) is currently writing (l) provides (m) helps
(n) is also looking
2. (a) were talking (b) wanted (c) noticed (d) seemed
(e) asked (f) told (g) had (h) went (i) was running
(j) had
3. (a) is studying (b) hopes (c) is (d) feels (e) has
(f) are constantly doing (g) mails (h) is always telling (i) is
4. (a) has (b) is working (c) improves (d) works (e) is
(f) takes (g) is cooking (h) eats (i) goes (j) realizes
(k) is taking (l) needs

EXERCISE 3

1. have believed
2. suffer
3. is
4. is
5. lies
6. involves
7. have been
8. have placed
9. possess
10. learned/has earned
11. are
12. have looked/look
13. accepted/accept
14. come
15. understand
16. don't have
17. had
18. were
19. have learned/learn
20. have given
21. had not considered
22. tend
23. had not published
24. have found/find
25. believe
26. is
27. learn
28. have scored
29. feel
30. havec ollected

EXERCISE 4

1. (A) b (B) b; c (C) b; b 2. (A) a (B) a (C) a 3. (A) a
(B) a (C) c (D) b (E) b; b (D)/(E)

EXERCISE 5

(1) will be (2) will have gone (3) will have spent (4) will
have (5) Will I be (6) will have changed (7) will not have
(8) will have spent (9) will be

EXERCISE 6

(1) have been (2) moved (3) took (4) got (5) used
(6) was (7) found (8) has been working/has worked
(9) have been trying (10) have gone/have been going (11) had
been looking/had looked (12) have been talking (13) had
planned/had been planning

EXERCISE 7

ACROSS 2. working 3. plays 6. are waiting 9. has run
11. stimulates 12. since
DOWN 1. finished 3. present 4. just 5. have been 7. is
taking 8. occurs 10. past

EXERCISE 8

(1) feels (2) are (3) has been (4) are (5) are studying
(6) are studying (7) are going (8) keep/have kept/have been
keeping (9) complains (10) is calling/calls (11) is trying
(12) have come (13) are still living/still live (14) has
supported/has been supporting (15) sends (16) mails
(17) has visited (18) looks forward

EXERCISE 9

(1) think (2) hear (3) are (4) was trying (5) exploded
(6) appeared (7) had been (8) have heard (9) sounded

(10) have heard   **(11)** have hosted   **(12)** deal   **(13)** is
(14) commits   **(15)** concern   **(16)** invented   **(17)** is   **(18)** appear
(19) had been   **(20)** woke   **(21)** had been   **(22)** concerns
(23) buys   **(24)** had run   **(25)** wrote   **(26)** have acquired
(27) has been looking/has looked   **(28)** concerned/concerns
(29) was dying   **(30)** needed   **(31)** has come

EXERCISE 10

ACROSS   **2.** running   **7.** progressive   **9.** will be
10. am going
DOWN   **1.** will have   **3.** have spent   **4.** comes   **5.** working
6. leaves   **8.** is flying

Unit 3

Subject-Verb Agreement

EXERCISE 1

The head noun is listed first; the verb, second.
(1) survey   is
(2) Americans   believe
(3) One   is
(4) subscribers   receive
(5) piece   is
(6) studies   have
(7) success   comes
(8) writers   have
(9) reading   is
(10) Neil Postman   has
(11) reading   remains
(12) look   leaves
(13) book   is
(14) books   have

EXERCISE 2

Head Noun/Modifying Phrase/Verb
(1) kind of fiction   [that each person likes to read]   is
(2) four most popular writers   [in the survey]   write
(3) One thing   [that most of the favorite books have in common]   is
(4) This designation   [which is made frequently by book sellers and reviewers]   is
(5) book   [that is unpopular with literary critics]   is
(6) this kind of book   [compared to books typically taught in college literature courses]   has
(7) review   [of books considered popular over the years]   shows
(8) Charles Dickens   [along with a number of other Victorian writers]   was
(9) Shakespeare's plays   [widely considered the paradigm of thoughtful literature in English]   were
(10) people   find

(11) eyeglasses   [as opposed to contact lenses]   help
(12) desire   [not any innate abilities]   makes

EXERCISE 3

(1) write   **(2)** their   **(3)** has written   **(4)** are   **(5)** major writers   **(6)** have   **(7)** appeal   **(8)** interests   **(9)** Has
(10) tell   **(11)** Do   **(12)** is   **(13)** a good choice
(14) appeals   **(15)** are   **(16)** good choices   **(17)** find
(18) their   **(19)** books

EXERCISE 4

(2) it   **(3)** is using   **(4)** is   **(5)** is   **(6)** are writing
(7) their   **(8)** is   **(9)** like   **(10)** comes   **(11)** helps
(12) like   **(13)** is   **(14)** has   **(15)** doesn't favor
(16) interests   **(17)** is   **(18)** tend   **(19)** do

EXERCISE 5

1. is   **2.** is   **3.** is   **4.** was   **5.** is   **6.** have been   **7.** is   **8.** are
9. was   **10.** is   **11.** are   **12.** were   **12.** is   **14.** is   **15.** was
16. is   **17.** are

EXERCISE 6

(1) were   **(2)** is   **(3)** deals   **(4)** were   **(5)** has
(6) knows   **(7)** seems   **(8)** has   **(9)** has   **(10)** are
(11) continues   **(12)** was   **(13)** was   **(14)** had   **(15)** were

EXERCISE 7

(1) has   **(2)** have   **(3)** are   **(4)** reveal   **(5)** feels
(6) face   **(7)** own   **(8)** insists   **(9)** say   **(10)** go

EXERCISE 8

(2) is   **(3)** is   **(4)** is   **(5)** are   **(6)** are   **(7)** are   **(8)** is
(9) are   **(10)** am   **(11)** am

Exercises for the TOEFL® Test

Units 1-3

1. A	4. C	7. D	10. B	13. C	16. A	19. C	22. A	25. C	27. A
2. A	5. D	8. C	11. A	14. B	17. A	20. B	23. D	26. D	28. C
3. B	6. B	9. B	12. C	15. C	18. C	21. C	24. D		

Unit 4

Passive Verbs

EXERCISE 1

1. was passed. **(B)**   2. have been neglected   **(D)**   3. was rejected **(A)**   4. were cracked **(C)**   5. are being taken **(C)**
6. can be found **(A)**   7. are damaged **(C)**   8. is driven **(A)**
9. will not be returned **(B)**   10. was moved **(A)**

EXERCISE 2

1. Driving events were added in 1904.   2. Swimming pools are clearly marked in competitive swimming.   3. Antiturbulence lane lines are used to separate the swimmers and keep the water calm.
4. In fencing, the sword tips are connected to lights by a long wire that passes underneath each fencer's jacket.   5. A bulb flashes when a hit is made.   6. Fungi, once thought of as plants, are now classified as a separate kingdom.   7. The status of women has been advanced by legislation.   8. Stocks are being bought and sold in a frenzy of activity today on Wall Street.   9. Thousands of photographs of the Great Red Spot will be transmitted by the next Jupiter space probe.   10. The old Barlow mansion on the hill was slowly being devoured by termites.

EXERCISE 3

Part A
Paragraph 1: were manufactured; are bought; is found
Paragraph 2: are made; are devoted; are . . . manufactured; are exported; are imported   **Paragraph 3:** are killed; are listed; are lost   **Paragraph 4:** was caused; are required; are found; are outlined; have been passed   **Paragraph 5:** is related
Part B
Stative Passive
is found; are devoted; are listed; are lost; are found; are outfitted; is related
Dynamic Passive
were produced; were manufactured; are bought; are made; are manufactured; are exported; are imported; are killed; was caused; are required; have been passed

EXERCISE 4

1. is made/D   2. are measured/C.   3. is known/H
4. is covered/B   5. are connected/(is) termed/F/H   6. is surrounded/H   7. (is) found/is considered/A/G   8. are used/E   9. are designed/E   10. are. . .termed/are found/H/A/

EXERCISE 5

(6) is reputed . . .   **(7)** is claimed . . .   **(8)** is said . . .
(10) is considered . . .   **(11)** is known . . . was believed
(13) is said . . .   **(14)** is conjectured . . .   **(16)** was recently reported . . . was seen   **(17)** is said . . .   **(20)** is supposed . . .   **(21)** were thought . . .   **(24)** must be admitted

EXERCISE 6

1. a   2. b   3. a   4. b

EXERCISE 7

1. **(d)** It was believed that if a toad crossed your path, you would have good luck. / A toad crossing your path was believed to be a sign of good luck.   2. **(h)** It was believed that if a cat sneezed, it would rain. / A cat sneezing was believed to be a sign that it would rain.   3. **(g)** It was believed that if a lizard crossed the path of a bridal procession, the marriage would have problems. / A lizard crossing the path of a bridal procession was believed to be a sign that the marriage would have problems.   4. **(a)** It was believed that if you saw a golden butterfly at a funeral, you would have a long life. / Seeing a golden butterfly at a funeral was believed to be a sign that you would have a long life.   5. **(c)** It was believed that if a weasel squealed, a death was imminent. / A weasel squealing was believed to be a sign that a death was imminent.
6. **(b)** It was believed that if a beetle crawled out of your shoe, bad luck would come to you. / A beetle crawling out of your shoe

was believed to be a sign that bad luck would come to you.
7. (e) It was believed that if a spier fell on you from the ceiling of a house a legacy would come your way. / A spider falling on you from the ceiling of ahouse was believed to be a sign that a legacy would come your way. **8. (f)** It was believed that if you fed horsehair to your children, they would do well in school. / Feeding horsehair to your children was believed to help them do well in school.

EXERCISE 8

1. It is expected that he will run in the primary elections. / He is expected to run in the primary elections. **2.** It is rumored that he is undergoing treatment in a clinic in Arizona. / He is rumored to be undergoing treatment in a clinic in Arizona. **3.** It is believed that the results of the lab tests were misinterpreted. / The results of the lab tests are believed to have been misinterpreted. **4.** The case is assumed to have been settled out of court. / It is assumed that the case was settled out of court. **5.** It is alleged that it was the work of arsonists. / It is alleged to have been the work of arsonists.
6. A major reshuffling of the White House staff is expected to be announced shortly. / It is expected that a major reshuffling of the White House staff will be announced shortly.

EXERCISE 9

1. It is thought that there are approximately 75,000 edible plants found in nature. / Approximately 75,000 edible plants are thought to be found in nature. **2.** It is estimated that the number of birds that are killed in collisions with TV broadcast towers each year is 1,250,000. / The number of birds that are killed in collisions with TV broadcast towers each year is estimated to be 1,250,000. **3.** The highest mountain in South America is known to be Aconcagua in Argentina. **4.** It is believed that the estimated number of unsolicited phone calls made by U.S. telemarketers each second is 200. / The estimated number of unsolicited phone calls made by U.S. telemarketers each second is believed to be 200. **5.** It is speculated that the amount of time reqired to set the table for a banquet at London's Buckingham Palace is three days. / The amount

of time required to set the table for a banquet at London's Buckingham Palace is speculated to be three days. **6.** It is reported that the maximum fine for parking illegally overnight in Tokyo is $1,400. / The maximum fine for parking illegally overnight in Tokyo is reported to be $1,400. **7.** It is believed that earth's population around 8000 B.C., when farmers began harvesting domesticated plants, was 4 million. / Earth's population around 8000 B.C., when farmers began harvesting domesticated plants, is believed to have been 4 million. **8.** It is said that thenumber of people born every 10 days in 1991 was 4 million. / The number of people born every 10 days in 1991 is said to have been 4 million.

EXERCISE 10

1. could be seen . . . were taken outside / Passive is used to maintain focus on subject—iguanas—and to create cohesion in the passage. **2.** has been estimated / Passive is used to maintain focus on subject—English words borrowed by the Japanese—and to create cohesion in the passage. **3.** can be read . . . is spoken / Passive isused to maintain focus on subject—Chinese writing first and then dialect—and to create cohesion in the passage. **4.** had been thought up . . . had been sold / Passive is used to maintain focus on subject—the crossword first and then the number of puzzles—and to create cohesion in the passage.

EXERCISE 11

1. Before Harvey's work was published in 1628, the role of the heart in circulation was not recognized. **2.** Lipids are built of carbon, hydrogen, and oxygen. **3.** The polar caps of Mars are made up not of water but of frozen carbon dioxide. **4.** Since that time, however, almost all of the early craters have been destroyed by the forces of erosion and weathering. **5.** These organisms are referred to loosely as "blue-green algae." They are believed to have been the first living things on Earth. **6.** This field is thought to reverse itself every eleven years.

Unit 5

Article Usage

EXERCISE 1

(1) The (2) the (3) a (4) the (5) The (6) the (7) a (8) Ø (9) the (10) an (11) Ø (12) Ø (13) The

(14) a (15) a (16) the (17) a (18) Ø (19) the (20) the (21) Ø (22) a (23) the (24) the (25) Ø (26) Ø (27) A (28) a (29) the (30) the (31) a

EXERCISE 2

1. <u>a</u> (C)   2. <u>The</u> (I); <u>the</u> (I); Ø (C)   3. <u>The</u> (I)   4. Ø (C); Ø <u>(C)</u>; <u>the</u> (I); <u>the</u> (I)   (5) Ø (C)   (6) <u>The</u> (I); Ø (C)   (7) Ø (C)   (8) <u>The</u> (I); <u>the</u> (I)   (9) <u>The</u> (I); Ø   (10) <u>a</u> (C); <u>the</u> (I)

EXERCISE 3

Answers will vary.
1. a cat   2. the articles   3. thrillers   4. the spelling checkers on the word processors   5. the long hours

EXERCISE 4

1. *the* second item/C; *the* auction/J   2. *the* subway/H; Ø friends/K
3. *The* end/F; *the* play/J   4. *The* moon/A; *the* trail/J   5. *the* candidates/E; *the* rich/G   6. *The* most challenging assignment/B; *a* physics project/K   7. *the* mall/I   8. *the* in-basket/J; *the* pile/J; *the* window/J; *the* fifteenth time/C   9. *The* function/F; *the* machine/J
10. *the* population/E   11. *The* main reason/D; *the* lecture/J; *the* most famous living poet/B   12. *the* ignorant/G; *the* state of bliss/F

EXERCISE 5

1. . . . for a heart-to-<u>a</u> heart talk   2. . . . meal is <u>a</u> breakfast.
3. . . . by <u>the</u> phone.   4. <u>The</u> time is <u>the</u> . . .   5. . . . during <u>the</u> day   6. . . . on <u>the</u> arrival   7. . . . take <u>the</u> heed
8. . . . mouth-to-<u>the</u> mouth   9. . . . on <u>a</u> horseback.
10. . . . to <u>the</u> church

EXERCISE 6

1. a   2. b   3. a   4. b   5. a   6. a   7. a   8. b   9. a
10. a

EXERCISE 7

1. Cheese is a noncount noun. / Correction: Cheese is made from milk.   4. Left-handed people is a plural noun. / Correction: Generally, left-handed people die earlier than others.   5. Diamond is a simple inanimate object. / Correction: A diamond is the hardest stone. / Diamonds are the hardest stones.   6. Hydrogen is a noncount noun. / Correction: Hydrogen is the first element on the atomic table.   8. Tie is a simple inanimate object / Correction: A tie is worn. / Ties are worn . . .   9. Arabian horses is a plural noun. / Correction: Arabian horses are prized for their speed and beauty.

EXERCISE 8

2. The Swiss are noted for their banks and their mountain scenery. **(h)**   3. Backpackers value lightweight equipment. **(k)**
4. Smokers believe they are being discriminated against today. **(f)**
5. (The) Hindus believe in reincarnation. **(c)**   6. The British had a vast empire in the nineteenth century. **(a)**   7. Marathon runners tend to be thin and wiry. **(e)**   8. (The) socialists advocate free universal medical coverage. **(j)**   9. The Navajos live in the Four Corners region of the United States. **(d)**   10. Jazz muscians like to improvise. **(l)**   11. (The) beetles are the largest group of insects. **(g)**   12. Computer programmers must possess excellent mathematical skills. **(i)**

EXERCISE 9

1. The cheetah   3. The photovoltaic cell   4. The compact disc
7. The liver   8. The potato   10. The stomach

EXERCISE 10

1. The heart pumps   2. (The) skin covers / Hair covers
3. The kidneys filter   4. The ears are   5. The tongue is / The mouth is   6. The scalp is   7. (The) muscles are   8. The brain enables   9. The lungs are / The nose is   10. The nose is

EXERCISE 11

1. A/The zebra   2. Telescopes   3. A/The hammer   4. Dentists
5. Baseball   6. A/The butterfly   7. Ice   8. Chewing gum
9. A/The broom   10. Glasses

EXERCISE 12

1. Rabies is   2. A cold is   3. The flu is   4. AIDS is
5. A heart attack is   6. An ulcer is   7. Cholera is   8. The mumps is   9. Leprosy is   10. A fracture is

Unit 6

Reference Words and Phrases

EXERCISE 1

ACROSS   1. it   3. country   5. these   7. this
DOWN   2. those   4. them   5. they   6. such   7. that

EXERCISE 2

Answers may vary.
1. these differences   2. This abasement   3. Men's names
4. This diminutive suffix   5. This suffix   6. This practice

7. Words with a negative connotation   8. Words   9. This problem   10. these rules

EXERCISE 3

Answers may vary.

1. This characteristic makes a person a giver.   2. These listening skills, some insist, are even more important than speaking skills
3. It goes on to examine the area of morale within organizations.
4. Or do these emotions and urges depend upon egotistical instincts?   5. Much of this redefinition will have to examine who our role models are.

EXERCISE 4

1. it   2. it   3. These desires/these issues   4. the Bulls/the Suns   5. the cars/them   6. (a) the words; (b) them/the plays
7. the silk melons   8. Their findings/These findings (or discoveries)
9. they/these foods   10. it/this (crazy) story

EXERCISE 5

Answers may vary.
1. (a) this   (b) that   2. those   3. That   4. these   5. That
6. These   7. This   8. those   9. That   10. This/That

EXERCISE 6

Answers will vary.
1. This feature   2. These promises   3. these tendencies
4. these phrases   5. These habits   6. These paintings

7. This practice   8. These conditions   9. These precautions
10. these excuses

EXERCISE 7

Answers may vary.
1. this/this game   2. it   3. This   4. this/that   5. it
6. that   7. This   8. it   9. that   10. this/this fine

EXERCISE 8

Answers may vary:
Paragraph 1: them, the question **Paragraph 2:** it; these species; them **Paragraph 3:** the species and habitats; those; those; these special places; It

EXERCISE 9

Answers may vary:
1. Such measures   2. Such expenses   3. such diseases
4. such a move   5. such a thing   6. Such actions   7. Two such birds (the only correct answer possible)   8. Such symptoms   9. no such person   10. Such dedication   11. Such people   12. Such actions

EXERCISE 10

Answers will vary:
1. . . . such senses   2. Such a . . .   3. It . . .
4. . . . this topic.   5. . . . this   6. . . . example of
7. . . . that   8. . . . that   9. . . . such   10. Such incidents are . . .

Unit 4–6

Exercises for the TOEFL® Test

1. D	4. A	7. D	10. B	13. A	16. B	19. D	22. D	24. A
2. A	5. C	8. C	11. C	14. B	17. B	20. D	23. A	25. C
3. D	6. A	9. B	12. C	15. A	18. B	21. D		

Unit 7

Relative Clauses Modifying Subjects

EXERCISE 1

1. that/Nauru   2. that/San Marino   3. that/Nauru
4. that/Nauru   5. whose currency/Liechtenstein
6. that/San Marino   7. that/San Marino   8. that/Nauru
9. that/the Nazis/San Marino

EXERCISE 2

1. . . . to which I gave money turned out to be a fraud. / . . . that I gave money to . . .   2. . . . that I bought last week is now on sale.   3. . . . whose employees are on strike is probably going to be sold.   4. . . . that I rescued from a tree has been hanging around our house.   5. . . . who tend to get sick often may have poor diets.   6. . . . who you saw in the hall with the dean is

actually working on a doctorate in mathematics.   **7.** . . . whose works were featured in last week's *Time* magazine just got another grant.   **8.** . . . <u>to whom</u> you gave your seat used to work with your mother. / . . . <u>whom</u> you gave . . .   **9.** . . . . <u>whose</u> employees are always complaining should take an honest look at itself.

EXERCISE 3

Answers will vary.

1. The man who is dressed in a shirt and tie and who is talking on the phone is a diplomat.   **2.** The students who are listening to a lecture are all honor students.   **3.** That man who is roller-blading by the lake tries to work out every day.   **4.** The woman who is on horseback and in uniform is a park police officer.

EXERCISE 4

Answers will vary.

1. A spouse who is patient and devoted is necessary for a long and happy life.   **2.** Housing that is uncrowded and clean is necessary for a long and happy life.   **3.** Children who are healthy and respectful are necessary for a long and happy life.   **4.** Friends who are there when you need them are necessary for a long and happy life.   **5.** Leisure time that is relaxing and satisfying is necessary for a long and happy life.   **6.** A hobby that is absorbing and educational is necessary for a long and happy life.   **7.** An education that is broadening and ongoing is necessary for along and happy life.   **8.** A boss who is courteous and trusting is necessary for a long and happy life.

9. A neighborhood that is clean, friendly, and free of crime is necessary for a long and happy life.

EXERCISE 5

Answers will vary.

1. The man [who is] dressed... [who is] talking...   **2.** The students [who are] listening...   **3.** That man [who is] roller-blading...   **4.** The woman [who is] on horseback...

EXERCISE 6

1. The manager we met was very polite.   **2.** The computer at the end of the row is out of order.   **3.** The crowd cheered the runner trying to regain the lead.   **4.** Dedicated students can be found in the library on Saturday nights.   **5.** No change.   **6.** The paintings we saw at the museum were impressive.   **7.** The president elected in November saw his popularity decline in March.   **8.** The parking place near the entrance is reserved for the employee of the month.   **9.** Angry workers confronted the union leader about the new contract.   **10.** Programmers experienced with UNIX systems will be given first consideration.

EXERCISE 7

1. You can't teach an old dog new tricks.   **2.** A bird in the hand is worth two in the bush.   **3.** A bad workman blames his tools.   **4.** People in glass houses shouldn't throw stones.   **5.** A rolling stone gathers no moss.   **6.** A watched pot never boils.

Unit 8

Relative Clauses Modifying Objects

EXERCISE 1

ACROSS   **1.** whose **2.** with **3.** whom **4.** about **6.** to
DOWN   **1.** which **3.** who **4.** at **5.** that

EXERCISE 2

1. . . . singer *whom* . . .   **2.** . . . . neighbors *with whom* we left our dog.   **3.** . . . . the mountain from *whose* summit . . .
4. . . . . my keys, *which* I thought I had put in . . .
5. . . . . dolphin *that* she had thrown some fish to. / . . . . the dolphin *to which* she had thrown some fish.

EXERCISE 3

2. A computer is a device that performs calculations.   **3.** Irrigation is a process by which water is artificially conducted to soil to promote growth.   **4.** A seismograph is an instrument that is used to detect and record seismic waves caused by earthquakes.   **5.** The Nobel Prize is an award that is given to individuals from all over the world who have made outstanding contributions in their fields.   **6.** Cobras are poisonous snakes whosenecks can be spread to form a hood when alarmed.   **7.** Entomology is a science that is devoted to the study of insects.   **8.** The tundra is a treeless plain in the Arctic Circle whose soil is a thin coating over permafrost.   **9.** Margarine is a spread that is prepared from vegetable fats.   **10.** The Kentucky Derby is a horserace in which three-year-old horsesrun over a one-and-one-quarter-mile course at Churchill Downs in Louisville, Kentucky.

EXERCISE 4

Answers will vary.

1. People were frightened of griffins which were part eagle and part lion and destroyed anyone who strayed into their territory.

2. The most frightening of the three Gorgon sisters was Medusa, whose head was a mass of coiling snakes and whose glance could turn a person into stone.   3. The gates to the underworld were guarded by Cerberus, which was a three-headed dog that threatened anyone who came too close.
4. As one of their tortures, the gods used the Harpies, which were vultures with the heads of women and whose claws tore at their unfortunate victims.   5. The monster that lay in wait for travelers on the road to Thebes was the Sphinx, which had the body of a lion and the head of a woman and dared those it stopped to solve a riddle or die.   6. Ulysses killed the Cyclops, who was a one-eyed giant who lived in a cave above the shore and ate sheep and men.   7. Ulysses was fortunate to escape from Circe, who was a beautiful witch whose pleasure was to turn men into swine.   8. Ships were often wrecked because of the sirens, who were beautiful nymphs who lived on treacherous rocks and whose irresistible song lured sailors to their doom.
9. Perseus was the hero who killed the Chimera, which was a fire-breathing monster that had the both a lion's and a goat's head and the body of a dragon, with a snake for a tail.
10. For the ancient Greeks, the only monsters that were essentially good were the Centaurs, which were half man and half horse and became rude and uncontrollable only when they became intoxicated with wine.

EXERCISE 5

1. I am often disappointed in movies made from books I have enjoyed.   2. We rented the same house our friends had lived in last year.   3. Look at the deer hiding in the shadows!
4. No deletion possible.   5. I felt overwhelmed by the papers scattered all over my room.   6. The trekkers walked down a narrow trail with a terrifying drop.   7. So far we haven't found a candidate competent enough to get the job.   8. Doris forgot to thank the woman she had received a gift from.   9. No deletion possible.   10. I went to the restaurant you recommended.

EXERCISE 6

1. No deletion possible.   2. No deletion possible.   3. No deletion possible.   4. A seismograph is an instrument used to detect and record seismic waves caused by earthquakes.
5. The Nobel Prize is an award given to individuals from all over the world who have made outstanding contributions in their fields.
6. No deletion possible.   7. Entomology is a science devoted to the study of insects.   8. No deletion possible.   9. Margarine is a spread prepared from vegetable fats.   10. No deletion possible.

EXERCISE 7

1. The Arabs have a culture of which they are justifiably proud.
2. It's a tiny office out of which they work.   3. I don't think there are any to whom we can award it.   4. This is a seminar in which we shall discuss nineteenth-century colonialism.   5. No change possible.   6. That's because she was a girl to whom nothing was ever denied.   7. Darwin was a scientist to whom we all owe a debt.   8. Apparently he was recluse about whom nothing is known.   9. Of course, they are all magazines to which I subscribe.   10. They are a family whom we just cannot put up.

EXERCISE 8

1. . . . I hope you will rise to.   2. . . . group your parents dislike.
3. . . . we have been warned about.   4. . . . man he owed some money to.   5. . . . everyone is talking about.   6. . . . letter she tried to hide.   7. . . . students the teachers failed.   8. . . . many Greek warriors sacrificed their lives for.   9. . . . no intelligent person can subscribe to.   10. . . . passage you are speaking about.   11. . . . man the children were staring at.

Unit 9

Nonrestrictive Relative Clauses

EXERCISE 1

Answers will vary.
1. (a) that I bought last week   (b) which are pervasive in many countries.   2. (a) that is in the library   (b) which is a very useful tool   3. (a) that is near the campus   (b) which was founded by Ray Kroc   4. (a) that lives in the house next door   (b) which is very commonly called "man's best friend"   5. (a) that form on the ground   (b) which she imagines are giants, castles, and other fabulous things   6. (a) that I wrote about the Nobel Peace Prize
(b) which took me two weeks to write   7. (a) that you ordered
(b) which was originally a Greek concept   8. (a) that have large hard drives and expanded memory   (b) which are becoming less expensive   9. (a) that is on the first floor of the office   (b) which is a marvelous invention that can transmit both words and images over telephone lines   10. (a) that won last year's Kentucky Derby
(b) which has very keen senses

EXERCISE 2

Answers will vary. The following phrases are suggestions. which has an enrollment of five thousand; who come from all over the world; all of which make for some stimulating discussion; which so far has been challenging and quite interesting; with whom I had a nice talk today at lunch; which is a place I've always wanted to visit; whose courses, I understand, are very popular; which is a pleasant community; which has four rooms in addition to a living room, kitchen, and bathroom; all of whom are students; which I check every day.

EXERCISE 3

Answers will vary.
1. A stethoscope, which is an instrument for listening to sounds produced within the body, is used by doctors and nurses.
2. A hammer, which is a hand tool consisting of a handle with an attached head made of a relatively heavy, rigid material, is used by carpenters.   3. A spatula, which is a small kitchen implement with a handle and a broad, flat, flexible blade, is used by cooks to lift food from hot pans and grills.   4. A hoe, which is a tool with a flat blade attached at a right angle to a long handle, is used for gardening.   5. Handcuffs, which consist of a pair of strong, connected hoops that can be tightened and locked about the wrists of a prisoner, are used by the police.   6. A compass, which is a device with a magnetic needle that is aligned with the magnetic field of Earth, is used by explorers, sailors, and hikers to determine geographic direction.   7. A tripod, which is an instrument with three legs that supports a camera, is used by photographers and filmmakers.   8. The periodic table, which is an arrangement of the elements according to their atomic numbers so that elements with similar properties are in the same column, is used in chemistry.   9. A wrench, which is a hand tool with a fixed or adjustable jaw for gripping, turning, or twisting objects such as nuts, bolts, or pipes, is used by mechanics, repair people, and plumbers.   10. A scalpel, which is a small, straight knife with a thin, sharp blade, is used in surgery and dissection.

EXERCISE 4

Answers will vary.
(1) which was wise.   (2) which was unfortunate   (3) which was foolish   (4) which was very distressing   (5) which was unbelievable   (6) which was really stupid thinking on her part   (7) which was very precious to me   (8) which annoyed me   (9) which I really appreciated   (10) which was inconvenient   (11) which was a relief

EXERCISE 5

Answers will vary.
(1) one of which   (2) none of which; all of which   (3) one of which   (4) many of whom   (5) two of whom   (6) both of which   (7) one of which   (8) one of whom   (9) a pair of whom

EXERCISE 6

ACROSS   2. all   3. whom   6. both   7. of   8. neither
DOWN   1. each   3. which   4. none   5. some

Exercises for the TOEFL® Test

Units 7–9

1. A	4. C	7. C	10. D	13. A	16. B	19. B
2. A	5. A	8. C	11. A	14. D	17. A	20. D
3. A	6. D	9. C	12. C	15. C	18. A	

Unit 10

Relative Adverb Clauses

EXERCISE 1

ACROSS   1. way   2. which   5. reason   6. during
DOWN   1. where   2. when   3. how   4. from

EXERCISE 2

1. The day *when* Christmas . . .   2. . . . reasons *why* December 25 . . .   3. . . . about *how* Zoroastrians . . .   4. . . . that *how* they overlapped   5. . . . Middle Ages, when it became . . .   6. . . . disliked how it was . . .   7. No change possible.   8. . . . December 6, when someone . . .   9. . . . reasons why the two . . .   10. . . . account for how December . . .

EXERCISE 3

Part A: 1. Ramadan is the period when Muslims . . .   **2.** Asian Lunar New Year is the holiday when most Asians . . .
3. The nineteenth century was the time when Queen . . .
4. 1969 was the year when Neil . . .   **5.** From noon to one

o'clock is the hour when many . . . 6. 1945 was the year when World . . . 7. winter is the season when people . . . 8. The Meiji Restoration is the period when the first . . .

Part B: 1. Downstairs is the place where a house is coolest.
2. Mecca is the city where every Muslim . . . 3. North is the direction where a compass needle points. 4. Saudi Arabia is the country where about one-third of all the world's oil is located.
5. The capitol is the building where a government meets.
6. A cemetary is the place where people are buried.
7. Argentina is the country where the 1978 and 1986 World Cup champions are from.

Part C: 1. A chance . . . is the reason why people immigrate.
2. . . . mileage is one reason why people buy compact cars.
3. . . . spelling is one reason why written English can be difficult.
4. . . . productivity is one reason why businesses use machines.
5. . . . behavior are the reasons why sharks have no natural predators. 6. . . . fluorocarbons is the reason why the ozone layer is healing. 7. . . . humor is the reason why people like Charlie Chaplin.

Part D: 1. . . . training is how athletes build strength. 2. . . . seed is the way you get coriander. 3. . . . conference is the way politicians disseminate information. 4. . . . minutes is how basketball games tied at the end are decided. 5. . . . details is one way projects fail. 6. . . . service is how clients are kept.
7. . . . fuels is one way the atmosphere will remain clean.

EXERCISE 4

Answers will vary considerably.
1. To get a better job is why 2. why there is so much aggression in the world. 3. 1947 was when 4. why English has so many complicated rules. 5. Around eleven is when 6. Cairo is where

EXERCISE 5

1. 1990 was when the Berlin . . . 2. Italy is where Ferrari . . .
3. . . . and 4 to 6 P.M. are when rush hour . . . 4. February 14 is when Valentine's . . . 5. ...February 19 is when Asian . . .
6. Evening is when people eat . . . 7. Nepal is where the world's . . .

EXERCISE 6

Part A: The best answers are from the following:
(from Exercise 3, Part A) 3 The nineteenth century is the time Queen . . . 4. 1969 was the year Neil . . . 5. From

noon to one o'clock is the hour many . . . 6. 1945 was the year world . . . 7. Winter is the season people . . .

(from Exercise 3, Part B) 1. Downstairs is the place a house is coolest. 2. . . . Muslim must make a pilgrimage to.
4. . . . the country about one-third of all the world's oil is located in. 5. . . . the building a government meets in. 6. . . . place people are buried in. 7. . . . country the 1978 and 1986 World Cup champions are from.

(from Exercise 3, Part C) 1. A chance . . . is the reason people immigrate. 2. . . . mileage is one reason people buy . . .
3. . . . spelling is one reason written English . . .
4. . . . productivity is one reason businesses . . .
5. . . . behavior are the reasons sharks . . . 6. . . . fluorocarbons is the reason the ozone . . . 7. . . . humor is the reason people like . . .

Part B: (from Exercise 5) 2. . . . country Ferrari . . . are made in. 3. . . . and 4 to 6 P.M. are the times rush . . . 4. . . . day Valentine's . . . 5. . . . the time Asian Lunar . . . 6. . . . time people eat dinner. 7. . . . country the world's . . . found in.

EXERCISE 7

1. (a) at time when   a
2. (a) the manner in which you have behaved   c
3. (a) when   g
4. (b) when   f
5. (a) why   g
6. (a) a second-hand store where   b
7. (a) A place where   d
8. (b) the cemetary where   b
9. (b) How   g
10. (a) when   f

EXERCISE 8

Answers will vary.
1. a time in which   2. where   3. a year in which
4. a time when   5. a place where

EXERCISE 9

Answers will vary.
1. a place known for its vastness and relentless dryness.
2. a century in which the Black Death raged.   3. a mountain on which many had died.   4. a time in which a huge population will have to deal with shrinking resources.   5. a place where many strange deeds had been done.

Unit 11

Correlative Conjunctions

Answers will vary.

1. Neither Andy nor Emily smokes. 2. Both Andy and his wife, Emily, work. 3. Neither their son nor their daughter lives with them at present. 4. The Morgans will buy either a Dodge or a Toyota within the coming year. 5. The Morgans subscribe not only to *Newsweek* and *The Atlantic Monthly* but also to *National Geographic* and *Home*. 6. They are going to spend their next vacation in either Mexico or Brazil. 7. Both snorkeling and walking are things they like to do on vacation.

1. No, neither Tony Perez nor Laura Park has . . . 2. Yes, both Tony Perez and Emma Singh can work in . . . 3. You could hire either Tony Perez or Laura Park, both of whom have training in microcomputer repair. 4. Yes, both Emma Singh and Laura Park have more . . . 5. She has not only a B.S. in electrical engineering but also an M.B.A. 6. Yes, both Tony Perez and Emma Singh are proficient in Pascal. 7. She is proficient in both Pascal and C. 8. Yes, both Tony Perez and Emma Singh can . . . 9. No, neither Laura Park nor Emma Singh has experience with . . . 10. No, neither Laura Park nor Emma Singh has applied to this company before.

Answers will vary.
1. You can take both linguistics and philosophy at the Wilmington Campus. 2. You can take either anthropology or economics.

3. You can take both English composition and linguistics. 4. We offer not only philosophy but also anthropology on Tuesday nights. 5. We offer technical writing both during the daytime and in the evening. 6. You can take it on either Thursday or Friday. 7. You can take it on either the Wilmington or the Philadelphia campus. 8. Neither astronomy nor physics is offered at times convenient for you. 9. You can take either linguistics or philosophy at the Philadelphia campus. 10. You can take either astronomy or physics at night.

Answers will vary.
1. . . . become a more responsible and independent person. 2. In the fall, I will take not only . . . 3. . . . hard at both my job and school. 4. You can either come with us now or come with Lisa later. 5. Not only Ismelda but also Nelson got into the honors program. 6. OK. 7. OK. 8. Marcus told me that he would either take his children . . . 9. You will need to present either a driver's license or major credit card . . . 10. OK. 11. In Britain and Australia, trucks are known as lorries and utes, respectively.

ACROSS   2. neither 5. respectively 7. both 8. either
DOWN   1. concise 3. not only 4. also 6. parallel

Unit 12

Sentence Connectors

ACROSS   2. although 6. example 8. consequently
10. furthermore 11. yet
DOWN   1. matter 3. however 4. fact 5. hand 7. before
9. whereas

1. an added idea 2. a contrast 3. a similarity 4. an example
5. a result 6. a contrast

1. *Furthermore,* she has a grasp . . . (Other possible connectors: all simple addition and emphatic addition connectors)
2. . . . painkiller *as well.* (Other possible connectors: all simple addition and emphatic addition connectors) 3. *In fact,* I've even . . . (Other possible connectors: all intensifying additive connectors) 4. *As a matter of fact,* when she's not . . . (Other possible connectors: all intensifying additive connectors) 5. *In addition,* the incidence . . . (Other possible connectors: all simple

addition and emphatic addition connectors) **6.** *What is more,* you have to . . . (Other possible connectors: all simple addition and emphatic addition connectors) **7.** We could *also* listen . . . (Other possible connectors: all simple addition and emphatic addition connectors) **8.** *Besides that,* I could . . . (Other possible connectors: all simple addition and emphatic addition connectors) **9.** *Actually,* I can't even . . . (Other possible connectors: all simple addition and emphatic addition connectors) **10.** *Moreover,* some patients tried . . . (Other possible connectors: all simple addition and emphatic addition connectors)

EXERCISE 4

2. Bob and Sheila are thinking about . . . Alternatively, / On the other hand, they might . . . **(h)** **3.** You already . . . On the other hand, / Alternatively, why don't you ask . . . **(a)** **4.** The new Fords . . . On the other hand, the Toyotas . . . **(i)** **5.** The city council . . . Alternatively, / On the other hand, they could have . . . **(b)** **6.** We might put up a . . . Alternatively, / On the other hand, we could plant . . . **(e)** **7.** The critics praised . . . On the other hand, the found . . . **(c)** **8.** To keep the insects . . . On the other hand, / Alternatively, consider using . . . **(g)** **9.** I guess I should . . . On the other hand, / Alternatively, maybe I . . . **(j)** **10.** Let's get a newspaper . . . On the other hand, / Alternatively, let's call . . . **(b)**

EXERCISE 5

Answers will vary.
1. **(a)** To illustrate **(b)** for instance **2.** in other words
3. in particular **4.** namely **5.** for example **6.** that is
7. Specifically

EXERCISE 6

Answers will vary.
1. Likewise, the Greeks feel that ties to land are permanent.
2. In the same way, eating with your left hand is incorrect in India. **3.** Similarly, Suraiya demonstrates her environmental awareness by recycling paper products and by composting organic matter instead of just throwing things in the trash.
4. Similarly, B-cells manufacture antibodies to help keep the body healthy. **5.** Likewise, in autumn you can find a breathtaking waterfowl concentration in California's Klamath Basin.

EXERCISE 7

Answers will vary.
1. Dandelion relieves rheumatic pain. Cayenne helps in the same way. **2.** One of the properties of echinachea is that it is a blood purifier. Likewise, one action of cayenne is that it purifies the blood. **3.** Dandelion is prepared by putting a few teaspoons of root into one cup of water, bringing it to a boil, and letting it simmer for ten to fifteen minutes. Echinachea is prepared in a similar way. **4.** Chamomile has a positive effect upon the stomach. Ginger likewise has a positive effect.
5. To prepare ginger, pour a cup of boiling water onto one teaspoon of the fresh root and let infuse for five minutes. In the same way, cayenne can be prepared by pouring a cup of boiling water onto one half to one teaspoon of powder and letting it stand for ten minutes.

EXERCISE 8

Answers will vary.
1. Dandelion relieves congestion of the liver and gallbladder. Cayenne, however, relieves colds and headaches. **2.** The flowers of the chamomile herb are used. In contrast, it is the roots of echinachea, ginger, and dandelion that we use.
3. Echinachea is prepared by boiling the root with water and letting it simmer. Ginger, on the other hand, is prepared by putting boiling water onto the root and letting it infuse.
4. Chamomile is taken as a drink. Dandelion leaves may be eaten raw in salad, though. **5.** Dandelion affects the liver, kidneys, gallbladder, and pancreas. Echinachea, however, affects the blood and lymph system.

EXERCISE 9

1. . . . so well, however / on the other hand / though
2. On the other hand / however / nevertheless / nonetheless
3. In fact / however **5.** Despite this / Nonetheless / Nevertheless / However / Even so

EXERCISE 10

Answers will vary.
1. The expedition encountered blizzards . . . Even so, they reached . . . **2.** He lost his parents . . . Despite this, he became . . . **3.** For many years he was addicted . . . With a lot of persistence and help from friends, however, he managed

to kick the habits and actually became . . . **4.** . . . community is often very challenging. In spite of the difficulties involved, there are the benefits of new . . . **5.** Our car broke down in Colorado . . . We got across the country nonetheless.

EXERCISE 11

Answers will vary.
Chart A: 1. Ariadne . . . gave Theseus . . . Thus, he was able to find his way. **2.** King Henry . . . wanted . . . Therefore, he divorced **3.** Adam . . . ate the forbidden fruit. As a result of this, they were . . . **4.** Tristan . . . drank the . . . Consequently, they fell . . . **5.** Inanna . . . descended into . . . Because of this, she brought her beloved . . .

Chart B: 1. The Aztecs were anxious to keep the sun in the sky and increase their crops. To do these things they believed they had to sacrifice prisoners of war. **2.** Ulysses wanted to hear the song of the sirens. To survive, he had his men plug their ears and had himself tied securely to the mast of his ship. **3.** James Bond felt he had a duty to save the world from megalomaniacs. with this in mind, he was ready to risk his life. **4.** Johnny Appleseed wanted to spread apple trees around the United States. For this purpose, he sowed seeds wherever he went.

EXERCISE 12

1. Similarly, **2.** remains, in fact, **4.** considerable; however, **5.** exploring, though **6.** For example, **8.** plants, for instance,

Exercises for the TOEFL® Test

Units 10–12

1. A	4. C	7. C	10. D	13. C	16. D	19. C
2. C	5. C	8. D	11. B	14. A	17. C	20. A
3. B	6. C	9. B	12. A	15. A	18. C	

Unit 13

Modal Perfect Verbs

EXERCISE 1

Part A **(1)** could have been **(2)** may have spent **(3)** shouldn't have expected **(4)** shouldn't have hung up **(5)** could have done

Part B **(6)** could have been handled **(7)** should have been told **(8)** might not have been **(9)** should not have been said **(10)** could have been avoided

Part C **(11)** must have been thinking **(12)** could have been hoping for **(13)** should have been paying

EXERCISE 2

Meaning-word clue / Modal
(1) annoyed / should / could / might have accepted **(2)** It was well within her abilities / could have done **(3)** thoughtless / could have worked **(4)** regretted / should have been **(5)** angry / could / might have called **(6)** rude / could / might / should have had **(7)** was perfectly able / could have helped **(8)** strongly criticized / could / might / should have told

(9) reproached / should / could / might have remembered
(10) thoughtless / could / might / should have thought

EXERCISE 3

(1) are to have **(2)** were supposed to have **(3)** were to have been **(4)** are we supposed to have **(5)** are to have **(6)** were we supposed to have **(7)** are to have **(8)** are supposed to

EXERCISE 4

Part A 1. must have **2.** should / would have **3.** must have **4.** can't have **5.** would have **6.** must have

Part B 7. should have **8.** must have **9.** can't have **10.** can't have **11.** wouldn't have

EXERCISE 5

Answers may vary.
(2) Could / might it have been someone else who looks like my client? **(3)** Could / might he have gone in the door of another

room?   **(4)** Could / might you have remembered it incorrectly?
(5) Could / might it have been later?   **(6)** Could / might you have been drinking?   **(7)** Could / might it have been a lot?
(8) Could / might you be an alcoholic?   **(9)** Could / might you have been drunk?

Answers will vary:
1. You may not have switched on the external drive first.
2. That could / may / might have been another cat.
3. You could / may / might have left it on another table.
4. You could / may / might have put on some weight.
5. That could / may / might be someone else's care he's driving.
6. They may / might not have sent cards to anyone this year.

(3) would have   **(4)** might / could have   **(5)** would have
(6) may / could have   **(7)** would have   **(8)** might / could

have   **(9)** might / could have   **(10)** would have   **(11)** might / could have   **(12)** might / could have   **(13)** might / could have

1. By 8:00 P.M. I will have been working for 12 hours.
2. By 2000, the Anderson family will have owned their farm for 100 years.   3. By June, Jason will have lost 60 pounds.
4. Two years from now, our club will have elected its second president.   5. By 2007, Hong Kong will have been part of China for 10 years.   6. By 2003, Lisa will have completed her bachelor's degree.

ACROSS   **1.** could   **3.** would   **4.** to have   **5.** have walked
6. may have   **7.** regret   **9.** irritation   **10.** Supposed
DOWN   **1.** contrary   **2.** must have   **6.** might   **8.** Should

Unit 14

Discourse Organizers

ACROSS   **2.** next   **5.** rhetorical   **7.** summary   **9.** sequence
DOWN   **1.** introduce   **3.** so far   **4.** first   **6.** there are
8. finally

1. a   **2.** b.   **3.** (A) a   (B) a   **4.** b   **5.** a   **6.** b   **7.** B

Answers will vary.
1. *To start with,* I always need more than I have.   2. *To begin with,* you have to draw up the plans.   3. *First of all,* I have to sweep the porch and the stairs.   4. *First,* boil some water.
5. *First of all,* get a good grammar book.   6. *In the first place,* you have to be attentive day and night.   7. *One of its causes* is overcrowding.

Answers will vary.
1. First of all, I'd buy my parents a house. Next, I'd buy myself a new car. Finally, I'd go traveling in Asia.   2. To begin with, you have to choose an interesting topic. Next, you have to narrow the

topic down. Then, you have to compile a list of books and journals to read. Lastly, you have to put your ideas and findings down on paper.   3. To begin with, the weather is usually fine. Then, the days are long. Finally, it's when I get my vacation.   4. To start with, you have to set aside a part of every day for exercise. Then, you have to exercise no matter what the weather is or no matter how you're feeling. Lastly, you have to be careful about what you eat.   5. First, I check the oil every week. Then, I check the other fluids. Finally, I have the oil changed every 3,000 miles.   6. To begin with, you encounter new words. Then, you often find new idioms. Finally, you see how grammatical structures are used.
7. To start with, you totally relax. Then, you dream. Finally, your body gets reenergized.   8. First of all, he/(she) is considerate. Next, he/(she) is caring. Finally, he/(she) has a good sense of humor.

Answers may vary.
1. There are; types; The first; The others   2. There are; kinds; One; The second; The last   3. There are; ways; To start with; Second; Next; Lastly   4. There are; theories; The first one; A second; Finally, there are   5. There are; properties; The first; Second; Third; Finally

EXERCISE 6

Answers will vary.
1. Briefly, I will survey different communities around the world and show how the warming of the atmosphere has led to some alarming changes   **2.** In short, my client is innocent of the charges that have been brought against him.   **3.** All in all, there was a lot more going on in the fifties than we normally think   **4.** As has been previously mentioned, the link between the smoking of tobacco products and lung cancer is well documented.   **5.** In summary, only in the preservation of diversity lies a healthy future for us all.   **6.** Overall, we've never been in a stronger position   **7.** In summary, pay particularly careful attention to the purity of your water and fresh food.   **8.** Briefly, plastic plays a vital role in our contemporary world.

EXERCISE 7

Answers will vary. Actual topics and sources of questions:
1. The text is about the diversity and development of animal life around the planet. (David Attenborough, *The Trials of Life,* 1990, Boston: Little, Brown)   **2.** The text is about the typical clutter that prevents us from being as efficient as we can be, and it makes suggestions about how we can become better organized. (Stephanie Winston, *Getting Organized,* 1978, New York: Warner Books)   **3.** The text is about a charitable foundation that is concerned with culture and the environment. (Cottonwood Foundation, by Genevieve Austin, *Buzzworm,* May/June 1993)   **4.** The text is a guide to computers that offer integrated features designed to satisfy the needs of all members of a family. (from *Home,* September 1993)   **5.** The text is a protest against overdevelopment in a community. (from a letter to the editor, *Newport Chronicle,* June 17, 1996)

EXERCISE 8

Implications: **1.** It's time you treated yourself to what you really deserve.   **2.** No one needs all that sugar.   **3.** Gadgets do not deliver the sound that you want.   **4.** There is no liberty. There is no peace.   **5.** This is exactly what you've been waiting for.

EXERCISE 9

Answers will vary
1. Shouldn't all young children be vaccinated? (They should.) / Isn't it our obligation to have all young children vaccinated? (It is.) / Don't we want to eradicate disease in the very young? (We do.)   **2.** Shouldn't the sales of powerful herbs be regulated? (They should.) / Isn't it time we did something about controlling the sales of powerful herbs? (It is.)   **3.** Don't we waste too much money on needless paperwork in our medical system? (We do.) / Don't we need to cut the high costs of medical care? (We do.) / Can't we save money by cutting wasteful administrative practices? (We can.)   **4.** Isn't winter a great time for a vacation? (It is.) / Don't you need a break from the cold weather? (You do.)   **5.** Isn't it better to be safe than sorry? (It is.) / Shouldn't you be safe? (You should.) / Doesn't it make sense to be safe rather than sorry? (It does.)

Unit 15

Conditionals: *If, Only If, Unless, Even Though, Even If*

EXERCISE 1

1. were . . . would . . . say   **2.** had taken . . . had studied / studied . . . could have had / would have had   **3.** look . . . will see / should see   **4.** had trained . . . would be   **5.** takes . . . is   **6.** smoke and eat . . . run   **7.** were . . . would not allow . . .   **8.** want . . . have to / will have to   **9.** had asked . . . would have helped.   **10.** had bought . . . would have been able   **11.** did not eat . . . did not get   **12.** had studied . . . would not have felt   **13.** graduate . . . will buy

EXERCISE 2

1. . . . will qualify . . . only if . . .   **2.** . . . will lose . . . only if   **3.** You should take . . . only if . . .   **4.** People were invited . . . only if they . . .   **5.** We got . . . only if . . .

EXERCISE 3

1. Only if / Not unless you change . . . will your engine run smoothly.   **2.** Only if / Not unless you keep . . . will the tread of your tires . . .   **3.** Only if / Not unless you live . . . do you need to add . . .   **4.** When . . . only if / not unless . . . will you obtain an accurate . . .   **5.** Only if / Not unless it was built before 1980 will your vehicle be . . .

EXERCISE 4

Sentences can begin with either *Only if* or *Not unless*
2. Only if I am totally exhausted can   **(e)**   **3.** Only if you are a serious photographer should you   **(a)**   **4.** Only if I exercise every day do I   **(d)**   **5.** Only if the book is overdue do   **(h)**   **6.** Only if the danger of frost has passed   **(i)**   **7.** Only if they are freezing

do **(f)** 8. Only if you ask and receive permission should you
(c) 9. Only if I washed it and cleaned it was I **(b)**

(1) unless **(2)** even if **(3)** Only if **(4)** only if **(5)** If
(6) even if **(7)** only if **(8)** unless **(9)** if **(10)** only if
(11) unless

EXERCISE 5

1. unless she knew word processing, she would have to spend a lot of time rewriting. **2.** unless we stop the timber industry / unless the timber industry is stopped, virgin forest will be destroyed. **3.** if she hadn't been so frank and outspoken, she might have gotten the job she wanted. **4.** if he hadn't found someone to practice French with, he wouldn't feel so confident. **5.** if we had not spoken only English, I would have understood more about my grandparents. **6.** If she were not such a great music lover, she would not have so many tapes and CDs. **7.** if it were harder to get a gun, the number of murders would decrease. **8.** If he had had health insurance, he would have gone to see the doctor by now. **9.** unless it rains soon, their crops will be ruined.

EXERCISE 8

1. Don't get on the tube in rush hour unless **(d)** **2.** Take the riverboat up the Thames to Hampton Court if **(h)** **3.** Don't rent a car unless **(a)** **4.** Go to visit the crown jewels on a weekend only if **(j)** **5.** Check to see that the flag is flying over Buckingham Palace if **(i)** **6.** Expect to pay 15% VAT (value added text) when you purchase anything except food or books even if **(b)** **7.** Be sure to visit the London Museum at the Barbican if **(e)** **8.** Be prepared to encounter accents and dialects that will perplex you even though **(g)** **9.** Always say Sorry when you bump into someone even if **(f)** **10.** Take a stroll on Hampstead Heath, London's largest park, if **(c)**

EXERCISE 6

1. Even though 2. even if 3. even though 4. even though
5. even though 6. even if 7. Even though 8. even though
9. even though 10. even if

EXERCISE 9

ACROSS: 3. despite 4. even 5. emphasis 8. contrary
11. though 12. Not
DOWN: 1. unless 2. were 6. might 7. hadn't 9. only
10. don't

Exercises for the TOEFL® Test

Units 13–15

1. D	4. B	7. A	10. B	13. A	16. B	19. C	22. D
2. C	5. A	8. C	11. D	14. D	17. D	20. C	23. A
3. B	6. D	9. D	12. A	15. A	18. A	21. D	24. A

Unit 16

Reducing Adverb Clauses

EXERCISE 1

While I am waiting for a helicopter to arrive / While waiting . . . After we spend a couple of days in Kathmandu / After spending / Having spent . . . When we started out / When starting out . . . After we had trekked for a week / After having . . . Before we climbed the high pass / Before climbing . . . while I was huffing and puffing my way to the top of the pass / while huffing and puffing . . . While he was scrambling over loose rock / While scrambling . . . Before I left the U.S. / Before leaving . . .

EXERCISE 2

Answers will vary.
1. Before signing up for a class . . . **2.** After having received your syllabus / After receiving . . . **3.** While listening to lectures . . . **4.** When hearing something you don't understand **5.** While taking part in discussions **6.** After finishing class **7.** After having finished your homework / After finishing . . .

EXERCISE 3

Not being very rich, Truhana had to go . . . *Having a long way to go*, Truhana had . . . *Daydreaming*, she began . . . *getting a good price for the honey*, I will buy . . . *"Loving lamb so much*, . . . *And making so much money*, I'll soon . . . *And being rich and respected*, I'll marry . . . *Taking so much pleasure in her fantasy*, Truhana began . . . *Seeing clearly now the ruin of her dreams*, Truhana . . .

EXERCISE 4

Answers will vary.

1. Alerted by Dr. Watson   2. Being experienced as a detective
3. Having noticed the curtains fluttering   4. Determined that evidence lay outside   5. Startled by a sudden noise   6. Scared out of his wits   7. Attempting to calm him   8. Wanting to get to the bottom of the matter   9. Realizing there was no way out   10. Having discovered that the boy had simply been trying to test him

EXERCISE 5

Answers will vary.

2. clutching a plank from the ship   3. Pulled by the currents
4. laughing and praying   5. Looking around   6. hoping to find food   7. After picking some fruit   8. while looking through the debris on the shore   9. using branches and the tools he had found.   10. startled to find footprints in the sand

EXERCISE 6

The ending of the story will vary.

EXERCISE 7

1. d   2. f   3. g   4. a   5. h   6. b   7. c   8. E

EXERCISE 8

ACROSS   1. frightened   4. shocking   6. pleasing
7. embarrassed   9. amused   10. puzzling   11. Boring
DOWN   1. frustrated   2. irritated   3. confused   5. intrigued
8. annoying

EXERCISE 9

Answers will vary.

1. While cleaning the yard, Sam spotted an opossum sniffing under the hedge.   3. After hiking all day long, I found the thought of a tent and a sleeping bag very attractive.   5. Having planted bulbs in the fall, we enjoyed many flowers in the sping.   6. Being late, Robert found the highway very long as he raced to work.
8. Frustrated by overly complicated questions, the students found the test infuriating.   9. After hoisting it up to the fifth floor with a heavy rope, the movers brought the piano in through the window.
10. After putting on sunglasses, he realized that the glare wasn't so bad.

Unit 17

Preposition Clusters

EXERCISE 1

1. count on   2. pay for   3. commented on   4. consented to
5. decided on   6. rely on   7. think about   8. approve of
9. complain about   10. believes in

EXERCISE 2

ACROSS   1. scowled   4. stare   5. winking   7. glanced
8. frowned   9. grinned
DOWN   2. looking   3. gazed   4. smiled   6. sneered

EXERCISE 3

Answers will vary.

1. My parents did not let me associate with troublemakers because they wanted me to succeed.   (a)   2. The police dealt with the suspect harshly to get him to confess.   (d)
3. Community members joined with each other to celebrate the end of the flood.   (e)   4. The administration consulted with the teachers about a change in the degree requirements.   (c)
5. I united with my neighbors in protesting the proposal to widen our street.   (g)   6. The minority political party would not cooperate with the majority to find a solution to the welfare problem.   (b)   7. My great uncle sided with the rebels during the Civil War.   (f)

EXERCISE 4

1.   (a) differ from   (b) retires from   (c) withdraw from
(d) detached from
2.   (a) escape from   (b) Fleeing from
3.   (a) dissented from   (b) separate from
4.   (a) deviated from   (b) shrank from   (c) recoiling from
(d) abstained from

EXERCISE 5

1. prays for   2. asked for   3. thirsts for / longs for / yearns for
4. is yearning for / is longing for   5. yearn for / long for   6. hope
for / ask for   7. longing for / yearning for [infinitive forms also
OK—to long for, etc.]   8. wish for

EXERCISE 6

1. afraid of   2. safe from   3. sorry for   4. ignorant of
5. unhappy about   6. homesick for   7. proficient in
8. enthusiastic about

EXERCISE 7

Answers will vary.
1. The World Wildlife Fund is interested in   (b)   2. MADD is
committed to helping reduce   (d)   3. The National Trust for
Historic Preservation is dedicated to   (d)   4. CARE is dedicated
to   (g)   5. The Sierra Club is accustomed to   (f)   6. The
March of Dimes is concerned about   (a)   7. The International
Eye Foundation is dedicated to   (c)

EXERCISE 8

1. On the   2. on   3. in   4. In the   5. in   6. in the   7. On the
8. On   9. In

EXERCISE 9

1. On account of   2. In the course of   3. With the exception of
4. On the strength of   5. at odds with   6. in return for / in the
process of   7. By means of   8. In the name of

EXERCISE 10

Answers will vary.
1. According to statistics   2. With respect to the computer
3. According to a recent poll   4. Based on the witnesses'
testimonies   5. Relating to your insurance policy   6. According
to several scientists   7. With respect to my grandparents
8. Based on what I have discovered this year   9. Speaking of
basketball   10. Pertaining to viruses

Unit 18

Gerunds and Infinitives

EXERCISE 1

(1) growing / object of preposition   (2) to grow and to adapt /
object   (3) maintaining / object of preposition; to think / subject
complement; to keep / object; getting / object of preposition
(4) improving / object of preposition   (5) memory training /
object of preposition   (6) to draw / object   (7) to mentally file /
noun complement   (8) memory training / object of preposition
(9) showing / object; asking / object; to recall / object
(10) to establish / object   (11) to associate / object
(12) to exaggerate / object; to superimpose / object
(13) To find / subject; calling / object of preposition

EXERCISE 2

ACROSS   1. producing   2. being   3. to stop   7. having been
10. received
DOWN   1. published   4. to find   5. having seen   6. been
fired   8. getting   9. to have

EXERCISE 3

Answers may vary.
2. To change / Changing old habits   (d)   3. Climbing mountains

(a)   4. To get caught cheating would be   (j)   5. Saving lives is
(c)   6. Paying the bills on time is   (e)   7. Before doing
anything inside a computer   (b)   8. To make a chocolate cake
(i)   9. To succeed in school was   (g)   10. To stay in good
shape   (k)   11. Trying too hard (f)

EXERCISE 4

2. Genghis Khan's desire was to   (c)   3. What Abraham Lincoln
is remembered for was emancipating   (g)   4. My personal
dream is to   (a)   5. The goal of the Peace Corps is to   (d)
6. One of the things Henry VIII is remembered for is beheading
(b)   7. The ambition of every rock group is to   (e)   8. One
reason to become a doctor is to   (j)   9. What a workaholic
enjoys is working   (f)   10. What everyone loves is receiving / to
receive   (h)

EXERCISE 5

Answers will vary.
1. to get well   2. to relax   3. to let go   4. to keep up   5. to
persist   6. to set aside   7. to create / to expand   8. to do /to
try to accomplish

EXERCISE 6

Answers will vary.
(2) to reach   (3) to get   (4) to make it   (5) to see   (6) to discover   (7) to find   (8) to turn back   (9) to stay   (10) to cross   (11) to be caught   (12) to have found the cave   (13) to set off again   (14) to have brought   (15) to be back   (16) to be alive

EXERCISE 7

1. I couldn't stop watching it.   5. I used to hate eating meat
8. Her lawyer advised her to drop the case.   9. I really appreciate your mentioning that   11. Would you hesitate to help
14. Gauguin hated living in France and yearned to paint   16. I don't deny visiting   17. She appears to be having trouble
18. He expected us to put in

EXERCISE 8

Part A   (2) to see   (3) to concentrate, to leave   (4) tutoring, reading   (5) hawking   (7) to operate   (8) to use   (9) to invent   (11) manufacturing   (13) experimenting, inventing
(14) to invent   (15) advancing   (16) making, making
(17) Moving, taking out   (19) to record   (22) perfecting, to replace   (23) to see   (24) passing   (25) to make and distribute, to design   (26) doing   (28) to flow, to pursue

Part B   (3) be unable / to concentrate; be forced / to leave
(4) begin / tutoring   (7) learn / to operate   (8) neglect / to use
(9) start / to invent   (11) begin / manufacturing   (13) devote (one's life to) / experimenting   (14) want / to invent   (15) care little about / advancing   (16) become absorbed in / making
(17) begin / taking out   (19) test (a way) / to record   (22) turn (one's attention to) / perfecting   (23) try (materials) to see
(24) try / passing   (25) exist / to make; go on / to design
(28) fail / to pursue

EXERCISE 9

Answers may vary.
1. to teach   2. to do / doing   3. to catch   4. experimenting, blowing up   5. to invent   6. to make / making   7. to work
8. to carry   9. inventing, advancing   10. to record   11. to replace   12. producing   13. to use

EXERCISE 10

1. Bob's   2. Maria's   3. the pool's   4. For a brand new car
5. Our candidate's   6. Eve's . . . for her family   7. The timber company's   8. Pieter's   9. the high school's

EXERCISE 11

1. Democracies insist on holding free elections on a regular basis.   2. Some democracies call for the people to vote whenever they want to determine the level of popular confidence in the present government.   3. The candidates argue about spending money for projects and programs.
4. The voters hope for their elected officials to do what they promised during their campaigns.   5. The people consent to accept the verdict of the majority.   6. People complain about elected officials forgetting their promises.   7. Elected officials often think about getting reelected.

EXERCISE 12

Answers will vary.
1. I had to put off going there until I could finish my work.
2. I can't put up with taking any more abuse from the new manager.   3. I'm looking forward to walking around Paris and sitting in cafés.   4. She did, but she decided to go through with having it again because her condition seemed to be getting worse.
5. I've given up drinking.   6. We've taken up reading and playing chess again.   7. Not much. I carried on studying till nearly dawn.

EXERCISE 13

Answers will vary.
1. James Watt was a Scottish engineer who is celebrated for inventing . . .   2. Robert Fulton was an American inventor who was successful in improving . . .   3. Samuel Colt was an American inventor and industrialist who was successful in pioneering . . .   4. Joseph Henry was an American physicist and educator who was proficient at guiding others in research that led to . . .   5. Enrico Fermi was an Italian physicist who was famous for building the . . .   6. Count Ferdinand von Zeppelin was a German aeronautical engineer who was celebrated for perfecting . . .   7. George Eastman was an American inventor and manufacturer who was famous for inventing . . .

Exercises for the TOEFL® Test

Units 16–18

1. B	4. D	7. D	10. A	13. A	16. D	19. C	22. A
2. C	5. A	8. B	11. C	14. B	17. B	20. A	23. B
3. A	6. C	9. C	12. A	15. A	18. B	21. C	24. A

Unit 19

Perfective Infinitives

EXERCISE 1

1. to have been   2. to have acted   3. To have wasted   4. to have made   5. (a) to have joined   (b) to have gone   (c) to have made   6. (a) To have dared   (b) to have done   (c) to have stayed.   7. (a) to have invited   (b) To have prepared (c) to have eaten   8. (a) to have seen   (b) To have resisted (c) to have put in

EXERCISE 2

Answers will vary.
1. to have finished all my research   2. for us to have undertaken
3. have shaken the hand of President Kennedy   4. to have learned how to use the computer   5. to have been one of the richest men who ever lived   6. to have seen the All-star game this year   7. to have attended my graduation   8. have attended grad school   9. us to have skate-boarded down that steep hil

EXERCISE 3

1. to have been / relative to the past   2. to have experienced / relative to the past   3. to have finished / relative to the past
4. to have been / relative to the past   5. to have written; to have changed / relative to the past   6. to have begun / relative to the present   7. to have made / relative to the future

EXERCISE 4

1. To have seen what is right and not to have done it is cowardice.
2. To have died for an idea is to have placed a pretty high price upon conjecture.   3. There are two tragedies in life. One is not to have gotten your heart's desire. The other is to have gotten it.
4. To have interpreted is to have impoverished.   5. The easiest person to have deceived is one's self.

EXERCISE 5

1. . . . consider America to have been discovered . . .   2. . . . not

to have been   3. . . . reported the high government official to have been selling . . .   4. . . . found all the jewels to have been stolen.
5. . . . people claim the Nazca lines in Peru to have been . . .
6. . . . low enough for them to have been accorded . . .   7. They promised all the work to have been done . . .   8. . . . expects their papers to have been checked . . .   9. She was thrilled to have been chosen . . .   10. The guerrillas claimed to have been educating

EXERCISE 6

1. . . . not to have tried . . .   2. . . . never to have heard . . .
3. . . . never to have given . . .   4. . . . not to have had . . .
5. . . . not to have investigated . . .

EXERCISE 7

Answers will vary.
1. I would love to have had more . . .   2. I would hate to have been discovered . . .   3. I would prefer to have been given . . .
4. I would like to have spent more time . . .   5. I would hate to have come . . .   6. I would prefer to have been able . . .   7. I would like to have known . . .   8. I would love to have been served . . .   9. I would like to have done even . . .
10. I would hate to have come . . .

EXERCISE 8

Answers will vary.
1. It was nothing less than a miracle for them to have escaped the burning wreckage alive.   2. It was really sweet of your mother to have sent a cake and gift for our anniversary.   3. We were shocked to have read about the latest international banking scandal that involved so many prominent figures.   4. It is generous of you to have spent so much of your free time doing volunteer work in the community.   5. It would have been totally unacceptable for anyone to have come to this gala event in ragged old clothes.   6. It must be thrilling to have gone hang gliding in the Alps.   7. It would have been tedious to have worked sixty hours a week on an assembly line, doing the same thing over

and over again.   8. For the whole family to have gotten together at Thanksgiving would have been marvelous.   9. It was incredibly annoying to have gotten caught in a ten-mile-long traffic jam on the freeway this afternoon.

EXERCISE 9

Answers will vary.
1. I seem to have left my wallet with my license at home.
2. The lead singer seems to have had too much to drink.
3. The waiter appears to have forgotten us.   4. The printer ribbon (or ink cartridge) seems to have been quite low on ink.
5. There appears to have been a mistake. I believe I asked for a nonsmoking room.

EXERCISE 10

Answers will vary.
1. By June, I expect to have finished all the courses I am presently taking, that is, Advanced English, English Composition, Accounting, Computer Science, and Calculus.   2. By the time I graduate, I plan to have played on the soccer team and contributed a few pieces to the College Review.   3. Before I make a job commitment, I plan to have visited Hewlett-Packard and

possibly Claris.   4. Once I was supposed to have helped my father paint the house but I injured my leg playing football.
5. Within the next five years, I hope to have gotten married and to have finished all my degree work and to have found a job I like.

EXERCISE 11

Answers will vary.
1. I drank enough coffee to have kept me awake twenty-four hours.   2. That horror movie was scary enough to have given me a heart attack.   3. The slide show of their last trip was boring enough to have put anyone to sleep.   4. The storm was snowy enough to have buried all the cars on the street.   5. After exam week, I was tired enough to have slept for days.   6. The salesman was convincing enough for me to have wanted to buy the stereo system right away.

EXERCISE 12

1. Derek's too serious to have gone to see . . .   2. Dr. Mayer's far too dedicated a teacher to have returned . . .   3. The border's too well guarded for them to have . . .   4. That lawyer's arguments were too convincing for him to have . . .   5. His excuses were somehow too contrived to have been believed.

Unit 20

Adjective Complements in Subject and Predicate Position

EXERCISE 1

Answers will vary.
1. to have carried someone on its back for such a length of time
2. giving its life to save a human being   3. an elephant could be so careful   4. the chickens are treated this way   5. to have found his way such a distance   6. camouflaging themselves in such intelligent ways

EXERCISE 2

Answers will vary.
1. I would be ready to take my first step.   2. I would be happy to be taken to a playground.   3. I would be eager to go to school.
4. I would be anxious for my friends to call me.   5. I would be eager to try something new.   6. I would be ready for a challenge to motivate me.

EXERCISE 3

Answers will vary.
1. It is insensitive . . .   2. It seems odd . . . is unfortunate

3. is sad   4. It is fascinating . . . is disturbing   5. will be helpful
6. It is compulsory   7. is wonderful   8. It is certain . . . is foolish   9. It appears likely . . . will be difficult.
10. is regrettable

EXERCISE 4

Answers will vary.
1. That Bokassa could be so self-indulgent is terrible.   2. That someone could have so many credit cards and such a wallet is quite amusing.   3. That someone could have lost so much money so fast is hard to imagine.   4. That someone could be so mean and callous is pathetic.   5. That such a disaster occurred is terribly tragic.

EXERCISE 5

Answers will vary.
1. It's frightening that two highly dangerous submarines could collide.   2. It's fortunate that the submarines that collided didn't explode.   3. It's unfortunate that a man died on the ship in the North Sea.   4. It's encouraging that more habitats are being set

aside for threatened species.   **5.** It's shocking that so many people may have AIDS.   **6.** It's good that some of Iraq's deadly weapons have been destroyed.

Answers will vary.
1. For carpenters to take no measurements would be unusual.
2. For scuba divers to dive without first checking their oxygen supply would be unusual.   **3.** For critics to write only positive

things would be unusual.   **4.** For vegetarians to order hamburgers at a restaurant would be unexpected.
5. For Buddhist monks to go hunting would be unexpected.
6. For ballerinas to play football would be unexpected.
7. For computer programmers not to like math would be unusual.

1. factual   **2.** potential   **3.** potential   **4.** factual   **5.** factual
6. potential   **7.** factual   **8.** factual   **9.** potential   **10.** Factual

Unit 21

Noun Complements Taking *That* Clauses

ACROSS   **1.** plan   **2.** to   **3.** for   **4.** motivation   **9.** reason
DOWN   **1.** permission   **2.** that   **5.** theory   **6.** news   **7.** fact
8. to say

1. rain on barren hills   **2.** indigenous people are forced to relocate   **3.** water supplies may dry up during dry seasons
4. the World Bank and other aid organizations have contributed to the destruction of fragile mountain habitats

1. a   **2.** a   **3.** a   **4.** b   **5.** B

Answers will vary. Examples:
1. The fact that Edison could spare only an hour for his marriage was proof of his complete devotion to his work.   **2.** The news that a polio vaccine had been discovered reduced the terror that people felt at the approach of summer.   **3.** The idea that a celebrity like Alexander Graham Bell could really be ill at ease in public belies the idea that all celebrities enjoy basking in the limelight.   **4.** The idea that Haydn had to resort to a devious method to communicate to his employer his need for a vacation is highly amusing   **5.** The belief that the mind was controlled by reason was brought into question by Sigmund Freud.

2. the fact   **5.** the fact   **7.** the fact   **9.** the fact   **11.** the fact
13. the fact

Answers will vary. Examples:
1. Carlos and Teresa are accustomed to the fact that their house is small.   **2.** Jorge is excited about the news that he has received two scholarship offers.   **3.** Jorge has had to put up with the fact that his little brother is noisy and messy.   **4.** Gloria is jealous of the fact that Jorge seems to get all the attention.   **5.** Julio is thrilled about the idea that the bedroom will soon be all his.   **6.** Guadalupe is concerned about the notion that her older sister is attracted to potentially dangerous situations.   **7.** Gloria is annoyed with the fact that her younger sister talks on the phone a lot.

Answers will vary. Examples:
1. I would remind them of the fact that they should always thank someone who has done them a courtesy.   **2.** I would remind them of the fact that they shouldn't smoke in a non-smoking area.
3. I would remind them of the fact that the windshield fluid is a completely different substance from the radiator fluid, which would only smear their windshield.   **4.** I would remind them of the fact that "enjoy" is followed by a gerund.   **5.** I would remind them of the fact that it is polite to say excuse me to anyone they bump into.   **6.** I would remind them of the fact that it is cold outside.   **7.** I would remind them of the fact that the speed limit is 30 mph or less.

1. OK   **2.** What explains the fact that in some cases . . .   **3.** ...was bizarre.   **4.** OK   **5.** She was conscious of the fact that they . . .
6. OK   **7.** . . . about the fact that he has . . .   **8.** OK   **9.** . . . . the notion that we   **10.** OK   **11.** . . . . supported the fact that the   **12.** OK

1. C	4. D	7. D	10. C	13. A	16. C	19. B
2. D	5. C	8. A	11. B	14. D	17. A	20. A
3. C	6. B	9. B	12. A	15. B	18. B	

Unit 22

Subjunctive Verbs in *That* Clauses

EXERCISE 1

1. John recommends that Bill (should) see an eye doctor.
2. They demand that the chief assign more police to . . .
3. They insisted that she get . . .   4. The memo stipulates that all personnel (should) wear formal . . .   5. Betty suggests that he / she try the house special.   6. The town planner proposes that they ban . . .   7. The teacher advises that he / she should check his / her figures again.   8. The librarian requested that we lower . . .   9. The president of the union insists they not lose hope.   10. She begs that he / she not send . . .

EXERCISE 2

1. He laughed at my suggestion that he ban students from chewing gum . . .   2. He smiled at my demand that the shops be closed . . .   3. he disregarded my request that he not print any . . .   4. She did not listen to my advice that she forbid . . .   5. He ignored my plea that he shut down . . . / that all weapons factories be shut down.

EXERCISE 3

Answers will vary. Examples:
1. Kurt's suggestion that he poison the dog was immoral.

2. Sally's proposal that he talk to the dog's owners again was worth a try.   3. Lisa's recommendation that he make friends with the dog might or might not work.   4. Rod's suggestion that he release the dog from its chain was somewhat risky.   5. Scott's advice that he buy earplugs was a good temporary solution.
6. Kate's suggestion that he get other neighbors to sign a petition was a good idea.

EXERCISE 4

Answers will vary. Examples:
PART A   1. That Matthew L. be hospitalized immediately   2. that Peter S. stop smoking   3. That Louise M. have a pregnancy test   4. that Greg A. apply a cold pack to his knees.   5. that Ronnie P. drink less coffee.

PART B   Students' original responses.

EXERCISE 5

ACROSS   1. build   3. vital   6. mandatory   7. stipulates
9. suggested   10. decision
DOWN   2. desirable   4. that   5. take   7. should   8. be

Unit 23

Emphatic Structures: Emphatic *Do, No* Versus *Not*

EXERCISE 1

no doubt;   Africa does;   no sight;   no small;   no sense;   no need;   do need;   Do that;   no package . . . no lazy;   no other;   Do make

EXERCISE 2

1. They <u>did</u> like   2. I <u>will</u> fix   3. They <u>have</u> made   4. I <u>certainly do</u> have   5. They <u>really are</u> going   6. I <u>did</u> notice   7. The senate <u>will</u> allow   8. Judy <u>has</u> learned   9. I <u>certainly do</u> understand   10. I <u>really have</u> seen

EXERCISE 3

1. **Meg:** Yes, I did remember.   2. **Nita:** Oh, then who did take the money?   3. **Ole:** Have you heard that Robert did manage to pass the chemistry exam? **Tuan:** I'm glad he did pass. Now he won't   4. **Paula:** It does seem that everyone in Darren's family has a major problem. **Rod:** Yes, he does have a dysfunctional family.   5. **Aziz:** No,

he never does send cards. **6. Hilda:** Not bad. Even though I don't usually like spicy food, I did find the flavors intriguing. **7. Sarala:** Of course. It's a bit wet after the rain. Do watch out for the puddles. **8. Taylor:** That's ridiculous. I did pay it. **9. Nick:** I do like watching golf on TV. **Nick:** No, I really do enjoy the suspense and the skill that you see. **10. Carla:** Did you hear that the Bonington expedition did make it safely to the top of Nanga Parbat? **Al:** That's great news! When I heard there were storms, I did doubt they would make it.

EXERCISE 4

had no time; had no comforts; had no warm room or soft bed; with no food, home, money, or job; had no way out; with no

friends; had no dress or ride; will have no husband; want no husband; is no princess

EXERCISE 5

Answers will vary.

There are no windows in our room. We have no hot water in our room. We have no clean towels. We have no air conditioning. There is no water in the swimming pool. The restaurant has nothing that we like. There is no private beach. There is no one around to help us. There is no taxi available to take us around. There is no grocery store within easy walking distance. There is nothing for the children to do.

Unit 24

Fronting Structures for Emphasis and Focus

EXERCISE 1

Fronted structure is underlined; inverted subject / verb is in **bold**.
1. <u>With great excitement</u> / Fronted structure. 2. <u>Seldom</u> **do we eat** / Fronted structure / Inversion 3. <u>Because we wanted to have a good view of the stage</u> / Fronted structure 4. No fronted structure. 5. <u>Rarely</u> **did my parents allow** / Fronted structure / Inversion 6. <u>To cut down on cholesterol</u> / Fronted structure 7. No fronted structure. 8. <u>Nowhere in the town</u> **could I find** / Fronted structure / Inversion 9. No fronted structure. 10. <u>Rain or shine</u> / Fronted structure

EXERCISE 2

Answers will vary.
1. **a.** Just after sunset **b.** With their arms waving 2. **a.** To find a lead **b.** in the living room 3. **a.** As the clock was striking twelve **b.** Because they wanted to know what was inside 4. **a.** In the valley below **b.** To their utter amazement 5. **a.** To find out how she's doing **b.** Twice a week

EXERCISE 3

(1) Little did I realize (2) Fluttering through the air (3) In the center of the village (4) Not for anything (5) Almost never (6) So weak (7) Around me (8) Not quite as bad as everyone feared (9) Never (10) Little did we suspect (11) No sooner

EXERCISE 4

1. (c) 2. (j) 3. (g) 4. (a) 5. (k) 6. (e) 7. (f) 8. (i) 9. (b) 10. (d) 11. (h)

EXERCISE 5

1. Under no conditions does that restaurant permit smoking. 2. Not once has he ever said he was sorry. 3. Not for anything would I take that drug. 4. Never had she felt so insulted. 5. Under no circumstances will the theater allow children to see that movie. 6. Not until recently did I realize the complexity of the health care dilemma. 7. In no way does this alter my opinion. 8. In no case can they leave the children unattended at home. 9. Not since I left home have I felt this way. 10. Nowhere have I seen such fascinating architecture as in India.

EXERCISE 6

ACROSS 3. not only 4. neither 6. nor 8. anyone
DOWN 1. will 2. sooner 5. either 6. not 7. could

EXERCISE 7

1. contrast of the structure 2. focus on the delayed subject 3. emphasis 4. emphasis 5. focus on the delayed subject 6. contrast of the structure 7. emphasis 8. focus on the delayed subject 9. emphasis 10. contrast of the structure

EXERCISE 8

1. *Nowhere have I heard of such high prices.* (form) 2. Fronted negative not appropriate for this context; scarcely should not be emphasized. (use) 3. Fronted negative not appropriate for this context; *little . . .* should not be emphasized. (use) 4. *Never have I been in such pain before.* (form) 5. No way = informal register. Inappropriate for context. (use) 6. *Under no circumstances can I take cortisone* (form)

Unit 25

Focusing and Emphasizing Structures: *It*-Clefts and *Wh*-Clefts

EXERCISE 1

1. It is / was Carl Jung who   (e)   2. It is in Chicago where   (i)
3. It is / was Florence that   (g)   4. It is / was Marco Polo who
(a)   5. It is /was at Versailles where   (h)   6. It is / was the
Wright Brothers who   (b)   7. It is / was in China where   (d)
8. It is / was the Black Death that   (j)   9. It is Wyoming that
(f)   10. It is the Haj that   (c)

EXERCISE 2

1. It was Thoreau, not Emerson, who lived . . .   2. It is the
students who have the . . .   3. It was in Toledo that . . .   4. It
is his thoughts of his children that . . .   5. It wasn't our cat who
killed . . .   6. It is Marjorie who will . . .   7. It is Ivor who must
have taken . . .   8. It is my aunt who has . . .   9. It's the
number three bus that you need to catch.   10. It was shrimp, not
steak, that I ordered.

EXERCISE 3

2. It was the German scientists Otto Hahn and Fritz Strassman
who demonstrated the process of nuclear fission in the winter of
1938.   3. It was to inform him about recent discoveries
concerning uranium and also about the possibility of constructing
a powerful bomb that Albert Einstein wrote a letter to President
Roosevelt in 1939.   4. It was to develop an explosive devise
based on nuclear fission that the top-secret Manhattan project
was established in August 1942.   5. It was in a squash court
beneath the stands of an abandoned football field at the
University of Chicago on December 2, 1942, that Enrico Fermi and
his colleagues produced the first controlled nuclear reaction.
6. It was J. Robert Oppenheimer who the Army chose in 1943 to
direct the lab in Los Alamos, New Mexico, where the atomic
bombs would be designed and assembled.   7. It was in huge
reactors and separator plants in Washington and Tennessee
where the uranium and plutonium for the bombs were produced.
8. It was on July 16, 1945, that the first atomic bomb was
detonated near Alamogordo, New Mexico.

EXERCISE 4

Answers will vary.
2. It's because they got buried under a heap of papers that I
forgot to renew them.   3. It's because the test was too hard
that I didn't get the grade I wanted.   4. It's because I was in a
great hurry this morning and wasn't paying attention to what I
put on that I am wearing two different socks.   5. It's because I
have some family obligations that I can't make it to class today.
6. It's because I was late to my sister's wedding that I was
caught speeding.

EXERCISE 5

Answers will vary.
1. It's my cousin Erik who is . . .   2. It's my friend Cheryl who
tends . . .   3. It's my nephew Alex who tends . . .   4. It is my
father who has traveled . . .   5. It's my mother-in-law who would
be . . .   6. It's my friend Mike who tends . . .   7. It's my friend
Beth who . . .   8. It's my cousin Galen who is . . .

EXERCISE 6

2. It is stamina   3. It is memory   4. It was stagefright   5. It is
inspiration   6. It was a drought

EXERCISE 7

2. It was out of a sense of honor   3. It is out of generosity   4. It
was out of malice   5. It was for his country   6. It was out of
frustration

EXERCISE 8

1. It was Sean Connery who starred . . .   2. It is Botswana that
is directly . . .   3. It was Abraham Lincoln who was elected
President in 1860.   4. It is the brain that is divided . . .   5. It is
Frankenstein that is the name of Mary Shelley's novel.   6. It was
Hernando Cortés who . . .   7. It is a vaccine that makes a
person . . .   8. It was the Bible that Gutenberg published in
1445.   9. It is the game of chess that ends . . .

EXERCISE 9

Answers will vary.
1. It was in 485 B.C. that Cincinnatus took command and
rescued the Roman army.   2. It was the prophet Mohammed
who fled Mecca for Medina, Arabia, in 622.   3. It was in
Armenia that Ashot I founded the Bagratide dynasty in 859.
4. It was in 1298 that Marco Polo began dictating his memoirs
in a Genoan jail.   5. It was in 1581 that Francis Drake returned
to England after a voyage of circumnavigation.   6. It was in
Vienna that Beethoven became Haydn's pupil in 1792.   7. It
was Frank Whittle who built the first jet engine in England in
1937.

2. It is just after midnight in Istanbul when the famous writer John LeCarré's plane lands.   3. It is in the Red Sea that oceanographer Jacques Cousteau prepares to dive at dawn.   4. It is during an avalanche on Mt. Makalu in the Himalayas that the mountaineer Peter Hillary finds himself wondering whether he should retire.   5. It is Colin Bragg, the gangster, who suddenly disappears in Nassau one day in February.   6. It is at the end of a long and intense week at the Sloan Institute that medical researcher Tsering Paldum first notices some rapid changes in a fungal culture.

Answers will vary.
2. Would you please tell me again how it is that gamma globulin types differ?   3. It told you yesterday that it was on the fifteenth, not the sixteenth.   4. Who was it that could have been calling so late last night?   5. He said it was because of a low pressure front coming in from the south that it was going to rain.   6. I don't understand what it is that I should fill out on this form.

1. What Kennedy said was   (e)   2. What made . . . was . . .   (i)
3. Where Tristan da Cunha . . . is   (k)   4. . . . planet is   (h)
5. . . . was crowned . . .   (j)   6. . . . revision easier is   (b)
7. . . . characteristics is   (c)   8. . . . iron mask was / is   (d)
9. What athletes have to do is . . .   (f)   10. . . . believed was   (a)   11. . . . noted for is   (g)

1. What follows the verb *forget* is an infinitive.   2. What Muslims cannot eat is pork.   3. What the Confederate army wore was gray.   4. Where the Olympic Games started was in Greece.
5. What all children need is love.   6. What *must* indicates is obligation.   7. What our galaxy is called is the Milky Way.
8. What Vincent van Gogh did was paint pictures.

Exercises for the TOEFL® Test
Units 22–25

1. B	4. A	7. D	10. B	13. A	16. C	19. B	22. A	24. A
2. C	5. B	8. D	11. C	14. D	17. C	20. B	23. C	25. B
3. B	6. A	9. A	12. D	15. B	18. C	21. C		

TAPESCRIPT

Unit 1 (Activity 1)

Passage 1
From when I was very tiny, my mother used to take me down to the *finca*, wrapped in a shawl on her back. She told me that when I was about two, I had to be carried screaming onto the lorry because I didn't want to go. I was so frightened I didn't stop crying until we were about halfway there. The lorry holds about forty people. But in with the people go the animals (dog, cats, chickens) which the people from the Altiplano take with them while they are in the *finca*. It sometimes took two nights and a day from my village to the coast. By the end of the journey, the smell— the filth of people and animals—was unbearable.

Passage 2
Any tree will do to make a house, but (I think this is part of our culture) only if it's cut at full moon. We say the wood lasts longer if it's cut when the moon is young. When we build a house, we make the roof from a sort of palm tree found near the foot of the mountains. We call it *pamac*. For us, the most elegant houses are made with cane leaves, because you have to go a long way to get them. You have to have men to go and get them to make the house. We were poor and had neither money to buy cane leaves nor anyone to go and get them. They're only found down on the *fincas* on the coast and they're very expensive. The landowners charge by the bunch . . . and it takes fifty bunches for a house.

Source: *I, Rigoberta: An Indian Woman in Guatemala*, Elisabeth Burgos-Debray (Ed.), New York: Verson, 1994. Passage 1: pp. 2–3; Passage 2: p. 21; Passage 3: p. 46.

Unit 2 (Activity 1)

Dr. M. was a distinguished musician. For many years he had been a singer; later he became a teacher at the local school of music. It was at this school that others began to observe Dr. M.'s strange problem. Sometimes Dr. M. did not recognize the faces of people he had known for a long time. Sometimes he saw faces where there were none: on a water hydrant, for example, or on the carved knobs of furniture. When Dr. M. finally went to Dr. Oliver Sacks' clinic, these events had been going on for years.

At the clinic, it was while Dr. Sacks was examining Dr. M.'s reflexes that the first bizarre experience occurred. Dr. Sacks had taken off Dr. M.'s left shoe to test his reflexes. He later left Dr. M. for a few minutes, assuming Dr. M. would put the shoe back on. When Dr. Sacks returned to his examining room, Dr. M. had not put the shoe on. Dr. Sacks asked Dr. M. if he could help, and Dr. M. said that he had forgotten to put the shoe on. Finally Dr. M. looked down at his foot and asked if his foot was his shoe. When Dr. Sacks pointed to Dr. M.'s shoe nearby, Dr. M. told him that he thought the shoe was his foot!

Later, as Dr. M. was getting ready to leave, he started to look for his hat. He reached for his wife's head and tried to put it on. Poor Dr. M. had mistaken his wife for a hat!

(Adapted with permission of Oliver Sacks for a first edition exercise from *The Man Who Mistook his Wife for a Hat and Other Clinical Tales*, Oliver Sacks, New York: Harper and Row, 1987.)

Unit 3 (Activity 1)

For many years, the Gallup organization has been asking Americans what their attitudes are about child raising. We will be summarizing some of this information in response to three questions asked on this topic. The polls we will mention were taken during the following years: 1947, 1973, 1980, 1990 and 1996.

The first question is: What do you think is the ideal number of children for a family to have?

Comparing four polls between 1973 and 1996, over 50% agree in all four polls that the ideal number is two. The next most popular number of children is three. There is a slight increase, however, in the number of people who think that three, rather than two children, is ideal in 1996 compared to those polled in 1990. In 1990, almost two thirds, or 67% say that two is the ideal number, with 18% saying that three is ideal. In 1996, only 57% think two is ideal and 21% believe three is ideal. One of the biggest differences between 1973 and 1996 is the percentage of people who think four or five children are ideal. For example, in 1973, 20% of the respondents fell into these categories compared to only 11% in 1996.

The second question is: Which do you, yourself, think is easier to raise—a boy or a girl?

Those polled had four choices to answer this question: a boy, or girl, no difference or no opinion. The responses reveal that more Americans today than in 1947 feel there is a difference in raising boys and girls. In 1947, 24%, or almost one of every four persons asked, say there is no difference. In 1996, only 12% feel there is no difference. More people in 1947 also had no opinion: 11% compared to 8% in 1996. More people in both time periods agree that boys are more difficult to raise than girls. In 1996, over half, 51%, say that boys are more difficult compared to 42% in 1947.

During both time periods, fewer than one third think that girls are more difficult to raise.

The final question is: Do you think children are better off if their mother is home and doesn't hold a job or are the children just as well off if the mother works?

A comparison between polls in 1990 and 1996 indicate that fewer Americans than before believe children are better off if the mother is at home. In 1990, 73% respond that they are better off if the mother is at home; in 1996 64% feel this way; 31% of the respondents in 1996 say that the children are just as well off if the mother works, compared to 24% in 1990.

* * *

Now you will hear seven statements. Listen carefully to each statement and decide whether it is true or false based on the notes you have taken.

1. Most Americans think the ideal number of children for a family is three.
2. In the 1973 poll, more Americans think that four or five is an ideal number of children than do respondents in the 1996 poll.
3. In the 1996 poll, the majority of respondents believe that there is a difference between raising boys and raising girls.
4. Almost three fourths of the respondents in 1996 say that boys are the most difficult to raise.
5. The majority of respondents to the 1990 and 1996 polls say that children are better off if the mother is at home.
6. If we compare the 1990 and 1996 polls, the percentage of respondents who believe that children are just as well off if the mother works increases.
7. In 1996 almost half of the respondents indicate that children are just as well off if the mother works.

Unit 4 (Activity 1)

When psychologists conduct experimental research with human subjects, they often don't tell the subjects the true purpose of the experiment because that knowledge may change the way the subjects behave. In the Milgram experiment, the real purpose was to see if people will obey an authority figure who tells them to do something that goes against their moral code. However, what the researchers told the subjects was that they would be participating in an experiment to see how punishing affects learning. More than 1,000 people participated in the experiment at various universities.

For this experiment the researcher told subjects that they would be in the role of "teacher." They introduced a man as a "fellow volunteer" who would be in the role of learner. However, the "learner" was actually someone who knew the true purpose of the experiment.

The researchers seated the subject in front of a machine that they said would deliver electric shocks when the subject pulled down a lever. They strapped the learner in a chair in an adjoining room where the subjects could see him. The researchers told the subject that the task of the "learner" was to recite a list of word pairs that he had memorized. They instructed the subject to give the learner an electric shock whenever he made a mistake. The shock levels as marked on the shock machine ranged from "Slight shock" to "Danger—severe shock" to "XXX", the most severe level. As the experiment progressed, the researchers told the subject to administer increasingly higher voltages. The learner-victim did not actually receive any shocks, but he acted as if he did whenever the subject pulled a lever. At certain levels, the victim shouted to the subject to stop or demanded to be set free. The results of the multiple experiments revealed that almost two thirds of the subjects beyond the researchers to the fullest, regardless of how much the learner-victim shouted or how much pain he seemed to be experiencing. Most subjects delivered what they thought were dangerous amounts of shocks to another person. Although most people protested to the researchers and sometimes implored them to stop the experiment, most of them did not disobey when the researchers ordered them to continue.

Unit 5 (Activity 1)

Today, I will be talking about computers. First I will provide a little background information, then I will tell you about how they work and their various sizes.

Historically, the earliest computing devise was the abacus used by the ancient Greeks and Romans and, interestingly, this device is still in use in the East today. There are mechanical devices using sliding scales, similar to the slide rule, which date back almost two millennia. These were used for performing various kinds of calculation, usually as an aid to navigation.

In 1642, the French philosopher-mathematician Blaise Pascal built a mechanical adding machine, and in 1671, a German philosopher-mathematician, Gottfried Leibniz, built a machine to perform multiplication. In 1835, the British mathematician Charles Babbage designed the first mechanical computer, the analytical engine. The work of another British mathematician, Alan Turing, in the 1930s, marked the next major milestone. He developed the mathematical theory of computation and, in particular, showed how a machine could be conceived which could perform any computation (the so-called Turing Machine). The digital computer is the direct descendant of these ideas. In the 1940s, American mathematician John van Neumann developed the basic design for today's electronic computers. Finally, with the development of the transistor in 1952 and the subsequent microelectronics revolution, the Computer Age was started.

Now, how does a computer work exactly? A computer is a collection of various components. At the heart is the CPU (central processing unit) which performs all the computations. This is supported by memory, which holds the current program and data, and "logic arrays," which help move information around the system. A main power supply is needed and, in the case of a mini- or mainframe computer, a cooling system. The computer's "device driver" circuits control the peripheral devices, or add-ons, which can be attached. These will normally be keyboards and VDU (visual display unit) screens for user input and output, disc drive units for mass memory storage, and printers for printed output.

Sometimes more intelligence has been attributed to computers than should be. A computer can only carry out tasks as commanded by the programmer, who translates instructions written in everyday language into a program that is a coded form matching the electronic coding within the computer's internal machinery. The program and data to be manipulated, that is text, figures, images, or sounds, are input into the computer which then processes the data and outputs the results. The results can be printed out or displayed on a VDU, or stored in a memory unit for subsequent manipulation. Whatever the task, a computer can function in only one of four ways: input-output operations, arithmetical operation (addition, subtraction, multiplication, and division), logic and comparison operations (for example, is the value of A equal to, less than, or greater than B), and movement of data to, from, and within the central memory of the machine. The programmer's role is to devise a set of instructions, an algorithm, that utilizes these four functions in a combination appropriate to the job in question.

Unit 6 (Activity 1)

Dialogue 1: A couple on their way to a party
Woman: I hate to say this, Mark, but I think we're lost.
Man: Lost? Nah, we're not lost. What makes you think that?
Woman: Well, I don't know how you define lost, but we've just driven by this corner three times now. Let's stop at the next gas station and get directions.
Man: Oh, we don't need to do that. I can figure this out. We'll just keep going straight for a while instead of turning again.
Woman: But I don't see how that's going to help. Why don't you slow down and I'll ask that woman coming down the street if she knows where Banks Avenue is.
Man: Hey, don't you trust me? I'll get us there. Don't worry. We don't need to ask anyone for directions.

Dialogue 2: A Couple at home

Woman: Hi, dear. You're home early!

Man: Yeah, I finished meeting with all my clients at 3, so I thought I'd beat the rush hour traffic. So how was your day? You were at the university all day weren't you?

Woman: Yeah, I had a really busy day! I had conferences with students all morning. Then I had to attend that seminar I told you about and two committee meetings in the afternoon. I thought the last one would never end!

Man: Huh...

Woman: And in between I was working on my presentation for the trip to Montreal next month. And guess what? I got a phone call from our old friend Rebecca. She's got a job now at a college in New Jersey. Remember her?

Man: Yeah.

Woman: So how about you? How was your day?

Man: Oh, fine.

Woman: (Pause, waiting for him to elaborate. He doesn't). Well, did you have a busy day too?

Man: Yeah.

Woman: (Pause again) So... what did you do?

Man: Oh, nothing important.

Unit 7 (Activity 1)

In the United States there are a number of ways to leave property to those you want to have it after your death. Fortunately, there are safe and understandable methods you can use that will save time and money when your property is passed on. A few terms are necessary in understanding the nitty-gritty details of "estate planning."

Estate planning is one of the more jargon-ridden areas of law. However, there are some legal terms that anyone who wants to learn about the subject must know. Some are euphemisms. For example, a dead person is referred to as a "decedent." Others are technical terms like the following:

"Testate" means to die leaving a will or other valid property-transfer device.

"Intestate" means to die without having left a will or any plan to transfer property.

"Realty property" is real estate, or in other words, the land and the buildings on it.

"Personal property" is every kind of property, from stocks to cash to furniture to wedding rings to your pet canary and your old magazines.

"Gifts" means property you transfer freely—that is, not by sale or trade—to a person or institution.

Finally, "estate" means all the property you own, minus anything you owe.

Unit 8 (Activity 1)

Second Chance

Kimi Tamura and Fred Escobar were born in the same year but in different cities in the U.S. When they were 12 years old, their families both moved to Los Angeles. The Tamuras and the Escobars moved to the same neighborhood near downtown Los Angeles. Coincidentally, the Tamuras lived on the third floor and the Escobars lived on the fourth floor of the same apartment building.

Kimi and Fred met each other for the first time in school. Kimi will never forget that day. She had long, beautiful braids which hung down her back. During the first hour, Fred had managed to tie her braids in a knot around the back of her chair. When Kimi got up to write an answer on the blackboard, her head tugged back and she screamed in pain. The whole class laughed at the joke, except the teacher who made Fred stay after school and wash the blackboards.

After this experience, Fred knew that. "It was love at first sight." He was glad he lived in the same building as Kimi. Fred continually thought of all kinds of excuses to knock on her door. "Could she loan him a newspaper?", "Did she have any paper he could borrow?", "Did she want to walk to school with him?", and so on. He did everything he could to see her as often as possible.

When Kimi and Fred turned 16, they started to go steady. They also gave each other special birthday gifts. Fred gave Kimi a ring which had the engraving "My true love forever." Kimi gave Fred a bright red model car. On the hood, she had painted the words "My heart races for you."

Kimi and Fred were sweethearts during the rest of high school. They were even the king and the queeen of the high school prom. This did not get in the way of their studies. They wanted to get married some day, but not then. They both had important career plans and wanted to wait a while. Kimi wanted to be a writer. She had dreams of writing The Great American Novel. Fred wanted to be an engineer. He had dreams of designing a famous bridge some day. Unfortunately, their preferred colleges were on different coasts (Fred in California and Kimi in New York) and for one reason or another, the two friends lost track of each other.

Fred ended up marrying a nurse he had met in one of his college classes. Kimi ended up marrying an artist she had met at her church. The years went by, both Fred and Kimi raised wonderful families. Unfortunately, when they were in their 50s, they became widowed. On his 60th birthday, Fred began thinking of his old sweetheart Kimi whom he had not seen for more than 40 years. He decided to try to locate her. He dialed a L. Tamura in the directory and fortunately reached Kimi's sister. She told him that Kimi was now living only a few miles from her family's original apartment in Los Angeles.

When he found this out, he nervously dialed her number and asked if he could meet her the next Saturday evening at 6:00 in the lobby of a Los Angeles hotel in which they had had their high school senior prom. Kimi was delighted to hear from him and immediately accepted his invitation. Not knowing whether they would recognize each other after so many years. they both agreed to wear carnations on the lapels of their coats.

On Saturday, Kimi arrived early to the hotel but realized that she had forgotten one thing-the carnation. She knew of a florist shop just around the corner, so she decided to make a phone call to see if by chance it was still open. As she sat in the phone booth making her call, she looked towards the front door and saw a large man with a red carnation walk in. Kimi could not believe her eyes—this could not be "her Fred." He was very unattractive: he was smoking a cigar and had a scruffy beard. His clothes looked filthy and he had gained a lot of weight. Kimi turned her back toward the door of the phone booth and started to dial.

Unit 9 (Activity 1)

1. We will begin our tour this morning with a bus ride past several interesting sites in Hong Kong. Flagstaff House, which contains a Museum of Tea Drinking, it's one of the finest surviving colonial buildings in Hong Kong. The House, which is open daily from 10 a.m. to 5 p.m., is on the east side of Cotton Tree Drive. As you can see, Cotton Tree Drive, which is a major highway, has very little in the way of pedestrian facilities. As we head up Cotton Tree Drive, on our right is the Victoria Peak Tram Terminus. The Peak Tram, whose construction we owe to a Scottish railway engineer, goes up a 45 degree incline to the top. Just ahead of us on Garden Road are the Botanical and Zoological Gardens, which you may want to walk through when you have more time. These gardens contain many tropical varieties of plants, some of which are over 100 years old.

2. Before entering the grounds of El Escorial, I would like to explain a few features, some of which may surprise you. The Monastery of San Lorenzo de El Escorial is a gigantic parallelogram which has four towers of 55 meters at each corner. It is covered by slate columns, on top of which are large metal globes with a weather vane and a cross. On the eastern side of the building, in the center, protrudes the upper part of the temple and the rooms of Philip II's Palace. Also projecting above the building are the twin bell towers and the magnificent dome of the temple, which reaches a height of 92 meters. In the building, the greater part of which is of Doric style and fashioned in granite, 9 towers rise up, and there are 15 cloisters, 16 patios, 88 fountains, 86 staircases, more than 1200 doors, and 2600 windows, all of which produce a dramatic display.

(Source: Serrano, M.L. *El Escorial.* Madrid: Editorial Patrimonio Nacional, 1972.)

3. Welcome to the Getty Center, which is lodged in the beautiful foothills of the Santa Monica Mountains! Today we will explore this scenic place designed by Richard Meier, who is famous for his contributions to architectural Modernism. All of you have just ridden up the hill on the tram, which was designed to make visitors feel "elevated out of their day-to-day experience." I hope you feel this way as we walk up toward the museum entrance on the travertine beneath your feet, a stone which was mined and transported from Italy. We will then take some time looking at the varied displays of paintings, sculptures, and artifacts within the museum itself. From here we will move on to the Museum Courtyard, which features a beautiful 120-foot fountain and then on to the Central Garden, which gradually circles downward to a magnificent round pool. Finally, The View South is a favorite for visitors, some of whom will see the panoramic view of Los Angeles for the first time. I hope you will give yourself some time to take pictures from this sight at the end of the tour. Well, let's get started!

Unit 10 (Activity 1)

1. the state to which you would go if you wanted to vacation at Yellowstone National park
2. the date on which sweethearts give each other valentines in the U.S.
3. the California city in which the Golden Gate Bridge is located
4. one of the months during which people born under the zodiac sign of Capricorn celebrate their birthday.
5. the reason for which Americans celebrate Memorial Day
6. the way in which you would spell the last name of the first President of the United States

7. the reason you would buy a jack to put in your car

8. the way in which you pronounce the state that the city of Chicago is in

9. the kind of store to which you would go to get a prescription filled

10. a reason for which you would call a hotline

11. the century in which Alexander Graham Bell invented the telephone

12. a country in which there are a lot of kangaroos and koala bears

13. the state in which you would find the Pittsburgh Pirates baseball team in their home stadium

14. the reason for which some roads have a double yellow line down the center

15. the day on which American children go trick or treating

16. the way in which you would get help from a telephone operator if you needed it while making a phone call

17. the country to which you would go to visit the Giza Pyramids

18. the month during which most U.S. schools have their graduation ceremonies

19. the reason for which you would multiply 1/2 the base times the perpendicular height of a triangle

20. the way in which you would spell the abbreviation for the National Organization for Women

Unit 11 (Activity 1)

Advisor: Welcome to New World Alternative College. My name is Ms. Sims and I'll be your college advisor for the next two years.

Student: It's nice to meet you I've been looking forward to getting into this school for many years. I guess it would be a good idea to know how to get out of the school as well! (Chuckle)

Advisor: To begin, I'd like you to look at the required and elective courses listed at the top of your Student Information Sheet. As we discuss your choices, I will write them down on your study plan. Is that all right?

Student: Sounds great to me!

Advisor: I would like to schedule you for four classes each semester so that you can complete your degree in two years. In order to take any humanities or environmental studies courses, you must take an English composition prerequisite and a life science prerequisite, respectively. I always like to have students do this during their first semester. Which English course would you like to take? It can be either Expository Writing or Technical Writing. For life sciences, you can take either Psychology or Biology.

Student: I'd like to take Expository Writing and Psychology during my first semester.

Advisor: Good. Now you have several choices for your two other courses during the first semester. I think it is good to get a firm grounding in math early on. Not only General Mathematics but also Computer Science is offered during fall semester only. Why not take one of these?

Student: OK. I took both algebra and trigonometry in high school. I would prefer taking Computer Science because I will learn something new.

Advisor: Great idea! Well, this semester seems to be a little heavy. Why not take one of your electives? Neither U.S. History nor World History is offered in the fall, so your only option is either Chinese or French.

Student: I guess I'd like to try French.

Advisor: Good, we are moving along nicely. Let's go on to spring semester. Not only World History but also U.S. History are offered in the spring. Would you like to take one of these?

Student: Yes, I would. I'd like to take World History. I'd also like to take both of my social science requirements in the spring.

Advisor: Oh, I'm sorry to tell you that neither Economics nor Geography is offered in the spring; however, both Anthropology and Communication Studies are.

Student: OK. Let's go for those. I guess I can choose one more class for this semester. What would you suggest?

Advisor: Why not take one of your environmental studies courses? Either the Greenhouse Effect or Air Pollution are good courses to begin with in this area.

Student: I think I'll choose the Greenhouse Effect.

Advisor: Great! Well, we have completed your plan for Year 1. Let's move on to your second year. You have completed not only your prerequisite English and life science courses but also your social science and other mathematics requirements. Why not take both of your humanities requirements for a change of pace?

Student: Is Linguistics one of the options?

Advisor: Yes, either Linguistics, Philosophy or Religious Studies.

Student: I am not very interested in religion, so I guess I'll take both Linguistics and Philosophy.

Advisor: OK. Now, let's see. You still need to choose two physical science courses. Either Astronomy or Physics is offered every semester, but Geology is offered in the spring only.

Student: Oh, I'd like to take both Astronomy and Geology. Please put me down for Astronomy in the fall and Geology in the spring.

Advisor: For the fall term, you still need to select one of your environmental studies courses. I would highly recommend either Air Pollution or Endangered Wildlife.

Student: Air pollution it will be!

Advisor: Now for the spring we already have you down for Geology. You must take Biology, your last life sciences requirement, and two of the following courses: Garbage Disposal, Hazardous Waste, or Acid Rain.

Student: I would like to take Acid Rain and either Garbage Disposal or Hazardous Waste. What can you tell me about these two courses?

Advisor: Garbage Disposal and Hazardous Waste, respectively, take local and global perspectives on the whole garbage problem. Are you more interested in the concerns of your own community or across the world?

Student: I guess for now, I'm more interested in the problems at home and will take Garbage Disposal. Thanks for that advice!

Advisor: Well, it looks as if we are finished with your study plan. I've enjoyed speaking with you today. Don't forget to stop by sometime either to visit or to discuss questions or problems.

Student: Thank you, Ms. Sims. I will!

Unit 12 (Activity 1)

Version 1:

Example: In the first version, Echo failed to win Narcissus' heart. Similarly, the young man in the second version rejected her love.

There once was a young man named Narcissus who was so handsome that all of the beautiful nymphs in the forest wanted to be with him from the moment they saw him. But Narcissus rejected all of them, breaking their hearts. Even the fairest of the nymphs, whose name was Echo, could not win Narcissus' heart. Echo was a favorite of Artemis, the goddess of the hunt. However, it happened that Echo made Hera, the queen of the goddesses, very angry one day and Hera punished her by never allowing her to use speech again except to repeat what was said to her. And so Echo followed Narcissus, unable to speak to him except to echo his word. One day Narcissus was calling to his friends and said "Is anyone here?" Echo called back "Here, here!" Narcissus then yelled "Come" and Echo, repeating him, responded "Come" and jumped out from her hiding place with her arms outstretched. But when he saw her, he proclaimed, "No, I will die before I give you power over me" and went on his cruel way. Echo retreated to a cave in shame, where she wasted away in sorrow until only her voice was left. But shortly after his meeting with Echo, another maiden who had been scorned by Narcissus made this prayer to the gods: "May he who loves not others love only himself." Nemesis, who was the god of righteous anger, heard this prayer and determined to bring about the request. And so one afternoon, when Narcissus bent over a pool of water to get a drink, he saw his own reflection and fell in love with it. He realized why everyone else was so in love with him, and he burned with a love for himself. But Narcissus knew he could never reach the beauty that he saw, because it was himself, and that only death would set him free. So he pined away at the edge of the pool gazing at his reflection until he died. Echo was there but she could only repeat Narcissus' words to himself: "Farewell, farewell," as he died. Although Narcissus had scorned all of the nymphs, they were kind to him in death and went looking for his body for burial. But in the place where he had lain gazing at himself a new and beautiful flower was blooming, so they named it Narcissus.

(Adapted from Edith Hamilton's *Mythology*, pp. 86–88, New York, Little, Brown & Co. 1969)

Version 2:

The lovely nymph Echo lived a carefree life until one day she saw the handsome Narcissus as he was hunting in the forest. She immediately fell deeply in love with him and, when he did not return her love, she became very upset. In her despair, she implored Venus, the goddess of love, to punish Narcissus by making him suffer the pain of love that is not returned. Then Echo wandered off to the mountains where she pined away until nothing was left but her voice. The gods, seeing this, were displeased with Echo's lack of pride. To punish her, they condemned her to haunt rocks and solitary places, and, as a warning to other maidens, to repeat the last sounds which fell on her ear. Only Venus remembered poor Echo's last prayer and waited for a chance to punish the scornful Narcissus. One afternoon, after hunting, Narcissus hurried to a lonely pool to get a drink. When he knelt over the pool to quench his thirst, he suddenly paused. Near the bottom of the pool he saw a face so fair that he immediately lost his heart, for he thought it belonged to a water nymph who was gazing up at him. With great passion, he reached toward the vision, but the moment he touched the water the lovely face disappeared. When the agitated waters became mirror-like again, the beautiful face, with curly locks, ruby lips, and anxious eyes staring up at him, reappeared. As Narcissus addressed what he thought was a water nymph, she appeared to be answering but he could hear no sound. Again he tried to reach through the water to her and again she disappeared. Hopelessly in love, Narcissus repeated his attempts to reach the nymph, who continued to gaze back with intense longing but who could never be touched. And so Narcissus lingered day after day at the pool, without eating and drinking, until he died, never suspecting that the nymph was himself reflected in the water. Thus, Echo was avenged. But the gods took pity on the beautiful corpse by the side of the pool and changed it into a flower bearing his name. Since that time the narcissus flower has flourished near quiet pools.

(Adapted from *Greece and Rome, Myths and Legends Series*, pp. 96–98, London:Brackenbooks, 1992)

Unit 13 (Activity 1)

Conversation 1:

(Two college-age females)

(sound of telephone ringing and someone picking it up)

A: Hello.

B: Hello, Mei? This is Lin calling. Do you have a minute?

A: Sure. What's up?

B: Well, I'm kinda upset. I got my first essay back from my composition instructor this morning and I got a D.

A: Oh no!

B: Yeah, I had no idea my paper was that bad! So at the end of class, when I was walking out, the instructor must have noticed I was upset 'cause she asked me if anything was wrong. And I said Oh it's nothing 'cause I couldn't think of what to say. I mean, it was a final grade for the paper so I can't change it and it would've sounded pretty silly to tell her I was bummed out about my grade. So what was I supposed to say?

Conversation 2:

(Telephone call. Two males; a customer and an airlines customer service employee. C = customer, E = employee)

(sound of telephone ringing and someone picking it up)

E: Good afternoon. Consolidated Airlines Customer Service, this is Mario Perez speaking. How may I help you?

C: Mr. Perez, I'm calling about a problem I had with your airline on a vacation I took last week. I was flying from Dallas to Miami and I didn't want to check my luggage so I brought it with me to the gate.

E: Uh huh...

C: Well, when I tried to board the plane, they told me that my luggage was too big to store in the overhead bins and that it would need to be checked separately. As it turned out, they checked the luggage on a later flight than the one I came in on. When I got to Miami I had no idea that the luggage wouldn't be on my plane so I wasted my time at the baggage claim.

E: Oh, I'm sorry . . . . The policy for . . .

C: Then when I found out it was on another plane, I couldn't wait for it, so I had to drive 15 miles back to the airport the next day just to get my luggage.

Unit 14 (Activity 1)

Who has not wished at some time for a photographic memory? It seems that this would be a great asset for recalling all the things we've worked so hard to learn in school as well as remembering our past experiences. In fact, however, a perfect memory is not the wonderful thing we might suppose. All in all, as I will explain, some things are better forgotten.

In the late 1960's, the Soviet psychologist Alexander Luria described a journalist (we'll call him "S" as Dr. Luria did) who had an amazing ability to remember giant grids of numbers and long lists of words after seeing them for just a few seconds. If you tried any of the short-term memory experiments in Unit 4 of *Grammar Dimensions,* you know how difficult this is to do. Even after a passage of 15 years, this man could reproduce the number grids and word lists both forwards and backwards. This ability did not come naturally, though. S. developed a variety of memory tricks to accomplish his feats; many of them involved forming visual images to recall the information. At first, this helped to impress other people with his recall abilities. Later, however, he could not forget. The images kept coming into his mind and distracting him. It made

him unable in some cases to carry on a conversation; in fact, Luria described him as "rather dull-witted." Finally, images began to interfere so much with S's ability to concentrate that he had to quit his profession; he supported himself by traveling from place to place as a performer, demonstrating his unusual recall abilities.

If you think about it, there are a number of problems that could result from a perfect memory. First of all, every time you remembered the past, you would not only remember all the good things, but also the negative aspects that you'd probably just as soon forget. We all have relationships that are probably better off because we have selectively forgotten some negative experiences. Would you really want to remember every painful experience, every angry argument, every embarrassing episode? Secondly, the act itself of remembering might take hours instead of minutes. A third problem might be the difficulty you'd have to organize all the information in your mind. Think of the clutter!

In short, a certain amount of forgetting is beneficial to our survival and our sanity.

Unit 15 (Activity 1)

Passage 1: How to Prevent Insomnia

Have you ever had trouble trying to get to sleep? The inability to

sleep when you are tired is called insomnia. Some people have chronic insomnia, that is, they often find themselves unable to sleep. Other people experience insomnia once in a while due to changes in lifestyle, illness, or other stressful situations. If you are temporarily troubled by insomnia, here are a few tips to help you: First, if you didn't get much sleep during the previous night, don't try to oversleep the next night to make up for it. It is important to get up at the same time each morning so that your body's inner clock is set for a regular time to get up. Another thing you might try is a light snack before you go to bed. People on a diet often have trouble getting to sleep because they are hungry. They would probably benefit greatly from a nighttime treat, according to Dr. Michael Stevenson, director of an insomnia clinic. A third way to combat insomnia is to stop worrying about getting enough sleep. You don't necessarily need eight hours of sleep to feel good the next day.

Now you will hear three statements. Choose the one that accurately paraphrases information from Passage 1:
    a. Don't oversleep even if you didn't get enough sleep the night before.
    b. Eat a light snack at bedtime only if you are not dieting.
    c. You should worry about getting enough sleep only if you don't get eight hours every night.

Passage 2: How to Prevent Sports Injuries
In one recent year, American hospitals recorded almost three million injuries that could be attributed to sports and recreation. Many sports injuries can be prevented with a little care and common sense. One important rule for preventing injury is to pay attention to pain messages. If your body starts to hurt, it is telling you to stop. But there are some measures you can take to prevent pain and injury in the first place. Warming up before you participate in sports, even if it is only for ten minutes, is one way to reduce injuries. Warming up can consist of a brisk walk followed by stretching. Conditioning is also important for sports. This consists of building muscle strength and flexibility. Many athletic trainers recommend weight training for all sports as it helps to develop good movement ability. In addition to warming up, cooling down is a crucial part of exercising. Especially after you have finished a strenuous activity, you need to return to a resting state gradually with moderate movement such as walking. It is dangerous to sit down or stand still directly after vigorous exercise, according to Steve Farrell, a research scientist. Farrell says that a failure to cool down after such exercise could result in a heart attack or even death in some cases.

Now you will hear three statements. Choose the one that accurately paraphrases information from Passage 2:
    a. You should warm up for a sport only if it is strenuous exercise.
    b. Unless you want to develop large muscles, weight training is not usually recommended for conditioning.
    c. Even if you are very tired, you should always keep moving for a short time after vigorous exercise rather than stopping.

Unit 16 (Activity 1)

Example: Swish, zoom, zoom. The propeller turning and engine roaring, the plane is ready for takeoff. The pilot radios the control tower for permission to move toward the runway. You are going for your first ride in a small plane. Your heart pounds as the wheels leave the ground, and you clutch your seat more tightly. Ascending higher and higher, you see nothing but white fog in every direction. Finally, the fog clears and you are astounded at the sight below.

1. Hiking for hours, you feel exhausted. Your mouth is dry and sweat is running down your forehead. You thought for sure you would be there by now. Hadn't they said to take the trail up to Conrad's peak and then head eastward for two miles? Shouldn't you be there by now? Sitting down, you lean back on a dustry rock and take a swig of water from your canteen. You close your eyes momentarily, but you are awakened by a sound off to your right.

2. You have awakened suddenly. Looking at your clock on your bedstand, you see that it is 3:25 A.M. The air is cool and you hear a soft rustling below your bedroom window. Could someone be trying to get into your house? Or is it just the large leaves and twigs falling loudly to the pavement below in the dead of night? Feeling too afraid to sleep, you decide to get up to investigate.

3. Everything is almost ready. Decorated with banners and signs, the auditorium looks welcoming. Volunteers have already put out more than 200 seats, arranged neatly in rows. The microphone stands ready for the heavy use it will receive. The noise level grows louder and louder. Suddenly, a woman appears on stage.

4. Having heard about the disaster, you were not sure what to expect. Piling supplies in the back of your van, you thought about the problems ahead. Would you be able to get there in time? Would you have the skills and knowledge to be of help? Being a professional, you knew your limitations. You stepped on the gas pedal and drove for hours it seemed. Finally, you reached what you had been looking for.

5. The village is awake and bustling. Standing on the corner, a woman tries to sell handmade baskets of various sizes. Calling for customers, an artist points to his three latest landscapes. An intellectual-looking man sits on his front porch reading a newspaper. Holding a baby in her arms, a woman crosses the street. But what captures your attention is the two children.

Unit 17 (Activity 1)

(Bold words are clues to answers.)

Contributions of John F. Kennedy on Policies in the U.S. and Abroad

In 1960 John F. Kennedy of Massachusetts was elected President of the United States. Kennedy's administration was **known for** promoting programs which would protect human rights in the U.S. and abroad. In the U.S., he **united with** Americans of all colors and religions by issuing an executive order which would allow all people equal access to government employment. Also a minimum wage bill was adopted which **resulted** in a raise of $.25 per hour (from $1.00 to $1.25) for interstate commerce workers. The elderly were **happy about** the Social Security Act of 1961 which increased old-age benefits and permitted the retirement age to be 62. **Regarding** school segregation, it was during Kennedy's administration that the first university, the University of Mississippi, was forced to admit the first Black student. Kennedy's administration made many attempts to develop international cooperation for peace. Many men and women **enlisted** in the Peace Corps to serve the world's underdeveloped countries. Volunteers **cooperated with** local technicians to build roads in Tanganyika, Africa. The U.S. also **joined with** Canada and eighteen European nations to form the Organization for Economic Cooperation and Development. Latin Americans were **enthusiastic about** the Latin American Aid Bill of $600 million which became effective in 1962. **On the strength** of the space programs of the U.S. and Russia, the two nations **consulted with** each other and decided to establish a cooperative program of space exploration.

John F. Kennedy **contributed to** many positive causes. It is difficult to know how many other good things he would have **succeeded in** doing if he had not been assassinated on November 22, 1963.

Unit 18 (Activity 1)

One of the longest and most expensive murder trials in Texas history involved the multimillionaire, T. Cullen Davis. Cullen Davis was the son of Kenneth W. Davis, known as "Stinky Davis," who made his millions in the oil boom of the 1920s. Cullen inherited much of this money after his father died.

As a young man, Cullen was not very conspicuous in public life. He had no accomplishments in high school, he dressed and acted conservatively, and he did not converse easily. This all changed when he met his second wife, Priscilla Wilborn.

Priscilla was a handsomely-figured platinum blond. She had been married twice and had born three children before she met Cullen. She was not from a well-off family and did not even graduate from high school. But, she did have a lively personality and wore racy clothing: cowboy boots, skin-tight hot pants, and bikini tops.

As a monument to their new life together, Cullen built a $6 million house on a 181-acre estate that Cullen's father had bought 30 years before. All seemed fairly well until Priscilla claimed that Cullen's violence had caused him to break her collarbone. He also beat her teenage daughter Dee and hurled her daughter's kitten against the kitchen floor and killed it.

Priscilla and Cullen were separated in July 1974. Priscilla stayed in the mansion while Cullen moved out. While waiting for the divorce, she entertained various characters at the mansion, from motorcycle bikers, construction workers, and alleged drug peddlers, some with criminal records. She claimed that she only did this to rehabilitate them. On the afternoon of August 2, a hearing on the divorce ended in the judge granting Priscilla an increase in support payments and $42,000 from Cullen to pay for her attorney fees.

That same evening a horrible tragedy followed. Priscilla and a boyfriend returned from a party and discovered Priscilla's 12-year old daughter murdered. Her story revealed that her former husband, Cullen, dressed all in black and wearing a woman's wig, stepped out and had both of his hands covered in a plastic garbage bag. In his hands he carried a revolver. She then claimed that he said "hi" to her and then shot her in the chest. Following this, he shot her boyfriend from behind a door and killed him. When Priscilla tried to run and escape outside the house, Beverly Bass and her friend "Bubba" Gavel were driving up the driveway. When they came to her aid, Cullen is reported to have turned and shot Bubba with a shot that ultimately paralyzed him.

The next day the police located Cullen at home and found four handguns in his car. However, none of the handguns matched the murder weapon. Cullen was charged with murder and trespassing and spent a year in jail before the case was decided. Because he had a lot of money, he hired the best criminal lawyer in Texas—Richard Racehorse Haynes. Much money was spent in pretrial investigations. Haynes tried to discredit all of the witnesses in the crime, especially Priscilla who had been known to associate with some "undesirable" people. Money was also spent in investigating potential jurors for the case.

In the closing argument of the trial, Racehorse Haynes tried to argue that Priscilla's reputation discredited her as a witness. Prosecutors for the case pleaded that Priscilla's character had nothing to do with the question of whether Cullen had committed murder or not. In the end, the jury deliberated just over four hours before arriving at the verdict of not guilty. After the trial, jurors admitted that they did not necessarily believe that Cullen was innocent, but they could not pronounce him guilty beyond a reasonable doubt.

Unit 19 (Activity 1)

Message 1
Hi, this is Patricia O'Connell calling. I'm having a party to celebrate the end of summer session and I hope you can come. It'll be on Saturday, the 25th of July, starting around seven at my house. Let me know if you can make it. You can reach me at 897-8533.

Message 2
Hi, it's Ray. I can't remember when you said you were getting back from your trip. Just calling to see if you got the birthday present I sent in the mail last week. Hope you like it. Anyway, give me a call when you get a chance.

Message 3
Hi, it's Immouna. I just wanted to let you know that I did find the books you needed for your project when I was at the library a few days ago, so I checked them out and brought them home with me. You can pick them up at my house whenever you want. If I'm not going to be here, I could leave them on the porch. Give me a call when you get back from your vacation. Hope you had a great time.

Message 4
Hello, this is Mr. Liu at the Student Services office. We've just finished reviewing our applications and interviews for the part-time administrative assistant position, and you were the top candidate. We would like to offer you the position. It would start on August 15th. Please let us know as soon as possible if you are interested in accepting our offer. You can leave me a message at 485-7269 any time.

Unit 20 (Activity 1)

1. (Conversation between friends)
X: Did you know that crazy guy, Tom Barker, will be going to Harvard next year?
Y: No, how can he afford it?
X: He got a $50,000 scholarship from one of the local service clubs.

2. (Lecturette)
Human beings and animals have existed side by side since the dawn of history. More often than not, however, human beings have dominated animals. This does not mean that they have not admired or even revered animals for their intelligence, beauty, loyalty, and strength. But it does mean that they have generally been willing to kill animals in order to feed or clothe themselves.

3. (Interview)
X: Professor, tell us how Los Angeles ranks against the rest of the nation in terms of charity.
Y: Well, the prognosis is not good. Los Angeles ranks near the bottom of all U.S. cities in per-capita giving. The hard facts are that half of all private giving goes to churches and synagogues for basic upkeep. Little to none transfers from the rich to the needy. By 2002, starvation, homelessness, illness, and death in Los Angeles County could resemble the conditions during the Great Depression.

4. (Newscast)
Newsflash. A unique fossil was discovered last week in the sands of Mongolia's Gobi Desert. Scientists discovered a fossilized rock of a carnivorous dinosaur nesting on its eggs like a bird. This is the first time anyone has learned anything about how the Earth's most fearsome parent may have tenderly cared for their young.

5. (Conversation)
X: I just bought a new pentium chip computer.
Y: That's great. I wish I could afford one. Does it have modem and fax capabilities?
X: It sure does. It also has a 16-megabytes of RAM and a CD-ROM drive.

Unit 21 (Activity 1)

S1: Thank you for allowing us to interview you today. We are seniors at May Valley High School and would like to know how students are actually admitted to the university.
A: Well, I'm happy to inform you about this. Now's the time to ask these questions—before you graduate from high school. In selecting students we look at two main things, your college entrance test scores and your GPA, or grade point average.
S2: (with an accent) My parents were immigrants to this country

and we don't live in the best neighborhoods. How can I pass the exams? How can I go to the university?

A: Well, that reminds me of another important point. Students who are economically disadvantaged can sometimes be admitted with a lower GPA or college entrance exam score than the other candidates. The reason for this I think is many of these students not only have had to work hard at their studies, but also they have had heavy family responsibilities, like babysitting, caring for the sick, translating maybe for loved ones, or taking on extra jobs. Special federal and state programs have been set aside to help these students get admitted to the university and pay their tuition.

S3: Does it make any differences how you get a high GPA?

A: (laughing) Good question. If you have a high GPA only because you have done well in non-academic subjects like PE, woodshop, auto mechanics, etc., then that could hurt you. We normally throw those courses out from the start and look carefully at your college prep English, math and science class.

S1: Are those the only things you consider—how about a student's involvement in student organizations on campus. For example, I am the editor of the school newspaper. Will that help?

A: It can only help in a split decision about a candidate. If a student's test scores and GPA are borderline, then supplementary criteria might be considered like involvement in clubs, athletic teams, debate teams and that kind of thing.

S2: Are you the only one who makes the decision about future students?

A: No, I am only one of a 15-member team who considers all of the evidence in order to make a decision. As you can see, the decision is always made very carefully.

S3: And fairly, it seems. Thank yu very much for your time.

S1 & S2: Yes, thanks very much.

A: You're welcome. Thank you. I hope to see your applications coming through anytime now. Good luch in your studies!

Unit 22 (Activity 1)

Dr. Laura: OK, we're ready for our first caller. what's you name, and what's your problem?

Caller 1 (woman): Uh, hi, my name is Sally. Um you know, my husband just lost his job and we're really strapped for money. Um, but the worst part is that (breath), you know, he's —he's home all the time. He's really getting on my nerves and I don't know what—

Dr. Laura: Uh, listen Sally, Sally. You married your husband—for better, for worse, it doesn't matter if he's getting on your nerves. You should stay with him and help him.

Caller 1: Well, wh, how? I mean, should I take another job? Uh well—

Dr. Laura: Well, that might help him, but I think most of all you should encourage him, help him get through the tough times.

Caller 1: But he's a pain in the neck!

Dr. Laura: OK. Thank you very much Sally. Next caller.

Caller 2 (man): Hi, this is David. Um, this is really embarrassing. I'm supposed to get married in three weeks and I'm-I'm not getting cold feet—

Dr. Laura: That's embarrassing?

Caller 2: No (laughing), that's not the embarrassing part. Um, it's not that I'm getting cold feet, it's just that I'm suddenly realizing that my fiancé and I have nothing in common. She—

Dr. Laura: Uh, do you love your fiancé?

Caller 2: Wh, yeah. I wouldn't—I wouldn't have proposed to her if I didn't love her.

Dr. Laura: I see, but you have nothing in common.

Caller 2: No, it's scary—

Dr. Laura: I think you've got a conflict here and I think you should take some time. I think you need to think things over.

Caller 2: You think I should postpone?

Dr. Laura: Yes, I do.

Caller 2: That so embarrassing, all of the invitations are out—

Dr. Laura: I think you need to get—I think you need to get to know your girlfriend a little bit better before you propose. I don't think you've taken enough time to think about this.

Caller 2: OK. Thank you.

Dr. Laura: You're welcome.

Unit 23 (Activity 1)

How to Create a Good Advertisement

Today I'd like to give some helpful hints about creating a good advertisement for your own company or store.

Every good advertisement needs just three main ingredients. First, the ad should include information about the product and its unique advantage. Next, don't razzle-dazzle your prospective customers but do give a clear statement of the information. Do respect your audience by giving a straight and simple message. Finally, do give a unique presentation. The first two ingredients make an ad good. The third one makes it great.

Now let's discuss three important features of an ad. First, do pay attention to the headline that you give to your ad. Always present features in terms of reader benefits. You do want to induce reader interest and stimulate further reading of the advertisement. Believe it or not, simplicity always wins. Don't be tricky. I recommend that you include no teasers, rhymes, double meanings, coined words, or humor because this really can confuse the customer.

The next consideration is the illustrations. Your illustration does need to capture the attention of the prospect. It does need to create a favorable impression of the product and clearly identify the subject being sold. Do make sure that the picture, drawing, or photo emphasizes any unique characteristics of the product in a positive light.

Finally, we turn to the body copy. The words in the body copy are very important because they are used to interest, inform, involve, help, convince, persuade, and induce a response from your audience. And we all know what that response does need to be: BUY, BUY, BUY, of course.

Adapted from Cassell, D. *How to Advertise and Promote your Retail Store.* New York: Amacom, 1983.

Unit 24 (Activity 1)

*In a recent survey, a number of well known Americans, including authors, media specialists, politicians and artists, were asked to name movies that they felt defined the American character. You will hear descriptions of two of these films. After you have listened to each description, choose the statement, a or b, which accurately paraphrases an idea in the description.
"Pollyanna"
    a. Americans have never hated or envied the rich.
    b. Americans have never hated the rich, just envied them.
"Mr. Smith Goes to Washington"
    a. Political corruption in Washington continues until an innocent man from the a small town arrives.
    b. Political corruption in Washington stops before an innocent man from a small town arrives.

Passage 1: Pollyanna
This movie, based on a novel, tells the story of a young girl named Pollyanna during the first decade of the 20th century. Since Pollyanna's parents have died, leaving her an orphan, she goes to live with her Aunt Polly, a wealthy woman in a small town. The town is filled with pessimistic people who tend to see the negative side of everything. Pollyanna, on the other hand, sees the good in every situation. Because of Pollyanna's charm, the townspeople are eventually won over by her cheerful optimism, and they, too, try to look for the positive in events that occur, even when the unfortunate things happen. According to Yale law professor

Stephen L. Carter, the film Pollyanna defines the American character because it "captures the American belief in the future as good and the individual as important." He also notes the values of American capitalism it embraces. Pollyanna's rich aunt, who owns everything in town, gets to keep all her property but learns the social obligations that accompany great wealth. Never have Americans hated the rich, claims Carter, but only envied them and wanted them to be nice.

Passage 2: Mr. Smith Goes to Washington
Another film that reflects America's belief that one person can make a difference is "Mr. Smith Goes to Washington." The theme of this movie, made in 1939, is that evil will triumph unless good people take action, and that the American political system works because, in fact, good people will not let it fail. In this film, not until an innocent young man arrives in Washington does political corruption stop. That man, Mr. Jefferson Smith, has been selected by the corrupt politicians to replace a deceased senator. They think he will unknowingly go along with a dishonest scheme that will put money in their pockets. When Mr. Smith goes to Washington, he believes that all politicians have the same unselfish goals that he has to help the American people. He comes to see that his idealistic views of the system are unrealistic, and he then sets out to expose the corrupt politicians who are trying to destroy the integrity of the government. Mr. Smith succeeds in his goal and the system is saved.

Unit 25 (Activity 1)

Note: when reading the a, b, c choices, begin each with "Is it . . ." or "Would it be . . ." or "Was it . . ." as appropriate (e.g., for number 1: Is it a. purple? b. brown? or c. green?)

  1. What color do you get when you mix the colors yellow and blue?
    a. purple
    b. brown
    c. green

  2. In what body of water would you find sharks?
    a. in a lake
    b. in a river
    c. in an ocean
  3. Who wrote the following symphony?
    a. Bach
    b. Beethoven
    c. Brahms

4. Which of the following American cities is most known for its rainy weather?
   a. Seattle
   b. Miami
   c. Minneapolis
5. What part of the body separates the chest from the lower part of the torso?
   a. the stomach
   b. the trachea
   c . the diaphragm
6. In what sport is a puck used?
   a. football
   b. hockey
   c. soccer
7. Which of the following is a bone disease that afflicts elderly people?
   a. halitosis
   b. thrombosis
   c. osteoporosis
8. Which word describes an excessive or illogical fear of high places?
   a. photophobia
   b. acrophobia
   c. claustrophobia
9. What does the "m" in the physics formula mc^2 stand for?
   a. molecule
   b. matter
   c. mass
10. Who invented the light bulb?
    a. George Westinghouse
    b. Rudolph Diesel
    c. Thomas Edison
11. What body part does the medical prefix "cardio" refer to?
    a. the lungs
    b. the stomach
    c. the heart
12. Listen to the following song. What is being played?
    a. the American National Anthem
    b. America the Beautiful
    c. Hymn to America
13. What does the abbreviation I.Q. stand for?
    a. intelligent question
    b. intelligence quotient
    c. intellectual quota
14. If you have just read the prologue of a play, which part did you read?
    a. the beginning
    b. the middle
    c. the end
15. In what popular board game do you buy hotels, railroads and utility companies?
    a. Risk
    b. Monopoly
    c. Go
16. Listen to the following music. What musical instrument is being played?
    a saxophone
    b. a violin
    c. a clarinet
17. In what field would you study if you wanted to learn about sedimentology?
    a. physics
    b. geology
    c. Linguistics
18. In what continent would you find the Amazon basin?
    a. Asia
    b. North America
    c. South America